Ordering Space

Types in Architecture and Design

ORDERING SPACE

Types in Architecture and Design

edited by

Karen A. Franck
New Jersey Institute of Technology

Lynda H. Schneekloth
State University of New York at Buffalo

Van Nostrand Reinhold
I(T)P A Division of International Thomson Publishing Inc.

New York ▫ Albany ▫ Bonn ▫ Boston ▫ Detroit ▫ London ▫ Madrid ▫ Melbourne ▫
Mexico City ▫ Paris ▫ San Francisco ▫ Singapore ▫ Tokyo ▫ Toronto

Printed in the United States of America
For more information, contact:

Van Nostrand Reinhold
115 Fifth Avenue
New York, NY 10003

International Thomson Publishing
Berkshire House
168-173 High Holborn
London WC1V 7AA
England

Thomas Nelson Australia
102 Dodds Street
South Melbourne, 3205
Victoria, Australia

Nelson Canada
1120 Birchmount Road
Scarborough, Ontario
Canada M1K 5G4

International Thomson Publishing GmbH
Königswinterer Strasse 418
53227 Bonn
Germany

International Thomson Publishing Asia
221 Henderson Road #05-10
Henderson Building
Singapore 0315

International Thomson Publishing Japan
Hirakawacho Kyowa Building, 3F
2-2-1 Hirakawacho
Chiyoda-ku, 102 Tokyo
Japan

International Thomson Editores
Campos Eliseos 385, Piso 7
Col. Polanco
11560 Mexico D.F. Mexico

Copyright © 1994 by Van Nostrand Reinhold
I(T)P™ A division of International Thomson Publishing Inc.
The ITP logo is a trademark under license.

Copyright © 1994 Chapter 5, "Farm Type in the American Midwest: A Reflection of Government Policy" by Hemalata Dandekar

Copyright © 1994 Chapter 7, "Terminologies and Types: Making Sense of Some Types of Dwellings and Cities" by Anthony D. King

Copyright © 1994 Chapter 16, "Getting to Know the Built Landscape: Typomorphology" by Anne Vernez Moudon

Copyright © 1994 Chapter 11, "An Artist's Perspective on Type" by Nancy Wolf

All rights reserved. No part of this work covered by the copyright hereon may be reproduced or used in any form or by any means – graphic, electronic, or mechanical, including photocopying, recording, taping, or information storage and retrieval systems – without the written permission of the publisher.

Typeset in Frutiger and Perpetua
Designed by Johanna Jacob

1 2 3 4 5 6 7 8 9 10 ARCKP 01 00 99 98 97 96 95 94

Library of Congress Cataloging-in-Publication Data
Ordering space: types in architecture and design / edited by
  Karen A. Franck, Lynda H. Schneekloth.
    p. cm.
  Includes bibliographical references and index.
  ISBN 0-442-01233-0
  1. Architecture – Classification. 2. Architectural design.
I. Franck, Karen A. II. Schneekloth, Lynda H.
NA2500.073 1994
720'.1—dc20
                                              94-21606
                                                  CIP

We dedicate this book to the memory of
Karen's father, Peter Goswyn Franck (1913–1989) and
Lynda's mother, Vera Eleanor Louise Oldakowski Hussmann Shookner (1913–1991).

Contents

9   Preface

15   **Chapter 1**
   Type: Prison or Promise?
      Lynda H. Schneekloth and Karen A. Franck

Part I   Species Typing

41   **Chapter 2**
   Notions of the Inhabited
      Lynda H. Schneekloth

61   **Chapter 3**
   Archetypes as a "Natural Language" for Place Making
      Mike Brill

79   **Chapter 4**
   A Built Landscape Typology: The Language of the Land We Live In
      Patrick Condon

Part II   Fixing Types

97   **Chapter 5**
   Farm Type in the American Midwest: A Reflection of Government Policy
      Hemalata C. Dandekar

117   **Chapter 6**
   Zoning as a Tool for Regulating Family Type in American Communities
      Marsha Ritzdorf

127   **Chapter 7**
   Terminologies and Types: Making Sense of Some Types of Dwellings and Cities
      Anthony D. King

Part III   Negotiating Type

147   **Chapter 8**
   Social Practice and Building Typologies
      Thomas A. Markus

165   **Chapter 9**
   Typological Thinking in Architectural Practice
      Martin Symes

179   **Chapter 10**
   The Question of Type
      Julia W. Robinson

Part IV Playing with Type

195 Chapter 11
An Artist's Perspective on Type
Nancy Wolf

209 Chapter 12
In and Out of Type
Jean La Marche

233 Chapter 13
Memory and the Making of Places
Frances Downing

Part V Type in Scholarship

253 Chapter 14
Type and the Possibility of an Architectural Scholarship
Guido Francescato

271 Chapter 15
Type as Analytical Tool: Reinterpretation and Application
Roderick J. Lawrence

289 Chapter 16
Getting to Know the Built Landscape: Typomorphology
Anne Vernez Moudon

Part VI Type and Social Practice

315 Chapter 17
Typification and the Building of Society: "The Absent Patron"
David Vanderburgh

331 Chapter 18
Just Not My Type: Gender, Convention, and the Uses of Uncertainty
Alice T. Friedman

345 Chapter 19
Types Are Us
Karen A. Franck

373 Contributors

377 Index

Preface

Humans do not occupy, imagine, or create an infinite variety of particular, idiosyncratic places. Instead, we structure environments by creating and using a multitude of categories of places and spaces, often called "types." With these types we group places that are alike together and we treat individual places as members of groups. This ordering of space into different kinds of spaces is an intrinsic and constituent part of life.

Types refer to abstract ideas, images of places, ideas about places, and to the particular, concrete spaces on the earth. Main Street, Peter Pan's Never Never Land, R1 zones, shopping centers, the sacred mountain, a phone booth, rain forests, heaven and hell, the frontier, and a colonial-style house are all types of places invented by human cultures. As this list suggests, place types are made and used in architecture, planning, policy, religion, research, popular culture, literature, and daily life. Our world is infused with place types. The spatial practices of any society both structure, and are structured by, the activity of typing.

The built landscape we inhabit in industrialized countries at the end of the twentieth century facilitates, and necessitates, quick movement between highly segregated activities located at some distance from each other. We no longer live in the layered and integrated world described in medieval literature, or as many native people in some parts of the world still do. We cannot live that way in "modern" societies (a different kind of type). Our social practices and our built landscape are structured by elaborate systems of place types, which enforce myriad distinctions and separations between different kinds of activities, people, and places that are often codified in policy and regulation.

This book begins to identify the ways that place type and typing operate in our society by revealing who uses them, for what purposes, and with what consequences. Types and ways of typing are used to produce and reproduce the material world and to give meaning to our place in it. Types help determine what we produce, modify, destroy, and preserve, and how we do so. They guide and constrain much of what we think and do, yet they remain implicit and largely invisible. The power of types in structuring beliefs, practices, and landscape, and the many physical, social, political, economic, and intellectual consequences that ensue, are rarely recognized or critiqued. Other categories, such as age, gender, race, and ethnicity, which also serve to organize society and were once taken for granted, have recently come under intense intellectual and social scrutiny accompanied by efforts to modify their meaning and use; the categories for ordering space are only beginning to receive this attention.

The problem is not that we use categories and distinctions in ordering space; categories and exemplars of categories are both necessary and beneficial. The problem is that we are often unaware of them and their advantages and disadvantages. We take types for granted, as given, and do not recognize that they are social constructions that further certain values and interests and restrict others. We may not see how much the distinctions that constitute the contemporary ordering of space enforce patterns of social domination and ecological destruction. If we wish to change these patterns, we need to modify the distinctions and separations that underlie them.

But types and typing are not only constraining; they are also liberating. In scholarship, design, and other creative endeavors they provide an essential means of gaining insight into what is and imagining what can be. Recognizing these empowering features is as important as recognizing the restrictive features. In this book we set out to do both.

So what is type? A type is a kind of thing and an exemplar of a kind of thing. Type is a conceptual construct that distinguishes similar from dissimilar so that we know that something is this kind of thing, not that kind of thing. Typing places exemplars into classes. Type is also the essence or the original of a kind of thing that makes it possible for us to understand the construct, image, or class. These categories for organizing the world are so important that they are taught to children both informally and formally. Remember the Sesame Street song "One of these things is not like the others, one of these things doesn't belong…"?

Types are used to identify empirically verifiable entities but, as often as not, they are imagined. Types are used to characterize what is here in the world (kinds of neighborhoods, rivers, or buildings), and also what has not yet been made and what can never exist in the world of matter (paradise or Never Never Land). Types exist physically in the material world, imaginally in our aspirations and hopes about our place in the world, and conceptually in our thinking and intellectual work. All the breadth, ambiguity, and power of typing as a human activity is carried by types used in the production of space and the making of places materially, imaginally, and conceptually.

The cover of this book, *Perfect Order* by Nancy Wolf, depicts an array of building and landscape types. The particular types or the organization of types identified in this illustration will differ depending upon the interests and concerns of the reader. Architects may point to the formal or architectural types of towers and detached houses, or to the architectural style (postmodern) of the towers, or to the steel frame and glass construction. Planners and geographers may identify the different kinds of neighborhoods; a zoning official may identify these neighborhoods by their technical zoning designations. An urban historian may see a representation of a U.S. metropolitan area in its contemporary postmodern condition, albeit exaggerated. A general reader may say these are office buildings, this is a highway, this is a park, identifying the most commonly understood building and landscape types of daily life.

Thus the types we recognize as important and employ in our endeavors vary significantly according to our purposes, according to our intended use for them. Researchers in many fields, including architecture, history, planning, urban design, and urban sociology, develop categories of places to describe and understand environments, and also, in some cases, to direct and prescribe future actions. Architects and others involved in the fabrication and modification of places use a wide array of different kinds of types to help them design places. Policymakers, officials in financial institutions, zoning officials, historic preservation commissions, and building inspectors refer to official codifications of types to regulate their fabrication, modification, and use. Developers, real estate agents, manufacturers, and advertisers use types to portray and present places and ideas, often in order to sell property or products. Social critics and artists of all media represent and interpret place types to us in their ongoing inquiry into meaning, often challenging accepted labels and textual readings as part of their explorations. And all of us, in the everyday practice of our lives, use our culturally and historically-bound, common-sense understanding of types to make sense of our surroundings, to imagine places, and to live in them. All of these activities locate us in the world and give meaning to our lives.

❏ ❏ ❏

No single, definitive reading of type or typing is given in this book. The collection of essays was developed precisely to offer diverse and, at times, conflicting perspectives on type as a form of knowledge, its locations in the human enterprise, and how we rely on types to invent, transform, and operate in and on the world. The division of the essays into six sections reflects the variable and contradictory features of types and typing. They are at the origin of our experience of the world and how we make sense of that experience (*Part I: Species Typing*). They map the world in ways that are difficult to change (*Part II: Fixing Types*) and they are also fluid and changing (*Part III: Negotiating Type*). While they are used self-consciously with precision in order to understand and analyze (*Part V: Type in Scholarship*), they are also used more loosely and more intuitively in design (*Part IV: Playing with Type*). And types are a constituent part of the social order, furthering dominant values and interests (*Part VI: Type and Social Practice*).

Chapter 1, "Types: Prison or Promise?" by Schneekloth and Franck, frames the question of type as a form of knowledge, demonstrating how it is woven into the material, imaginal, and conceptual worlds we find and create. The chapter describes five type operations: occupying, naming, imaging, inventing/modifying, and representing, and suggests how these different ways of interacting with type allow us to create and transform both knowledge and places. Further, the introductory essay describes some of the ways type both enables and limits our ability to be active readers and creators of the world.

Part I: Species Typing contains three chapters concerned with typing at a fundamental and species level in our interaction with the world of nonhuman nature. This series of essays, in addressing some of the ways we as humans are more alike than different in our endeavors to live on the earth, starts from an idea of beginnings and the typing of earth/human relationships. The separation of the sacred from the profane, the distinction between what we consider part of ourselves and what we exclude, and the types of landscapes that have evolved over thousands of years of gradual manipulation are all basic orderings reflected on the face of the earth and in our interactions with it. Although the three chapters posit different views on humans and the nonhuman world, they each strive to understand the place of our constructed world in relationship to the found world.

Schneekloth, in "Notions of the Inhabited," uses science fiction to explore the (re)emergence of an ecological imagination and what that might mean in the late twentieth century. The conceptualization of the world into a duality of "us" and "not-us" has permeated our world and the places we make; this division marks what we attend to and care for, and what we discard and consume. She suggests that this culturally conceived division in Western industrialized societies works to the detriment of ourselves, our places, and other species, and may require a conscientious re-imaging to construct a world less appropriated by humans and more appreciative of many others.

Brill, in "Archetypes as a 'Natural Language' for Place Making," also reaches into human/earth interactions to present a theory/story of the emergence of special places which he describes as "charged." Some of these places are personal, some cultural, and some appear to be species wide, archetypal, and fundamental to the way humans have inhabited the earth and made their places meaningful. He suggests that designers can use an expanded awareness of place archetypes, and demonstrates this process in the design exploration of a burial ground for radioactive waste.

Condon also explores place types through design, using a typology of landscape types he has developed. In "A Built Landscape Typology: The Language of the Land We Live In," the author proposes that built landscapes — that is, human interventions into the found world — express the dialectic between the human need for order and nature's indifference to formal order of any kind. At the approach of the next millennium, we live in a world that has been transformed from mostly found to mostly constructed. Condon explores some of the implications of this radical spatial change for human experience of the world.

The essays in *Part II: Fixing Types* demonstrate ways that Western industrialized societies have developed types and typologies to direct and control social and economic structures locally, nationally, and globally. Dandekar's chapter, "Farm Type in the American Midwest: A Reflection of Government Policy," describes the evolution of U.S. midwestern farms in relation to changes in government policy that both responded to and created market transformations. The place types of farm and farmscape have changed radically in the last 200 years, and are fast disappearing into corporate businesses. They will continue to do so as long as the place types are shaped by current U.S. regulation and the international political-economy.

The creation of zoning by function in the early twentieth century allowed the dominant culture in the United States to protect an ideal of family type. The ideal of a nuclear family was merged with the ideal of a place type — suburban home — and the single-family residential unit was made the "highest" form of use. Ritzdorf, in "Zoning as a Tool for Regulating Family Type in American Communities," elaborates on the development of zoning and the rulings that created the rights of some groups of people to exclude others. Further, she offers suggestions on how zoning and the current patterns of settlement might be transformed in the interest of social justice and the emerging diversity of American families.

King, in "Terminologies and Types: Making Sense of Some Types of Dwellings and Cities," addresses a different form of type fixing in the practices of naming and representing as they occur in the real estate market and urban scholarship in the university. Through an analysis of various texts, among them real estate ads, photographs, and scholarly books, he critiques the socially and politically constructed meaning systems that both represent and transform the material world.

The three chapters in *Part III: Negotiating Type* describe how different interpretations of type come together and how the meanings and uses of types are negotiated by various players both during and after the design and construction of buildings. Markus, in "Social Practice and Building Typologies," examines the relationships among the production of buildings, their use, and the writing of texts about them, all of which are forms of social practice. He argues that the meaning systems of place types are constructed and mediated through language. The language of building types serves to create and maintain commonly understood social relations, particularly important in the rapidly changing and fragmenting world of places in the late twentieth century.

In "Typological Thinking in Architectural Practice," Symes presents three case studies in which different kinds of types common in the professional practice of architecture are negotiated. In one case, he explores the type of method employed in the provision of housing. In another case, the transformation of a known type, the riding stable, to accommodate disabled riders raised difficulties when the client/design team attempted to build maximum flexibility into the design process. In the third case study, it is the type of precedent that is questioned: Is the place being built a clinic or a hospital? Symes's piece illustrates the implications of type and typing for the social enterprise of architecture.

"The Question of Type" by Robinson speaks to the power of typological thinking when type is used as a question in design inquiry rather than as an answer. Type becomes a question when a given type, applied to a specific problem in a specific location, is transformed, or when a new type is required, as in the emergence of group homes. Because architects belong to (at least) two different domains — the profession of architecture and the shared common culture — they use both basic (shared) and classificatory (professional) type systems in their making of places. Treating type as a question can improve architects' ability to understand and integrate the basic cultural system of place types and the more elaborate classification systems of architecture. This will enhance communications between designers and clients, and facilitate the development of new place types.

The chapters in *Part IV: Playing with Type* reveal the fluid conceptualizations of type that occur so often in the making and unmaking of places and in our ideas and images of them. In "An Artist's Perspective on Type," Wolf gives a critique of the last 30 years of architecture, and, through a manipulation of types, questions the vernacular landscape. In text and images, she re-presents the different types of places modern architecture, postmodern architecture, and deconstructivism have imagined and constructed. In her drawings we recognize, sometimes with horror, kinds of places we have occupied and conceptions of the world we hold. Wolf challenges Western industrialized society's creation of a built landscape that is devoid of feeling and discourages human occupation.

La Marche, in his chapter "In and Out of Type," illustrates the many ambiguities and limitations of type and typing both through his own text and through extensive invited commentary from others. By presenting his own short but very dense propositions and initiating an extended conversation with readers, his critical piece becomes a composition of many voices, designed around, and sliding in and out of, ideas of type and typing.

Downing, in "Memory and the Making of Places," explores the many ways that types are framed and used in the design process. By playing with types, and ordering and reordering their memories, experiences, and images, architects form conjectures of what future places might be. Downing suggests that during design inquiry it is this facile manipulation of type through analogous and metaphoric thinking that results in innovation in typing.

Part V: Type in Scholarship offers insights into the ways that type is, or could be, used in scholarly work within the domains of architecture, planning, environmental design, environmental/behavioral studies, and other place-making practices. Each of the authors describes an approach that can facilitate inquiry and subsequent knowledge about type and typing. Francescato, in "Type and the Possibility of an Architectural Scholarship," poses the question, "Can the idea of type suggest which characteristics are unique to architectural knowledge as opposed to knowledge in other domains of human experience?" He answers this question by exploring the nature and methods of the architectural enterprise, the nature of the objects it produces, and the forms of knowledge on which it depends. He makes a plea for an instrumental scholarship in architecture that is grounded in typological thinking.

Using his research on the development of urban rental dwelling units in the French-speaking cantons of Switzerland between 1860 and 1960, Lawrence develops the argument for "Type as Analytical Tool: Reinterpretation and Application." Because type can be considered a corpus of shared knowledge, the analysis of places typologically and historically through a wide array of texts and representations can reveal spatial practices and transformations. These incremental and rapid developments change society's structure of living in and perceiving the world. Type, as an analytical tool, has the potential to uncover social, spatial, and temporal dimensions of the built environment, as well as interactions between these dimensions.

Vernez Moudon presents an overview of typomorphological inquiry as it has developed in the Italian, French, and English schools in this century. "Getting to Know the Built Landscape: Typomorphology" provides a cogent overview of the perspectives and debates in and among these schools. In doing this, the author demonstrates the power of this kind of type analysis to improve our comprehension, and indeed, our construction, of the urban environment.

The last section, *Part VI: Type and Social Practice*, struggles with the uses and abuses of typing as a form of social practice that empowers us to make places but that often, at the same time, disempowers others through processes of exclusion and social control. In his chapter, "Typification and the Building of Society: The Absent Patron," Vanderburgh revisits the proliferation of new buildings types in the nineteenth century at the beginning of modernity. He reconstructs a history of place types framed by an "absent patron" – the newly emerging middle class. He suggests that the concept of functional building types, such as the prison, were attempts to build a society without an acknowledged or traditional center, substituting pattern for patron. The very certainty of the new forms were reassuring to a rapidly transforming society that searched for cues to keep the social order intact by tightly controlling the structure of space.

Friedman, in "Just Not My Type: Gender, Convention, and the Uses of Uncertainty," critiques the convention of type as a device for the conservation of the dominant culture (class, race, gender relations), and recounts a brief history of architecture from the perspective of the location of knowledge as reified by conventions. She then offers two cases in which the convention of gender was disrupted by powerful women clients: Farnsworth as a client of Mies, and Barnsdall as a client of Wright. In these two circumstances, the projects were both successful and unsuccessful, depending upon the perspectives of the viewer. The dislocation of expected types – whether building type, client type, or profession type – offers the opportunity of challenging the dominant social order.

Franck's chapter, "Types Are Us," presents a reconceptualization of type that approximates a mutable web of interwoven form, use, and meaning constellations rather than a fixed container. The process of revealing the current webs of place types and the purposes behind their creation is important intellectual work, as is the work of experimental investigations in art, architecture, and social theory that critique and propose alternatives to our current understanding and making of place types.

The structuring of knowledge about place into varied and complex types is an ongoing conversation about making the world in our minds and on the land. There are no "givens." In this conversation we select diverse and often contradictory aspects of the material, imaginal, and conceptual worlds for attention, deliberation, and possible modification. We hope to offer some insight into the process of place making through a revelation of the scope of this activity. From a reading of this book, it may appear that type is about everything, thus opening the idea of typing to the criticism that if it is everything, it is not useful. We contend that typing is a fundamental human activity that is, indeed, about everything. Therefore, like life itself, it is a profoundly important human enterprise to engage.

□ □ □

We wish to thank all the authors who worked so hard in the creation of this book. Not only did each one prepare a chapter but many read and commented on the work of other authors, as can be seen in the side comments next to the author's initials. We would also like to thank our colleagues and students who have engaged in ongoing conversations and debates about type. Thanks also to Rachel Schneekloth and David Herzberg for their insightful and careful editing. And a thank you to Wendy Lochner of Van Nostrand Reinhold who trusted that this would be a good book and gave us latitude in the preparation of the text.

Chapter 1

Type: Prison or Promise?

Lynda H. Schneekloth and Karen A. Franck

Types organize thinking, communicating, and acting in all domains of life. Types and acts of typing allow us to make distinctions between things and to divide them; they allow us to recognize similarities between things and to collect them. Humans use systems of thought to name and group experiences and objects into loose categories important to their cultures and times. Types and typologies are pervasive constructs that are communicated and reproduced generationally.

The ordering of space into different kinds of spaces is a form of typing that is an intrinsic and constituent part of life in any society and historic period. Place types, like other categories, structure knowledge. Without place types of some kind we could not know or act; we would have no way of recognizing similarities or patterns of differences, or of creating such patterns. We would have no way of structuring space or practices in space.

Spatial structures and our ideas about them constitute a form of knowledge, a way of knowing the world. The power of this knowledge is the power to make, to dwell, to create, to understand, and to transform. Typing as a practice is a profound human enterprise that is as much a part of human cultures as the rituals and practices surrounding the production of food. The ways we produce food – how we organize landscapes to accommodate this form of work (including finding rather than producing food), who is responsible for the activity, what the food is, how the food gets distributed and shared, and where it is eaten – may differ radically across societies. But the spatial structuring of the land to provide sustenance and the social practices associated with its sharing are essential to human existence. Types operate in the same manner. Although the structure of types varies across cultures, the activity of typing frames knowledge and facilitates living within all societies.

A small toddler, just learning to talk, sat on his father's lap while their plane taxied down the runway in preparation for take-off. The two were looking out the window at planes moving along the runway behind them. "Airplane," *the father says.* "Car," *responds the child.* "No, it's an airplane," *corrects the father. Undaunted, because he knows that airplanes fly in the air and vehicles move on the ground, the child repeats,* "car."

Nathaniel, age two and a half, has just arrived in Washington for his first visit to his great aunt's apartment. He is well acquainted with apartments and apartment buildings; he lives in one. While driving by the United States capitol his mother asks,
  "Is that where Mary Averett lives?"
  "No," *he replies without a moment's hesitation.*
  "Why doesn't she live there?"
  "Because it's not a house."
  "What is it?"
  "It's a big building."

Typing enables us to create order in the world and to make sense of our lives as individuals and as groups of people. It is the way we produce and reproduce the material world that we inhabit. Through the process of typing or even the grasping of operating types, we place ourselves in the world and in specific communities of people. And yet, every structure of place type we create to make sense of the world, to study the environment, and to fabricate material places in the world, hides other possible structures and ways of living. We cannot live in ways we cannot order, or in ways we have not yet ordered.

"Knowing" specific spatial practices and their physical manifestations makes it difficult to imagine other ways of typing and living, particularly as we reproduce what we already know and formalize the spatial practices and the place types to support them through policy and legal regulations. We insure that the spatial practices are concretized and almost impossible to change. Further, the power to construct knowledge through typing and untyping is not equally distributed. In these ways, the human enterprise of typing which enables us to understand and make the world also limits and constrains our habitation. This tension is one of the themes of this text.

This chapter introduces the diverse meanings and operations of type and typing presented in this book. Our goal is not to generate a definitive understanding of type as it operates in space and place, or to give a comprehensive overview of all the literature related to type. Rather, our intent is to uncover the variety, multiplicity, and complexity of types and typing. To begin that process, we first explore the location of types in human experience. Place types exist in the material world; they exist imaginally in our aspirations/hopes/fears about the world and our place in it; and they exist conceptually, in our thinking, ordering, analyzing, and reading of the world. We then discuss how place types operate and are operated on: that is, how they are experienced, produced, and reproduced through the activities of occupying, naming, imaging, inventing/modifying, and representing. Finally, we expand the theme of type and typing as both constraining and empowering.

Our motivation for working on this book has been to understand type and typing more fully by inviting others to write chapters, by reading what they have to say, and by pondering the issues ourselves. We wrote this chapter, "Type: Prison or Promise?" after working with the other authors; the ideas and insights in it were developed over the course of reading and commenting on many versions of all these essays. We have tried to craft a book that embraces disparate views and an introduction that points to their differences and their commonalities.

Place Types in Human Experience

When we group places into categories or treat places as members of categories, we are making place types with our minds. We also make place types with our hands and our machines; that is, we physically construct material places that possess the characteristic features of the types in our minds. The physically constructed types are made by human minds, human hearts, and human hands. A place called a "house," even the house I live in, is a mental construct which differentiates it from other aspects of the built landscape. It is also an imaginal dwelling *and* a

1-1
House on Wall Street
(photo by Karen Franck)

material place on the earth that possesses a certain cluster of formal characteristics, meanings, and social practices. Other place types, not physically constructed, are nonetheless mentally and socially constructed so that they too are imbued with imaginal and conceptual content and also possess assigned meanings and social practices. All place types possess some degree of abstraction and embody hopes and fears about the way we wish the world to be.

Thus, place types exist in the material world, and they exist imaginally and conceptually as well. They draw content and qualities from these worlds: they possess material, imaginal, and conceptual aspects. Material types are the socially constructed, usually named, kinds of places we occupy or observe in the world. Imaginal place types, including archetypes and ideal types, are made of words, ideas, and beliefs, representing imagined, remembered, or otherwise cognitively constructed places. Conceptual place types, including classification systems, typologies, and typological analysis, are the intellectual constructs used for description, explanation, and prescription.

1-2 Safiya's Houses (drawing by Safiya; photo by La Tosha Hay)

These aspects of type – the material, imaginal, and conceptual – are not separate; they are part of the same constellation of use and meaning. Any type classification system designed, any new type generated in the built landscape, any accepted type of building endlessly repeated, any policy or regulation developed, and any place found in science fiction all borrow from these three conditions. However, we often address primarily one of these aspects, and only secondarily the other two. A particular example is considered a material type when, in that context and for that purpose, its material aspects are considered most important even though it also has both imaginal or conceptual content. In another context and for another purpose, it may be treated as an imaginal or a conceptual type. For ease of discussion, we treat these aspects as three different kinds of typing, while recognizing that the categories of material, imaginal, and conceptual are not pure or independent. Instead they reflect differences in the orientation and focus of the activity we are pursuing, and reveal which aspects are receiving our attention and consideration.

What is of interest to us are the ways in which material, imaginal, and conceptual aspects of type intersect to form meanings and spatial practices. Some of the authors in the book offer the premise that our ideas emerge from our experience of the material world and our continual interaction with it. Brill, Schneekloth, and Condon attempt to demonstrate how it is *from* this condition of being in the world that we construct imaginal and conceptual types, such as archetypes and a typology of landscape types, and reproduce certain kinds of landscape spaces. Others, such as Franck, Markus, and Vanderburgh, work to uncover the ways that material types are organized by and into conceptual types to protect humans from too much meaning, from contradictory meanings, and in some cases, from each other. These systems of typing are never neutral – some groups of people benefit and others do not.

Many of the authors start with type as a conceptual system that structures the world into categories or classes. These categories and classes are reinforced in various domains such as architecture, real estate, scholarship, land use policy, and regulation. The fabric of the material world, the world described by Lawrence historically and by King through real estate listings, is framed, limited, contested, and transformed by the mental categories into which we place the actual artifacts. The meanings associated with dwelling types or class differences layer material existence with imaginal aspects. The meanings are further reproduced through the conceptual categories of type into which the artifacts are placed. Systems of type, often presented as value-free systems, are actually built on imaginal constructs formed of the hopes and fears of peoples and eras. These constructs often serve to maintain power relations, to support certain economic and political structures, and to structure the use of public space, that is, who uses it and how.

Each of the chapters, although entering the discourse of type through the imaginal, the conceptual, and/or the material aspects of type, demonstrates how these aspects intersect, often in invisible ways, to make a certain perspective appear "true" or appropriate.

Material Aspects of Type

Material place types, or the material aspects of types, exist in the world of matter. Many, but not all, material place types are physically produced through fabrication or some intervention in the landscape: soccer field, national park, city, school, bedroom, farm, street, and lighthouse are examples. Wolf's *Perfect Order* on the cover depicts material place types at different scales: suburban, downtown, and urban residential neighborhoods; park, highway, single-family houses, and office buildings. Other material place types, such as forests, deserts, rivers, and prairies, are socially constructed and materially present, but not physically constructed by humans, although they may be physically maintained.[1]

Because material place types have names, meanings, and uses associated with them and because they often embody meanings and beliefs, they have much imaginal content. They also belong in the conceptual domain because they are often designed, constructed, and regulated, and their practices prescribed.

Material place types are probably the most widely recognized and commonly used categories of places among professionals and the public. They are the ones we all observe, occupy, and refer to in conversation. Because these types are so widely understood, at least within a given culture, architects and others are able to converse with clients about the kind of place they wish to construct, modify, purchase, preserve, and so on.[2] Material place types are often called "functional types" or "building types," although this term excludes many landscape types such as forest and meadow, and places that are not enclosed, such as highways and gardens.

1-3
"The Covenant,"
Jeffrey Fama, 1993

1. See Wilson (1991) for a presentation on the transforming culture of nature; Harrison (1992) about the role of the nonhuman world in the construction of western culture; Merchant (1989) for an analysis of the ecological transformations that occurred in the United States with the advent of Europeans; and Jackson (1984) on the American vernacular landscape.

2. Robinson, Downing, Symes, and Franck all address the ways that types are (1) employed as general cultural categories commonly shared among members of a society, and (2) developed and used by designers.

1-4
Field
(photo by Lynda Schneekloth)

It is likely that in all cultures at all periods people have distinguished different kinds of spaces or places in the landscape and have assigned different uses and meanings to those kinds. The world is thus spatially and socially structured or mapped. In most societies, physical interventions are made to support particular activities and meanings in particular kinds of places. These interventions can be slight or transitory, as among Aborigines and nomads, or extensive over time and space as in the construction of Hagia Sophia, Hoover Dam, the pyramids, or New York City. In all cases, space is organized by category and therefore into categories. Even where there is little or no intervention in the landscape, assigning meaning and possible uses to a certain kind of place is the social construction of a type, as is the creation of a "national forest," a material place type as much as a church is. Material place types, like all types, are inventions, even when the subject matter of their invention is found in the world.

Today most material place types are complex social, economic, cultural, and physical constructions.[3] Almost all of the places we occupy are the result of some physical intervention in the landscape. Today, as before, the material place types created by a society represent and reproduce the dominant order and values of that society at that time. Material place types are created or modified to shape people's activities, relationships, and beliefs in particular ways, and to further particular values and interests.[4]

Imaginal Aspects of Type

Woven into the social and physical construction of material types are imaginal types. Imaginal types are in our minds, hearts, and senses; they are often represented and approximated in the world but they do not exist materially. We cannot physically construct or physically occupy imaginal types, although there are many material places that approximate imaginal types and may be viewed or treated as examples of them. Or, conversely, perhaps we *only* occupy imaginal types since there is no human habitation without interpretation.

Material places can be like imaginal types but they cannot be identical with them. Frontier, utopia, the American Dream, Dante's inferno, the ideal home, and my memory of my childhood neighborhood are imaginal places, as are heaven and hell. Each of the material types depicted on the cover of this book does exist in the world, but this particular exaggerated arrangement of them — this perfectly ordered city — does not exist. At the same time, the image depicts a significant and powerful imaginal type of place that guides contemporary planning and zoning of cities.

---

3. The social production of material place types is a growing field of research. Notable works are King's anthology (1980), Hayden's history of feminist designs of U.S. homes and neighborhoods (1981), Cranz's history of U.S. parks (1982), Cromley's history of New York apartment buildings (1990), Jackson's history of suburbs (1985), and Horowitz's history of some campuses of U.S. colleges for women (1984).

4. Researchers are exploring the social, cultural, political, economic, and technological forces that shape the design and use of the built landscape. One of the clearest and most succinct case studies of such forces is Silverstein and Jacobson's (1985) study of the supermarket.

Recently, more attention is being given to the political and economic interests that material place types serve. Barna (1992) looks at the corporate architecture of Texas in the 1980s; Zukin (1991) looks at several built landscapes around the United States; and Vale (1992) focuses on the urban design of Third World capitals. Sorkin (1992) and Davis (1990) discuss different parts of the contemporary U.S. landscape of malls, suburban subdivisions, gated communities, and corporate enclaves.

Imaginal place types significantly influence beliefs and actions regarding material places. We may seek out or create material places that approximate the imaginal place and occupy or treat material places as if they were, indeed, the imaginal place. We often imbue material places with meanings and associations drawn from imaginal places so that we experience the place both materially and imaginally. Imaginal places may be represented in images and text so powerfully that they inspire the subsequent creation of material places. Edward Bellamy's city in *Looking Backward* ([1888] 1983) inspired the establishment of many utopian communities. Le Corbusier's 1925 *Plan Voisin* and other drawings influenced the design of a generation of housing developments including Coop City and Lefrak City built in New York in the 1960s. Bentham's Panopticon as the ideal institution was referred to again and again in the design of prisons that were built in England, the United States, and France. The frontier in J.F. Cooper's novels helped spur the westward flow of Europeans across the American continent.

Imaginal types, including ideal types and archetypes, reflect one of the earliest meanings of the word type:

> Originally, the way *typos* was used in Greek gave it the meaning of an empty or hollow form for casting… From the beginning of its use by Plato and Aristotle the word had a sketchy, incomplete relief or outline character that emphasizes a visible shaping quality rather than a sharply struck definition (Hillman 1980, 6).

Further,

> The very impurity of types in experience therefore necessitates "ideal" types which are not intended to be evidentially verified, but which are required as purely imagined backgrounds for understanding human experience… The act which forms an ideal type is a *Wesenschau*, an insight into essence, and not a statistical averaging (norms) or a logical reasoning (classes) (Hillman 1980, 7).

"Ideal types" appear in architectural discourse, particularly in reference to the idea of paradise or the hut and the temple.5 Imaginal or ideal types may prefigure or inspire the design of actual places, but the quality that the imaginal and the actual places share is not exact. The imaginal cannot be copied; it is more general, more elusive. In describing the arguments made by Quatremère de Quincy in the eighteenth century, Vidler writes that "Quatremère posited the notion of the *ideal* type, never realized, never tangibly visible, and never to be slavishly copied, but nevertheless the representative form of the principle or idea of the building" (1977, 105). It is precisely the elusiveness and potential richness of ideal types that makes them such potent sources for making and interpreting the world.6

Material types may serve in design or other creative endeavors as subject matter for the creation of imaginal types (as in Wolf's *Perfect Order*), just as imaginal types serve as subject matter or inspiration for the creation of material types. Thus imaginal and material types can act as generators: the type becomes a seed, the origin of something else. It transforms into another type, another thought, an action. Type suggests, expands, grows beyond itself. This aspect of types has been noted in architecture. Eighteenth-century theorists "were referring not simply to a designation, a static classificatory term but rather to an active principle, a mode of design in itself…" (Vidler 1977, 99). In psychology, Hillman notes that Jung did not intend his system of personality types to be used as a classification tool but as a critical tool, an "explanatory basis and theoretical framework for the boundless diversity" (1980, 23).

Several contributors to this volume explore imaginal types and their connections to material types. Schneekloth uncovers the fundamental, although changing, distinction that is made between *us* and *not us* and the beliefs that currently accompany this division. This distinction generates imaginal types that frame our understanding and experience of the world and helps shape the material place types we create. Brill draws upon the idea of archetype and archetypal experience to describe the essential qualities and mythic themes of material places. In examining the design process of architects, Downing describes their use of remembered and imagined places and shows ways in which the imaginal in architects' minds shapes the making of actual places. Wolf's essay and her art suggest the kinds of images architects have seen and drawn upon over the past 30 years, resulting in significant changes in the design of material types.

The layering and framing of the material world by and through imaginal content is both enlarging and delimiting. Our experience of the world is made richer and more compelling by the hopes, desires, fears, and wishes we hold.7 Yet

---

5. See McClung (1983) and Rykwert (1972) for the role of these imaginal archetypes in the history of architecture.

6. In his chapter, Francescato explains several important implications of Quatremère's thinking for understanding the value of the idea of type as a composite of form and function.

1-5
Erie Beach (photo by Lynda Schneekloth)

7. See for example Bachelard (1969), Tuan (1974), Berman (1989).

8. Schneekloth, Brill, and Wolf speak to this condition and its alternatives.

in the contemporary built landscape we have created many sterile and standardized places that do not resonate with the imaginal aspects of our being. We have reified a false separation between the "objective" and the "subjective" so that both the material world and the imaginal become depleted by our attempted severance of their interconnections.[8]

Imaginal types can also become quite singular and controlled, and work to protect us against other imaginal types. Franck demonstrates how the idealization of separation between different kinds of users and uses has helped generate the highly segmented and segregated environments of contemporary life represented in Wolf's drawings. The ideal of separation serves as an imaginal type that guides, and constrains, our making and experiencing of the material world. Once the material version of imaginal types become codified into law, the possibility of realizing other versions or other imaginal types becomes even more limited, as Ritzdorf shows in the zoning of the single-family neighborhood in the United States, which enforces a single idealization of the American house and the American family.

Conceptual Aspects of Type

Professionals and academics in many fields perform intellectual work around and upon material and imaginal place types. We organize and present information about them and we classify them for the purposes of description, explanation, or regulation. We create abstracted versions as ideas or as analytic models to help describe and explain, or as prototypes to be copied. Concepts of place types — individually, in loose collections, or in systems called typologies — are the intellectual constructs we develop to do this work. The particular structure for thinking about type we offer here, as well as categories of land use in a zoning ordinance, the identification of archetypes and housing types, and discourses on the idea of type in architecture, are all about conceptual aspects of type.

The purposeful development and use of classifications to categorize and compare items mark a self-conscious attitude toward types. These conceptual types and systems of types based on empirical criteria are a fairly recent invention in western society, beginning in the seventeenth and eighteenth centuries when taxonomies were first used in the natural sciences (Foucault 1970). These systems posited clearly defined and mutually exclusive classes. The intention of this kind of typing is not to describe the essence of the items in the class, as ideal or imaginal types do, but to describe their relationships to each other, to items in other classes, and to the criteria of the classification system (Schneekloth and Bruce 1989).

It was also during the eighteenth century that such self-conscious and empirically derived classifications were adopted in architecture. In 1771 Blondel listed the major building types of the period and their programs — theaters, halls for dancing and festivities, fountains, exchanges, baths, slaughterhouses, etc. — and designated the appropriate "character" for each (Vidler 1977). Following Blondel, J.N.L. Durand developed techniques of descriptive geometry allowing him to move beyond a descriptive classification of building types to analyze their significant similarities and differences (Vidler 1977).[9]

Durand introduced the possibility of using type as a means of analysis. Abstracting particular features from a set of material types allows the analyst to focus on specific generalizable characteristics of material places, to present and compare those features in a generalized and standardized way, and to ignore other features — to do typological analysis. Since Durand's teaching and his 1801 book *Recueil et parallèle des édifices de tout genre, anciens et modernes*, architects have made much use of this and other techniques for analyzing the spatial and formal features of place types. Currently architects use typological analyses to understand and to compare existing buildings, to design future buildings, and to understand changes and continuities in building and settlement types over time.[10]

The opportunity that typological analysis offers to abstract information from empirically observed cases can help reveal commonalities and differences that were not previously apparent. Hillier and Hanson (1984) have developed diagramming techniques that uncover spatial relationships in buildings that are not immediately apparent through observation of the buildings. Both Markus and Robinson employ this kind of diagramming method in their chapters. Moudon describes other methods used in Italy, France, and England for analyzing buildings and settlements together. The spatial, functional, managerial, and cultural characteristics of building types and their interactions can all be studied together as they change over time, as Lawrence demonstrates.

Robinson, Moudon, Lawrence, and Francescato all suggest that design researchers would do well to employ various systematic methods in their intellectual work for conceptualizing and analyzing material place types. This would not only be valuable for guiding and enriching research, it would also make the findings more accessible to architects and other design professionals who orient much of their work around material, imaginal, and conceptual types.

Durand's classification of building types in 1801 was not only descriptive; it was also intentionally prescriptive. It was to be a guide to how buildings should be designed: they should follow the prototypes he presented. The imperative to map elaborate classifications onto the landscape was reinforced with the development of many new building types in the nineteenth century. As suggested by Vanderburgh, many of these types and the classifications they embodied responded to the spatial anxieties of the middle classes, intent on creating and maintaining spatial practices designed to control, remove, and protect.

Today all kinds of explicit and systematic classifications and accompanying requirements prescribe and regulate the development, use, and appearance of material types. These classifications are mapped onto the landscape, resulting in predictable, controlled types of places. This is done through zoning ordinances, building codes, regulations on historic preservation, financial and government policies and programs, and architectural programs for buildings. For instance, the midwestern farmscape takes much of its pattern from the division of townships and sections of land into plats of fixed size that were codified by Congress in the 1780s (Dandekar).

Classifications often have a significant and influential imaginal content that is not immediately apparent. The way academics classify cities is guided by very influential Eurocentric assumptions (King). The typologies prompted by Durand and other French theorists assumed and reinforced the continuation of conventional social, including gender, relations (Friedman). Many building types developed in the nineteenth century enforced and protected class relations, confirming the social standing of the middle class (Vanderburgh). This continues today in land use planning and development that attempts to enforce particular patterns of gender and class relations.

9. As pointed out by Lavin (1992, 238), even though Durand did not use the word "type" but rather *genre* or *species*, the use of the word *type* in reference to categories of buildings and their functions is traced to him. Pevsner's (1976) history of architecture organized into such categories continued that tradition, as he himself noted. Much of the research in architecture and environmental design is now organized by building type.

10. See, for example, Sherwood (1978); Glassie (1975); Holl (1980); Polyzoides, et al. (1992); Tice (1993); and Moudon (1986).

Architects and others engaged in the designing and building of places refer to myriad classifications in their work. As illustrated by Symes's case studies, the design process is often a series of choices and negotiations revolving around selections from different classes of material types. Classifications referred to by professionals in the design process, which Robinson calls "classificatory types," may confuse clients, thereby generating difficulties for responding to their needs. The line between classifications for description versus prescription is indistinct and changeable. Even when conceptual types are ostensibly intended exclusively to describe, they exert a powerful influence on the actions we take regarding the places so described. Technical classifications of types used by architects to make choices in turn generate particular configurations and features of the material types they design.

The landscape of material types generates conceptual types and, conversely, the conceptual types generate the material world and our spatial practices in it. What Markus has said of the space of buildings is also true of other spaces in the landscape: they are embodiments of classification systems that organize objects, people, and activities (1987, 467). These systems are presented linguistically in written texts that describe or prescribe spaces and their relationships (Markus). Written texts that classify and describe places are provided to assist the public in finding places for services and entertainment, for visiting, for renting or purchasing property, and so on. The many classifications we all refer to in daily life are not neutral or inconsequential any more than the technical classifications used by architects. Their content, wording, and organization, as well as what they exclude, reinforce existing material and imaginal place types and the dominant social practices of our society.[11]

We know about the world because of type and typing, and the intersection of material, imaginal, and conceptual aspects embodies knowledge about the world. Our power to generate and transform knowledge about ourselves and our relationship to the landscape and each other lies in our ability to work with, operate on, modify, and transform all these aspects of type.

Type Operations

We think, conceive, represent, and talk of places in and through categories, and we fabricate, occupy, and regulate places in categories as well. We find ourselves in a world of existing types that frames the way we see, experience, imagine, and produce the world. In other words, types operate through us. But at the same time we actively operate on types when we interact with, accept, challenge, transform, make, and unmake them. The work in this volume illustrates at least five different ways that imaginal, conceptual, and material types operate in our society: through (1) occupying, (2) naming, (3) imaging, (4) inventing and modifying, and (5) representing.

Occupying

We live *in* the world, we inhabit spaces, and we make places. Our knowledge and understanding of our lives, as individuals and groups of people, start with our experiences in the world, mediated and interpreted by others. We are grounded in our physical occupation of space, and we carry on activities and make meaning out of the fabric of our habitation.

The designation of different kinds of places, of place types, emerges from our occupation of them: certain kinds of places are best for carrying out certain kinds of activities and are not so good for carrying out others. For millennia, places in the landscape have been distinguished for qualities that make them good places for fishing, for growing crops, for seeking refuge, for a lookout point, for dwelling during particular seasons, for burial, for special ceremonies, and so forth. The uses and meanings of many kinds of places are codified in religious practices, written laws, and regulations.

Physical interventions are made in the landscape to mark places and to support the activities associated with them. In doing this, societies have produced a vast array of specialized building and settlement types. These place types, just as the field or the good place to gather nuts, are generated from (and designated by) the activities or spatial practices associated with them. The most fundamental way we produce and reproduce place types is by occupying them, by pursuing particular spatial practices in particular kinds of places.[12]

---

11. One interesting example is *Places: A Directory of Public Places for Private Events and Private Places for Public Events* by Hahn and Stoumen (1991).

12. Within the academic domains of planning and social theory "space" has been reintroduced in an attempt to understand modern and postmodern spatial practices. See Sorkin (1992), Jameson (1991), and Lefebvre (1991), among others.

Spatial practice is not only the pursuit of an activity such as planting crops, taking a walk, or worshiping a god; it is also the manner of doing so. That includes who does it, the specific pattern of actions and interactions in space, the objects used, the timing, and so forth. The places we physically construct are designed to support these culturally defined practices. While many activities such as producing food have always been present, the spatial practices for doing so often change significantly. As Dandekar demonstrates, radical changes have occurred in the ways that crops are grown, stored, and marketed in the midwestern United States, and the farmscape has changed accordingly to sustain these new practices.

Spatial practices do not always require specialized types to support them. For some cultures or during some periods, caring for the ill did not take place in a building type designated solely for that activity. Eventually, a place type that we now call "hospital" evolved for housing the activity. Over the past two centuries, the spatial practices associated with caring for the ill have changed and the design features of hospitals have changed accordingly (Forty 1980). Other spatial practices, such as watching a movie from your car, may decline in popularity or profitability. Drive-in theaters are torn down and the land redeveloped, or they are transformed into flea markets or other marginal uses.

As our ways of occupying the world change, so do our interventions in the landscape and the place types we physically construct. At the same time, however, practices and meanings can change without significant physical changes in place types. Often spatial practices associated with a given place type are changed temporarily to accommodate radically different needs. A school may be used as an emergency shelter after a hurricane, or a street may be closed to traffic to be a farmer's market. When the links between the physical features of place types and their uses and meanings are loose, they can accommodate emergency, temporary, or transforming human needs.

The designation or construction of places for particular activities is usually made by agents with the political or economic power to do so. Today many of these decisions about what place types shall be created and how they shall be designed or used are regularly contested by the public and by special interest groups. These conflicts make it very clear that spatial practices constitute social/political/economic life. In reproducing spatial practices, we are continually making a specific form of social order that privileges certain practices and place types and neglects or restricts others. If people's actions conflict with the meanings and uses prescribed by the dominant social order, they are viewed as disruptive of that order and the actions may be curtailed or forbidden.

The Laws of Enclosure and the struggle that followed in sixteenth-century England resulted from changing economic conditions which made it profitable for the landed gentry to raise sheep instead of subsistence crops. They no longer required serfs on the land to do this work, and the new laws passed insured that people were moved off the land into the cities to fuel the new industrialization. The Robin Hood stories embody the radical transformation of spatial and social practices occurring at this period in history.

1-6
Outhouse
(photo by Tony Holmes)

Occupying places in ways that conflict with the dominant uses and meanings of place types is often used as a form of resistance, as in political and religious demonstrations, sit-ins, and urban insurrections. Conflicting interpretations of acceptable spatial practices in particular place types are frequently heard in the courts over issues such as the right to beg on subways, the right to proselytize in bus stations and airports, and the right to demonstrate in front of post offices or in front of a person's home.

1-7
Home for the Houseless (photo by Gwen Howard)

The use of the name of one material or imaginal place type to describe the qualities of another may become so common as to alter its meaning. Recently the New York Zoological Society decided to omit the word "zoo" from the name of all its facilities in New York. They are now to be called "Wildlife Conservation Parks" in order to avoid the secondary meanings of zoos as places that are confused and disordered, and to communicate the new purpose of conservation rather than display.

When homeless people live on the street, in train stations, or build shacks in parks or under bridges, those places become their homes as they sleep, wash themselves, and store their belongings there. Since these uses are not intended for these place types, regulations are created to inhibit or forbid the spatial practices of "domestic life" in "public" spaces (more type designations). Restricting sleeping on benches (or removing the benches), and forbidding the building of shacks, are ways spatial practices in place types are regulated to maintain the existing social order. The occupation of space is not uncontested; it is often differentially interpreted, acted upon, and enforced. Place types are both the subject and the tool of these actions.

Naming

Place types are also made by naming material and imaginal places, and by labeling the categories of place types. When naming a place type we give it meaning by suggesting the formal characteristics and the spatial practices it accommodates; in doing so we also limit the potential for other meanings and practices. The name given to a place type shapes our images of it, how we create or modify an actual place to match the name, and how we occupy it or otherwise interact with it.

The proliferation of the modern high-rise office tower was not only dependent on scarce urban land, appropriate technology for construction, and uses that could occupy such space, but also on the power to *name* the space, the era, the form, and the spatial practice. Often the naming, or the meaning of the name, is a gradual invention as the material place is developed over time. The emergence of the apartment building in New York City in the last century as a place of residence for middle class families demonstrates the evolution of a place type and the narrative of its name (Cromley 1990).

Frequently the names of imaginal place types are used to describe the qualities of material places. The Lower East Side of Manhattan is often called a "frontier," which suggests that newcomers are "pioneers" settling a dangerous, if not hostile, territory (Smith 1992). The names of place types are very useful and provocative in this regard: they generate, with one word, all kinds of images and information associated with one place type, now applied to another, analogously or metaphorically. The power of the names of place types to generate a host of information and images is crucial to the design process and to communications between architect, client, and others engaged in planning and building places (Downing, Symes, Robinson).

When we occupy a place, its name and the meanings attached to the name shape our understanding of the spatial practices that are appropriate. This is well illustrated in adults' admonishments to children when they explain the appropriate behavior for a given place type. "Shh, this is a... (church, hospital, library). You must be quiet," or "Don't ride your bicycle in there! That's a garden." The name of a place type can be changed, and accordingly new spatial practices adopted, often with little or no modification of the physical features of the place. Spatial practices may also change while the name remains the same. For example in the nineteenth century, before the advent of many public parks, cemeteries were the sites of picnicking, promenading, and other leisure time activities. The links between the name, the spatial practices, and the material aspects of place types are not tight or fixed (Markus, Lawrence, Franck).

When a place has no name to designate its type, there may be confusion or lack of consensus on how it is to be used. Its use and meaning may be contested with little opportunity for the dominant social order to determine the spatial practices that will serve that order (until they name it or change it). The wide open space surrounding apartment buildings in public housing projects in the United States is one example of a nameless place. Although it once included playgrounds and parking spaces, between these named places are large stretches of anonymous space with no clear intended use (or name).[13]

The naming of place types inscribes a social order onto the landscape. Markus writes that the consistency of the meaning of the names of building types over time provides one reliable way to make sense of the many new, and otherwise confusing, types that are emerging. King also sees naming as a way that we secure a sense of order in an increasingly disordered world, but also points out that the naming may be an unreliable ordering that misrepresents or distorts existing circumstances, as in the naming of different types of cities.

The creation of a new type name for a category of existing places, such as "edge city" (Garreau 1991) or "defensible space" (Newman 1972) can serve to identify features of these places that previously had not been noticed or understood. The names and the concepts they stand for then become the grounds for subsequent debate, analysis, and new social and physical constructions. Similarly, in promoting the adoption of a new place type, naming it in a way that captures its features in an accurate but also compelling way is important. One example is the term "cohousing" for a form of communal housing that originated in Denmark (McCamant and Durrett 1988). A new name frames new ways of seeing, under-

1-8
Inside/Outside
(photo by Karen Franck)

Overheard in a NYC train station:

"Well, what if we've made a mistake and this is not a station? What if it's really a mental ward and these are patients? The chairs are the same and look how weird everyone looks. And there (pointing to the ticket booth) is the nurse's station."

"Or, it could be a restaurant."

"That too, but where are the waiters?"

A colleague asked, with some annoyance, if "imaginal" is in the dictionary. This is one example of using a word that is not widely adopted to capture ideas and meanings that are otherwise elusive. Someone, somewhere, invents words to frame emerging ideas and practices. Some are quickly adopted such as Ms., cohousing, defensible space.

standing, and imaging the world. The conservative nature of language, that it changes slowly, is an anchor in our making meaning of the material world. It is also a constraint. Without new or modified words we may limit our ability to portray new or different imaginal, material, and conceptual worlds.

Imaging

We picture material and imaginal places in images in our minds. These images are fueled not only by our own experiences of places, but also by the representations of these places in religion, art, literature, and popular culture. Images of place types may lead us to seek out or create actual places that resemble the image, and the image of the place may significantly affect our experiences of place. In fact, place images are so strong that they sometimes supersede the actual experience of place, or form a pattern we constantly seek to reproduce in our living in the world. The ability to have common images, such as an image of suburban living, is crucial in the ability to actually make places, such as "suburbs." Hillman writes:

> Now by imaging a type in our minds, instantly the type moves into images that display it. Instead of our having to multiply instances to prove the type, the type multiplies images out of itself… types have now become empty casting molds, out of which a pattern of images flows, and the mind, by generating examples, moves from type to image (1980, 23).

The connection between type and image is very close. In describing the design process in architecture, Schön refers to this same highly generative aspect of types, to "their fullness, the richness of imagery, ideas, and common places associated with them" (1988, 183).

Designers and others responsible for the making of places have large repertoires of images that they call on when they are engaged in placemaking because their task is to make something that does not yet exist. As Downing describes, architects transform the images they have in many different ways to address the design problem at hand. Often these images are then represented in drawings and models and become actual, material places; sometimes they do not. But all of us have place images that guide our daily spatial practices like buying a home, rearranging the furniture, or choosing flowers for the garden. All of these activities depend to some extent on imaging a place that does not (yet) exist and transforming the world into the place of our image.

1-9
Outside/Inside
(photo by Karen Franck)

The name or other representation of a type generates images that are connected somehow to that type for an individual, group, or society. In recognizing that a particular place is an exemplar of a given type, we are matching the example with our image of the type. "We see types by seeing images; or rather, when we see a type, actually we are seeing an image" (Hillman 1980, 16). Sometimes a given, material place does not match the predominant or conventional image of that type; this may leave us confused or disappointed. Dandekar, for instance, describes how the farm buildings designed today to meet the requirements of agribusiness and its spatial practices do not conform to the traditional images of midwestern barn and silo. As new place types are invented, as the design of existing ones change substantially, or as new architectural styles emerge, our repertoire of images for identifying place types is caught short and we may be uncertain what type these places are (Markus).

Inventing and Modifying

Although humans are born into communities of people who have established patterns of spatial types, the uses and meanings of types and the distinctions between them were, and are, invented, passed on, modified, and discarded by cultures. Even as we live in the world as we find it, we also engage in a continuing process of inventing, modifying, and reinventing the physical world, both in our imaginations, and in our thinking and studying the world.

---

13. In his chapter Lawrence notes the evolution of a similar, unnamed type of space in rental housing in Switzerland.

Acts of ordering and reordering the world into different categories are acts of invention that can have radical implications for how we structure the material world and our spatial practices in it. Within a society, material place types are invented and developed to accommodate a particular spatial practice, or to support a social structure or stratification that is perceived by some to be a social good, at least for some members of the group. Once the landscape has been structured to support certain practices and certain interests, or building types have been adopted to support a certain stratification, it can be very difficult to question or to change this order and the assumptions behind it. For example, one of the most difficult landscapes to transform is the ubiquitous parking lot, once people become habitual users of it.

Similarly, imaginal types that evolve can be difficult to uncover and modify (Schneekloth) as are conceptual types (King). Although types and the way they structure the material, imaginal, and conceptual worlds are cultural inventions, they become so deeply embedded in our lives and environments that we may simply assume that they constitute the only way, or the best way, of ordering.

That the meanings and uses of place types also change over time points to their malleability and negotiability.[14] Indeed, at times we seek to invent a new type to accommodate a newly recognized social need. The recent proliferation of group homes for previously institutionalized people was a conscious invention of a place type. This place type continues to evolve and to be modified as arguments continue about what is a "normal home" (Robinson). At the same time that we create a new type such as a group home, we will probably find that these "new" types maintain the same kinds of distinctions and separations between types of people that began with the proliferation of new building types in the eighteenth and nineteenth centuries (Vanderburgh, Franck). They continue the imperative to create ever finer social and spatial distinctions.

Some of the forces that shape the invention and modification of material types are explored in this book: radical changes in class structure at the dawn of modernity (Vanderburgh); market forces and the commodification of space (Franck); changing government policy, agricultural methods, technology, and market forces (Dandekar); changing therapeutic philosophies (Robinson); changing architectural styles (Wolf); and changing intellectual discourses (La Marche). Authors also point to recent changes that could generate new or modified types: a more ecologically thoughtful perspective (Schneekloth), changing gender relations (Ritzdorf, Friedman), and increasing awareness of the inadequacy of mutually independent categories (Schneekloth, Franck).

A very significant part of intellectual and academic practice is the invention, modification, and critique of imaginal and conceptual types. In this book, for example, each author describes the constituent elements of her or his respective concept of type. In some instances, possible applications of type in research, scholarship, or design are presented. There are critiques of the conceptual types now in use, and a questioning of the very act of ordering. Other authors posit imaginal types as the foundation for our apparently technical rendering of the world into typologies with the aspiration of better understanding typing and our experience of the world. All of this is hard intellectual work: we struggle with how and what to order while we also do the ordering; and simultaneously we live in a world that is itself ordered in multiple, complex ways. Our intellectual practices engage, invent, and modify the world as surely as does the decision to invest in suburban shopping malls over urban main streets.

The arguments that rage over the most appropriate structure of knowledge are often arguments of type and typologies. These debates range from discussions of the most appropriate societal response to problems of deviance to discourses on the relative merits of formal versus functional type categorizations. Some of the responses authors have made to each other's chapters in this book illustrate substantial differences in opinion of how best to conceptualize and to apply ideas of type in understanding and studying the world.[15] What one author sees as valuable and significant, another author may view as trivial, obvious, or misguided. These conversations show very clearly how important the position of the categorizer is in shaping the categories he or she generates and advocates. Types and type systems are selected, invented and/or modified for the ends they serve, whether they privilege material, conceptual, or imaginal aspects. And we are necessarily invested in those ends.

14. See chapters by Robinson, Vanderburgh, Markus, Lawrence, Franck, and La Marche for discussions of the negotiability and malleability of type.

15. See particularly comments in chapters by Brill, Markus, Symes, La Marche, Francescato, and Franck.

Representing

Place types are also produced and reproduced through the representation of material and imaginal places in words, images, and fabrications. Representations in drawings, diagrams, sketches, models, text, film, video, and in the design of places are a significant part of the process of typing. How places are re-presented can significantly influence subsequent choices and actions.

Representations are forms of power in that they influence others. This occurs when an architect seeks to convince a client that this particular scheme is the most appropriate response to their program. It occurs when realtors describe properties in text and photographs. It occurs when fashion designers seek to sell clothes by presenting them in exotic far-off places in their advertisements. Power companies, including the nuclear industry, try to convince people that they are ecologically minded by showing us pictures of beautiful landscapes in their advertisements. And the representations of the city in the media contribute to the anti-urban bias of the United States and the continual disinvestment in the cities in favor of suburban living. The list is endless.

Representations and images operate in tandem. Images of paradise are portrayed in the ongoing evolution of the garden place type. Archetypal images continue to dwell in our minds and souls and we seek to reproduce them – at times even by creating places for non-habitation through the representation of a place as forbidden (Brill).

The relationship between building type and image has been a frequent topic in architectural discourse from the eighteenth century until today. The concern has often been that buildings, through their outward appearance, should convey their intended uses and meaning, that the image they create should portray what building types they are. Sometimes, however, image takes precedence over all else and the connection to the purpose or context of the building is lost. Goode (1992) argues that in the United States, postmodern architecture's preoccupation with image has neglected and distorted the other aspects of type and typological theory as it has evolved in Europe. Types are seen and treated *only* as image, and as singular images at that. Buildings are presented as isolated architectural objects with no social or architectural context. This single and superficial interpretation of type as merely image is a useful marketing device. During the early 1980s,

> the imagery of plazas and arcades was appropriated as an instrument of representation by architects in the service of the developers and corporations who are the real shapers of the American City. Such imagistic appropriation masks the role of space as an instrument of control, social stratification and exclusion (Goode 1992, 8).

Wolf's drawings of building facades that lie around like so many stage sets depict the postmodern preoccupation with, and abuse of, image.

1-10
Photomontage, Martha Rosler, 1993

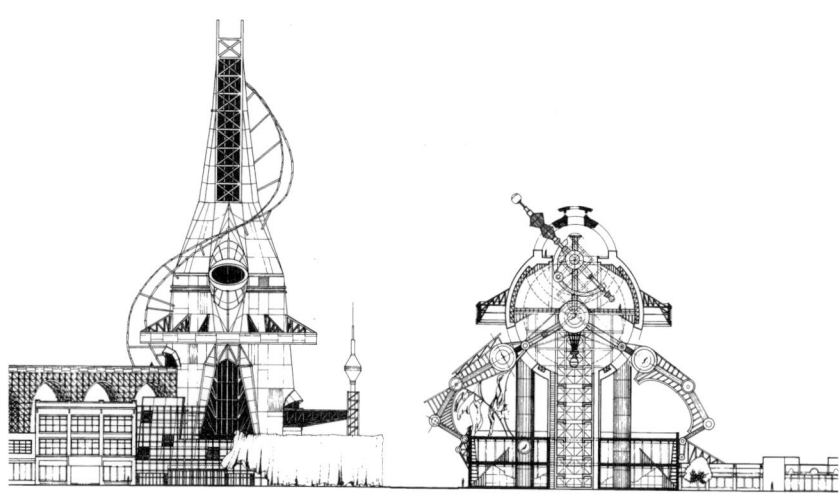

1-11
Main Street, Alan Makalinao, 1993

Representations of place types can be seductive and misleading. They are also instructive: we learn from written and visual representations. Sometimes what we learn from a representation, the meanings we glean, were not intended by its maker. In fact, many messages in representations are below levels of consciousness, or offer dominant cultural norms without a conscious intent. For example in advertisements, the intent may be to sell children cereal, but the presentation of the mother in the kitchen doing the serving carries messages of proper gender roles in addition to the instruction about why this cereal is better than any other.

Representations offered to uncover hidden beliefs are a form of critique because they expose the underlying messages that are not intended to be openly read. The particular reading of science fiction described by Schneekloth, and the images created by Wolf and Rosler (Figure 1-10), reveal circumstances that exist in our material world that we may not *see* because they form the media of our culture. The use of various forms of representation to bring our attention to, and therefore our questions to, these beliefs is an act of resistance.

Representation, a powerful tool of critique, also powerfully re-envisions present places and potential places. Architects, landscape architects, and urban designers have this power – to re-present to us both what is in the world that we had not noticed or appreciated and to present to us what is possible for the future. This ability, and obligation, needs to be more fully acknowledged and more widely employed.[16] As Pignatelli observes,

> Architects ought to be the Masters of Imagination, that is, of the capacity of grasping the value of phenomena, the inner trends of collective conscience, the capacity of proposing new images of and for the town (1985, 42).

In some instances, representation as critique and proposition by architects may have no specific client and no real world problem or project posited by a client.[17] Sometimes such works are dismissed as "paper architecture" or architecture that is not "social." This reading denies the power of the imaginal; the images and text can reveal aspects of our own material, imaginal, and conceptual worlds and their intersections that we had not seen or thought about before. Visionary drawings, imaginary clients and programs, and dramatic narratives and characters tell us much. Indeed, they reveal as much as scholarly research and other more conventional methods of discovery precisely because they are attuned to, and use, the imaginal aspects.

The Prison *and* The Promise

Type is enormously useful. It explains the world to us, it makes sense for us. And it does this, usually, without our having to think about it: we accept knowledge of the world structured and interpreted through type. Type is suggestive rather than true. This is its power, but also its problem. We assume truth, and we assume agreement when, in fact, this is not in the nature of typing nor of the struggle to form and change spatial practices.

---

16. For example, in working with citizens groups to develop a "vision plan" for the city of Des Moines, Iowa, Diana Agrest and Mario Gandelsonas discover aspects of the city which they point out to residents who then *see* their city in new ways. The architects then propose various ways of transforming what is there. See also *Roanoke Vision: Comprehensive Development Plan for Roanoke, Virginia, 1985-2005* (Buckhurst Fish Hutton and Katz 1985).

17. Recent examples include Spiller Farmer Architects (1990), Nesbitt (1991), Woods (1992), and Darden (1993).

"Oh, you're doing a book on type. Are you for it or against it?"

1-12
House mailbox
(photo by Tony Holmes)

18. These contrasting meanings of type as essence and type as class appear in the earliest discourses on type in architecture. Whereas Quatremère de Quincy adopted a view of type as essence, Durand approached type as class (Mead 1983). These two views continue but may not be clearly distinguished and, more importantly, may often merge.

Still living in the modern period, however, many people expect some definitive understanding that is rationally derived and can be widely agreed upon. We have been asked why, if we have been working so many years on this topic, we don't yet have a definition of type. And we have also been told, repeatedly, "That is not type, that is… (metaphor, building type, life)." These comments reveal the underlying modernist assumption that type is only one thing, and often a static, imprisoning thing at that. This perspective in itself is an act of typing, where the mutually exclusive categories – pro-type and anti-type or type and not-type – become the prison.

But it is in the very nature of type and typing that they are many things and take on various, contrasting meanings and uses. Types are essences and classes; the boundaries between types may be open or closed; types are universal and culturally and time bound; they fix and control while they are fluid and changeable. One of the prisons we create and inhabit is an intellectual one: expecting and searching for fixed, clear, and separable definitions and applications of type and typing where, instead, we could recognize and value their variable and contrasting meanings and uses.

Closed and Open Boundaries

Type as a way of thinking is appropriate to the task of world making because typing as an activity and type as a form of knowledge are impossible to confine. Their fluidity and ambiguity defy definition. Type can refer to ways of structuring the built landscape where the boundaries are blurred and categories overlap. These type categories are fluid, the embodiment of essence, often emerging from the experience of the world, and respecting differences and overlaps in specimens. Other systems of ordering such as "class" are formed for specific purposes and accommodate an "either/or" designation. These types are more highly defined and idealized, a system against which specimens are compared.[18]

Within the discourse of place types, many types of type operate in the structuring of the world. Some types, such as the imaginal types of archetypes and ideal types, partake very much of essence and ambiguity. Yet when they are made manifest in the world in conceptual systems or in endless repetition of the same material types, they often take on more of the features of classes. Indeed, one might say that building types are a blending of type as embodiment of essence and type as class.

Type is almost entirely classlike in building codes, zoning ordinances, and government programs where the categories of place types are highly defined and independent. Because of these features, it is difficult to introduce a new type/class into the regulatory structure without affecting the entire typology since the structure is already a system whose rules include all built form. It is intended that every piece of land be named in a zoning plan; no building can be constructed that does not fit some designation.[19] Design guidelines and policy recommendations are more loosely structured; some things are allowed to remain slippery and uncategorized because they are perceived to be relatively unimportant, or perhaps so well understood that they need no explanation.

The condition of open borders between types in some practices facilitates the gradual transformation of one type or the borrowing of some aspects of an existing type in the making of a new place type. For example, the recent introduction of the "industrial campus" represents such a borrowing where the setting type of the university has been used without the accompanying social practices. The condition that incidences within a type share some qualities but do not have to be alike in other ways permits evolution and gradual change. Each specimen can be a little different from the next until the type becomes something else. The transformation from the Victorian vertical house to the suburban ranch style demonstrates how changes in some elements over time (amount of land, transportation infrastructure, government policy, verticality, size, methods of production and construction, etc.) create a new thing, a new place type. Further, each type — police station, strip development, park, frontier — carries meanings that overlap with other types. These shared meanings may be called forth, or ignored, depending upon one's purpose. Transformations often occur when a different set of meanings is emphasized or when an unusual type designation is made. Within the design disciplines, place types are appropriately ambiguous and new types are easily introduced for discussion and experimentation. Exercises for students often use emerging type, mixed type, or no type programs to encourage students to question the mindless reproduction of the existing built landscape.

Stable and Changing, Universal and Different

Types contain or collect to themselves *and* they generate and grow beyond themselves. Type as holder/collector gives us continuity, predictability, and a sense of stability. Type as generator becomes the origin of something else; a thought, an action, another type. Here type is dynamic; it suggests and expands. Type is probably always both container and generator, but, depending upon how types are used, they can become more of one than the other. Type as holder/container gives us named and recognizable building and landscape types that allow us to know what should happen where and how to be. The imaginal type of the American Dream of a privately owned home is a holder/collector, providing a kind of unifying theme in this culture, a shared idea. At the same time, it is also a generator, stimulating thoughts and actions, highly amenable to all kinds of manipulation.[20] And over the years this imaginal type has been the generator of different kinds of material place types called houses.

That types and their naming provide stability, some continuity, and a continuing frame of reference is important. It may be that some types, such as archetypes, are timeless and species wide. And, at the same time, types also change over time, varying considerably between cultures and between different groups within the same cultures. Depending upon what kind of type we are considering or what features we address, we can point to continuity and universality or to change and difference.

Repressive and Transformative

Typing is powerful and flexible, pervasive and useful; it enables our comprehension of, and living in, the world. But type thinking is also a prison that limits our inhabitation. Too often we forget that type is a constructed overlay on the world, that we (or others) made it and thus remake the world everyday. We assume that our accepted and reified structure of types is somehow "real" and we are therefore unable to restructure the world to support alternative visions of human culture. Although types are being used all the time to further specific goals and interests that we may seriously question, we are neither sufficiently aware of this process nor do we make effective use of types to reach alternative goals and serve other interests. While changes in types can be transformative, supporting a more socially just and ecologically sound world, the changes can be, and often are, repressive and unjust.

Fixing the inherently ambiguous boundaries of type through codification and reification can cause problems. As these boundaries become institutionalized

---

19. The recent introduction of "multiple use" buildings into the codes is an interesting case that starts to push at the underlying system of categorization by function.

20. See Dovey (1993) for a discussion of how archetypes are manipulated in the making and marketing of new housing.

1-13
Waste treatment plant
(photo by Lynda Schneekloth)

In response to a proposal to slow down traffic on a residential street in the city and make it safer for children who play in and near the streets, the Traffic Engineer replied "But streets are for cars, not for people."

21. The role of the imaginal, as represented in novels, on the making of the material places, is explored by Bender (1987) in *Imagining the Penitentiary: Fiction and the Architecture of Mind in Eighteenth Century England*. The portrayal of the material *and* the imaginal as represented in novels is explored by Chandler (1991) in *Dwelling in the Text: Houses in American Fiction*.

22. Architects who are planning and designing alternatives to the post-World War II suburb are doing precisely this. See the work of Duany and Plater-Zyberk (1992), Solomon (1992), and Calthorpe (1993).

through policy and legal structures, regulation and land use controls, and religious beliefs and mythic structures, places become only one thing and are no longer able to sustain other forms of spatial practices. The knowledge that is embedded in place types and typing becomes frozen and the places and social practices become difficult to unmake and remake. Types then become highly restrictive, resistant to change or transformation, indeed a prison that does not invite, or even permit, alternatives. This is true of imaginal, material, and conceptual types. Thus, the material form of the imaginal type called "highway" has become fixed and regulated: its material version has precise and limited characteristics, restricting our legal (and our imaginal) ability to realize this archetype in other forms.

To transform material place types, we need to recognize their connections to imaginal types. In the modern world of "facts" (surely an imaginal world if there ever was one), we have not realized the power of imaginal types to frame the world, and to give us meaning. Place types embody myths and identities we seek to reproduce. We need to discover what the imaginal types are and how they operate.[21] The power of imaginal types is evident in the works of utopian thinkers and science fiction writers and in the visionary drawings of artists and architects. To make a new world one must make a different place.

The "American Dream" has been interpreted and reproduced all over the United States in a single type – suburbia. It has been built as predominantly single-family, detached houses in purely residential settings, separated from all other land uses, forcing a dependence on cars and limiting our ability to use any other modes of transportation, including walking or bicycling. The suburb is a place of physical and psychological safety, the house in the garden. It is also a place of exclusion and its proliferation across the landscape is ecologically very costly. The materialization of the dream doesn't work nearly so well as it does in the miniaturized Main Street of Disneyland, the imaginal collage of the American psyche. Further, the type, suburb, is only one possible manifestation of the American Dream. To construct alternatives we must understand the power of this imaginal fiction and the hopes and fears embedded in it. It is quite possible to make places that realize the dream in different ways and to do so may not require changing the imaginal content. There are also other imaginal types, such as town, that can be drawn upon to develop alternatives.[22] For a type to be transformed, both critique *and* proposition are required. Fortunately, it is precisely around type in its material, conceptual, and imaginal aspects, that such work is possible and valuable.

TYPE: PRISON OR PROMISE? 33

New Work on Type

Type is emerging as a serious subject of inquiry and debate as part of the deconstruction of the edifice of modernity, just as it was a serious topic at the dawn of this era.[23] It is argued that the conscious employment of type is part of the old "new world order" that began with the Enlightenment and industrialization, now under siege. What is powerful and wonderful about the current intellectual work on type is that we are beginning to understand a little more about type as a form of knowledge, about the role it plays in human experience, how it operates, and about its power to make and unmake spatial and social practices.

Within the messy terrain of praxis the work of the world gets done. We acknowledge that type contains and limits our making of knowledge about and action in the world, and yet often we don't attend to the ways in which types are generated and used in place making. The world of practice has not been seen as a legitimate arena for inquiry because of its typological assignment as the place where knowledge is "applied," which is far less important than the place ("science") where it is generated. The expansion of the concept of knowledge to include practice offers new insight into the process by which places are made and judgment exercised in selecting types for production. This work is, in fact, a form of knowing and constructing knowledge. We know so little about how types are constructed and created; that is, the processes by which we incessantly reproduce the world without consciously constructing or deconstructing the types we are using.

Typing is inherently a reductive process. We take particular discrete places, ideas about places, and fantasies about places, and select and discard aspects of them. Without this editing, types could not exist. The naming of something is an act of power; it calls forth something out of the world, a place or kind of place, as different and distinctive. The naming constructs a concept, a bundle of intersecting meanings and conditions into a thing that we can know while it excludes bundles of other meanings and possibilities in the process of collecting and separating.

The types that a culture invents and passes on and the names it uses to do so reflect and reinforce its stance toward the world and humans' place in it. We live in a culture that is preoccupied with nouns and naming things. In contemporary western society, the typing we do by naming removes places from their embeddedness in the world and creates a distance between us and our sensual experience of the world. Sardello describes it thus:

Another culture's system of typing can make us much more aware of our own. Robert Pirsig, in his novel, Lila: An Inquiry into Morals *(1992) describes four people, among them John, a Native American, walking down the dirt road, when "one of those raggedly nondescript dogs that call Indian reservations home came onto the road and walked pleasantly in front of them. They followed the dog silently for a while...*
"What kind of a dog is that?"
John thought about it and said, "That's a good dog" (Pirsig 1992, 465).

"None were left now to unname, and yet how close I felt to them... They seemed far closer than when their names had stood between myself and them like a clear barrier..."
(Le Guin 1986, 193).

23. *Type and the (Im)possibilities of Convention* (Rockcastle 1991) has many excellent essays. For additional discussion of the idea of type in architecture see also Argan (1963), Vidler (1977, 1987), Moneo (1978), Coloquhoun (1981), Morris (1982), Pérez-Gómez (1983), Oeschslin (1986), Goode (1992), Lanvin (1992), and Tice (1993). Aldo Rossi's buildings and writings have also been influential.

"An anima mundi *perspective begins by calling attention back to the 'great repressed'... the things of our industrial world as well as to the things of nature. After this re-calling, this re-specting, comes the development of a pluralistic listening through which we are imaginatively taught by the things themselves" (Bishop 1988, iii).*

Nominalism [naming with nouns] affects language by reducing words with inherent power to implements of the mind, to concepts – purely subjective realities... Noun language does defend us against the display of colors, edges, curves, surfaces, hardness, softness, gloom or brightness, fixity, texture, gravity, working in combination and discombination, piling on top and alongside each other making thing as image (1985, 29).

In typing, late twentieth-century modern, postindustrial countries assign a passive role to world. Our culture deanimates things, denying the active participatory role played by the world in our construction of it. Sardello calls it "a cultural repression" (1985, 30). The representation of the world as the passive container of human drama is a fiction of modernity and industrialization which requires the unlimited use of the earth to fuel progress.

Within the places, ideas, and hopes that are discarded or ignored in the naming of types lie unexplored ways of knowing and living. The conscious exploration of type recognizes the power of typing as the unraveling, weaving, and reweaving of the web of the world. Typing the world can be a collaborative activity in which many perspectives, including the world itself, participates.

□ □ □

Type will always be a prison and a promise because it will always be open and closed at the same time. While attending to some things we will find ourselves not attending to others. Each closure opens something new, each understanding contains the ground that slips away. Typing limits change and this is good; typing limits change and this is bad. Types change often without attention to the implications of those changes, such as the human and ecological cost of making the American Dream in suburbia. Typing empowers groups of people, as with the emerging type of community-based group homes. And types serve powerful interests as with the designation of "urban enterprise zones" which often ignore the existing social and spatial practices of marginal groups.

In bringing the implicit values, forms of knowledge, and concepts to explicit levels of discourse, we hope to open a space for dialogue about place types and their meanings in diverse communities. We can negotiate and transform the world through these conversations.

1-14
Clearing on Madelaine Island
(photo by Lynda Schneekloth)

The world – our material, conceptual, and imaginal constructions of it – is the place of dwelling; it is the ground within which we try to place ourselves, to make sense of our lives. The ongoing discourse of typing is of cosmic importance because it is about finding a way to understand the place of humans in the world, and at the same time, finding ways to live wisely in the world of streets, gas stations, forests, fields, and homes.

Some of the figures used in this chapter represent work done by students under the direction of Karen Franck or Lynda Schneekloth. "Safiya's Houses" (Figure 1-2), is taken from the term paper, "City: Friend or Foe" by La Tosha Hay for the course "Architecture and Social Change," NJIT, 1993. "The Covenant," by Jeffrey Fama (Figure 1-3), was done in a graduate architectural studio at SUNY/Buffalo, 1993. "Home for the Houseless" (Figure 1-7), is a part of a Master's Thesis in the Department of Architecture, SUNY/Buffalo by Gwen Howard, 1993. And "Main Street" (Figure 1-11), is a drawing by Alan Pena Makalinao for his Master's Thesis, Department of Architecture, SUNY/Buffalo, 1993.

References

Agrest, Diana and Mario Gandelsonas. 1994. *Agrest and Gandelsonas, Architects*. New York: Princeton Architectural Press.

Argan, Guilio. 1963. On the typology of architecture. *Architectural Design* December: 564-5.

Bachelard, Gaston. 1969. *The Poetics of Space*. New York: Beacon.

Bandini, Micha. 1984. Typology as a form of convention. *AA Files* (no. 6) May: 73-82.

Barna, Joel. 1992. *The See-Through Years: Creation and Destruction in Texas Architecture*. Houston, Tex.: Rice University Press.

Barth, John. 1988. *The Floating Opera and the End of the Road*. New York: Doubleday.

Bellamy, Edward. [1888] 1983. *Looking Backward*. New York: Bantam Books.

Bender, John. 1987. *Imagining the Penitentiary: Fiction and the Architecture of Mind in Eighteenth Century England*. Chicago: University of Chicago Press.

Berman, Morris. 1989. *Coming to Our Senses: Body and Spirit in the Hidden History of the West*. New York: Bantam Books.

Bishop, Peter. 1988. The soul of the bridge. *Sphinx 1: A Journal for Archetypal Psychology and the Arts* (London).

Calthorpe, Peter. 1993. *The Next American Metropolis*. New York: Princeton Architectural Press.

Chandler, Marilyn. 1991. *Dwelling in the Text: Houses in American Fiction*. Berkeley, Calif.: University of California Press.

Colquhoun, Alan. 1981. Typology and design method. In *Essays in Architectural Criticism*, by A. Colquhoun, 43-50. Cambridge, Mass.: MIT Press.

Cranz, Galen. 1982. *Politics of Park Design*. Cambridge, Mass.: MIT Press.

Cromley, Elizabeth. 1990. *Alone Together: A History of New York's Early Apartments*. Ithaca, N.Y.: Cornell University Press.

Darden, Douglas. 1993. *Condemned Building*. New York: Princeton Architectural Press.

Davis, Mike. 1990. *City of Quartz: Excavating the Future in Los Angeles*. New York: Verso.

Dovey, Kimberly. 1993. Dwelling, archetype, and ideology. In *Dwelling*, ed. R. Mugerauer, 9-21. Austin, Tex.: University of Texas Press.

Duany, Andres and Elizabeth Plater-Zyberk. 1992. The second coming of the American small town. *Wilson Quarterly* Winter: 19-48.

Durand, J.N.L. [1801] 1982. *Survey and Comparison of Buildings of all Types*. New York: Princeton Architectural Press.

Forty, Adrian. 1980. The modern hospital in England and France. In *Buildings and Society*, ed. A. King, 61-93. London: Routledge & Kegan Paul.

Foucault, Michel. 1970. *The Order of Things*. New York: Pantheon Books.

Franck, Karen and Sherry Ahrentzen, eds. 1989. *New Households, New Housing*. New York: Van Nostrand Reinhold.

Garreau, Joel. 1991. *Edge City: Life on the New Frontier*. New York: Doubleday.

Glassie, Henry. 1975. *Folk Housing in Middle Virginia: A Structural Analysis of Historic Artifacts*. Knoxville: University of Tennessee Press.

Goode, Terrance. 1992. Typological theory in the United States: the consumption of architectural "authenticity." *Journal of Architectural Education* 46 (1): 2-13.

Hahn, Hannelore and Tatania Stoumen. 1991. *Places: A Directory of Public Places for Private Events and Private Places for Public Events.* New York: Tenth House Enterprises.

Harrison, Robert. 1992. *The Forest: The Shadow of Civilization.* Chicago: University of Chicago Press.

Hayden, Dolores. 1981. *The Grand Domestic Revolution: A History of Feminist Designs for American Homes, Neighborhoods, and Cities.* Cambridge, Mass.: MIT Press.

Hillier, Bill and Julienne Hanson. 1984. *The Social Logic of Space.* New York: Cambridge University Press.

Hillman, James. 1980. *Egalitarian Typologies Versus the Perception of the Unique.* Dallas: Spring Publications.

Holl, Steven. 1980. *The Alphabetical City.* New York: Pamphlet Architecture.

Horowitz, Helen L. 1984. *Alma Mater: Design and Experience in the Women's Colleges from Their Nineteenth-Century Beginnings to the 1930s.* New York: Knopf.

Jackson, J.B. 1984. *Discovering the Vernacular Landscape.* New Haven: Yale University Press.

Jackson, Kenneth T. 1985. *Crabgrass Frontier: The Suburbanization of the United States.* New York: Oxford University Press.

Jameson, Frederick. 1991. *Postmodernism, or the Cultural Logic of Late Capitalism.* Durham: Duke University Press.

King, Anthony D., ed. 1980. *Buildings and Society: Essays on the Social Development of the Built Environment.* Boston: Routledge & Kegan Paul.

Lavin, Sylvia. 1992. *Quatremère de Quincy and the Invention of a Modern Language of Architecture.* Cambridge, Mass.: MIT Press.

Lefebvre, Henri. 1991. *The Production of Space.* Cambridge, Mass.: Basil Blackwell.

Le Guin, Ursula. 1986. She unnames them. In *Hear the Silence: Stories by Women of Myth, Magic and Renewal,* ed. Irene Zahava, 192-4. Trumansburg, N.Y.: Crossing Press.

McCamant, Kathryn and Charles Durrett. 1988. *Cohousing: A Contemporary Approach to Housing Ourselves.* Berkeley, Calif.: Habitat Press.

McClung, William Alexander. 1983. *The Architecture of Paradise: Survivals of Eden and Jerusalem.* Berkeley, Calif.: University of California Press.

McLeod, Mary. 1984. Review of *The Architecture of the City* by Aldo Rossi. *Design Book Review* Winter: 49-55.

Markus, Thomas. 1987. Buildings as classifying devices. *Environment and Planning B: Planning and Design* 14: 467-84.

Mead, Christopher. 1983. Buildings of all types: Jean-Nicholas-Louis Durand. Review of *Survey and Comparison of Buildings of all Types* by J.N.L. Durand. *Design Book Review* Summer: 12-15.

Merchant, Carolyn. 1989. *Ecological Revolutions: Nature, Gender, and Science in New England.* Chapel Hill, N.C.: University of North Carolina Press.

Moneo, Rafael. 1978. On typology. *Oppositions* 13: 23-45.

Morris, Ellen K. 1982. Architectural type and institutional programme. *Journal of Architectural Education* 35 (2): 17-25.

Moudon, Anne V. 1986. *Built for Change: Neighborhood Architecture in San Francisco.* Cambridge, Mass.: MIT Press.

Nesbitt, Lois. 1991. *Brodsky and Utkin.* New York: Princeton Architectural Press.

Newman, Oscar. 1972. *Defensible Space.* New York: Macmillan.

Oechslin, Werner. 1986. Premises for the resumption of the discussion of typology. *Assemblage* 1 (October): 37-54.

Pérez-Gómez, Albert. 1983. *Architecture and the Crisis of Modern Science.* New York: Cambridge University Press.

Pevsner, Nicholas. 1976. *A History of Building Types.* London: Thames and Hudson.

Pignatelli, Paola C. 1985. The dialectics of urban architecture: Hestia and Hermes. *Spring* 1985 (Dallas, Tex.): 42-45.

Pirsig, Robert. 1992. *Lila: An Inquiry into Morals.* New York: Bantam Books.

Polyzoides, Stefanos, Roger Sherwood and James Tice. 1992. *Courtyard Housing in Los Angeles.* 2d ed. New York: Princeton Architectural Press.

Relph, Edward. 1987. *The Modern Urban Landscape.* Baltimore: Johns Hopkins University Press.

Roanoke Vision: Comprehensive Development Plan for Roanoke, Virginia 1985-2005. Prepared by Buckhurst Fish Hutton and Katz with Thomas and Means and Margaret Grieve. Roanoke, Va.: Office of Community Planning.

Rockcastle, Garth, ed. 1991. *Type and the (Im)possibilities of Convention.* Midgård Monographs of Architectural Theory and Criticism 1 (2). New York: Princeton Architectural Press.

Rossi, Aldo. 1982. *The Architecture of the City.* Cambridge, Mass.: MIT Press.

Rykwert, Joseph. 1972. *On Adam's House in Paradise: The Idea of the Primitive Hut in Architectural History.* New York: Museum of Modern Art.

Sardello, Robert. 1985. Saving the things or how to avoid the bomb. *Spring* 1985 (Dallas, Tex.): 28-41.

Schneekloth, Lynda H. and Ellen Marie Bruce. 1989. Building typologies: an inquiry. In *Proceedings: EDRA 20,* eds. G. Hardie, R. Moore, and H. Sanoff. Oklahoma City, Okla.: Environmental Design Research Association.

Schneekloth, Lynda H., Marcy Feuerstein, and Barbara Campagna, eds. 1992. *Changing Places: ReMaking Institutional Buildings.* Fredonia, N.Y.: The White Pine Press.

Schön, Donald. 1988. Designing: rules, types, and worlds. *Design Studies* 9 (3): 181-91.

Sherwood, Roger. 1978. *Modern Housing Prototypes.* Cambridge, Mass.: Harvard University Press.

Silverstein, Murray and Max Jacobson. 1985. Restructuring the hidden program. In *Programming the Built Environment*, ed. W. Preiser. New York: Van Nostrand Reinhold.

Smith, Neil. 1992. New city, new frontier. In *Variations on a Theme Park: The New American City and the End of Public Space*, ed. Michael Sorkin, 61-93. New York: Noonday Press.

Soja, E. 1989. *Postmodern Geographics: The Reassertion of Space in Critical Social Theory*. New York: Verso.

Solomon, Daniel. 1992. *Rebuilding*. New York: Princeton Architectural Press.

Sorkin, Michael, ed. 1992. *Variations on a Theme Park: The New American City and the End of Public Space*. New York: Noonday Press.

Spiller Farmer Architects. 1990. *Burning Whiteness, Plump Black Lines*. London: Penna Press.

Tice, James. 1993. Theme and variations: a typological approach to housing design, teaching and research. *Journal of Architectural Education* 46 (3): 162-75.

Tuan, Yi-Fu. 1974. *Topophilia*. Englewood Cliffs, N.J.: Prentice Hall.

Vale, Lawrence. 1992. *Architecture, Power, and National Identity*. New Haven, Conn.: Yale University Press.

Vidler, Anthony. 1977. The idea of type: the transformation of the academic ideal, 1750-1830. *Oppositions* 8 (Spring): 95-113.

Vidler, Anthony. 1987. From the hut to the temple: Quatremère de Quincy and the idea of type. In *The Writing of the Walls*, by A. Vidler, 147-64. New York: Princeton Architectural Press.

Wilson, Alexander. 1991. *The Culture of Nature*. Toronto: Between the Lines.

Woods, Lebbeus. 1992. *The New City*. New York: Touchstone.

Zukin, Sharon. 1991. *Landscapes of Power: From Detroit to Disney World*. Berkeley, Calif.: University of California Press.

Part I

SPECIES TYPING

Chapter 2

Notions of the Inhabited

Lynda H. Schneekloth

Humans structure the world in a fundamental way by making a boundary between *us* as human beings, and *the other,* that is, the things that we make, the places we inhabit, and the world-as-given. This fundamental typological distinction between us and not-us not only structures the material world, but frames the way we think about and re-present this world. The boundary secures us, places us in our habitats; it infuses the world and us with meaning.

Out of the *not-us*, we construct place types which give purpose and meaning to the nonhuman world, places such as nature, city, house, farm, toxic dump, wall, power plant, or outer space. Some place types support human activities such as agriculture, dwelling, and waste disposal. Others refer to the things and the devices we use to make places, such as walls and bridges, or to the technologies we have created to extend ourselves into the world, like electricity or institutions. Some place types are said to be natural and therefore "given;" others are artificial, meaning we perceive them to be constructed by us – our creations. Places, the material world, and our beliefs and fictions about them, are locations of inhabitation for our species.

The names we create for places call forth the *other*, meaning the *not-us*, situating the places, the namers, and the relationships that bind them. This suggests that type names embody self/place relationships. The characteristics assigned to

2-1
Sarah's front porch, Monteverde
(photo by author)

places – habitable or uninhabitable, civilized or primitive, sustaining or threatening – separate and connect us to our places. Types tell us as much about ourselves as they do about the world because each *other* constructed by us locates not only the place, but us. Further, and importantly, each name refers not only to the possibility of physical inhabitation, but always to an imaginal dwelling, that is, the thinking, dreaming, and re-presentation of being in the world.

Even as the self/place distinction orders the world to support our human dwelling, the boundary shifts. What is included as *us* is transformed in different times, reflecting different beliefs of the place of humans in the world. And place types, the typology of which further structures and names the world, carry diverse meanings across, and even within, one culture. The meanings are constructed and used with different intention. In this sense, they are not "true" or "real" descriptions of the world; instead they are re-presentations of the world that reveal bounded times and places. Place types are particular truths that belong to particular people and serve the purposes of cultural ideologies. They are noninnocent ways of organizing the world, however broadly we draw the circle around the *us*. Yet, in spite of their constructed and located specificity, place types carry mythic power because they embody shared beliefs, values, and information that are tacit.

The power to construct place types sets the boundary of us/place relationships in the imagination of given times through the process of inclusion and exclusion. And because of this power to structure cultures and individual lives, place types are always contested and problematized. Today, the struggle over the us/place boundary is evident in the ongoing discourse about the relationship of humans to "nonhuman nature." The current paradigm has placed us over, above, and outside the rest of the universe. The fiction that humans stand apart and are superior to all *others* in the world has enabled us to appropriate freely and colonize the earth through destruction and consumption, even if we acknowledge that human beings are utterly dependent on the gifts of the sun, water, and plants. The effect of this particular story – the world as *not-us* – has evolved and dominated western thought. It has been disastrous for the nonhuman world, and as is now being revealed, for our species as well.

The mythology of humans as somehow separate from the world is being challenged by the science of ecology, the environmental and green movements, and fantasies presented in diverse representations of the late twentieth century. Every day the texts of our times – newspapers, television, radio, films, books –

2-2
The Concrete Central Peninsula, an abandoned industrial wasteland, Buffalo, New York
(photo by Per Pederson)

MB: *As you set out your argument for the non-innocence of type and boundaries, it is one that for many readers may be new, and shocking in the sense that it reorders (or de-orders) their world. Without any examples (of, say, a type that is a "particular truth" serving a "particular cultural ideology") you ask the reader to accept a strongly argued position, without permitting them much of an "Oh, I see what she means."*

LS: *Mike, you are right. I am asking people to accept the idea that type is non-innocent without any evidence, and that may be asking a lot at the beginning of the chapter. But because this idea is central (especially the particular "truth" about what is "us" and what is "not-us"), and is developed throughout the chapter, I hope the readers will, as Coleridge says, "suspend their disbelief" until they get into the chapter.*

HD: *For the 1,000-plus-acre potato farmer from Michigan, the perception of land as just one of the several "factors in production," co-equal with labor, capital, and technology, fits with the mind-set described here. It liberates such farmers to move to another location when the profit equation does not work out. This is in stark contrast to the postures of subsistence farmers from a village I have studied in some detail, in Maharashtra, India, who will not exchange an eighth of an acre of ancestral land even though the exchange would give them better quality or contiguous land parcels that would be easier to cultivate. To them, their land is primordial to cultivation, and particularized, specific in its relationship to each farmer, his family, and his ancestors.*

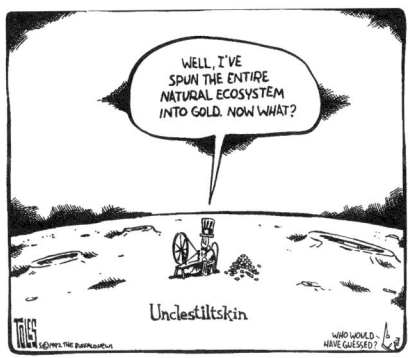 

2-3
Cartoons challenge our cherished myths about the place of humans in the world.
(courtesy of Tom Toles and *The Buffalo News*. Cartoons originally appeared April 24, 1990 and May 31, 1992.)

"From its beginnings, science fiction has been the mythic vehicle of one particular culture, the rational, materialistic, weigh-and-measure, science-and-technology minded culture that has arisen in Europe and America since the Renaissance — so-called modern Western Civilization" (Panshin and Panshin 1989, 3).

"Opposition is not enough. In that vacant space after one has resisted there is still the necessity to become — to make oneself anew" (hooks 1992, 51).

remind us of the destructive effect we are having on the earth as habitat. The actions that led us to this condition are not, in one sense, the evil deeds of amoral people so much as they are the ongoing practices of people acting from within the dominant cultural story which assigns meaning to the boundary between us and not-us. The urgency and strength of the current struggle over this boundary suggests that we are renaming our relationship with the world, and that a different boundary will frame a new fiction for the next century.

As part of this discourse, this chapter seeks to explore underlying beliefs about the *not-us* that structure the way we think about places. The practice of constructing and reproducing place types materially and imaginally creates fantasies of the world and our place in it. These are powerful fictions, stories that reveal beliefs that engender and hold truths. They frame the activities of humans in the world.

Our various acts of representation in the arts and other media reveal stories about place types — which are really stories about us. In this inquiry into the construction and deconstruction of us/place relationships and place types, I will be using the genre of science fiction. Science fiction is often located outside legitimate forms of representation because it contains popular rather than elitist fantasies of the world and popular forms of representing it, forms rich in their construction of places. In this form of fiction we create worlds, homes and frontiers, and *others* to which we must relate. This type of representation is a powerful device for seeing ourselves and our habitats; it provides us with dreams and nightmares of what our dwelling might be(come).

In this chapter I am using science fiction because it both reflects and challenges our beliefs about us/place relationships. I seek to uncover the ways in which we have constructed places as locations of domination and destruction, *and* to explore ways of representing human/place relationships differently. The construction of imaginal fictions engenders new beliefs and the possibilities of new relationships. It is an act of resistance and empowerment, and opens the possibility for a location more appreciative and less appropriating of all others. This ongoing activity, remaking and renaming the world and our relationship to it, is of intense and urgent interest for our species and our place in the world.

Homelessness and the Ravaged Earth

Human beings evolved on this earth, and, to the best of our knowledge, have always lived on this planet; our imagination springs from our experiences in this world, and our very lives depend on the earth for sustenance. Therefore, to make the claim that the human species is homeless reveals that our living on the earth, our inhabitation, is somehow damaged:

> Provided human society does not lose its memory in the meantime, the last decades of the twentieth century will one day be remembered as among the most critical in history – a time when humanity as a whole was violently projected into a new, utterly divergent, millennium. The scale of the transformations we are witnessing today has no precedent either in natural or cultural history. The global uprooting of both nature and humanity makes each and every one of us a refugee of sorts. How long we will remain refugees on earth no one can say, but the fact of homelessness has by now become obvious even to the most privileged or protected members of the human family (Harrison 1992, 238).

In many science fiction texts, humans are represented as homeless either through the total destruction of the earth, for example by aliens to make room for an intergalactic highway as in *The Hitchhikers Guide to the Galaxy*, or by humans who now live on a ravaged and threatening planet as in the *Road Warrior* films. Our myths and fictions, whether couched in the language of heaven, other planets, or the frontier, locate *elsewhere* as the place to be and remove us, figuratively, from the places where we now find ourselves.

This condition, this imaginal homelessness, has resulted from many forces working over centuries beginning with the removal of the soul, the immanence, from the earth and the displacement of the god(s) from the world in all material things to the heavens (Giegerich 1985). This was a beginning of the leaving of earth in western culture and the displacement of desire to heaven – an early frontier of our imaginal inhabitation.

As God was removed from the earth, the soul of the world was endangered. The invention of "life" in the sixteenth and seventeenth centuries dealt the final blow to an animate world (Foucault 1970). Until this time, the earth was commonly understood to be immanent, alive, and all of the world to have soul includ-

MB: *Isn't the reverse as true (that our experiences in this world spring from our imagination)... in fact, doesn't much of your discussion about structuring a world through naming and through imagining suggest that?*
LS: *Yes, both are true – our imagination springs from our evolutionary and personal experiences of the world, and the world(s) we live in is/are the world(s) of our imagination. These ideas are not oppositional, as they might be framed in some discourses, but rather depend on each other. We simultaneously are dependent on the world, and the world we inhabit is dependent on our construction of it.*

2-4
The historic Fisherman's Wharf Building being demolished in Buffalo, New York
(photo by author, 1993)

MB: *This "de-animating" of the world and its places is certainly being contested through recent conjuring of "spirit of place," "genius-loci," explorations of affective places (including despair), and Jungian analyses of home and person. In our desacralized world, these probes into "re-animation" do not seek to reanimate all the world in the archaic way, with a spirit in every rock, but only certain places. Perhaps this is an attempt to create "difference," the precondition for a world that can have sacred places because it has profane ones. But to have a healing, we need to see the sacredness in the profane, and to care for it all. Some of our vernacularists and appreciators of commonplace landscapes help us see this wider embrace.*

LS: *As you suggest, the consciousness of an animated world really never disappeared from our culture, even when logical positivism and rational thinking were most dominant. There has always been an oppositional voice that has refused to be disconnected, refused to forget the shadows, and some very interesting work is being done, as you mention, in understanding the sacred of the every day. Yet we remake beliefs and ideas to suit our era, make truths convenient to a time. For example, when you suggest that those probing this idea don't reanimate "all the world in the archaic way," you are pointing out a boundary critical to our culture. We call a different consciousness "archaic" as a way of distancing ourselves from it, implying that our view is somehow more evolved, more true, more real. And the question I would ask is why the distinction between life and non-life (especially in light of the difficulties that scientists have in actually creating a definition) is so important to us — what is the difference set up to do?*

ing rocks, trees, animals, and the heavens. The invention of biology, and the distinction between life and non-life that emerged from the newly forming faith in science as the arbitrator of truth, resulted in the subsequent de-animating of everything that did not fit our newly conceived category of life.

The stories of science have filled our imagination, displacing biblical faith. The proposition of evolution destroyed 6,000 biblical years of dwelling on the earth. The displacement of the six-day homocentric creation story with the billion-year story of evolution demanded that we construct a history in which we are newcomers and inconsequential participants. Further, the discovery that the earth is not the center of a rather small universe, but a speck on the outer reaches of an insubstantial galaxy, demanded that we re-represent ourselves in the place of the cosmos. This task, understanding our place in the extraordinary new dimensions of time and space, has occupied our imagination for the last 200 to 300 years.

As long as the human soul had God in the heavens, and God had given us the earth, we were securely placed *and* relieved of the responsibility of guiding the world — we were only following orders. Once our de-animating imagination began, however, it was not long before we discovered that God was also dead. We adapted to this loss by transforming our myths about the origin of intent and located "will" in the human species. We changed our story from salvation in the heavens in the afterlife to salvation through the perfectibility of "man" to be achieved through the myth of progress powered by our belief in science and technology. This means we are in charge of the earth, and our will is to make it "better":

> Just as the doctrine of divine transcendence took away the pervasive divine presence to the natural world, so the millennial vision of a blessed future left all present modes of existence in a degraded status. All things were in an unholy condition. Everything needed to be transformed. This meant that anything unused was to be used if the very purpose of its existence was to be realized. Nothing in its natural state was acceptable… This compulsion to use, to consume, has found its ultimate expression in our own time (Berry 1988, 115).

In our new fiction of human perfectibility and belief in our power to transform the world, we have lived as an isolated and alienated species in an immense universe of dead material with which we have only a consumptive relationship. The dominant mythology we have constructed to understand this particular relationship to the earth has rendered the planet inconsequential, and expanded the fantasy of the frontier as the place to occupy, and the future as home. In other

"For reasons that remain altogether obscure, Western civilization has decided to promote institutions of dislocation in every dimension of social and cultural existence. The international hegemony of these institutions — metropolis, economy, media, ideology — has led to an aggravated confusion about what it means to dwell on earth" (hooks 1992, 199).

words, we are never at home and never satisfied where we are, but are always going to the next place or the next time in which the world will be better through our activities.

To be dissatisfied with where we are now makes us yearn for the *frontier*. The place type, frontier, is an extraordinary space, a thin edge between the shifting distinctions of civilization and wilderness, that always disappears and is transformed as soon as it is occupied. Inherent in the idea of frontier is the idea of leaving home, both literally and figuratively. This will to leave is complemented by the interpretation of home as unsatisfactory, "unholy," confining, unimportant, and hence discarded. The frontier has been literalized in the colonization and appropriation of the Americas, Africa, and the Far East by Europeans, the "go west, young man" movement in North America, and currently in the exploration of space and the preoccupation with virtual realities. One can even interpret the flight from the rural agricultural existence into the cities as a gesture of frontier thinking, just as the suburbs became the frontier between the out-of-control city and the rural countryside. Today we speak of "urban pioneers," upper middle class people who are brave enough to repopulate our wild, uncivilized cities.

The preoccupation with the frontier in space and time, and our condition of homelessness, have influenced the way we represent our world and our place in it. One imaginal fiction we see and hear consistently is the fantasy of the consumed, discarded, and ravaged earth. Film, fiction, TV, science, environmental politics — all of these texts convey the possibility of non-inhabitation. In this fiction, we erase the earth through our consumption, be it a nuclear holocaust, gradual poisoning, or insidious and unending resource depletion and waste disposal. The earth is represented entirely as a wilderness, a location beyond the "civilizing" influence of human society.

The *Road Warrior* films demonstrate that the world can be an inhospitable place filled with violence and occupied by "out-laws" and fantasies of survival of the fittest, a capitalist interpretation of Darwinism. In films such as *Brazil*, a "Big Brother" bureaucracy imposes a thin veneer of order on an explosive, terrorist-infused, disintegrating social world where people inhabit anonymous, unscaled buildings, nuclear cooling towers, and ruins. Or consider *Blade Runner*, in which polluted, dark, drizzly cities are presented as crumbling shells of deconstructing material except for the places of the privileged few who live far above the streets. Only mutants, outlaws, robots, and otherwise useless people will be left on the earth as everyone else tries to move "off-world." Curiously, in both *Brazil* and

MB: *The frontier is where the Homeless and the Rootless meet, with different agendas. The Homeless (from war, famine, economic necessity, oppression) are, they hope, really just passing through in their search for home. The Rootless, the moderns, travelers, believers-in-progress, and adventurers, claim the frontier as locale, because it is always Other, interesting and even exciting, but Otherness as an "experience." For them, the widespread commodification of adventure decreases the probability of having any, increasing its already inflated value.*

The real frontier is often lawless and disordered, where (otherwise repressed) cunning and/or fierceness, boldness, and fortitude have high utility — not a place for the highly socialized. So those who seek the frontier find real danger or a sham, and there are rapidly fading opportunities for frontierness in general. They find there is no "away," no "there," and have sad dreams of Virtual Reality as their next frontier.

"The fears of our modern society are given shape and substance by such urban dystopias. The city has become the id of the modern imagination, the place where civilized behavior is vanishing. In the late twentieth century, the big city fulfills the same role as the howling wilderness of the sixteenth and seventeenth centuries; a place of base instincts, ugly motives, subterranean fears and unspoken desires, a place which reveals the savage basis of the human condition and frailty of civilized society" (Short 1991, 48).

"Catastrophic fantasies haunt us: they announce the end of the world... The fantasies of the literal end of the world announce, however, the end of this literalist world, the dead, objective world" (Hillman 1982, 90).

2-5
The U.S.S. *Enterprise*, the federation starship from "Star Trek: The Next Generation," meets the Borg/Ship. The mission of the *Enterprise* is "to boldly go where no one has gone before."
(drawing by Jeffrey R. Livingston)

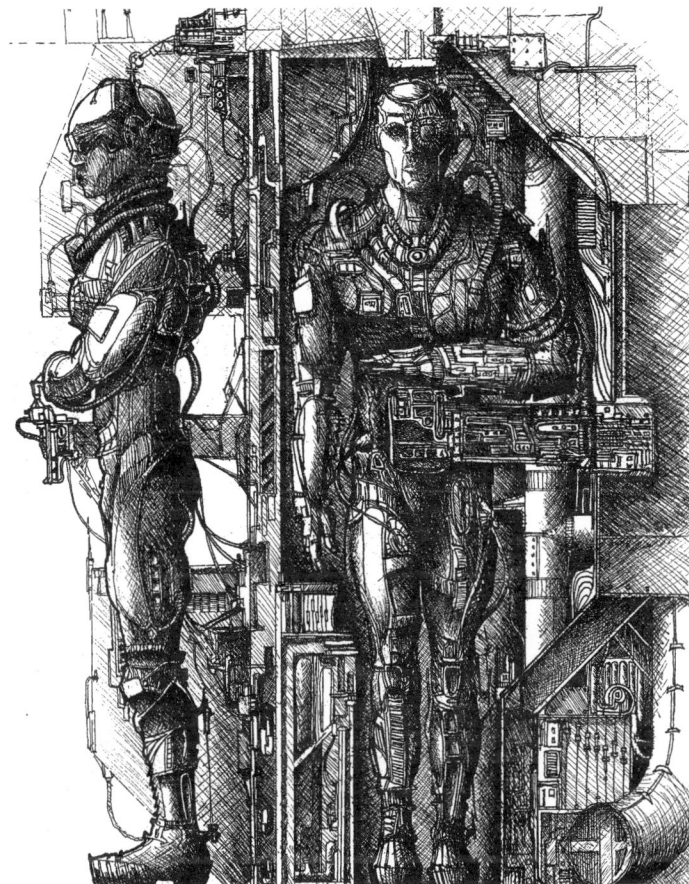

2-6
The Borg/Ship, one of the sentient entities from "Star Trek: The Next Generation," is a merger of self and place.
(drawing by James Magnuson)

Blade Runner, salvation is still imagined to exist in the pastoral countryside, the place of humanly constructed and maintained nature, outside the disintegrated city. In these films, it is *us* who have ravaged the earth.

One of the more poignant representations of our consumptive relationship with the earth is the invention of The Borg on the television program "Star Trek: The Next Generation." The Borg travel through the reaches of far space in their/its space cube habitat, searching for consumables. It/they mindlessly and amorally take whatever it/they want. The "ship" appears as a maze of machines where humanoid borg components plug themselves in. It is all corridor; a beehivelike world with no spatial hierarchy for orientation. It is computer as dwelling.

The Borg's first meeting with the U.S.S. *Enterprise*, the Federation starship out to "seek new worlds," almost results in the complete destruction of the crew and the *Enterprise* (the ship as "frontier home"). A subsequent meeting between the Federation and The Borg destroys much of the Federation fleet and barely stops The Borg from assimilating the life and technology of the earth. The monotone computer-generated voice repeats: "Resistance is irrelevant. Self-determination is irrelevant. We will assimilate your technology and life-forms."

The Borg embodies many of our fears. The entities have a humanoid form but are representations of confused boundaries. They are cyborgs, part human and part machine, sentient robot creatures, a piece of the ship. They are unindi-

2-7
Love Canal, Niagara Falls, New York. Love Canal, the symbol of contaminated communities in the United States, was a neighborhood built over toxic waste. It was evacuated in 1978, and current attempts to resettle the area by the State of New York are being contested by many groups.
a. The Fence.
   (photo by Suzanne Musho)
b. Interpretation of Love Canal. (graphic by Robin Bean)

2-8
Abandoned industrial lands in Buffalo, New York.
(photo by Greg Usewicz)

viduated, absorbed by the collective consciousness where self/other boundaries are totally erased. As an *Enterprise* crew member explains, "the ship thinks what it wants and it just happens," hence the confusion about whether The Borg is a single functioning unit, or made up of separate parts – an "it" or a "they." This lack of boundary, this fusion between the collective and the individual, is a source of great anxiety as is revealed in many texts in our culture, from the fear of communism in the political cultural domain to dystopian literature of this century. The story of The Borg describes not only the fusion of self with other, but of self with place; self, other selves, and place are indistinguishable and one.

The Borg theme is explored in subsequent episodes of "Star Trek." In one story, the *Enterprise* saves a component Borg and repairs or heals it/him. Through various interactions with the crew of the starship, the entity begins to have a consciousness, making it self-aware. It/he begins to form an individuated self and speaks beyond the totalizing "we." The Borg unit, now with a name, Hugh, has achieved a new level of consciousness. This is offered as a heroic achievement and significant developmental feat, but we must ask if this represents a good, or if the story presents, once again, the appropriation of an *other* into *us*?

The Borg are capable of destroying everything without regret, seemingly without even knowing they are doing violence. Their oblivion to the consequences of their actions demonstrates a form of intelligence/consciousness that is either unaware or uncaring of any other thing or being outside itself except as it is consumable. Hugh, the rescued Borg entity, cannot comprehend that the people of the starship do not want to merge. The Borg's oblivion to the consequences of its activities is terrifying to us not because of its alien nature, but because it is a mirror of our own actions in this world.

The fantasy of totally ravaging and consuming any other, of being the ultimate consumer, appears not only in our fictions. Its presence in our imagination demonstrates that it is one interpretation of our relationship to the earth. To name this frightening possibility, as is done through The Borg, is to bear witness to what is relentlessly unfolding before us. Through mindless consumptive activity humans are transforming all *not-us* into *us*, believing that everything unused must be transformed by us to have meaning. Our construction and deconstruction of the world not only appropriates the earth, it literally threatens to consume it and create an uninhabitable world.

The Fantasy of a Loving World

Through our meanings and practices, we have constructed a dead universe in which we remain the single, lonely shred of consciousness, "one brave and tattered shred of spirit in a universe otherwise made of dead matter…" (Panshin 1989, 8). The earth is presented as an inert globe in a universe of dead space, composed of minerals, vegetables, and animals – forms of life to use as resources for our habitation. Not only have we rendered the earth dead and all other life-forms insentient in our fictions, we now have the capability of truly killing it and ourselves in nuclear war or through a gradual poisoning.

Like many science fiction texts, Octavia Butler's trilogy, *Dawn* (1987), *Adulthood Rites* (1988), and *Imago* (1989), begins after the great killing. The stories are set some centuries after a nuclear war has destroyed life on earth. An alien species, the Oankali, arrived immediately after the nuclear war and rescued the few humans they found alive on the earth and brought them to *Chkahichdahk*, their home/ship orbiting the earth. The Oankali have healed humans and begun a very slow process of introducing themselves to them.

In *Dawn*, the Oankali are patiently and carefully reconstructing the earth by interpreting, modifying, re-creating, and implanting genes of diverse life-forms on earth. Over time the radiation-damaged earth will heal and reappear as the earth through the reconstruction practices of the Oankali. The extraterrestrials (the out-of-earthers) are compelled to preserve, heal, and comingle with all forms of life wherever they find them; they are gene traders. In exchange for mixing life, they lovingly protect and preserve all that they encounter. This is their life, their destiny, to come together with others, always becoming something other, to interbreed and create new forms of life. They are intensely attracted to human beings because they find this species to be so full of life – and death.

Chkahichdahk, the imagined world/ship of the Oankali, is also compelled to preserve life at all costs, to love the other. Butler presents us with a type of inhabitation that nourishes, protects, and cares for its inhabitants. In this world, the habitat actively participates in dwelling, as this sequence shows:

> [H]e walked over to one of the walls and touched it… a dark spot appeared on the wall where he made contact. It became a deepening, widening indentation, then a hole through which Lilith could see color and light… There was space, vast space. The hole in the wall widened as though it were flesh rippling aside, slowly writhing. She was both fascinated and repelled.

2-9
A visualization of the Oankali, sentient beings from Butler's (1987) *Dawn* (drawing by James Magnuson)

"Is it alive?" she asked.

"Yes," he said.

She had beaten it, kicked it, clawed it, tried to bite it. It had been smooth, tough, impenetrable, but slightly giving like the bed and table.

"What is it?" she asked.

"Flesh. More like mine than like yours. Different from mine, too, though. It's... the ship."

"You're kidding. Your ship is alive?"

"Yes. Come out" (Butler 1987, 27-28).

Lilith, the person selected to work with the Oankali in preparing humans to return to earth, discovers that she has been living inside a sentient "tree" that made space for her, fed her, and watched over her. Her jail, where she had slept for over 250 years, was alive. As she walks along with Jdahya, she carefully avoids stepping on snakelike extrusions rooted in the earth. These, too, are the ship, producing food to sustain other life-forms. The ship has an intelligence, and it can be induced to be very active through chemical communication. But more than that, claim its inhabitants:

> [T]he human doctor used to say it loved us. There is an affinity, but it's biological – a strong symbiotic relationship. We serve the ship's needs and it serves ours. It would die without us and we would be planetbound without it. For us, that would eventually mean death (Butler 1987, 33).

The ship/being provides for the needs of itself and inhabitants – food, oxygen, waste disposal, transport, storage, living space, work areas. And when the Oankali need new spaces, they grow them by communicating their need through touching the being/ship. It keeps track of its inhabitants, alerting others to dangers. *Chkahichdahk* participates fully and intimately in life.

The same growing world has been brought to earth from the "ship" to restore it as a habitat for humans. *Adulthood Rites* and *Imago* take place on this renewed earth. And although the Oankali's reconstruction of the earth takes care of humans just as the ship does, the humans persist in traditional human activities such as growing familiar foods and working the land. Some, "the resisters," reject the Oankali completely and live and die in the wilds, the unhealed portions of the planet.

These stories reveal our ambivalence toward a loving, active world. The idea of being at one with the earth, of recognizing the healing, loving possibility, is compelling and attractive. Yet the shadow of oneness is annihilation, alteration, erasure. Many humans refuse to live with or reproduce with the Oankali. They refuse to participate in making a new life-form, of engaging with the other. They will not be embraced by a participating, nurturing world because they fear absorption or transformation. This fear reveals the modern fantasy of exaggerated individuation, the carefully constructed idea of self that must be protected from violation by others.

In yet another way, Butler's trilogy is a thoroughly modern tale. It is the story of severance, of loss, of seeking reunification and restoration. The humans in the story are separated from their home and, in a fundamental way, from each other. To speak of such complete separation is always and already to know loss. The representation of this knowledge reveals a longing and grieving for wholeness, completeness, and the fantasy of innocence.

To contemplate severance in the late twentieth century is to consider seriously not only the annihilation of life on earth as we know it, but to imagine the possibility of extinction, the ultimate separation from place. Species obliteration grips the human consciousness:

> Species have become extinct throughout the Earth's history... But no species has ever been forced to contemplate the distinct possibility of its own extinction. "Extinction," "annihilation" crush imagination. It is difficult to view as fantasy the prospect of immediate extinction of the human species, to see it psychologically (Bishop 1986, 64).

The possibility of complete severance with life and the earth is an alien thought, and so the story of reunification must be alien as well. In Butler's work, the reunion of humans with earth is mediated through another kind of being. The self/place relationships we have constructed, both technically and imaginatively, have created the conditions of our leaving. Yet, it seems, we do not know how to come home. The insertion of the Oankali in this science fiction text, an *other*, is required to imaginatively re-connect humans to the earth.

Pre-severance, being at one with the world, recalls the myth of original unity which places humans inside nature, as one, together. It posits oblivion and

"Love is the extremely difficult realization that something other than oneself is real" (Iris Murdoch).

> *"We might consider our intimate and compassionate presence to earth as originating ultimately in the curvature of space, as it is presented in modern science. The entire earth community is infolded in this compassionate curve whereby the universe bends inwardly in a manner sufficiently closed to hold all things together and yet remains sufficiently open so that compassion does not confine, but fosters, the creative process" (Berry 1988, 20).*

2-10
Active industrial site next to a landfill (photo by Greg Usewicz)

innocence. But Butler transforms the myth of original union to offer a possibility of a different relationship with a friendly world which does not require the forgetting of the distinction between self and place. The Oankali are both within and outside *Chkahichdahk*, their world. They recognize that they cannot exist without the nurturance of their world; they acknowledge their dependency. "It would die without us and we would be planetbound without it. For us, that would eventually mean death" (Butler 1987, 33). But the Oankali retain their uniqueness; they remain separate but also connected beings, as a species and as individuals. The Oankali are not the possessors of their world, and their world does not possess them. Here is a fiction of a loving world that places beings in more than one location. This fiction displaces the either/or fiction of the modern world.

The Ecological Imagination

The texts of science fiction reveal our current paradigms of being a separate and alienated species and they present possibilities for resistance to this fiction. Embedded in many science fiction stories is an ecological imagination, a way of seeing the world as connected and related rather than as fragmented and separate. This fiction locates human beings and our makings within the world.

The word *ecology*, coined by zoologist Haeckel in the 1870s, countered the paradigmatic perspective in biology that focused on a species independent of its habitat. The term, within the discourse of science, has transformed not only the practice of science, but public policy and wilderness preservation. The idea of ecology provides an opportunity for a fundamental revisioning of human/place relationships because ecology, like other theories, represents a healing fiction rather than a literal truth:

> The idea of ecology – no matter how sophisticated, how pertinent and "right" it seems for these desperate times – is an imaginal fiction. Nevertheless, the creation of such a fiction, such an important symbol, is a major psychological event. Through this symbol, concern for images of the *other* is becoming more important than concern for images of *self* (Bishop 1990, 3).

A new fiction, emerging at a time when we find ourselves increasingly preoccupied with homelessness and the possibility of species extinction, offers us a new way to imagine ourselves in the world. How this new ecological imagination might work is one theme of resistance in text of science fiction.

The Prime Directive: the Appreciation of Other

One of the more radical features of the series "Star Trek: The Next Generation" is the "Prime Directive." This is a foundational law of the Federation that decrees that it will not intervene in the unfolding and ongoing history of any people, change any historical happening (important because time travel is a part of their lives), nor intervene with the "good" of any other life-forms as determined by that life-form, not by human beings. This is a manifesto of noninterference. The Federation will neither make the first gesture of communication with species that do not know of its existence, nor will it intervene in their lifeworld. Other beings, their lives, and habitats are to remain undisturbed by the world of humans.

I have called this radical because we have come so recently to this ecological imaginal fiction in our relationship with others. The last great taking, the colonization of continents and subjugation of other human cultures by Europeans, is only 500 years old – a mere minute in time. When Columbus landed in the Caribbean in 1492, he began an unparalleled incursion on the American continents.

The right and desirability of appropriation is the premise of the founding of the "new world" and this manifesto has had mythic power in our culture. Through this assumption we have lost people, cultures, languages, worldviews, animals, plants, knowledges. Everything in the found place – the frontier – belonged to the people who discovered it and claimed it based on the assumption of superiority of the race. And today, although the right to appropriate peoples, cultures, and land is questioned, it still occurs daily through various institutionalized forms of racism, sexism, and classism.[1]

The appropriation and erasure of nonhuman nature has not been sufficiently problematized in the industrialized world. Environmentalists fight to save whales, elephants, and old growth forests. But they are still an oppositional voice struggling against the dominant culture's interpretation of our relationship to nonhuman nature. Nash (1989) offers the analogy between radical environmentalists today, and abolitionists in the last century who fought to redefine the accepted possibility of humans as property. The abolition of slavery was a redrawing of the boundary between what is *us* and *not-us*.

The idea of the Prime Directive is an act of resistance against the erasure of the earth and nonhuman species, literally and imaginally. In episodes where the *Enterprise* meets humanoid species, it is not difficult to understand the meaning of the Prime Directive – do not disturb either the life-forms or their habitats, because to destroy or even alter a place of inhabitation is a form of species murder.

2-11
Elevators of an abandoned grain elevator in Buffalo, New York
(photo by author)

"Here we are, born yesterday (from an evolutionary perspective). We need to present ourselves to the planet as the planet presents itself to us, in an evocative rather than a dominating relationship. There is need for a great courtesy toward the earth" (Berry 1988, 14).

"A person kills somebody, and then mourns the victim. In more attenuated form, someone deliberately alters a form of life, and then regrets that things have not remained as they were prior to the intervention. At one more remove, people destroy their environment, and then they worship nature. In any of its versions, imperialist nostalgia uses a pose of innocent yearning both to capture people's imaginations and to conceal its complicity with often brutal domination" (Renato Rosaldo in hooks 1992, 189).

1. See Churchill (1992) and hooks (1992), respectively, for discourse on representations and appropriations of Native American and black cultures by white society.

"The inertia of objects is deceptive. The inanimate world appears static, "dead," to humans only because of our neuromuscular chauvinism. We are so enamored of our own activity range, that we blind ourselves to the fact that most of the action in the universe is unfolding outside our range, occurring at speeds so much slower or faster than our own that it is hidden from us as if by a... veil" (Robbins 1990, 69).

"ENVIRONMENTALISTS ARE GRAVE THREAT TO MANKIND The fundamental goal of environmentalists is not clean air and clean water; rather it is the demolition of technological/industrial civilization. Their goal is not the advancement of human health, human happiness, and human life; rather it is a subhuman world where 'nature' is worshiped like the totem of some primitive religion" (Berliner in The Buffalo News, *11/11/90).*

"Is it not time that inanimate objects — and plants and animals — resume their rightful place in the affairs of the world? How long can humankind continue to slight these integral pieces of the whole reality?" (Robbins 1990, 88).

It becomes much more difficult with sentient life-forms that are totally alien, so alien in fact that life is not immediately recognizable. One episode takes place on a small planet on which no life-form was discovered. Here, the Federation has begun the process of "terra-forming" — that is, making the planet habitable for the human species. They run into some problems, and at one point, a scientist is killed. The team from the *Enterprise* discovers a replicating crystal in the sand of the planet. As this form replicates itself, it attempts to destroy others on the *Enterprise*. Through the communication magic possible only in science fiction, they make contact with these tiny crystalline structures/beings, which call the humans "ugly sacks of mostly water." These strange creatures are defending their place from what they perceive to be an invasion that is destroying their habitat. Instead of "overcoming" the aliens and persisting in terra-forming, the *Enterprise* leaves the crystal forms and their planet. The crystals defined their own good — not the good defined by humans of the twenty-fourth century.

In this incident the Federation can be excused for their habitat destruction; they had not identified the space as a place of habitation. They did not recognize the sentient life-form which called this place home. It was an ignorant act against others, but one which was rectified as soon as the error had been discovered.

The ecological imagination inherent in the Prime Directive stands in stark contrast to our current practices in the world. Compare the ecological imagination reflected in this directive to our attitudes about a species and their habitat we not only recognize, but profess to value highly — human beings. We are daily destroying our own places of habitation through active destruction and neglect. The continued use of fossil fuels, logging, unsound waste disposal, and even the ongoing urbanization and global inhabitation of the earth by one species, *Homo sapiens*, is destroying the habitat not only for other species, but for ourselves. An interesting demonstration of a nonecological imagination is revealed in our current attitudes toward health and sickness in the western world. At some level and in some discourses we "know" that many of our dis-eases have, like cancer, an environmental origin, and yet we continue to fixate on healing the *bodies* of human beings instead of restoring our habitats. Here, we draw again an impervious line between us and our places, building up the wall that continues, nonetheless, to crumble before our eyes.

The environmentalists of the late twentieth century, although still struggling to understand the fictions they are attempting to create, implicitly recognize the imperative of in-habitation. They are calling us out of our culture's fixation on the individual species and mobile, sentient creatures such as mammals at the expense of the communities of creatures and homes of these species in the world of vegetation, the fabric of rooted and invisible life that nurtures all of us.

The much discussed and argued spotted owl controversy in the northwest of the United States demonstrates the crude tools we have created to think about habitat. The fragmentary language of "endangered species" and the preservation of isolated creatures is inadequate to the question of life on earth. The only accepted argument to be made from a legal, and therefore culturally appropriate, perspective about the preservation of an ancient web of life – the old growth forests – is that one species, the spotted owl, may become extinct if this habitat is not preserved. We have come far to be able to recognize that the preservation of a bird may be an important cultural act. But this act, which reveals the ecological connection between the bird and its home, still conceals our relationship to the bird and *our* home.

In a very fundamental and material sense, the destruction of habitat is the ultimate terror. Without the place of dwelling and sustenance, we are all "the living dead." The us/place dualism that we attempt to maintain is a fiction that thoroughly and completely pervades the ways we maintain ourselves and treat the world. The anomaly that confronts us every day is that we *are* our places, our habitats, the earth – and our places are us. The destruction of our habitat is therefore an act of suicide.

The possibility of an ecological imagination is explored in the Prime Directive of "Star Trek: The Next Generation." It challenges our willingness to insert ourselves into the world of other species and habitats, erasing and colonizing them for our "good." Yet even in the virtual world of television, it is not always possible to follow this directive or to understand its implications. Sometimes the Federation interferes; sometimes it does not recognize the species and habitats. But regardless of the Federation's errors, the Prime Directive is an imagination uncompromisingly directed toward the appreciation of, rather than the appropriation of, the other.

2-12
Regenerating shoreline, Buffalo River, New York. The Buffalo River, which flows through the city of the same name, is one of the 42 toxic hot spots in the Great Lakes Watershed. (photo by author)

"We shall not cease from exploration
And the end of all our exploring
Will be to arrive where we started
And know the place for the first time."
(T.S. Eliot, "Little Gidding")

2. *Always Coming Home* (1985) is the title of an "historical" science fiction book by Ursula Le Guin in which she explores the rhythm and importance of home, our leaving and returning, always.

Always Coming Home[2]

If we view science fiction as a mythic structure for our times, the stories tell us that we have made a world in which, we tell ourselves time and time again, we do not belong. In much of the western world, we move around from one place on the earth to another, often finding ourselves far from the home of our parents and their parents. We are no longer connected to the spot where the genealogical tree had its beginning, nor the ancient burial grounds of our ancestors (Harrison 1992). This is new in human history. In this situation,

> [Home] loses its limits, its definition, its meaning, and for the first time in cultural memory an increasing proportion of people in Western societies are not sure where they will be buried, or where they should be buried, or even where they desire to be buried (Harrison 1992, 198).

Not to know where you will ultimately rest is a profound expression of dislocation and detachment from places, from habitation in the earth. In human cultures, the burial of the dead has long defined the place of dwelling and the connection with past communities and peculiar places of memory. We have become a species disassociated with particular places on the earth, nostalgic for the fantasy of home and rootedness.

Since the inception of modernity, western culture has been experiencing a great moving, seen in the wave of migrations from Europe and Asia to the American continent, and ongoing dislocations of people all over the world because of war, famine, or work. Metaphorically, this era could be thought of as a time in which humans left the idea of place as ancestral burial grounds, and even the earth as home, to explore other realms of experience. The invention of ways to travel quickly across the globe and into space, the idea of the frontier as the most exciting place to inhabit, and the creation of stories and myths such as science fiction are all about this leaving. Yet, perhaps leaving and the preoccupation with, and occupation of, the frontier have been peculiar gifts. Perhaps to recognize and appreciate our home we had to leave it:

> [I]t is essential in human life to address the "other." And in order to do that you must, in a figurative and in a real sense, leave home. You must leave the security of your own language, the security of your form of government, and the security of all the psychological cushions built into your culture and your way of life. In other words, if you come face to face with the other you can come home and see the dimensions of the familiar that make you love it (Lopez 1990, 53).

Having left, can we return home to the earth of our dwelling to explore new dimensions of self/place relations? If humans choose to reinhabit the earth in a fundamental sense instead of living off the earth, we will have to acknowledge that we are not the same as when we left. We have lost the oblivion of unconscious habitation. The coming home will have to express and acknowledge this experience of separation and alienation. We may be interconnected and dependent on the evolving earth and its life, but we cannot, in some sense, lose ourselves in it, or be totally immersed in it. We now recognize ourselves as *the other* and realize that our fantasies of being outside nature are a truth.

We are not the same as we were before this imaginal leaving; nor is the earth the same. In our travels into space, we have created a new image of a wholistic earth; we have seen the photographic representation of the small blue-green globe floating in the blackness of space. This image has signaled a radical relocation of us and the earth that suggests a different comprehension of our dwelling: *we are one with the planet earth*. Bishop writes:

> The abrupt creation of this idealized image of wholeness, the "Whole-Earth" fantasy, is an event in industrialized cultures… [portraying] the Earth as a discrete evolutionary unit in an immense cosmic drama (Bishop 1986, 59).

The intense debates that emerged at the beginning of modernity which transformed our sense of time beyond the short story embedded in biblical truth, and our understanding of space beyond our geocentric imagination, now have new meaning. It is almost as if we have come full circle – from the earth as unique in the heavens and the center of the universe, to a sense of the earth as simply one among many celestial bodies, to a realization that the earth is, indeed, unique and precious. The fate of the earth is our future as it has been our past. We now have an image of the earth as habitat, and through our discourses in science, we know again (re-cognize) that our well-being is dependent on the resiliency and diversity of the whole fabric of the earth systems – geosphere, atmosphere, hydrosphere, biosphere, and the mindsphere (Berry 1988, 19). This image, the re-presentation of the whole earth, grounds the realization that we have no other place to go, no other home, now or in the foreseeable future. The prodigal children, the human species, have in one sense returned home changed by our experiences, although we still have much to learn about the implications of the creation of the new image of the wholistic earth.

It is ironic that at the same time that we have engaged a new understanding of our interconnectedness with the wholistic earth, we are experiencing an upswelling of localized, place-related affinities all over the world. In the face of the modern global village, people are claiming their right to live in particular, culturally remembered places, challenging layers of colonizers and images of being colonized. The nostalgia for connection to place as we have imagined it to exist in more rooted cultures is asserting itself with violence, framing our modern tale of severance and loss. The claiming of place is being fought with a sense of desperateness that suggests it may not be possible for us to regain this imagined relationship between people and place, if it ever existed. Perhaps the longing for the ancestral burial grounds and the sense of placelessness so evident in modern life are less literal experiences than they are individual and cultural inabilities to re-imagine what places are and can be (Bishop 1992).

The idea of returning home as a responsible species to communities of people/places opens up the possibility of a *beloved place*. The revisioning of home as beloved place transforms the concept from the place we find ourselves because of an accident of birth to a place where we choose to live, committing ourselves to particular peoples, a specific place, and many *others* we would call friends:

> What is wanting is the return to the beloved community, or to the possibility of one. That would return us to a renewed and corrected awareness of our partiality and mortality, but also to healing and to joy in a renewed awareness of our love and hope for one another. Without that return, we may know innocence and horror and grief, but not tragedy and joy, not consolation or forgiveness or redemption (Berry 1990, 78).

Will we ever be able to create and live in beloved places — to overcome our fear of totalizing commitment and our terror of being consumed? This would demand a sense of ourselves as individuals, as cultures, and as a species. It would require that we be unafraid of comingling, of engaging others and reemerging changed, but not obliterated. This would be a sense of ourselves revealed in Butler's story of the Oankali.

The search for *particular* beloved communities and the earth as *one* may appear to be contradictory activities. Can we simultaneously recognize our dwelling in the emerging comprehension of the "whole earth," and be attached to our discrete, ancestral burial grounds? Can we learn to locate ourselves in two places, perhaps even more, as people committed to specific communities in pecu-

MB: *The current violent Balkanization throughout the world is creating a true lawless and disordered frontier, but horribly, "one right here at home" — and this in cultures that normally reject "frontierness," cultures less comfortable with modernism, who hold more traditional place attachments. They are making an otherness they do not want. Contested homelands are destroyed, creating more lawless frontier, and more homeless, and more contention for homelands. And there is really the possibility of these too-violent frontiers leading to a monstrous event creating a post-apocalyptic world of* only *frontier.*

Nobody seems to get what they want at, or from, the frontiers they seek or inadvertently create. As your paper suggests, a radical re-inhabitation *may be a sustaining project for both the Homeless and the Rootless and, perhaps, all. And one great value of the pop artistry of sci-fi, of the made-up, is to provide us with vision(s) of the possible.*

2-13
The Old First Ward, a community set among the gigantic grain elevators, historic home to the Irish residents of Buffalo, New York
(photo by author)

liar bioregions and cultures of the earth, and as a species connected to many others and the whole, interdependent earth?

Another question emerges from the consideration of an imagination directed at returning home. If we view the whole earth, even the universe, as our home, then we must ask, where is the frontier, modernity's residence of choice? We constructed many frontiers to which we could escape from the burdensome confinements of home. Yet now we know that both the denigration of home and the leaving for the frontier have had enormous costs, and have been ultimately unsatisfactory.

To come home means we must re-image our construction of home as "confinement" and frontier as "away." It is time to remind ourselves that as humans we have always been located in that space between the world-as-given and culture. Our myths and stories reveal that since the evolution of consciousness, we have experienced a tension between ourselves and the world, and have struggled to mediate that tension. Perhaps the evolving image of frontier offers us a new fiction for addressing this tension, of making a place for ourselves that acknowledges our *in-between-ness* and habitation of many places:

> Wherever we stand, in the Gila Wilderness or in Times Square, we stand at the intersection of nature and culture. We belong to both worlds at once, or we belong to neither (Dobb 1992, 46).

It is not only possible to redraw the boundaries between us, place, home, frontier, and other domains of dwelling and to inhabit them simultaneously; it is our responsibility to engage in that effort.

Concluding Thoughts

The us/place relationships revealed in science fiction confound our clearly bounded typological distinction between the world and us. These texts identify the boundaries between home and frontier, between animate and inanimate, between civilization and wilderness, and ultimately between us and other, as fictions. Our anxiety about endangered species and the loss of the forest in the environmental discourse is much more than just the fear of losing biodiversity and wildlife. The fear is about the disappearance of the boundaries we know, the shadow against which our dwelling has been grounded. "Without such outside domains, there is no inside in which to dwell" (Harrison 1992, 247). Can we create a fiction about

---

"Humans have always — at least since the invention of language — distinguished nature from culture and have been aware of a deep tension, even a measure of estrangement, between themselves and the rest of nature. If they have often managed to achieve a measure of harmony between nature and culture at the ecological and psychological levels, this is not 'natural' in the sense of being unself-conscious. Rather it is an achievement — actually a work of art. People have always *had to find their way back into the sunflower forest" (W. Jordan in* Restoration and Management Notes*).*

HD: *I think your reference to the worlds created in science fiction is a clever path in that it gives us, architects/planners, permission to consider utopian constructs about social relationships. This is an arena which we in the architecture and planning professions have relinquished under the constant, and relentless, pressure to justify and argue in the scientific, rational mode. The positing of constructs was a domain we once proudly claimed, and are now often embarrassed into disowning.*

ourselves and others that is not hierarchial and oppositional? Can we be located in many different imaginal, social, and geographical places? These are fertile explorations of the ecological imagination of connections and relationships.

If the type distinction between us and place opens, becomes less rigid and more overlapping, then it follows that the place types we create and name must also be vulnerable, because each place type locates not only a place of habitation, but locates us and our relationship to it. Once we engage in the struggle to relocate and rename *us* and *other*, and to reconstruct our types of habitation, many confusions emerge that demand our attention.

Where do we locate *away* – the places of non-inhabitation such as landfills, toxic rivers, and discarded inner cities? If there is no *away*, but only *here*, we will have to rethink the production, consumption, and disposal of our things and places. Waste lands, wasted things, waste products, and wasted people are not that which we discard from the self, that is, they are not the *other*; they are a part of us that we must find some way to address.

If we choose to reinhabit the world because the image of the wholistic earth reverberates in us, nature is no longer out or over *there and other*. It must always and already be *here and us*. We may invoke the Prime Directive by not consuming old growth forests, tiny remnants of prairie, and areas of rain forest, but we cannot pretend that we are therefore heroically saving the world. We are only caring for ourselves and our home. And if nature is no longer far and away because it is both us and not-us, then our own constructions – our cities and things – are natural and deserve to be as beautiful and protected as nature preserves and tropical forests (Hillman 1982). The boundaries blur between that which is green and organic and that which is gray and constructed.

The ecological imagination (re)invents an interconnected, relational world in which the action of any element has the potential to transform the entire world. It reoffers the possibility of an animate world, a world that presents itself to us if we attend to it/us. The earth includes us as part of its activity – we are not "outside" the fabric of the relationship. The ecological imagination defies the fiction of our independence and the fantasy that we stand above and not within. And more than any other fiction recently constructed, the insertion of ecological imagination into a wide range of discourses – from science to literature – acts as opposition and resistance to our continued preoccupation with separate, dislocated species living in isolated, discrete place types.

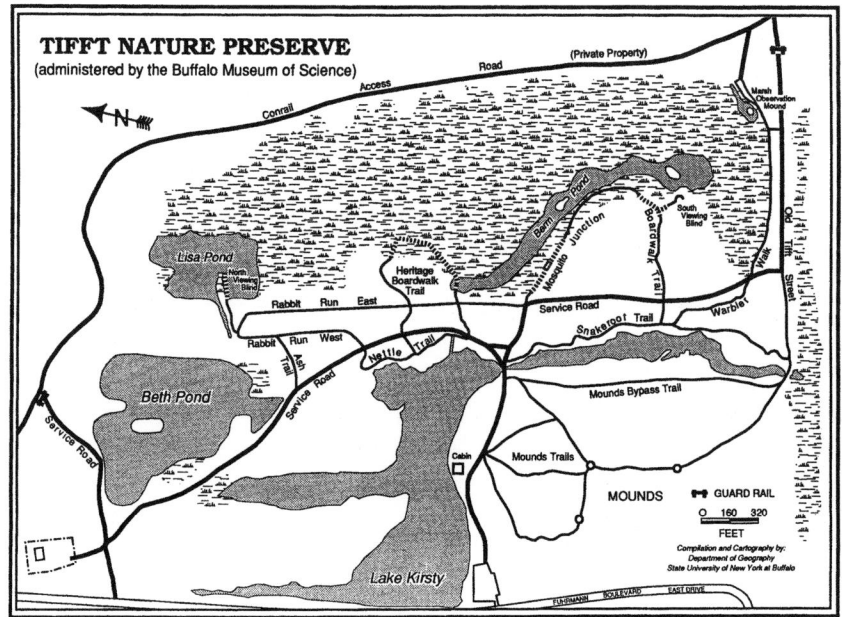

2-14
Tifft Nature Preserve is located on abandoned industrial wastelands. The area identified as "mounds" is a landfill (courtesy of Buffalo Museum of Science and Tifft Nature Preserve)

"Critical affirmation is a concept that embraces both the need to affirm one another and to have a space for critique. Significantly, that critique is not rooted in a negative desire to compete, to wound, to trash" (hooks 1992, 58).

"It is the knowledge that one has already lost whatever there is to lose and that life is therefore given, or forgiven, gratuitously... a fact of life awakens to the fact that there is something rather than nothing, that nature is without a human reason for being, and that we dwell in the givenness of loss. This knowledge, this self-knowledge alone, is freedom" (Harrison 1992, 231).

MB: *Just read your chapter "Type meets Sci-fi." An initial read resulted in "what is this doing in a book on type?... it is really stretching it." Upon reflection, it really starts the concept, for me, of a psychoanalytics of type, and of categories, and their differences. Both category and type include and exclude, and obviously require recognition of otherness, as defined by some criteria deemed relevant. What is nice about the piece is that it shifts the notion of type (and category, but less so) into the non-innocent realm, the creation of "useful" truths. The leap from "excluded other" to ideas of hierarchy, dominance, exploitation, and subjugation seems to me to be both amazing and critical to what you say... and it seems to be, cognitively, a shift in perspective from "mere" typing or categorization. It serves something that, clearly, has darkness in it, but like all pervasivenesses in us, it must serve something other than darkness as well.*

If "category" is a hard boundary, a binariness of belonging and excluding, it holds so little promise for us to understand anything in truly human terms. "Type," however, with its soft edges, its "live" boundary, its frontier, makes a place not in or out, a place that itself has no hard boundary, a place in which the self and other are other, or in which the self and other are one... or in your terms, "appreciated."

So it is type that opens the possibility of non-exclusionary vision. And type remains in the domain of resistance, or is the domain. This rambling is my way of including your piece as a piece on type, by stepping into that frontier where I can see both what I thought type was, and was not.

The ecological imagination problematizes our current myths; it does not, however, answer the question of the relationship of humans to the world, the fundamental typological distinction between self and other. To act from within the world does not mean that we "belong" within; to be one species among others does not mean we are a continuation, much less the apex.

Our story of the expulsion from the Garden of Eden manifests a knowledge we are only coming to understand, that we have stepped outside of the givenness of the natural world and cannot return to oblivious inhabitation of a world of only cycles and renewal. We know our death, our finitude, our outsideness. As we come to know ourselves as *the other*, capable of consuming, appropriating, and truly destroying the earth, we find that we may have "failed to think the discontinuity between humanity and nature radically enough" (Harrison 1992, 200). The invention of a place type like the frontier, set at the edge and between other places of habitation, is one possible fiction for reinterpreting our habitation of the earth as home and our world-making practices such as place types.

The ecological imagination presents us with a different world and a new relationship — one that has the potential of being less destructive to the others with whom we share our places. But even if we restructure our images of the world, inserting place types such as the frontier and others yet to be imagined, are we still not the sole constructors of the world, are we not simply inscribing it differently? Creating a fiction can be an act of liberation and/or a continuation of appropriation, and we thereby know that there is no salvation embedded in this new story. It is, however, much less important that we come to some new truth about the us/place typology than it is to continue to engage in the struggle to create stories of possible relationships of humans and the world — new imaginal fictions for dwelling in the earth.

Relationships with *others*, with that we imagine to be *not-us*, can be forms of domination, whether we want the other to be like us through appropriation and colonization, or literally through consumption of the other as explored in the image of The Borg. But relationships do not have to be defined by hierarchy and domination. They can also be acts of connection and love, of intense curiosity about a nurturing, animate world and the *otherness* of the beloved other as in the story of the Oankali. The tension between appropriation and appreciation can be embraced as we play with the new ecological myth as it problematizes and challenges the boundaries of place types and the very existence of the fantasy of self/other type distinction.

Our underlying beliefs and cultural stories structure the way we physically and imaginally inhabit and represent the world through our type-making practices. The emergence of an ecological imagination is an act of resistance to current distinctions between humans and the world. Its construction through various discourses, including science fiction, suggests new ways to bound and unbound us/place relationships in our continual search for ways to dwell in the earth.

I would like to thank Karen Franck, Rachel Schneekloth, Bob Shibley, and Mike Brill for their reading and comments on this chapter. Also thanks to Stephan Klein, my students, and family who continued to urge me to write about science fiction.

2-15
John's garden, Monteverde (photo by author)

References

Adams, Douglas. 1979. *The Hitchhiker's Guide to the Galaxy*. New York: Pocket Books.

Berman, Morris. 1984. *The Reenchantment of the World*. New York: Bantam Books.

Berry, Thomas. 1988. *The Dream of the Earth*. San Francisco: Sierra Club Books.

Berry, Wendel. 1990. Writer and region. In *What are People For?*, 71–87. San Francisco: North Point Press.

Bishop, Peter. 1986. The shadows of the holistic earth. *Spring* 1986: 59–71.

———. 1990. *The Greening of Psychology: The Vegetable World in Myth, Dream, and Healing*. Dallas, Tex.: Spring Publications.

———. 1992. Personal correspondence 21, October 1992.

Bladerunner. Directed by Ridley Scott and produced by Michael Deely. Screenplay by Hampton Fancher and David Peoples. The Lad Company, 1982.

Brazil. Directed by Terry Gilliam. Embassy International Pictures, 1985.

Butler, Octavia E. 1987. *Dawn*. New York: Popular Library.

———. 1988. *Adulthood Rites*. New York: Popular Library.

———. 1989. *Imago*. New York: Popular Library.

Churchill, Ward. 1992. *Fantasies of the Master Face: Literature, Cinema and the Colonization of American Indians*. Edited by M. Annette Jaimes. Monroe, Maine: Common Courage Press.

Dobb, Edwin. 1992. Cultivating nature. *The Sciences* January/February.

Foucault, Michel. 1970. *The Order of Things*. New York: Vintage Books.

Giegerich, Wolfgang. 1985. The nuclear bomb and the fate of God. *Spring* 1985 (Dallas, Tex.): 1–27.

Harrison, Robert Pogue. 1992. *Forests: The Shadow of Civilization*. Chicago: University of Chicago Press.

Hillman, James. 1982. *Anima mundi*: the return of the soul to the world. *Spring* 1982 (Dallas, Tex.): 71–93.

———. 1985. Natural beauty without nature. *Spring* 1985 (Dallas, Tex.): 50-55.

hooks, bell. 1992. *Black Looks: Race and Representation*. Boston: South End Press.

Le Guin, Ursula K. 1985. *Always Coming Home*. New York: Bantam Books.

Lopez, Barry. 1990. Paying attention: an interview with Barry Lopez. *Orion* Summer: 50–53.

———. 1991. The rediscovery of North America. *The Amicus Journal* Fall: 12–16.

Lovelock, James E. 1979. *Gaia: A New Look of Life on Earth*. New York: Oxford University Press.

Nash, Roderick F. 1989. *The Rights of Nature: A History of Environmental Ethics*. Madison, Wis.: University of Wisconsin Press.

Panshin, Alexei and Cory Panshin. 1989. *The World Beyond the Hill: Science Fiction and the Quest for Transcendence*. Los Angeles: Jeremy P. Tarcher.

Road Warrior. Written by Terry Hayes and George Miller with Brian Hannant. Kennedy Miller Entertainment Pty. Ltd. & Others, 1981.

Robbins, Tom. 1990. *Skinny Legs and All*. New York: Bantam Books.

Short, John Rennie. 1991. *Imagined Country. Environment, Culture and Society*. New York: Routledge.

Star Trek: The Next Generation. Produced by Gene Roddenberry. Episode Eighteen: "Home Soil" by Robert Sabaroff, directed by Corey Allen; Episode Forty-two: "Q Who" by Maurice Hurley, directed by Rob Bowman; Episode Seventy-four "The Best of Both Worlds," Part 1 and Part 2 by Michael Pillar, directed by Cliff Bole. Premier Fall 1987.

Wilson, Alexander. 1991. *The Culture of Nature: North American Landscape from Disney to the Exxon Valdez*. Toronto: Between the Lines.

Chapter 3

Archetypes as a "Natural Language" for Place Making

Mike Brill

Many people have experiences filled with feeling and meaning that are clearly related to particular places. These experiences occur in relatively few places, but in those places relatively frequently. The places feel "charged;" they excite the spirit. The feeling of "charge" may be a reverberation of that particular place experience with something already in us, like a template in the mind of form and meaning bonded together – an archetype. These archetypal meanings are about significant aspects of our lives that are expressed through the forms of these places. In conveying these meanings, the physical forms of these places may act as a "natural language," natural for it is one that we are born knowing.

This essay is an inquiry into these possibilities, all of which suggest one way that places communicate meaning. The exploration is an architect's search for more understanding of what may be a universal, spirit-driven, and active principle in place experiencing. It is intended to add to our repertoire of ways for place making, to enrich and inform it.

In this exploration my methods have been qualitative, speculative, and interpretive, as they must be, for they focus on the revelation of meaning in places, on feelings and emotions, and on the activity and products of our spirit, all of which tend to bypass our usual circuits of knowledge.

LS: *There is an assumption about what constitutes the "usual circuits of knowledge" left unspoken here. What is considered "legitimate" knowledge and who gets to decide? I assume you are speaking about knowledge derived through the tenets of science and rationality which is currently being challenged in many discourses, particularly in feminist theory. See Harding (1991)* Whose Science? Whose Knowledge? Thinking From Women's Lives, *Ithaca, Cornell University Press; and Haraway (1988) "Situated knowledges: the science question in feminism and the privilege of partial perspective," in* Feminist Studies *14 (3).*

Charged Places and Archetypes

Almost everyone has had the experience of being in a particular place and feeling very moved or "charged," almost in an electrical sense. Of all our places, relatively few are charged, and those that are often become special to us. Some examples are the Acropolis, the pyramids, Hagia Sophia, the Chrysler Building, a deep forest, a clearing in that forest, a lonely beach, the Zen garden of Ryo-anji, the Vietnam Veterans Memorial, rural New England cemeteries, a ruined barn, or a bare orchard in winter snow.

Along with the "charge," these places seem to engage us physically, sensually, and emotionally through our body and senses, and imaginatively and rhetorically through our mind. Feelings of connectedness and flickers of revelation suggest that they engage us through spirit as well. It feels like an intensification of reality. The places are not necessarily beautiful, the feelings not necessarily pleasurable. Feelings can be of nurture, contentment, and connection, or of awe, foreboding, fear or isolation, or that tranquility tinged with terror we call the Sublime.

The charge is often accompanied by a variety of experiences: a floating reverie or a liveliness of imagination and flickers of meaning; a coming together of our individual senses into one whole, fully engaged and very alive; an enhanced feeling of connection to something important; a slowing of time, or a feeling outside of time; a feeling that this place is a center of being, or has no real location; and even when other people are present, they fade out and you are alone – but not lonely. These seem to be almost automatic responses to a charged place and mark the place experience vividly. These sensations recur again and again in charged places, and people return to them often for this reason.

Some charged places are only charged for one individual and not for others. These are often places with strong personal associations, like "my grandmother's attic." There are also places charged only for people of a particular culture and no other, like the Gettysburg Battlefield. Such a place is only charged if you know its story. I cannot conceive of place experiencing in which culture does not shape the experience in some part. But in charged places, culture may account for very little.

There are, in other words, places that may actually be charged for our species. Many people of many cultures and times have been moved by the painted caves at Altamira and Lascaux, the Moorish gardens of the Alhambra, and the great stone circles wherever they appear. Because you do not have to be of the time or culture of these places to feel their charge and sense their meaning, it may be a patterned response that transcends the boundaries of particular times and cultures – a species-wide experience.

While many people have similar responses to charged places, not everyone does, nor is it always the same, nor is any place charged for everybody. But the pervasiveness of this phenomenon still suggests that something fundamental to humans as a whole is at work. The feeling of charge may be a reverberation between that moment's place experience and something already in us. Many have called what is already in us "archetypes."[1] I believe most of the charged experiences people have are simple affirmations of the presence of archetypes.

Ideas about archetypes have been offered continuously for more than 25 centuries. Because they reside in the *inaccessible* unconscious, these ideas seem untestable through empirical methods. Sometimes posed as theories, they have more the character of stories that we use to try to explain the origins and workings of phenomena that are strong in our experience. However, they are parsimonious and attractive theory-stories, and I accept them as reasonable. They suggest that an archetype is an inherited memory, an inborn template in the mind, what some call a "natural symbol" of meaning bonded to form. Some ancient scholars saw archetypes as ideas of which actual phenomena are mere imitations or shadows. Jung (1969) spoke of them as inherited memories, derived from aeons of common experiences that are now present in the collective unconscious of all individuals. In all these, archetypes exist for many phenomena in human experience including, but certainly not limited to, places.

One example of a probably worldwide archetypal experience is that of dark and light, some of whose significant meanings are: a reassurance of stability in the

---

1. Beliefs in archetypes and other universals are rejected, or at least questioned, by many, especially those who see sameness as a threat to the potential of human uniqueness, or as the result of aeons of psychic and political oppression. (Is it not the tension, play, and dialectic between sameness and uniqueness that makes us most human?) A review of the literature done by the anthropologist Givens (1982), as part of the government's research in preparation for the far future radioactive waste burial project discussed in this chapter, finds a wide variety of psychosocial universals, findings that at least sustain the possibility of archetypes. And since archetypes supposedly reside in a "collective unconscious," they remain quite inaccessible to individuals, but probably are accessible in some way… Jungian analysis and the Rorschach test are examples.

LS: *The unconscious as the location of all that we cannot explain and access is a modern construction and one that we should question. It is an interesting assumption that all things ought to be clear and explainable and that we therefore construct a shadow place, a waste place, a holy place, of the things that we do not understand.*
MB: *Are there not different ways of knowing? Why deny the use of the categories of "explainable" and "inexplicable" (within the frame of a particular construct of knowing)? For me, the categories themselves do not carry a value. Assigning a value to each category is an act of ideology, argument, or caprice.*

LS: *The idea that the experiences of the world are imperfect or incomplete representations of some ideal has always been a fascinating notion to me in two ways. First, embedded in the idea is that the world is imperfect and flawed, and that our thoughts are perfect and more "true." Second, it assumes that the idea is somehow separate from the manifestations of the world rather than emerging from them.*
MB: *If our ideas only emerged from the world, what then of imagination, dreams, fantasy, and desire. With these we create a world different from the one we "find." Because it is different does not automatically imply the one we "found" is imperfect or flawed. Imagining is like breathing in that you cannot stop it, and it is an act of spirit.*

cyclical constancy of the sun, moon, and stars, the "makers" of dark and light; fear of the dark, and comfort in the light; attributing to light and the sun divinity, warmth, birth, closeness, life, and joy… to the dark, sleep, death, distance, and evil… and to the moon, cold, mystery, and madness; feeling uplifted at the light's daybreak rise, and saddened at a sunset; light and dark as metaphors for understanding and intellect, as in a person's being "bright" or "dim," "dull" or "in the dark." Light and dark give meaning to simple directions: east, the light's home, the beginning of things, the most sacred direction; and west, about ending, darkness, the location of the land of the dead. And there are many more. These first meanings of light and dark still pervade our feelings and language, myth, religion, and the arts.

My review of theory-stories about this idea-with-many-names suggests that archetypes have several characteristics. Archetypes are themselves never seeable or knowable. They are hidden from consciousness and are manifested only in specific instances through real phenomena in the world, but even then only incompletely or imperfectly. We cannot make them, we can only sense their presence through the feeling of charge. Archetypes probably only exist for phenomena experienced "in the beginning" as significant and meaningful. There may be no new archetypes. They are the "original" and "most perfect" conditions or forms of these significant and meaningful phenomena. Archetypes have been primary content for all the symbolic forms of human expression – myth, language, religion, and art – and may have preceded and guided their development.

Many different manifestations may spring from the same archetype; the archetype is generic. Given the great range of phenomena for which there can be archetypes, relatively few are at core physical forms, even when their particular manifestation is in a physical form, such as a built place.

Relatively few of our experiences are charged and thereby felt as manifestations of an archetype. But when it is charged, an experience is profoundly altered. The archetypal phenomena are not necessarily desirable or nice; our fear of monstrosities is based on archetypes even more monstrous, in fact "perfectly" monstrous. Some archetypes are more active, and others more latent, within the domain of cultures or in individuals. Active ones shape much of our feeling and outlook; latent ones do so much less. But all are there and all can be awakened.

Archetypes are both products of and magnets for the spirit. They originate in that activity of the human spirit that imbues certain aspects of the world with significance. They are a mechanism for the spirit's excitation, evidence of the presence of spirit, and a way for its continuous elaboration.

Theory-stories of Archetypes

Several theory-stories suggest that early in the human species's beginnings, our senses were highly sensitive, far more than now, fully open, integrated and unified, and totally unselective.[2] The torrent of undifferentiated sensations coming in from the world may well have dominated all our experience, creating a stimulus overload unimaginable to us now, a true Chaos. Through some peculiar workings of the human sensorium and the brain and its mind, perhaps to escape domination by the senses, something rose within us and confronted this chaos of sensory impressions with an opposing, vital, and animating force of expression, making sense of a world that had been just sensation. This animating, vital force was the human spirit.

Our spirit opposed uncontrollable and meaningless sensation by experiencing (and later, expressing) certain things as both significant and meaningful and others as not, creating a world and a life filled with feeling and meaning. This process transformed forever all things in the world by making them, at least partially, products of our spirit – creations like Nature, the Divine, and Evil. These phenomena, given meaning by our spirit, became archetypal, and when manifested in a particular form, are experienced as charged. And, in a great energizing loop, like Eliade's (1954) "eternal return," experiencing this reverberant charge re-excites and re-affirms the spirit that first gave those phenomena their meaning. So archetypal significance and meaning come to us in the forms of a particular experience. It intensifies that experience, and makes us feel more "real" than that type of experience normally does, making it both particular and transcendent.

The focus of most bioevolutionary adaptive mechanisms is survival of the body and, through it, species continuity. What an archetype is, and does, suggest that it has an adaptive value, but one that is for survival and elaboration of the human spirit rather than the body. Yet most ideas about early human relationships to place imply that the most critical human activities were related to nourishment, safety, and procreation. Essentially about physical survival, these assumptions echo Hobbes' sad vision of humans in a state of nature as "[in] continual fear and danger of violent death; and the life of man, solitary, poor, nasty, brutish and short."

Yet the evidence of our intense early concern for matters of the spirit, our choosing and committing great resources and much attention to sacred places (many of which are not survival places of safety or nurture), intimates that something is operating here that is at least as powerful as somatic and species survival, and it suggests that a spiritual life is necessary for the survival of humans. This, in

LS: *This theory-story suggests that Homo sapiens are somehow discontinuous with other species and it places us (again) outside of evolutionary processes. To the best of our knowing, no species experiences the world as undifferentiated or chaotic, if only in its ability to be able to differentiate what it can and cannot eat. Why should we posit that humans are fundamentally different?*

This story does serve some purposes. It serves to reinforce the differences rather than continuity between humans and other life-forms which we know have contributed to the current environmental crisis. And it serves to remind us of our power to construct and order the world so that it makes "sense" to us. My question is whether or not this story at this place in time helps or hinders our dwelling on the earth.

MB: *In turn, I question the need always to meet broad social purposes in the offering up of ideas. That implies a pre-editing, a decision about the good, and about goodness that I am not sure I can/should/want to make.*

---

2. Various theory-stories seem to conjure human development as if it were in strands… some emphasize survival of the body, some elaboration of the spirit, others development of consciousness and cognition, or a dialectic formed by travail. We probably think in strands because it seems easier to disaggregate experience and "hold it still" rather than to embrace the terrifyingly complex wholeness that is our true experience of the world. I hope that ultimately we can find a way to wed the more body-based theories to ones more welcoming of spirit … to seek a wholeness in our thinking that tries to be an analog of our experience.

turn, suggests several things: that people with great spirit were selected in evolution; that places for the spirit were of critical importance in habitat selection; and that group survival has always been dependent on those with vision and visions.

In the realm of *architectural built form*, most theories that try to explain innate feelings and meanings emphasize the role of body experience in human development, and tend to de-emphasize any role for the spirit. Walter (1988) suggests that a primary way of knowing a place as a whole is through "haptic perception." Some of this perception comes through our actual touching of the parts of places, but more comes from the body's non-contact projection of touching, through our bodies' feelings of the properties of a place, its rhythms, edges, size, mass, completeness, and directions. This haptic perception is not based in a particular organ (as hearing is to the ear), but rather on the entire body as it feels things through its own inner articulations related to geometry, gravity, and tensions.

Harries (1983) hypothesizes the existence of natural symbols derived through millennia of common, transmitted experience of how the body senses a place. He posits some fundamental dialectics as natural symbols in human experience: our bodies' six directions, its center, and the polarities experienced through our senses of vision, hearing, touch, gravity, and location. These polarities are dark-light; loud-soft; rough-smooth/hard-soft/cold-hot; heavy-light; here-there/inside-outside. All are analogous to our experience of our own bodies. These meanings are not simple one-to-one relationships between form and meaning but are more complex. So, for example, a building aspiring verticality can be felt as a body's movement towards the spiritual, or as bravura, risky arrogance, or more ambiguously and richly, both.

Thiis-Evensen (1987) links bodily feeling more directly, almost empathetically, to the primary physical elements used in making buildings. From a fundamental dialectic of the balance of the forces of inside and outside, he derives the archetypal physical elements that delimit spatiality. Primary are the wall, floor, and roof, and then the door, window, and stair, all of which mediate between inside and outside. He argues that our body senses meanings through its felt relationship to three characteristics of each element: its motion, weight, and substance. Motion is the element's dynamic nature, felt as expanding, contracting, or balanced; weight is its relation to gravity; and substance is the character of material – hard-soft, warm-cold, etc.

Most current theories about our innate preferences for types of *landscapes* also suggest that such preferences are bioevolutionary adaptive mechanisms. By their nature these theories emphasize survival of the body and deemphasize any role spirit might play (Appleton 1975; Dubos 1965, 1968, 1980; Kaplan 1975, 1979, 1987; Orians 1986; Orians and Heerwagen 1992). Condon (1988) has a more spirit-welcoming theory about innate responses to landscape. He suggests these responses were forged during the millennia when humans remade the land and nature to meet their needs, during the process of which their own natures were changed in a dialectical and continuingly interactive relationship.

The meanings and feelings we have about our developmental and mythic landscapes and their attendant skyscapes are strong: the different characters of the celestial bodies, their mysterious regularity with occasional awesome interruptions; the forest's intimate immensity and the fear-filled certainty of being lost amidst dark spirits; the bosque or grove, a piece taken out of the forest, more knowable, filled with lighter spirits; the clearing making a "here" in an immensity of "there"; the solitary tree, a condensation of shelter and a connection to the gods above.

Landscapes, both natural and worked, loom large in any analysis of archetypes, and in every culture. Landscape archetypes may be so powerful because the vast bulk of evolution took place *in* landscape. They were "imprinted" over a period of time far longer than we have had built form. About 99 percent of human development took place in unworked landscapes, while only one percent took place in settlements, buildings, and made landscapes. So the forms, rhythms, and "stories" of early landscape and skyscape may well be part of the very structure of human consciousness. Other reasons for the power of landscape archetypes may be that, for the species, their imprinting happened during the period of the mind's greatest openness to imprinting, during the development of consciousness, and especially of the mythic consciousness. This was at a time of full-sensorium integration where the body was a far more sensitive "receiver," in a situation of the most profound participation in nature as a life-unity. Significantly, in landscapes there exists a strange situation in which the archetype and the actual place are often the same. That is, an experienced hominid ecosystem or territory is both the encoded template *and* the signal recalling the template, a kind of "doubling" or densification of the primary experience.

LS: *To suggest that innate preferences for landscapes on a bioevolutionary perspective is about the body and not the spirit continues the fracture between the two so skillfully articulated by Descartes. Is the spirit not of the body? For a fascinating discourse on this topic see Drew Leder (1990),* The Absent Body, *Chicago: University of Chicago Press.*
MB: *One vision of the spirit is that it is a desire and a way to make something that has no corporeality or mortality, that is both ephemeral and enduring, a way for us to live more easily with the tragedy of our transiency.*

LS: *Is the fear of death as we currently propose it a modern theory-story? Is it possible that humans have not always had the same fear of death and the desire to "escape from our body's vulnerability?"*

These may be good reasons why original landscapes loom so large in archetypal experience, but they do not explain the great archetypal power still found in built forms, both architectonic and made-landscapes. Several kinds of explanations seem plausible. For example, Orians and Heerwagen (1992) suggest that archetypes manifested in built places are derived from those in the original natural landscape, that the built forms have physical qualities like those in landscape.

It is also possible that some built forms have such potency for us because they embody a most fundamental archetype – mortality and immortality. We humans have always dreamed of an escape from our body's vulnerability, from our own mortality, from death, from what Harries (1982) calls the "terror of time." He argues that our body's dream always fails, but for the spirit, building seems to vanquish time and mortality. Built forms can embody spirit and they endure, some seemingly forever. And some are ideal and perfect forms and thus immortal or even divine.

Our original place experiences of vast forest and largely open savanna, the chancy nomadism of game chasing and food foraging, and nature's intransigence may have felt unprotected and vulnerable in an uncontrollable world. Some 10,000 years ago we began to domesticate both space and nature, physically and spiritually. Space became "place" when we set it aside, marked it off, changed it, used it, got to know it, and endowed it with values and meaning. Through this making of places, we try to lessen our physical vulnerability, and gain spiritual and psychological control over our mortality. Through the stability and durability of built *architecture*, we try to banish change. Through the use of perfect geometries in our important constructions, we try to give them a perfection that is timeless and immortal. Through built *landscapes* and their tending, we try to hide, control, frame, beautify, or objectify nature's intransigence and sublime indifference to us. And, even in our softer domestications, the quiet garden and dwelling, we make places to shelter reverie and daydreaming, more humble attempts to escape from time's terror.

So our need to change the physical environment is not just for protection in a physiologically hazardous world, for we also seek psychological control through making places that project, protect, and excite our *spirit*. And this may be true even in our most body-nurturing places. The corner, attic, cellar, and nook that Bachelard (1969) calls "images of intimacy" all certainly give a sense of nurture, but something else as well. Even Bachelard argues that the primary purpose of these sought-out places is for *daydreaming*, a projection of the spirit – a spirit floating. And, many of his "images of intimacy" offer, in their physical form, both a comfort spot *and* an outward prospect, an opening for vision(s) and the flight of the dreaming spirit.

Archetypes of Our Original Places

Certain phenomena that humans experienced repeatedly have become archetypal, such as gender, divinity, number, dark and light, terrifying creatures, force, birth, death, and place. In experiencing these, place may matter little or much; in some, place is the core significance of the experience, and these may be our original place archetypes. These few may have special power because of their great age and significance in the development of consciousness.

Given this, I speculate that there is a small set of archetypes that are places at their origin. The set might include: the place of mystery and fear; the sacred place; the forest; the grove or bosque; the clearing; the sky; still and wild waters; the settlement of The People; the gathering place, probably the dancing ground; the fire circle; the sleeping enclosure; the dwelling and its place in the sun; the place to be alone with spirit; the land of the dead; the garden of plenitude; and the journey.[3] Note that none of these conjure specific forms, and that many are landscapes. This suggests that any reasonable theory about place archetypes cannot be about specific physical forms, and must strongly embrace landscape.

Archetypes as Mythic Themes in Places

In contrast to the case described above where place itself *is* the archetype, a place can be the *medium* through which archetypes are expressed. One way places express archetypes is through the physical embodiment of and the "telling" of mythic themes. Myths are among the earliest human expressions; similar ones developed everywhere, and we still express mythic themes through all our symbolic forms, including place making.

---

3. One story that particularly interests me is the archetypal one that may be embodied in the gathering place. If we speculate that the "dancing ground" is the primal communal experience with its rhythmic, body-linked experience of individual and group ecstasy, that could inform our thinking and feelings about today's issues of public and private, and public places and public life, and life-with-strangers, and design for all these.

There seems to be a worldwide set of common myths, ones that have very similar basic structures while differing largely in specifics. While people only experience cultural or ethnic variations, and never the archetypal myth at the center, remarkable structural commonalities attest to that center. Some very common myths are: the creation of the world from a chaos of Nothing; the fire-theft; the great mother; virgin birth; the plenitude of Eden and the beauty of paradise; the chaos-again of the flood or deluge; the land of the dead; the dying and resurrected deity or hero; the questing journey or pilgrimage; and sacrifice, suffering, and redemption.

One example of a mythic theme embodied in place is the *sacred place*, probably one of our first places of significance. Scholars suggest that all sacred places embody the same myth of the deities' first creation, of the first place, of the making of an ordered and harmonious world out of our original chaos of nothingness (Cassirer 1955; Eliade 1957; Rapoport 1982). The pivotal act of most world creation myths is the creation of the first difference, marking a location, a place. This acts as a center, a "here" from which cosmic order can spring, although surrounded by a "there" that remains chaos. It is the beginning of an order that *is* our world, giving humans a harmonious place to dwell.

The forms of sacred places try to embody and "tell" about this making of a centered, ordered, stable, and protected world out of Chaos. In them we often see a prominent center from which the four cardinal directions spring, each different; the center strongly marked, with light, and with divinity-seeking verticalities; celestial order and harmony embodied in symmetries and rhythms; a strong difference between the sacred place and the profane world that surrounds it; a sturdiness of boundary for holding back the still-present chaos; a strongly marked entry, enhancing the importance of passage between the sacred and the profane (for we must live in both to have either); chiaroscuro, where the light of clarity and order grapples with the dark of mystery and chaos; our sacrifice and appreciation embodied in materials of value, often lovingly worked; and our continual care and maintenance, made into sacred work, for it keeps disorder from returning.

By embodying elements of this schema in its form(s), sacred places are, in some sense, the myth of creation presented in built form, rather than in a linguistic narrative.[4] Other archetypal places may embody other mythic themes.

The Essential Qualities of Place

All of our symbolic forms of expression, like myth, religion, and the arts, use archetypes as primary content. And within each expressive medium – stories, ritual, dance, drawing, self-mutilation, enriched speech, and place making – any archetype may be conjured and expressed in more than one way. While space and place are certainly among our earliest significant experiences, they are only one category of many in significant human experiences. This suggests that of all our archetypes, relatively few are places, and that there are two kinds: the few that *at their origins* are places (like Paradise or the deep forest), and those archetypes that are *expressed* spatially and through places, like trying to touch the Divine through the building of a spire or through the making of geometries that are ideal, un-natural, and crystalline perfect.

Our sensing of forms that embody archetypally significant meaning suggests that such forms can act as natural symbols, or as a natural language. In speaking of archetypes as a natural language I feel somewhat trapped by language itself, for it is not a good enough vehicle for conjuring archetypes, or any other nonlinguistic ways of expressing meaning. Archetypal meanings just do not work like language. Nor, of course, do meanings in dance or painting. A *linguistic* narrative is sequential; its words have fairly precise meanings and these must be learned; it has a beginning and end; the ear hears and the mind understands. Conversely, meaning experienced through the medium of *place* is in an unlearned or natural language. These meanings come through all the senses, body movement and posture, and the mind, but are more felt than understood. They are not precise meanings, but rather flickers, bundles, even a mosaic of meanings. They are more simultaneous than sequential. No direct linguistic translation is possible; places speak in another way. But you are reading a text I have written, so we will both make do with language.

I believe that the most robust expressions of meaning for each symbolic form spring from those qualities that distinguish it from the other symbolic forms. These are the qualities that constitute it, its particular essence, that which makes it what it is. The essential qualities that distinguish made places from the other symbolic forms should give rise to certain expressive capacities that only places have,

---

4. As one interesting inquiry into the nature of sacred space, I developed a set of "design guidelines" for sacred places, using a composite of many world creation myths as a kind of pre-design program (Brill, 1985b).

Table 3-1 Essential Qualities that Constitute All Made Landscape and Built Form

Landform and topography	Purpose and use by the one and the many	Orientation and direction	Order	Location	Materials, materiality, and workmanship
Geophysical materials (land and water), plant materials and its cycles	Approach, passage, and movement through	Relationships to natural cycles and celestial activity	Rhythm and sequence	Fixity	Surface manipulation and color
Character of available energy (wind, sun...) local alternating of climate	Views to and from	Light, dark, and chiaroscuro	Centers and boundaries	Markedness	Entropy, maintenance, and care
Relationships to the near environment... context			Dimensions and sizes	Stability	
			Parts and wholes	Substantiality	
			Joints and continuity		
			Scale relationships/human(s) to place		
			Geometry and shape		
			Mass and hollowness		
			Enclosure and openness		

or that places have most robustly. Table 3-1 shows what may be the essential qualities of all made places, both architectonic built forms and made landscapes.

If each symbolic medium's most vigorous expressions are those that stem from its essential or defining qualities, then place making, which focuses on these essential qualities of places, should conjure certain meanings more easily than others, ones especially suited to the medium of place. Yet it seems that no one of these essential qualities has a sole or unique relationship to a particular feeling or meaning. For example, "protection" and "vulnerability" are archetypal feelings well suited to expression through place, yet it is clear that *many* of the previously mentioned essential qualities of place could be used in their expression: how threatening the near environment or context is; how light and dark are arranged, especially light *out there* and dark *in here*; how firm the place boundaries are; what the degree of enclosure and openness is; scale relationships, the sizes of things related to humans; and the character of approach, passage, and movement through the place.

These essential place qualities are major components of expression in all places. But they become something more in certain places, places that recall the few Original Places, and places that embody mythic themes. Another set of places that feel like "more" are those that engage a dialectic of *tones*.

LS: *To suggest that we understand the world by making distinctions is to privilege separation over connection. We understand the world both by differentiating and by relating, but our current worldview privileges one over the other.*

MB: *Yes, the western world currently overprivileges differences... invention over convention... the particular over the universal... the new over the old. An exploration of archetypes may be a way of integrating the particular with the universal, the new with the old. And we need* both *differentiation and similarity to even have the idea of dialectic, of tension, of integration.*

Archetypes as a Dialectic of Tones

The essential qualities of place (e.g., mass and hollowness, light and dark) suggest that one way places can be strongly expressive is through a *dialectic*, but a dialectic that focuses less on the constructed dualism of its polar terms than on their wholeness as continua, or the area of experienced tension between them. In these terms, I have started to explore those dialectics that seem most robustly related to place.

One such dialectic is our constructed separation of body and spirit, the flesh and the soul. Our spirit reaches, makes meaning, and is immortal; our body is grounded, feels, and is mortal. All our symbolic forms have expressed both the tension and the integration of this lived dialectic. Some of our "charged" places resonate more with our body, some more with our spirit, some more with the tension between them, and some profoundly integrate them. So, for example, a tall *spire* aspires to touch the divine spirit in light… a *cave* nurtures and protects the sleeping body in its dark womb… and the *pyramid* of Egypt tries to do both, its form a tension between its vertical and spirited aspiration and the downward slump cause by the great stones placed there to guarantee an eternity of protection for a sacred body.

In trying to understand archetypes, I have examined certain recurrent and common place forms, ones that seem frequently charged, and then tried to sense their archetypal content. Among these are the cave, the spire, the labyrinth, the pyramid, the stone circle, the orchard, and the mound. Certain dialectically opposed pairs of meanings began to emerge with some frequency. I call them *tones*. There are certainly more tones than I have found, and the work continues. The first tones are two pairs of apparent opposites.

> contentment ………………aspiration
> nurturance ……………………….risk

Each or several of the tones can be emphasized in places, and seemingly opposed tones may both be present in a place's forms with a resulting integration, a new term, or a re-cognition of an original (and more whole) term.

Each of the tones above has a "dark" and a "bright" side. While nurture and contentment feel desirable, an excess of either may hamper personal growth. And aspiration, often a drive towards virtue, may sometimes reflect an excess of pride. Risk taking, while necessary for development, can be dangerous to health and longevity. All of these, as feelings, can be sources of great pleasure. But aspiration and risk carry a sense of incompletion, desire, and need for fulfillment. So each tone can serve us well and/or poorly, depending on the values we hold. By directing us toward or reminding us of what we can be, these tones engage what Harries (1983, 1985) has called the "ethical function" in place making.

LS: *I have a serious problem with the proposition that some place archetypes may be more spirit and some more bodily. To suggest that a cave nurtures "the body" in its womb and the spire attracts our "spirit" to the divine is a peculiarly male (and therefore modern/western) interpretation. The problem arises not only from the dualism that this represents (which is constructed and which we now experience as real), but because it denies one of the most powerful parts of these "tones" - and that is their integrative power. These experiences of archetypal places make sense to us because they do not split our world, because they challenge these convenient constructions which serve other purposes.*

LS: *To call great expanses of forest or the ocean "inhospitable" speaks more to our lack of understanding of these places than to any characteristics of the place. Some peoples understand the forest to be a place of intense intimacy and nurturance.*

Aspiration

Aspiration is about spirit. It is future oriented, ambitious, desiring, about becoming more, moving toward virtue, toward the divine. Some of aspiration's obvious *forms* are the endless staircase or ladder-to-heaven, the spire, obelisks, bell towers, radio towers, Simon Rodia's Watts Towers, the rocket, Gothic cathedrals and Gaudi's cathedral, and the great telescopes – all pure verticality, light seeking, gravity fleeing, desire as direction. Aspiration's forms are generally uninhabited.

Risk

The primordial form of risk is separation from nature and from the mother. Yet risk is a necessity for individuation and for culture. It is precarious, perilous; a gamble, a mystery engaged; an exploration, a necessity for learning, and for growth. Risk's adrenalin rush sharpens the senses. Because it is an engagement with danger, it accepts the possibility of bodily hurt and is thus a devaluation of body life.

Risk requires at least the possibility of success. The charge felt in places of risk may be the tension of a simultaneous bodily attraction *and* repulsion. The attraction is the lure of challenge without which growth cannot occur. The repulsion is leaving that which is familiar, protective, and nurturing, and venturing into the unknown. Attraction and repulsion bonded together is much like Edmund Burke's ([1757] 1958) concept of the "sublime," and many sublime landscapes are clear embodiments of body risk, like Niagara Falls or the Grand Canyon.

Risk's archetypal forms require inhabitation or at least human presence. The forms embody separation, distance, attenuation, and infinity (no-thing, nowhere). Examples are a great expanse of inhospitable nature such as the forest or the ocean, or precipitous ones, like a great waterfall or canyon edge. In social terms the open expanse of empty plaza is a risk form, where you are fully exposed to the gaze of others; in physical terms, a delicate bridge; in behavioral terms, the journey (which, when it has aspiration toward virtue, becomes a pilgrimage) (Munro 1987).

The slender tower is a risky disconnection from earth, and an isolation, with a place at its top inhabited by a special person, a lonely one, a risk taker, a seeker and seer – like the minaret, the lighthouse, the bell tower, the glider.

5. Setha Low, Clare Cooper Marcus, and others have reported several times very similar findings from their own classes, in workshops at several annual conferences of the Environmental Design Research Association.

Niagara Falls, a place of risk, is beautiful in the postcard; sublime at a middle distance, but terrifying close up, for your body aches to join it, to be one once again with fierce water, to experience primordial chaos, undifferentiated, formless, unstoppable power. Wild water is about risk: the torrential rain stirring real fear of another deluge; surfers taking risk-pleasure in riding high Pacific surf, becoming one with a wave. The risk becomes institutionalized and tamer in the amusement park's water ride and in Larry Halprin's wild-water urban plazas. Boogie-boarding is tamer yet; tamest, the bubbling backyard birdbath.

The Labyrinth is a place of risk, through unresolvable ambiguity, where distinctions are lost between inside and outside, here and there, open and closed, leaving and entering. In it there is no particular place, only a permanent state of being lost, where all space is the same under the featureless sky. The space is shaped for movement, not habitation, a journey made almost permanent, where the only achievement can be a return to the not-lost at its beginning or by finding a valuable center.

Contentment

Contentment suggests that a person has been successful in limiting, accepting, or assuaging need, and is thankful, gratified, and comfortable. It is often accompanied by some inertia, indifference, and risk-aversion. It is a state to which contemplation, reverie, and daydreaming come easily, all of which are flights of the spirit, suggesting some available openness. Places of contentment seem to enclose the body while opening to an outside.

Many people have places they go to for contentment and reverie. During several years of teaching design studio I asked my students to describe "places that were important to them." Analysis of a large number of their thoughtful responses show that over 90 percent were small, tranquil, inhabitable, single cells of space, really "places" more than spaces in Tuan's (1977) sense. They were held in great affection; none of them were "architecture," all were humble and unprepossessing; they were generally experienced alone, and frequently returned to for reverie, solace, and contemplation.

Although the particular places had a variety of actual forms, my analysis suggests that only two forms underlay them all. Half were small outdoor places in a natural or unclaimed setting, and half were much like a small, quiet hut. Bachelard (1969) has called these "images of intimacy." I have called this special category of charged places "embracing places."[5]

Nurturance

Nurturance refers to sustenance, nourishment, and plenitude; connection to and physical closeness of significant others; and maternal, embracing protection. It is about body and bodies.

Some archetypal forms of nurturance are the cave, the dwelling, and the burial mound; the kitchen garden and the farm; savanna-like habitats; corpulent granaries, storehouses, and markets; and places that bring people together face-to-face, as in walled circles, "greens," or "commons." Places of nurture tend to eschew any idealized geometry, have a noninsistent form, use relatively unworked materials, enclose and support family or small community behavior, are protective and secure, signal surplus or plenitude, and are ordinary, repetitive, and familiar.

Walled circles like Stonehenge and palisades are open places that make a fixed center on the earth, bringing bodies together and saying "we are here," making and marking off inside from outside, and where the circle is pierced, framing a "there" from a protected "here;" they create an inward-focused nonhierarchical sturdy safeness for a group's gathered contemplation. Open above, they expose and elevate the groups' concerns by embracing the sky's cycles of celestial theater and the play of dark and light.

The burial mound is about nurture. The weight of great natural protection laid over a treasured body below, returning it to the embracing earth; it has a soft, permissive, and giving form, with no aspiration to an otherworldly divine. The body and the marking mound are left alone to return to natural processes.

I am exploring the meaning in forms of some other dialectics which seem to be very appropriate to place. In doing this work, I select places that are frequently felt as charged and then try to sense or understand what significant themes seem to be embodied in the forms of the places. Some additional tones that seem to recur frequently are:

        dwelling......................placelessness
        community........................solitude
        order.................................chaos
        valued...........................disdained
        immortal spirit..............mortal body
        power..........................subjugation

I purposefully used several of these tones and archetypes in the design and development of Landscapes of Peril, a recent design project.

An Example of Using Archetypes in Design

This design project resulted from the intention of the U.S. Department of Energy (DOE) to bury some 500,000 barrels of radioactive waste one-third of a mile below New Mexico's shifting sand desert, in a geophysically inert thick salt formation. The waste will remain dangerous for 10,000 years. Analysis suggests that the highest probability of releasing these dangerous contaminants is through human intrusion, probably in the far future. The DOE is ethically committed to placing a permanent marking at this burial site, warning of its dangers, to help prevent inadvertent release of radioactivity into our descendants' food chain, water supply, and air. The criteria for success of such a warning mark are that it must endure, be discovered, and be understood.

Linguists predict that even 1500 years from now none of today's languages will be spoken, or even readable, except by scholars. Although it always has been and still is a fairly desolate area, research suggests that there will be many successive cultures at the New Mexico site, with very different characters, some possibly quite primitive. Mineral-search drilling, the perilous event that is most probable, does not require very sophisticated technology, nor an advanced culture. The U.S. government does not believe it can commit to any policing or institutional control beyond 100 years from internment of the waste. America's government and its state boundaries and those of nation-states will probably change markedly over the 10,000-year period.

In 1991, the DOE, through Sandia National Laboratory, conducted a search process and selected two teams of six experts each. Each team was asked to explore and propose a solution. On one team were an anthropologist, an astronomer, a materials scientist, a linguist, an archaeologist, and myself (an architect). In our first meeting, I suggested that the use of archetypes in place design could bypass the far future communication problems of not knowing anything about the language or the culture of future people at the site. The team accepted the idea that there is an enduring human propensity to experience meanings in the physical forms of many things, including places. Nonlinguistic, species-wide archetypes probably came before or with culture, can work independently of it, and will exist even after any apocalyptic cultural discontinuity, as long as humans remain relatively biologically unchanged.

LS: *Have humans always created places of non-inhabitation as part of their place making? Or is this a peculiar new type which has evolved as part of modern, western culture?*
MB: *I think it is a very old type. Some places have always been set apart, some sacred and some taboo. They were often uninhabited, or inhabited only by a few, the very spiritually privileged or outcasts.*

3-1
Landscape of Thorns
(drawing by Safdar Abidi)

As a result, the site and all the structures on it are proposed to be designed as a multimodal system of communication, with the primary effort to design the entire site as a warning, using archetypes as a natural language of form and meaning bonded. Conceived of as a system of communications, the site's overall design is complemented by: many and obvious places with short inscriptions in seven languages; bas-reliefs of faces with the universally recognized expressions of horror and sickness; protected but findable buried rooms with lengthy messages inscribed in stone, supported by astronomical diagrams locating this burial in time, and a periodic table identifying the buried radioactive elements. All this was based on multidisciplinary research culminating in a substantial set of design guidelines.

The archetypal images selected for the site's design are of perils that we believe place design can strongly express: wounding of the body; dangerous emanations; keeping something buried that must not escape; and poisoned, destroyed, and dead land. Seven alternative test designs, called Landscapes of Peril, were developed; each embodies one or more of these archetypes while also responding to the design guidelines. All the landscapes entirely cover and thus clearly mark the extent and the boundaries of the square-mile interment area, called "the Keep."

Landscape of Thorns is a random field or forest of concrete thorns (or oddly shaped claws), some 50 feet high, whose shapes suggest punctures, wounding to the body, all rising up from below and reaching out like an uncontrolled growth of something dangerous, like mutations.

3-2
Menacing Earthworks
(drawing by Safdar Abidi)

3-3
Black Hole
(drawing by Safdar Abidi)

Menacing Earthworks are immense lightning-shaped earthworks radiating from an open-centered Keep, emanations of danger seen best from the air, or from vantage points on top of the highest earthworks. At ground level, the massive earthworks crowd in on you, cutting off the horizon, suggesting a loss of place. The square sandy Keep is open, vast, and desolate, except for a walk-on map locating the many other radioactive waste sites in the world in relation to the one here.

Black Hole is a black masonry slab, evoking an enormous "black hole," an immense no-thing, a void, land removed from use, worthless. Uninhabitable, because it is often exceedingly hot, for its blackness absorbs the desert sun's heat and reradiates it. The slab's many thermal joints have an irregular pattern, like the crazy cracks in parched and dead land.

Spikes Bursting through Grid is a regular grid (about house sized) inlaid in a masonry slab that covers the Keep, yet the heavy and ordering lid cannot stop wounding energy bursting from below. The spikes/teeth/barbs first ripple the Keep's cover, then deform it, then puncture it, and finally the grid's reliable and human-imposed order is destroyed by a more powerful force, chaos.

3-4
Spikes Bursting through Grid
(drawing by Safdar Abidi)

3-5
Rubble Landscape
(drawing by Safdar Abidi)

3-6
Forbidding Blocks
(drawing by Safdar Abidi)

3-7
Spike Field
(drawing by Safdar Abidi)

Rubble Landscape: Under the sand is a layer of stone. A square outer rim of it is dynamited into boulders and bulldozed into a crude pile over the Keep. This makes an enormous rubble-stone cover that is different in height, material, and vegetation from the surrounding desert. It feels like a massive effort to keep something dangerous contained in its underground lair. Its top of broken rubble makes it a place that feels destroyed, rather than one that has been made.

Forbidding Blocks: The under-the-sand stone is dynamited, cast into house-size concrete and stone blocks, and dyed black. The blocks are set in a deliberately irregular square grid, with five-foot-wide "streets" running both ways. The streets are hot, ominous, lead nowhere, and are too narrow to live in, farm in, or even meet in. It is a massive effort to deny use, uninhabitable, crudely ordered, forbidding and uncomfortable.

Spike Field: Large stone spikes pierce the sand, coming up and out of the Keep, moving in various directions, uncontrolled, and chaotic. The whole area is bounded by a wall, the spikes contained in it, making the outside safe.

This project was a very conscious effort to use designed forms to affect the unconscious of others, through archetypal images of peril and fear, and through visceral or haptic responses conjured by threatening and alien landscapes of human-diminishing scale. The works of artists often touch our unconscious and act viscerally and haptically. I maintain that this project is not an attempt to make art, but to be a specialized communication "device." As a communication, it encodes and sends as unambiguous a message as is possible, and as such is manipulative.

Archetype and Type

In some discourses about type, an archetype is spoken of as if it were a special type of type, one that is original and fundamental, older and deeper, a type that lurks beneath type and perhaps generates it. In many instances this may be probable, but the differences between type and archetype are also important to discuss.

In this discussion I accept, in general, Quatremère de Quincy's ([1825] 1977) concept of type as something never actually knowable or seen, but manifested in the general forms of particular places. It is an idea about the forms of places, but insufficient to describe or model the form of any particular place. An archetype shares with type this quality of being unknowable and hidden, and revealed only generally, and only through particular instances.

Type, then, acts as a shadowy pattern for certain places that share characteristics. Using this pattern, we sense these places as members of a set, conjuring the type. The set is fluid in its number of members, and the individual members differ in other characteristics. But the type does evoke an image sufficient to sense particular places either as excluded from, or as members of, the set, through their resonance with the type.

In *architectural* terms, type is usually about *form* (a domed drum) or about *use* (a stadium), and sometimes about both (a domed stadium). Even in types mostly about use, we have an image of form. In *landscape* terms we also find use type and form type. For example, Condon's (1988) development of fundamental landscape types posits form types like the bosque, the allée, and the single tree, and use types like the street, the cloister, and the natural theater.

Types are cultural productions, generic images of physical forms that are produced through their recurrent historic manifestations. Types may also be a particular culture's variant of species-wide archetypal experiences. There are important divergences between archetype and some normative concepts of type. In type, the *form* is emphasized, does not vary much, and meaning is de-emphasized. In archetypes, *meaning* is emphasized more than form, and the forms that express the meanings can vary quite widely, although there may be certain forms that are more robust than others, and appear more frequently. For example, all the easily recognizable "perfect" geometries (like the circle and the square) can express the same archetype – that of perfection, the ideal, and, by extension, the Divine. *But the forms are not the archetypes, only their medium of expression*. The archetype is divinity.

Type's forms may act as symbols and carry meaning, but the meaning is most often related to the cultural history of the configuration of such places and/or their physical function. For people outside that culture, such forms may mean little, or may mean something different. Since type depends on a cultural history of manifestations in form, and an archetype does not, archetypal place experiences happen often in strange places, places outside of one's own culture.

The tendency to construct type seems cognitive, a way to categorize, repeat, and know, while the tendency toward archetypes seems more spirit driven, a way toward an intensification of reality. Experiencing a manifestation of type is seldom felt as a charged experience, while the excitation of charge is the very mark of experiencing an archetype.

Because type is largely about physical form, it overprivileges the visual sense, and diminishes (relatively) the value of the other senses. Conversely, one characteristic of an archetypally charged experience is that it seems to integrate *all* the senses. Archetypes can be called up by senses other than the visual, from the smell and humidity of places, their acoustic quality, or the feel of the air. We must remember that the different senses are really distinguishable only in reflection and analysis, and not in direct experience.

So, in archetypes (as compared to types) there is no single form that lurks beneath, but many. That does not mean that form is unimportant or irrelevant to experiencing an archetype. Rather it suggests that form is very important to the production of meaning, but not invariant or particular forms.

Value of Thinking about Archetypes

The experience of using archetypes as a premise for design work, along with ongoing conversations with students in seminars and design studios, leads me to speak of archetypes not within the discourse of style, nor even method, but rather as an attitude. It is *one* way, not *the* way. It is not intended to supplant other ways of thinking about place design, but to augment them.

While archetypes may reside only in the unconscious, they are confirmed often by the simple intensity of their presence and by the way they impress themselves upon consciousness. Just talking with students about charged places seems to legitimate place experiences that they, and so many other people, would otherwise tend to keep to themselves. It suggests an enriched way of place knowing in the world, a way, perhaps, of resacralizing the world.

This essay does not twinkle with citations, but that does not reduce my great debt to the many from whose thoughts I have learned, most notably: Joseph Campbell, Ernst Cassirer, Mircea Eliade, Karsten Harries, Carl Jung, Yi-Fu Tuan, E.V. Walter, and, quite directly, from Patrick Condon and Bob Riley.

The essay builds on ideas presented at the workshop entitled "Beliefs, Intentions & Built Form" held in Miami, Florida in October 1991 and then as the 1992 Daniel Urban Kiley Lecture at the Landscape Architecture program of the Harvard Graduate School of Design, April 1992. I am very indebted to Irwin Altman for his late 1990 cogent critique of all my work in this area, and to Bonnie Ott for her frequent thoughtful reviews of work-in-progress.

It is also an entrancing subject for a place designer, because it more clearly links place making to some of humanity's basic questions: Who are we? Where have we come from? Where should we go? and What does it all mean? It makes the act of place making feel more central to our humanness. It even suggests that architecture and landscape architecture might be taught as if they were a branch of the humanities, one of those ways we re-present ourselves to ourselves, like ethics, history, and philosophy.

And finally, there is value in the idea that, somehow, place archetypes connect us to others and can be a means of shared experience and knowledge. Our modernity carries with it an emphasis on privacy and private life, alienation and isolation, a loosening of communal bonds, and a desacralization of our world. There remains, however, a longing to reconnect with the others and to have places that touch our spirit. And that longing may be satisfied, in some small way — even if for a moment — with each experience of a charged place, and the archetypal meanings that connect us as we share them.

References

Appleton, J. 1975. *The Experience of Landscape*. London: John Wiley & Sons.

Bachelard, G. 1969. *The Poetics of Space*. Boston, Mass.: Beacon.

Brill, M. 1985a. Sacred places and embraced places: using design-as-inquiry to understand the difference. An address given to the C.E.L.A., Council of Educators in Landscape Architecture, September 20, University of Illinois, Urbana, Illinois.

———. 1985b. Using the place-creation myth to develop design guidelines for sacred space: A peculiar method. An address given to the C.E.L.A., Council of Educators in Landscape Architecture, September 20, University of Illinois, Urbana, Illinois.

———. 1989. Using archetypes in the design of "charged" places. An address given as the Horace Cleveland Distinguished Fellow, April, Landscape Architecture Program, University of Minnesota, Minneapolis, Minnesota.

———. 1990. Personally important experiences of "charged" places. (Unpublished).

Burke, Edmund. [1757] 1958. *A Philosophical Enquiry into the Origin of Our Ideas of the Sublime and the Beautiful*. Edited by James T. Boulton. Notre Dame, Ind.: Notre Dame University Press.

Campbell, J. 1959. *The Masks of God*. London: Pitman Press Ltd.

Cassirer, E. [1923] 1973. *Language & Myth*. New York: Dover Publications.

———. [1925] 1955. *The Philosophy of Symbolic Forms: Vol. 2. Mythical Thought*. New Haven, Conn.: Yale University Press.

Condon, P. 1988. *A Designed Landscape Space Typology*. Minneapolis, Minn.: School of Architecture and Landscape Architecture, University of Minnesota.

Dubos, R. 1965. *Man Adapting*. New Haven, Conn.: Yale University Press.

———. 1968. *So Human an Animal*. New York: Scribner's Sons.

———. 1980. *The Wooing of Earth*. New York: Scribner's Sons.

Eliade, M. 1954. *The Myth of the Eternal Return*. Princeton, N.J.: Princeton University Press.

———. 1957. *The Sacred and the Profane*. New York: Harcourt, Brace & World.

Givens, D. 1982. From here to eternity: communicating with the distant future. *etc* 30 (2), 159–79.

Harries, K. 1982. Building and the terror of time. *Perspecta* 19: 55–69.

———. 1983. Thoughts on a non-arbitrary architecture. *Perspecta* 20: 9–20.

———. 1985. The ethical function of architecture. In *Descriptions*, eds. D. Ihde and H.J. Silverman. Albany, N.Y.: State University of New York Press.

Hildebrand, G. (1991). *The Wright Space*. Seattle, Wash.: University of Washington Press.

Jung, C. 1969. *Man and His Symbols*. New York: Doubleday.

Kaplan, S. 1975. An informal model for the prediction of preference. In *Landscape Assessment*, eds. E.H. Zube, R.O. Bruch, and J.G. Fabos. Stroudsburg, Pa.: Dowden, Hutchinson and Ross, Inc.

———. 1979. Perception and landscape: conceptions and misconceptions. In *Proceedings of Our National Landscape*, eds. G.H. Elsner and R.C. Smardon. Pacific South West #35. Berkeley, CA: Pacific Southwest Forest and Range Experimental Station.

———. 1987. Aesthetics, affect and cognition: environmental preference from an evolutionary perspective. *Environment and Behavior* 19 (1): 3–32.

Lobell, M. 1983. Spatial archetypes. *Revision* 6 (2): 69–82.

McCully, R. 1987. *Jung & Rorschach: A Study in the Archetype of Perception*. Dallas, Tex.: Spring Publications.

Munro, E. 1987. *On Glory Roads: A Pilgrim's Book about Pilgrimage*. New York: Thames and Hudson.

Orians, G., 1986. An ecological and evolutionary approach to landscape esthetics. In *Landscape Meaning and Values*, eds. E. Penning-Rowsell and D. Lowenthal. London: Allen and Unwin.

Orians, G., and J. Heerwagen. 1992. Evolved response to landscapes. In *The Adapted Mind*, eds. J. Barkow, L. Cosmides, and J. Tooby. New York and Oxford: Oxford University Press.

Pitt, D. 1990. Evolution and the avant-garde: A transactional reconciliation of conflicting landscape value systems. In *The Avant-garde and the Landscape: Can They Be Reconciled?* eds. P. Condon and L. Neckar. Minneapolis, Minn.: Landworks Press.

Quatremère de Quincy, A.C. [1825] 1977. Type. With an introduction by A. Vidler. *Oppositions* 8 (Spring): 148–50.

Rapoport, A. 1982. Sacred places, sacred occasions and sacred environments. *Architectural Design* 52 (9/10): 75–82.

Thiis-Evensen, T. [1987] 1989. *Archetypes in Architecture*. New York: Oxford University Press.

Tuan, Y. 1977. *Space and Place*. Minneapolis, Minn.: University of Minnesota Press.

Walter, E.V. 1988. *Placeways: A Theory of the Human Environment*. Chapel Hill and London: University of North Carolina Press.

Chapter 4

A Built Landscape Typology:
The Language of the Land We Live In

Patrick Condon

The chapter that follows is divided into two parts. The two parts cover the same topic; however, their mode of generation is quite different. One part, "Reason," is written in a *reasonable* way. The other part, "Imagination," is written in an *imaginative* way – or at least such is my hope.

I make no claim of competence in either of these modes of thought. In fact, using the two different voices is more an act of desperation than of hubris. I have struggled for several years to construct a simple and clear argument in support of my view that there is a commonly understood language of landscape space types. I feel that presenting the topic in two different modes may be the best way for me to convey my point of view.

Any language system functions at the point of intersection between the mind and the natural world; language is the medium of that exchange. As a bridge between the two realms, language exists half in the realm of *reason* (thinking, ordering, computing, concluding) and half in the world of natural phenomena (sensations, visions, pleasure, pain, stimulation, need). The world of natural phenomena impresses the sensibilities and produces images in the mind; that is to say that the natural world exists in the realm of the *imagination*. I am cognizant that the words, reason and imagination, can be used in many other ways. I am using them as expressed above.

Type is a language system and, as such, it too exists half in reason and half in imagination. My previous attempts to explain landscape type by reason alone felt incomplete – the image was left behind. On the other hand, a descriptive study of a particular landscape type, as it presented itself to the imagination, did not provide me with *reasons*, i.e., *explanations* for why the space was so beautiful and affecting.

Consequently, I here attempt to do both at the same time. I suggest that the reader engage the two parts simultaneously, jumping from reason to imagination, then back again. Others may prefer to read them in turn, first all of reason, then all of imagination (or the reverse).

Reason

In this chapter I argue that the human creative spirit is expressed in the landscape in the form of identifiable types. I am using the same definition of the human spirit that Mike Brill develops in this volume: a creative force that charges forth to confront the chaos of uncontrolled and undifferentiated sensory im-pressions with an equal and opposite power, a power of ex-pression.[1] This power of expression is conceptual (holding a thought in the mind and in that way naming things), physical (making things), and social (sharing a language and making things together). An important product of this expressive naming and making is a shared language of designed landscape space types.

As the title suggests, the focus of this chapter is on *designed* landscape *space* types. By designed I mean any landscape that manifests a *human design,* whether the space is productive, like an orchard, or restorative, like a cloister. By landscape space I mean any landscape that we can *be inside*. The street is a landscape space; the garden gate is not.

I am suggesting that basic types of designed landscape space exist and are commonly appreciated. I believe that they are commonly appreciated because they strike the beholder as meaningful in a fundamental, almost primal way. To the extent that they are meaningful in this fundamental way, the landscape space types constitute a basic language of landscape experience.

The Dialectical Landscape

Most existing work on environmental type and typology comes from the discipline of building architecture. In applying this body of inquiry in landscape architecture we can rightfully ask: Are there essential differences in the way that the local spaces and fixed forms of buildings are experienced versus the way that the open and continuous spaces of the landscape are experienced?

I answer yes. The experience of landscape space types is special because the connection between humans and the landscape is dialectical. Since the idea of this dialectical connection is at the core of my argument, I will devote some space to explaining what I mean by it. To do so I thread together the thoughts of a few individuals who are, in my view, significant figures in the development of dialectical thought in the west. They are Robert Smithson, Maurice Merleau-Ponty, Karl Marx, and the philosophers of the English Romantic Movement: Edmund Burke, Uvedale Price, and William Gilpin. I link together their different but related

Imagination

Some landscapes are made by nature without human help: natural landscapes.

Some landscapes are made by humans out of the living and inert materials that nature provides: built landscapes.

Natural landscapes are the ones we haven't had the audacity or the desire to reshape yet.

We are born into built landscapes. We die into built landscapes.

The story of my life and your life is unfolding in built landscapes.

Humans have been hard at work turning natural landscapes into built landscapes for a half-million years. More and more men and women were born, so more and more room was needed.

This half-million years of beating back natural landscapes will probably be finished within the next 50.

Nature doesn't care. Nature has other planets to work on.

At first, the room belonging to the forest was made into rooms belonging to humans.

The first room was the clearing.

Next the corridor through the forest was cut: an allée.

Many other types of rooms were cut from a reluctant nature by unrelenting humans: the orchard, the terrace, the street, the square, the yard, the cloister.

---

1. See Mike Brill, Chapter 3, this volume. I take this occasion to express my debt to Mike Brill for this and other insights that he has freely shared with me.

Over time these rooms became more and more comfortable for humans. We worked to make them look a certain way, give them a certain order. When we ordered nature's materials and bent nature to human purpose, we no longer needed to be afraid of nature.

Over time nature's meaning changed. Nature the omnipotent, the unreasonable, the jealous, and the terrible became nature the inspirational, the kind, and the nurturing. It became pleasurable to behold the nature we had transformed. Framed inside the order of the rooms, nature the terrible became nature the beautiful – the vine that appalled in the bramble became the vine that captivated on the arbor.

Over the millennia the orderly rooms fashioned of nature's materials became a predictable framework for human experience in space. Consequently there was no need to take specific note of them anymore. The pleasurable and secure sense they conveyed persisted, but these sensations sank comfortably into the subconscious, their important characteristics obscured behind the veil of the habitual. Nature the horrible was safely sequestered in "far-off lands" while nature the nurturing was our loyal, dutiful, and dependable companion.

In some parts of the world this situation remained stable for almost 2000 years. But about 200 years ago some especially sensitive people noticed that there were so many rooms being cut from nature that both nature the horrible and nature the nurturing were disappearing – only the human order remained. They started to paint pictures of the "room in nature" before nature vanished entirely, leaving the room a barren white shell. They thought that the rooms for human activity should have walls woven of nature's materials, and that without them the human body, mind, and spirit would freeze. I am thinking of painters like George Inness and Frederic Church.

Eighty years ago a different group of people came along. They said that in this Modern Age, people were tough enough to live in bare white rooms. People need not

dialectical notions of landscape/human interaction to propose a way of thinking about designed landscape typology – a way that may be useful for practice.

I illustrate my contention that the designed landscape space types that structure our everyday experience are, in Merleau-Ponty's terms, "practical categories" (Merleau-Ponty 1974, 180) that are manifested in the landscape when we, as Marx would put it, "oppose nature and thereby change our own nature" (quoted in Fromm 1966, 40). I argue that this interdependent opposition of humans and nature is an identifiable aspect of form in the landscape, and that this dialectical opposition produces an aesthetic "charge." *Beautiful*, human-initiated *order* is one side of the dialectic; *sublime* nature's *complexity* is the other (Smithson's and the Romantics' idea). Finally, I choose particular designed landscape space types for inclusion in this typology if they powerfully manifest this dialectic in physical form.

Robert Smithson: Earth Artist. The American artist Robert Smithson is best known for his earth sculpture, the *Spiral Jetty*, built on the shore of Nevada's Salt Lake in 1970. He died in 1973 when his plane crashed while he was photographing the site for his *Amarillo Ramp* project; he was 35 at the time.

During the last few years of his life, Smithson devoted much of his creative energy to developing an idea he called the *dialectical landscape* (Smithson 1972, 1973). The dialectic of which he spoke was not the dialectic of Hegel; it was not the purely internal process of the mind by which a thesis is changed into an antithesis, and the contradiction thus engendered resolved in a higher form of truth, the synthesis. He used the word dialectic in the older, more basic, sense of two conceptual categories (words and the things that they signify) that are mutually dependent on each other for definition. Thus, night and day, man and woman, right and wrong, life and death, mind and body, inside and outside are all defined in relation to their opposites.

When Smithson retreated from the galleries of New York to the landscape, he erected an intellectual redoubt from which to attack an entrenched enemy: the art of static, dead, abstract, metaphysical, timeless, and ideal "truths" holed up in hermetically sealed galleries and museums. Smithson felt that nature, with all of its contradictions and complexities, was a more significant issue for artists to wrestle with precisely because "nature is indifferent to any formal ideal" (Smithson 1973, 63). He meant that nature presents a picture to our eyes and mind that resists the absolute clarity, purity, and completion of a pure and unam-

4-1
Chaotic and ordered at the same time, the ponderosa pine is indifferent to any formal ideal. (photo by author)

biguous idea, or form.[2] In his view, artists of his time were paying too much attention to the isolated, the elevated, the pure, and the unblemished — i.e., paying too much attention to the "formal ideal." In order for such a pure art to reach its idealistic goal, it was necessary to remove it from the world's complexities — make it an autonomous art. But an art with no worldly meaning is useless! Simthson thought that it was absurd to confine the contemplative act (i.e., the transfer of meaning and impressions between the art work and the person experiencing it) within the atemporal vacuum of the museum so that the works were without reference to the actual phenomena of nature, and without geographical context. He argued that such art was isolated into "a metaphysical void, independent from external relationships such as land, labor, and class" (Smithson 1979, 219):

> Occult notions of "concept" are in retreat from the physical world. Heaps of private information reduce art to hermeticism and fatuous metaphysics... Art's development should be dialectical and not metaphysical (Smithson 1972, 39).

When Smithson refers to the metaphysical, he means metaphysical in the sense of the *immaterial*, or the *incorporeal*. For him, art that does not refer to the material, corporeal world is nonsensical. It is completely sealed off from the world, and is consequently without general value.

Because he believed that art's development should be dialectical and not metaphysical, he was drawn more and more exclusively to the landscape. The problem, as he saw it, was to join the *experience* of nature with the *material* of nature, with the "thing itself." He wanted to join physical nature *with* the meta-

freeze because we have invented "machines for living." That took care of the body. As for the spirit, "no problem, that's just an old myth. The sooner we do away with the spirit the better!" The mind, on the other hand, was a different matter altogether! There was no limit to what the mind could become if humans could throw off their chains to nature. The mind could be like a god!

These people thought that the landscape could become the location for the machine. They thought that the landscape of rooms in nature was not a suitable setting for the machines for living. They wanted it changed. They banished the landscape of space and they were glad of it. I am thinking of architects like Le Corbusier and Mies van der Rohe.

About 35 years ago, other people thought again about the rooms in nature. By this time the rooms in nature had nearly disappeared entirely, and our spirits had nearly disappeared along with them. The modern city of no-space and no-place had made the spirit moribund, they said.

They said that we should rebuild the rooms of our old house on earth. A new structure of rooms cut into the earth, the forest, and the city, would warm our souls, they said. I am thinking of Jane Jacobs, Christopher Alexander, Rob Krier, and Christian Norberg-Schulz. They struggled to recapture the names of the forgotten rooms. They started in the heart of the city and agreed that there were stoops, yards, streets, and squares. I think that they were right. There are other rooms in nature that

---

2. Viewed from one perspective, humans are transient nothings in the face of nature's eternal persistence. Viewed from another perspective, the human mind and spirit are endowed with the ex-pressive and creative capacity to make a cosmos out of a chaos — to order the physical world in a way that makes it meaningful. Smithson seems to revel in these contradictory readings: humans as nature's excrement versus humans as nature's transcendent.

we can suggest. They are rooms that we order from nature's materials for human ends, rooms that have persisted throughout the millennia and are therefore so commonly recognizable that they are now unremarkable. They are rooms but not a combination of rooms (a park is a combination of rooms, a garden is a combination of rooms). I wonder if these are the names of the rooms: the single tree, the clearing, the cloister, the square, the street, the front yard, the backyard, the allée, the orchard, the bosque, the theater, the stair, the terrace, and the promontory. It might be that these are the rooms of our house on earth — our house in nature. I would like to express my impressions of some of these rooms.

The Clearing

Making the clearing makes a room in the unrelieved immensity of the forest. The sun now strikes the ground and brings forth a teeming horde of new plants and insects. The stable life of the forest hemorrhages. The forest edge appears, a dynamic and productive place. The settler builds the cabin at the edge — the deer browse at the edge — the birds feed at the edge.

The act of making the clearing begins the dance of oppositions. The light that floods the clearing betrays the true darkness of the surrounding forest. The forest is alternatively gloomy and depressing, or shady and inviting. The clearing is alternatively brilliant and open, or scorching and exposed. As the sun arcs across the ceiling of the sky, the shadows lengthen. Nightfall extinguishes the opposition, along with everything else, in the total blackness. The duality of the clearing has made it a magnet for meanings. Clearings figure prominently in the myths of many peoples from forested landscapes.

Nature greedily wants to take back what humans have changed. The forest dispatches billions of seed minions to reclaim lost territory. Other species seek to confiscate the fruits of this human labor. But human labor to maintain the clearing is orderly and efficient. Humans defer gratification. Humans plan for the harvest and engineer a

physical mind. His "dialectical landscape" was all about structuring an opposition between the physical world and the sensibilities of the mind. Within this structure, all the inherent oppositions and contradictions between the mind and the world would be maintained intact.

Smithson carefully stipulated that his definition of the dialectic differed from other more metaphysical definitions. His was a "real world dialectic," specifically opposed to Hegelian dialectics that "exist only for the mind" (Smithson 1979, 128).

The Beautiful, the Sublime, and the Picturesque. Smithson's view was not new and he knew it; in the eighteenth and nineteenth centuries others had said the same thing. Smithson supported his argument with the long, moribund, and at the time completely disreputable aesthetic theory of the *picturesque*. He claimed that his art and the art of America's great nineteenth-century master of the picturesque, the landscape architect Frederick Law Olmsted, were in the same tradition. Both were trying to conjoin, and by this means express, the dialectic between the expressive, creative, naming, ordering, *mind/spirit*, and the im-pressive, dynamic, fecund, and chaotic processes of the *physical landscape*. Both men did their work in open landscape locations that were subject to all the influences of "land, labor, and class" (Smithson 1979, 219). Smithson argued that both he and Olmsted tried to make the dialectic *palpable* — experienced in the body as well as the mind, with all its contradictions intact. According to Smithson this kind of art is *picturesque* by virtue of the oppositions and contradictions it exposes (Smithson 1973).

Both Smithson and Olmsted were familiar with earlier theories of the picturesque and its antecedents, the theory of the beautiful and the sublime. Olmsted admonished his employees to understand these theories as their first task upon joining the firm: "You are to read these seriously, as a student of law would read Blackstone," he would tell them, referring to the works of William Gilpin and Uvedale Price (quoted in Smithson 1973, 63). Smithson attributes similar importance to this earlier aesthetic theory. He summarizes the evolution of these theories, beginning with the publication of Edmund Burke's *A Philosophical Enquiry into our Ideas of the Sublime and the Beautiful,* first published in 1757:

> Burke's notion of "beautiful" and "sublime" functions as a *thesis* of smoothness, gentle curves, and delicacy of nature, and as an *antithesis* of terror, solitude, and vastness of nature, both of which are rooted in the real world, rather than in a Hegelian Ideal (Smithson 1973, 63).

4-2
View of the late eighteenth-century picturesque landscape of Lancelot "Capability" Brown at Harwood House, North Yorkshire, England (photo by author)

The picturesque, articulated by Uvedale Price (1810), provided the synthesis. Smithson said that the picturesque synthesis is:

> related to chance and change in the material order of nature. The contradictions of the "picturesque" depart from a static formalistic view of nature. The picturesque, far from being an inner movement of the mind, is based on real land; it precedes the mind in its material external existence… Central Park is a ground work of necessity and chance, a range of contrasting viewpoints that are forever fluctuating, yet solidly based in the earth (Smithson 1973, 63).

To the extent that this synthesis remains "forever fluctuating," it departs from Hegelian notions of synthesis. In Hegel's synthesis the opposing forces of the dialectic solidly congeal into a higher form of being. Smithson suggests that in the picturesque synthesis of the landscape dialectic, the vibrancy and tension of the beautiful and the sublime are retained intact; they never congeal.

In Smithson's interpretation of the dialectical landscape, the aesthetic power (and consequently the meaning) of Central Park, and by extension of any landscape, is found in the relationship between the "beautiful" of human originated formal *order*, and a nature that is "indifferent to any formal ideal" (Smithson 1973, 63). In Central Park the *sublime* Ramble, an im-pressive, terrifying labyrinth where nature's dynamic processes seem indifferent to human formal order, connects to and collides with the Bethesda Fountain, where nature's materials are composed in a *beautiful* ex-pression of human formal order.

landscape that conforms to the human body — row on row, one foot *apart. When the human dies and is not replaced, the forest returns, indifferent to the temporary disruption, unmoved by the order that was struck.*

The Bosque

What the clearing is to the forest, the bosque is to the open landscape. The bosque of trees, in the open landscape, fixes a sacred vortex in profane doldrums. The bosque was the first temple, with the gods ensconced in the sanctuary, the sanctuary protected by phalanx after phalanx of guarding tree trunks.

Trees are so big, so alive, so unearthly. *They touch and block out the sky. Nearly all cultures* were *certain that the trees of the bosque or the grove were, in actual fact, gods (or at the very least* inhabited *by gods). One need only remove the post-Enlightenment blinders from our eyes even momentarily to re-experience this original truth.*

You are in the grove. Observe the tree. The elephantine torso of the tree splits repeatedly until it is an infinity of impossibly thin fingers, grasping azure. The syrupy air, never completely at rest, is palpable in the grove. The massive tree waves its wooden arms. Its tortured limbs groan out a melancholy exchange with the vagrant zephyrs whispering through the branch tips. The trees of the grove heave, roll, and surge en masse, an infinitely precise dance, the choreographed phenomena of an animated planet. The observer is transported. Edges between air and solid matter lose their crispness. Vitality billows into the space in stupefying waves — the sky, the air, the wood, the grass, the self, become unconsolidated.

Humans make the bosque, the copse, the wood lot, the plantation, the grove. Sometimes the purpose for the bosque is pragmatic: to produce the long timbers only possible in densely planted groves; to grow wood to feed the winter's fire. Sometimes the objective is sensual pleasure: to create a protected space to eat; to create a shaded space to sit. Sometimes the goal is spiritual: to invite the ancient Greek deities; to provide a setting for a Christian revival meeting. Pragmatic, sensual, and spiritual purposes can coexist in the bosque. Wherever it is, the bosque establishes the dance of oppositions between what nature gives, the expanse and the seed, and what humans impose, the bosque.

The bosque is a pattern chosen by humans. It may be a grid as in the plantation; this will insure that the trees will all have straight trunks and mature at the same time. It may be a random order; this will insure that trees will have varied girths and mature at different rates. A widening may be imposed; this will make an entry, a path, and a center. Framed inside this subtle order, the terrible forest becomes the beautiful bosque.

The Orchard

The orchard is a most powerful example of how humans make rooms for living out of nature's materials. When humans cultivate an orchard, they choreograph a dance with nature. Humans arrange nature's trees in a geometric pattern on the cleared land. Nature's sun plays against the pattern in a daily fertility ritual, a ritual that culminates on the day of the harvest.

The orchard is a paragon of how and why humans order nature's materials. Over time, humans came to understand the fruiting capacity of the tree and vine. This understanding suggested an order; the order structured the space. Arranging the trees in a grid insures that each tree gets a maximum of exposure to the sun as it arcs across the ceiling of the sky. Humans prune the trees (a radical hacking away, in fact) so that the remaining energy of the plants is directed toward fruiting. The land must be at least well chosen for this aspect or, at most, terraced and shaped to hold the rain.

Human cultivation of the orchard must be continuous or nature will retake it. Continuous cultivation makes the orchard a powerful metaphor: it is employed repeatedly in both the old and new testaments of the Bible where "God tends the vineyard" of humanity.[3]

Smithson's remark on nature's "indifference" does not suggest a lack of insight into nature's profound systems of order. Rather, he means that believing nature *in general* to have a formal *intention* indulges in a soothing but uncritical anthropomorphism.

The thoughts and work of Smithson and Olmsted help suggest how we might distinguish landscape *types* from the open and continuous landscape within which they must necessarily find their place. Smithson and Olmsted were both earth artists. As artists they brought to light a crucial but generally unrecognized property of human experience in typical landscapes – its dialectical quality. It follows that this dialectical quality would be a crucial and discernible feature of designed landscape space types.

The dialectical basis for this typology can now be summarized. As our human spirit emerged and confronted the chaos of our environment, we were both acted on by that environment and, in turn, forced to act back. To create a meaningful world, to distinguish the important from the unimportant, the sacred

4-3
Humans acting on the environment; the environment acting back. A beech tree slowly heals the wounds of words, marking the years. (photo by author)

4-4
The Rockery, by Frederick Law Olmsted, North Easton, Massachusetts. Olmsted maintains the tension between the order of the arch and the chaos of its apparent decay, apparent because the Rockery was designed to look like a ruin when new. (photo by author)

from the profane, the good from the bad, and the useful from the useless, required thousands of years of human effort. This work is still underway. In this millennial process nature became, on the one hand, understandable and nurturing (the garden, the orchard), while its incomprehensible and terrible aspect was suppressed but not eliminated (tornadoes, snakes, bottomless pits, AIDS).

The nurturing aspects of nature and our ex-pressive capacity to order nature for human purpose are manifest in the landscape of the *beautiful*, i.e., in formal order – the field, the lawn, the allée, the arbor, the house – all of them representing stability and predictability. But nature is *indifferent* to formal order. Nature in its essence is incomprehensible and terrible. It is the im-pressive landscape of the *sublime*, i.e., of chaos – the bramble, the landslide, the forest fire, the volcano. It is one giant elm tree in flower with a billion buds bursting forth a billowing pollen explosion. Nature is a state of constant change and threat, an ocean of aggression and overkill, a chaos of unpredictabilities that only lets up, for us, on the day we die.[4] Human life occurs in the landscape of the dialectic between the beautiful and the sublime, between order and chaos, between mind and matter. Both Smithson and Olmsted recognized this middle ground as the ground for their art. I am suggesting that the meaning and impact of landscape types result from this relationship between the beautiful and the sublime, between the beautiful *order* of the arbor structure and the *chaos* or s*ublime indifference* of the vine.

Other Voices. It is interesting that others who were working on political and philosophical problems recognized the importance of this middle ground between the inner world and the physical world. Karl Marx thought of this middle ground as *labor*:

> Labor is, in the first place, a process in which both man and nature participate, and in which man of his own accord starts, regulates, and controls the material reactions between himself and nature. He opposes himself to nature as one of her own forces, setting in motion arms and legs, head and hands, the natural forces of his body, in order to appropriate nature's productions in a form adapted to his own wants. By thus acting on the external world and changing it, he at the same time changes his own nature. He develops his slumbering powers and compels them to act in obedience to his sway (quoted in Fromm 1966, 40).

It was left to Maurice Merleau-Ponty, the influential postwar French philosopher, to extract the implicit aesthetic that is grounded in Marx's notion of the

4-5
Apricot orchard in summer. Okanagan Lake region, British Columbia, Canada (photo by author)

The ordered structure provides a predictable and comforting framework for the pleasurable experience of the orchard. Viewed through this frame we can contemplate and appreciate that which would otherwise repel. The orchard is, in fact, a riot of generational, annual, seasonal, daily, and even minute-to-minute changes, violent and excessive. The orchard remains stationary only as a human order. During the eight weeks that bracket the spring equinox, the orchard passes from a state of apparent frozen death, perpetually encased in a twilit bluegray landscape, to an absurdity of sensual richness of overwhelming chromatic intensity. A superfluity of tantalizing blossoms overwhelms the most insatiable mob of pollinators. Their haste is apt; the next cycle of the sun finds the ground all round paved with points of pink – an insolent gust ripping petals from their seats and raining them down. Nature's lurid display is ephemeral and indifferent to our voyeurism. Nature's indifference leaves us feeling overwhelmed and abandoned. While these and other equally violent disruptions go on, only the unchanged lines of trunks linked to the base of land reassures us, integrates us, holds the self inside the skin.

The Cloister

The cloister has gone by many names: Persians called it the walled garden; Greeks called it the agora; Romans called it the forum. The square of the cloister orients to the cardinal points – in this way it re-presents the four quarters of the world. The cloister is the clearing transcendent. The clearing carves out the trees of the forest and lets the sun come down; the cloister walls out the world and lets the spirit fly up.

The cloister is a clearing with nature's dynamic flux congealed. The trunks, branches, and leaves of the forest edge are petrified, they are the columns, the arches, the carved adornment of the arcaded edge. If the clearing is the least emphatic ordering of nature's materials, the cloister is the most. Nearly all of nature's violent dislocating transformations are frozen in stone. Only the arcing sun is admitted, the rational, predictable, and constant sun, the gentlest possible weaving of nature's phenomena into the solid fabric of the cloister.

But even this one force, the razor vector of the sun, can still transport. One does not cross the open center of the cloister; rather, one walks through the perambulatory, around the edge. The sun angles through the screen of the colonnade, projecting a radiant filigree on the warm stone floor ahead. You walk with dignity through alternating membranes of hot and cold air. The pulsing slap of

---

3. See Mathew 20: 1–16; Mathew 21: 33–43; Mark 12: 1–12; Luke 20: 9–16; and Isaiah 5: 7 for just a few examples.

4. This view of nature as aggressor is elaborated by Camille Paglia (1990) in *Sexual Personae*, New York: Vintage Books.

human/landscape interaction. In his essay "Marxism and Philosophy," he suggests that:

> It is... understandable that the introduction of the notion of the *human object*, which phenomenology has... developed, was reserved for Marx. Classical philosophies dissociated this notion; for them, streets, fields, houses were complexes of colors in all ways comparable to objects of nature and merely encased with human significance by a secondary judgment. When Marx speaks of human objects, he means that this significance adheres to the object as it presents itself in our experience... The spirit of a society is realized, transmitted, and perceived through the cultural objects which it bestows upon itself and in the midst of which it lives. It is there that the deposit of its practical categories is built up, and these categories in turn suggest a way of being and thinking to men (Merleau-Ponty 1974, 180).

When we think about the designed landscape space types that structure our everyday experience, we are actually thinking of the practical categories that Merleau-Ponty describes. These landscape space types are manifested in the landscape when we "oppose nature and thereby change our own nature" (quoted in Fromm 1966, 40). This interdependent opposition of humans and nature is discernible in space as the opposition between humans' own "beautiful" order, and nature's own "sublime" complexity (Burke [1757] 1958; Condon 1991). The result of all this effort over the millennia is a set of "practical categories," i.e., types, that manifest their mode of development to our aesthetic sensibilities as a tension between the beautiful of human formal order and sublime nature which is "indifferent to any formal ideal" (Smithson 1973, 63). The different designed

4-6
The beauty of human order opposed to nature's sublime complexity in the Reflection Garden at the Bloedel Reserve, Bainbridge Island, Washington (Reflection garden by Richard Haag, photo by author)

landscape space types should therefore quite markedly *manifest in form the dialectic between the human compulsion for the beautiful formal ideal and nature's sublime indifference to formal ideals of any kind.*

In my reflections and in my own observations of the world since I first became interested in landscape type, the above hypothesis has, for me, held up. I invite you to reflect on this hypothesis and make your own observations with this hypothesis in mind.

Landscape Archetypes

Most writers on the topic of building typology suggest that types are the building blocks of an edifice of commonly understood meanings. It is also generally postulated that this edifice sits upon the foundation of natural *archetypes* — i.e., archetypes are the invisible but crucial basis for types. Brill, for example, suggests in his chapter that a shared natural language of *landscape* archetypes slowly took root in a millennial process involving millions of human spirits, all of them intent on making a cosmos out of chaos.

Aldo Rossi suggests that building and urban typology rests on a foundation of natural archetypes. In *The Architecture of the City* (1982), his section on "Typological Questions" begins with the following:

> The city as above all else a human thing is constituted of its architecture and of all those works that constitute the true means of transforming nature (1982, 35). I am thinking of Francesco Milizia's definition of the essence of architecture as the imitation of nature: "Although architecture in reality lacks a model in nature, it has another model derived from man's natural labor in constructing his first house" (1982, 27).

Anthony Vidler, in his 1977 historical overview of type, recalls how Ribard de Chamoust, writing in 1783, argued that:

> I mean by this word type, the first attempts of man to master nature, render it propitious to his needs, suitable to his uses, and favorable to his pleasures. The perceptible objects that the Artist chooses with justness and reasoning from Nature in order to light and fix at the same time the fires of his imagination, I call archetypes (quoted in Vidler 1977, 97).

In this same sense I am suggesting that the designed landscape space types find a basis in natural landscape space archetypes. The archetypes are the natural forest and the natural clearing.

4-7
Cloister at Durham Cathedral, Durham, England (photo by author)

heat on your cheek and sunshine on your retina initiates an inexorable and hypnotic meter, in step with your footfalls and your heartbeat. In time this oscillation loosens the grip of the self, gives rope to the spirit. But the unchanging beat does not threaten us with disintegration; we will not wander too far from reason in such a space.

The Single Tree

In undifferentiated forest landscapes, the clearing opens up and connects the warming sun to earth. In undifferentiated open landscapes, the single tree focuses an awful and undifferentiated plane on a center. It makes a here *and a* there *out of a* nowhere. *Rooted in the earth, the single tree* explodes *out of the indifferent ground, fueled only by a voracious appetite for space. Humans watch their whole life away while she unfolds and extends her constantly cleaving spine, while she dances her hundred-year solo. The single tree is a space for performance. The measure is order. The rhythm is chaos.*

The single tree is a miniature ecology. The tree does not relent until it has ordered all *the dynamic flows of sun, soil, air, and water within its compass.*

The single tree is an evident cosmology. Come the fall equinox, the tree "dies." Come the spring equinox, the tree is "reborn." The single tree draws life from base earth, but connects to immortal sky. Life force, *somehow miraculously locked in the seed, forces the union. Such a centering, ordering, and unifying power has made the single tree a magnet for meanings. The single tree figures most prominently in the myths of many peoples from both forested and dry landscapes.*

4-8
Single tree (American Elm), West Union, Iowa (photo by author)

The Forest and The Clearing. By *natural forest* and *natural clearing* I mean forests and clearings that occur through natural, ecological processes, prior to human intervention. This proposition is supported from a number of quarters. René Dubos (1980) postulates that since the savanna landscape, the cradle of our species, is a landscape that is neither completely forested nor completely clear, but rather a complex tapestry of forests and clearings, human beings are drawn to replicate the conditions of this original landscape when they take up residence elsewhere – planting groves in the desert and clearing openings in the forest. Jay Appleton (1975) extracts an aesthetic from this principle in his "prospect refuge theory." He postulates that when humans are in re-created or natural savanna-type landscapes (the landscape of forest and clearing, a dialectical pair) they will normally experience a feeling of aesthetic satisfaction. He suggests that this feeling of satisfaction comes from a built-in capacity to recognize that their biological need for food and protection can be assured in such a landscape.

Sir George Frazer (1951) provides evidence of how important the forest and the clearing were in the development of the human spirit. In his exhaustive study of mythology, he convincingly shows that the Sacred Tree, the Sacred Grove, and the Sacred Clearing are the organizing feature *of* and landscape locus *for* the world's oldest myths. He finds this to be true across cultures for mythologies that developed independently. This suggests that when the human spirit charged forth to repel the chaos of sensory im-pressions with creative ex-pressions, it quickly conjured a meaning and role for the forest and the clearing and made the forest and the clearing crucial elements of the embryonic cosmology.

Taken together, the works of Dubos, Appleton, and Frazer support the proposition that the forest and the clearing, understood as a dialectical pair, are the archetypal landscape space foundation upon which the edifice of a designed landscape space typology can be erected. In forested landscapes, the natural clearing can be seen as nature's gift to humans. Imagine yourself thrashing through the trackless forest wilds. Suddenly you burst forth into the light and space of the clearing. Finally you are free of lurking threats (i.e., free of evil). You look up into the open sky and are thankful.

In open landscapes, the natural forest – or more appropriately the woods or the grove – can be seen as nature's gift to humans. Imagine wandering through the sun-bleached expanse, exposed and visible to predators and enemies from all quadrants. Suddenly you "make" the grove. Now you are invisible to and protected from approaching threats. You look up into the diaphanous green ceiling of the trees and are thankful.

4-9
Natural forest/natural clearing landscape in the Okanagen Lake region, British Columbia, Canada. This complex tapestry of openings and enclosures is typical of savanna-type landscapes. (photo by author)

The Land.   The dynamic interaction of the natural forest/natural clearing dialectic takes place on *land*. Land, of course, is almost never completely flat. The particular topographic situation will alter the character and quality of the forest and clearing.

Designed landscape space types must somehow take their places, i.e., arrange themselves, within the continuum between the completely open natural clearing on the one side, and the completely closed natural forest on the other. The form of the land influences the continuum between the completely open and the completely closed. Land is either flat or steep or somewhere between. The land is either concave (inward facing) or convex (outward facing) or something between.

The Social Dimension.   So far I have suggested a way to arrange the types relative to the morphological properties of the natural landscape archetypes on the one hand, and the morphological properties of the land on the other. This is useful; however, the human dimension is not yet incorporated. Humans interact with nature at many levels; the most direct would be the body in motion, hewing the forest, making the clearing, and bringing order to the chaos of nature. But as the clearing becomes a "thing for us," through stabilizing our sensual relations (such as hunger) with the environment, so too does the *street,* as a human thing, become a "thing for us." The street stabilizes our relations with nature. But the relations with nature that are manifest in the street are relations with nature's other humans, or to put it another way, other natural creatures behaving in conformance with their

Humans plant, nurture, and protect the single tree. Sometimes the purpose is pragmatic and sensual: to provide a cool and shady space under its broad dome for human comfort and company. Sometimes it can mean more. Imagine a rocky promontory, on it the single tree, and in the shade of the tree a stone altar. Think of the "Liberty Tree" in Philadelphia. Picture a single tree the size of the Pantheon, quietly marking the changing centuries from its fixed place in an Aegean village square.

The Backyard

The backyard makes the transition and connection between the sanctuary of the shelter and the chaos of nature. The backyard can be as small as a porch with a flowerpot and still be a backyard (remove the pot and the transition evaporates and along with it the backyard).

Thinking about how backyards assert themselves in agricultural landscapes can be instructive. North American farmers can configure their yards in whatever way they wish since they control all the land around the house. The farmer usually cuts a regular form, like a rectangle or a square, out of the fabric of the surrounding fields and forests to make the backyard. This seems to echo an ancient compulsion. In nearly all the world's cultures, humans mark the "four quarters" of the world by marking the square district. Apparently they do so to "make a world," to make a cosmos out of a chaos (Eliade 1959).

In the backyard, humans make the quarters *for their family. The quarters comfortably* frame *and control nature's transformations. The quarters, marked out on the ground, extrude a space up to the sky — like the cloister or the clearing. Inevitably other elements are imposed to reenforce the quarters: fences, hedges, perennial beds, trees, orchards, garden plots. Each human intervention seems aimed at projecting an ideal order, a formal order, on an indifferent landscape.*

Nature's response is cool to this human toil. Nature will go where directed if this requires no extra effort. But

no matter how much energy humans expend, the feral habits of wind and rain, of sun and cloud, of plants and insects, provoke an onslaught of aberrations. This natural dissonance can only be sublimated, not obscured, by the power of the backyard's formal frame. The backyard with its tended plants and its fixed boundaries maintains the dream of nature the nurturing and wards off the menacing nightmare of nature the corrupting.

This most domestic and intimate of landscape spaces often expresses an imbalance in the life of the resident. In one backyard the battle with nature is lost, the backyard frame that fixes the image of "nature the nurturing" collapses. Nature the unreasonable, nature the downright ugly, reclaims it. Nature wallows drunkenly with the beer cans and old rusting wagons choking out everything that was once of value. In the other backyard the fight is obsessive. The family digs weeds out, days spent on knee pads, the bluegrass is "perfect." Nature is haughty and will not be bothered. Nature says from the heavens: "Your fears will be realized, your work notwithstanding."

The relationship between the resident and nature seems more balanced when it is less like a battle and more like a dance. The backyard gardener guides nature's forces; accepts nature's lead, then responds with her own thrust. She knows she's the frail one, but she still starts the music. Her pluck makes her special. She is the creator, no animal like her. Nature admires her for this, makes her lord of the flowers and says to her mildly "till you die we'll be partners."

The Promontory

The promontory is the place marked for elevated view. The promontory becomes a promontory when humans order it as such. It has a floor suited to the footfalls of humans. It has walls, real or implied, scaled to humans. The room of the promontory has walls made of rock, of trees, of air. The extent of the space is palpable even when it lacks solid definition. The promontory, like the single

essential social nature. Therefore, another continuum along which landscape types might be arranged is conceivable. This pole would have *human-to-nature* designed types like the clearing on the one end, and *human-to-human* designed types like the street on the other.

Landscape Types and Their Arrangement. The three dimensions of the model I am proposing are: (1) the clearing to the forest continuum; (2) the human relations to nature continuum; and, (3) the landform continuum. These three dimensions are arranged on a three-dimensional model as shown in Figure 4-10. The form is that of a cone.

The *clearing to the forest* continuum moves around the base of the cone. This continuum begins at the rearward edge of the cone and progresses in one direction, clockwise. The progression begins with the landscape space types that, for me, have the deepest association with the natural clearing; it ends with the types that seem to have the strongest association with the natural forest. In this progression we move generally from the most open landscape space types to the most enclosed.

On the *human relations to nature* continuum the progression begins in the same spot, at the rearward base of the cone; however, here the progression operates in two directions. One stream moves clockwise, the other counterclockwise,

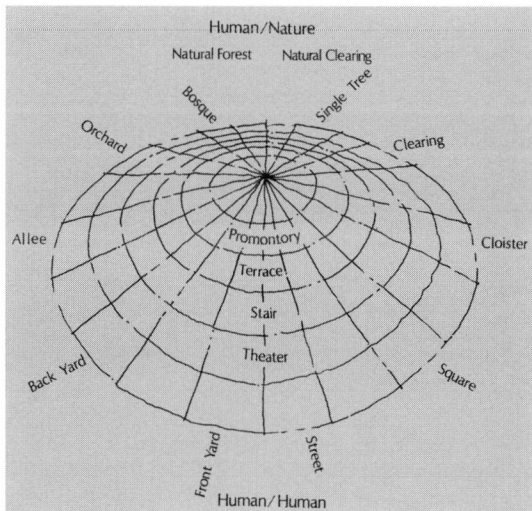

4-10
Order

the two streams ending and joining at the forward base of the cone. Thus the bosque, the single tree, and the clearing are all types that, in my view, hew order out of the chaos of nature; they are all about human relations with nature. That is why I have located them near the *human to nature* rearward base of the cone. Opposite these types are those that seem to be mostly about humans behaving naturally in conformance with their essential social nature — types such as the street and the front yard. These are located near the *human to human* forward base of the cone. Between the stream ends are types like the allée situated at the left side of the cone, and the cloister situated on the right. For me the cloister and the allée seem to manifest a similar degree of human interaction with nature. However, they are quite different with regard to the forest to clearing spectrum, because they have very different spatial structures, and very different degrees of enclosure.

The *landform continuum* is quite simple. There seem to be certain types of designed landscape spaces that are *all about* landform. They are the theater, the stair, the terrace, and the promontory. The theater is virtually all about human relations to other humans. At the other end of the scale, at the pinnacle of the cone, is the promontory. The promontory seems to be virtually all about human relations to nature. The stair and terrace arrange themselves on the human relations to nature gradient between these two extremes.

The following is a list of the types in this designed landscape space typology. In the landscape they can be found singly, in combination, or in some complex superimposition. They can be thought of as the armature of our typical landscape experiences, or, more precisely, the armature of our experiences in beautiful and meaningful built landscapes. They are: the single tree, the clearing, the cloister, the square, the street, the front yard, the backyard, the allée, the orchard, the bosque, the theater, the stair, the terrace, and the promontory.

These designed landscape space types have been included because, after long reflection, it is sufficiently apparent that they meet four criteria. First, they manifest, in form, the dialectic between the human compulsion for the beautiful formal ideal and nature's sublime indifference to formal ideals of any kind. Second, they are the products of human intervention in the landscape. Third, they are not logically reducible to a more essential space. Fourth, they are valid as types by virtue of what they have persistently represented. For example, the single tree has a long history as a symbol for life and female fecundity in Greek and Roman mythology. The orchard (as vineyard or olive grove) has a long history as a symbol for humanity in the Judeo-Christian tradition.

tree, is a connection between the undifferentiated plane and the immortal sky.

The plane rises up a hand to cup the promontory. A "lookout" without this earthly lift and embrace is an alien appendage and is not a promontory. We require the embrace of the earth, a signal of its acquiescence to our conceit, before we can relax our vigilance in the face of nature's power. Protected by the walls and framed by the windows of the promontory, nature the terrible becomes nature the beautiful.

In the promontory we are more than a mortal, less than a god; we are like the Greek Castor and Pollux, who were one day defiled, the next day exalted. From our Olympian heights we command the landscape. Our heart swells with power; but our gut trembles with anxiety — we are diminished by nature's vastness.

From Mount Olympus in ancient Greece to Capitol Hill in Washington, D.C., it's always the same. Most cultures find, make, use, and ascribe meaning to the promontory in this way. In the sense that I am using the word, any "sacred mountain" that has been climbed and has had a promontory position identified is a promontory. The promontory has equal status with the sacred mountain that embraces it. Promontories are important locations *for most religions and governments; promontories are important* symbols *for most religions and governments.*

When we make and then go to the promontory, it means we care about nature. We hope that nature will notice. We march up on nature's shoulder to cement a friendship, to insure no love lost, to give our homage.

Obviously this list excludes many types of built landscape spaces that do not conform to these criteria. The parking lot and the interstate highway do not, for me, manifest the dialectic. The park and the garden are, for me, reducible to more basic space types. The ball field is more a function than a space; at best it is a function that takes place within a clearing. Is the alley a designed landscape space type? I am not sure; perhaps others would say yes. How about the path? Again, perhaps, to some.

I am aware that any listing of types, no matter how deeply embedded in the conditional tense, may seem incomplete at best and presumptuous at worst. Nevertheless I think that the list has value. It is a *beginning* design vocabulary – only words. It is up to the designer to write the sentence. Type by itself is nowhere near enough. The designer must also understand the specific material language of the site, the design language of the site's history (past and future), and the design language of the human activities proposed. If, then, the designer uses type as the armature upon which the other more particular languages are fastened, the result can be a poem in space.

4-11
The beautiful human interventions in the farmscape can suppress but cannot entirely obscure nature's sublime complexity. USDA Soil Conservation Service aerial survey of Scott County, Minnesota

Conclusion

Every day we spend in the landscape is another day spent inhabiting a narrative. This narrative is half real, half invented. The real part, the part that is not a human fabrication, is the messy, horrible, and incredibly *sublime* physicality of nature itself. This is a nature that for the most part remains invisible. The invented part, the part that we as humans make up as we go along, is the order that we impose on nature to domesticate it. It is the idealized, abstract, and *beautiful* order of our lawns, our farms, our streets, even of our freeways and our shopping malls. This is the part that we see all too well, so well that we seldom experience directly the sublime nature that it suppresses.

Designed landscape space types are the words in this narrative. Like the narrative itself they are half sublime, half beautiful – half real, half invention. This language is truly alive. Its vitality springs from the sublime force of violent nature. Humans lash and leash this violent nature in the straps of beautiful human order.

The story of our lives is written with the words of this vital, beautiful, and sublime language when we shape, then experience, our yards, streets, clearings, groves. Since each of us simultaneously acts out and watches our story unfold, the narrative continues to fascinate us. But if the language of our world is shattered, we are helpless. Our communication channel with nature is closed; our communication channel with other people is impeded.

Designers of landscapes should take note; they contribute more than most people to building our shared world. Designers should understand and use the shared language of designed landscape spaces as the *typical words* of their *unique sentences*. In this way our communication channel with nature is kept open. The dance of oppositions between nature and the mind, between the beautiful and the sublime, between the arbor and the vine, endures.

References

Appleton, Jay. 1975. *The Experience of Landscape*. London: John Wiley & Sons.

Burke, Edmund. [1757] 1958. *A Philosophical Enquiry into the Origin of our Ideas of the Sublime and the Beautiful*. Edited by James T. Boulton. Notre Dame, Ind.: Notre Dame University Press.

Condon, Patrick M. 1991. Radical Romanticism. *Landscape Journal* 10 (1): 3–8.

Dubos, René. 1980. *The Wooing of Earth*. New York: Scribner's Sons.

Eliade, Mircea. 1959. *The Sacred and the Profane*. New York: Harcourt, Brace & World.

Frazer, James Goerge. [1924] 1951. *The Golden Bough: A Study in Magic and Religion*. Abridged ed. New York: Macmillan.

Fromm, Eric. 1966. *Marx's Concept of Man*. New York: Frederick Unger.

Merleau-Ponty, Maurice. 1974. *Phenomenology, Language and Sociology: Selected Essays of Maurice Merleau-Ponty*. Edited by John O'Neill. London: Heinemann Educational Books Ltd.

Price, Uvedale. 1810. *Essays on the Picturesque*. London: J. Mawman.

Rossi, Aldo. 1982. *The Architecture of the City*. Cambridge, Mass.: MIT Press.

Smithson, Robert. 1972. Cultural confinement. *Artforum* 11 (2): 39.

———. 1973. Frederick Law Olmsted and the Dialectical Landscape. *Artforum* 11 (6): 62–68.

———. 1979. *The Writings of Robert Smithson*. Edited by Nancy Holt. New York: New York University Press.

Vidler, Anthony. 1977. The idea of type. *Oppositions* 8: 95–115.

Part II

Fixing Types

Chapter 5

Farm Type in the American Midwest: A Reflection of Government Policy

Hemalata C. Dandekar

The grandeur of farm architecture as it has evolved in the midwest and the prairie states of the United States holds a special appeal for architects. Current architectural journals feature projects derived from the local vernacular of farmscapes; big barns and silos offer forms that are considered essential elements of a "regional" architecture.[1] Susana Torre, while presenting her contemporary Firestation Five project at the College of Architecture and Urban Planning at the University of Michigan, projected images of farms in the Columbus, Indiana region and commented that farm buildings constituted some of the most significant architecture in the area (Torre 1988).[2] In the early 1960s, as a foreign architecture student visiting the American midwest for the first time, I, too, unexpectedly found that the big barns, silos, and farmhouses in the midwest vied for my attention with the Wright and Mies architecture I had come to the United States to study. The "organic" siting of these American farm complexes — in isolation on the expansive land holdings of farms on the flat grain-belt plains, or clustered more closely on the smaller holdings of the dairy and diversified production farms of the midwest — was aesthetically pleasing. The traditional agrarian structures exuded a sense of fit, a sense of belonging and rootedness to the terrain that was scenic and memorable.

5-1
Charles Moore brings to TRINOVA Headquarters a translation of midwestern rural form. (courtesy of Gary Quesada/Korab Ltd.)

1. For example Charles Moore, raised in Michigan and trained at the University of Michigan, brings to works such as TRINOVA Headquarters near Toledo, Ohio (Bleznick 1991) a special translation of midwestern rural forms. See also Minneapolis-based Stone and Scherfleth's design center for Herman Miller in Graafschap, Michigan, and the works of Peter Landon Associates (Keegan 1989).

5-2
Farm house and its big barn, Allegan County, Michigan (photo by author)

The physical layout of the American farmstead, the shape of its buildings, and the patterning and division of farmland have been transformed by pressures not just internal but also external to the farm enterprise. Historical changes that shaped the agricultural system were followed by changes, at times dramatic, in the physical form of the individual agricultural buildings themselves and in the overall layout and configuration of the typical homestead. An examination of this evolution of American midwestern farmsteads reveals the many significant ways that

5-3
Old and new structures coexist compatibly.
Dairy farm on Waters Road, Washtenaw County, Michigan (photo by author)

It was only years later, in the mid-1980s, when I undertook some systematic examinations of midwestern barns, that I began to realize that the evolution in type represented by these farm clusters in the United States was unique to North America.[3] On the vast landscape of the midwestern and prairie states, towering turn-of-the-century gable- or gambrel-roofed bank barns, painted red and sporting lean-to additions, were often surrounded by smaller, ancillary buildings and tall silos. The apogee of this vertical silo technology, the Harvestore silo, glinted a magnificent and improbable metallic blue in the summer sun and spoke of modernity and science. At times the traditional and the scientific structures were compatibly, and at times uncomfortably, juxtaposed with the modern, low-profiled, metal-sided sheds of the new, mechanized corporate farm. In most rural areas of the world, particularly those involved in traditional agriculture, profiles of farms and their buildings appear unchanging. In contrast, in the midwest and other regions of the United States, particularly where agricultural production continues to be a viable and significant part of the economy, the configuration of the rural landscape and its agrarian structures have been dynamic and evolving.

2. Another architect who has drawn on the farm vernacular as inspiration for contemporary projects, such as a house for his parents on Washington Island, Wisconsin, is Frederick Philips (Davidson 1990).

3. Some of my earlier work on Michigan farms and their buildings has been supported by a Michigan Council for the Humanities Mini-Grant (1986) and Regular Grant (1988), and Phase 1 (1988–89) and Phase 2 (1991–92) of a Michigan Bureau of History project on preservation of big barns in Michigan.

AK: *The point about "government policies" is well taken, but there is a real need to distinguish the political elements in government. In the United States, how do Republican and Democratic governments change agricultural policies over time? And if they don't, why not?*
HD: *I have found it difficult to attribute particular postures and inclinations regarding the shape of U.S. agricultural policy to the two major political parties in the United States. The characterization of the Republicans as free-market oriented and the Democrats as populists, oriented towards equity and distribution, although comforting to academics, proves far too simplistic when one looks at any particular sector of the economy, such as agriculture. In this sector too many other factors affect the decision-making process of policy formulation, adoption, and implementation. First is the question of who is in power and in what positions. Over the last four or five decades it has become clear that in any four-year presidency, the House and the Senate have been controlled by a varying combination of parties. Furthermore, within the House or the Senate the relative importance and posture of the representatives from the "farm states" have swayed decisions regardless of which party was in power. Their power, or an upcoming presidential election, could make for decisions quite "uncharacteristic" of the incumbent party regarding government purchase and pricing of commodities. In addition, even if a particular policy can be characterized as quintessentially Republican or Democratic in its ideological premise, the vigor (or lack thereof) of policy implementations by career staffers in agriculture, down to the county extension officers, can be variable and uncertain. It is not a simple matter, therefore, to identify who is really in charge of shaping agricultural policy during any particular time frame.*

Secondly, agriculture in the United States is affected by two significant forces that the political parties can neither predict nor control: the climate and global politics. Good weather and a breakthrough in the development of a particularly successful corn hybrid can result in a glut of government stocks. The political and environmental realities in Europe, the former Soviet Union, China, or India can dramatically influence price and global markets for U.S. agricultural products. This can result in very pragmatic shifts in U.S. agricultural policy quite separate from ideological, partisan positions. Cochrane and Runge's concise history of the U.S. agricultural commodity program, in Chapter Three of their Reforming Farm Policy: Towards a National Agenda, *leaves in question whether change in one administration or another makes any difference even at the level of one program, let alone a whole sector of the economy.*

Leaving the task of broader political attribution and causality to braver spirits, in this chapter I have endeavored to identify and describe a separable phenomenon: agricultural policy as it has impacted the U.S. midwest and identifying the ways this has shaped farm form and the rural built environment. This is an interesting and "doable" task that warrants much further work.

government policy has influenced these changes. Government actions have affected land ownership, transport modes, and thus agricultural markets. Government sponsorship has stimulated an agriculture-related education that has influenced farming. The government has been a major force in both creating technological advances and educating farmers about potential applications of new technology. Technological changes have had a direct influence on shaping the farmstead. Government policy in other related social and economic spheres has affected the costs of various factors in agricultural production including credit, support services, and inputs such as seed and fertilizer. These, in turn, have influenced what farmers produced and the buildings they constructed, with consequences for the aesthetic, visual, and physical characteristics of rural communities. Too little attention has been paid to this active government role in analyses of rural built form.

Type Analyses of the American Farm Building

Various authors have delineated typologies of American farm buildings including farmhouses and big barns, approaching the topic from many disciplinary perspectives. At the scale of individual architectural units, such as the farmhouse (McAlester and McAlester 1984; McLennan 1987) or barn (Tishler 1986; Tishler and Witmer 1986), type analyses have focused on plan, layout, construction detail, materials, and styles of overall form and ornamentation. A typology of midwestern barns based on an analysis of their structural, skeletal characteristics and the architectural quality of the enclosed volume is provided by Dandekar, Darvas, and MacDonald (1992). Hubka (1984) links the changes in the lives of New England farmers to changes in the form and layout of their farm buildings, describing how buildings were modified and relocated on New England farmsteads to meet the practical needs of the farmer. He classifies the characteristics of the buildings that are shaped by environment, economy, and culture, but also points out those that accrue from the individual choices made by the farmer functioning as a designer.

On a national scale the regional diversity, variation, and substantial evolution of farm buildings in North America are described by Noble (1984). Noble's book is a significant contribution to obtaining an overview of big barn evolution from a material, cultural geographer's perspective. In a similar vein, Noble and Seymore (1982) delineate a typology of barns in the northeastern United States based on the visual form and organizational elements of a barn structure. They consider the external form and envelope of the big barn, the number of levels and height of its structure, its roof lines and internal layout. They suggest ethnic antecedents as one explanatory variable of farm form.[4] But Dandekar and Schoof (1988), in their typology of Michigan farms, posit that the influence of ethnicity in the configuration of early barn types in the United States has given way in subsequent periods to design decisions based on a very American sense of economic, technical, and functional rationality.

Taking the farm cluster as the unit of analysis, Dandekar and Schoof organize Michigan farmsteads into five types, divided into specific physical attributes of layout, profile, and composition of component units. The types range from farms serving a local market to those producing for the international, global market. As is illustrated in Figure 5-4, the types derived from: (1) the geographic extent of the market for which they produced; (2) the agricultural commodities they produced and the structure of the farm enterprise; (3) the mode of production and the extent of mechanization; and (4) the changes in the technology of buildings. The typology spanned approximately 150 years of continuous transformation of physical structures. The types, named after their markets, were called subsistence, regional, national, international, and corporate farms. A particular farm rarely fit exclusively into one or another "pure" type, as structures were modified continuously with alterations, additions, and "tack-ons" of different vintages. At any given time, farms locked into a market and production pattern of an earlier period still continued to be viable, coexisting with subsequent types. The typology provides a useful heuristic to help observers understand farmstead evolution by linking the consideration of form to use and relating changes in building forms to changes in function or technology. But it does little to underscore how the use itself is shaped by actions of government at the federal, state, and local levels. In fact, much of the work on farmsteads ignores or de-emphasizes the link between changes in physical form and changes in government policy, and rarely connects evolution of form to specific government actions. Taking the case of the midwestern farm as an illustration, this essay seeks to explore these connections.

In many countries, particularly those involved in traditional agriculture, the twentieth-century evolution of North American agriculture — the epitome of scientific farming — has represented a paradigm worth emulating to solve chronic, global food shortages. Internationally, the United States is acknowledged to be one of the most open and *laissez-faire* economies in the world. But even a superficial historical examination reveals that the shape of farms and farming in the

LS: *Ethnicity is one of the subtexts of the cultural discourse. When I read about the influence of ethnicity on the configuration of early barns I am reading about the influence that a previous culture brought to a new landscape in the settlement of the United States by Europeans. To assert that subsequent periods of typological development of farmsteads in the United States are based on the "American sense of economic, technical, and functional rationality" raises many questions about the nature of the newly emerging ethnicity; that is, the American culture.*

4. Noble and Seymore (1982) discuss the influence of three basic ethnic influences, the English, German, and Dutch. By correlating the distribution of three basic barn types and their variations with the predominant ethnic origins of the farm community, they present a regional scale of analysis which speaks to the spread of ideas about, and choices in, design of barns in the northeastern United States.

United States from the subsistence cultivation of the pioneer to the high-tech, mechanized, computerized, agro-industry of today's corporate farm is not solely the product of free-market forces, but has also been significantly affected by government interventions. Though ignored in national rhetoric related to free enterprise, the role of the government in shaping U.S. farming is generally noted and accepted in the literature pertaining to American agriculture (Rasmussen 1960; Cochrane 1979). In fact, Cochrane delineates a broad and inclusive set of categories in which the American government has been active, and categorically states that the "government has been involved in almost every aspect of agricultural development" (1979, 227).

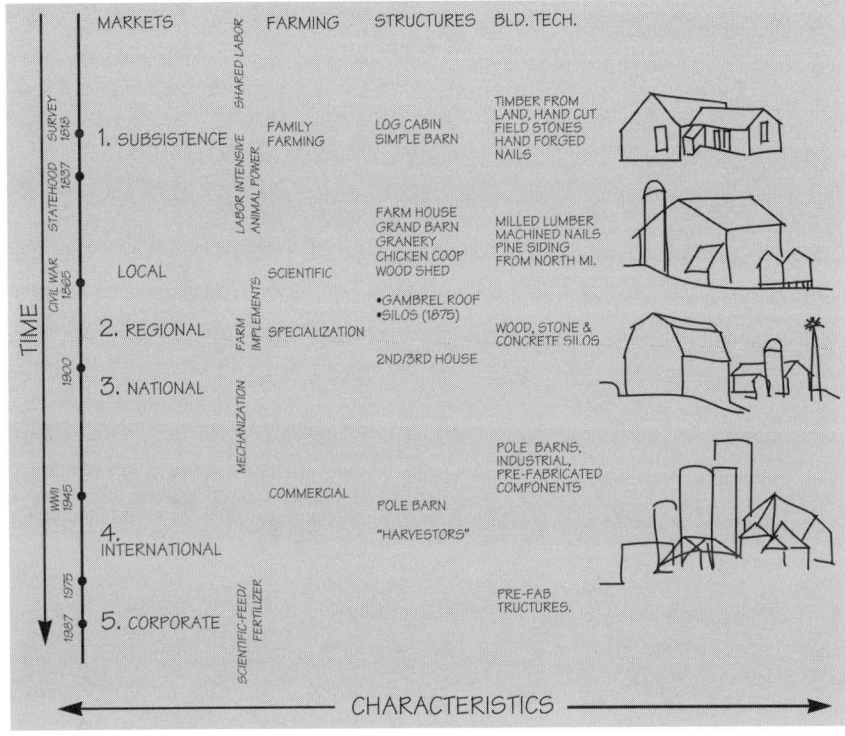

5-4
Typology of barns by Dandekar and Schoof. In this typology the evolution of farm form is related to changes in markets and the technologies of farming and building. (source: Dandekar and Schoof 1988, 62)

This paper will address three sets of the most significant of these government policies and actions. The first set consists of policies that affect overall settlement patterns and the configuration of built form. These policies affect land ownership, land settlement, and transport in ways that imprint the American landscape to this day. The second set consists of policies related to agricultural education that nurtured the modern science-based agriculture that rendered American farming so notable in the 1950s and 1960s. Public institutions such as land grant colleges and the U.S. agricultural extension service encouraged this scientific farming and had a great impact in shaping the physical structures that were built to facilitate that effort.

The third set consists of more recent government policies regarding price subsidies, production ceilings, credit, and grain reserves that have significantly affected the size, output, and product mix of American farms. These policies have affected the prices farmers are required to pay for materials and inputs, and the profit they can make from selling in various markets, local or global. They have indirectly, and, at times, quite directly affected the choices American farmers make about how to use their land, what crops to raise, and the technology to support this cultivation. These choices have affected the configuration of the buildings farmers build to shelter their harvest and the machinery they use for cultivation.

Examining the interconnections between government policies and the shape of farms in the midwest makes transparent the typology of rural farmsteads in North America, and helps reveal the information encoded in the spatial patterning of the rural landscape. In this analysis of farm type, I have considered elements beyond the morphology of the specific farm buildings. These elements include size, function, and layout of farm buildings; land division patterns; technology of building and agriculture; and the nature and characteristics of materials used. In this essay I select the government interventions in agricultural development most significant for farm form; those that illustrate how policy at the national, state, and local levels has helped shape farm activity in America and thus molded the face of the American farmstead. In so doing, this exercise reveals the ways in which government policy can affect the evolution of building types on the American landscape in very tangible, spatial ways. It substantiates the claim that social and economic constructions are central in the evolution of building types. It also illustrates that technical and economic rationality, overriding principles in shaping built form, are in themselves shaped by government actions.

Phase I: Early Settlement Period

The most dramatic effect of government policy on land division, and therefore on farmstead configuration, begins in the early settlement and expansion period of U.S. history that followed early colonial rule. The early European settlers to North America – the Spanish, French, Dutch, and British – brought with them their own ideas of how the land should be divided up and used. Hart (1975) discusses the different land division patterns that occur as a result of different land survey systems used by these early colonizers.

Following the consolidation of British rule in the northeast, a land distribution pattern evolved in New England based on a nucleated village of residences and fragmented land parcels around it. A number of such parcels of different soil quality and topography constituted an individual farmer's land holdings. This mix of soil types and land configuration allowed the farmer to grow a diversified mix of crops that served as insurance against loss of production in one or another, providing the farm family a self-reliant subsistence. The homes were clustered together in the village, allowing the enforcement of a uniform code of morality and austerity. The surrounding land was used judiciously in a way that reflected the British and New Englanders' resistance to amassing material goods as an end in itself (Hart 1975).

The American Revolution brought far-reaching changes in land ownership that displaced the feudalistic land law that had prevailed under British rule (Cochrane 1979). The land policies adopted by the 13 founding states, although differing in emphasis from state to state, resulted in the establishment of a freehold land tenure system. By 1853, territorial acquisitions westward resulted in a country that covered 1.9 billion acres, some two-thirds of which consisted of land in the public domain. Initially, the views of policymakers, who wished to dispose of the land in relatively large units in order to raise cash for the new government, prevailed. The speculation in land that resulted from this often ended in financial failure because, typically, the small pioneer settler, from whom early land speculators hoped to profit, had no money. Defaults were prevalent. In response, the government slowly liberalized the legislation regulating the terms of sale of public land.

MB: *Our Eurocentrism often has us start our histories at places that are self-validating, while other starting places might be even more illuminating. I would like to see the chapter* before *this one too, to glimpse the farming and husbandry practiced on the lands we took from Native Americans, and the transitions we might see if we examined their practices using this essay's triple lens of land ownership and use, ongoing education about methods of sustenance provision, and group attitudes towards the exchange value of food.*

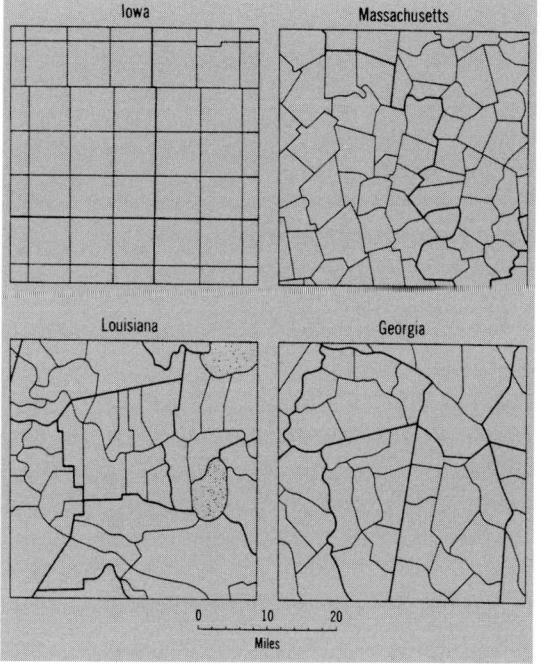

5-5
Land division in selected areas of states in America. The different land division patterns that resulted from colonial and postcolonial approaches to surveying and dividing the land are illustrated in this diagram. (source: Hart, 1975, 50)

LS: *The foundation of land speculation presented here challenges one of the great myths of American history — that of available, accessible, and affordable land for all people, meaning home and livelihood for all. Even while the myth persists, the principle of speculation continues today in governmental responses to home and livelihood in that they continue to be not available, accessible, or affordable. It is perhaps hopeful that at one time governmental policies were developed to counter speculation and make land available to people without resources.*

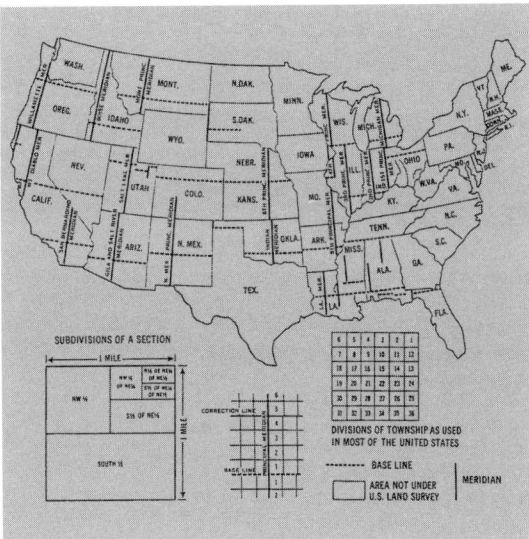

5-6
Division of land in the United States by the Government Land Survey (source: Cochrane 1979, 43. Courtesy of the University of Minnesota Press)

Land Survey Ordinance of 1785

In the Ordinance of 1785, Congress approved a land survey of the public domain to facilitate the sale and distribution of public lands (Cochrane 1979). Government surveyors were directed to establish, on unsettled lands, horizontal east-west lines called "baselines," and vertical north-south lines called "meridians." From these lines, tiers of townships were laid out, with each township containing 36 sections. The land was to be sold to individuals in minimum lots of 640 acres, for cash, at public auctions at a price of not less than one dollar per acre. One section in each township was reserved for the support of a public school.

For many reasons, but most importantly because the early pioneers did not have $640 to invest, the disposal of public land was slow. Again speculation in western land became rampant. In an effort to remedy this, the land law of 1820 reduced the minimum acreage an individual could buy to 80. As Cochrane points out, although this law and the administration of it had many shortcomings, it did enable many people to become landowners. He notes that "such a mass distribution of land to those who tilled the soil was unique in the history of the world up to that time" (Cochrane 1979, 57).

There was pressure on Congress from several quarters to distribute public lands to settlers free of charge. Among those pressing for such change were reformers who wanted to alleviate the poor economic conditions of urban factory workers. Legislation introduced in 1852 to this end failed. A Homestead Act passed by Congress in 1860 was vetoed by President Buchanan, who was responding to various pressure groups including the southern plantation farmer. The Homestead Act was enacted on May 20, 1862, with the south in rebellion. It enabled any person to file for 160 acres of unappropriated public land if he or she met certain conditions of citizenship or intended to acquire citizenship in the United States. Residence on the land for five years, becoming a citizen, and paying a small fee (a mere ten dollars in the early years) gave ownership. The original act allowed those who did not wish to live on the land for five years to buy it for $1.25 per acre if they lived on it for six months and made small improvements on it.

The survey system and these land purchase provisions served to make the grid system of land division the dominant pattern for the bulk of the landmass of the United States. It formed the quilt-like, regular, squared pattern of land holdings that is a noted and unique aspect of the U.S. landscape. In addition, the philosophy of land ownership as vesting freehold in an individual, and the technical survey system adopted to divide the land and enable this philosophy to be implemented, served to establish the unique American tradition of yeoman farmers and farm families scattered in a regular pattern, each in isolation, on their own individual pieces of land. This isolation mandated that granaries, smokehouses, water, and later windmills, milk houses, and enclosures for small animal husbandry that allowed for self-reliant living and subsistence cultivation had to be built on each farmstead. The long distances between farms made it essential that each farmstead set up a judicious system of windbreaks, fences, and woodlots to protect itself from storms and allow the family to heat and shelter themselves. The size of land divisions encouraged the planting of individual family orchards and kitchen gardens to supply daily foodstuffs. This was a very different configuration of settlement and land pattern from that of the nucleated villages of New England and their antecedents in Europe. The development in the United States is one very clear instance of how government actions concerning an essential resource – land – and the terms of access to it imprinted a landscape on a very grand scale, creating a unique pattern, or type, that persists in the midwestern landscape today.

The early settlers' choice of land across the United States often resulted from a scientific assessment of land attributes. Hart (1975) notes that early immigrants to North America were well aware that the vegetation on a given plot of land was an excellent indicator of what might be expected from other plants if they were grown there. Handbooks from the nineteenth century explained the significance of the different hardwood tree species as indicators of soil quality. Settlers initially avoided prairie lands, primarily because of the difficulties a treeless area created for people who relied on wood to build their houses, their barns, their fences, and their fires. This rational and scientific approach to choosing land was expanded to other aspects of cultivation and habitation, and characterized most aspects of later farming practices. American immigrant farmers rapidly shed the customs and traditions of building structures in the lands they had left and began to construct farmsteads that were uniquely "American." In this they were influenced by the constraints and the availability of local resources, most importantly the land itself and its vegetation, water, and topography. In addition, they responded to the amenities in the immediate area that were often shaped by the laws and policies influencing both the availability and price of services, products, and materials.

LS: *The structure of the landscape also framed the cultural pattern of independence and primacy of the nuclear family, rather than struggle to create community. Here, already, space was used as the mediator of conflict.*

5-7
The quilt-like pattern is sustained when farms grow and there are additions. Aerial photograph of farm west of Ann Arbor, Michigan (photo by Kenneth Baird)

Michigan: An Illustrative Case

Early settlement and land patterning in Michigan during the period of large-scale government surveys and disposition of public lands illustrate the influence of government policy on the pace and shape of early settlement. Surveyors began their work in the state in 1815, and made sufficient progress by 1818 that a land office was opened in Detroit. The Erie Canal, opened in 1825, helped move settlers to Michigan. By 1831 the survey of ten million acres was completed, facilitating the public sale of lands. Over four million acres were sold in 1836, constituting a land boom made possible by government actions.

As codified in the Northwest Ordinance, Michigan land was divided into six mile-by-six mile plots of 36 square miles called townships. Each township was divided into a six-by-six grid that yielded 36 one mile-by-one mile plots of land called sections. Along these boundaries, Michigan's original road system was constructed and, to this day, the grid retains its imprint on the organization of Michigan's rural landscape. In heavily agricultural areas the main roads are still regularly spaced, one mile apart. The typical plots granted or offered for sale by the Territorial Government of Michigan were quarter sections, or 160 acres, a size and pattern of land division continued with the passage of the Homestead Act in 1862. The quarter section was considered manageable farm size for a family to work. The plots were bounded by roads on two sides, which were useful for the transportation of goods and produce. "Crossroads" or "four-corner" towns began to dot townships, built by private entrepreneurs but facilitated by public or communal construction of roads and various infrastructures such as drainage systems. Later, waves of immigrants who purchased land from the original homesteaders often received 40 or 80 acres, i.e., a quarter or a half of the original quarter section. Usually at least one side of the purchased plot fronted on the section road. Thus the original pattern remained intact, becoming more detailed in its subdivisions. Even today, this pattern holds to a great extent, making identification of specific properties on a map by their legal, descriptive title rather simple. The origins of the system remain apparent in the rectilinear configurations of individual holdings delineated on a plot map.

The early period of settlement and subsistence farming in Michigan, as elsewhere in the midwest, was characterized by family farms that produced nearly everything needed for family consumption, as this was necessary for survival. Roads and transportation were poor and trips to nearby towns were made only occasionally. Labor-intensive, general farms raised a diversity of crops. There was

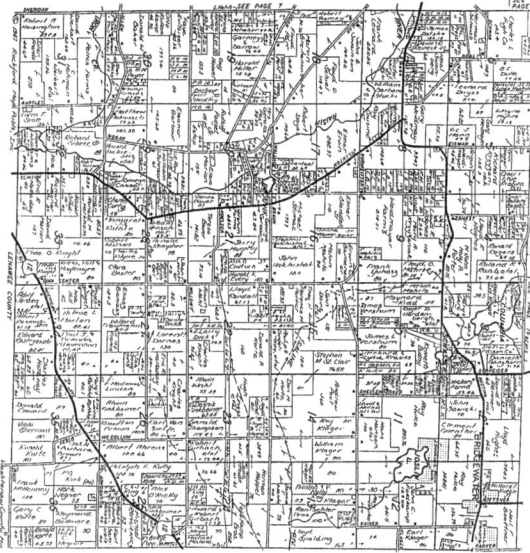

5-8
Current plat map of Bridgewater Township, Washtenaw County, Michigan illustrates the existing road pattern.

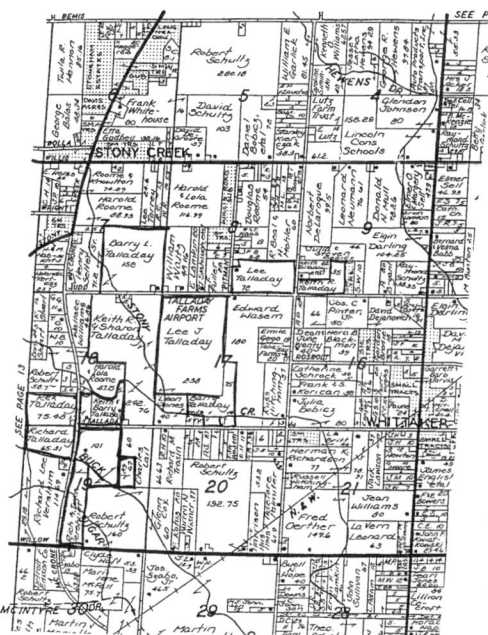

5-9
Individual holdings today are imprinted by the original government survey. This piece of a plat map of Augusta Township, Washtenaw County, Michigan is typical of plat maps in the midwest and illustrates how the typical subdivision of land makes individual holdings that are squared and grided.

small-scale animal husbandry: a few cows, pigs or sheep, and chickens, primarily for home consumption. The widespread adoption of horse- or ox-drawn labor-saving technology occurred in the 1850s (Cartensen 1980). Even so, all family members were assigned chores, and the work load was still such that even at the end of the nineteenth century and into the early twentieth century, it was extremely common for neighbors to exchange labor during the harvest season.

The hewn-log house was one of the first structures the early settlers built. Unlike log cabins, which were designed for temporary or partial use, these log houses were built as permanent homes. An outdoor privy or "outhouse" was the major convenience. Log houses and, later, timber-framed houses, sometimes functioned as the main family residence into the 1940s and 1950s. As a family became wealthier, their house was modified and expanded. An original log house in Gratiot County, Michigan built in the 1870s, with later wood frame additions of kitchen and tool room, was occupied without other structural changes until the mid 1950s. This persistence of early farm structure and type is characteristic of the early settlement period. In the upper peninsular area of Michigan, where settlement took place much later, I have photographed log houses and frame houses built in the early 1900s by Swedish, Finnish, or Slavic immigrants that are similar to those built much earlier by German or English settlers in southeastern Michigan. Even in the more urbanized and industrialized Michigan counties the transformation to "modern" housing and life-styles has been relatively recent for many farm people.

The division of the landscape into sections greatly influenced the overall layout of each farmstead. Rather than the cardinal points, the section road was the critical orienting factor in the placement of the farmhouse and access drive. The house generally faced, but was set back from, the section road. The other agricultural buildings were clustered separately but adjacent to and behind the house. Unlike Europe, land was abundant and could be used less economically in such a scattered site plan.

The house was invariably a subordinate structure, both in size and visual impact, to the most important structure of the farm — the main barn. The barn enjoyed a prime location on the most elevated and well-drained site. It was thoughtfully oriented to the cardinal points and its windows and doors were carefully designed to maximize benefits from the elements and minimize the costs. Barns dominated the surrounding landscape and were a measure of a farmer's wealth and success. They indicated stability, permanence, and a family's control

5-10
Log House in Washetenaw County, Michigan, occupied into the 1930s (photo courtesy of Clarence Hammond)

"I am bewildered by our casual use of space…"
(J.B. Jackson 1984, Discovering the Vernacular Landscape, *154*).

5-11
Log barn, Upper Peninsular, Michigan (photo by author)

over the surrounding land. The barn was built of hand-hewn doweled timber frame, and was wood sided with a gabled roof. It was used to house the animals and to store hay and grains. The wealthier farmers built subsidiary structures such as chicken coops, granaries, pigpens, smokehouses, and icehouses as part of the subsistence farm complex.

Farm buildings were constructed with a great deal of family labor, using materials obtained from the family land. When log houses were being built, much of the lumber used might have been felled to clear the land for cultivation. Stones and boulders found during this clearing were crafted by stoneworkers into foundation walls for the barns and other structures. The best hard wood was reserved for structural members; the rest was used in fencing, siding, flooring, and shingles. All this was achieved with the most basic of woodworking tools such as the adze, axes, hatchets, mallets, and saws. The whole activity of building was quite localized and individualized. Thus the structures of this period often have the imprint of the personal style and proclivity of the master barn builder or carpenter who constructed them. The folk traditions of the builders are apparent in the structures, and there is little direct evidence of government influence at this micro scale of building design. The major impact of government policy on farms in this period was on the patterning of land and its division, as well as the placement of services and amenities in the community.

Phase II: Railroads and Commercial Agriculture

Throughout the nineteenth century great emphasis was placed on building the physical infrastructure of transportation systems in America. The position of the public sector was that the survey and sale of government land had to go hand in hand with efforts to build up infrastructure. The rationale was that this infrastructure would facilitate bringing settlers and the supplies they needed into the hinterland, and getting agricultural production out. Early road and bridge building in the United States did not receive significant federal or state aid. But the canal era, which was sparked by the success of the Erie Canal (authorized by the New York state legislature), set off nationwide canal building in which governmental units were involved at various levels. However, it was in the construction of the railroad system that federal, state, and local governmental involvement was most significant. The efforts of states such as Missouri, as early as the 1850s, to fund the construction of a railroad system with state credits and local bonds is described by Riegel (1926). The precedent of federal aid, primarily in the form of land grants, was set by the passage of a bill in 1850 that gave the state of Illinois a land grant for the use of the Illinois Central (Riegel 1926). Land grants for railroad construction were administered by the Land Office in the Department of the Interior. When the railroad determined its route, a map was sent to the Land Office, which then withdrew from public settlement the land which the grant gave to the railroads. This put the railroad companies in the powerful position of being able, almost, to determine the location of settlements and thus to influence land prices.

During the latter part of the nineteenth century, an improved railway system stimulated the growth of a number of cities along its lines. Private railroad companies, which received various incentives from local governments to expand the rail system, were responsible for much of the growth of the rails. During this period the small four-corner and marketplace towns that responded to the early settlers' need for services flourished or died on the whims of where the railroads chose to locate their lines and stations. Hudson (1985) describes the impact the railroads had on the visual aspects of the landscape in states such as North Dakota. The grain elevators that sprang up at the bulking centers on railroads efficiently captured the grain production of an eight-mile radius around them and had tremendous visual, political, and social significance for the region.

The distribution and location of these centers resulted not from concerns about farmer efficiency but from the priorities and objectives of the private railroad companies (Hudson 1985). In midwestern states such as Michigan, the advent of the railroads created regional market opportunities for some farmers, allowing them to compete with neighboring states such as Ohio, Illinois, and Iowa. It also affected the crops Michigan could sell in the marketplace. Wheat, the predominant cash crop, reverted to a subsistence crop, while dairy cattle, sheep, and pigs became increasingly important. New buildings or additions and modifications to older structures were needed to house these animals. Portions of the farm acreage were maintained as woodlots for fuel and building materials. Farmers also continued to raise horses and cattle, but for their own use. The family-owned general farm remained the norm, but the size of the farm increased in order to allow for surplus production for commercial sale. The cultivation of more acreage by one family unit was made possible by the technological development of laborsaving machinery which, in turn, needed to be housed and sheltered on the farmstead. The scarcity of male labor during the Civil War had stimulated the innovation and use of laborsaving farm machinery such as the steel plow and the wheat binder. Now, as the Industrial Revolution drew labor from the countryside to the city, farmers again had to innovate and adopt new, efficient laborsaving devices to compensate for the resulting farm labor shortage.

Even with these transformations of agriculture, farm families, remarkably self-sufficient, continued to produce most of their own food. However, the effects of industrialization, mechanization, and improved roads and transport were apparent in their consumption patterns. Products such as butter began to be processed outside of the farm, making it cost-effective for the farm family to elim-

AK: *Land division in the United States reflects the essentially colonial nature of settlements. See especially Chapters 7 and 8 – "Rural Division of Land" and "European Farmlands" – in A.J. Christopher 1988,* The British Empire at Its Zenith.

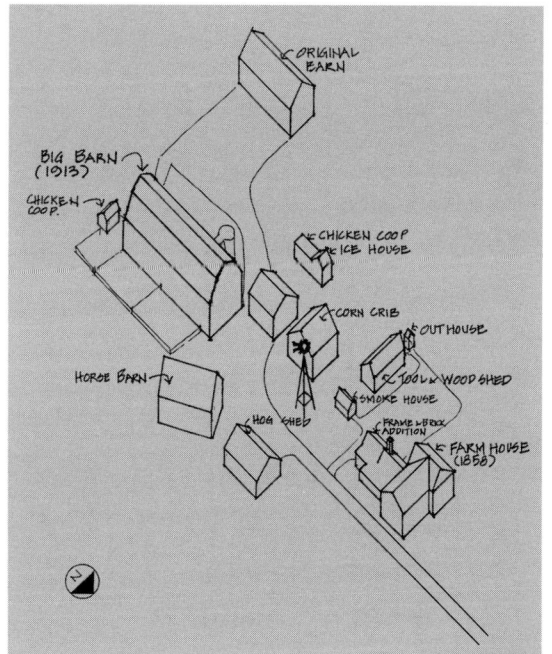

5-12
The Raab farm buildings. This drawing of existing structures on a farm in Bridgewater Township, Michigan, illustrates the types of farm structures one might expect from this period.
(courtesy of Mary Bockstahler)

inate the chore of churning butter and buy it instead at the general store. Articles such as shoes and clothing were increasingly bought at nearby market towns. This cost-effective approach left its mark on other areas of farmers' lives, but the innovations and advances of the late 1800s did not make them rich. More efficient and increased production went hand in hand with steadily declining prices for farm products. The farmer of this time found himself under duress. Consequently, farmers turned to farm organizations with nationwide affiliations to fight in state legislatures and in Congress against the big railroad and grain elevator corporations. Local granges often operated cooperative stores and elevators. By 1875 there were 600 local granges in Michigan (Dunbar 1965). These grange halls can still be seen throughout various townships in Michigan.

As markets increased in range with improvements in transportation modes, farmers began to specialize in the crops they produced. The farmers that prospered consolidated their wealth by increasing the type and size of farm structures they built. Big, three-level banked barns with gabled roofs were constructed on these more prosperous farms. Animals were sheltered in the lower level, which was often bermed to the north to take advantage of the earth's insulation against the chilling north winds. Doors opened out at the lowest level on the south side where the animal yard captured the sun's warmth during the winter. The second level was used for threshing, winnowing, tool storage, and as a granary. On the third level were mows for storing hay. The foundation was made from rubble stones obtained from the land. The structure was timber-framed, doweled, and mortice and tenon jointed, and the roof, shingled gable. The timber frame might have been constructed from lumber from the family land, but the siding was often white pine brought by railroad from northern Michigan.

As a successful farmer became wealthier, the size of the barn he needed increased. To construct it required more labor than the family could provide. A barter system developed in which neighbors and the whole community participated in building these grand barns. In these traditional "barn raisings" everyone contributed in some way, regardless of age or gender. New types of farmhouses were built to replace the log houses or to add to them. These were usually of frame construction, larger than the original, and had separate kitchens and bedrooms. The wealth of the family was reflected not only in the size of their house, but in the materials they used (brick being more expensive than wood), and in the refinement of the architectural detailing. A carriage house to shelter the carriage and tools, horses, and feed might have been added, and so might corn cribs, designed and constructed to deter rodents. Thus the development of effective transportation systems with public grants and assistance led to the commercialization of agriculture, to farm prosperity, and to the consolidation of this wealth in larger, more elaborate, and more numerous farm structures.

Phase III: Technology and Scientific Education

The period of 1900 to 1945 was one of transition and transformation in agriculture to cash crops produced primarily for sale in larger regional markets. In the midwestern states it was characterized by a shift from animal husbandry and cultivation of feed crops for family subsistence and sale in local markets, to cash crops. Market demand became the principal factor in the selection of crops to be raised. While the small labor-intensive family-owned farm was still prevalent, farmers began to experience the early stages of capital-intensive agribusiness. At the same time, the development of the automobile began to kill off farmsteads in the ever-expanding peripheries of growing cities. Motor vehicles and improved roads made journeys to cities a matter of minutes rather than hours or days, and carriage houses were converted to garages or to housing for other animals. Farm families abandoned their homesteads as urban, industrial jobs became more attractive. Farmhouses and barn complexes were left behind to decay.

Urban and industrial growth and the resulting demand for labor in the city greatly affected farming, drawing many sons of farmers away from the farm. The development and adoption of new technology to lower production costs, such as the internal combustion tractor and the combine, led to less need or demand for labor. Thus the relationship between mechanization and migration from the countrysides was due to both push and pull factors. The substitution of inanimate mechanical power for animate horsepower was most apparent in the countryside in the adoption of the now ubiquitous tractor. Tractors appearing on farms in the early 1900s were initially steam powered, but the proliferation of the internal combustion engine made tractors commonplace by the 1920s. Initially able only to cultivate or plow, tractors soon were modified to haul wagons, harvesters, and combines (Stadtfeld 1972). Tractors were also used to power threshers and silo fillers, which chopped whole corn and blew it into the silos. Sheds were built or barns modified or enlarged to house and repair tractors, and the horse barn began to be obsolete.

One of the most important technological innovations of this period was the silo, first developed in 1875. The earliest silos were made of wood, were square in plan, and were sometimes built in the corner of an existing barn. Later, with "barrel-making" technology, they were constructed in the more familiar round plan when it was discovered that this cut down friction-drag on the inside surface and thereby reduced spoilage. Silos were used to store succulent "green fodder," principally feed corn, which is rich in both nutrients and water. There were several advantages of "silage." Corn had greater food value than the more traditional dried hay and stored grains, thus making it feasible for a farmer to care for more livestock. Also, silage kept cows "fresh," that is, able to give milk throughout the year instead of only six or seven months. The silo increased the efficiency of a dairy farm tremendously and, with it, the chance for higher profits. It also changed the image of the farmscape tremendously as it proliferated throughout the midwest. By 1924 Wisconsin had the greatest number of silos with more than 100,000, while Michigan had 49,000. The soaring cylindrical tower was placed beside the large barn, often hovering over the barn's already high peak. The modern silo was not an American innovation, but, as Dandekar and Savitski (1989) have documented, the activities of public institutions such as the Illinois Industrial University, the Missouri Dairy Commission, and the State Board of Agriculture were a significant factor in making broad-based adoption of silo technology and the refinements in its design primarily an American endeavor. These institutions published and disseminated technical bulletins that analyzed and lauded the efficacy of silage and provided detailed designs and plans for building "scientific" silos. A boom in silo construction resulted.

Thus the adoption of new methods of cultivation or machinery had the effect of adding new structures on the farmstead or requiring substantial modifications or additions to existing buildings to make them functional for new needs. The mechanization of this period also served to push the farmer further into cash crop agriculture. This is illustrated by the effect of adopting of the mechanical thresher. Various threshing machines were reported to have been invented in Michigan, some as early as 1835, but commercially manufactured threshers only became available during the 1920s (Chase 1922). Like tractors, early steam-powered threshers were replaced by ones with internal combustion engines. Since the steam engines drew power from products grown on the land including stumps, straw, and other combustible material used as fuel, they allowed the farm to be self-sufficient. But to use the internal combustion engine, the farmer had to purchase kerosene or gasoline. This forced the farmer to cultivate cash crops for sale.

Other laborsaving devices developed during this time included spraying equipment, self-propelled harvesters, hay choppers, and hay loaders. Land grant colleges such as the Michigan State Agricultural College, as well as state and county farm bureaus, aided in this "scientization" of agriculture. They helped farmers increase their crop yields and make farming more efficient and, therefore, more economically viable. Government support for the educational institutions was provided quite early on. State colleges of agriculture were established after the passage of the Morril Land Grant Act of 1862, which was a notable step in the advancement of American agriculture. But the more advanced research and graduate level work in agriculture occurred later, with the establishment of agricultural experiment stations to provide a scientific basis to the agricultural undertaking. The first state-supported agricultural experimentation station was established in 1875 in Connecticut. In 1887 the Hatch Act provided a yearly grant to each state for the support of an agricultural experiment station. Within a decade every state had an agricultural station devoting itself to the work of basic agriculture research (Rasmussen 1960). The impact of this legislation on shaping the scientific base of modern American farming was highly significant.

A less scientific but equally innovative trend occurred in the building technology of this period. Standardized milled lumber – the ubiquitous 2 x 4s, 2 x 6s, and 2 x 8s of our current construction palette – became available in the late 1800s, as did standardized nails with reliable strength and dimensions that replaced the hand-forged ones used in earlier periods. These ushered in the era of the billowing gambrel roof so familiar to any barn observer. While barns had already become quite large in plan, the gambrel roof, replacing the typical gabled roof, increased their volume appreciably, allowing the farmer to store more hay and straw in the loft. Farm building "pattern books" from this period feature both the gambrel- and gable-roofed structures. In 1910, a peak barn-building period in Michigan, most of the new structures – some of which used lumber from the earlier gable-roofed barns – were gambrel roofed. Agricultural extension stations' technical bulletins to farmers facilitated such transformations by informing farmers of new building types such as the round barn, and explained how to make the construction of existing buildings more cost and space effective.

A review of the extension bulletins and publications of the agricultural experimentation stations of the midwestern states by Dandekar, Darvas, and MacDonald (1992) reveals the promotion of six major structural barn types (see

LS: *Was there no controversy regarding the scientization of farming? Were there voices in the discourse which challenged the technical, rational ideology and the idea of progress?*

Figure 5-4). In these six types, arrayed chronologically, there is an increasing efficiency in the amount of wood needed for construction and a freeing of the internal spatial volume so as to accommodate new, larger machinery. This typology, based on the promotional literature of the experimentation stations, has proved to be very useful in identifying the types of barns that were actually built in many areas of Michigan, illustrating the power of the government agencies to influence the type of buildings that were actually erected.

Technical rationality prevailed in the evolution of agrarian building forms during this phase. The agricultural extension bulletins that addressed the optimal layout and design of specialized farm structures are a graphic illustration of the dictum that "form follows function." In this tradition the development of more corporate forms of farm production, involving shifts in technology, resulted in quintessentially pragmatic changes in the size, shape, and materials used in American farm architecture. The growing size of individual farm holdings was made possible by these new agricultural technologies. The research underlying these technologies often occurred in the publicly supported land grant colleges. Thus government policy affected the number and distribution of farmsteads on the landscape and rendered many earlier farm structures obsolete. Dandekar and Savitski (1989) provide some examples of the impact of this phenomenon on the physical plant of a large family farm in Michigan.

Phase IV: Modern and Corporate Farming

Direct government intervention in agriculture through legislation which specifically affects the price of farm inputs and the allowable level of farm production is a 1930s, post-Great Depression, phenomenon. Emanating from the New Deal thinking of the Roosevelt era, the Agricultural Adjustment Acts were approved, litigated against, redesigned, and finally accepted as portions of the Second Agricultural Adjustment Act in 1938. The eventual passage of this landmark act enabled the passage of various pieces of farm legislation that impinged on current farm operations. A central theme underlying these legislative efforts was the perceived need to stabilize prices and income in the agricultural enterprise. There is a vast literature and ongoing debate on the efficacy, nature, and extent of this legislation, and that which built on it, which has influenced subsidy payments to farmers, taxation to raise revenue for agriculture, programs to reduce production, price support measures, and commodity storage (Cochrane 1979). One of the major consequences of governmental programs was the periodic accumulation of huge stocks of grain. Often these were an unwanted side effect of adopting high price supports without constraining production. In other cases it was justified as the conscious building of stocks in good years to be used to buttress consumption and decrease price increases in poor crop years. Farmers played a major role as investors in structures, such as cylindrical steel bins to store these grains on their farms. Many of the structures would not exist but for government-induced stocks of grain and subsidies for their storage.

It is neither possible nor useful to address in detail the various effects of government interventions on the shape of farms. It is enough to note that it is this body of legislation that still shapes modern farmers' decisions about production and helps determine the size of farms that are economically efficient. By and large this legislative effort has reduced the risk in farming and therefore allowed American farms to become more specialized. Farming has changed from a mix of production to mono-cropping or cultivation of two or three specialized crops. This has affected the kinds of structures erected in recent times on the American farmscape. A two-step evolution can be observed: the first from about 1945 to 1975, resulting in what Dandekar and Schoof (1988) have termed "modern farms," and the second since 1975 or so, resulting in what have been called "corporate farms."

Modern Farms

During the period of 1945 to 1975 specialized farming for national and international markets became the norm for many American farmers. There were several significant reasons for this: rapid advances in national/international transport; the emergence of the United States as a major world power and the corresponding change in its domestic and foreign policy; tremendous advances in scientific/technological farming in the United States including development of high-yield hybrids, fertilizers, pest controls, and large-scale mechanization. An agricultural boom followed World War II; returning soldiers often came back to the family farmstead, greatly increasing available labor on the land and, along with it, new capital. This capital was used to purchase new, larger, more efficient, and specialized machinery. Large-scale farming, particularly in the Great Plains states, became common.

With the technological advances in farming, the farmscape began to change dramatically. New baling machinery bundled hay tightly into huge bales, allowing them to be left in the fields through the winter rather than being stored under the gambrel roof of the big barn. On farms where the new balers were used, the big wooden barns became less essential and began to disappear, bulldozed for safety either to save on taxes or for their lumber or allowed to decay from neglect.[5] Too costly to build and ineffective for modern farming practices, the wooden barns gave way to prefabricated, sheet metal pole barns. Farmers have adopted the new low-slung pole barn with enthusiasm. It can be easily and speedily constructed and, with an open floor plan, is extremely adaptable. New machinery, varied in size and shape, can be easily accommodated. However, these sheet metal buildings have no folk antecedents, no cultural or ethnic roots. They are stimulated by the ease of mass production and lowering of cost. Large and rather ungainly pole barns are added to the farm for their efficiency, but their industrialized color and form lack the traditional, romantic aesthetic of the farmscape. The results can be jarring to the aesthetically sophisticated eye.

The enlarged market also changed the nature of farming. Farmers no longer produced for family subsistence except in the most casual way. One such farmer, Mr. Wing, whose farm is just on the outskirts of Ann Arbor, Michigan, and who cultivated grains and dairy cattle, confessed that he did not sell one bean in Ann Arbor and bought his milk in gallon containers at the supermarket, "just like everyone else" (Wing 1987). Mr. Wing's family has been farming on this particular farmstead since the 1850s. He recounts that in his father's time they raised cows, sheep, and chickens, butchered their own meat, and had a large garden. Now he buys his milk from the supermarket and raises grain for the international market. The constraints of large-scale, specialized farming and government regulations regarding the quality and standards in food production – for instance milk – are such that it is not cost-effective for him to produce for his subsistence needs. Instead, the emphasis of farm policy is on producing for the global marketplace. In the course of several interviews including a conversation on August 18, 1991, Mr. Wing has become increasingly vociferous in his complaints about the government's role in farming. He feels that there is an undue and unfair intrusion of governmental presence in the form of regulations and control over his farm enterprise. He is of the opinion that government activities place his modern, family-owned farm in a compromised position relative to the corporate farm.

---

5. Dandekar and Bockstahler (1990) describe how local governments control property taxes and have a propensity to raise taxes on property that is well maintained. This predisposes owners of barns that have no economic function to allow them to become dilapidated or to demolish them.

LS: *One could argue, on the contrary, that this is the new American vernacular landscape having deep roots in "American" culture (see J.B. Jackson's* The Vernacular Landscape, *1984).*

LS: *This pressure to produce for the international market is being felt throughout the world. Farmers in many "Third World" countries who had raised food for subsistence and for a local market are being pressured by government policy to raise export crops for the international market to relieve the debt pressure on the country. At the same time, more food is being imported. The pressure is very great and, as Mr. Wing suggests, it is almost impossible for farm families to choose a different method of farming.*

AK: *It's interesting that in the United States there seems to be less resistance to these changes (perhaps because of the scale of the American landscape), whereas in Europe, especially the United Kingdom, there is immense resistance to change in "the countryside," which is seen as a cultural, social, and political resource — not just as an economic one.*

Corporate Farms

Triggering the shift from modern to corporate farms were changes in the U.S. role in world affairs and in its foreign policy. The emerging posture of the United States as a leading proponent of global free trade meant that U.S. farms were seen as the "world's breadbasket." Farmers produced crops for India, Russia, and other countries previously unknown to the small family farmer. Advances in national and international transport aided this expansion of the market. This was a period of "green revolution" technologies, leading to unexpectedly large crop yields. Phenomenally high-yielding hybrids as well as super fertilizers and pest controls were developed. Specialization was accentuated and mono-crop farms became common. In using the new products and machinery, farming became energy intensive, but the cost of energy was kept low and this evolution seemed reasonable.

Starting about 1975, large corporate farms registering sales of over five million dollars a year, of which there are over 1000 or so in the United States, have been changing the face of American agriculture. In the early 1960s farms with at least $100,000 in sales represented only 1.1 percent of the 3.5 million farmers growing the nation's food. These large farms accounted for almost 25 percent of all sales of farm products but earned only 10 percent of the profits. By 1982, however, 1.2 percent of farmers had increased the value of their sales tremendously, grossing more than $500,000 each. Three years later, in 1985, the total number of farms had declined to 2.2 million and the largest 1.2 percent produced nearly 33 percent of the total sales for all farms, and their profits had multiplied even more quickly, to over 55 percent of the total national farm profit (Robbings 1987).

The technically sophisticated, blue fiberglass Harvestore silos, 61 feet high and 20 feet in diameter, which provide effective and efficient storage for the large amounts of feed that were formerly kept in the traditional barn, are now threatened on the corporate "superfarm." Economies of scale on the corporate farm have resulted in greatly increased numbers of cows and cattle. The increased silage these farms require has made a horizontal type of silo called a "bunker silo" a more efficient and preferred structure. Big vertical silos have become obsolete. The bunker silo, a large, six- or seven-foot-high rectangular enclosure of wood or concrete retaining walls, stores silage that is densely compacted by driving heavy machinery over the top. Because a greatly increased volume of silage is stored in this silo, the increased spoilage at its sides and top represents only a small fraction of the total silage. According to Green (1988) and Talladay (1988), the loss is considered negligible by modern farm standards.[6] Lacking the grandeur of the vertical silo, bunker silos possess a quite ordinary, even ugly, appearance. Over time, if they continue to be the silo of choice for large-scale farming, the midwestern landscape will lose the towering presence of the vertical silos whose scale dominated the rural landscape of the past century, and whose symbolical importance in representing farms was equal to that of the big red barn of an earlier era.

Corporate superfarms are changing the rural landscape tremendously. Mechanization of animal husbandry, prefabrication of buildings, and computerization of accounting, feeding, and delivery systems are characteristics of this new agriculture. Row after row of look-alike, gleaming metal buildings shaped like industrial structures are constructed to house chickens, hogs, or cattle. The farm factories of the future are a reality here. For many generations the image of farms and farmscapes has been one thing: the big red barns and the silos. For the next generation it may be quite another: industrial structures that look like factories.

Conclusion

The dynamic changes in the form of American agricultural architecture have received critical impetus from a variety of government policies and actions. Few countries in the world have demonstrated so directly, and at such a large scale, the impact of rapid experimentation, adoption, and diffusion of technology in the spatial configuration of the agrarian landscape and forms. The changes have primarily been scientifically driven. However, given a global concern about the sustainability of various types of development, this phenomenon has come under increasingly critical scrutiny. Questions are being raised about the widespread and heavy use of chemicals, hormones, pesticides, fertilizers, and additives. There is concern about residues in the food chain and groundwater contamination from farm runoff. There is discomfort with genetic and cloning experimentation in livestock, and questions about where such manipulation might lead. These and other matters of concern, long debated in the organic farming movement, have moved into the mainstream of American public opinion.[7] Recent academic work on the relative inefficiencies of large-scale, high-tech agriculture versus more traditional approaches may result in a shift of federal policy and subsidy in agriculture to one

MB: *Aesthetic judgments are made here about certain types of structures, and about the farmscape as a whole: bunker silos have an "ugly appearance"… and pole barns are "rather ungainly"… and "lack the traditional romantic aesthetic of the farmscape… jarring to the aesthetically sophisticated eye." These judgments feel like a longing for the "picturesque" and seem strangely out of place in this otherwise remarkable history of a "quintessentially pragmatic" landscape, a history that so clearly shows how new methods, new machinery, and new policies have always affected both physical form and infrastructure, and quite directly. This entire history is one that traces adaptations driven by efficiency, bereft of romance. Even so, the farm, a supposedly pragmatic landscape type, holds our hearts in ways very different from, say, how machines (also quintessentially pragmatic) hold them. While intellectuals may not, I assume that many farmers see their farms as machines for controlled production of edible commodities. But, of course, how we see and feel about landscapes changes. As these landscape types change and become corporately enormous and sprout "ugly" pole barns and bunker silos, might not their effect change as well… perhaps from a nostalgic "picturesque" to the more forbidding but powerful "sublime?"*

MB: *Coming to the end of this dazzling panorama of the consequences-in-form of government policies and attitudes towards farming, it really wants to be in pictures, a movie really. I want to see the changing physical aspects of the farm and buildings in the form of the "flip-books" of my youth, those hand-held soft booklets made of maybe 50 sequential and slightly different drawings, creating a minimovie when swiftly riffled through.*

AK: *This paper locates types in relation to the ever-larger space economies to which such types belong (and also help to constitute). The narrative treats the process of change as somewhat too "natural" whereas it is, essentially, a political process in which some people (and countries) are winners and others losers. There are real (corporate) interests involved here! The ideology of government is strongly influenced by extremely powerful corporate interests. Also, much more attention needs to be given to the "politics of resistance" here — on moral, aesthetic, social, political, and health grounds.*

6. M.M. Green runs a family-owned corporation whose farm and herd consist of 4000 acres of land, 3000 head of registered Holstein, of which 1500 are milk cows. Lee Talladay runs a family-owned corporation of 1500 acres and 250 beef cattle.

7. For example, Keith Schneider wrote a front page article in the *New York Times* (9/11/89) entitled "Weaning Chemical Use: Seeds of Revolt on Farms," in which he referred to the National Academy of Science Report that urges a change in federal policy to encourage farmers to switch to "alternative agriculture" – which appears to be a turn to more natural farming techniques.

more sympathetic to the traditional, diversified family farmer. Consumer concerns related to the state of the global environment may cause some shifts in the technology and processes used in American agriculture and result in substantial changes in the form and structures of American agricultural architecture. But currently the trends that have been described here continue to hold true and may persist despite efforts to change their direction.

Whatever the outcome, it is clear that in determining the future of farming and farm structures it will be government policy and institutions that shape the broad-based changes. Perhaps in today's United States this holds true for other building types as well. This essay has attempted to make clear that evolution in form in the United States is not merely "natural" or derived from free-market forces and the social/cultural proclivities of the designer/builder, but rather take strong directives from the government and public sector apparatus. Very strong political, ideological, and economic interests are played out in local, state, and national/international governments when policy is formulated. The result is a legislative environment that can warp and shape the "technical rationality" equation of any design decision. In the case of farms and farm structures, the model of scientific rationality and the global marketplace that has been endorsed by the U.S. government has resulted in an increasing loss of community and autonomy at the level of the individual farmer. My impression is that with the evolution to corporate farms, the quality of life and the aesthetics of rural environments have been degraded. In addition, urbanites enjoy the benefits of low prices and reliable food supply, but face the consequences of high-tech scientific agriculture in the residues and additives that reach them through the food chain. Despite the damage to the environment and the demise of family farms accruing from government actions, to date little government attention has been given to keeping the social and economic fabric of the rural United States intact.

I believe that architects and physical planners cannot afford to restrict their professional attention to the analysis of the morphology of building form. To take such a spatial and technical view simply because that is our specialty dooms us to being spectators of changes that vitally affect what *is* our domain — the nature of our physical environment and the quality of life that accrues from, and is embedded, in it. My research on farm structures has led me to question many of the assumptions that have shaped farm policy. It has led me to critique the technical and economic rationality that endorses the current evolution to corporate farm.

A type analysis of building form that leads one to take a stance and argue for a position about "how things ought to be" needs to be an essential component of our professional agenda. By all means, through type analysis, we should help ourselves and others to understand the built world and how it came to be shaped the way it is. But the exercise must also help us reach a multifaceted explanation of why it is that way, and lead us to some conclusions about what and how it might or should be changed. To do less is to abrogate our social and ethical responsibilities as professionals who help shape the physical environment.

AK: *The question of "building, architecture, and the new international division of labor" is discussed in King 1990,* Urbanism, Colonialism, and the World Economy.

I would like to thank Glenn Nelson for his extremely valuable insights about U.S. agriculture, for critical commentary on earlier drafts of this chapter, and for pointing out useful work in the literature on U.S. agriculture.

References

Bleznick, Susan R. 1991. Midwestern vernacular: Charles Moore's TRINOVA headquarters rephrases agrarian form. *Inland Architect* 35 (4): 54–55.

Carstensen, V. 1980. An overview of American agricultural history. In *Farmers, Bureaucrats and the Middlemen: Historical Perspectives on American Agriculture*, ed. T.H. Peterson, 18–19. Washington, D.C: Howard University Press.

Chase, L.S. 1922. *Rural Michigan*. New York: Macmillan.

Cochrane, Willard W. 1979. *The Development of American Agriculture: A Historical Analysis*. Minneapolis, Minn.: University of Minnesota Press.

Dandekar, Hemalata C. and Daniel F. Schoof. 1988. Michigan farms and farm buildings: 150 years of transformation. *Inland Architect* (January/February): 61–67.

Dandekar, Hemalata C. and John A. Savitski. 1989. The silo: a century of experimentation on the Michigan farm. *The Chronicle* (Historical Society of Michigan) 25 (3): 2–5.

Dandekar, Hemalata C. and Mary Bockstahler. 1990. The changing farmscape: a case study of German farmers in southeast Michigan. *Michigan History* (Bureau of History, Michigan Department of State) 74 (2): 42–47.

Dandekar, Hemalata C., Robert Darvas and Eric MacDonald. 1992. *Michigan Farm Building: Phase II*. Report to the Bureau of History, Michigan Department of History.

Davidson, Cynthia C. 1990. The psychology of small. *Inland Architect* 34 (2): 32–33.

Dunbar, W.F. 1965. *Michigan: A History of the Wolverine State*. Grand Rapids, Mich.: W.B. Eerdmans Publishing Co.

Green, M.M. 1988. Interview with author. Green Meadows Farms, Elsie, Michigan.

Hart, John F. 1975. *The Look of the Land*. Englewood Cliffs, N.J.: Prentice Hall.

Hubka, Thomas C. 1984. *Big House, Little House, Back House, Barn: The Connected Farm Building of New England*. Hanover, N.H.: University Press of New England.

Hudson, John C. 1985. *Plains Country Towns*. Minneapolis, Minn.: University of Minnesota Press.

Keegan, Edward. 1989. Peter Landon Associates. *Inland Architect* 33 (2): 40–42.

McAlester, Virginia, and Lee McAlester. 1984. Folk Houses. In *A Field Guide to American Houses*, 75–101. New York: Knopf.

McLennan, Marshall. 1987. Vernacular architecture: common house types in southern Michigan. In *Michigan Folklife Reader*, eds. C.K. Dewhurst and Y.R. Lockwood, 15–47. Ann Arbor, Mich.: Michigan University Press.

Noble, Allen G. 1984. *Barns and Frame Structures*. Vol 2 of *Wood, Brick, and Stone: The North American Settlement Landscape*. Amherst, Mass.: University of Massachusetts Press.

Noble, Allen G. and Gayle A. Seymore. 1982. Distribution of barn types in northeastern United States. *The Geographic Review* 72 (2): 155–170.

Rasmussen, Wayne D. 1960. *Readings in the History of American Agriculture*. Urbana, Ill.: University of Illinois Press.

Riegel, Robert E. 1926. *The Story of the Western Railroad: From 1852 through the Reign of the Giants*. Lincoln and London: University of Nebraska Press.

Robbings, William. 1984. Down on the superfarm. *New York Times*, August 4.

Stadtfeld, C.K. 1972. *From the Land and Back*. New York: Scribner's Sons.

Talladay, Lee. 1988. Interview with author. Talladay Farm, Augusta Township, Michigan.

Tishler, William H. 1986. Fachwerk construction in the German settlements of Wisconsin. In *Winterthur Portfolio* 24 (4): 275–92. Chicago: University of Chicago Press.

Tishler, William H. and C. Witmer. 1986. The house barns of East-Central Wisconsin. In *Perspectives in Vernacular Architecture*, vol. 2, ed. Camille Wells, 102–19. University of Missouri Press.

Torre, Susana. 1988. Invited lecture at the College of Architecture and Urban Planning, March 3, University of Michigan Ann Arbor, Michigan.

Wing, Leroy. 1987. Interview with author. Ann Arbor, Michigan.

Chapter 6

Zoning as a Tool for Regulating Family Type in American Communities

Marsha Ritzdorf

One of the fundamental value assumptions implicit in American zoning and land use policies is the "rightness" of the single-family lifestyle. The single family is assumed to be a traditional nuclear family consisting of a stay-at-home mother, a working father, and children. Although 1990 census statistics reveal that only 13 percent of American families conform to this norm, it is still embedded in our cultural mythology and reinforced in our patterns of land use. A single-family detached home on its own piece of land, located on a quiet, tree-lined street far from the bustle of the city, is the metonymic representation of the American Dream.

Zoning is the tool that bonds this spatial metaphor to the landscape, and the mechanism that fuses the household type of the traditional family to a housing type – the single-family home. Zoning ordinances, which overlay types of uses onto the landscape, purport to protect the public welfare of the community. However, what they actually do is protect various, politically powerful subcultures, including suburban families who are intent upon maintaining the exclusivity of their neighborhoods and who wish to promote "family values."

The assumption of "family type" is built into the design and planning of many residential districts. In these exclusively single-family districts, it is expected that "traditional" nuclear families, or their municipally sanctioned alternatives, will be the only occupants. Until the twentieth century (a few historical anomalies aside), this was a reasonable assumption to make about upper and middle class life in the United States. In contemporary America, however, "the popular vision of the typical household of father, mother, and two or three children is fast assuming the proportions of folklore" (Houston 1981, 73), as the census figures for 1990 reflect.

Regardless of these recent changes in the American family, most zoning laws remain basically unyielding in their nostalgic interpretation of "correct" community land patterns in which work, home, and services are spatially separated. This interpretation glorifies the creation of isolated suburban environments; the more distance between a residential neighborhood and jobs, services, and people of a different socioeconomic status, the "better" that neighborhood is (Ritzdorf 1987).

Through restrictive family definitions, certain types of family relationships are legitimized and others are not. The language of family, and in particular the language of the traditional nuclear family, permeates zoning ordinances. Not only do these ordinances contain family definitions, they also present a hierarchical typology of family dwellings from single-family to multifamily. In all cases, it is assumed that the definition of family will create sociophysical spaces that reflect this stratified and value-laden classification.

The purpose of this chapter is fourfold: to discuss the cultural ideal of the family and its linkage to municipal zoning ordinances; to examine the practical workings of this linkage, specifically how the ordinances work to enforce the cultural ideal; to analyze briefly the role the courts have played in supporting this activity; and to suggest some strategies for change.

The Cultural Ideal of "Family"

Traditional familial relationships are highly valued in all cultures. However, cross-culturally, family form is so varied that it is impossible to argue for the existence of universal psychological, sociological, or biological relations. The nuclear family, so important to white, nineteenth- and twentieth-century European and American cultural norms, is not always the central point of reference elsewhere or for minority groups in the Euro-American context (Coontz 1988). However, all societies define family in some way:

> Despite wide variety in the organization and even the definition of families, all known societies of any significant size or complexity seem to use this concept to institutionalize and legitimize certain special, socially sanctioned relationships among various members of the group (Coontz 1988, 22).

The concept of family provides a framework within which a society captures the relationship of a group to society as a whole. It helps set the rules by which the society and the group called "family" will interrelate. Therefore, when groups which represent life-styles alternative to that practiced by the majority of a society are sanctioned, it allows them to cross boundaries which have heretofore been forbidden. Since in America the nuclear family represents the cultural norm of the white middle class – the dominant social group – the entry into a neighborhood of groups who live together but are "not like us" is a threat. The neighborhood, regarded as providing a sphere of protection, is violated (Perin 1988).

In 1977, Perin interviewed the significant actors in the land use arena (bankers, planners, architects, developers, and local officials) in several major U.S. cities. She documents their belief in a specific set of ideas about the structure of society and the spatial rules that they employ to assure its perpetuity. Central to all of them is the homogeneous single-family neighborhood. In a more recent book, *Belonging in America: Reading Between the Lines* (1988), she further develops her theme using interviews with over 100 suburban men and women. The relationship between U.S. cultural values and the appeal of the homogeneous suburban neighborhood remains strong even in an era when home ownership is a fading dream for many young families: "the house as a symbol of the single-family ideal loses none of its power despite both high divorce rates and high housing prices" (Perin 1988, 98).

The presence of a male to head the household is intrinsic to the nuclear family: "family also depends on husbands and fathers for its legitimacy, and mothers and children have their place derivatively" (Perin 1988, 40). Historically, in western Europe, nuclear family households were associated with high degrees of independence and the connected possibility of rapid economic mobility (Coontz 1988). In nineteenth-century America, as home and workplace drew apart, the nuclear family unit took on a more significant social meaning, continuing the belief that the "monogamous family (is) the outcome of evolution from lower forms of life and is the final divinely ordered form" (Lund 1937, 410). It is no wonder that America would embrace residential patterns that protected the "one socially legitimate family."

The absence of a man breaches the middle class norm of family, a norm with which many women identify more strongly than they identify with their gender. In general, women have continued to support a system that ultimately stigmatizes them because the definition of family is fundamentally defined by gender-assigned roles (Perin 1988). Men who are divorced or widowed are not considered deviant because the male head is maintained. It is only the absence of a man that breaches the norm of family, for its definition insists on the presence of a man. Prior to 1990, the U.S. census acknowledged only two family types: "families" and "female-headed households." While the census now acknowledges a variety of family types in their data, the traditional stereotypes are still played out in zoning regulations.

The language of housing types reinforces stereotypes about the appropriateness of a family based on the size, quality, and location of the dwelling that houses it. "A family home," gushes the real estate agent as she/he describes a stereotypical single-family suburban home, "it's just the place to raise your children." However, the external nature of the neighborhood or the "traditionalness" of the form do not guarantee the quality of life within. For example, mounting statistics related to the frequency of and the nature of the perpetrators of child/wife sexual and physical abuse show that these are crimes that occur in all economic classes and are primarily the crimes of "family men." Yet the reliance on outdated stereotypes remains at the heart of the public land use agenda.

Preoccupation with the nuclear family unit is not limited to the planning profession, but permeates all public policy-making in the United States The concept of "the family ethic" is advanced by Abramovitz to explain this historic pattern:

> As a dominant social norm, the family ethic articulates the terms of women's work and family roles. According to its rules, proper women marry and have children while being supported by and subordinated to a male breadwinner. Even through major changes in the political economy, the family ethic has persisted... Since colonial times, social welfare policies have treated women differently based on the extent to which their lives conformed to the terms of the family ethic (Abramovitz 1988, 2).

The family ethic shapes municipal land use patterns. The age-old patterns that dictate that it is the role of women to maintain the private sphere of home and family have not changed as women enter the work force in massive numbers. Instead, women are responsible for both maintaining the family's private domain and helping support it by paid labor force participation. Land use patterns based on the traditional family ethic serve contemporary families poorly, especially women and their children, and do not reflect changing patterns of work, play, residence, and travel. In addition, they have never reflected the needs of alternative families. As more middle class women find themselves downwardly mobile through divorce, they are hard-pressed to find their appropriate identity.

Judicial Perspectives on the Meaning of Family in Zoning Law

The right of U.S. municipalities to enact ordinances regulating land use through zoning was established in 1926 (*Village of Euclid v Ambler Realty Co.* 272 U.S. 365, 1926). Since that case, the Supreme Court has consistently upheld zoning to protect and maintain the character of single-family residential areas. Alternative living arrangements have been dealt with harshly. As early as *Euclid*, the court spoke of protecting neighborhoods from multifamily housing:

> With particular reference to apartment houses, it is pointed out that the development of detached housing sections is greatly retarded by the coming of apartment houses, which has sometimes resulted in destroying the entire section for private housing purposes; that in such sections very often the apartment house is a mere parasite constructed in order to take advantage of the open spaces and attractive surroundings created by the residential character of the district (272 U.S. 365, 114, 1926).

According to the zoning scheme worked out by the court, the main purpose of zoning was the protection of single-family neighborhoods. Valuing single-family dwellings as "the highest and best use" became the common local method of prioritizing land use. Although, in the original sense, the phrase *single family* was a designation of a physical structure, it was a short leap to the municipal interpretation of it as a regulation on the type of dwelling occupancy – occupancy by the traditional nuclear family unit.

Historically, federal and most state judiciaries (once the constitutionality of the act of zoning was established) have supported the supremacy of local level control, meaning that political decisions directly affecting specific communities should be decided only by those communities. In zoning practice this is enforced to the extent that those not living in an area are not even allowed to speak at a zoning hearing. Indeed, after 1928, for 46 years the Supreme Court refused to review a zoning case.

Between 1949 and 1955, appeals were dismissed, or appeals for certiorari were denied in all 21 cases involving planning or zoning matters. Richard Babcock, observing with barbed pen, wrote in 1966:

> I would like to believe that among the justices of our higher court, conservative or liberal, Democrat or Republican, Southerner or Yankee, corporate lawyer or ex-professor, there has been a consensus on only one point: if we cherish our equilibrium, never agree to review a zoning case (Babcock 1966, 109).

In 1974, the court broke its 46-year silence on the matter of zoning. The case was *Village of Belle Terre v Boraas*, and the broad issue was the legitimacy of including a definition of family as a facet of a local zoning ordinance (94 S.Ct. 1536, 1974). Belle Terre, a small village on Long Island, New York, imposed restrictions on the number of unrelated people who could live together as a family in a single-family residential district. The zoning ordinance permitted a family of any size related by blood, marriage, or adoption, and any two people not so related, to occupy a single-family dwelling. The owners of a house rented to six students challenged the restriction. The District Court upheld the restriction, the Court of Appeals reversed it, and the matter went to the Supreme Court, which upheld the ordinance. Justice Douglas, writing for the court, summed up the constitutional issues on which the ordinance was being challenged:

> The present ordinance is challenged on several grounds: that it interferes with a person's right to travel; that it interferes with a person's right to migrate and settle within a state; that it bars people who are uncongenial to the present residents; that it expresses the social preference of the residents for groups that will be congenial to them; that social homogeneity is

KAF: *This leap was very significant. "Single family," which started out as a designation of a dwelling* type, *also became the designation of an occupant* type. *Zoning ordinances have, very successfully, intertwined (1) a form type (detached house on a lot of particular size and configuration), (2) an occupant type (nuclear family), and (3) a use type (exclusively domestic activities of that household). The phrase "single family" now stands for the fusion of all these types, both at the level of the house and the neighborhood.*

not a legitimate interest of government; that the restriction of those whom the neighbors do not like trenches on the newcomers' right to privacy; that it is of no rightful concern to villagers whether the residents are married or unmarried; that the ordinance is antithetical to the Nation's experience, ideology, and self perception as an open, egalitarian and integrated society (94 S. Ct. 1536, 1974).

The majority opinion, upholding the ordinance, clearly regards the fundamental question of the case as one involving the local power to protect residential areas from disruptive intrusion. In finding that the ordinance did not violate the appellees' fundamental rights of travel, association, or privacy, the court required only that the ordinance bear a "rational relationship to a permissible state objective." Justice Douglas found that permissible state objective in the village's desire to preserve traditional family and environmental values.

> A quiet place where yards are wide, people few, and motor vehicles restricted are legitimate guidelines in a land use project addressed to family needs. The police power is not confined to elimination of filth, stench and unhealthy places. It is ample to lay out zones where family values, youth values and the blessings of quiet seclusion and clean air make the area a sanctuary for people (94 S. Ct. 1536, 1974).

The *Belle Terre* decision in 1974 was not surprising. There is a well-established legal tradition affirmatively recognizing the traditional family. Writing in 1970, Justice Wollenberg stated:

> The traditional family is an institution reinforced by biological and legal ties which are difficult or impossible to sunder. It plays a role in educating and nourishing the young which far from being "voluntary" is often compulsory. Finally, it has been a means for uncounted millennia, of satisfying the deepest emotional and physical needs of human beings (*Palo Alto Tenants Union v Morgan*, 321 F. Supp. 908, 1970).

This view has generated a substantial body of family law devoted to the definitions, regulation, and protection of family interests. In a definitional analysis of the development of "the legal family," Einbinder concluded that the definition of family has remained relatively stable in the cases involving insurance and welfare laws and become more turbulent in the areas of marriage and zoning (Einbinder 1974).

An exchange from the *Belle Terre v Boraas* oral arguments emphasizes this point. Justices are not identified in the recording of oral arguments. Mr. Sager is the attorney representing the opponents of the village ordinance.

Question: And you say that the Village, in this case, at least, has no constitutional power to define the family, the way, at least the way they did?

Mr. Sager: I think that's right.

Question: And could not define it to, what I think what sociologists now call a nuclear family. Is that it?

Mr. Sager: …the familiar bond which satisfies this (ordinance's) test can be a good deal more remote than the nuclear family. It can be, for example, a remote cousin, uncle, grandfather.

Question: Well, tribal. They can't define it in tribal terms.

Mr. Sager: Tribal terms may be more accurate, Your Honor.

Question: Well, your clients do not form a family, do they?

Question: By your definition they do, don't they?

Mr. Sager: They do not – I think we'd have to ask whose definition was being drawn on, Your Honor. By sociologists' definition, I'm not sure; by the Village of Belle Terre's, certainly not. By mine, they certainly formed a single housekeeping unit. As a practical matter, their dinner was –

Question: My question was: Is it a family, f-a-m-i-l-y?

Mr. Sager: They are not what I would call a family, Your Honor (cited in Perin 1977, 91).

Although the Belle Terre zoning ordinance may represent an extreme and narrow view of family, 18 years later the term "family" has still not been defined in any consistent manner within municipal zoning ordinances. While the state courts tend to be far more liberal in their interpretation of family (three now forbid outright numerical family definitions), many still use *Belle Terre*, the reigning federal case, as the bench mark of their decision making. For example, in August of 1991, the Connecticut Supreme Court upheld a family definition limiting unrelated individuals sharing a household to three. Quoting directly from *Belle Terre*, the justices rejected the arguments of the plaintiff and an *amicus curiae* brief filed by the American Planning Association and the Connecticut Civil Liberties Union, who argued that "Stratford's definition of family reflects a bygone era," called the regulation exclusionary, and said the town could achieve its objectives in a less restrictive way (*Dinan v Town of Stratford* 220 Conn. 595, 1991).

Zoning Out Differences

Zoning regulations attempt to separate deviant living arrangements from the neighborhoods called "single-family" where the mythical nuclear family resides. Perin (1988), in her study of the relationship between land use and social order in the United States, states that Americans find the very presence in their neighborhood of those of different status to be an unsettling experience. In commenting on her own work she writes:

> I found that Americans see renters, blacks, children, the elderly, people with low incomes, together with the signs of them in housing and geographical locations as being culturally unsettling. I suggested that, like the people of many ancient and exotic societies, Americans attribute dangerous social Powers to whatever and whomever are seen as being marginal to or in transition between clearly defined social statuses... *the low cultural rating bequeathed to renters, minors, women, blacks and central cities sharpens the definitive achievements of their opposites and makes more crisp the attainments of the categories of owner, adult, white, male and suburb, sweetening the struggle to achieve in so categorizing a world* (Perin 1988, 40; emphasis added).

JR: *This raises the interesting question of the extent to which like-minded people have the right to live together and to exclude others.*

Beginning with the colonists, European immigrants emphasized their cultural differences by limiting membership in their local communities to like-minded people (Norgren and Nanda 1988). Those who did not support community values could leave voluntarily or were driven out. This exclusiveness was focused on the sentimentalized nuclear family unit after the transportation systems that evolved during the industrial revolution made the separation of work and residence a reality for a broad spectrum of the middle class. The model of the home-based wife and the single-family detached home became emblematic of the American Dream. The physical separation of economic classes and the spatial separation of difference was codified in communities through covenants and zoning.

In the nineteenth century, restrictive deed covenants were used to protect the spatial exclusivity of neighborhoods within the larger community, and in the twentieth century, zoning added a public tool to help insure not only neighborhoods that are homogeneous as regards the use of the land, but are protective of lifestyles based on traditional nuclear family relationships. Further, the courts, as arbiters of values, have exhibited a consistent pattern of willingness to protect the rights of communities to perpetuate their homogeneity of lifestyles (Norgren and Nanda 1988).

AK: *Both here and throughout the paper I have the impression that "family" is being used as a metaphor for property.*

Zoning functions by dictating the spatial structure of the land, permitting and disallowing what can happen where. But as importantly, through family definitions, it also defines "who" can happen where. These definitions dictate the composition of the family, limiting or forbidding those who are unrelated by blood or marriage from living together. Family definitions have been included since the first zoning codes were written and implemented in the early twentieth century. Early definitions tended to use a simple standard, defining family as "one or more individuals sleeping, cooking, and eating on the premises of a single housekeeping unit" (Bassett 1936, 189). However, since the 1960s, there has been a move in American communities toward more restrictive family definitions.

Faced with changing life-styles in the 1960s (especially the move towards communal living and the deinstitutionalization of the mentally ill), and a strong desire to preserve the small nuclear oases they had created, local governments began to incorporate stricter family definitions into their ordinances. The new post-1960 definition of family began to limit the number of unrelated individuals (and in some cases the number of related but nonnuclear family members) who could live together (Ritzdorf 1985). In a 1983 study of the Seattle-Everett metropolitan area, for example, all the communities had family definitions that had been passed since 1950, and 74 percent had been passed or substantially revised in the 1960–1982 time frame. Nine (29 percent) of the communities allowed no unrelated individuals to live together. While eight were small suburban communities, the ninth was Everett with a population in excess of 50,000 (Ritzdorf 1983).

Various criteria have been used to define family in municipal housing in the United States. These include the relationship of the household members, the number of individuals in the unit, control by a single head, performance, the nonprofit character of the household, and common use of the kitchen (Shilling 1980). The definitions fall into four broad categories:

(1) No Definition: Some zoning ordinances contain no definition of family. These, however, are rare.
(2) Broad Definitions: An ordinance which defines a family as a "single housekeeping unit." These are also rare.
(3) Moderate to Restrictive Definitions: Zoning ordinances which define family as the traditional family related by *blood, marriage, or adoption*, and/or a set number (usually two to five) of unrelated individuals sharing a single housekeeping unit. The majority of communities in the United States have and enforce family definitions which are in this category (Ritzdorf 1985).
(4) Very Restrictive Definitions: Those definitions which restrict family to a group of people legally related by blood, marriage, or adoption only (Ritzdorf 1983).

A wide variety of reasons and rationalizations have been advanced by courts and communities for restricting household composition. These justifications have included preservation of property values, preservation of rent structures, prevention of parking or traffic problems, preservation of neighborhood safety, control of population density, the prevention of noise and disturbance, and the control of immoral or antisocial behavior (Shilling 1980).

The power of a municipality to deny the rights of extended families and unrelated individuals to live together represents a potent form of exclusion, affecting not only the minority and poor members of society, but all who live alternate life-styles, either through choice or necessity. Single parents and the elderly are two groups for whom the benefits of home sharing are obvious. Ironically, by forbidding or limiting this option, communities are denying them what may be their only opportunity of continuing to live as a family in the house, neighborhood, and community with which they are familiar.

Restrictive family definitions can also be self defeating to innovative housing and preservation policies. Older, overly large homes can be reused in many innovative ways if the definition of family is not used as a roadblock. The "catch-22" of many supposedly liberal accessory apartment ordinances, for example, is a rule that the total number of occupants of all the units cannot be more than the family definition allows for the home if it had only one unit. While this makes the ordinance more palatable to the citizens, it does nothing to encourage an increased density in large dwelling units that are underutilized.

In 1984, I conducted a nationwide random sample survey of American suburban and urban communities to gather information about how municipal land use planning and zoning policies were dealing with the needs of the "new traditional family." The local ordinances and the returned questionnaires were examined for what they revealed about five issues. The first was an examination of the municipal family definitions to assess whether municipalities were attempting to limit the right of unrelated people to live together. For example, could two single-parent households combine and share a living space? The second was an inquiry into the ways in which people were limited or prohibited by local ordinances from combining economic and domestic responsibilities by working in their homes. The third was an evaluation of how communities were regulating day care, both in homes and centers, and in what types of neighborhoods they were permitted to locate. The fourth was an examination of the treatment of accessory apartments in single-family residences. The last was a look at whether or not municipalities were allowing discrimination against children in local rentals (now forbidden under the Fair Housing Act Amendments of 1988).

The results of the survey affirmed the fact that communities were doing little or nothing to respond to the changing needs of the families that reside in their neighborhoods (Ritzdorf 1987). While a longitudinal follow-up of the survey is needed and planned, it is unlikely that it will reveal major changes in municipal zoning patterns.

In addition to defining family membership, zoning ordinances make explicit that certain homes and neighborhoods are more appropriate domestic environments than others. Zoning divides housing into categories called *single-family* and *multifamily*. An examination of a typical zoning ordinance will show further divisions based on lot coverage, number of units, etc. For example, a single-family neighborhood may be more or less dense, with some neighborhoods having minimum lot sizes far bigger than others. In multifamily zones, some may only allow duplexes while others may allow high-rise apartment buildings.

JR: *I guess the whole purpose of prestige is to restrict access to only a few including "oneself". If prestige can be legally sanctioned, can it also be legally restricted?*

AK: *Questions of prestige relate to the realm of the social, but they are embedded in, and shore up, the basic principle of private ownership of property and the differential values that are placed on it.*

JR: *Density is often framed as a fire code issue. These structures are used as accessory apartments illegally, which raises questions about selective enforcement of regulations. Why enforce these fire codes when so many other violations are ignored?*

JR: *This is very interesting. Can we begin to change values by creating places that look like the past but actually permit "deviant" uses? This is a real opportunity to create diversity!*

KAF: *Zoning ordinances, as they are presently written and enforced, operate at several levels. In single-family neighborhoods, they operate at the level of the individual house, the block, and the entire zone in which that house is located. In this example, zoning not only requires certain physical, spatial, and social characteristics for the individual house, but ensures that all other houses in that zone will have the same characteristics. Moreover, if several neighborhoods have the same regulations, in the same or adjacent municipalities, then these characteristics are repeated across the landscape. In this way, zoning can and does remove differences in dwelling type, occupant type, and use type not only from individual neighborhoods but from entire regions.*

Each of these zones carries a multiple set of cultural messages about owning and renting, more prestigious and less prestigious neighborhoods, etc. Moreover, the actual uses allowed in each of these zones varies according to the "prestige" of the zone. While living in a single-family zone is generally the most prestigious in most communities, the larger the lot required and the fewer the number of other uses besides housing allowed add another layer of prestige to ownership in that zone or community. Indeed, there are communities that incorporated solely for the purpose of insuring that absolutely no other use than large-lot (one acre or more), expensive housing would be allowed. These small communities have no services at all (Ritzdorf 1983).

The average municipal zoning ordinance enforces these types in a variety of ways. For example, current residential land policies in many communities exclude the combining of home and work; exclude the location of child care, shopping, or services in residential neighborhoods; forbid the remodeling of large expensive older homes into more than one unit; and exclude other forms of affordable housing such as modular or manufactured units.

Places that are experimenting with more integrated community design are few and, for the most part, exclusive and expensive developments. The essence of these "postmodern" communities is their replication of "ye old village" through the use of rigid neighborhood development codes. While the stated goal is to break down traditional single-family zoning patterns, they appear to be merely architecturally and culturally nostalgic. More study is needed to see whether the claim that they will be accessible to nontraditional and low-income households is actualized in future developments. Research is also needed to investigate whether or not these rigid codes allow work within the home (including home-based, not center-based, child and elder care), accessory apartments, and other innovative uses of residential space.

It is municipal zoning and land use regulation that regulate and enforce separate physical spheres at the community level in the built environment. If buildings, as Torre (1977) argues, are the symbolic form that embody a cultural ideology about how people live and the kind and hierarchy of values which should be fostered by them, zoning ordinances are the rules which make sure that the same types are nurtured and created over and over again. This leads to a community where physical design is defined as the constant re-creation of the status quo (Torre 1977).

Conclusion

The type, family, as used in municipal zoning ordinances, is a culturally bound discourse. The language both persuades and informs us about values and attitudes. It presumes a specific type of social tie, the nuclear family type – parents living at home in a unit unrelated to the workplace – as the apocryphal norm. The relatively narrow range of choices this creates in most environments in the United States needs to be changed to meet the needs of a changing population, while preserving some shared standards of behavior that are believed to be intrinsic to American middle class life.

Even if we were to accept the assumption that this is the model life-style to which American families should aspire (an assumption that will be challenged in the late twentieth century again and again), it ignores the lives of those who are not middle class and/or not white. Women from or heading families without means have consistently been part of the work force and have worked outside the home in substantial numbers throughout U.S. history. Additionally, they have taken people into their homes as boarders or lodgers and conducted business from their homes in an attempt to help meet the economic needs of their families.

For people who are both poor and of color, race becomes a "second axis of oppression." Traditional municipal rules often benefit whites while exploiting or diminishing the life chances of persons of color. This has been absolutely true of zoning, which has consistently been used to prevent the spatial extension of people of color into white, middle class America.

One of the challenges of twenty-first century planning and design will be to change and enhance the scope of the boundaries that shape U.S. (read: suburban) communities. The housing type, single-family home, and the myriad symbolic images that are attached to it, will remain a societal norm for the indefinite future. Yet, it is possible to restructure local zoning to allow a more flexible attitude toward both dwelling type and size, and the character of the family that dwells within.

These changes should include the elimination of discriminatory family definitions and their replacement by reasonable standards for neighborhood densities that apply to related and unrelated groups of individuals. They should include a restructured meaning of the use parameters of the dwelling type, "single-family" home, to include home occupations, child and elder care, and reasonably designed accessory apartments in all residential zones. Integrated design solutions and social arrangements (such as cohousing) should be encouraged and supported. All these uses can be and are reasonably integrated in exemplar communities scattered around the United States.

The social structure of society is manifested in the spatial design of its communities, "and, although those whose activities are facilitated may not be aware of the power inherent in the physical arrangements, it is clear to those whose options are limited by them" (Salem 1986). Innovative planning and design solutions that can realistically and sensitively respond to the changing demographics of American society are not possible without the retrofitting of existing zoning regulations. American communities are in far more danger of decline from policies that limit a continued experimentation with alternative forms of family and that frustrate housing innovation than they are from the presence of families and dwelling units in their communities that represent diverse types of lifestyles.

References

Abramovitz, M. 1988. *Regulating the Lives of Women: Social Welfare Policy from Colonial Times to the Present*. Boston: South End Press.

Babcock, R. 1966. *The Zoning Game*. Madison, Wis.: University of Wisconsin Press.

Bassett, E. 1936. *Zoning: The Laws, Administration and Court Cases During the First Twenty Years*. New York: Russell Sage.

Coontz, S. 1988. *The Social Origins of Private Lives: A History of American Families*. New York: Verso.

Dinan V Board of Zoning Appeals of the Town of Stratford. 220 Conn. 61, 595 A.3d 864, 1991.

Einbinder, M. 1974. The legal family: a definitional analysis. *Journal of Family Law* 1973–74 (13): 781.

Houston, L., Jr. 1981. Market trends reveal housing choices for the 1980s. *Journal of Housing* 38: 73–76.

Lund, R.S. and H.M. Lund. 1937. *Middletown in Transition: A Study in Cultural Conflicts*. New York: Harcourt, Brace & World.

Norgren, J., and S. Nanda. 1988. *Cultural Pluralism and the Law*. New York: Praeger.

Palo Alto Tenants Union v. Morgan. 321 F. Supp. 908, 1970.

Perin, C. 1977. *Everything in its Place: Social Order and Land Use in America*. Princeton, N.J.: Princeton University Press.

———. 1988. *Belonging in America: Reading between the Lines*. Madison, Wis.: University of Wisconsin Press.

Ritzdorf, M. 1983. The impact of family definitions in American municipal zoning ordinances. Ph.D. dissertation, University of Washington, Seattle, Washington.

———. 1985. Challenging the exclusionary impact of family definitions in American municipal zoning ordinances. *Journal of Urban Affairs* 7 (1).

———. 1987. Planning and the intergenerational community: balancing the needs of the young and the old in American communities. *Journal of Urban Affairs* 9 (1).

Salem, G. 1986. Gender equity and the urban environment. In *The Egalitarian City: Issues of Rights, Distribution, Access and Power*, ed. J. Boles. New York: Praeger.

Shilling, B. 1980. *Exclusionary Zoning: Restrictive Definitions of Family: An Annotated Bibliography*. Montecello: Council of Planning Librarians.

Torre, S. 1977. *Women in American Architecture: A Historic and Contemporary Perspective*. New York: Whitney Library of Design.

U.S. Bureau of the Census. 1990. *Household and Family Characteristics: March 1990*. Current Population Reports, Population Characteristics, Series P-20 No. 447. Washington, D.C.

Village of Belle Terre v Boraas. 94 S. Ct. 1536, 1974.

Village of Euclid, Ohio v Ambler Realty Corp. 272 U.S. 36547 S.Ct. 114, 1926.

Chapter 7

Terminologies and Types:
Making Sense of Some Types of Dwellings and Cities

Anthony D. King

the beginning of all understanding is classification
    Hayden White 1978, 22

Questions concerning the origins, social meanings, and the economic, political, and cultural significance of building types can be approached from many different directions. Any question we may choose raises even more fundamental issues in regard to classification systems, folk taxonomies, or the social construction of knowledge.

From a sociological perspective we may consider the social production of building form, addressing the way social forms, differences, and relationships are not just mapped onto space but acquire a degree of permanence from the conferment of a particular, and sometimes exclusive, type of building form. However, this prioritizing of the social over the spatial tends to understate the extent to which space (including the forms and configurations of particular building types) is actually *constitutive* of the social.

The obvious problem here is in providing the right degree of hermeneutic precision. We can speculate about the correlation between built forms and social forms but there is little to confirm, incontrovertibly, what social meanings are supported by spatially different building types.

In this context, terminological systems and taxonomies, as representing the social and cultural distinctions of the social formation in question, can provide some valuable insights: they show how particular building types, both in their topology as well as their internal spatial divisions, map important culturally relevant social differences (King 1974, 1980; Markus 1982, 1987, 1993). These approaches have also demonstrated how the discourses of particular populations, within an overall distribution of power (Foucault 1980), not only result in the production of new building types (though appearing in different architectural forms), but that the types and forms, as well as the design and building process itself, are essential to the constitution of the discourse (Metcalf 1989; Prior 1988; Rabinow 1989; Scull 1981).

As methods of inquiry, however, the mapping of a society's terminological systems onto its building types and their subdivisional spaces cannot be unquestioningly accepted as a mirrorlike "reflection" between two domains of human and social activity. As Lefebvre has put it,

> does language, logically, epistemologically, or genetically speaking – precede, accompany, or follow (the production of) social space? Is it a precondition of social space or merely a formulation of it? The priority-of-language has certainly not been established (1991, 16).

The ontological questions of whether everything that is named actually exists and, more importantly, whether everything that exists is actually named, are paramount. We might also think about questions of power concerning who or what is naming, in addition to questions about who or what is building and producing the space.

These two domains of inquiry – the social production of building form and the social production and appropriation of language as a means of differentiating building forms and spaces – are both fundamentally related to the social production of building types. By *type*, I refer to the socially classified, and usually terminologically distinguished, forms of building such as monastery, gas station, or city hall. Building *form* refers to the spatial and built form characteristics given to buildings, including those that may be needed to produce a particular building *type*. Let me turn now from the question of production to that of consumption.

It would seem logical to assume that there is a reciprocal relationship between named categories of space in any social formation (including differentiated building types) and their regular social reproduction, both in mental constructs and in language, as well as in a material sense. Social meanings are constructed in relation to particular spaces in the built environment, which then help to reassert and reproduce the concepts and spaces from which the social meanings derive (though not without interpretation). Here we might recognize, in everyday language, the way in which sociospatial categories are continually used as social metaphors, from "suburban lifestyle" to "Manhattan type," from "ghetto mentality" to "semidetached existence." People who speak metaphorically about "building bridges between communities," or who refer to "the White House position," assume the prior existence of a material reality from which the metaphor is drawn.

The main point, however, is that buildings, building types, architectural symbols, and forms have no permanent social meaning beyond the history, society, and culture – maybe only the speech community – in which they exist. Meanings are not stable. It is the constantly changing social order that forever inscribes, and reinscribes, its socially and culturally differentiated categories onto the built environment. In the same way, those categories are then inscribed onto the subjectivities of different social selves.

A further point is that, irrespective of their meanings, the very existence of type serves to signal some kind of difference. To take the simplest example: no matter how similarly two houses are constructed, they always exist in relation to each other (i.e., on the right or left, near or far). Dependent on the social order of which they are a part, they will always be invested with degrees of similarity and difference. I will draw on two different sets of data to illustrate the relationship between the terminological systems in which taxonomies are both constituted and expressed, and the building and urban types constituted by and through these taxonomies and terminologies.

The first case I examine is the public discourse of participants in the housing market in a particular city in northern England, especially that of the realtors (or house and estate agents, as they are known). This draws on research undertaken in the early 1980s. The material suggests that the concept of dwelling type, and the features and characteristics that are chosen to distinguish between and elaborate different types, operates in the economic domain as part of the process of commodification and marketing of dwellings. "Dwelling type" is the generic social science term I shall use to refer to what estate agents generally call a property, and which in the public realm is usually referred to as a house (rather than a home, as is often the case in the United States). In this generic sense, a house may have one, two, or more stories, though usually no more than four. As indicated in Figure 7-1, all classes are referred to, in the language of estate agents, as "residential property," as opposed to "commercial property" (offices, retail shops, etc). "Residence" (as in the ubiquitous description, "desirable residence") belongs especially to the language of estate agents. It is a term heavily invested with social meaning and is used by estate agents either to describe a detached (that is, freestanding) dwelling of above-average proportions, and standing "in its own grounds" or, as a marketing ploy, to represent a detached house as such.

Type, and the attributes by which one example of it is differentiated from another, is an essential mechanism for the operation of markets. However, this process clearly rests on a set of social and cultural meanings which have their own level of determinacy *outside* as well as inside the economic domain. They are also meanings that change over time.

The second set of studies examines the terms used by academics to classify types of cities, with the discussion focusing on the way different disciplinary discourses (in English) are mapped onto a variety of forms of urbanism in order to produce a range of classifications incorporating different city types. One objective is to raise some basic questions concerning the consistency and inconsistency of the criteria. More importantly, however, by foregrounding the general Eurocentricity of the categories, I wish to bring out the crucial importance of position-

Dimensions of Contrast Used to Compare Dwelling Types in West Yorkshire, England, 1980–82.		
1. District/locality	9. Location	16. Equipment/appointments
2. Price	a. transport and other amenities	17. Constructional aspects
3. Dwelling type (see Fig. 7-2)		18. Size/living area
4. Number of bedrooms	b. social appraisal	19. Materials of construction
5. Central heating?	10. Site	20. Age/year of building
6. Garage/accommodation for car	11. Appearance/visual attributes	21. Style
	12. Overall quality	22. Land/plot area
7. Listing of rooms (e,g., kitchen, hall, dining room, etc.)	13. Degree of individuality	23. Rateable value/local tax
	14. Physical/social attributes	24. Color of bathroom suite
8. Garden	15. Condition/standard of maintenance	25. Other special interior features

7-1
Table based on advertisement by estate/house agents and private vendors in the *Yorkshire Evening Post*. This list includes, in order of frequency, the most often mentioned items.

JR: *In the United States, residences are often places where a group of people who are dependent live together in supervised settings, e.g., residences for the... (blind, elderly, indigent, etc.). That the term "residence" means different things in different countries reinforces your point about speech communities.*

ality, or situatedness, whether temporal, spatial, cultural, or ideological, in the generation of all systems of classification. Classification systems are all what anthropologists call "folk taxonomies" (Conklin 1972), though the folk differ from place to place, time to time, and in their command over social power. The systems that get adopted are those that, in any discursive field, belong to the groups with the most social and political clout.

Housing: Social and Cultural Categories

Recent conceptualizations of culture in relation to dwelling forms have emphasized the symbolic element in socially constructed systems of meaning. In *Housing, Culture and Design* (1989), Low and Chambers discuss housing under four definitions of culture: as a political and economic structure, as cognition, as a meaning system, and as interpretation. Here, I want to encompass the last three conceptualizations by reference to an earlier source. A society's culture, according to Goodenough, consists of

> whatever it is one has to know or believe in order to operate in a manner acceptable to its members... It is the forms of things that people have in mind, their models for perceiving, relating and otherwise interpreting them (quoted in Sturtevant 1972, 131).

Other conceptualizations of culture emphasize the notion of a set of rules, of models, and, particularly, the idea of a shared system of classifying phenomena.

One aim of the ethnoscientific approach I use in this chapter — which has some affinity with the tenets of discourse theory and the notion of the "interpretive community" (White 1978; Fish 1980) — is to discover and describe the system of classification of a given culture in its own terms or, as Frake (1972, 192) writes, "discerning how people construe their world of experience from the way they talk about it." A second aim is to identify the principles on which the system is based. And in discovering folk taxonomies, it is obviously essential to use the discovery procedures relevant to the culture being investigated. For example, the fact that Hopi Indians believe that owls exert a favorable influence on peach trees is, as Lévi-Strauss pointed out, essential knowledge in understanding their classification of trees (cited in Sturtevant 1972).

An equally important task is to discover, for any given culture or subculture, which are the most culturally relevant domains. Some cultures have a very elaborate understanding of some areas of experience (e.g., food, weather, health states) but not others, and these differences are reflected in native terminology. Thus, while certain domains in particular cultures have a relatively small and weakly terminologized vocabulary (such as taste and smell in English), others have a much more developed one. Ethnoscience attempts to explain why this is so.

Cultures can be classified as richer or poorer according to the formal properties of the reference systems they appeal to in erecting their classificatory structures (Sturtevant 1972). In the context of the present discussion, this suggests that people constantly invest meanings in housing, or the built environment more generally, as a way of inscribing cultural difference along socially meaningful lines. This is how they create social distinctions among themselves (Bourdieu 1984). As Frake says,

> The greater the number of distinct social contexts in which information about a particular phenomenon must be communicated, the greater the number of different levels of contrast in which that phenomenon is categorized (Frake 1972, 198).

Hence, a large number of "dimensions of contrast" used in classifying social phenomena is some indication of their social significance.

With regard to housing, since no two houses are exactly alike in every discernible feature, the act of placing them into either the same, or different, classes requires the selection of only those features that are seen as significant for making a distinction between them. The way that people learn which features are significant to understanding a taxonomy, and which are not, is obviously not just derived from the houses themselves, but is absorbed as part of a person's social and cultural equipment.

Taxonomies make possible a regulation of the *amount* of information about an object in a given situation by providing a hierarchical ordering of categories. Part of the professional equipment of botanists, librarians, or estate agents, taxonomies are obviously also part of our everyday life, a fundamental principle of human thinking. To cite a well-known example: How, and by what criteria, is a hamburger distinguished from a hot dog, one kind of beer from another (Hage 1972), or a bungalow from a single-story cottage? And what is the significance of the principles to which these criteria refer?

In classifying dwellings, therefore, we need to know the criteria by which houses are put into one category rather than another and, within these, what are the "dimensions of contrast" by which they are compared. It is a question of knowing not simply the national, regional, or local language, but, in Goodenough's phrase, "whatever it is one has to know or believe in order to operate in a manner acceptable" to the members of a given culture. What matters, in short, is the social, cultural, and historical meanings that are invested in both the terms and the objects to which they refer. Thus, what does the English prospective buyer need to know to make sense of the following German advertisement?

> PRIVAT. DHH. Kiefersfelden/Obb.Wfl.ca. 160m2. Grd. ca.500m2. Bj.80/81. Alpenstil am Berg. NN 500m, eingez. Gart., Treibh., Gerateh., u.a. Terrasse14m2, Sauna, Treppen u. Flur Marmor, Einbauk, Hobbyr. 32m2, Waschr., Vorratsr., 5 Zi., Garage, VB 440 000,-DM (*Die Welt*, 31 July 1982).[1]

Or the German buyer of the following?

> Gildersome. Immaculate, larger than average Detached Double Fronted Dormer Bungalow. Promt. Corner position in qt. Cul-de-sac. Extd. Comprising Entr. Hall with Spanish style doors, kit., lounge with feature Marshal-lite fireplace, Georgian bay. 3 bedrooms (one with fitted louvred 'robes); tiled bathroom, with coloured suite. Artexed walls and ceilings and many extras. Gar. with pit. Easy level garden. Realistic price at £25,000 (*Yorkshire Evening Post*, 7 August 1982).

It will be obvious, at least to the English reader of the above, that much of the knowledge about our classification of experience and the selection of relevant features in describing social and cultural phenomena is generally outside of awareness. Except when explaining to a nonnative, the information is taken for granted.

The distinctive social and cultural meanings attached to dwelling types, and to the domain of private housing in general, obviously become more apparent when data are treated comparatively. This might be undertaken in a number of ways: (1) historically, in one society, with taxonomies considered over time; (2) within one society, but between two or more different socioeconomic classes or groups; (3) within one society, between two matched social class groups but between different regions; and (4) between two different language communities and cultures with attention given to social and economic comparability of samples. In the following exploratory discussion, some impressionistic rather than systematic comparisons will be made, especially along the second and third of these dimensions.

---

1. In the context of my discussion, a "translation" of this is redundant, unless each term is extensively elaborated in the context of its own historical and cultural significance.

DV: *These advertisements are fascinating objects. They are as similar as they are different, because both form a part of the subculture that includes sellers, financiers, advertising media, and buyers of "homes." As first-time buyers quickly learn, it is difficult to conduct any transaction without accepting the real estate agent's strange calculus of value and appropriateness. In this sense the market is not free, because choice is strongly inflected by mediating interests.*

JR: *In my research in the midwestern United States, with a different purpose and a random selection of all kinds of housing within the city limits, I found that the categories people use to identify the types are based less on architectural detail and more on gross physical differences (categories like hospital, dormitory, house, institution). The status that is involved in these categories is less linked with stylistic attributes and more engaged with attributes that affect use, such as how many people share a room, how much control residents have over visitors, or who else occupies the building. This reinforces the importance of context in any exploration of type and illustrates the complexity and variety of the types we all use on a daily basis.*

AK: *Yes, it is an important point that the* context *of classification can alter how types are defined and classified. (Try buying a used car...)*

Words, Dwellings, and the Property Market

Without considering the complex topic of valuation, it can be assumed that, in free market societies, the market value of a dwelling is primarily governed by location, for dwelling types similar in every respect except location differ in price. Yet where market forces constantly work to create or maximize value by commodifying specific attributes and "putting a price on them," those attributes of dwellings must have social and cultural meaning, and significance, for the potential purchasers. In a society whose members share certain expectations and norms, material advantages in a dwelling such as central heating, double glazing, or number of rooms will, other things being equal, be reflected in the market price. However, other features will only have meaning, and hence, economic value, to *some* social groups in any one society (including class, ethnic, racial, gender, or age groups, and their regional variations), or to members of one society or culture rather than another. Thus, "gesunder Bayerische Waldluft, Apotheke in der Nahe" ("in the healthy Bavarian wood air, pharmacy in the vicinity") may be attributes worth paying for to a health-conscious German buyer looking through the housing advertisements in *Die Welt*. But she or he would have little interest in, or even knowledge of, the social importance of a "stone-fronted, neo-Georgian link semi, not on estate," which might be found advertised in the *Yorkshire Evening Post* in northern England. It is these socially and culturally specific attributes and criteria that are explored below.

Like all social and cultural phenomena, housing is classified into types or categories. The criteria used to construct these, and the degree of differentiation between them, are obviously related to the purposes for which the categories are created. In the United Kingdom, for a variety of social and economic policies and other reasons, dwellings are frequently classified into five or six types. Official government statistics recognize the following ones: (1) detached houses and bungalows, (2) semidetached houses, (3) terraced houses, (4) flats and maisonettes, and (5) other accommodations.

These same terms (and types), as well as others, are also used by estate agents and the general public. A further distinction is sometimes made between purpose-built and non-purpose-built flats, or the number of stories that high-rise flats contain (e.g., Department of Environment 1978, 1, 4; HMSO 1980, 1990).

The Building Societies Association, representative of the principal institutions advancing loans to house purchasers, uses six types: (1) bungalow, (2) detached house, (3) semidetached house, (4) terraced house, (5) purpose-built flat, and (6) converted flat. It regularly publishes tables of average dwelling price according to type and region, i.e., the 12 standard regions used in government statistics (*Building Societies Association* 1980, 1985, 1990).[2] That no information other than type, price, and region is given highlights the taken-for-granted assumption that, irrespective of size (floor or plot area), location, site, number of rooms, facilities, or any other factor, dwelling types *as such* have both social significance as well as a distinct market value. This is also born out by the *Bulletin*'s comment accompanying the table:

> The figures... cannot, of course, necessarily be taken to indicate differences in the prices of comparable dwellings. Terraced houses can range from luxury town houses in Chelsea to very modest dwellings suitable for first time buyers, while detached houses can range from huge mansions to small cottages. Nevertheless, the figures do usefully indicate differences in house prices for different types of houses in the various regions (*Building Societies Association* 1982, 22).

Finally, while some house or estate agents advertising dwellings in the press rank them according to price or sometimes district (location), in this part of northern England, at least, others classify them according to type. The assumption is that potential purchasers, presumably because of the social cachet attached to it, are *primarily* interested in buying a particular *type* of house in a city or suburb, and only secondarily interested in the location. It is common knowledge, then, that house types as such have economic and social importance in the United Kingdom; they are taken-for-granted social and cultural categories in which people think. Despite this, compared to the extensive research undertaken on questions of tenure or on social area, relatively little is known about types' social, as distinct from their spatial or geographical, significance (e.g., Carter 1983). With this in mind, the following section constructs the beginnings of a folk taxonomy of English dwelling forms, though one specific to the Yorkshire region.

Types: Signifiers of Social and Cultural Difference

The following study was undertaken in order to gain some insight into the corpus of dwelling types in one particular society, the terms that distinguish them, and the way both are used for the inscription and maintenance of social difference in Britain.

Information on dwelling types was taken from newspaper advertisements for the sale of private dwellings inserted both privately by individual vendors, or on the vendor's behalf by estate agents. These are the normal practices followed in Britain. Terms used to describe dwellings, together with all other information given, were collected and classified from two different sources in the same month in 1980 and 1982.

The most comprehensive analysis was made on the basis of house advertisements from an evening newspaper, the *Yorkshire Evening Post (YEP),* with a large regional circulation in West Yorkshire, and especially in the large (population 705,000) postindustrial metropolitan district of Leeds. This sample may be taken as representative of a number of regional cultures in the United Kingdom, though in the early 1980s it had a somewhat larger "skilled manual" social class component than did England and Wales as a whole (43 percent compared to 36 percent). It had also a smaller "middle class" (professional and "intermediate" groups) population than in England and Wales generally (19 percent compared to 27 percent) (Reid 1977, 65). For historical reasons, the region has a large proportion of what might be termed typically English industrial housing, in the form of terraced and especially back-to-back dwellings (Muthesius 1982).[3]

A more impressionistic analysis was made of property advertisements in *The Times* on the same occasions. Given the predominantly middle/upper class readership of this newspaper (Reid 1977) and its larger circulation in the southeast of the country (28 percent of the region's population in professional and "intermediate" classes, compared to 19 percent in Yorkshire and Humberside), a class as well as regional dimension can be assumed in the results.

---

2. American "equivalents" of these terms would be one-story single-family house, single-family home, duplex (or two-family), row house, purpose-built, and converted apartment. That the material on which this account draws is from the early 1980s should not detract from the general argument being made; the overall conclusions still apply. A second study is planned to document changes that have taken place over the last decade.

3. Here it is necessary to distinguish between a "through terrace" property, which runs right across the width of the terrace and where occupants can literally go in at the front door and out at the back door, and the back-to-back. In this case, two quite separate properties, joined by a common wall, exist "back-to-back" on either side of a terrace. The distinguishing feature of an inner terrace back-to-back house is that it has windows and door only on *one* of its four walls, the other three forming part of the adjoining properties, being blank.

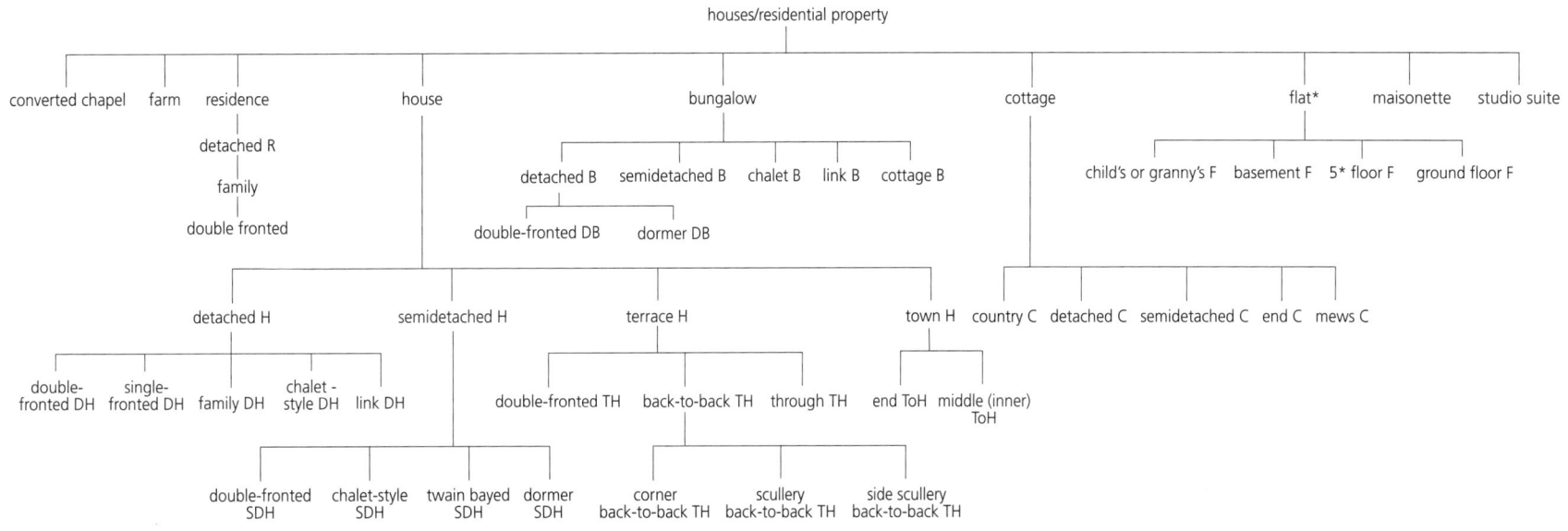

7-2
Taxonomy based on advertisements by estate/house agents and private vendors in the Yorkshire Evening Post. This taxonomy refers only to privately owned residential property. Public sector housing types are not discussed in the text.
R=residence H=house DH=detached house SDH=semi-detached house TH=terrace house ToH=town house B=bungalow DB=detached bungalow C=cottage *F=flat (occasionally referred to as apartment)

Compared to the eliciting procedures prescribed by careful ethnoscientific methods which use oral information from "native informants," the results discussed here are obviously more limited. This work is concerned with the "public terminology" of estate agents, though an analysis of private advertisements indicates that the terms and categories used there are similar. The sample represents "public language," specifically the categories and native terminology used when advertising and marketing property. Investigating how estate agents or individuals *actually* classify and talk about houses among themselves would obviously require different eliciting procedures.

The basic data from the study are presented in Figure 7-1 and Figure 7-2. In the *YEP* sample, dwellings are distinguished and compared by up to 25 main criteria or "dimensions of contrast." The shortest advertisement includes reference to only *three* of these – locality, type, and price (e.g., "Garforth, semi. £21,000") – again indicating the social importance of type. Figure 7-1 lists, according to approximate frequency of reference, the principal criteria used. In the following section, these are illustrated and, where significant for the discussion, briefly commented on. As the first two items in the table, locality and price, are the two primary determining criteria governing the prospective buyer's decisions, the discussion begins with these types.

Figure 7-2 provides a broad taxonomy constructed from the entire corpus of terms. This shows that whereas some 12 to 15 terms (and types) are commonly utilized, such as "town house" or "detached bungalow" (lines 2 and 3), other features are selected and given meaning, such as "twin bayed" or "side scullery" (lines 3, 4 and 5), to generate a taxonomy of over 40 identifiable types, all of which exist and are in regular use. These, in many if not all cases, can then be contrasted over some 20 to 25 dimensions (Figure 7-1). Advertisements also often include photographic images of the dwellings on sale. The combination of both image and description, which also includes some of the categories in the taxonomy and reference to some of the dimensions of contrast, is illustrated in Figures 7-3 and 7-4.

Figure 7-3 Photographs and captions taken from handouts prepared by estate agents illustrate the type of advertisements used in the *Yorkshire Evening Post*.

"2-bedroomed stone built double-fronted back-to-back end terrace house within easy walking distance to town center"

"Economical family town house situated in secluded woodland setting"

"Large double-fronted stone built semidetatched Victorian villa adjoining greenbelt to the rear yet within easy flat scenic walking distance of a railway station"

"Traditional through terrace property enjoying convenient location close to schools, shops, and public transport"

"Delightful stone cottage dating back approximately 200 years"

"White-rendered double-fronted five-bedroomed detached residence set on a corner position"

"Spacious 1940s semidetatched property located in a good residential area with access to local amenities"

"Attractive first-floor apartment ideal for first-time buyer, professional, or retirement couple set in maintained gardens"

"Superb individually built detached bungalow standing in private and enclosed grounds approaching one third of an acre"

134 ORDERING SPACE

Ostensibly, the inherent distinction between detached, semidetached, terraced houses, bungalows, maisonettes, and flats, is based on criteria of physical form or design, and indicates, among other factors, varying degrees of physical separation from the neighboring household or family, whether on one side (as in the semidetached), on both sides (terrace), or above or below (flat). Within this frame, the detached house, and especially the bungalow, gives the greatest degree of physical-spatial (and potentially, social) separation. Other terms, such as "double-fronted" or "through house," also refer to physical design properties but, like the earlier terms, also have spatial or accommodation implications. More important, they also carry implicit information about location, age, condition, and especially the social characteristics of the location.

The relevance of this information to our understanding of type is that there would be no point in having such an elaborate system of classification unless it served some social purpose. As to why it exists, two explanations may be offered. The first, a purely economic reading, suggests that, as in all market economies, specialization and difference are utilized to differentiate properties on the basis of price. Though such an explanation is clearly plausible, it overlooks the distinctive social meanings attached to dwelling type, each of which takes its place in both a nationally and regionally constructed, carefully differentiated hierarchy of social meaning and status. It is especially in the context of these social and cultural meanings that the economic value is given to the dwelling.

DV: *Yes, and this explanation also overlooks the social meanings surrounding the purchasing act and the price itself.*
AK: *I agree.*

That particular dwelling types in Britain have distinctive meanings associated with class position is borne out in a wide range of literature, from studies of working class dwellings through a variety of other types, from the bungalow and "semi" to the country house (Girouard 1971; Jackson 1973; King 1984). In this hierarchy, a detached house has more social cachet than a "semi;" a double-fronted detached house (i.e., with one or two windows on either side of a central entrance door) is preferred to one that is single fronted; a corner back-to-back or end terrace (in Yorkshire) has a social edge on one that is mid- or inner terrace. In this system the highest degree of social clout is determined by the greatest degree of "detachedness" or separation. At the top of the social hierarchy is the country house which is, as one advertisement aptly put it, "totally protected by its own land."

For the working and middle class *YEP* readers of the urban North, social difference is invested into dwelling types that historically and more recently are mass produced. For the upper and middle class readers of *The Times* in the more affluent

South, class distinctions are displayed not only by more rural, ex-urban locations, but by association with more individualized types of dwelling. Thus, in addition to the standard "common culture" types of detached, semidetached, terrace, or bungalow (though not the regionally specific back-to-backs of Yorkshire), social and architectural differentiation is constructed by the deployment of such terms, and residence types as hunting box, country cottage, retreat, crofter's house, garden flat, villa, manor house, penthouse, rectory, mews cottage, country home, vicarage, mill cottage, studio residence, barn, boathouse, wing of mansion, riverside flat, castle, mansion flat, artisan's cottage, apartment, and lodge.

Here, distinctions are constructed not only by the fact that the dwellings are singular examples and not mass produced but, to draw on Bourdieu (1984), by the different cultural capital invested in different types. As indicated by Frake, taxonomies are elaborated along horizontal lines of discrimination, according to "the variety of cultural settings within which one talks about the objects being classified" (1972, 198).

It is important to see how dwelling types are elaborated along different dimensions of contrast. Here, I shall draw selectively on the research to refer to information on appearance, age or style, construction materials, and location in relation to the two populations. While both *YEP* and *The Times* populations are interested in the appearance of dwellings, and what I shall call their degree of individuality and difference, the range of terms on which they draw is not the same and gives some insight into the socially distinctive speech communities in the sample. For *YEP* readers, the visual referent is represented by "charming, really nice, delightful, attractive, appealing, eye-catching," and the "degree of individuality and difference" described as "unique, exceptional, distinctive, or individually designed." For *The Times* population, the appearance of dwellings is characterized as "pretty, elegant, lovely, enchanting, glorious, picturesque," and the degree of individuality and difference as "of great character, most interesting, impressive, outstanding, intriguing, and unrivaled." In referring to the physical and social characteristics attributed to dwellings, *YEP* populations refer to their being "most impressive, very prestigious, superior, imposing, substantial." For *The Times* readers, a more developed terminology applies which points to the spatial distinction in their settings. Dwellings are "secluded, isolated, in a commanding or prominent position." Dwellings are also invested with anthropomorphic qualities: they are "dignified, of great character, and proudly poised."

JR: *It is interesting to see how different these categories are from those in the Minneapolis* Star Tribune. *A quick perusal of the Saturday Real Estate Section reveals that type names are used in ads for houses but less often than descriptive terms (three-bedroom, two-story, stucco). The type names used do have class connotations but seem less overtly class oriented (Cape Cod, colonial, contemporary, rambler, town home, Tudor, twin house, split-level).*

DV: *This is a fascinating case of a motivated construction of types to provoke the circulation of cultural and financial capital. One easily imagines sellers and agents, thesaurus in hand, rooting out new euphemisms for previously undesirable properties (e.g., the venerable "handyman's special").*
AK: *As indeed they do.*

"Unique, idyllic Gothic style cottage in excellent condition, set in a delightful secluded garden"

"Listed Georgian country house set in attractive gardens and grounds"

"Most attractive, historic listed former rectory of Jacobean origins occupying a delightful position in lovely mature gardens, parkland and wooded gardens"

7-4
Photographs and captions taken from handouts prepared by estate agents illustrate the type of advertisements used in *The Times*.

For each population, dwellings exist in different times and spaces. Though both *YEP* and *The Times* readers live in historical worlds, the histories they occupy are not necessarily shared. To indicate that a dwelling is "100 years old" is not the same as stating that it is "built in 1894." The historical and cultural capital which *The Times* vendors bring to the description of their dwellings is more elaborate than those from *YEP*. For these, a relatively undifferentiated periodization and set of style categories is used. Allowing for the fact that "pre-war" and "post-war" may refer, for example, either to style, date of building, or quality of construction, the styles and histories occupied by *YEP* vendors are those delineated by "17th, 18th, and 19th century, Victorian, Edwardian, 1929 built, prewar, postwar, modern, Georgian, traditional, older type, mock Tudor, mature, Georgian style, traditional" or simply "period." *The Times* vendors and readers, however, live in more finely differentiated historical times, which may begin in the "15th century, 16th century" and even in "ancient" and "medieval" times. Temporal precision is also more critical for them, as in "early 20th century, c. 1840, built 1895." The range of periods and styles runs from "Tudor, Elizabethan," through "William and Mary, Queen Anne, and early Georgian," to "early, mid, and late Victorian, Edwardian" and "designed by Baillie Scott, a member of the Arts and Crafts Movement, in 1904." Additional historical meaning (and economic value) is bestowed by the accolade "Grade I (or II, III) listed," indicating an officially approved designation on the national register of "historically" or "architecturally significant" buildings.

In the context of these advertisements, materials have a social meaning rather than a constructional one. They also have regional and cultural significance. Hence, in appealing to local identities, references to "Yorkshire stone front" are frequent. In virtually all cases, stone (as the most expensive material) is preferred over brick.

As signified by the terms, the space occupied by *YEP* vendors tends to be either functional – "close to amenities, access to motorway, convenient for town, easy access to shops, adjacent to the golf course" – or it provides opportunities for social appraisal: "popular residential area, at head of private cul-de-sac, small exclusive idyllic development, good class residential area, one of the premier residential areas in executive area of H_, premier residential district, the village where people of influence live." By comparison, explicit social appraisals are less evident among *Times* vendors, for whom the important dimensions of contrast are socially and culturally specific representations of particular environments: "in a beautiful park with a lake, half a mile down a bumpy lane in loveliest countryside, by unspoilt medieval village, superb position overlooking the Green, in beautiful undulating countryside, tree-lined round and near park and village green."

In this particular market society, dwelling types and the terminology by which they are known are a culturally significant resource that socially differentiated subjects use in establishing their identities, which are mainly, though not only, those of class. Types are constantly differentiated from each other and social meanings put into them according to the regionally distributed characteristics of the population that inhabits them. Though dwelling forms and peoples' taste for them are typically conservative, market forces constantly aim to create new demands, or desires, by exploiting class differences and inventing new features and types. In this sense, new types and styles of housing are in the same category as new flavors of yogurt, or new designs of cars.

Although this discussion may suggest that the category system is very rigid, this is not necessarily the case. Over time, though dwellings remain largely the same, the social characteristics of their occupants may change. In the last decade, for example, the city region from which this material was taken (Leeds) has become the second largest financial center, after London, in the United Kingdom (*Times Educational Supplement* 2/24/93), with consequent effects on the occupational structure of the city. In the nineteenth and early twentieth centuries, when many of the central and inner suburban dwellings were built, the city was a major textile and engineering manufacturing center; in the mid twentieth century, it became the principal location for the ready-made clothing industry in Britain. It was the tail end of these industries that attracted, in the postcolonial era of the 1960s and 1970s, a large number of immigrants from South Asia and the Caribbean. In more recent years, the expansion of higher education has brought an increasing number of students to the city, partly attracted by the lower rents or costs of terrace housing. These broad economic and demographic developments reshaping the social and cultural structure of the city also contribute to the changing social meanings that dwelling types acquire over time. It is also true, however, that the differential nature of both the types of dwellings and their spatial distribution provides a ready-made grid for the reinscription and maintenance of social and cultural difference.

Typologies of Cities

In the previous section, I discussed how terminologically distinguished dwelling types are used as a way of inscribing social, regional, and cultural identities within one nationally defined society. I now turn to the way city types are used by members of an English-speaking, academic community to inscribe their national, disciplinary, and ideological differences.[4]

Systems of classification are a way of "making sense" for the individuals and populations doing the ordering. The city, which might be seen as a relatively uncontroversial phenomenon, poses classificatory problems not only of a different kind but also on a very different scale. As James Donald writes,

> The city does not just refer to a set of buildings in a particular place. To put it polemically, there is no such *thing* as a city. Rather *the city* designates the space produced by the interaction of historically and geographically specific institutions, social relations of production and reproduction, practices of government, forms and media of communication, and so forth. By calling this diversity "the city," we ascribe to it a coherence or integrity. *The city*, then, is above all a representation... I would argue that the city constitutes an *imagined environment*. What is involved in that imagining – the discourses, symbols, metaphors and fantasies through which we ascribe meaning to the modern experience of urban living, is as important a topic for the social sciences as the material determinants of the physical environment (Donald 1992, 6).

It is obvious from Donald's position, and especially from Michel de Certeau's (1984) essays on "walking in the city," that there may be as many representations of "the city" as there are individuals to make them. Be that as it may, for the academic purpose of attempting to *understand* "the city," the political objective of *controlling* or planning the city or, indeed, the economic or political purpose of *producing* the city (Holston 1991), scholars and others have generated both individual types as well as broad classification schemes in order to capture and control the phenomenon – as well as the phenomena – of the city. On the Foucaultian principle of power/knowledge, the conceptualization and classification of "cities" not only represents real relationships of power, but such representations emerge from specific political, historical, geographical, cultural, and social positions.

DV: *It is worth asking why "the city" as a conceptual unit is so attractive to power/knowledge. As Raymond Williams has observed, it is not easily separated from its various social and physical contexts. Yet as you point out, it has served as a locus for many cultural and conceptual struggles – perhaps this is its only purpose?*

AK: *But it also acts as a more sublime metaphor, e.g., the heavenly city...*

JR: *It is fascinating to see the rich variety of descriptions, almost all of which create an image of a city that has some physical content. How can we keep all of these categories in our heads? Which categories do we apply ourselves and which do we only respond to and in which situations?*

AK: *Your comment points to the importance of our own subjectivities (as class, gendered, professional or other selves) in appropriating the space(s) of the city.*

---

4. This section develops arguments first set out in "Culture, Space, and Representation: Problems of Methodology in Urban Studies," in *Urbanism in Islam: Proceedings of the International Conference on Urbanism in Islam*, October 22–28, 1989. Middle Eastern Culture Center, Tokyo, Japan. Vol 5 (Supplement), 339–74.

They also reflect the location of the classifiers in a global political economy of knowledge.

Consider some of the more common ways cities are categorized in the academic literature in English. Figure 7-5 lists some of the common and, from number 26 on, less common categories for describing cities and forms of urbanism either in the titles of known monographs or in texts on cities and the urban. At least 20 to 25 major systems of classification or frames of reference are in common use, each suggesting at least one overriding variable or characteristic categorizing, or purportedly "explaining," the city or the quality of urbanism. Moreover, many of these classes of city (such as continent, nation, and geographic site) would also subsume data and analytical themes from other systems.

The list of descriptors ranges from technology, energy base, and mode of production, through national or cultural identity and religion, to the level of economic development, ethnicity, and location. In that context, it is clear that for scholars attempting to investigate or write about these different representations of "the city," an equally wide range of methods would be required to address even these conventional categories.

Systems of classification based on one attribute are not necessarily used, nor would be seen as applicable, for all cities or all forms of urbanism. An example is religion/culture: an explanation is sought for the characteristic features of what is called the "Islamic/Muslim city," and for the ancient Hindu city, but not for the Buddhist or, today, the Christian city – though we may take note of urban analysis within particular cities in terms of Protestant/Catholic differences (for example in referring to Belfast), and Shiite/Sunni/Maronite ones (for example in referring to Beirut). As Abu-Lughod (1987), Brown (1986), and others have pointed out, the application of predominantly religious/cultural criteria to the analysis of something designated the Islamic city is largely the outcome of Orientalism (Said 1978).

For what and whose reasons are such categories being constructed, at what period, on the basis of what information, where, and by whom? If Krautheimer (1983) discusses the "Christian City" in medieval Europe, very few contemporary (European) scholars would use this label for these European cities today. Yet from the perspective of other religious groups, such a category might still make sense.

If we speak of the "Islamic City" in the early twentieth century, is this still the most appropriate label for the cities subsumed under that label today in light of the large number of alternatives offered by the categories? Are there other cities

Classifications of Cities Arranged According to Criterial Attributes.

1. **Technology/Energy Base**
   Preindustrial cities
   Industrial
   Postindustrial
   Electronic
   *Postelectronic
   *Solar
   *Electric
   *Nuclear

2. **Mode of Production/Political Economy**
   Precapitalist
   Capitalist
   Postcapitalist
   *Presocialist
   Socialist
   Postsocialist
   PostFordist
   Finance
   Communist
   Postcommunist
   Mercantile capitalist
   Industrial capitalist
   Monopoly capitalist
   Precolonial
   Colonial
   Postcolonial
   *Preimperial
   Imperial
   Postimperial

3. **Continent/Geographic Region**
   African
   North American
   South/Latin American
   Asian
   Middle Eastern
   Far Eastern
   European, etc.

4. **Nation/State Culture**
   Canadian
   German
   Japanese
   Korean, etc.

5. **Religion/Culture**
   Christian
   *Buddhist
   Hindu
   Islamic
   *Jewish
   Sikh
   Religiosity/Secularity
   Sacred
   *Agnostic
   Secular
   Holy

6. **Ethnicity**
   Arab
   Hausa
   Yoruba
   *Bedouin
   English

7. **Economic/Social**
   *First World
   *Second World
   Third World
   Generative
   Parasitic
   Rich
   Poor

8. **Race**
   Apartheid
   Black
   White

9. **Geographic Scale**
   Local
   Regional
   National
   Global
   World
   *Universal
   Metropolis
   Ekumenopolis
   International
   *Planetary
   *Earth
   *Moon
   *Mars

10. **Ideological**
    Premodern
    Modern
    Postmodern
    *Postpostmodern
    Traditional

11. **Ethnogeographical (outside region or continent)**
    *Eastern
    Northern
    *Southern
    Western
    Occidental
    Oriental

12. **Geographic Location**
    Coastal
    Hillside
    Mountain
    *Underground
    *Submarine
    *Aerial
    *Extraterrestrial

13. **Population Size (including demographic characteristics/density, etc.)**
    Large
    Medium
    Small
    (in terms of given numbers)
    Growing
    Static
    Declining

14. **Cultural Orientation**
    Orthogenetic
    Heterogenetic
    Multicultural
    Unicultural

15. **Functional**
    Administrative
    Capital
    Commercial
    Educational
    Industrial
    Recreational
    Religious, etc.

16. **Chronology (Western Calendar)**
    15th Century
    18th Century
    19th Century
    etc.
    Ancient
    Medieval
    Early Modern

17. **Level of State Intervention**
    Planned
    Unplanned

18. **Urban Segment/Spatial**
    Outer
    Inner
    *Upper
    *Lower
    Edge
    Inside Out

19. **Gender/Sexual Orientation**
    Gay
    Women's
    *Men's
    Feminist
    *Postfeminist
    Lesbian
    Boys'
    Girls'
    *Masculine
    *Feminine
    Non-Sexist

20. **Class**
    Working Class
    Middle Class
    Underclass

21. **Transport**
    Walking
    Streetcar
    Freeway

22. **Climate**
    Tropical
    Mediterranean
    Sunbelt
    Frostbelt
    *Hot
    *Cold
    *Windy
    *Wet

23. **Social Pathology**
    Vice
    Crime
    Murder
    *Crimeless

24. **Season**
    *Spring
    Summer
    *Fall
    Winter

25. **Dynasty/"Period"**
    Tudor
    Windsor
    (reign)
    Georgian
    Elizabethan
    Federal
    Antebellum
    Progressive
    Victorian

26. **Science Fiction**
    Cities of the Dead
    Imagined

27. **Morality**
    Sin
    Immoral
    Good
    Evil

28. **Cosmology**
    Of "Four Quarters"
    Mayan

29. **Visionary/Utopian**
    Garden
    *"Green" (ecological)
    Ideal

30. **Cognitive (construction of city/urbanism)**
    Silver (photography)
    Cities of the Mind

31. **Age**
    Ancient
    Middleaged
    New
    *Young

32. ***Construction Material**
    *Bamboo
    *Brick
    *Concrete
    *Mud
    *Stone
    Timber

33. ***Height**
    *Tall
    *Short
    *Flat

34. ***Weight**
    *Heavy
    *Light

35. ***Orientation (social/cultural)**
    *Creative
    *Destructive
    *Hedonistic
    *Repressive

36. ***Culture (arts/media)**
    *Artistic
    Music

37. ***Senses**
    *Noisy
    *Silent
    *Tasty/less
    *Smelly
    *Tactile
    Unseen
    *Visual

38. **Metaphorical**
    *Running
    *Dying
    *Blue

7-5
* Asterisked items are those which, to the author's knowledge, do not exist in the literature.

that are becoming more Islamic? Perhaps Paris? Or Bradford (Yorkshire) in England, with its large proportion of Muslim inhabitants? Or is it a postindustrial, late capitalist Islamic British city, or do we, lazily, simply label it as an example of the postmodern?

Likewise, while studies by "First World" scholars proliferate on the "Third World city" and "Third World urbanization" there are, as far as I know, no studies by "Third World" scholars of "First World" cities (in those specific terms of classification). As with other categories, the act of classification belongs to those with the power to classify. Similarly, scholarly literature frequently refers to "western" cities or urbanism, but not (outside specific nations or continents) to eastern, northern or southern ones, although Max Weber's (1958) categories do include Occidental and Oriental cities. Whereas there are studies of socialist urbanization and cities (Scargill 1979; Forbes and Thrift 1987), so far there are none of the postsocialist city, though they are no doubt in the writing.

As Edward Said has pointed out, "the one human history uniting humanity either culminated in or was observed from the vantage point of Europe or the West" (1986, 223). So-called "world knowledge" is communicated through the language and conceptual categories of the first colonial language, English, or the two other principal world (and colonial) languages, French and Spanish. Thus, the main defining terms for and classifications of cities and urbanism stem from Euro-America. They relate to the critical and defining characteristics of such "western" cities – "industrial," "capitalist," "socialist," or "modern." The City of the Other is defined in difference. Hence, "non-western" cities are classified according to what a particular city is *not*, rather than to what it *is*. Likewise, the "traditional" city in regions of colonial control became defined as such only in the context of the colonial "modern" city juxtaposed alongside it (Hamadeh 1992). "Economic levels," in terms of "First" or "Third World," similarly stem from "the West." Concepts of time, historicity, and periodizations are similarly Eurocentric. The "now" of secular, "social scientific" knowledge is the "now" of Europe and North America (Fabian 1983). How would cities be classified from other eschatological perspectives? What would the "non-African," "non-Indian" or "non-Islamic" city be like?

A number of categories indicated in Figure 7-5 are based on geographical criteria with the boundaries defining types of cities or urbanism being spatial (nation, continent), and the city being located in geographic space. In these contexts, the classification system works by "moving sideways," across space. At first this may seem quite logical (i.e., Japanese cities are those located in Japan). However, this framework does not account for colonial cities like nineteenth-century Shimla in India or early twentieth-century Rabat in Morocco, which are at least as British or as French as they are Indian or Moroccan. Nor does it describe cities exhibiting high levels of external cultural influence, whether this is Hispanicization, Americanization, or Islamicization.

By what criteria are contemporary cities to be classified? Today, many cultures exist far from their points of origin, modifying the cities of their hosts. Similarly, capital is international, transforming space and environments wherever it chooses to settle, though subject to local cultural and political constraints. We might therefore ask whether a city is "Asian," "western," "Latin American" or "Islamic" primarily because of its geographical location, its majority population and institutions, its social, cultural, religious, and political life, or its physical and spatial built environment and architectural forms. Is Bombay the most "western" city in India or the most "Indian" city in "the West"?

Other types of cities are not located in space but in time, such as the nineteenth or twentieth century, or at some stage of a social, economic, or political process sometimes characterized by "pre" and "post" such as preindustrial or postcommunist. Other types indicate a change from one mode of production to another, or from one dynasty to another. In this context, the classification system works not by "moving sideways" but, in a linear concept of time, by moving "forwards and backwards." What this demonstrates is that, from the viewpoint of a single reader, all kinds of taxonomic inconsistencies are present. "The nineteenth-century city," a frequently used stereotype of American or British scholars, assumes in the first place a Christian, as opposed to an Islamic, or Orthodox calendar. But it also generally assumes an industrializing context that takes no account of a colonial world system of production and consumption, including the "nonindustrial" cities of Rio or Calcutta, without which the British or American "nineteenth-century city" cannot be understood (King 1990a, 1990b). Equally enigmatic and stereotypical is the category of "the modern city," which presents even greater conceptual problems in terms of its location both in time and in space (King 1994).

Apart from the obvious ethnocentricity of these designations, there is a problem of their sheer operational utility as representations and models. The internationalization of major "western" cities (e.g., Los Angeles, New York, London, Paris, Berlin) in the last two decades has seriously undermined earlier models of these cities. Similarly, in so-called "Third World" and "Islamic" cities, it is likely that there are as many "modern," "First World," "western," or "postindustrial" sectors as there are "traditional," "Third World," "eastern," "preindustrial," and "Islamic" parts in contemporary "western" cities.

The figure highlights a further point. Gender, particularly in relation to the social, behavioral, and spatial activities of women in the city, has typically been a criterion for evaluating the distinctiveness of so-called Islamic cities by non-Islamic, usually male, scholars. Yet feminist studies of cities and urban space in Europe and North America in the past two decades have pointed out many gender specific dimensions of social and spatial life, as well as architectural and building form, in these places (Hayden 1984; Matrix 1984; Little, Peake, and Richardson 1988).

Finally, though there are "quality of life" classifications of cities regarding public safety, levels of pollution, noise, and health indicators (Population Crisis Committee 1990), no one has found methods of examining the comparative creativity provided by the conditions in different cities, or which affect their cultural output.

Conclusion

Language, and terminological systems in particular, are critical to the construction of classification systems in any given society. Yet language alone is by no means sufficient to understand and make sense of particular taxonomies and the types to which they refer. As the illustrations of dwellings included in this chapter make clear, visual information provided by images is also required. It may also be the case that olfactory and aural information is needed to identity particular categories of space and type. Even this may not be sufficient, without a native informant, to distinguish between the subtle social and cultural differences by which particular populations constitute the various types identified in their physical and spatial environment.

The discussion also points to the equally important significance of the physical and spatial environments themselves, through which such socially, culturally, and politically constituted taxonomies are constructed. *Classification systems,* to use the Foucaultian term, and the types and categories that they generate, are necessary and integral parts of a discursive formation. The material reality of the built environment, the physical and spatial world in which those systems have been constituted, is an essential part of the discourse.

Juxtaposing the two systems of classification – dwellings and cities – demonstrates how arbitrary, culturally specific, and incomprehensible some categorizations can be. Placing names on phenomena is an act of generalization. Yet as Abu-Lughod points out,

> Generalization is inevitably a language of power applied to people who stand apart from, and outside of what is being described. Generalization produces effects of homogeneity, coherence, and timelessness, flattening out differences among people in a community (Abu-Lughod 1991, 139).

The same may be said of nonhuman phenomena. By comparison to the finely grained taxonomy represented by mapping terminological systems on the quite small-scale spaces of dwelling types, the taxonomies applied to the vastly different spatial scale of cities seems almost grotesque.

Shared assumptions about type and terminologies are fundamental to social and cultural thinking. Yet the mental constructions of such types and the classification systems to which they belong stem from a particular position in time, space, history, and culture, as is evident from the discussion on cities. The radically changing nature of our contemporary world, an outcome of "time-space compression" in Harvey's words (1989), has led to the destabilization and redundancy of many categories which we use to understand it.

As I have emphasized throughout this chapter, categorization is about social power. It is the power involved in naming, and it is power exercised on a global scale. The western invention of the "postmodern" is, on one hand, a testament to the desperate human desire to control our uncertainties by placing them under a category. Its rejection, on the other hand, as the latest symptom of crisis management in "the history of the epistemic violence of imperialism" (Spivak 1988, 172), is ample demonstration that the power to classify is at the center of contemporary cultural politics.

This paper has a long history. I am indebted to Frank Duffy, John Worthington, and Alan Lipman for their comments on a much earlier version, to Deryck Holdsworth for his input in the section on cities, and especially to Karen Franck and Lynda Schneekloth for their many valuable editorial suggestions. Frances King has my many thanks for numerous photographs from which those included have been selected. As always, the responsibility for this version is entirely my own.

References

Abu-Lughod, Janet. 1987. The Islamic city – historic myth, Islamic essence, contemporary relevance. *International Journal of Middle Eastern Studies* 18: 155–76.

Abu-Lughod, Lila. 1991. Writing against culture. In *Recapturing Anthropology: Working in the Present*, ed. R. Fox. Santa Fe, N. Mex.: School of American Research Press.

Bourdieu, Pierre. 1984. *Distinction*. London and New York: Routledge.

Brown, Kenneth L. 1986. The uses of a concept: "the Muslim city." In *Middle Eastern Cities in Comparative Perspective*, eds. K.L. Brown, M. Jole, et al., 72–81. London and Atlantic Heights, N.J.: Ithaca Press.

Building Societies Association. 1980. *BSA Bulletin*. London: Building Societies Association.

Carter, Harold. 1983. *The Study of Urban Geography*. 3rd ed. London: Arnold.

Conklin, Harold C. 1972. *Folk Classification: A Topically Arranged Bibliography of Contemporary and Background References*. New Haven, Conn.: Department of Anthropology, Yale University.

de Certeau, Michel. 1984. *The Practice of Everyday Life*. Berkeley, Calif.: University of California Press.

Department of Environment. 1978. *English House Condition Survey*. London: HMSO.

Donald, James. 1992. Metropolis: The city as text. In *Social and Cultural Forms of Modernity*, eds. R. Bocock and K. Thompson, 1–54. Milton Keynes: Polity Press in association with the Open University.

Fabian, Johannes. 1983. *Time and the Other: How Anthropology Makes its Object*. New York: Columbia University Press.

Fish, Stanley. 1980. *Is There a Text in This House? The Authority of Interpretive Communities*. Cambridge, Mass.: MIT Press.

Forbes, Dean, and Nigel Thrift, eds. 1987. *The Socialist Third World: Urban Development and Territorial Planning*. London: Blackwell.

Foucault, Michel. 1980. *Power/Knowledge*. New York: Pantheon Books.

Frake, Charles O. 1972. The ethnographic study of cognitive systems. In *Culture and Cognition: Rules, Maps and Plans*, ed. J.S. Spradley, 191–205. San Francisco and London: Chandler Publishing Co.

Girouard, Mark. 1971. *The Victorian Country House*. London: Country Life.

Hage, Per. 1972. Munchner beer categories. In *Culture and Cognition: Rules, Maps and Plans*, ed. J.S. Spradley, 263–78. San Francisco and London: Chandler Publishing Co.

Hamadeh, Shrine. 1992. Creating the traditional city: a trend-enterprise. In *Forms of Dominance: On the Architecture and Urbanism of the Colonial Interlude*, ed. Nezar Alsayyad, 241–59. Aldershot, U.K.: Gower.

Harvey, David. 1989. *The Condition of Postmodernity*. London and New York: Blackwell.

Hayden, Dolores. 1984. *Redesigning the American Dream: The Future of Housing, Work and Family Life*. New York: Norton.

HMSO. 1980, 1990. *Social Trends*. London: Her Majesty's Stationery Office.

Holston, James. 1991. *The Modernist City*. Chicago: University of Chicago Press.

Jackson, Alan A. 1973. *Semi-Detached London*. London: Allen & Unwin.

King, Anthony D. 1974. The language of colonial urbanization. *Sociology* 8 (1): 81–110.

———, ed. 1980. *Buildings and Society: Essays on the Social Development of the Built Environment*. London: Routledge & Kegan Paul.

———. 1984. *The Bungalow: The Production of a Global Culture*. London and Boston: Routledge & Kegan Paul.

———. 1990a. *Urbanism, Colonialism and the World-Economy*. London: Routledge.

———. 1990b. *Global Cities: Post-Imperialism and the Internationalization of London*. London: Routledge.

———. 1994. The times and spaces of modernity. In *World Order/Cultural Difference*, eds. M. Featherstone, S. Lash, and R. Robertson. London, Newbury Park, and Delhi: Sage.

Krautheimer, Richard. 1983. *Three Christian Capitals: Topography and Politics*. Berkeley, Calif.: University of California Press.

Lefebvre, Henri. 1991. *The Production of Space*. Cambridge, Mass. and Oxford, U.K.: Blackwell.

Little, Jo, Linda Peake, and Pat Richardson, eds. 1988. *Women in Cities: Gender and the Urban Environment*. London: Macmillan.

Low, Setha and Erv Chambers, eds. 1989. *Housing, Culture and Design: A Comparative Perspective*. Philadelphia: University of Pennsylvania Press.

Markus, Thomas M. 1993. *Buildings and Power*. London and New York: Routledge.

———. 1982. *Order in Space and Society: Architectural Form and its Context in the Scottish Enlightenment*. Edinburgh: Mainstream Publishing.

———. 1987. Buildings as classifying devices. *Environment and Planning B: Planning and Design* 14: 467–84.

Matrix, ed. 1984. *Making Space: Women and the Man-made Environment*. London: Pluto.

Metcalf, Thomas. 1989. *An Imperial Vision: Indian Architecture and Britain's Raj*. Berkeley, Calif.: University of California Press.

Muthesius, Stefan. 1982. *The English Terrace House*. New Haven, Conn.: Yale University Press.

Population Crisis Committee. 1990. *Cities: Life in the World's Biggest Metropolitan Areas*. Washington, D.C.: Population Crisis Committee.

Prior, Liam. 1988. The architecture of the hospital: a study of spatial organization and medical knowledge. *British Journal of Sociology* 39 (1): 86–113.

Rabinow, Paul. 1989. *French Modern: Norms and Forms of the Social Environment*. Cambridge, Mass.: MIT Press.

Reid, Ivan. 1977. *Social Class Differences in Britain*. London: Open Books.

Said, Edward. 1986. Orientalism reconsidered. In *Literature, Politics and Theory*, eds. F. Barker, P. Hulme, M. Iverson, and D. Loxley. London and New York: Methuen.

———. 1978. *Orientalism*. New York: Pantheon Books.

Sapir, Edward. 1912. Language and environment. *American Anthropology* 14: 226–43.

Scargill, David I. 1979. *The Form of Cities*. New York: St. Martin's Press.

Scull, Andrew T., ed. 1981. *Madhouses, Mad-Doctors and Madmen: The Social History of Psychiatry in the Victorian Era*. Philadelphia: University of Pennsylvania Press.

Spivak, Gayatri C. 1988. *In Other Worlds: Essays in Cultural Politics*. London and New York: Routledge.

Spiwak, H.J. 1951. *International Glossary of Technical Terms Used in Housing and Town Planning*. Amsterdam: International Federation for Housing and Town Planning.

Spradley, James S., ed. 1972. *Culture and Cognition: Rules, Maps and Plans*. San Francisco and London: Chandler.

Sturtevant, William C. 1972. Studies in ethnoscience. In *Culture and Cognition: Rules, Maps and Plans*, ed. J.S. Spradley, 129–67. San Francisco and London: Chandler.

Tyler, Stephen, ed. 1969. *Cognitive Anthropology*. New York: Holt, Rinehart & Winston.

Weber, Max. 1958. *The City*. Toronto: Collier Macmillan.

White, Hayden. 1978. *Tropics of Discourse*. London and Baltimore: Johns Hopkins University Press.

Part III

Negotiating Type

Chapter 8

Social Practice and Building Typologies

Thomas A. Markus

The production of buildings, their use, and the writing of texts about them are three forms of social practice. Like all social practices, they are ways of constructing reality. They not only change the material world but also the way it is perceived, that is, its meaning. The built environment, constructed in this way by the community of builders, users, and speakers, has a meaning reflecting the nature of their own relations. The meaning of buildings concerns the social relations that produce and are produced by social practices.

The meanings are experienced when we use buildings; when the meanings are communicated through language, this experience is shared. The infinite variety of such experiences is structured by a stable, simplifying framework. Named building types are the language categories that constitute this framework.

Material History

This discussion is about society, language, meaning, and the process of creating, writing about, and using buildings. The relationship between these concepts depends, naturally, on an underlying theory concerning the individual people, or subjects, in society who have material histories. Subjects are treated here as historically formed, not only by the ancient forces of evolution, genetics, and language-learning and language-speaking abilities, and the more proximate one of early environment, but by their continuous growth in the process of interacting with their societies.

Subjects have an inner world that structures and gives meaning to the outer, material world. In part this inner world is unique to each individual – Husserl's (1970) "lifeworld" – and in part shared with others. But all of it is formed within a historical process and is rooted in material existence. The aspect of materiality that matters for those who study buildings is that of bodies located in space, much of the time in built space created for a purpose.

Subjects, individually, in groups, and in institutions, produce and reproduce their societies. These productive processes change the material world as well as its meaning. They are social practices, and through them the inner and outer worlds meet; that is, the outer world acquires meaning. These meanings are our social relations. The most universal social practice, which can be used to define human beings and distinguish them from other creatures, is the ability to speak a language and use it consciously to produce social relations.

In Figure 8-1 subjects (who experience buildings or read texts about them), social practices, and social relations are represented as three domains. They are enclosed by a common domain of society-in-history. Social practices include three of specific relevance to our discussion. One is the use of ordinary language; another is the production of texts about buildings; the third is the actual design and production of buildings. A subject experiences, through use, a building, and through this experience discovers its meaning as signifying a type of social relation. This is indicated by the three points connected by the triangle.

KAF: *Isn't the use of buildings and spaces one of these social practices? As you have said, we also "construct reality" through our use of buildings. So we construct types through our ways of occupying them.*
TM: *I agree.*

Though this chapter specifically addresses the connection between spoken or written language and building types, it is important to recall that buildings convey meaning primarily through other languages, those of forms and spatial structures. These systems of signs and metaphors speak of social relations and through them we come to understand a building. Though they signify in *ways* that ordinary language cannot – T.S. Eliot calls poetry a "raid on the inarticulate" – nevertheless *what* they signify, the meaning, has to be capable of articulation in spoken or written form. Otherwise it is impossible to communicate about these meanings and hence to share them; there would be no language-sharing community. And the aspects of ordinary language that we shall be concerned with have to do with use and function. When the forms and spaces signify meanings that are at variance with use and function, then contradictions are created which result in loss of meaning.

RL: *Do the contradictions always result in a loss, or do they sometimes lead to a transformation of meaning?*
TM: *Sometimes they result in transformations. It depends on the extent to which the structure underlying a tradition is used in the transformation.*

Social Practice and Buildings

The designing, constructing, and using of buildings are major social practices of all developed societies, as are speaking and writing about them. Buildings acquire meaning as objects that organize space so as to produce social relations. It is not necessary to bring about material change in the physical environment for it to acquire meaning. For Australian Aborigines a Dreaming site, as found in nature, carries meaning about the "Dreamtime" when the world was created. Through storytelling, song, dance, and painting this myth is kept alive; that is, the meaning of the place is kept alive.

RL: *That "buildings acquire meaning as objects that organize space so as to produce social relations" is not wholly valid in all situations (e.g., buildings for storing implements).*
TM: *Such implements are tools of a productive process; someone owns the land and tools, consumes or sells the produce to someone, etc. The whole process, including the storage of the implements, is the economic base of a set of social relations.*

The use of spoken or written language is a universal social practice. Texts about buildings are a special case of language use; they can be descriptive, about existing buildings, or prescriptive, about buildings yet to be designed and built. Especially potent elements of the language about building space are the words that refer to use: function-language. Such apparently simple words as "museum," "liv-

KAF: *Even in an "unstable building culture" the names may arouse these expectations but the expectations may not be met. We may continue to use the same words, even though the form and use of the buildings change.*
TM: *True. But I prefer not to qualify it further because what happens in* un*stable cultures is too problematic to deal with at this point.*

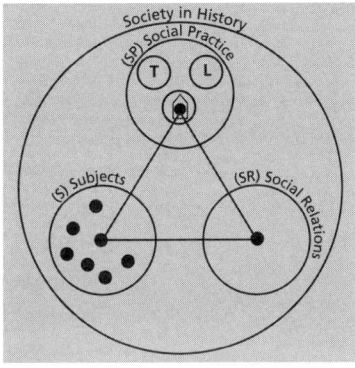

8-1
Diagram showing relations between subjects, social practices, and social relations

T = texts about buildings
L = language
⌂ = designing and producing buildings

KAF: *If we want to change the power relations in a given time and society, then we also need to change the buildings.*
TM: *But power relations can be changed without any change to buildings. For example, in the French Revolution abbey churches were converted with little or no material change to be revolutionary* tribuneaux. *It is precisely this reuse which, symbolically, was so powerful, for it stated that the privileged spaces of the* ancien regime *could be used to embody entirely new power relations. The reinvestment of space/place with new meanings, by new uses, is a traditional way of transforming relations. It is rather like eating your enemy to absorb his power!*

ing room," or "atrium" describe a rich set of entities, purposes, and relations. In a stable building culture they have connotations that go far beyond use. They arouse expectations about the form of the building, about its spatial structure, and about the range of activities to be found there.

Social Relations and Buildings

Social science has long familiarized us with social relations of power. These are based on the partitioning of finite resources — land, capital, energy, raw materials, skill, labor, knowledge, productive capacity, weapons, and so on. This is basically a cake-slicing operation, the zero-sum game so beloved of operational research. More here is less there. The distribution of power in society is governed by formal and informal political processes and relies on supporting ideologies. Its critique is justice.

Alongside power relations there are, in all human groups, those that Gorz (1989) calls "bonds." They are independent of law, contract, or rewards for production. It is for this reason that he calls them "subversive" and he cites the relation between a mother and her infant as one of its most striking examples. Poets and theologians speak of love; in politics it is known as solidarity; and in everyday life we experience it as friendship. Bonds are, in a strange way, infinite, the inverse of power relations: the stronger they are between individuals or within a group, the more there is to give away.

There is no human society, no matter how oppressive (asymmetrical) its power relations may be, in which bonds are not created. But the greater the asymmetries of power, the more sacrifice is involved in maintaining bonds. Primo Levi's picture of Auschwitz is eloquent testimony to that. Buildings are among the most powerful material instruments for creating, sustaining, and controlling power relations. They also affect the formation of bonds by creating responsive space or by allowing for such relations in "interstitial" or unprogrammed space.

Use of the word "social" to describe all human relations may, at first sight, appear to diminish them to those capable of empirical observation. But it is intended to include more; not only those that we experience both as socially formed and forming subjects, capable of outside-in analysis, but those unique to each individual (Husserl's "lifeworld"). It is philosophy, linguistics, art, poetry, and psychoanalysis that point to the possibilities of inside-out analysis.

In both power and bond relations there are at least three levels. The first is that which deals with the relation of self-to-self, the relation that is at the root of self discovery, that continuously provides clues to the answers to such questions as "who am I?" "Where have I come from?" and "Where am I going?" The second level is that of self-to-others, for which "social" is normally reserved. And of course this points to the first relation too, for it is in interaction with others, in speaking and listening to them, that the self is created. And it also points outside the self, for it involves an awareness (and, for the student, a study) of the relation of others-to-others. The third level is the relation of self-to-*other* — those cosmic schemes that are conceived as lying outside history. In different cultures they have taken form in a range of ideas and beliefs: reason, science, nature, explicitly religious schemes, art, or justice.

For Marx, economic asymmetries have resulted in the opposite of relation — alienation. And he defines the same three levels of alienation, from the self, from others, and from nature (the only *other* which a materialist perspective can admit).

RL: *So self and social identities are interrelated?*
TM: *Yes. We get to know ourselves* in *others; there is no other way of becoming a "self."*

RL: *At which level is the type of building: at the level of eating places or at the level of canteen, pub, cafeteria, mess, café, etc?*
TM: *Both. Types have a hierarchical structure.*

Architectural Discourse and Social Practice

The social relations that any analysis must address are those of power and bond formation, each of which is both socially constituted and in the domain of the inner "lifeworld." And both are stratified into the three levels that have just been described. To understand the meaning of buildings, that is, the way they embed these social relations, the social practices that produce buildings have to be examined. The evidence is contained in the materiality of buildings, in the processes by which they are designed, produced, and used, and in the texts about them. There are appropriate analytical tools for each of these. Of course these have to be based on sound theory; but more than that, they must address those features that experience tells us are significant.

Immediately there is a difficulty. Although our experience of buildings appears to have a unity, in fact it consists of distinct elements that, to a great extent, are independent of each other. This is true of our experience of other people too. There is no reason why physical appearance, intelligence, or a sense of humor should in any way cohere. We know that these aspects of people's personalities occur in a wide range of combinations. And yet we also know that for any specific person of our acquaintance, the way they cohere with each other and with other traits is precisely what makes that person unique. Creative authors have the ability to

KAF: *We also choose or create our own functions which may not be those that were intended. We are not always following a script of actions written by others. We also write our own.*
TM: *Yes. But here I'm discussing how we* interpret *buildings, not how we* change *them. I'm concerned more with a passive response than an active one.*

invent characters whose traits cohere in such powerful and fitting ways that they become *archetypal*. Falstaff's combinations of body and face, wit, and intelligence is powerful enough for "Falstaffian" to have become a generic description of character.

Form, Function, and Space

What are the distinct elements of our experience of buildings which, despite their apparent coherence in specific cases, have independence? I shall work on the assumption that the three most significant are form, or what things *look* like (and to a lesser extent, what they feel, smell, and sound like); what people do in the building and its individual spaces, or what it is *for*; and how we sense *where* we are, next to whom or what, in what relation to other spaces, inside and outside the building. These three sets of experience underlie almost everything that is said about buildings, so it is reasonable to speak of form, function, and space as being the three discourses of architecture, each with appropriate techniques for its analysis.

Clearly the experience of form is immensely powerful. It is immediate and direct. Methods for its analysis in architecture have traditionally descended from art-historical methods and focus on the geometrical composition of plans, elevations and volumes, articulation of surfaces, the iconographic program of ornament, painting or sculpture, underlying properties of rhythm, scale and proportion, color, texture, the flow of light, opacity and transparency, and the use of stylistic systems or languages such as classical orders.

Of the three, this is the one that tradition has made most familiar. Almost all architectural criticism and historical scholarship is committed to the view of buildings as art objects. In both the UDC and the Dewey Decimal library classification systems "architecture," at 720, is in the "fine arts" class of 700, squeezed between "landscape gardening" at 710 and "sculpture" at 730. The places where architecture students work are "studios." The subject is covered in the media on "arts" programs or pages. Architecture-as-art is classless – it spans from Prince Charles to the humblest tenants' organization on a municipal housing estate.

The experience of function is at its most direct when we are participants or actors in what is going on. At one remove, we may merely be observers of other actors using a building. If even that evidence is not available, we deduce function from all kinds of material clues: the form, spatial structure, and location of an entire building, or any one of its spaces, the furniture, content, or equipment in a space, or the inscriptions on buildings or room doors.

In the absence of any such evidence, functions can be discovered from texts that describe them. The lexicon of words used in these texts, the function-language, is part of normal everyday speech. We communicate almost everything of importance about the daily use of buildings and their spaces in such language. We can do that because the words describe much more than a simple material process. "Canteen" is more than a place for eating; after all, restaurant, mess, nightclub, pub, cafeteria, beach picnic hut, and café also denote eating places. What each of these words does with great success is to distinguish different relations between eaters, and between them and the providers and servers of food. That is, each has a distinct meaning that, within a culture, signifies a known set of relations, and within a stable building tradition implies a limited and easy-to-recognize range of forms and spatial structures. Such words denote *types*.

The coherence of this tradition was evident in the predictable relation between form and function. From a given form the function of a building could be safely predicted, and the converse was also true. The situation held till about the mid-eighteenth century, when it was fractured by the Enlightenment and then the French and Industrial Revolutions. There was an explosion of new building types; architects no longer necessarily came from the same ruling class as that of major clients, and the universal language of classicism began to give way to a whole range of new stylistic sources. The consequences of this will be examined later. But theorists did not give up without a struggle. One of the last and most powerful defenses of the form-function link was by Blondel (1771-77), who set out a range of *genres* or functional types. For each *genre* there was an appropriate character suitable to it and it alone. This theory came to fruition in the *architecture parlante* of Lequeu, Boullée, and Ledoux, in which allegorical and metaphorical forms were created to express the finest nuances of purpose. This is how Boullée (1781–97) defends his design for a place of justice over a prison:

> It seemed to me that if I placed this august palace above the shadowy lair of Crime, I should not only show to advantage the nobility of the architecture on account of the resulting contrast, but I should also have an impressive metaphorical image of vice overwhelmed by the weight of Justice (1974, 98).

Spatial structure refers not to the geometrical or volumetric properties of space, experienced and capable of analysis through their forms, but to the topological properties of adjacency. A building's spaces are permeable to each other in specific ways. One space opens into another or several others. A space can be reached directly from the street, or after passing through only a few others, or many spaces may have to be traversed before reaching it. There are graphical techniques and precise methods for quantifying such topological relations, many of which have been developed by Hillier and Hanson (1984) and their colleagues. Where there are no choices of route, the space has a treelike, branching structure. Where there are alternative routes there are rings. Spaces near the entrance are shallow, those at the end of a long sequence are deep. These properties of trees, rings, and depths can be shown to relate to density of encounters between people, and to social phenomena of control and being controlled, privacy, isolation, and surveillance.

Spatial properties too, like form, were governed by a stable tradition that related to familiar function in a predictable way. Coupled to the gradually evolving language of classical forms, the overall result was that form, function, and space signified a coherent and unified meaning. In other words, if the meanings of each discourse had been mapped separately onto the domain of social relations, they would have converged at a single point. It was not necessary to do this; it was possible to think of architecture as having its own, inherent discourse that yielded meanings without the need to refer to any external domain. After the eighteenth century this possibility became more and more difficult to ignore. It became clear that any apparent cohesion was based on the existence of a community of building users, designers, readers, and speakers – a community that shared a language game – and this community was disappearing. The old cohesions were fragmented and it became clear that recovering meanings would involve mapping individual properties of buildings onto the domain of social relations.

It is relevant to note that recently Eco (1986) has developed architectural semiotics to identify "social exigencies" *external* to architecture as the field where innovation can occur. These are "systems over which [the architect] has no power," (Eco 1986, 82) and they can be equated with social relations.

If form, function, and space are indeed the critical properties, then the task of understanding buildings, of discovering their meaning, begins to look like archaeology. The archaeologist is faced with remnants of a building, from which he or she reconstructs its form: the geometries of its spaces, the kind of ornamental and iconographic program, and the use of any stylistic conventions. Coupled to other evidence of any found artifacts – bone, hearth, utensils, functional evidence per se – and spatial evidence about the way rooms are connected to each other and to the outside, a picture of culture, use, and social relations can be constructed.

Buildings Shape Social Relations

Each of the three discourses of architecture is at work in shaping relations of power and bonds at each of their three levels. It is not difficult to see power at work in the production of buildings. Ultimately its source is the possession of the resources to undertake building projects in the first place. Private individuals or enterprises, cities, or the state, who do control such resources, will always have an unwritten agenda beneath their overt programs, whether these are healing in a health center, productivity in an office or factory, or display in a museum. This covert program is designed to ensure that their political power, as controllers of these resources, is reproduced in all the building's features.

Clearly those in the centers of power will determine who is appointed as designer. In much more subtle ways, through their influence on education, the professions, and the media, they will have shaped the discourse of architecture itself. They will have determined the language, structure, and, above all, the silences of the brief.

The fact that a building's forms speak the language of the sponsors in no way diminishes their emotional or artistic impact. It merely explains *whose* language of forms, whose imagery, is used.

The first and major act of control over function is to decide to build at all, and for what purpose. Moreover, since resources of land, capital, and labor are limited, these also determine what is not built, that is, what functions are excluded from the city or from within a building. Lest there be any doubt about the functional program, the sponsors write, or control the writing of, the brief. Much effort is put into giving such texts the appearance of technical, neutral, or "objective" documents, free of values and hence beyond debate.

In spatial structures, depth, asymmetries of trees, limitations on rings, control over access from public space, and other devices ensure the desired distribution of power. This is graphically shown by Hillier and Hanson (1984) in their idea of spatial "inversion." In normal buildings to which the public ("visitors") have access – for instance ships, banks, libraries, bars, theaters, churches, or town halls – the public is limited to the occupation of outer, shallow zones. So the street side of a shop, the banking hall, open shelving of a library, drinking lounge, auditorium, nave, or public enquiry office are separated from the shopkeeper's space, the bank staff's offices, the librarian's quarters and the book stacks, the serving area behind the bar and the drink storage, the stage and the dressing rooms, the chancel and the sacristy, and the town officials' offices. The separation is by counters, doors, and spaces beyond which, in the depth of the building, lie the "inhabitants'" spaces. It is they who control the entire functional program. Increasing depth signifies increasing power. So the "holy of holies" exists not only in sacred buildings, but in the form of a rector's office in a university reached at the tip of a branch after passing through corridors, stairs, and outer offices.

The typical "inverted" building is the institution such as a hospital, asylum, or prison. Here the inhabitants are located in the outer, shallow, space and the visitors (even though a "visit" may be a 20-year prison term!) in the depths. Depth now signifies loss of power; the most controlled and weakest groups in the asymmetrical structure are at its deepest point.

But form, function, and space are relevant also to the formation and maintenance of bond relations. Imagery can sustain or symbolize them, often by decreasing the uniformity of large-scale orders, or providing the means for the continuous creation of local images by the users or owners of parts of a spatial system. Functions can be defined in an open-ended way, in which the brief becomes easy to redefine, and the rules can be designed to accommodate changing roles and activities as the spirit moves the occupants, with minimal organizational or material barriers. The spatial structure can be such that communication is easy, free, and leads to many chance encounters, at the same time allowing freely chosen privacy.

Function Language of Builders

The labels that denote use work if they are woven into the everyday language of those who use the buildings. Using and speaking are then both natural and contextually bound. If a function is torn out of its context, not only is it difficult to interpret its meaning, but the entire spatial structure into which it is placed loses meaning. One has only to imagine a school classroom and its activities placed in an art gallery or a railway station. Not only would it be very difficult to understand the purpose and meaning of the classroom, but the normal clarity of pur-

KAF: *But functions are not this tightly fixed to particular contexts. People are quite flexible in pursuing activities outside their conventional locations.*
TM: *Yes, but some disjunctions are at least inappropriate, if not outright nonsensical. There are limits to the amount of "re-structuration" people can cope with. I do not consider stability as so stultifying and negative as you do. I place great value on tradition — especially since it is that which allows one deliberately to make a break for conscious, radical reasons.*

pose of the art gallery or railway station would also be eroded. While it is possible to do this with the space and its activities, whatever bizarre reason there might be for doing so, it is not possible to do it with the word "classroom." It refuses to be torn out of its language structure; context means precisely that — context, bound into the text of use and language. Function language is the secure structure which protects meaning through the established words for types.

One of the characteristics of this language, like all human language, is that it employs categories — for naming natural and artificial objects, food, events, feelings, people, roles, and areas of knowledge. These categories are organized into groups, usually in a hierarchical way, to become taxonomies, and, in their fully developed form, classification systems. All cultures use language for this, and anthropology and linguistics have shown how these classification systems represent a view of the world. They are the social constructs through which the world is given meaning.

Obviously some specialized practical tasks depend on classification systems; it is difficult to imagine how any library, museum, social security, or educational system could operate without using them. But the need is far more profound than that. Because our experience of the world is infinitely varied, and each part of it is unique, the only way we can cope with this flood of rich material is to locate each unique part within a stable, general structure; to pigeonhole, or group it, with others that it resembles in its essentials. This overall structure is a classification system that we carry in our heads and whose conceptual elements are defined in language. The pigeonholing makes the world familiar and stable

KAF: *The "classroom" links function with form, but "holding a class" is an activity and could (and does) take place in a variety of different places without losing the meaning or purpose of classes. I try to show in my chapter how physical attributes of place are often only loosely linked to use and meaning.*

TM: *All nonspatial language about activities, like "holding a class," is free in this way. It is only when it is transformed into spatial language, like a "classroom," that it becomes embedded into material experience of real bodies in real places. If "holding a class" takes place, say, for soldiers in a trench, or pregnant mothers in a prenatal clinic, then it is precisely that social (relational) context, defined by a new place, that makes it meaningful. "Classroom" really means "holding a class for a group of children, in the context of other groups, in an organization dedicated to that purpose with its own dedicated complex of spaces, usually called a 'school.'" This is precisely the beauty of the shorthand that a "type" based on use really is.*

KAF: *But doesn't "holding a class" have a very clear spatial dimension? It is an activity that takes place in a space, and the phrase suggests particular relationships and particular tasks that are organized in space. Admittedly the material aspects of the space are undefined in this phrase but the spatial aspects are suggested.*

TM: *Yes, "holding a class" certainly has a spatial dimension. My point is that its spatial context and its linguistic context normally go hand in hand. However, the spatial can, willfully or in ignorance, be fractured, but the linguistic one cannot because it is so much more deeply rooted in culture. So when the spatial context is fractured, it is precisely the resulting dissonance with the linguistic context — the expected spatial connotation of "holding a class" has not materialized in real space — that causes the loss of meaning.*

KAF: *Language also allows us to explore and represent differences. Metaphors and other figurative language reveal similarities between experiences that at first appear completely different. Lynda Schneekloth shows how science fiction does this: we see ourselves in alien beings. Language helps us discover what we did not see or know before. In doing so, it can make the world seem less familiar and less stable.*

TM: *Yes. I like your inclusion of differences alongside similarities. But it is only the structuring achieved through categories of similarities that allows the contrast of differentiation to work.*

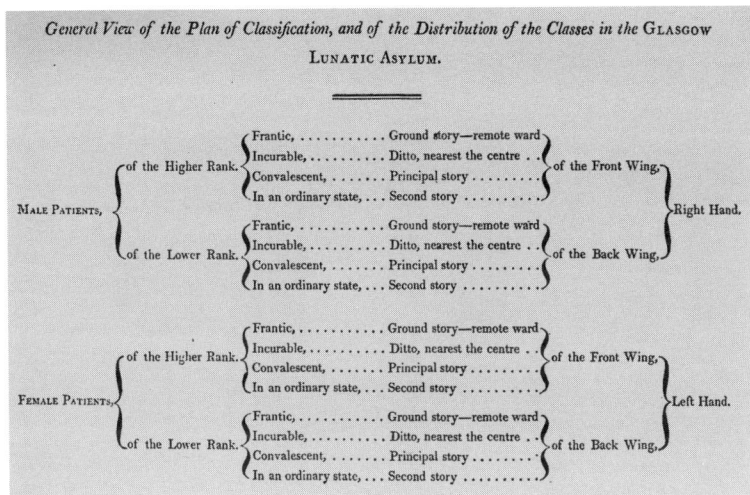

8-2
William Stark's diagrammatic representation of the brief for the Glasgow Lunatic Asylum (1807) on which he worked as architect (source: W. Stark 1807. Courtesy of the Glasgow District Council Libraries Department)

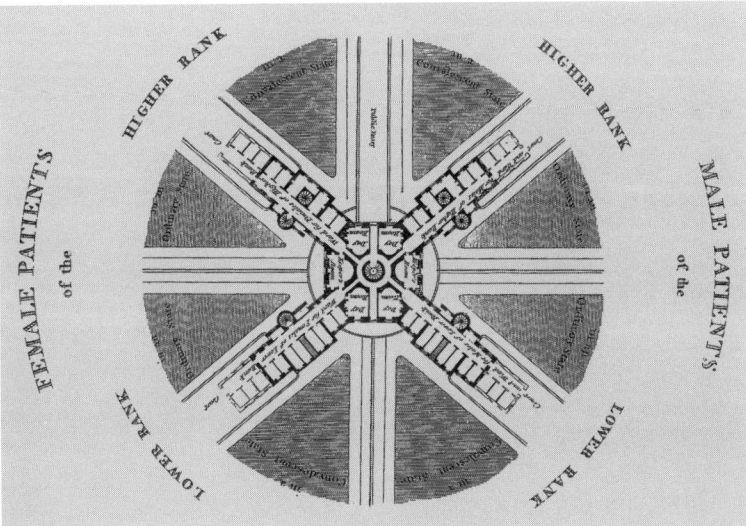

8-3
Plan of Glasgow Lunatic Asylum (source: W. Stark 1807. Courtesy of the Glasgow District Council Libraries Department)

and, while it is socially produced like the specialized classification (a conscious task), it is completely unconscious.

This use of language permeates the entire social practice of building production. Texts are the main means of educating those engaged in the process. They also form the substance of building regulations, design guides, competition and other briefs, critical descriptions, and management rules.

Prescriptive Texts

Two examples will show the formative rules of prescriptive texts in briefs. In many ways, they design a building even before a designer appears on the scene. The first goes back to 1807, when the architect William Stark was commissioned to design Glasgow's first lunatic asylum (Stark 1807). He translated the brief he had been given into a diagram, which forms the left-hand side of Figure 8-2. The whole asylum population was divided by gender. It was then divided again according to patients' economic means – those who could pay fees, being "of higher rank," and the paupers from the surrounding counties, being "of lower rank." Finally each class was divided into four diagnostic classes – "frantic," "incurable," "convalescent," and "in an ordinary state." This classification by gender, economic class, and medical condition – in fact, productive capability – accurately reflected in microcosm the class structure on which the society of the developing Industrial Revolution was based.

The right-hand side of the diagram mapped each of the 16 classes into zones at various distances from the center and on various floor levels. The eventual outcome, a four-armed Greek cross plan, with central inspection over which was a dome (Figure 8-3), was really an inevitable outcome.

The second example is the 1970 competition for Glasgow's Burrell Art Gallery. This was financed from a bequest by the shipping magnate Sir William Burrell. The competition attracted 242 entries and was won by Meunier, Gasson, and Andresen. Even a simple analysis of the text of the brief reveals some interesting features that affected the finished project and, indeed, all the entries.

In Figure 8-4 the brief is represented by blocks, each proportional to a piece of the text in the brief. The blocks are arranged in a descending tree according to the division of the brief into headings, subheadings, sections, and paragraphs. The diagram shows two things: the degree of elaboration of each part as measured by the volume of the text, and the degree of discrimination as shown by the varying depth of the tree branches for various sections.

SOCIAL PRACTICE AND BUILDING TYPOLOGIES 155

It can be seen that three issues are developed to the deepest, fifth, level. The first, a listing of the reasons for disqualifications of submissions, represents a "gate" through which all valid submissions had to pass. Secondly, the clauses setting out the legal rights of the Trustees, and other parties with the associated control over funds, represent the overall power exercised over a project by any sponsor. Third is the development in great detail of two parts of the schedule of accommodation. One (small) part deals with general rules about all areas; the other (large) part deals with ever-finer subdivisions of European art by chronological period. Although there is a splendid collection of ancient oriental and Middle Eastern art, only the art that is recognized as coming from "home" is seen as capable of being discriminated into further classes.

In the built project and in all the submissions that qualified, the labeled spaces, their size, grouping, and sequence, are material reproductions of the classification built into the schedule of accommodation whose structure is represented in Figure 8-4. The plan (Figure 8-5) is, in fact, a materialization of a specific theory of art and history, and a specific art-scholarly technique. Above all, the requirement in the brief that Burrell's residence at Hutton Castle in Berwickshire, in the form of a central courtyard, hall, dining room, and drawing room, all with their original furnishings, be reproduced, ensured that the gallery became a statement of the relation between the wealthy private collector and art. This was in the tradition of the Renaissance princes. Finally, the insistence of the Trust Deeds on a rural site (the eventual choice falling on Pollok Park) and the juxtaposition of the wooded landscape and the art objects separated only by a transparent screen on the northern edge, made another important statement: art and nature are partners in innocence and both can be isolated from history and society.

Convergence of Meanings

As long as tradition produced predictable and stable convergences between the three discourses in the domain of social relations, that is, as long as the points in that domain could be described by using function-language, there was no problem about meanings. The classification of functional types conserved, in an authentic and reliable way, the meaning of buildings in terms of social relations.

Of course there was not only a single, specific design that carried the meaning of, say, "museum" to a *given* subject. A range of solutions would carry similar meanings, and these can be represented as a "cloud" around a point that represents a specific kind of social relation (Figure 8-6a). By the same reasoning, a given

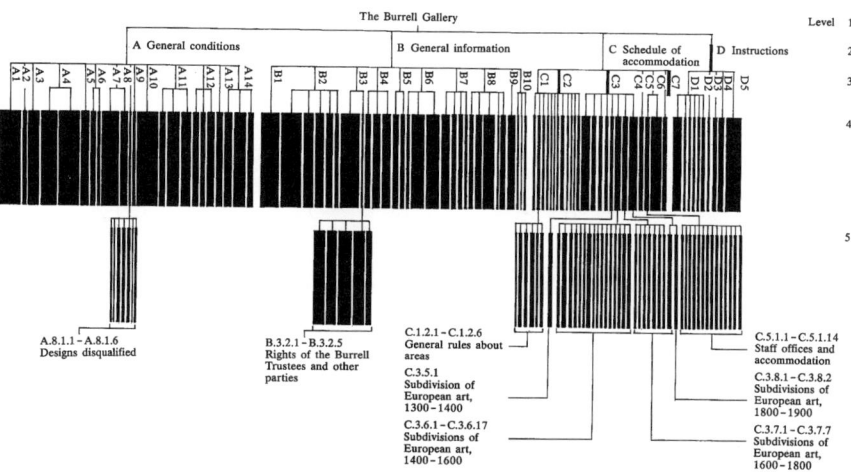

At levels 4 and 5 the length of the bars is uniform and their width is proportional to the length of each bit of text. Therefore the area of each rectangular block is a scale representation of the volume of text in the corresponding section. At levels 2 and 3 the text is merely a series of headings and subheadings with the exception of the four marked in thicker lines, which represent a small amount of text accompanying the heading or subheading. Only European Art is classified down to level 5; all other parts of the collection remain classified at level 4. This is the author's diagram, but is based on, and gratefully acknowledges, work by one of his students, Salman Othman, who in his Special Study Project "A Case Study of the Burrell Collection", 1985 (Department of Architecture and Building Science, University of Strathclyde, Glasgow) made the first attempt to analyse the Burrell Gallery brief.

8-4
Text structure of Burrell Gallery brief (drawing by author. First appeared in Markus 1987)

KAF: *The social relations were also stable and predictable. Classifications may become extremely important just when societies become less stable and less predictable. David Vanderburgh talks about this in his chapter on the emergence of new building types in nineteenth-century France.*
TM: *Yes, I agree.*

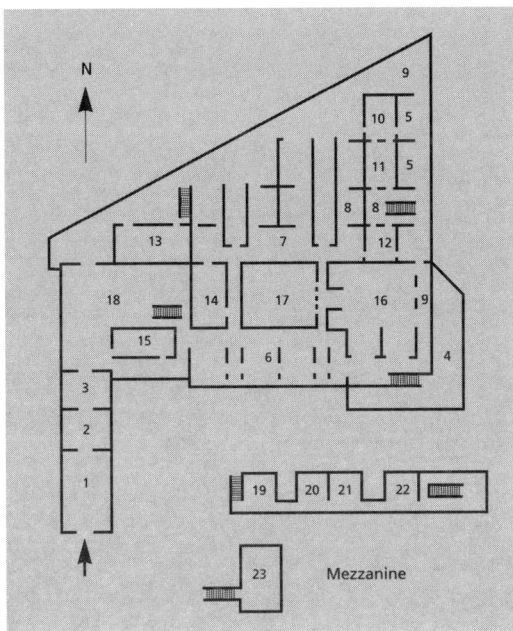

8-5
Plan of Burrell Gallery, Glasgow (1970–83).

GROUND FLOOR
1. lobby, cloaks, wc's
2. inner lobby
3. shop
4. restaurant

Oriental Art
5. carpets and Near Eastern ceramics

Medieval and Post Medieval European Art
6. stained glass and furniture
7. tapestries
8. needlework and lace
9. sculpture

Period Galleries
10. Elizabethan room
11. 17th- and 18th-century room
12. Gothic domestic room

The Hutton Castle Rooms
13. drawing room
14. hall
15. dining room
16. temporary exhibition area
17. lecture theatre
18. courtyard

MEZZANINE
Paintings and drawings
19. old masters
20. 19th-century French
21. pastels: Degas and Manet
22. special displays from the collection
23. school room

KAF: *Language changes more slowly than building functions and forms, but this does not seem to cause as much confusion as you suggest. People figure out the intended purposes and uses by observation, and they often create meanings with or without names for the building types.*
TM: Eventually *people figure out new function-form relations. "Figuring out" is another way of saying that they understand it, i.e., they* can *name it. Until this takes place, I believe any concepts arising from experience — as all, intrinsically do — are fuzzy, ambiguous, and contradictory.*

building could carry a range of similar meaning to *different* subjects, thus creating another "cloud."

The form-function link that Blondel struggled so hard to maintain in the eighteenth century made it possible to define a type by using its functional label in the assurance that it implied an appropriate form. Indeed, it also implied an appropriate spatial structure, though this remained, of the three discourses, the one that was least explicit. The labels were a shorthand for an immensely rich social and architectural description, though they could not, as Blondel had hoped, reconstitute the specific meaning of an individual building. For that there was no substitute for direct experience.

There are two patterns of typological evolution. The first has the branching characteristics of biological evolution, with ever more specialized types growing out of more primitive ones. This occurred, for instance, with the evolution of hospitals, asylums, and prisons from the catchall eighteenth-century poorhouse, workhouse, and bridewell. Similarly the club, hotel, and stock exchange can be traced back to the coffeehouse. But another form of evolution was, so to speak, in reverse — the fusion of previously separate types into new complexes whose component parts lost nothing of their earlier specialization. This, in nature, is impossible. The post-1834 workhouse of the New Poor Law brought together not only hospital, prison, poorhouse, and asylum components, but also elements of the mill or factory, school, and farm.

These changes signified new social relations in new kinds of space. Once their novelty had worn off, the meanings of these spaces became unambiguous. But it was not always the case. Foulston's surprising Theater Royal in Plymouth (1811–19) amalgamated to the theater a hotel, a ballroom, a club, an assembly room, and an Athenaeum to house the local Literary and Philosophical Society. What did the elite users of this complex make of it? What did they call this place with its variety of functions that had been forced into one spatial complex, but which refused to converge into a recognizable pattern and for which no word existed? If the complex was difficult to name, it would also be difficult to use and to manage.

Shifts of Meaning

The Theater Royal conglomerate obscured meaning as a result of its scattered elements from within one discourse, that of function. There is an even greater slippage of meaning when all three discourses are themselves comprehensively scattered.

Medieval monastic churches were turned into the courthouses of the new State early in the course of the French Revolution with little or no material change. The bishop's throne was replaced by the judge's seat in the apse, and hanging behind it instead of the huge wooden crucifix was the *tricouleur*. The altar could be reused as the judge's table. The lateral spaces of the choir could now house lawyers and court officials. Witnesses and accused could be located where the pulpit and lectern had been, and the public could occupy the nave. Yet the change from church to courthouse soon became understandable and recognizable (even if frightening). And the change in label completely represented it. The survival of space with sacred imagery and iconographic features that had not been destroyed or defaced was a striking manifestation of the power of the new ideology to transform the old. The new function "dragged" the formal and spatial discourses with it to a new, convergent position (the dotted lines on Figure 8-6b represent this). Forms and spatial structures with established meanings in sacred, liturgical, and communal functions were abruptly reused for the new function and, apparently, seen as appropriate.

KAF: *Why were these changes seen as appropriate whereas other changes you describe were not?*
TM: *There are boundaries to the degree of change that can be tolerated. There is room for argument about where this boundary is, but I think one has to accept that the boundary is not infinite. If it were, one could never call a place/space "inappropriate." No loss of meaning could be critically approached, as anything could be called an "enlargement" or "enrichment."*

Another kind of change, though of the same type and from the same period, may, for many users and observers, have been resistant to such redefinition. They found it difficult or impossible to accept the reuse of a splendid building for an oppressive, squalid purpose, as when Fontevraud Abbey was converted to a huge prison. There is evidence that the new function and the old forms and spaces refused to converge. Observers as well as users sensed the prison function as fitting uneasily into the monastic complex. There was a contradiction, which is represented by the gap between the two points in Figure 8-6c.

This is analogous to the situation in which someone's facial expression, gestures, and words are contradictory. Modern drama has exploited this technique as a way of probing everyday behavior and relations. But when the experiments leave the stage and are reenacted in the street to become the norm, they lose their significance. Meaning is lost rather than illuminated.

KAF: *Previous meanings are lost but often new meanings emerge. They may emerge gradually over time as the uses and names of the building types develop.*
TM: *Yes. The drama I refer to does, over time, enlarge the meaning of everyday experience. But it is when the everyday is regarded as an experimental stage that confusion occurs. Instead of enlarging experience, it constricts it by making it less comprehensible. There are no shortcuts.*

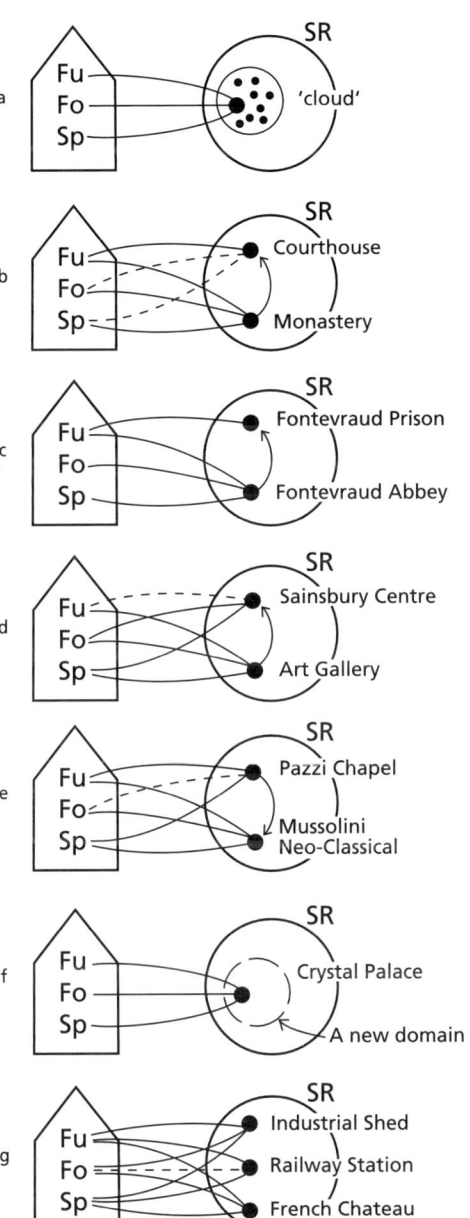

8-6
Diagrammatic representations of meaning in various cases.
SR = Social Relations
Fu = function
Fo = form
Sp = space

Sometimes the power residing in space and form is used to redefine completely the meaning of a traditional function. The use of forms derived from the high-tech imagery of industrial buildings and machines, and spatial structures derived from the supermarket, in the Sainsbury Center at the University of East Anglia, makes it possible to redefine art objects as commodities in an industrial market economy. The location of the exhibits on shelves or in recesses, their lighting, the neutralization of their background and their grouping into "departments," make them accessible in quite a new way. Figure 8-6d represents this shift, successfully achieved for ideological purposes. Formal and spatial elements from production and exchange spaces combine with a redefined function of "art gallery" at a new point in the domain of social relations. It has been possible to redefine art in this way because to most observers, unless they analyze what is going on, the experience is innocent of contradiction, all the more so since in formal terms it is innovative and elegant.

A similar case occurred in a British university department when a community of students and scholars was placed into a new building with a controlled single entrance, lift-centered vertical access to six floors of long double-banked corridors with private staff rooms on either side, and seminar rooms at their ends. This lacked the possibilities of chance encounters, free formation of informal small groups, and easy links with those who worked outside the building. Its deep, treelike spatial structure had all the characteristics of an institution in which, despite the rhetoric of creative intellectual freedom, the community's traditional function is eroded by introducing features associated with surveillance, control, and the absence of communication.

Occasionally an individual's or an entire generation's experience of an architectural form is so overwhelmingly associated with a historical disruption that its conventional meaning is irretrievably obliterated. For those who lived through Mussolini's use of classicism, the harmony which the Pazzi Chapel signified to them, and continues to signify for many other people, may never again be recoverable (Figure 8-6e).

When a radically new function creates entirely new forms and a new spatial structure, a new point appears in the domain of social relations. The Crystal Palace (Figure 8-6f) said something quite new about nature, art, machinery, and labor relations. And even though it had little in the way of precedents, and no successors as pure in their intentions, it did seem to carry these meanings to the majority of visitors. This was genuinely revolutionary. It created meaning not by

SOCIAL PRACTICE AND BUILDING TYPOLOGIES 159

disrupting and re-fusing traditional elements, but by new inventions on every front. Its functional program, certainly on this scale and with this degree of organization, would be completely novel. Equally novel was its glass, iron, and wood technology, transferred and vastly developed from its modest glass house and conservatory roots. And though its spatial structure, defined by columns on a modular grid, had real precedents in certain markets and mills, it was only in the imagination of Durand 50 years earlier that a grid had ever achieved such a scale, hierarchical articulation, and combinatorial richness.

One more shift is worth considering: producing a new meaning by the juxtaposition of two previously disparate but unambiguous types. The classical or Gothic facade building hiding the shed behind reached its epitome in Scott's French *château* in front of Barlow's great train hall at St. Pancras Station. While at first, as at Euston, such curious combinations may have been puzzling, they soon became the pattern *par excellence* for the major railway stations of Europe. It signified a division that was deeply embedded in the urban tradition. The city street had never been bounded by industrial buildings. The mills, factories, sheds, and machines on which the industrial revolution was based were peripheral, on town edges, or hidden behind the conventional civic and commercial fabric, as were the lives of those who worked in or with them. Engine and train sheds, designed by railway engineers, were part of that industrial world. If for commercial reasons they had to be placed in the very heart of the city, they too had to be camouflaged by "polite" structures designed by architects. This differentiated between a building with a technical function to shelter (moving) machinery – the *loco*motive – from a building to receive, classify, and control the human elements of the system – the passenger. When a designer such as Cubitt wanted to expose the shed to the street, without a "polite" screen, *this* was seen as *a*typical. It was a contradiction not between two discourses, or two different types, but between one and the absence of another, a void (Figure 8-6g). It is no coincidence that his daring experiment, at King's Cross terminus, was built in the same year as the Crystal Palace, where this technological hinterland or underworld was polished up, placed in a park, and combined with works of art. But for urban stations it was not accepted as the way forward.

These contradictions, slippages, and disjunctions offer new creative possibilities; they can be used to camouflage otherwise unacceptable meanings; or they can be, quite simply, bizarre. For instance Tschumi's "little red cubes" in the Parc la Villette in Paris are objects not unlike the sculptures of the Russian Constructi-

RL: *What is the basis for this affirmation (and others in this chapter) that are not supported by evidence such as bibliographical references?*
TM: *This particular comment on the Crystal Palace is based on contemporary descriptions by visitors.*

8-7

One of Piranesi's *Carceri* etchings: No. V, Second series, 1760 (courtesy of National Galleries of Scotland, Edinburgh)

KAF: *But this does not stop people from using the cubes or enjoying them. Their meaning may be ambiguous, but that seems to cause few problems for visitors. Indeed, their ambiguity may be pleasurable.*

TM: *If buildings are thought of as sculptures, then these cubes work in a quite delightful way. But I don't accept buildings as sculptures or toys for individual use; they are objects of social use. And if use is to be "inscribed" in this totally free way, then what one is really saying is that one builds a sculpture/toy and* **turns it into a building through inventing uses for it. On rare occasions this might work. But in general this can only be done by deliberately removing all signification from buildings and allowing** *individuals to invest meaning in them by inventing uses. So it ceases to be a social object. As soon as a group or community invents a shared use, then any individual's freedom is removed.*

KAF: *Who experiences it as gibberish? Observers do not only discover meaning; they also create it. They even create or assign meanings to what* **appears** *meaningless.*

TM: *I experience it as gibberish! Assigning meanings to meaningless objects is a defense mechanism against being submerged by chaos. Of course we all do it so as not to drown. But to go out of our way to create this stress for others, and I'm talking about architectural objects, not art objects, seems to be irresponsible and dangerous.*

vists. But here these are supposed to be buildings: they enclose what is usable space. However, devoid of a defined functional program, for ideological reasons based on deconstructionist philosophy, they lack any recognizable point of reference in public life. In their most extreme versions such buildings are the architectural equivalents of gibberish.

The deep desire for connections in the discourses of architecture, achieved through connections with our social domain and "lifeworld," is a desire for a certain predictable order. Architecture has always been a matter of order-making through rules. So long as these rules behaved like language rules, made up and understood by a community of language speakers, with a firm structure that nevertheless allows each speaker the freedom to say something new every time he or she speaks, they were needed and acceptable. One aspect of the rules is the way they define types. It is when the rules become a straightjacket that creative thinkers react. Piranesi's *Carceri* etchings have nothing to do with real prisons. In many of them there is a light, rational upper world of classical order, sitting on an underground that is dark and full of paradoxical space and figures (Figure 8-7). It is that upper world and its rigid rules which imprisons the underworld of creative imagination and freedom.

Toward a New Typology

From Venturi to Derrida, conscious attempts have been made in recent decades to "deconstruct" function from form. With an ever-increasing emphasis on form, silence over space, and relegation of function to certain simple-minded notions of material processes, these attempts have partly succeeded in making the everyday street, urban industrial zone, and individual building as contradictory as were the early experiments.

On rare occasions the ability to disconnect and reconnect enables shatteringly new things to be said. This is possible even when, as in Scarpa's Verona Castelovecchio museum, the historical context of an existing building that needs to be conserved could so easily have imposed severe limitations. More often this freedom is either experienced as gibberish, or it leaves the door wide open to exploitation by any dominant ideology. I have already described the use of high-tech forms to redefine art.

Neoclassical language has been used in an attempt to convince us that the fly-by-night financial enterprises of London's Docklands have a solidity rooted in ancient culture. Of course to an extent this has always been true, especially in the use of the classical language. What is new is that the meanings are now much more difficult to unravel. At best, users of the new townscape have to construct, and live with, multiple typologies. They might have to remember, or try to communicate, this kind of experience: "I work in a clinic that has a classical temple entrance; its intestinal interior (full of shiny tubes and struts) feels like a factory or aircraft hangar; and I am in an office deep in space, to which I can get by a single route after passing through everyone else's space." Such multiple types are messy. And though they appear fragmented, each component is still rooted in the experience of use and hence in function-language.

So far the domain of social relations has been described as if it were two dimensional, so that it was possible to place a point in the circle of Figure 8-6. In reality it is multidimensional, and a point lies at the intersection of them all.

What is new is not that there are multiple dimensions of relationships — that has always been the case — but that the three architectural discourses are inadequate to represent new relations. If a cooperative workshop feels more like a community broadcasting station than a "factory," despite its machinery and processes being identical to those in the latter, then the designer is faced with having to match forms, functions, and spaces that are each associated with quite disparate meanings. The problem is to bring them together to produce unified and understandable meanings signifying the new relations of the workshop.

There are several steps in resolving this problem. First, it is necessary to be clear about the nature of the many dimensions present in social relations. Here is a suggestion for just a few dimensions: power/bonds; closed/open; constrained/free; hierarchical pyramids/nonhierarchical nets; centripetal/centrifugal; cooperative/competitive; conforming/subversive; traditional/innovative; tightly defined/loosely articulated; productive/existential; local (and spatial)/global (and transspatial); and institutional (strongly programmed)/negotiated (weakly programmed).

The second step is to find the correspondence between function words and points in this multidimensional space. Whether the word is an established one, such as "school" or "museum," or a new one, such as "cooperative workshop" or "health club," there are choices about what its meaning in terms of social relations should be: What is the intention? That is another way of saying that there is freedom about which point in multidimensional space the building should represent, and what *type* of building, with what *name*, represents this point.

KAF: *As long as it is understandable, does it have to be "unified"? Aren't multiple meanings acceptable if they seem to make sense and are not contradictory?*
TM: *The condition for "understanding" is convergence. Multiple meanings sounds like a euphemism for no meaning. And no meaning, in general, is not a good thing!*

RL: *Yes, languages do evolve, but not necessarily in tandem with other characteristics of human culture, including buildings. I think the disjunction between them could be discussed more. It is important not to accept the dogma that "the social" is necessarily mirrored by "the spatial." To me this kind of determinism underlies Hillier and Hanson's work, but this chapter suggests new avenues and new means to overcome this straightjacket approach.*
TM: *But the argument behind space syntax is exactly the opposite of this kind of "mirroring." It is that the organization of space, the creation of spatial structures, their use, and their interpretation are all social actions per se; they don't "mirror" anything. It is the main way in which society produces and reproduces itself in the material world, a primary social phenomenon in its own right.*

This chapter appears by permission of Routledge, London. It is a condensation of, and substantially the same as, Chapter 2 in Buildings and Power: Freedom and Control in the Origin of Modern Building Types *by the author, published by Routledge, London, 1993. It also draws on material from "Language Structure and Building Types" in the journal* Hordisk Arkitekturforskning *(1993) 4: 35–48.*

KAF: *Clearly the fragmentation has its advantages: it provides opportunities for change, variety, and flexibility. There is an increased possibility of new or modified types that are responsive to new social relations.*
TM: *The opportunity that fragmentation provides is for a creative new synthesis of the bits. Change, variety, and flexibility are not desirable per* se. *They are desirable means to the ends of new discoveries — i.e., new syntheses.*

The third and final step is to find typical conjunctions of form, function, and space that can both be described by a commonly used and understood function word, and that represent an intended point in the multidimensional domain of social relations. None of this is yet possible. We are not yet on the threshold of a new typology. On the one hand, traditional function words are being redefined; they are beginning to mean new relations. On the other hand, words for the new functions are not yet rooted in language. And as long as there is ambiguity from either cause about the words, the search for suitable conjunctions of form, function, and space is bound to remain highly tentative. Just what form and spatial structure should a "museum" or "health club" have? What functions do, or should, these words signify?

The daily experience of buildings, and ordinary language, do not yet converge either to encompass the relations of new functions or to encompass the new relations of old functions. The fragmentation has given immense freedom as well as immense opportunities for chaos. For the time being we are stuck with fragmented typologies. But language remains the safe anchor that enables us to make a response to authentic innovation while protecting us against those that threaten self and society with disintegration.

References

Blondel, J.F. 1771-77. *Cours d' architecture… donnée en 1750 et les années suivantes*. Paris.

Boullée, E.T. [c.1781–97] 1974. *Architecture: Essay on Art*. Translated and edited by H. Rosenau. London: Academy Editions.

Eco, U. 1986. Function and sign: semiotics of architecture. In *The City and the Sign: an Introduction to Urban Semiotics*, eds. M. Gottdiener and A.P. Lagopoulos. New York: Columbia University Press.

Gorz, A. 1989. *Critique of Economic Reason*. Translated by G. Handyside and C. Turner. London: Verso.

Hillier, B. and J. Hanson. 1984. *The Social Logic of Space*. Cambridge: Cambridge University Press.

Husserl, E. 1970. *The Crisis of European Sciences and Transcendental Phenomenology: An Introduction to Phenomenological Philosophy*. Translated by D. Carr. Evanston, Ill.: Northwestern University Press.

Levi, P. 1962. *If This Is a Man*. Translated by S. Wolf. London: New English Library.

Markus, T. 1987. Buildings as classifying devices. *Environment and Planning B: Planning and Design* 14: 467–84.

Stark, W. 1807. *Remarks on Public Hospitals for the Cure of Mental Derangements, etc.* Edinburgh: James Ballantyne and Co.

Chapter 9

Typological Thinking in Architectural Practice

Martin Symes

This chapter discusses the ways in which architects use typological thinking in professional work. It identifies for this purpose three particular components of design practice: the adoption of a design method or approach, the use of spatial types, and the use of functional typologies. The first provides a way of defining the architect's relationship with a professional context; the second provides vehicles for the storage and transmission of architectural knowledge and experience; the third provides a framework for the codification of user needs. The interaction between these various kinds of type are illustrated with three case studies. The case studies focus on moments of transition between stages of the design process, because the use of types is especially helpful to designers when such transitions prove problematic.

Designers first choose an approach. This may be to make rational decisions, to involve users in design participation, or to follow subjective experience. Then designers must explore the variety of spatial forms they may propose and also consider the various functions the anticipated building may contain. Their task is to use the chosen approach to bring the spatial and functional "futures" into a meaningful relationship with each other. Thus architects typically try to negotiate a match of some kind between use and spatial organization within the professional

JR: *To what extent designers consciously "choose" their modus operandi is not clear. In fact, few designers seem to be able to discuss their methods clearly because only* some *architectural decisions are made consciously. Very often conflicts are resolved through insights that appear to be without roots in conscious, rational decision making.*

position they have adopted. They have a certain kind of relationship with their clients, they may be predisposed to follow one of a number of compositional principles, and the functional specification may be for new or established needs. Architects' use of types helps them bring these aspects of the design problem together: this is their professional skill. In exercising it they achieve the wider goals of economic viability, social legitimacy, and personal self-expression.

The case studies presented in this chapter are drawn from an ongoing program of research into the changing shape of architectural practice. The life histories of a selection of architectural firms have been established and the design development of a number of their projects has been reported. In this chapter, various incidents from these projects have been selected for further analysis.

These case studies suggest that design processes do not flow continuously or easily from one day to the next. They are by their nature discontinuous, with times of ready or easy development and times of difficulty, confusion, delay, and conflict. In these breaks between different phases of a design process, a great deal can be learned about the thought process involved. The use of typological thinking can be most readily identified and assessed at these times of transition.

Type and the Professional Practice of Architecture

In architectural practice, each project is divided into a number of sub-tasks. In each of these, standards and norms can be identified. Concept design competitions may, for example, be won by adopting an established and well-regarded outline design concept. Feasibility studies usually depend on applying knowledge gained from previous experience with the same building problem. Early phases of interior design make assumptions about the standards that will be applied in planning small areas. The development of construction details often hinges on the study of current technology; legal requirements are embodied in codes of practice; communication with building contractors is facilitated through drawing conventions; building materials are ordered with standard specifications. All these are examples of typological thinking and can be seen as having some of the strengths and weaknesses that derive from it.

The moments of transition from one sub-task, or phase, of a project to another are often problematic. At these points in time a design project can come to a crisis. The approach to professional practice may suddenly seem problematic. The compositional principles adopted and the functional programs developed may

GF: Perhaps the most valuable contribution of a typological view of architecture is that it substitutes unity *of form and use for the duality implied in the concept of organizing a "match" between the two. Architectural types embody that unity and the architect's principal skill is not in reconciling varied and often contradictory requirements, but in proposing forms that contain both the redundance of known environmental configurations/uses and the challenge of new ones.*

MS: I understand the word typology *to have two meanings: the study of types (i.e., their classification and description) and the study of a type (i.e., its investigation and interpretation). It is quite clear that in practice architects do both these things and do them with respect to various objects (e.g., client requirements, building forms, etc.). Some types of architecture may make it easier for architects to resolve the conflicts between, for example, types of client requirement and types of building form than others; you mean that these are better* types of architecture.

JR: It is an open question to what extent the identifiable sub-tasks relate to actual decision making and to the criteria used to make decisions. Stated typologies may reveal or hide what is actually going on. It is important to compare actual actions with expressed typologies to discover matches and disparities.

GF: These are examples of typological thinking in that categorization and classification are used. But in this sense all thinking is typological! In architecture, the concept of type inevitably retains the taxonomical kernel that lies at the root of the term, but is carried well beyond it through the link between architectural form and its historical precedent — with all this implies for the social and cultural significance of the architectural object.

MS: Of course, architectural objects are socially and culturally created: so too, probably, are the typologies we can use to describe them. But this applies outside architecture as well. On the other hand, many societies and cultures allow us to think non-typologically as well.

JR: *If designers do define an "irreducible core," this could be very revealing. It would be interesting to study what is left out when this core is defined by a given designer. That would go a long way toward defining the values and approaches of a particular architect or group of architects.*

GF: *That the* idea *of type is simultaneously "vague and precise" has been often remarked. But it does not follow that types themselves lack specificity. On the contrary, as Muratori pointed out for urban typologies, architectural types cannot avert specificity because they are developed in particular geographic, social, and cultural contexts. True, Quatremère de Quincy regarded type as "more or less vague," but by this he clearly meant to stress the difference between type and model, the first embodying the "rules" for the generation of the object, the latter the mere reproduction of an object. The reason that a type permits modification, adaptation, and ultimately even its own expiration in the birth of a new type is not its vagueness, but rather the fact that a type is not a model.*
MS: *The argument I am putting forth here is that types* are *specific as well as general and that this characteristic is useful for practice. On the second point, I prefer a rather different meaning for the word model: namely, that it is a simplified description of reality.*

unexpectedly begin to conflict. When these problems arise it may seem that further progress on the design has been blocked. One of the best ways of overcoming such a crisis is for the designer to simplify the set of design decisions that have already been made until only an irreducible core remains. The new perspective that is needed for the development of the project can be built upon the basis of this core, which becomes a framework within which other details can then be reconsidered.

Such core decisions should be concerned with types. The approach to the project should be thought of as a *type of practice*. The physical arrangement should be considered as a *spatial type* and the functional specification as a *type of use*. Then the essential basis of compatibility between these aspects of the design can be more clearly identified. The approach can be simplified or refined. Spatial details and details of use can be reconsidered and a way forward can be found for the development of the design. The clarification of fundamentals offered by typologies of approach, space, and use makes them essential to practice. The flexibility of detailed development that they allow is of considerable value to modern practice. The use of typological thinking offers great advantages in the solution of complex design problems.

Schön (1988) described the rules sometimes used in design protocols as deriving from "underlying types... that serve as 'holding environments' for... knowledge." Types summarize and hold together a whole range of already interpreted information about the detailed implications of possible actions. They offer a "shortcut" that can be economically sensible for producing a form, educationally satisfactory for explaining ideas to clients, and personally reassuring to the professionals themselves if they fear the risk associated with innovation.

Another, and complementary, advantage of typologies to design practice is to be found in Vidler's discussion of the notion of type in architectural theory. This is its adaptability, or lack of specificity. Vidler's article begins by characterizing "the idea of type in architectural theory... (as having an)... omnibus meaning of concept, essential form, and building type," and continues with the comment that "the word 'type' [is] a term whose peculiar etymology and history of use lent itself especially well to an idea that was vague and precise at the same time" (Vidler 1989, 147).

Vidler means to refer to the philosophical origins and theoretical uses of the word *type* in the architectural discourse of the late eighteenth century. But today's reader might also note that ideas that have that combination of vagueness and precision to which Vidler points undoubtedly have some value for problem solving in practice.

The precision of a type allows one to make an urgent decision and carry on with the design process; to put further marks on the blank sheet of paper even though problems have set in. But the vagueness of a type allows such a decision to be incomplete, and as yet poorly perceived, only a starting point for considering further decisions. A skillful and successful design firm will develop the ability to know when and how to exploit one of these characteristics in its use of types, and when another.

The evidence reported in the following case studies suggests nonetheless that this flexibility can also bring certain difficulties to contemporary practitioners. A typology can always be debated and its constituent types questioned. If it lacks conviction, the approach taken or the matching of function with form that has been proposed will become problematic. Progress on resolving design dilemmas will become more difficult rather than less. Typologies bring ambiguity as well as flexibility to architectural practice. For designers looking for certainty, or needing to display confidence to their clients, there can be great disadvantages to typological thinking. Advantages and disadvantages of typological thinking can be found in all three of the aspects of design practice mentioned in the introduction to this chapter.

In their design approach an architectural firm will probably mix rational decision making with consultation, team work, and precedent analysis. They can use their experience to judge which should predominate in a given professional context. When the design process reaches key stages they may be challenged to justify these choices. Then it should be possible for the designers to fall back on key decisions taken by their own, or their clients', preferred method. Those that fall outside this type may have to be abandoned, or reconsidered. Such moments include the beginning of the project, when the designer faces a blank sheet of paper and must consider how it is to be filled, as well as later stages in any lengthy construction process.

Buildings take between one and 12 years to design and build. Hospitals are the most complex, but even a small house may stay on the drawing board for many years if the client's dream to build is not backed up by sufficient funds. A typology of design approaches can suggest methods of keeping design development on track during this time and of progressing to the next stage when there have been interruptions or delays. Equally, without some method for tracking design, there is a risk that the selected type of approach will be abandoned at an intermediate stage, and that experience stored up in the results of the earlier process will be forgotten.

GF: *From the perspective of a typological theory of architecture, it is impossible to talk about advantages and disadvantages of typological thinking since it holds that architectural thinking is always typological. Moreover, placing the idea of type in the context of convenience or expediency seems to trivialize it whether or not one subscribes to typological theory.*
MS: *Even if all architectural thinking were typological, and that could only be the case if architecture were defined very narrowly, expedience and convenience are far from trivial reasons for its use.*

JR: *Presently, I am not aware of a "typology of design approaches." However, having a typology of approaches seems like a good idea for your research. If these could be developed, and I am not sanguine about the ease of this task, they would be very useful for designers because they would present the opportunity for more conscious selection of modes of approach.*

JR: *You seem to suggest that there is one kind of typological thinking. I suspect you are talking here about "normative" typological thinking where types are taken to be immutable and unchanging.*
MS: *No, I'm thinking of the kind of research that tries to find the dimensions by which a range of possibilities can be elaborated. Changes in context may sometimes mean that research has to be reconsidered. Whether or not it is used normatively, or even becomes a norm itself, is a rather different question.*

JR: *The choice between adopting an established type or starting again is one of the modern fallacies. There are other ways of using types. They may be redefined; they may be combined. Types, in my view, are not immutable but changing, and in fact evolve to reflect change. This too is an interesting subject of research. Think of the single-family house in Victorian times and today.*
MS: *By "starting again" I include "altering," which you quite rightly say often occurs. When a type becomes "established" this means, usually, that its use is very strongly reinforced by social pressures or customs. I suppose professionals are often caught in a dilemma here: whether to follow the customs of their peers or to declare their independence! Would not this have applied to Hawksmoor as well as to Frank Lloyd Wright?*

GF: *Not surprisingly, type has often been confused with an architecture of convention. Yet nothing in the idea of type suggests the formula or the recipe. In fact, because type represents a bound entity of form and use, adopting "the same physical form for a whole range of building problems" is an inadmissible solution from a typological viewpoint.*
MS: *It should be clear that I am using the word* type *generically and do not mean to imply a specific, metaphysical connection between particular typologies. The great thing about people is that they often operate quite flexibly. Thank goodness most architects can be included in this statement.*

The use of functional types also has its advantages and disadvantages. Advantages clearly accrue when one statement of the design requirements for a building function can become the model for the programming of other projects. A statement of use type can provide a starting point with general validity even while many applications can be made to specific building tasks. The rationalism of modern architectural theory has supported this approach.

There is a functional typology for mass housing, schools, railway stations, and department stores. Each type within them can be adapted to site conditions, budgets, and local patterns of need. Economy of effort and a sense that the acceptability of the built result can be predicted are obvious benefits. So too are the possibilities of establishing long-term building plans and of training practitioners to specialize in particular kinds of use.

But typologies of use can also become outdated and redundant. Changes in society's expectations have thrown millions of hours of work on housing types into question; fundamental changes in medical or educational technology can do the same for hospital and school typologies; even developments in computing equipment can have quite radical effects on our thinking about types of office space. In these circumstances, typological thinking becomes a drag on problem solving instead of a stimulus to it.

It may seem difficult to evaluate the part played by spatial types in the work of the architectural profession. We recognize that many architectural firms come up with roughly the same physical form for a whole range of building problems. There are, again, advantages for the firm and for the client in this phenomenon. The firm can market itself and the client can select a designer. Design and building times can be predicted with some degree of accuracy, and costs can be estimated more reliably. Even architectural critics value the opportunities designers create for refining their buildings' aesthetic. But history is also replete with examples of tired applications of inappropriate formulae to architectural production. One sign of a successful professional may be the skill to know when to adopt an established spatial type and when to start again.

These paragraphs have outlined certain major advantages and disadvantages of typological thinking for three key aspects of architectural practice: the adoption of a design method, use of spatial types, and use of functional typologies. It can be argued that referring to existing types is not strictly necessary: that it is always possible to think every problem through from the beginning, to create a fresh solution to each challenge, and to take high risks of being unable to carry an idea through.

Sometimes architects do indeed dare to do just this. But the culture of architecture as a practical profession is made from mixing such innovative creativity with the use of standards, norms, and models. A number of recognized typologies inform this mixture; their use seems to help architects work in a complex modern society. The case studies that follow will show some of the ways this happens.

Case Studies

An ongoing series of research projects has included the development of case studies of architectural design practice. Of special interest here are incidents that show how the typological choices made by a firm solving practical problems in different aspects of a single project are linked to each other. The first case shows this kind of connection.

Experience in researching architects' behavior has suggested that the clearest picture of the choices they make emerges from studying crises in the design process. These are times when there are real difficulties in reaching a decision, but there is an urgent necessity to do so. The second case study concentrates on the use of types on such an occasion.

Typologies that are both precise and vague allow decisions to be made that close off certain options at the same time that they allow further flexibility in developments which are to follow. The third case study shows how, *in extremis*, the ambiguity of typological choices can even lead to the abandonment of a project's original ideals.

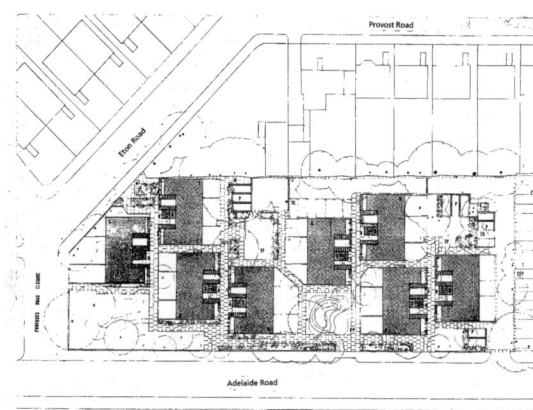

9-1
Site Plan of Adelaide Road, Chalk Farm, Camden
(source: Marmot and Symes 1987a)

Adelaide Road

The first case study is drawn from a participatory design approach to public housing in central London in which special spatial form was developed for the project. The case shows how these two choices of type interacted with each other.

Over the last 30 years there have been many calls for a more sensitive approach to housing design for low income groups by involving users in the design of their residential environment. This has happened largely in response to protests by outraged communities who found that their homes were to be demolished, without consultation, as part of a slum clearance program. They objected to the breaking up of communities, to the need for many people to try to find replacement housing without assistance, and to the lack of choices in the location and type of new council housing that they were allocated.

Public participation has become a common type of planning process in Britain. Large-scale housing projects cannot now be implemented without some form of consultation; but the active involvement of residents in the design of their own houses is still rare. It is argued that only the very wealthy can afford the luxury of a custom-designed home, so most people must be content to select their homes from the highly conventional types of solutions offered by private developers or from the often idiosyncratic conversions undertaken by private landlords.

Although architects in the public sector may think they have an opportunity to improve on this situation, they are sometimes told that residents cannot be involved as it is impossible to identify them in advance and design for their needs. There are very few examples of new local authority housing where the residents have been actively engaged in design or construction. The Greater London Council's most publicized participatory scheme was that at Adelaide Road, derived from Nicholas Habraken's (1972) ideas about "support structures."

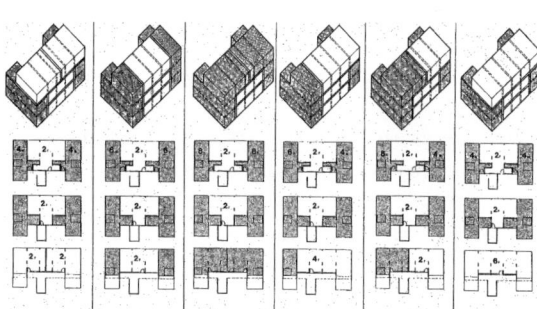

9-2
Diagram showing different possible dwelling mixes in standard block, Adelaide Road
(Source: Marmot and Symes 1987a)

JR: *It is interesting to speculate whether this is a spatial type or a construction type. I would argue for the latter.*

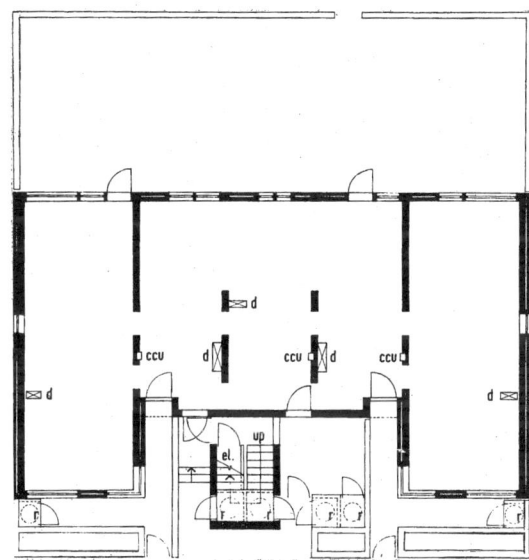

9-3
Plan and model of PSHAAK's basic structural shell, Adelaide Road (source: Marmot and Symes 1987a)

Adelaide Road was developed as a spatial type, as well as a type of approach for this type of function, by Nabeel Hamdi while he was a student at the Architectural Association. The spatial solution involves the separation of the main structure of the building (support structure) from the internal fitting out of the dwelling (assembly kit). With the use of the adjustable parts of the kit, the number and size of rooms in a dwelling could be modified to accommodate the functional type of each family, at the same time satisfying the need for a participatory approach.

The Adelaide Road scheme, now known as Beaumont Walk, was built between 1976 and 1979. It is located next to a conservation area, with good transport services by bus and underground. Primrose Hill and Regent's Park are nearby.

The approach necessitated an incremental design process. The first participatory step was to invite a number of families from the council's waiting list to a meeting at which the principles of the scheme were described. The building shells were already nearing completion, but no decisions had yet been made about interior layout. At the meeting, the opportunities and limitations of this spatial type were pointed out. Until potential residents accepted these limitations and agreed to continue with the process, no detailed functional types could be specified. Only very general ideas of the broad area requirements of council tenants had been known.

Those potential tenants who still wished to take part were issued a manual comprising a step-by-step explanation of what was involved in the design process and a detailed checklist that asked for their requirements. They were given a simple set of drawings of their allotted space on which to sketch their ideas. After a couple of weeks, small groups of residents met the architect on site to discuss these proposals for interior design.

The combination of a participatory approach to housing design with a "shell and scenery" spatial solution produced certain problems. The architect found it was extremely time-consuming to deal personally with the tenants, many of whom kept changing their minds up to the last minute. Dealing with fire and building regulations was also quite complicated due to the variety of layouts, and the council departments involved showed resistance to this new way of working. The architect claimed that there should be a minimal difference in costs between this type of building and traditional methods; savings in design and construction time would be possible by the use of simplified procedures; and in the long term, savings should be considerable as the system easily lent itself to modification and modernization. But these advantages were never quantified.

This example of typological thinking in the design approach, as well as in the generation of functional and spatial solutions, suggests that one role for the architect is to keep developments on each aspect in balance as the design progresses. It is perhaps not surprising, therefore, that the designer here saw his task as that of a negotiator or enabler, using his special expertise to interpret people's needs and marry them with regulatory and constructional possibilities.

Northwick Park Hospital

The second case is drawn from the bureaucratic design process of a large hospital complex in the northern suburbs of London. To begin with, there seemed to be a clear position at the level of design approach and building function. Difficulties emerged, however, when it became necessary to find spatial types for certain parts of the complex. The case deals with one of these problems; specifically, the design of the consulting area of the outpatients' department. It shows how a core spatial decision had to be clarified before progress could be made on specifying the functional type in more detail.

A novel feature of the 800-bed Northwick Park Hospital as a functional type was that it combined a district hospital with a large clinical research center supported by the Medical Research Council. This composite functional type was intended both to give patients the benefits of access to the latest developments in diagnostic and treatment facilities, and also to give research workers the advantage of ready contact with everyday medical problems. Detailed design required innovative layout solutions to many of the specialist areas as well as lengthy negotiations with the different groups involved in decision making.

Despite the fact that its bureaucratic approach had to cope with unusual spatial types, the design of this vast, complicated, and expensive building project seemed to proceed remarkably smoothly. Northwick Park's architects, Llewellyn-Davies and Partners, had long been concerned with the need to provide an "indeterminate architecture," which resulted in "multistrategy" buildings. Everyone on the building team was committed to seeing the building on the ground as quickly as possible and had accepted a very general design type with enthusiasm. But as more detailed spatial decisions began to be discussed, team consensus appeared to break down. Administrators did not always agree with doctors, doctors had different ideas of their space requirements, and the nurses had different ideas again. The agreed-upon design began to seem problematic.

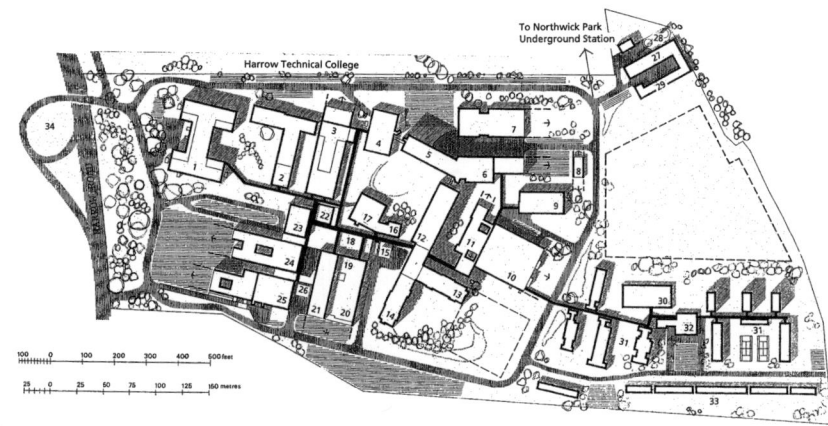

9-4
Site plan, Northwick Park Hospital (source: Marmot and Symes 1987b)

1 Maternity unit
2 Psychological Medicine (Psychiatry)
3 Rehabilitation unit (Physical Medicine)
4 Library, Lecture hall
5 Medical illustration
6 Clinical Research Institute
7 Animal house (Animal accommodations)
8 Radiochemistry (Radiochemical laboratory)
9 Isolation unit
10 Operating theatres
11 Recovery unit
12 North wing (Clinical Research Centre wards)
13 East wing (Medical/Surgical wards)
14 South wing (Medical/Surgical wards)
15 Chapel
16 Clinical lecture theatre
17 Staff dining rooms
18 Central kitchens
19 Pharmacy
20 X-Ray: Central supply under
21 Pathology
22 Shopping square
23 Administration: main entrance
24 Outpatient department
25 Accident and Emergencies: Mortuary under
26 Supplies delivery
27 Boiler house
28 Oil storage
29 Maintenance department
30 School of Nursing (Nurses' training school)
31 Staff residences
32 Common rooms
33 Staff houses
34 Flyover

One of the main buildings on the site was to be the outpatient department. It was close to the main hospital entrance and administration, to the accident and emergency department, and to the diagnostic and pharmacy building. It had been sited to permit future expansion to the west, should the need arise. Patients would come to the outpatient department to consult a specialist before admission as inpatients, for consultation after they had been discharged, or for specialist diagnosis without ever being admitted to the hospital. The unit at Northwick Park would have to handle 150,000 attendances each year – i.e., 300 patients, on average, were to be seen during each half-day session. The spatial solution would have to reconcile the needs of patients, doctors, and nurses, and be flexible and economical.

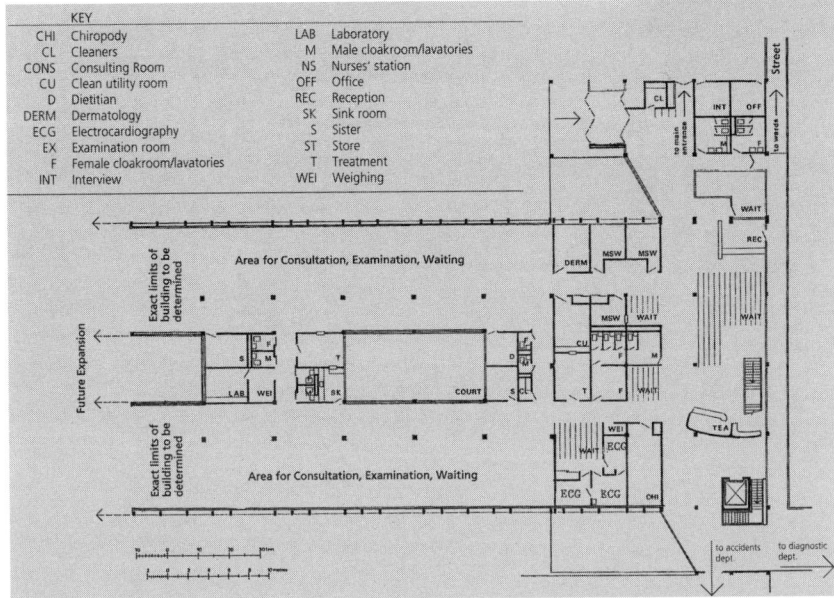

9-5
Plan of Out-Patients' Department, Northwick Park Hospital (source: Marmot and Symes 1987b)

9-6
Generic arrangements of consulting and examination areas, Northwick Park Hospital (source: Marmot and Symes 1987b)

JR: *It is debatable whether the solution is spatial in that it seems to involve plan relationships rather than three-dimensional spatial ones. These could also be called functional solutions since they are dealing primarily with functional relationships that are manifested in spatial terms.*

During the debate it emerged that opinions on the functional requirements were not unanimous. An important research study favored a system of identical consultation/examination rooms grouped as intercommunicating suites. This arrangement, it was felt, gave maximum flexibility of use for different specialties. It might also give patients the advantage of continuous consultation with their doctors. This was the form of room used in private consultancy, and was therefore assumed to be the most comfortable for patients. Doctors who tried using this

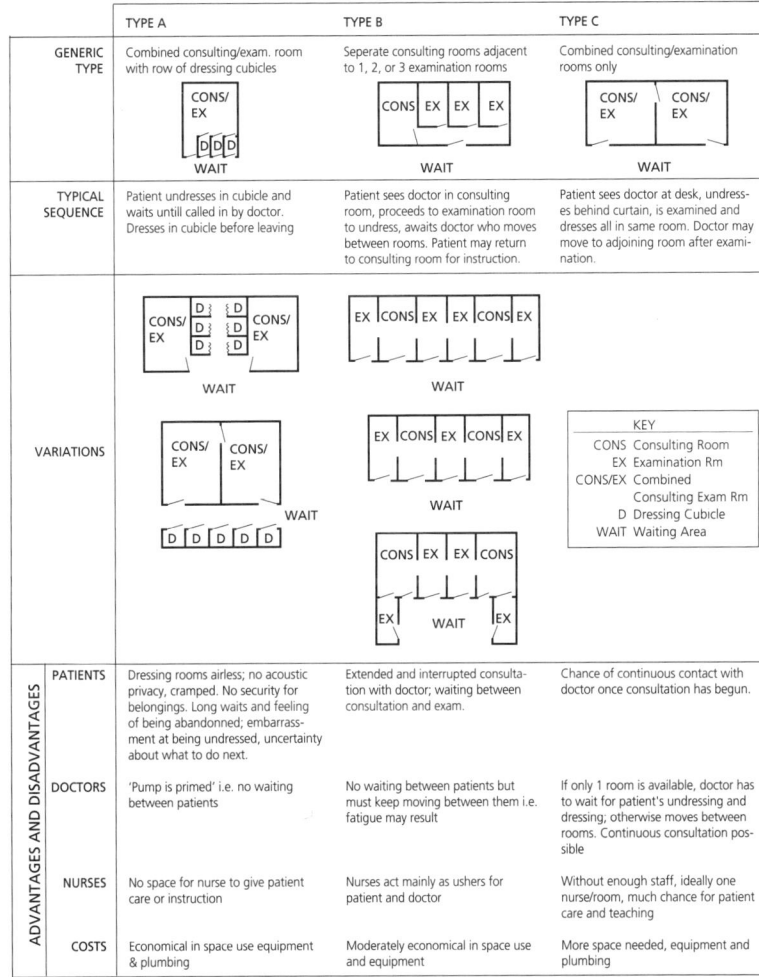

TYPOLOGICAL THINKING IN ARCHITECTURAL PRACTICE   **173**

arrangement, instead of one where they moved between consulting and examination rooms, were surprised to find that they were able to use the time patients took to undress or dress quite effectively by writing notes, and that they were considerably less fatigued at the end of a session than when moving several times between patients in the course of each consultation. Rather than wasting time waiting for patients, some doctors were able to increase their patient load each session.

The department of the English government financing the hospital favored a second spatial type with examination rooms separated from an office for consultation. However, the Scottish Health Department (SHD) had concurred with the research study in selecting the former type. In making that recommendation, however, the SHD assumed a third functional type. They wanted all procedures involving the patient to be carried out in one room, but expected the doctor to move between rooms if necessary. A nurse would be allocated to each room to help patients in dressing and undressing and to ensure that the doctor's advice was correctly understood. However, this was by far the most expensive solution and the architects were not sure that the arrangement would be accepted by other members of the project team. If they could not recommend a suitable spatial solution, they might find themselves unable to help their clients settle their functional priorities and the project might be unacceptably delayed.

Ultimately, the architects suggested what seemed like a compromise: divide the outpatients' area into two parts, with one part planned in the way suggested by research, and the other part planned using the cheaper type favored by the client ministry. At a more fundamental level, however, the overall building design concept, a "street" with a number of different sections of accommodation attached to it, could be maintained. The "core" spatial type could be seen to be sufficiently robust to accommodate a variety of detailed spatial types in different parts of the complex. With this framework established again, the functional crisis could be settled.

Riding for the Disabled

The third case is drawn from a crisis of confidence that arose when the contract between a design-building firm and its community service client came due for renewal. It had appeared that approach, function, and spatial types had been settled, but in the end, all three had to be altered. The disadvantages of flexibility outweighed its advantages in this instance.

The building project had as its client a Bristol-based charity, The Avon Riding Center for the Disabled, or RDAvon. This was, in turn, affiliated with a national charity whose aim was to promote riding for disabled people. The organization had plenty of experience to draw on, but few resources. Its advisers were mainly volunteers, and they sought innovation in the type of approach adopted as well as in the functional program and, by implication, spatial arrangement. They first approached a local design and building firm, Form Structures, to prepare a feasibility study, examining a number of sites in and around Bristol where a center could be built. At the same time they set up local "disabled" and "building" subcommittees to negotiate with Form on the functional and spatial details of the project proposals. On these committees, RDAvon had a range of people with a wealth of valuable experience and contacts in different areas. There were architects on each of the subcommittees, solicitors, estate agents, etc. RDAvon set up an office on Form's premises, and appointed a fund-raiser to obtain funding for the new building, and a member of staff to liaise with Form as the project got slowly off the ground. But the unusual spatial type adopted stretched the abilities of this elaborate and underfunded approach to architect-client organization interaction too far. The flexible solution types selected early in the process eventually had to be abandoned and replaced by tried and tested methods.

The Riding Center's successfully completed first phase consisted of an indoor riding school, access arrangements, and initial landscaping. The master plan Form Structures prepared showed additional facilities on the site and RDAvon now had to consider whether they should continue with the future phases.

The approach adopted had been as follows. After site feasibility studies and briefs had been drawn up, and a design solution prepared and costed, Form Structures's cost consultant deducted the following: first, the cost of labor, since the project was to be built with labor funded by the Government's Manpower Services Commission, and second, a sum to cover savings they thought could be made on site. The drainage, for example, was costed very cheaply because the contractor was able to use the site as a demonstration area. To this rock-bottom price was added only a percentage fee for overhead. There were obvious advantages to this degree of flexibility, provided it could be combined with a sound judgment of the possibilities for completing the project to the functional standard required.

JR: This seems to be a purer example of spatial type in that it is clearly a fully three-dimensional concept.

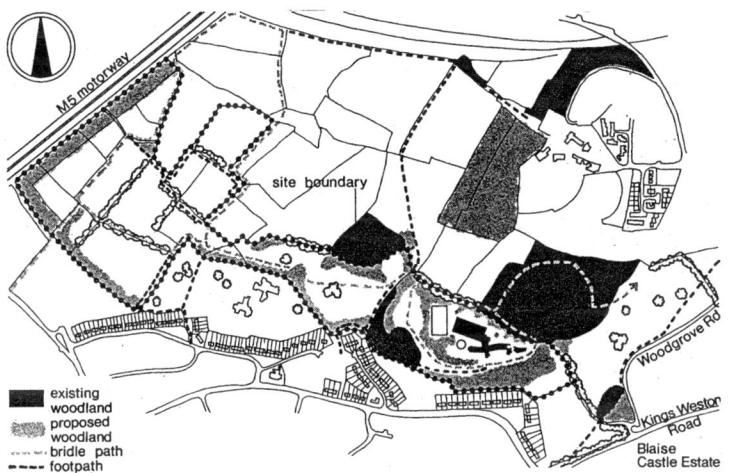

9-7
Plan of the riding school complex for Avon Riding Center for the Disabled (source: Clelford and Symes 1987)

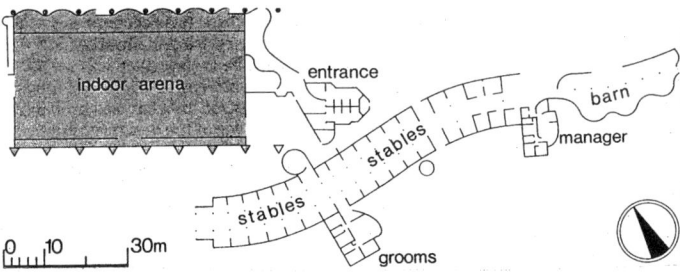

9-8
Ground plan of buildings for the riding school as proposed. Arena as built shown shaded (source: Clelford and Symes 1987)

During the construction of Phase I, Form Structures continued to alter the details of the spatial solution when they could make savings of money or time. For example, they were able to obtain cheap steel components for the roof trusses and have them bolted together on site by a relatively inexperienced labor force instead of having them professionally prefabricated off site. Unfortunately RDAvon had never really known what building would result, and was concerned that the functional type they were expecting would not materialize. Form Structures's flexibility seemed too great to them.

The first phase of the Riding Center was handed over with public acclaim and much mutual backslapping, but, at the time when decisions were needed about Phase II, it was not yet open for use. Some basic facilities still had to be provided; for example, stabling and viewing seats had been considered either as additions to the building contract or as emerging out of somebody's goodwill and generosity in a temporary form. These and other facilities were to have been provided more permanently by the subsequent phases of the building program, but this could not start until the client had raised the money. And to raise the money, RDAvon needed to have an "operational" building as a showpiece – potentially a vicious circle. The building was "finished but incomplete." Its functional type was, in practice, changing from prestige stadium to neighborhood shed.

There was a strong challenge to Form Structures's initial approach. The client's "disabled" subcommittee claimed there were major and possibly insoluble design flaws in the spatial scheme for Phase II previously agreed upon. It argued that more design work and amended planning and building regulation approvals would be needed. The "building" subcommittee became concerned about window details and about a lack of space between the stables and the arena entrance. Then RDA's national sponsor, the disability advisory committee, said they required an enlarged treatment room, additional special bathrooms, and a new draught lobby and exit. It was also suggested that horses should be mounted from the right, not the left. The original design approach, and functional programming, were seriously questioned through these attacks on the spatial form.

At the beginning there had been consensus. The initial stage of the building was planned to Olympic space standards, agreed upon by all. The problem now was that the rest of the premises had to provide sufficient facilities (in scope, size, and quality) to service it. That would mean an extended commitment of time, money, and effort by all concerned, and not just for new building work, but for external works like the nature trail, landscaping, and other work in future stages.

More work would also be required for the eventual staffing and running of the Riding Center. For the client, this would mean years more of fund-raising and construction work. The expert and the professional members of the RDAvon sub-committees all had their own ideas about where time and money could be saved, both on the design and during construction. It was difficult for their lay colleagues to appreciate that architecture or good design need not cost more. They saw the need for a different approach altogether: for conventional tendering and for the use of standard designs, even a greatly simplified functional program.

There was also a feeling that the subsequent phases of the work should be seen publicly to be "value for money," and that this would result from the use of more traditional methods. Of course, the charity would still want to take full advantage of the goodwill of individuals or firms, of grants, government aid, etc. Like every building purchaser, they understandably wanted, and justifiably expected, the most for the least outlay. Of course, the designers and the local authority wanted a building of obvious merit on a prominent and environmentally important site. It seemed that the innovative design approach was not satisfying these expectations. The level of uncertainty was too great. More familiar functional and spatial types would have to be selected.

Form Structures was thus persuaded to redesign Phase II of their RDAvon project. They adopted more conventional building plans and put the construction contract out to competitive tender from other companies. Types can give flexibility, but they must be defended when necessary on the basis of the store of established knowledge they transmit. In this case, that defense could not be sustained, and the types adopted had to be replaced.

Conclusions to the Case Studies

These incidents, drawn from case studies of architectural practice, indicate the kinds of occasions in which design problems arise. In broad terms, this is when the process moves from one level of detail to another, or from one stage to the next. Types must be clarified at these points in time. The cases show how a participatory, a bureaucratic, and an innovative cooperative approach coped with such moments of crisis.

In the example of Adelaide Road, the architects had to innovate to produce well-designed participatory housing. They convinced a client body that this was a viable approach when conventional wisdom might have suggested otherwise. They used a participatory housing solution developed by other architects to do so, but gained personal satisfaction from defining their own role in its implementation creatively. They established a clear position for the project, linking types of approach, function, and spatial solution with each other.

The incidents also show that design processes include a sequence of problem-solving activities. These often consist of defining the relationships between different aspects of the project in ever more detail. The knowledge stored in types must be brought out and specified so that those concerned can be certain they can remain on track. The cases show that this detailed development may originate in a lack of understanding of a spatial principle, in an argument over functional preferences, or in disappointment over the results of a design approach. Thus the spatial flexibility in the design of Northwick Park concealed a functional problem which could only be resolved at a late stage in the process, when detailed design was under way. The bureaucratic approach to this complex project seems not to have impeded the clarification of types necessary to allow this to happen.

In addition, the incidents raise questions about the advantages and disadvantages of the use of typological thinking in architectural practice. Types seem to underlie much of what architects propose, and this sometimes makes communication with clients of various kinds easier than it otherwise might be. On some occasions, the flexibility of a type sets the scene for the resolution of difficult programming or design problems.

But on other occasions that very flexibility becomes a liability; excessive ambiguity leads to uncertainty and confusion. Types have many virtues but also some vices. The prime example given here is that of Form Structures. In overcoming their crisis with RDAvon, they changed contractual methods as well as building designs and the functional program. They replaced the innovative types used earlier with more conventional methods. It could be argued that the flexibility of those initial types meant that when a serious crisis arose, all could be changed. On the other hand, perhaps it was their lack of detail that made redesigning necessary.

Implications of Type for the Social Enterprise of Architecture

These conclusions lead us back to a discussion of the place of typological thinking in helping architects overcome the difficulties of achieving their psychological, social, and economic goals. Three particular observations seem relevant to this perspective.

JR: *The idea of typology assumes, I would think, that the idea of a type is shared. But here you seem to call that into question. To what extent and in what ways do the visions concur or differ?*

MS: *What I am suggesting is that when different social groups operate independently, they may develop different typologies, but when they work together they may have to negotiate new ones.*

9-9
Riding school interior in use by local mounted police force (source: Clelford and Symes 1987)

The first is that although individual architects naturally aim to gain some sense of satisfaction from doing the job well, they cannot always gain this from believing that their design is all artistry, that personal interpretations of a problem must always be developed, or that personal expressions of a possible solution must always be offered. Clearly, for a designer working on a number of projects over a period of time, it is unlikely that each project will allow, or demand, the same level of subjective intervention. If personal satisfaction is to be achieved from a different kind of creative involvement, it may derive in part from the feeling that designers can both draw on, and contribute to, a fund of knowledge they can use, and adapt. They can develop their personal vision within a tradition to which others also contribute. Indeed, a typological understanding of design approaches suggests that the ideas offered by building owners or users (through design participation), by other professionals (in design negotiations), or by objective criteria generated from other aspects of the context (in rational decision making), all allow for designers to build on the experience of others.

A second observation is that any design organization, whether working in the private market or the public sector, must legitimate itself. It must be able to justify its right to offer its particular services to others. Here, a typology of building functions helps. A firm may claim to work well with housing residents if it is their needs which generate the design requirement; it may claim to integrate its own design concepts well with those of other businesses if it is charged with creating workplace design; or it may say that it offers well-informed and scientifically valid methods if it has to tackle complex urban problems. In general, an architectural firm may say that part of its skill is in knowing enough about previously produced solutions to advise on when they may be applied, without further ado, to a new building task.

A third important observation on the value of typological thinking to architectural practice is concerned with its economic viability. Each designer or design group (and of course, one of these may consist of hundreds of highly trained people) must survive: it must be able to maintain itself financially, or to be maintained by others. A design group cannot always expect those representing users of a future building to pay the full cost of a design thought out from first principles in all its parts. A design group cannot always expect to be paid for the full costs of considering the impact on its design of the constraints imposed by planners, engineers, surveyors, and contractors. A design group cannot always persuade its patron that a comprehensive set of investigations should be mounted before any design decision is made. It can – and arguably should – benefit from its experience of other similar design problems, or learn from appropriate precedents. It will clearly do this by its use of types.

The need for designers to be satisfied with their artistry, for society to recognize the legitimacy of their services, and for the economy to support it, also encourages the use of types in architectural practice. The case studies included in this chapter suggest that the main virtues of types are their ability both to hold a store of experience and to permit a flexible response to the complex design problems architects often face. Architects and their clients should, nonetheless, be aware that in some circumstances a type's ambiguity will confuse decisions and negate these benefits.

The case study material was prepared in collaboration with Alexi Marmot and Anthony Clelford. This work formed part of a research project which received financial support from the Nuffield Foundation and from the Architects' Registration Council of the United Kingdom.

References

Habraken, Nicholas. 1972. *Supports: The Alternative to Mass Housing*. Translated by E. Valkenburg. London: Architectural Press.

Clelford, Anthony, and Martin Symes. 1987. Design-build collaboration. *Architectural Case Problems* 7. London: Bartlett School of Architecture and Planning.

Marmot, Alexi and Martin Symes. 1987a. Public participation in design. *Architectural Case Problems* 2. London: Bartlett School of Architecture and Planning.

Marmot, Alexi, and Martin Symes. 1987b. Conflict and interest groups in design. *Architectural Case Problems* 3. London: Bartlett School of Architecture and Planning.

Schön, Donald. 1988. Designing: Rules, types and worlds. *Design Studies* 9 (3): 181–90.

Vidler, Anthony. 1989. *The Writing of the Walls*. London: Butterworth Architecture.

Chapter 10

The Question of Type

Julia W. Robinson

Building type is an idea that is fundamental to architecture; its nature raises basic architectural questions.[1] In the design process, however, the notion of type has been taken for granted and type is treated as an answer, the solution to a problem, or the assumed end point. In this chapter I discuss why the idea of type should remain a question and why type should be treated as a point of departure or a temporary destination rather than as an end point.

When type is treated as an answer, the selection of a building type drives subsequent design decisions. Type then plays a normative role by providing an image of a typical outcome that has associated with it countless prescriptive ideas. If we designate hospital, we have delimited not only a functional type but also ideas of siting, size, structure, materials, and even the kinds of windows and doors, lighting, heating, and furniture (Robinson 1991). In this way notions of type generally are fundamental to any building process. Their normative use thus promotes the status quo by generating conventional solutions.

However, it is possible to see type as a question in at least three ways. First, when applying a building type to particular circumstances of a given architectural problem, the existing type or prototype must always be adjusted to those circumstances. In this case the type itself raises a question about what is to be retained and what changed; for example, in the application of the typical single house to a hilly site, the type is transformed into a split-level scheme. Second, because the building types that we take for granted are not fixed, but change over time, their nature cannot be assumed to be fully understood, but remains a constant question. For instance, as the typical American single-family house constructed in the United States changed from a bungalow to a ranch house, split-level and pseudo-Victorian, the idea of house type has altered to encompass the new concepts and forms. Third, in situations where no applicable type seems to exist, the question of what needs to be built arises in the context of the existing types, and asks what attributes of what existing building types can be useful in this situation. As will be discussed later, the response to deinstitutionalization has created a new building type, group home, that draws upon the single-family house and the institutional residence but is different from both.

A very important role for architects is criticism of the normative patterns of building, and development of alternatives to what is ordinarily done. In this role, the architect must be cognizant both of the normative patterns and of ways to analyze them. In architecture, however, the word *type* is often used as if there were only one way to categorize buildings by type. There are, however, at least two dif-

---

1. This chapter brings together some new ideas with those from previously written papers, especially Robinson (1989, 1991).

ferent kinds of architectural types: those used in everyday parlance by all members of a culture, here called *basic types,* and those used by the profession to describe formal and other differences between buildings, here called *classificatory types.*[2] Confusion between these two has resulted in a lack of appropriate criticism of architectural types. Designers need to know when they are using which type, and how to use them appropriately.

The following discussion addresses the importance of type as a way of making sense of the physical world, and, relative to architecture, explains the complementary roles of the basic and classificatory types in creating appropriate architecture. Finally, in the discussion of group homes, it is shown how the use of type as a question can play an important role in the proposal and critique of new architectural forms.

About Type

Types are the categories that we use to define the world around us.[3] They are idealized forms with generally agreed-upon names that stand for a set of concrete objects. Associated with each idealized form and name are concepts and physical elements that characterize the type. According to this usage, any group of objects that possesses a mental image and name is a type. Since the act of communication involves reciprocity between name and object, the type name generates an idealized physical object and a consistent set of characteristic elements, and conversely, the object of a given type consistently conjures up the type name.

Although, or perhaps because, types are ubiquitous in our thinking, we tend to take them for granted. Whether or not we choose to become aware of them, type categories seem to form and re-

AVM: *This is a good distinction, but could be said in simpler ways, for example, popular versus scholarly understanding (re: Henry Glassie).*
JR: *Glassie's terms are an excellent addition to the discussion. Here I am attempting not only to characterize the differences as Glassie does so effectively, but also to qualify how* they *are different.*

AVM: *Do you mean "conceptual"? Wouldn't idealized forms be called archetypes?*
JR: *Idealized in this sense means images that represent ideas. Archetypes are one kind of idealized form that derive from the hypothesized collective unconscious. Types are idealized forms that are meaningful at a conscious level within what Anthony King calls an "interpretive community." See Stanley Fish (1980),* Is There a Text in This Class? The Authority of Interpretive Communities *(Cambridge, Mass.: Harvard University Press), especially pages 167–73.*

AK: *Only for members of the same "interpretive community."*
JR: *Exactly so.*

2. The term "basic type" is used as developed by Rosch and others. See for example Rosch, et al. (1976) and also Rosch (1978). In the terms used by Amos Rapoport (1990), basic types would be polythetic because they have many defining characteristics, while what we are calling "classificatory types" would tend toward being monothetic, which Rapoport rejects as not being useful. The polythetic categories developed by Rapoport to describe ideal types are neither basic nor classificatory in the sense developed here, but rather seem to combine the two in a new analytic form. This suggests that in addition to the two type categories discussed in this chapter, others not presently found in architectural thinking may be useful to develop. But I disagree with Rapoport about the uselessness of monothetic categories, because in my view the differences between monothetic and polythetic categories makes them complementary. An important consideration when addressing types may well be the extent to which a type is defined by its central point or by its boundaries: both basic types and Rapoport's polythetic types are defined by their central conditions, whereas classificatory types are defined by their boundary conditions. The nature of categories defined by their central conditions is to permit ambiguous edges, thus to remain open to change and redefinition. Those defined by their boundaries are relatively clear and fixed. Due to this difference, the more fixed classificatory types permit analysis of the more flexible and variable polythetic types, such as basic types.

3. Categorization is used here in contradistinction to classification. By categorization I mean the general placing of items into groups; classification refers to the placing of items into groups (or classes) on the basis of consciously structured criteria developed to make clear distinctions between groups.

AK: *I have no idea what a "law school" might look like. Identification obviously depends on an audience drawn from the same interpretive community.*

AK: *There seems to be an assumption here that "the viewing subject" is an architect or architectural student in the United States. If so, it should be stated.*
JR: *No, this is not the assumption. In the draft that you responded to, the identity of psychology students as study subjects was not made clear, and from this study as well as my own (e.g., Robinson, et al. 1992), I conclude that type is as powerful for nonarchitects reading architecture as it is for architects, although their interpretations will likely differ in many instances.*

AK: *What about the differentiated social and cultural meanings that "people" as well as "architects" invest in the visual appraisal of buildings, which result in a range of differentiated types? Only under certain controlled or limited conditions could type be accepted in such a twofold category.*
JR: *Your point is well taken. This is clearly an overstatement. Certainly there are many kinds of cultural categories related to architecture that are not basic types, and that are not professional categories. But I would argue that if they are not basic types, they will tend to be classificatory types, such as the real estate types in your chapter. As I am focusing on architects' use of type, I will retain the ambiguity for this chapter.*

form in our minds unconsciously as patterns of thinking, and then structure our subsequent thought. An example of the power of type to influence the perception of buildings is in the work of Danford and Willems (1975), in which four groups of people were asked to evaluate the character of a place based on different kinds of cues: a guided walk, a slide representation with knowledge of the type of place, a slide representation without knowledge of the type of place, or the name of the type of place. All four groups gave essentially the same responses to the varying stimuli. Although the article intends to make a somewhat different case, the reported data make it clear that regardless of the form of the information given on the building (a law school), the building type could be identified. In this particular case, where the building must have been typical for its type, the name alone generated the same response as the representational cues. This suggests that in certain instances type is so powerful that it may dictate how we interpret what we see. It is easy, by extension, to see how such basic types contribute to the structuring of expectations for places, cuing normative patterns. The power of type to direct attention, combined with its ubiquitous nature, indicates why it is so important to consider its effect upon design.

Types seem to emerge in one of two ways: relatively unconsciously, as a human response to the need to order objects for functioning in daily life; and more or less consciously, in response to the need to describe and analyze an object for a specific reason. In architecture, *basic type* is what people ordinarily use, and represents a way of understanding architecture as sets of generalized, identifiable objects. The second kind of type in architecture, *classificatory type*, represents the professional attempt to make distinctions and clarify relationships. In the first approach, type represents a point of convergence of objects (house, apartment). In the second, type is used to delineate and differentiate between objects, defining boundary conditions (single-family, multifamily housing). These seem to be related to two different ways of understanding: a normative, associational understanding from accumulated direct experience, and critical, analytical, organized understanding. These two perspectives generate different but complementary and often overlapping sets of categories. Thus the particular architectural object that is simply "house" in one context is "single-family house" or "prefabricated housing" in another. The process of design seems to require the use of both of these kinds of type, the first as a way of understanding the full nature of the type selected, the second as a way to adjust, respond to, or replace an ideal type when applying it to a real circumstance.

Since designers use cultural categories, including basic types, in everyday life as well as in the professional context, the application of basic architectural type in design is often uncritical. Similarly, the classificatory types learned in the professional context may be applied habitually. A compounding problem is that a basic type is broad and ambiguous because it contains large amounts of information, whereas a classificatory type is most useful when it is narrow and clear, containing limited information. Therefore when designers use basic types as a way of generating designs, their elasticity is often very useful, but not for classification; the classificatory types, tending to focus on limited attributes, if inappropriately applied may lead to incorrect analyses. The debate about type is derived largely from the failure to differentiate between these two approaches to type. The question addressed here focuses on the roles played by these two kinds of type, and the differences between them.

Basic Types and Architecture

Certain psychologists have found that there is a basic level of types, that is, a level where there is general agreement about the name of a particular object (Rosch, et al. 1976; Rosch 1978). When viewing the object in Figure 10-1, most people in the United States will name this object "apartment building." Conversely if someone says "apartment building," we imagine an object that may not be identical to the illustration, but that has many of the same characteristics. This exemplar of apartment building also belongs to a superordinate category "building," and to a subordinate category "low-rise apartment." But in terms of a superordinate category the apartment can also be called "multihousehold dwelling," or as a subordinate category it can be called "walk-up apartment." Subordinate and superordinate categories are less consistent than basic categories, being more context bound than is the basic category. Therefore, if this particular apartment building is seen by itself it will be called "apartment building," but if seen with other housing types (see Figure 10-2) it will likely be given a name differentiating it from them. If seen with single houses and high-rise apartment buildings, the group may be given a more general name such as "housing" or "building."

Basic types are useful for communication because they allow us to consider a limited set of objects that we can agree about. Categories need to be specific in order to contain useful information, but too much specificity creates impractically large numbers of categories. The basic-level category balances the need for informative categories with the need for small numbers of categories. Basic types are general enough that they can account for broad sets of objects, but specific enough that sets can be distinguished from each other (Rosch, et al. 1976, 382).

Several researchers have explored the ways that physical environments are perceived and named by lay people.[4] Among these, Tversky and Hemenway (1983) found that the basic types for environments were room types, buildings types, and landscape types. This was supported in my own work, in which photographs of housing interiors and exteriors were evaluated by lay people (Robinson, et al. 1992). I also found that the type categories useful for differentiating between kinds of housing from a design perspective are not necessarily relevant nor identifiable to lay observers. Contrary to expectations that all of the images would be grouped into building type categories, images were grouped into room type as well as building type. Exterior images were generally grouped in building types whereas interior images were grouped in room types. Contrary to expectations by the initial researchers that most would be identified, only some of the diverse set of building types were consistently named: hospital, dormitory, house (or home), and apartment building. This was far fewer than the ten types designated in setting up the study (hospital, nursing home, dormitory, group home, rooming house, mid-rise apartment, walk-up apartment, row house, and single-family house).

The power of a basic architectural type derives from two sources: it is shared within a given cultural context and it encompasses multiple modes of categorization. Schön (1988), apparently referring to basic types, argues that type is a powerful design tool precisely because it packs so much information into one icon. Basic types represent simultaneously: (1) a set of architectural attributes that

10-1
An architectural object that calls to mind a type

4. The standard technique for eliciting user categories is the sort of study where people are asked to place images of objects, places, etc. into groups in any way that makes sense to them, and are then asked to name the groups. For examples, see Rosch, et al. (1976) and Tversky and Hemenway (1983).

AK: *Nothing is said of the characteristics of the "lay people" here. What common characteristics are being assumed here?*
JR: *The characteristics of lay people assumed here is that they are not architects. Whether the student subjects, typically middle class people, can be said to represent all lay people is, of course, subject to question. In Tversky and Hemenway's study some of the psychology students might be design students, although in our study design students were explicitly excluded.*

AK: *Who, or what, is this monolithic category of "lay observers"? Aren't they differentiated by gender, age, region, race, ethnicity, income, class, experience, etc.?*
Also, this discussion assumes that all building types are new, purpose-built — but in most parts of the world (outside of the United States) many types (e.g., hospital, nursing home, housing) are adaptations from earlier, obsolete building forms with other functions. As far as terminology is concerned (as well as the designed object to which it relates), all of these are culturally specific American (maybe even U.S. regional) types.
JR: *The student group that evaluated the images in our investigation were students of psychology at a midwestern United States university, a mix of men and women, largely middle class, clearly a limited group. They were evaluating settings from their own urban context, settings that are limited (due to the relative youth of the city) to twentieth-century buildings, mostly purpose-built and not new. Having interviewed beyond this group of people, however, I hypothesize that relative to building type, the responses from others in this region would not be significantly different, and based on the way that ideas are communicated globally today I would suspect that the responses would be similar for others exposed to normative U.S. images (i.e., Canadian and U.S. Americans, and possibly television watchers from around the world). In any case, the point is that lay people use categories differently from the way that architects use them for professional purposes, and that when left to categorize things in their own way lay people use fewer, broader categories than do professionals.*

10-2
Architectural objects in the context of others may be differentiated by superordinate category, by basic category, or by subordinate category.
a. superordinate category: building vs. model
b. basic category: apartment building vs. house
c. subordinate category: low-rise apartment building vs. high-rise apartment building

can be described; (2) a set of rules for construction and for organization of space; (3) a set of behaviors and defined roles that take place within it; and (4) a set of qualities it should exhibit. Its usefulness in design, then, is that it immediately gives boundaries to the problem at hand, prescribing ways to think about and address it. If type is seen as an answer, these boundaries form limits to thinking. If type is seen as a question, these boundaries provide reference points for further exploration. The question of type forms a substantial issue for designing, whether used in conventional ways or in ways that challenge convention.

The basic architectural type normally carries the functional name of the building or space, but does not only engage the functional characteristics.[5] When linked to the basic type, the functional term or token refers to the complete set of characteristics. This integration of the various modes of categorization makes the basic architectural type appropriate as a *subject for* analysis rather than a *technique of* analysis.

In architectural parlance, basic types are commonly used to denote the normative physical form of built environments. In delimiting the design context, architects use basic categories such as factories, schools, stores, churches, nursing homes, hospitals, and hotels; superordinate categories such as educational, recreational, commercial, institutional, industrial, and residential; and at the subordinate level, categories like high-rise, low-rise and mid-rise, or congregate and full-time care, or cancer, heart, or children's. Categories such as these are not clearly defined or overlapping but seem instead to follow normal cultural usage in reference to the physical form.

In this usage there is apparent convergence between the approach of designers and lay people. Nevertheless, even though the terms are culturally shared, and therefore provide a potential point of convergence between the two groups, what they mean to each is not identical. While the difference is not enormous, it is important to be explicit about it: when lay people think about a basic type, such as dormitory, they may be cued by a formal icon, but the icon generally represents a set of human issues first, and a set of physical forms second. To a designer the type is first a set of physical building forms and second a set of human issues. This impairs communication between the two groups. These differences need to be examined and understood so that designers can better respond to the lay view. For example, a common reason lay people do not readily accept innovative design is that the buildings look unfamiliar. A sensitive designer may be able to discover innovative forms that retain enough familiar features that people will find them interesting rather than repellant.

AK: *If we are speaking historically about "the Modern Movement," there were/are many "basic types" of dwelling that existed in different countries prior to its introduction.*
JR: *This is true, and I suggest that these were operative in the minds of architects as they proposed the new style, and that the new forms were made as figures against the ground of the existing basic types.*

AK: *Is this the way all architects design? Don't at least some of them think about the problem to be solved and then think of ways, which may not be design ways but organizational ones, to solve it? (See Francis Duffy 1992,* The Changing Work Place). *Don't some of them look at the changing social/political/economic processes that are producing building types?*
JR: *There is no statement here that says building type is the only way that architects design. But I think the evidence is profound that when building form is thought about, the normative building types are generally used as reference points for change. Thus when Duffy is discussing the workplace as something other than an office building, he recognizes that he must differentiate his position from the normative. He therefore works in juxtaposition to the office building.*

AK: *Isn't a dormitory primarily representative of social issues? Another very U.S. way of looking at things: what most European societies refer to as "social services" are referred to in the United States as "human services," for obvious political reasons.*
JR: *I gather that it represents such to you. However, from my observation, most practitioners and architectural theoreticians, in the context of architectural design, think primarily of the form of a building type such as a dormitory, rather than seeing it as representing human issues. This is the central point of this chapter.*

The basic category also demarcates the place where professionals and users who share a culture can agree upon what is normally done. An American house, for instance, has certain necessary characteristics such as being free-standing and containing at least a living room, kitchen, bedroom, and bathroom. While architectural styles have changed radically, basic building types have remained far more stable; since they require informal consensus they usually change slowly. Even when interests like that of the Modern Movement focused on substantive reconfiguration of building forms, the basic category remained a force for cultural continuity. Le Corbusier's houses, for example, retain the same basic public-private organization of spaces as traditional houses, and even have most of the same kinds of room divisions. As such, however, the basic type provides a locus for critique and improvement of the fit between cultural ideals and the design of environments.[6]

5. The general use of building types to name building exteriors is not only supported by the research discussed, but also by observation of common usage and by the work of Tversky and Hemenway (1983).

6. This idea of a fit between cultural ideals and the design of environments is called cultural responsiveness by Rapoport (1987, 10–15).

7. Morris lists three divisions of architectural types: (1) functional or programmatic taxonomy, (2) formal or configural taxonomy, and (3) imagerial or iconic taxonomy (1980, 40). Wallace identifies three scales used for classification: (1) epistemic, concerned with the properties of phenomena; (2) genetic, concerned with presumed causes of phenomena; and (3) functional, referring to presumed effects of phenomena (Wallace 1983 cited in Rapoport 1990).

8. The first way of classifying environments, by physical properties, is Wallace's epistemic mode and Morris's formal or configural type. The second way, how environments are made, is analogically related to Wallace's genetic code, a category not proposed by Morris but warranted by common use of construction and other techniques as a way of categorizing buildings. The third way, how environments are used, is Wallace's and Morris's functional mode. And the fourth way, how environments are understood, is a symbolic/associational mode, similar to Morris' imagerial or iconic mode and perhaps a subcategory of Wallace's functional mode.

Classificatory Types in Architecture

Architects design physical places for intended purposes. While the process of providing physical places often raises interesting questions about their given purpose, the primary role of the architect in addressing the relation between built form and purpose is to discover an appropriate physical design for a given circumstance. It follows, therefore, that the classificatory types developed by the architecture professional emphasize physical form, or "formal" aspects of buildings, over other attributes.

The complexity of architectural form is not widely appreciated, nor is the complexity of basic types. The myriad classifications in architecture suggest the depth of the challenge to create built form; they indicate how many different variables must be taken into account. Additionally, since every one of these variables is embedded in basic types, these types are very rich. Thus, whether or not they agree with the values it represents, for most Americans "house" captures not only a generalized building form, but ideas about lawns, walkways, entries, mailboxes, doors, construction method, dimensions, walls, floor and ceiling materials, plumbing fixtures, furniture, wall and ceiling mouldings, lighting, and much more. The substance of the basic type represented by the visual image is not simple.

There seem to be four ways to classify environments; the first three derive from a generative mode (how architecture is made), and the last comes from a responsive mode (how architecture is received by the audience).[7] The first way represents what normally comes to mind when typology is discussed in architecture, that is, the classification of environments by their *physical properties*. The second way deals with *how the environments are made*, the third with *how environments are used*, and the fourth responds to *how environments are understood*.[8] The professional categories that have been developed use these approaches both individually and also by combining them in ambiguous, overlapping ways. I propose these four ways not because they are pure groupings, but because they raise interesting contrasting purposes and reveal something about the nature of architectural categories. By separating how environments are used from how they are understood, for instance, we can distinguish the two ways of classifying, acknowledging that they operate differently.

Physical properties include such taxonomic categories as materials, arrangement of spaces, style, size, geometric order, sub-elements, and construction system. Buildings are sometimes categorized by construction (wood frame, metal frame and panel, pre-stressed concrete and masonry infill); by plan and space configuration (courtyard building, atrium building, skip-stop elevator high-rise, duplex apartment); and by style (Tudor, Georgian, medieval, postmodern). Sometimes they are classified by precedent (Corbusian or Miesian, New England village green versus Italian piazza); or by size (high-rise, mid-rise, low-rise); or by sub-elements (bay window, skip-stop elevator, tower). These formal categories allow efficient discussion of alternative formal arrangements relative to known outcomes. They focus on specific attributes of forms without requiring the entire set of questions about the form to be engaged at once.

But as makers of environments, designers are also concerned with the *rules and processes* that generate forms (how environments are made). Some of the rules and processes are implied by the formal characteristics of environments, like plan configurations. Some relevant categories are linked to material (which often overlap with form categories, as in the cases of concrete construction and brick construction), or may be linked to style (also overlapping with form, but in this case responding to rules of combination). Functional intentions and expectations may also be generative, thus potentially linking generative ideas to actual functioning. Regulation categories are not only generative, but also respond to use characteristics; for instance, "intermediate care facilities for the mentally retarded" is a category of housing responding to federal regulations. Other rules and process types relate to financing and construction (fast-track projects, speculation office buildings), and to client relationships (governmental building, community participation projects, developer housing). By focusing on these generative processes, the methods of construction and regulation may be clarified and be dealt with as a distinct set of issues relative to architectural form.

The set of *use characteristics* is at least as rich as the others. We can classify buildings by the people they serve (elementary and high schools), by the functions that they perform (school, hospital, stadium, museum, or educational, health, recreational, cultural), by the way they perform their service (group homes and rooming houses versus dormitories, hotels versus motels, first-class restaurants versus fast-food places), by the operation of environmental control system or other system used (forced air versus hot water heating), or even by cost (moderate-income versus upper-income housing). There may be considerable overlap with rules and processes, for certain uses are linked with regulations and financing structures (speculation office buildings link formal outcome, purpose, and financing; and nursing homes link regulations with purpose and formal outcome).

The last taxonomic category, *how environments are understood*, is value laden and qualitative. The source of the values may be cultural or personal but the category itself is associational and symbolic. It includes more general qualitative categories such as satisfactory, powerful, homey, confusing, or stark. While not normally considered to be types, these qualities emerge as one way people categorize places. If someone says "a cozy house," we share with others an idealized notion of what kind of house they mean, although it may be imprecise. On the other hand, if someone says "a tall building," we have a more distinct notion, certainly as distinct as if they had said "a brick building." These qualities are not necessarily functional or tied to building use, although they may be. To be useful as architectural categories, however, these need to be linked by research to architectural form.

The variety and diversity of classificatory types in architecture reflect the very large number of physical variables represented by any one architectural project, as well as the many ways that environments can be understood. When considering types, it is important to recognize that basic types embody particular classificatory types in a single icon, reflecting normative notions of such things as codes, materials, and style for a given cultural context and time. Because of their dynamic nature and complexity, types cannot be taken for granted and are necessarily a question for study. Furthermore, in considering any particular design, the question of selecting the appropriate classificatory types is also a question that must be addressed.

Type as a Question, the Group Home as Subject

If basic types are the figures that influence architectural choices, then classificatory types frame the ground against which basic types can be understood. Classificatory types provide a way to isolate and criticize the formal aspects of the normative and otherwise overly complex basic types. That there are many classificatory types permits the analysis of architectural form from many vantage points. To illustrate how classificatory types can elucidate basic types we will examine an evolving American building type, the group home, relative to basic types that presently are informing its evolution, and in the light of classificatory types defined using Hillier and Hanson's gamma analysis (1984, 143–63).

AK: *If there is such a variety of buildings and purposes, where is the "basic type" going to come from?*

JR: *The basic type, if one does emerge, will come either from shared knowledge about the program and form of housing that works best, or from government regulation or policy (such as fire codes or sponsorship of construction) that requires the definition of building type. At present there are considerable differences between states and regions, largely in response to the variation in regulatory practices. To the extent that there is a national interest in these buildings, the type will emerge more quickly. To the extent that a more informal kind of consensus develops, the process will take more time or will not occur at all.*

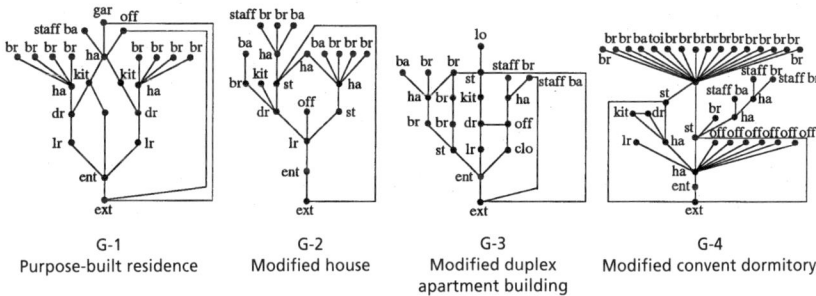

10-3
Spatial structure of four group homes (graphics by Hank Liu)
ba=bathroom br=bedroom clo=closet dr=dining room ent=entry ext=exterior gar=garage ha=hall kit=kitchen lo=lounge lr=living room off=office st=stair toi=toilet

9. The idea of the institutional building as being reversed was developed by Hillier and Hanson (1984, 183–97), based on their gamma analysis of buildings, and is further developed relative to various housing types in Robinson (forthcoming).

The generally understood name *group home* describes a building that houses a number of people who need some kind of supervisory care. However, since there is a great variety of buildings that serve this purpose, there is now no clear formal icon that represents this idea. For this reason, the existence and character of the potential basic type, group home, remains a question that we will explore here.

The classificatory types that frame this discussion are institutional or reversed buildings, and ordinary housing.[9] While Hillier and Hanson (1984) defined the term "reversed buildings" using examples from England, my analysis of examples of nursing homes, hospitals, and dormitories as well as single-family houses found in a midwestern United States city supports their basic hypothesis of a fundamental structural difference between the institutional or reversed building and the ordinary house. The reversed or institutional building is controlled by a nonresident group, due to their occupation of spaces at the entry of the building, with the residents occupying places distant from the entrance; ordinary housing is controlled entirely by the residents, with all spaces occupied by them. Another attribute of institutional space is the placement of social spaces in locations that do not support social interaction. Additionally, in the institutional building, the privacy gradient found in most ordinary housing is abrogated either by placing spaces intended for intimate activities directly adjacent to very public spaces, or by housing large numbers of people together (Robinson forthcoming).

The four groups homes selected are: a purpose-built shared house serving eight physically handicapped adults (G1); a modified single household dwelling serving nine youths (G2); a modified duplex apartment for seven youths (G3); and a remodeled convent housing 30 developmentally disabled adults (G4). These examples do not represent the full range of approaches to group homes, but were randomly selected from cases within the city of study.

In these four examples three basic housing types are operative: house, apartment, and dormitory. These types play two different roles: that of conceptual model, and that of physical container to be modified. *House* is the conceptual model that guided design, or redesign, in the first three cases (G1, G2, and G3). *Dormitory* is the conceptual model in the fourth case. Existing exemplars of house, apartment, and dormitory were the physical containers modified to accommodate three of the group homes (G2, G3, and G4); only one was new construction. The difficulties in adjusting the existing buildings to meet code and lifestyle requirements of the new housing form indicate just how powerful the physical type is in perpetuating certain kinds of activities and inhibiting others.

In looking at the emerging building type group home as a question, especially as a question about how group homes could or should be designed, the analysis of the existing buildings both in terms of their classificatory institutional type and in terms of their original building type becomes a productive proposition. Gamma analysis provides an etic, or professional view of the structure of the types and reveals a number of interesting physical relationships that are linked to social ones (see Figure 10-3). The comparative analysis also reveals the role played by building type in delimiting the choices available to the designer.

Although at first glance the building type of origin may seem somewhat arbitrary, there does seem to be a correlation between the building types selected as models, the types selected to remodel, the willingness to invest monetarily in change, and the societal attitude toward the population housed. Three approaches correspond both to three different populations and to assumptions about the relative "deviance" of the residents: physically disabled adults are provided a new purpose-built residence, problem adolescents are placed in the remodeled residences, and developmentally disabled adults are housed in a minimally remodeled institution.[10]

The residence for physically handicapped adults, G1, represents a considerable economic investment, as it was designed specifically to serve as a group home for this type of resident and responds to code requirements, which require more space and better materials than might be required of an ordinary dwelling. On the other hand, the provision of substantial space for staff reflects an assumed dependence, and the provision of a setting substantially different from an ordinary dwelling in appearance, if not structure, implies an acceptance of certain institutionalized features for this group. The settings for problem adolescents, G2 and G3, approximate the type of housing they would have if at home, but are modified to meet code and care requirements: a larger number of residents are housed, more exits are provided requiring some reconfiguration, and space is provided for staff. These first three settings are normalized, as opposed to being normal settings, in that they are modified to meet code and care requirements but are otherwise as close as possible to an ordinary dwelling. The residence for developmentally disabled adults, G4, represents a somewhat out-of-date idea for housing this population, although many similar places continue to serve these groups.[11] This setting, clearly institutional, reflects an assumed dependence of the residents on staff, and an assumed need to segregate this group from access to ordinary housing, or a willingness to accept a compromise for this population.

AK: *If we speak of the etic view, doesn't this also imply reference to the emic?*
JR: *Yes, but in this case the lay people evaluating the buildings were not able to identify the group home as a building type, because while it is a useful social category it doesn't have a single building icon that represents it. The only way then to study the group home is to use classificatory types as a reference. In other words, since there does not seem to be a clearly developed emic view, the etic description becomes the useful approach.*

AVM: *In which way relative to house as type? Isn't house the basic type anyway? Why don't you use the distinction between basic and classificatory types for this analysis?*
JR: *I am using this distinction. Basic types served to frame the way these buildings were designed and redesigned, but are the subject of analysis, rather than the tool for analysis, because they are too diffuse. The classificatory types I use describe basic categories relative to a single formal variable: the links between spaces. Basic types, unless reduced as in this case to diagrammatic descriptions such as gamma analyses, are too complex to be a useful device for analysis since they contain too many variables. In other words, basic types are the question; classificatory types provide ways to address it.*

10. While the state where the study took place is progressive in terms of the design of small group homes for developmentally disabled people (housing six to ten people), at the time of the study in 1984 — and today as well — the city in question retains many larger settings that house developmentally disabled people.

11. The documentation of these buildings took place in 1986, and since then many similar residences have been replaced by housing more closely approximating the settings for adolescents I describe here.

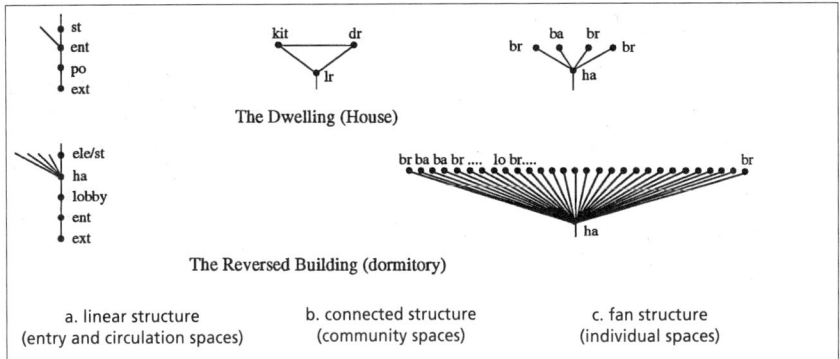

10-4
Spatial structure of the dwelling and the reversed building (graphics by Hank Liu)
ba=bathroom br=bedroom ele=elevator ent=entry ext=exterior ha=hall kit=kitchen lo=lounge lr=living room po=porch st=stair

Examination of the building types of origin and of the changes made to the buildings raises additional questions about the relationship between building type and social values. The selection of a given building type as a point of departure is made in response to assumptions about the residents. And once selected, the type delimits the range of possible alterations and outcomes. Although every building represents a kind of compromise with the ideal, it must be assumed that the final design represents an acceptable level of compromise with the ideal or the building would not be inhabited. The kinds of compromises that exist in each of the buildings can therefore be seen as a message about the values held toward the residents.

In order to explore this further, it is necessary to explain some key attributes of the classificatory types — typical midwestern dwelling units and reversed buildings — represented by house and dormitory. In general, as illustrated by Figure 10-4, the dwelling unit, whether apartment or house, reflects a privacy gradient.[12] The semiprivate entry sequence is linear; the private spaces (living room, dining room, and kitchen) are organized in an integrated relation (although

---

12. In addition to Robinson (1993) see also Alexander, Ishikawa, and Silverstein (1977) for a discussion of what they term the "intimacy gradient."

13. These terms are used as defined in Robinson (1993).

---

this is more variable than the other two organizations); and the semi-intimate (bedroom corridor) and intimate spaces (bedroom and bathroom) are structured in a fan shape.[13] The linear structure of the entry sequence controls and directs the visitor; the integrated nature of the living room, dining room, and kitchen permit informal flow of activities between them; and the location of the semi-intimate corridor at the nexus of the fan shape restricts access to the intimate bedroom and bathroom areas. This is in contrast to the design of the dormitory, also illustrated in Figure 10-4, where the linear sequence of the entry sequence is similar, but there are no integrated relations, and the social spaces are treated as segregated in the fan-shaped relation. The significantly greater numbers of rooms organized in the fan shape create a hall that no longer functions as a semi-intimate space, but rather as a semipublic area. Here then there is no gradient between the intimate bedroom and the semipublic corridor, and the path between bedroom and bathroom is semipublic rather than semi-intimate as in the dwelling unit.

The two residences for adolescents are both renovated ordinary dwellings. The house, G2, and the duplex, G3, are the kinds of residences in which many adolescents would ordinarily dwell, and for this reason it seems reasonable to assume that they would be appropriate for a group home. In both buildings, the social spaces are located appropriately close to the entrance, without intervening staff space. Since the adolescents are dependents, it is appropriate that in each building the staff occupies a place near the entrance, and that the adolescents themselves occupy areas farther into the residence. The fact that almost all the adolescents share a bedroom with another resident and share a bathroom with six or seven others compromises privacy, but no more than many family situations. In fact, the remodeled house, G2, has a structure identical with other houses except that the added fire stair increases accessibility to the outside and the staff bedrooms increase the number of spaces. In G3, on the other hand, the need to meet code restrictions has compromised resident privacy. Since some bedrooms are located in what was the living room of the former upstairs apartment, and since access had to be provided to an additional stair, four of the six resident bedrooms are in an integrated relation rather than being related to a corridor and bathroom in a fan shape. Occupants of one bedroom must pass through another bedroom to have access to the bathroom or to exit. This violates the privacy of the bedroom. Organized for two-bedroom apartments, the structure of the duplex did not allow the ideal bedroom relation to emerge when remodeled. This compromise of the privacy of the adolescents was, nonetheless, permitted to take place.

THE QUESTION OF TYPE 189

The remodeled convent shows compromises of a different order. First of all, the existence of five offices in the building, and their location closer to the entrance than to the residents' social space, signifies that it is a building controlled by the staff, a workplace as much as a dwelling. Second, the number of bedrooms is larger than that typically found in ordinary dwellings, and the 30 residents must share a single communal bathroom as well as other areas for eating, recreation, and so on. Third, the privacy gradient is the locus of a significant compromise. While most residents share a bedroom with one other person, one bedroom is shared by six. This room was a work area when the building was a convent. Furthermore, in order to use the communal bathroom, a room that has multiple toilet stalls and sinks (itself a significant compromise of privacy), the occupants of the room for six must traverse the downstairs public corridor and go upstairs. Although the bedrooms, with the exception of the downstairs one, are in a fan shape, corridors shared by 30 people are semipublic, so that the intimate spaces of bedroom and bathroom are separated by a semipublic territory. By negating resident control and the privacy gradient, this institutional building is a radical compromise of resident needs.

The group home for physically handicapped adults, G1, seems to have been structured like a set of paired single-household dwellings joined at the front to share an entrance, at the rear to share staff space, and surrounding an atrium at the center. Living rooms are at the point of entrance, and the staff spaces do not control the residence. The design creates the privacy gradient normally found in dwellings, while at the same time permitting a much higher level of egress to the exterior as well as access to the staff without interfering with the daily patterns of the residents. While clearly different from the typical dwelling, the structure of the building reflects its key attributes. The purpose-built group home shows that it is possible to structure housing for dependent people in a way that maintains the privacy gradient and resident control. But as discussed earlier, the structure is only one part of the architectural design. For example, the appearance of this particular building leaves something to be desired. In order to create architecture that responds to needs, we must go beyond the use of one or two classificatory types in order to develop a holistic design.

Although they share a name, architecturally the four group homes resemble their building types of origin more than they do each other. They are alike only because of the purpose they serve and the way they serve that purpose. But in considering the group home as a question, we also examine the nature of the single dwelling, the duplex, and the institutional building. In the process of comparing the structures of particular group homes using a classificatory type, we discover important architectural differences we may not have otherwise observed, and also uncover the different values they represent.

Building type both reflects and projects societal conceptions of the group of people to be housed. As the building type group home evolves into a predictable form, assuming it eventually comes to be an idealized architectural configuration, it will represent such cultural attitudes. The building configuration that would best solve the situation projected by the (verbal) term "group home" thus remains a question, or perhaps the end product of a quest for a good fit. Such a fit represents selected underlying values. Certainly the way that the four residences illustrated are presently structured reflects the kind of staffing considered suitable and the amount of control over the residence given to the resident, as well as the level of investment considered desirable, and a host of other things, not all of which are reflected in the structure as analyzed here. But whether the basic type we consider as a question is undefined, as in the case of the group home, or is defined, as in the case of the single residence, the forms of building type continue to change and evolve. Therefore the nature of types remains a question to be continually studied and reassessed.

Conclusion

Today, much of the architectural profession, and especially theoreticians, tend to think about architecture almost exclusively in classificatory types and elements, focusing on formal attributes of architecture. This causes difficulties in that formal changes almost always have social effects, which can only be dealt with if they are understood, requiring a more holistic approach than classificatory types can provide. If architecture is to be meaningful in the daily functional world, and to the lay person, there is a need to understand what the normative cultural architectural ideas are so that they may be appropriately addressed. By paying attention to the sources of the categories they are using, applying both classificatory and basic categories, potential innovators will discover that their work is more effective in the marketplace of ideas.

AK: *The type projects the social views of those groups in authority, making these social/architectural decisions.*
JR: *I think I finally understand how you and I differ in our perceptions of how a society works. I am willing to go beyond particular racial, ethnic, cultural, gender, etc. subgroups of a society to make general statements about what a society does, because I believe that if a group of people sanctions leaders to make decisions for them, the decisions de facto reflect the overall societal ideas at that time. Thus, if no one is changing the circumstances for injustices that are in the public's knowledge, these can be said to represent societal ideas. Certainly, within a given society there are competing notions, and that is, for example, why there are presently many versions of group homes. But there does seem to be a tendency for some ideas to converge so that patterns of behavior emerge that are shared (although other patterns persist that are definitely not shared). Here, I am interested in the relationship between the shared patterns that represent consensus and those that remain diverse, and how they reflect contradictions and conflicting values.*

AK: *Is the commodified nature of ideas implied by "marketplace" intended?*
JR: *Not necessarily. The marketplace of ideas in this context refers not only to the economic marketplace, but to the cultural marketplace, in which certain ideas are adopted or rejected for noneconomic reasons as well.*

Existing cultural categories in general, and basic architectural types in particular, derive from a combination of direct responses to values and perceived needs, and an arbitrary holdover of vestigial forms. While values and perceived needs change over time, architectural forms often remain unchanged, or are only partially altered in response. We have remnants of the past, equivalent to the necktie, or shutters on a house, that are not essentially related to our current ways of doing things. In some cases, like the necktie or shutters, these features have some pleasant associations and are neutral to the new values, but in other cases, like high heels or single-paned windows in cold climates, they may inhibit desired societal changes. If we accept basic types as a subject for study, we can identify those forms that are not necessary to a given intent, but simply came along for the ride in what might be called attribute carryover; we may identify those environmental forms that are desirable to maintain; and through the generation of new form alternatives, we may also create better environmental solutions than presently exist. This identification and improvement requires using categories that contrast with basic type.

Recently researchers such as Groat (1988), Hillier and Hanson (1984), Krampen (1979), and Robinson (1988) have been investigating the relationship between formal categories and lay perceptions of environments. These studies, although not widely known in the architectural community, set the groundwork for ongoing research and have the potential to educate designers about the perspectives of the nondesigning citizen. But architects can also become more sensitive to their own cultural knowledge, for they are not only members of the architectural subculture, but are also participants in the normative culture. Alertness to the cultural messages of the basic types can help designers create buildings more responsive to users' hidden agendas. The relationship between ordinary and professional understandings of buildings is central to the wise use of type. Classificatory types permit the study of these issues because they describe concrete physical characteristics that can be defined and thus provide a frame of reference for analyzing basic types and generating changes in them.

Basic categories are powerful in their gathering of many ideas into one icon. They are rich and complex. While they change slowly, they do evolve over time, and their nature at any given moment should not be taken for granted. Because they frame our way of seeing the world, basic categories are essential to understand; because they evolve and change, they remain a continuous question, open to reinterpretation.

It is useful to distinguish between basic and classificatory types because the question of the nature of basic architectural types can be analyzed using a variety of classification systems. Classificatory categories offer several ways to develop perspectives on basic categories: to understand the nature of the existing types; to understand how they may need to be adjusted as they are applied in particular circumstances; and finally to develop design possibilities by identifying individual attributes of existing types that may be recombined in new ways. By understanding that type is a question and not an answer, the designer can be more effective in understanding, responding to, and changing normative cultural patterns.

Working with me on this endeavor have been several students: Keith Nicholls, Tom Melville, and Hank Liu. Funding for this project has come from the University of Minnesota in the form of the Undergraduate Research Opportunity Program and the International Student Opportunity Program.

References

Alexander, Christoper, Sarah Ishikawa, and Murray Silverstein. 1977. *A Pattern Language.* New York: Oxford University Press.

Danford, S. and E.P. Willems. 1975. Subjective responses to architectural displays: a question of validity. *Environment and Behavior* 7 (4): 486–516.

Gibson, J. 1950. *Perception of the Visual World.* Boston: Houghton Mifflin.

Groat, Linda. 1988. Contextual compatibility in architecture: an issue of personal taste? In *Environmental Aesthetics,* ed. L.J. Nasar. Cambridge, U.K.: Cambridge University Press.

Hillier, Bill, and Julienne Hanson. 1984. *The Social Logic of Space.* Cambridge, U.K.: Cambridge University Press.

———. 1990. Defining vernacular architecture. In *Vernacular Architecture,* ed. Mete Turan, 67–101. Aldershot, U.K.: Avebury.

Krampen, Martin. 1979. *Meaning in the Urban Environment.* London: Pion.

Morris, Ellen K. 1980. The discourse of type. In *Language in Architecture: Proceedings of the ACSA 68th Annual Meeting,* ed. John Meunier, 34–47. Washington, D.C.: Association of Collegiate Schools of Architecture.

Rapoport, A. 1987. On the cultural responsiveness of architecture. *Journal of Architectural Education* 41 (1): 10–15.

Robinson, Julia W. 1988. Institution and home: linking physical characteristics to perceived qualities of housing. In *Looking Back to the Future/Se Retourner vers L'Avenir Vol 2: Proceedings of the IAPS 10 Conference,* eds. H. Herbert van Hoogdalem, et al., 431–40. Delft, the Netherlands: Delft University Press.

———. 1989. Typology and the interplay of form and function. Paper read at the 20th Annual Conference of the Environmental Design Research Association, Blacksburg, North Carolina in the symposium "Architectural Theory as a Basis for Environmental Design Research: An Emerging Paradigm?" organized by Linda Groat.

———. 1991. Representation, mind & body: architecture and the use of the plan. In *Reflections on Representation Conference Proceedings,* eds. A. Chen, J.W. Robinson, and E. Steinfeld, 19–27. Buffalo, N.Y.: School of Architecture & Planning, State University of New York at Buffalo.

———. 1993. Messages from space: privacy and power in housing. *Power by Design: Proceedings EDRA 24.* Oklahoma City, Okla.: Environmental Design Research Association.

———. Forthcoming. *Architecture Through the Looking Glass: Beyond Institution and Home.* New York: Van Nostrand Reinhold.

Robinson, Julia W., John Klensin, Julio Bermudez, and Michelle Johannes. 1992. Probing terminology for cultural categories: institution and home. In *Metamorphoses: Proceedings of the IAPS 12 Conference,* eds. A. Mazis, C. Papageorgiou, and K. Tsoukala. Thessaloniki, Greece: Artisotle University of Thessaloniki.

Rosch, Eleanor. 1978. Principles of categorization. In *Cognition and Categorization,* eds. E. Rosch and B.B. Lloyd. Hillsdale, Ill.: Erlbaum.

Rosch, Eleanor, et al. 1976. Basic objects in natural categories. *Cognitive Psychology* 8: 382–439.

Schön, D.A. 1988. Designing: rules, types and worlds. *Design Studies* 9 (3): 181–90.

Tversky, B. and K. Hemenway. 1983. Categories of environmental scenes. *Cognitive Psychology* 15 (1): 121–49.

Part IV

PLAYING WITH TYPE

Chapter 11

An Artist's Perspective on Type

Nancy Wolf

For an artist, questioning the accepted definitions and uses of building type is liberating. This process challenges our understanding of the built environment and our relationship to place and space.

The drawings, paintings, and prints reproduced in this essay are a critique of the changes I have witnessed over the past 20 years in urban forms and spaces in the modern landscape. The descriptions of the pictures are an attempt to put into words my visual responses to our rapidly changing environment. Intuitively I feel that the buildings and urban spaces that are most successful are animate. They are externalized forms of our inner selves. They express our hopes, dreams, and social beliefs as well as our physical requirements. However, all too often contemporary buildings and the spaces that surround them reflect little more than modern technology and consumer demands.

In recent years I have traveled and lived in nonwestern cultures for extended periods of time. In Nigeria, Nepal, and India I have seen some of the extraordinarily powerful buildings and spaces these societies have created to integrate people's most intimate physical and psychological needs and beliefs with their external world.

Sundarshan Raj Tiwari, a Nepalese architect, describes how the traditional Nepalese builders have used the "blissful qualities of tinkling bells tuned to varying wind speeds of dawn and dusk to give a sonic backdrop to the pilgrim" (Tiwari 1989, 102). Kofi Awoonor, a Ghanaian poet, poignantly refers to the "gods who cried again from the hut in me" (Egudu 1977, 69). In contrast, urban sociologist Richard Sennett observes that:

> Whereas the ancients could use their eyes in the city to think about political, religious, and erotic experiences, modern culture suffers from a divide between the inside and the outside. It is a divide between subjective experience and worldly experience, self and city. Moreover, our culture is marked by hard struggle whenever people seek to make inner life concrete. This sets us off not just from our origins but also from non-European cultures nearer in time whose masks, dances, ceremonials, shrines, sacred grounds, and cosmologies connect subjective life to physical things (Sennett 1990, xii).

In the middle of this century Lewis Mumford wrote that "Man grows in the image of his gods and up to the measures they have set" (Mumford 1961, 575). Twenty years ago, when I began drawing and painting people in relationship to their architecture, the defining gods of type, place, and space were utility, efficiency, commerce, style, technology, and the grandiose urban renewal schemes built to serve them. I watched with dismay the psychological impacts the resulting types and spaces had upon the people for whom these forms were created. I saw the new types of urban space and forms lead increasingly to desolation, isolation, and despair within ourselves and our communities.

A 1974 drawing, *Entrance to the City,* is loosely based upon Corbusier's vision for La Ville Radieuse. Enormous, repetitive office towers, significant features of the urban redevelopment projects of that time, dominate the skyline. These schemes destroyed many cities' intimate spaces and expressively detailed buildings essential to maintaining a sense of neighborhood. The highway depicted here, which links the city to its suburbs, divides many of the delicate and important transitional neighborhoods between the suburb and the city. The disrupted social

11-2
Future City #5, 1972
(etching collage on plexiglass, photo by Nancy Wolf, courtesy of Marsha Mateyka Gallery, Washington, D.C)

11-1
Entrance to the City, 1974 (pencil on paper, photo by Nancy Wolf)

patterns of those neighborhoods contributed to people's despair and the eventual abandonment and destruction of their homes and communities.

In *Future City #5,* an etching collage of that same time, I portray mass-produced housing as labyrinthine dwellings, stacked on top of one another or extended along the roadside. These forms created ominous depersonalized corners into which people withdraw, rather than creating cozy niches or front door stoops from which to watch the street, gossip, or enjoy the sun. This "future city" has no central square in which to meet with friends and exchange ideas over a cup of coffee, or to gather for communal festivities.

California Coastline is the suburban counterpart of *Future City #5.* Here too the suburban houses and mobile homes provide no intimate feelings of shelter from the relentless, sun-filled, treeless terrain. Nowhere is there a sense of meaningful progression through space. Power plants, power lines, gas tanks, tract houses, and mobile homes all are undifferentiated forms, neutral in their impact on the observer. The observer is quickly repelled by this sterile vision of the suburban landscape.

The form of planning underlying many modern cities and suburbs is the grid. The grid fulfills the needs of both the urban planner and the architect. It gives the urban planner an efficient, rational form upon which to work. It offers the architect a convenient device by which he or she can translate precast modular forms into monumental towers. The grid can be infinitely expanded. While the limitless vision of the grid can and often does fill the vast American horizon, it cannot fulfill the smallest and most pleasing details of everyday life. The grid becomes a tangible expression of the modern way of thinking about our environment. *Prisoner to a Grid* (1973) is a visualization of the failure of this thinking. The anonymous grid of modern architecture envelops this Victorian town house which it will soon replace.

11-4
Prisoner to a Grid, 1973
(charcoal pencil on paper with mylar and metalized mylar overlay)

11-3
California Coastline, 1974
(pencil on paper, photo by Nancy Wolf)

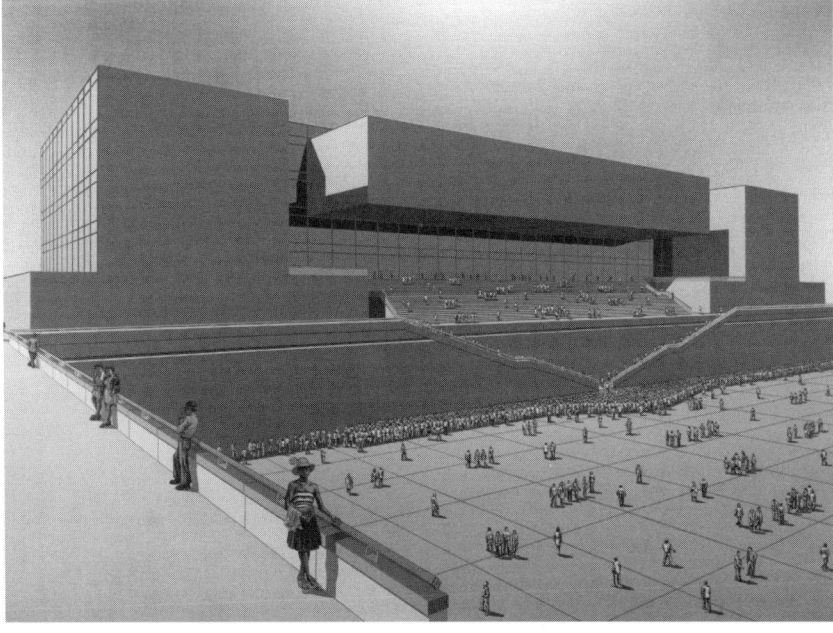

11-6
Journey to a New Place, 1979
(pencil on paper, photo by Nancy Wolf)

11-5
Tax Court, 1977
(oil on canvas, photo by Lance Wyman)

The 1977 painting *Tax Court* is based on the United States Tax Court designed by Victor Lundy as part of an urban redevelopment scheme in Washington, D.C. This painting questions what should be the appropriate scale and placement of a building in an urban context. The building is situated with its back to the city and its front facing a depressed expressway. It becomes a graphic example of how the arbitrary spaces created by urban removal and renewal allow a monolithic building serving a very specific function to override and ignore so many other urban considerations and concerns.

Following my years of visual comments on modernist architecture, in the late 1970s I began a new series of drawings about our abandoned urban buildings. These drawings portray building types dissolving into ruins. They express our sense of despair over the loss of connection between ourselves and our environment which I had witnessed taking place in the 1960s and 1970s. But I also felt that through this dissolution of type into formlessness we were being forced to reassess our values.

In *Journey to a New Place* (1979) I covered the modern monolithic buildings on the horizon with the scaffolding and shrouds I saw so often draped over partially dismantled and destroyed buildings in our deteriorated inner cities. I piled the garbage of that other city of shame around the bases of these new buildings. However, in *Architect's Dilemma* (1981) I argue that within the rubble of the partially destroyed buildings one might find the flexibility of forms to allow for diversion and dalliance. The drawing asks if there might be the suggestion for a solution in this rubble of despair. Around the base of the modernist high-rise in the distance I depict the formal and rigid behavior of people caught within the vacuum of the modernist city.

198 ORDERING SPACE

11-7
Architect's Dilemma, 1981
(pencil and colored pencil on paper, photo by Nancy Wolf)

As the inner cities decayed and were gradually abandoned, architects and their critics tried to understand the reasons for our failures. When I saw the new buildings created in response to the criticisms of modernist architecture, it seemed that architects had not yet understood some of the underlying problems. Responding to the critics' and the public's concern that modernist architecture and urban spaces were cold and impersonal, architects adopted artifice, style, and historical allusion for their solutions to the sterility of their forms. But in postmodernist buildings architects merely altered the facades of the modernist buildings. They did not change the type. They had failed to understand that how they thought about building type had helped to create the buildings and public spaces that were so profoundly isolating.

11-8
Hidden Longings, 1987
(conté pencil on paper, photo by eeva-inkeri)

Hidden Longings is an interior view of a modernist building to which an ornamented surface has been superimposed in an attempt to camouflage the endless grid at the top. Even with the addition of this artifice of traditional architecture, the space invokes no sense of place. People stand passively, alone or in lines. Their purpose for being in this space is unclear. They are portrayed here as they often appear in modernist spaces. I have suggested the more intimate worlds of the Greek temple and the African hut behind the barred, plate glass doors — alluded to in the title of the drawing — but these worlds are inaccessible.

In *Tempietto of San Pietro Inside the Walls,* Bramante's Chapel serves as the focal point of a modernist scheme. The drawing comments on the lack of interplay and integration between these two building types. It is a parallel statement to the earlier *Prisoner to a Grid*: in both cases the historical forms are imprisoned. The Victorian house was destroyed, as I witnessed so often in the urban renewal schemes of the 1960s; in the postmodern scheme the Bramante Chapel is enshrined, becoming lifeless in its modernist surroundings.

O. M. Ungers's German Museum of Architecture in Frankfurt is the subject of the drawing *Das Haus Im Haus,* executed in 1986. The drawing is meant to challenge Ungers's use of type. Ungers's *House*, a sophisticated space rich in artifice and irony, is constructed inside a gutted turn-of-the-century villa. But what is a house? What should be its function? Coolly neutral, what purpose does Ungers's house serve? The homeless huddle anonymously around and within it, tolerated but not comforted. Commedia dell'arte figures in the foreground play out their flirtatious roles, oblivious to the suffering nearby. Underneath the house stream masses of people. Their destination is unclear. The clouds above reflect the scene below.

11-9
Tempietto of San Pietro Inside the Walls, 1987
(conté pencil on paper, photo by eeva-inkeri)

11-10
Das Haus Im Haus, 1986
(pencil on paper, photo by eeva-inkeri,
courtesy of Marsha Mateyka Gallery,
Washington, D.C.)

The drawing on the cover, *Perfect Order,* completed in 1988, is my interpretation of a bird's-eye view of our contemporary urban environment. Buildings, spaces, and their inhabitants are defined by and consigned to their own clearly differentiated areas. It is an order that reflects how we think about ourselves. In the center are the megalithic postmodern corporate signature buildings, headed by Philip Johnson's famous Chippendale (AT&T) Building. These buildings tower over grandiose formal gardens. High walls insulate and isolate the wealthy and powerful from the ruined city of the past on the right and the tangled web of highways marking the "edge cities" of the suburbs on the left.

In the early l980s challenges to this order of space and place were discouraged. Few people asked how these architectural types of buildings and spaces could offer solace to enlighten and encourage the human spirit. Even fewer people perceived the loss of a sense of pilgrimage or progression from one place to another. There were scarcely any intimate places to delight the eye and stimulate the mind. In this setting, however, one clearly observed the homage paid to wealth and power in our society.

We had lost the understanding of what the real functions of buildings and spaces should be. The society, and the architects who served it, had created corporate signature buildings, ornamental malls, and escapist Disneyesque fantasy architecture. They remained cloistered behind walls of indifference to those around them. Despite the sterility and coldness of modernism, the best modernist architects had a utopian dream of providing light and air for all who inhabited their spaces. In contrast, postmodernism seems self-conscious and self-absorbed.

11-11 *New Realities,* 1990 (pencil on paper, photo by D. James Dee)

The AT&T Building became the signature building of the postmodern movement. Its construction was watched with great interest. It was written about and analyzed at length. But at street level, it seemed, the architect's ideas had failed him. Enormous arches created a dark and foreboding public space, which appeared even more cavernous with the addition of diminutive gray wrought iron tables and chairs. One thought of the fascist architecture of an earlier era. The SONY corporation, which now owns the building, has renovated the street level spaces.

In the IBM building, Edward Larrabee Barnes has created one of the livelier public spaces in New York City. A transparent space grid admitting sun and light spans a large courtyard. Trees and flowers flourish in this space. Food is served from gaily colored carts, and there is seasonal entertainment. The space adjoins two heavily used office and commercial buildings. Sometimes there are no seats available.

□ □ □

After the enthusiasm for the utopian dreams of modernism and the contextual historicism of postmodernism waned, a new movement was built upon the "erosion of what might be called architectural certainty" (Giovannini 1988, 43). Deconstructivist architecture encourages us to examine the "disparate texts and parts" of buildings by locating the "inherent dilemmas" within them (Johnson and Wigley 1988, 11). I have extended these "inherent dilemmas within buildings" to include the inherent dilemmas between buildings in order to examine the effect one building type can have upon another.

The drawings *New Realities,* based on a constructivist composition by Iakov Chernikhov, and *Delicate Balance* show the uneasy relationship that exists between the high-technology buildings in midtown Manhattan and the old industrial and commercial buildings of the Cast Iron District in lower Manhattan. The imposition of the cast iron buildings onto the overscaled high-rises in these drawings emphasizes the enormous changes of scale and attitudes towards the construction and uses of buildings in our society. The high-rises are primarily built by speculators to house large corporations and sophisticated computer technologies of the mid-twentieth century. The cast iron buildings were constructed in the nineteenth century to house small, often individually owned, dry goods businesses, textile manufactures, and warehouses. These buildings were "objects of great pride to their owners" (Gayle and Gillan 1974, vi).

11-12
Delicate Balance, 1990
(conté pencil on paper, photo by D. James Dee)

The theatrical facades of *Billboard Dreams* (1989) have Helmut Jahn's One Liberty Place in Philadelphia as their focal point. This work was in part inspired by the eighteenth-century Italian *chinea* (fireworks machine). Pierre Jean Grosley wrote at the time about these machines: "each evening the decoration changes. The last is always the most brilliant, and none resembles those of preceding years" (quoted by Myers and Boorsch 1971, 239).

Like the dislocated and partially dismembered structures of the buildings of the abandoned city, deconstructivist architecture with its dynamic and unorthodox use of materials can offer new possibilities for architects, urban planners, and their critics to re-examine how we look at place, space, and type. It enables us to question our relationship to our environment and challenges us to ask how architecture might better fulfill human dreams and aspirations. As a homeless man explains simply in Patricia Leigh Brown's article in the *New York Times* about the homeless, "a home is the idea of who you are" (*New York Times*, March 28, 1993). Herbert Muschamp in his review of the recently completed Holocaust Museum in Washington D.C. states in universal terms, "A place is a form of knowledge" (*New York Times*, April 11, 1993). We may inquire what contributions we must make to the environment so that our surroundings will reflect our hopes and dreams. How can we bring to the surface, from within ourselves, those things that we value, and how can we translate them into architectural type? Do we need speed or do we need connection? Do we want style or do we want urban serenity?

11-13
Billboard Dreams, 1989 (conté pencil on paper, photo by D. James Dee)

11-14
Pilgrimage, 1993
(acrylic on canvas, photo by Tony Holmes)

By exercising choice, we can redefine type. The parking lot can become a plaza or a sports park; the gas station, a meeting place; the billboard a marker for the spirit; the grid, a mandala; the industrial floor of an abandoned factory, an artist's studio; the highway along a riverbank, a park for strolling. In *Pilgrimage* (1993), "a city on a city," I explore some visual possibilities for reversing our order of values to see how connecting our communities might appear in a modern landscape. The architectural critic Wolf Von Eckardt wrote:

> It has been all but completely overlooked that the shadow of human identity is cast by the light of human community. Community, in turn, except in its most abstract sense, relates to its physical setting as the soul relates to the body. A community with which to identify and from which to receive identity cannot very well exist without its buildings and locus, the physical place which this mutuality creates (Von Eckardt 1967, 31).

Walking through traditional Nepalese towns, I have felt that real connection is created by hundreds of small reminders to be seen at every turn of one's glance and at every corner of passage. These reminders are at one's feet and at the rooftops as one gazes to the heavens. They are in the tinkling of wind-bells and in the exquisite detailing of a temple sculpture. They are made of time and timelessness.

References

Brown, Patricia Leigh. 1993. The architecture of those called homeless. *New York Times*, 28 March.

Egudu, Romanus N. 1977. *Four Modern West African Poets*. New York: Nok Publishers.

Gayle, Margot and Edmund Gillan, Jr. 1974. *Cast Iron Architecture*. New York: Dover Publications.

Giovannini, Joseph. 1988. Breaking all the rules. *New York Times Magazine*, 12 June.

Johnson, Philip and Mark Wigley. 1988. *Deconstructivist Architecture*. New York: Museum of Modern Art.

Mumford, Lewis. 1961. *The City in History*. New York: Harcourt, Brace & World.

Muschamp, Herbert. 1993. Shaping a monument to memory. *New York Times,* 11 April.

Myers, Mary, and Suzanne Boorsch. 1971. Grand occasions. *The Metropolitan Museum of Art Bulletin* (29) 5: 236–43.

Sennett, Richard. 1990. *The Conscience of the Eye: The Design and Social Life of Cities*. New York: Norton.

Tiwari, Sundarshan Raj. 1989. *Tiered Temples of Nepal*. Kathmandu: Mrs. Sunita Tiwari.

Von Eckardt, Wolf. 1967. *Crisis in Cities*. New York: Delacorte.

Chapter 12

In and Out of Type

Jean La Marche

Jose Buscaglia
Elizabeth Cromley
Michelle Fisher
Kenneth Frampton

Bruce Goodwin
Karen A. Franck
Alice Friedman
John Knesl

and commentators:
Nicholas C. Markovich
Thomas Mical
Lynda H. Schneekloth

This chapter is presented as a collection of notes for several reasons. These include the attempt to fabricate an analogous demonstration, in written form, of Aldo Rossi's intentions in architecture; it is an attempt to parallel Rossi's "forgetting architecture" with a repetition in thinking and writing about architecture. The text mimics and repeats. It explains as well as demonstrates, and the demonstration is both spatial and temporal. (I use the term "text" in two senses: (a) its popular sense of the main body of a manuscript, book or newspaper and, more importantly, (b) the sense that experience in general can be treated as if it were a "reading" and, therefore, can be analyzed by means of literary, linguistic, and semiotic criticism).[1]

JK: *Can/should experience be subjected to "reading," is it justified to refer to "reading" spaces, drawings, Rossi's statements, others' statements about Rossi… as "readings" or would it be important to work out the differences between these modes of perceiving, thinking, uttering?*

JK: *…as in making space for repetitions, and other texts.*

1. One of those having an influence on the transformation of "text," Jacques Derrida, treats it in a way that parallels, metaphorically, Rossi's idea of type which I try to delineate in the body of my text. Robert Bernasconi describes Derrida's position: "Deconstructive or double reading… is not an attempt to provide a reading of Rousseau which goes further than previous readings in exhausting the texts. Rather, its concern is with the *relation* between the 'new' reading and the readings which preceded it. Indeed, the 'new' reading emerges in the attempt to see what commands the dominant reading: logocentrism does not show itself as such except from elsewhere. In this way, Derrida regularly engages with and in that way keeps alive the memory of previous — and to his mind one-sided — interpretations of the texts he examines. His reading of Rousseau is no exception. It is no accident that he begins his discussion of the *Essay on the Origin of Languages* by entering into the controversy about the date of its composition. Previous interpretations cannot

The text is spatialized not only in the conventional separation of material into a main body and other information in the form of footnotes, citations, and references (not to speak of allusions and associations). (I claim responsibility for the original text, although I maintain that it also was, and remains, a palimpsest of voices).

The text is also spatialized by means of the build-up of other voices, repetition, and certain graphic manipulations.[2] The space of the text is intended to demonstrate correspondences between Rossi's intentions in a typology of "forgetting" and literary theory and criticism involving the power of the author. The text attempts to be a demonstration: a spatial analogue and a concrete prose repetition of Rossi's idea of type.[3]

The temporality of the text concerns the reader's sense of time, the *tempo* of a dialogue as opposed to a monologue, and the temporality of the trace that the original 55 notes, some of which have disappeared, and the conversation around them leave as history or memory. The time involved in reading a text of this sort is quite different from that of a conventional text. The tempo of reading is affected by the number and quality of the voices that it presents and the ways in which those voices are engaged.

The chapter, therefore, attempts a demonstration – an analogy in writing to Rossi's "forgetting architecture." The power of the author presented in the structure and origin (architecture) has a relationship with the conventionally-marginalized-and-now-elevated-as-text criticism of others (life). The commentaries compete with the original text, sometimes overtaking it as if in a figure/ground reversal.

MF: *The repetition is the falling away (forgetting) of the structure and the imposition, the presence of a more recent history (life).*

MF: *Comprehension (in this text) comes from reading back and forth (repetition) and presence of absence (what is latent). Forgetting is related to being latent. If authorial presence provides a strong structure or construct in which the critical voices can present themselves as vehicles for the reader, the author will be forgotten and remembered by the reader. The author will be latent.*

TM: *Nietzsche appears to be an author here: in* On the Advantage and Disadvantage of History for Life, *he isolates the necessity of forgetting as crucial to action, to living, as a deliberate and brief suspension of memory.*

JB: *To the extent that this text allows other voices to overtake it, to erase it through commentary, the work can be considered a counter-text or, perhaps more appropriately, a counter-monument similar to Rossi's intentions in "forgetting architecture." Because of what they understand as the inherently fascist nature of monuments, Jochen and Esther*

be ignored. On Derrida's account, those readings come to belong to the text; they are interwoven into it. In consequence the text is to be defined as the history of its various readings. A new reading which 'holds' is not only added to the previous interpretations it addresses, but supplements them, in Derrida's Rousseauian sense of adding *and* substituting. Hence commentators on Derrida who focus only on the new interpretation that Derrida adds, fail to recognize the more complex juxtaposition which constitutes double reading as 'one divided but coherent movement'" (Bernasconi 1992, 147). Rossi's perspective concerning the history and architecture of the city parallels Derrida's position in relation to textual readings.

MF: *How can previous readings mark a text except by imprinting the reader? The text then has a life outside its own margins – expanding in a collective of readers who write and speak.*

JK: *Rossi comes from urban geography/realism/hermeneutics/dialectics but has not the intention of deconstruction (?).*

2. The voices are JB: Jose Buscaglia, EC: Elizabeth Cromley, MF: Michelle Fisher, KF: Kenneth Frampton, KAF: Karen A. Franck, AF: Alice Friedman, BG: Bruce Goodwin, JK: John Knesl, NCM: Nicholas C. Markovich, TM: Thomas Mical, and LS: Lynda Schneekloth.

3. The relationship between this text and Rossi's work engages various complex issues, including the idea of type as origin which was one of the most significant Enlightenment interpretations of type. Notwithstanding the fact that the "original" 55 notes were made up of the many voices that any text presents, their remainder in this text is treated as a single, uniform set of notes designed to elicit the voices that build up in any writing and in/on every architecture. If the process of exchanges between commentors continued, a history would develop in which the final text might contain none of the "original" notes. Origin would have slipped into absence.

Gertz designed and built a Gegendenkmal for the city of Hamburg, a counter-monument whose fate is to disappear, sinking slowly into the ground, as passersby write comments and inscriptions on its walls. This Monument against Fascism, War and Violence — and for Peace and Human Rights *is a monolithic text against itself, an artifact that, instead of relieving the collectivity from the responsibility of remembrance — it is proposed — will make people reclaim and face their memories. The ideas behind the erection/burial of the Gegendenkmal are similar to the intentions of this text: "... its aim is not to console but to provoke; not to remain fixed but to change; not to be everlasting but to disappear; not to be ignored by its passersby but to demand interaction; not to remain pristine but to invite its own violation and desecration; not to accept graciously the burden of memory but to throw it back at the town's feet" (Young 1992, 277).*

JK: *See Benjamin's/Bergson's distinctions re memory: Gedachtnis vs. Erinnerung (approx.: memory vs. remembering).*

TM: *Foucault establishes a distinction between two objects of memory — the monument and the document. The spatialization of memory implicates a question of power structure(s).*

MF: *It seems impossible that an object, a form, can be independent of meaning.*

TM: *As stating that one does not engage in politics is still a (radical) political statement, so too perhaps a form without meaning engenders an/other meaning.*

BG: *Perhaps Tafuri hoped that Rossi's was "an architecture in which form had lost its meaning," but surely this is not what Rossi felt, or hoped. He is explicit about that in "The Analogous City."*

MF: *What we are trying to escape leaves its imprint on what we obtain. Structure is inescapable, contingent.*

BG: *You say that type "was one of architecture's clearest structuralist manifestations," and I think that in a way this is quite an astute and provocative observation. I would agree in the sense that the structuralist looks for what lies below the surface, for what is constant behind superficial variations. But it is my understanding that it is a primary goal of structural linguistics and structural anthropology to uncover the structures of the mind itself through the study of the patterns in those phenomena, as you point out quite concisely later on, in Note Thirty-two. I think that, for Rossi, typology is basically a way of organizing knowledge, and however profoundly that knowledge might be connected with our history and experience it does not imply a structure of the mind in the way that (for example) language does. Eisenman was certainly after the sort of cognitive structure that language seems to imply, but I think Rossi is interested in the way that meaning is culturally constructed, not innate.*

Introduction

In the late 1950s, the Italian architect Aldo Rossi assisted in the resurrection of the idea of type in architecture. Emerging from behind the eliding surfaces of modernist works, the resuscitation of type recalled the history that it had enjoyed in academic theory and practice and breathed new life into old questions of origins, principles, and laws that modernist positions had arrested or circumvented. Rossi established a new type, one that manifested the poetic objectives and the materialist convictions that he pursued relentlessly and that became both the evidence of and the conditions of life. Thus his convictions and interest provided the materials for an architecture of both reason and memory (Moneo 1978) or an introduction of memory into objects (Eisenman 1982). It was an architecture in which form had lost its meaning and, therefore, type was the ground upon which the life of the community would become figured.

The revival or renovation of type in architecture paralleled, and cited for legitimation, the many versions of structuralism: it was one of architecture's clearest structuralist manifestations and thus proposed certain structures by which thinking and making architecture could/should be undertaken.[4] This "should" contained a political agenda as did, ultimately, the specific idea of type that Rossi put forward. That agenda and other issues in relation to type in general, and to the work of Aldo Rossi more specifically, will be explored in the text that follows.

□ □ □

One

The original meaning of type, from the Greek, was concerned with "impression," "figure," and came from the verb "to beat."

Two

Aldo Rossi seems to reverse this: type is ground.[5] Type can be formulated in a binary relation to atypicality or non-type, or, in Rossi's work, to life (the "events" of the life of the community). But what does atypicality mean in relation to type? What is not-type? While life can be viewed at some generic level as atypical, it is important for us to ground this in some specificity. In Rossi's work it appears to mean the alterations that take place over time. The unadulterated condition of type is the ground upon which figuration – the events lived by people in their daily lives – takes place. The contingencies and surprises of everyday life (Rossi's "unforeseen") create the poetic excrescence that builds up on type.

Three

The meaning of Rossi's "unforeseen" ["In some of my recent projects, or ideas for projects, I try to stop the event just before it occurs, as if the architect could foresee – and in a certain sense does foresee – the unfolding of life in the house" (1981, 6)] is constituted in imagining, for example, "the effect produced by a person who leaves a room unexpectedly" (1981, 35). This is one of the ways that the latent poetic of Rossi's work can be sighted, as in the "Plan for a Villa with Interior," a project that haunts his sketches for many years. Rossi's typology, therefore, is a set of architectural "pieces" – steps, corridors, and arcades – that provide a background or setting against which the events of life could become figural.[6] It is an architecture of the theater and a theatrical architecture. In order to be able to produce such an architecture, it is important to "forget architecture."

JK: *So to speak: beaten into the plastic material of space,* then *receding.*

JK: *Non-type does not equal life; did he not rather maintain that to miss the type meant to miss "life"?*

EC: *The word type points to (1) different forms of buildings as figures in the cityscape (figure), (2) different events inscribed on the mute surfaces of those buildings.*

MF: *There are ways in which I can imagine the ground re-figured by the events of everyday life. More commonly I think it becomes worn down, smoothed over, rounded, except in one's memory. Certainly this is a layering which builds up/on type.*

TM: *Filmic montage, as postulated by Eisenstein, locates meaning exactly at the "gap" where two images are abutted. Though this image is more akin to the works of the Japanese filmmaker Ozu, it implicates process gaps that invite projection of meaning through the unstable line between present and absent.*

NCM: *Rossi presents the ultimate Italian vision of drama, Verdi's* Nabucco. *The magnificence of simple elegance, a type of life, emotional, passionate, spectacular.*

JK: *I think he means: architecture as theater on its own.*

TM: *The process of forgetting, as relayed by Henri Bergson in* Matter and Memory, *is tied to the question of duration(s) – one never achieves a complete erasure.*

4. There were other manifestations, such as Peter Eisenman's early work which assumed a limited set of autonomous, architectural archetypes and an interest in Noam Chomsky's structural linguistics (Eisenman 1987). See also Eisenman (1975a and b).

12-1
City Hall, Muggio, Italy, Competition Design, Aldo Rossi, 1973
(Note: all Rossi drawings courtesy of Studio di Archittetura)

5. I use the term *ground* in two ways in the text: (a) as background (as in the gestalt concept of figure/ground), and (b) as the foundation upon which our ideas are constructed. The first use agrees with Rossi's assumption of an analogous relationship between architecture and theater: architecture is a stage, a backdrop and thus a background for the events of life. The second use reflects some post-structuralist architectural projects. Eisenman, for example, has attempted a critical architecture that challenges architectural metaphors in philosophy such as "ground;" he does so in various attempts to literally cut at the ground — as in the Cannaregio Project, the late Houses (for example, Fin d'Ou T Hou S), Checkpoint Charlie (the ground was excavated to reveal the major urban histories of the Berlin site), and the Wexner Center at Ohio State University at the rear of which architecture and landscape become confused. The two uses, however, are not mutually exclusive.

6. Rossi has indicated often his youthful interest in film and theater. The following quote, which immediately precedes the one in the text, indicates the significance of performing arts in Rossi's view of architecture: "Of course, whether a corridor or a room, it is inevitably a place in which someone will say sooner or later, 'Must we talk about all this?' or 'See how things have changed!' and other things that seem to be taken from some screenplay or drama… The corridor was a strip of space that seemed surrounded and gripped by private acts, unforeseeable occasions, love affairs, repentances. And especially by images which do not leave their imprint on film but which accumulate in things" (See Libeskind 1980).

Four

Rossi's theoretical project is ultimately more humanist and classical than the reductive imagery of some of his work might suggest.[7] His architecture is intended to accept, actually and metaphorically, the additions, marks, and memories that accrue to its frame, its body. This is the excrescence which the events of life on/in architecture generate and it is the basis for his argument to forget architecture.

KAF: *How do you know the architecture is intended to accept? The imagery doesn't seem to invite addition, marks, memories.*

JB: *As in this text, Rossi's architecture is to provide the frame upon which the excrescence will grow or be adscribed. But if type is ground for Rossi, in accordance with the Marxist model of base/superstructure, how much does the frame or ground determine the nature of the excrescence and is it ever possible for this excrescence to appropriate and fundamentally alter the frame that supports it? "Forgetting architecture" is the response to a phenomenon where the excrescence validates the frame, a process that seems to negate the more complex tensions that a parasitic or symbiotic relationship between frame and outgrowth might generate.*

Five

Rossi argues that by analyzing cities over time we can understand those "elements" that either support or obstruct the interests of the collective will. He analyzed various cities by means of techniques, such as figure/ground Nolli maps, that privilege form and composition. The analyses reduced cities to a limited array of simple types and compositional strategies. It is precisely by means of this analytic that the excrescence is lost, erased, eliminated. Can type contain a history of the city – of the events that constitute the many histories – if it is to be the ground against which these appear? We might wonder about a process that is motivated by an interest in life yet erases it as it sets out to pursue its goal.

JK: *He wants to find the "strong" types (that can support those "excrescences").*

MF: *Isn't this a technique that allows one to begin but does not erase backward glances?*

Six

Rossi's early work was concerned with a materialist architecture (attention to or emphasis on material objects, needs, and considerations with a disinterest in, or rejection of, spiritual values). This appears in the forms and compositions in the city.

BG: *The term "materialist" is of course confounded with connotations from Marx to Madonna.*

Seven

Through the analysis of the structure of the city Rossi arrives at an "autonomous" architecture expressed in the development of a typology of relationships between architecture and the city. As Grahame Shane suggests, Italian contextualist theory was patterned after the traditional materialist attitude that dictated that "the design must fit with, respond to, mediate its surroundings, perhaps completing a pattern implicit in the street layout or introducing a new one" (1976, 676).[8]

MF: *How can type be established in a single time line history?*

TM: *Type as a tightrope walker? Perhaps Virilio's model of technological time (dromology – the logic of the race) is more productive than single linear time.*

7. See Knesl's (1988) conclusions concerning the classicism at the heart of Rossi's project.

MF: *Are the rationalists correct in their conclusion? Is meaning "other," empty? Is it not a double reading?*

JK: *"Other" does not mean empty – quite the contrary.*

JB: *When Erwin Panofsky equated Renaissance perspective with critical philosophy and Greco-Roman perspective with skepticism, he was facing the question of the draining of meaning from form. As he explains, the spatial concept of infinity which was central to the construction of the linear perspective significantly contributed to the development of a detheologized conception of the universe. "The result," Panofsky writes, "was a translation of psychophysiological space into mathematical space; in other words, an objectification of the subjective" (Panofsky 1991, 66). Is Rossi's call to revive the classical vocabulary a way of circumventing the banality and triviality of modern science? Is it an attempt to deviate from the reign of constant distortion implicit in modern perspective and to return by analogy to the possibility of re-creating a psychophysiological space where form and thought would not be mutually exclusive?*

BG: *Your question gets to the heart of what I believe is central to rationalism and most interesting and powerful about it: the importance of the collective memory, which in the case of architecture is unconscious (cf.: Benjamin's discussion of architecture as experienced in distraction).*

JK: *Rationalism attempts to establish a field of relations* within, *it admits a limited number of meanings, at minimum that of* clarity *("strength?") from which new insemination can occur…*

8. There are several definitions of autonomy operative in architectural discourse. See a discussion (Editors 1985) concerning two contrasting positions in the work of Rossi and Eisenman. Rossi's autonomy depends on the idea that elements refer only to their own nature… and their geometries are neither scientific nor technical but essentially architectural. Eisenman's autonomy is based on his assumptions concerning modern sensibility, i.e., a sensibility in which objects are seen as ideas independent of "man."
JK: *The "old" man (of humanism)?*

Eight
Through their analysis of the city, the neorationalists "trace the destruction of the classical system of order in the industrial revolution" and, subsequently, conclude that form is "drained of any signification of meaning…" (Shane 1976, 678-9). This view leads Rossi to conclude that we can "revive the historical vocabulary of forms and solutions of existing cities… [and] accept as given the past forms and typologies and design with them – but by analogy only" (Shane 1976, 678). Reflecting the European tradition for purist geometry, rationalists, like the architects of the Enlightenment, define architecture as an expression of thought. What is the difference between form expressing thought and form drained of meaning?

Nine
There is a fundamental assumption in the neoclassical tradition, as in Boullée's theory and in Le Corbusier's writings, that "connotations of… neoclassical form are well established in the collective subconscious" (Goodwin 1980, 119). How is the possibility of a "collective subconscious" and its invention and maintenance central to the rationalist position in the twentieth century? Is signification of meaning different from connotations in the subconscious?

☐ ☐ ☐

Ten

Rossi's early work is concerned with the collectivist values that his theories promote. As an "autonomist," "it is precisely through architecture that society can express its civic and public manifestations. The genuine value of the autonomy of architecture is that it allows for an expression of society in which architecture is an indispensable instrument for the production of the framework necessary to civil life" (Moneo 1976, 19).

Eleven

Is there an assumption in neorationalist arguments that "type" is a "natural" social representation, presentation, or demonstration? Or that its relationship to society is the only and proper concern of architecture? Rossi states that type-forms reflect the collective will of the people. Does this assertion acknowledge the political issues involved in the making of architecture? Does it overlook the question: Who controls production? Surely not "the people" unless we reinstate the nineteenth-century concept of *volksgeist*.⁹ Rossi's idea of the city is based on the assumption of an established and pre-existing relationship between architecture and "the people," a relationship that is "embodied" in the material conditions of the city.¹⁰

KF: *If by type one means (1) classical type, (2) institutional/monumental type and, finally, in relation to (1) and (2) above, urban type, then quite obviously it is the cultural and political precondition of the civic (Moneo); the pre-condition that is of Arendt's "space of public appearance" as* the political space.

JK: *He says: we (architects) certainly do not control it, nor should we pretend or aspire to do so...*

JK: *The question to ask Rossi: How does this relation establish itself, how can one deduce it is valid to continue as a "type"?*

12-2
Apartment Block, Gallaratese quarter, Milan, Italy, Aldo Rossi, 1973

9. Rossi's argument contains complex, late modernist residues of nineteenth- and twentieth-century *zeitgeist* legitimations. Given the similarities between the *volksgeist* and *zeitgeist* arguments — the nature, structure, and rhetorical significance of each — it is possible that they both play a role in his work.

10. Boullée's conviction that "speaking monuments" were an "essential component of a well-ordered republican society" is repeated in Rossi's arguments but with a Marxist inflection. According to Vidler, "Boullée stated the theory of typical character in a way that stressed not so much the symbolic nature of the form, but the metaphoric, or allegorical mode, in the service of making the building speak to the society. For Boullée and many of his peers, 'speaking monuments' were an essential component of a well-ordered republican society..." (Vidler 1977, 103). He goes on to declare the death of symbolic type and, thus, lays a ground for Rossi's form without meaning: "the ultimate futility of this [architecture parlante] symbolic project was revealed. In an age of consumption, no symbol could achieve more than momentary, personal significance" (Vidler 1977, 103).

NCM: *Is it not true that the exaggeration of the rational leads to the surreal, to de Chirico, to the dream?*

KF: *The disintegration of the typological/institutional as a traditionally determined, received trope is obviously connected to the privatization of the late modern world and the tendency to reduce all objects, including buildings, to commodity status. This only too real situation probably accounts for Rossi's estrangement and his propensity for the romantic compensation of the sublime. As he puts it somewhere, "deprived by history of achieving any large tasks... etc." One is reminded of Clement Greenberg: "Having been denied by the Enlightenment of all tasks they could take seriously... they [the arts]... could save themselves... only by demonstrating that the kind of experience they provided was valuable in its own right and not to be obtained from any other kind of activity" (1973, 67–8). Thus Rossi, like Philip Johnson, is a disenchanted figure of the late Enlightenment – the failed Enlightenment, as is evident from the joint global failure of reason and socialism.*

JK: *I think that the absence of traces of "life" in the images/spaces is what is to call forth life (the laundry on the balcony) – a dialectical strategy.*

TM: *...or thoughts too sophisticated to operate by dialectic.*

LS: *This is a critical question. Tension is revealed and accepted but not resolved. How can we simultaneously be aware of context because it is peculiar and specific (and of which do we speak?) and always use the same geometry?*

JK: *The response is in the judicious application of the types...*

NCM: *Yes, it is the dream where one wanders alone, lost in the fog.*

TM: *To be alienated is to be alienated from something. The question concerning alienation is more accurately a question of "what is being excluded/suppressed?"*

JB: *It would appear that it is the self that assumes peculiar and specific form in the architect's conceptions of both context and of the collective. Tension is revealed and accepted at the theoretical level but, behind this gesture, as Denis Hollier would propose, there is no uneasiness: "Architecture is society's authorized superego; there is no architecture that is not the Comendatore's" (Hollier 1989, ix).*

11. There is an interesting parallel to the emptiness or alienating qualities of Rossi's work in the reductive and diagrammatic architecture produced by architects trained in the academic modernism at Harvard. See Herdeg (1983).

Twelve

As a rationalist, a romantic proclivity he shares with Boullée whose *Treatise* he translated and prefaced, Rossi is in the "tradition of the sublime." One of Rossi's characteristics is "his estrangement from the real, understood as everyday occurrence" (Moneo 1976, 18). The reductive, formalist consequences of this propensity are evident in such haunting images as the Gallaratese Housing project, the Modena Cemetery, and the School at Fagnano Olona. But the "everyday occurrence" is what Rossi's architecture is intended to allow and support. Is Rossi's work the most powerful emergence/eruption of the rational in the heart of the real? Can the metaphors of specifically visual binary techniques, such as the gestalt concept of figure/ground, be used to measure or characterize other, non-visual relationships?

Thirteen

Rossi constantly repeats the same "monumental type-forms and purist geometry" (Shane 1976, 678). The monumentality is evident in the Gallaratese Housing project in which, according to Martin Filler, "the simple, relentlessly repeated square windows and wall openings of the lateral facades give it a gravity and a formality that make some critics uneasy" (1980, 104). The same unease is evident in many of Rossi's projects including the Modena Cemetery. Is the alienating experience of Rossi's works the inevitable consequence of his theoretical constructions and intentionality?[11]

□ □ □

Rossi's work attempts to exclude all but the most general types and to avoid the circumstantial. Particular figures are used... because of their power to suggest archetypes... (Colquhoun 1986b, 199).

□ □ □

TM: *Rossi's drawings carry his "signature," yet they are circumstantial. Is his architecture that which excludes the circumstantial, or merely banishes/"forgets" it into representation?*

Fourteen

Rossi tells the story of his attempt, early in his architectural education, to draw the plans of a piazza based on the lengths and angles from a survey he and other students had done. He recalls his pleasure in the failure to "close" the triangle: "I found in this inability to close the triangulations... something mythical, like a further spatial dimension" (1981, 49). Something escaped the otherwise exhaustive control of rationality: "Whenever I draw a triangle I always think not only of the difficulty of closing it, but of the richness implicit in the error" (1981, 81).

Even his pleasure in the problems that rationality has faced in its post–World War II decline, however, does not obscure Rossi's interest in an architecture of reason:

> The unsuccessful attempt to close the triangle was an affirmation of a more complex geometry, which, however, proved to be inexpressible and could demonstrate only the most elementary facts (Rossi 1981, 49–50).

He continues: "Perhaps from these experiences my early projects for the bridge at the Triennale and the monument at Segrate were born" (1981, 49). If so, his early work failed to fulfill his hope of expressing "a more complex geometry," one that he never defines.[12]

TM: *Is this discrepancy a trace of the circumstantial re-exerting its presence on the type (the document)? Nietzsche's writings prophesied makers of new myths. How does the immanence of the circumstantial become equated with the mythical?*

MF: *"Proved" presumes exhaustible.*

TM: *This "inexpressible" recalls the problematic of representation of the sublime.*

TM: *Perhaps this mode of re-presentation and construction blocks this possibility: the sketch (as text) and building (as text) propose discontinuous type/ologies.*

NCM: *There is an element of intuition and unpredictability even in the most rational of lives.*

Fifteen

The analytical method which Rossi and others employed in the Italian rationalist movement is based on preoccupations with the Gestalt concept of figure/ground relationships in the urban plan. It is a technique that ultimately produced international studies of building typologies, a taxonomic propensity central to neoclassicism.[13]

JK: *I thought that the internal organization of buildings arrayed on the ground of the city was far more important for him than a figure/ground pattern.*

12-3
Study for the
Geometry of the Memory,
Aldo Rossi, 1978

12. Rossi's early effort to express that which eluded him, the inexpressible, is related to Lyotard's position concerning the relationships between rationality and what he refers to as the "inhuman," "indeterminate," and the "unpresentable." In a critique of photography in the modern world, Lyotard states that the "indeterminate, because it cannot be forecast, has to be, if not eliminated, at least limited to the capacities of the apparatus…" (1991, 122). He also raises the possibility of both an answer to Rossi's dilemma and the source of his pleasure: "As if reason had no doubt that its vocation is to draw on the indeterminate to give it form, and that it cannot fail to succeed in this. Yet it is only at the price of this doubt that reason reasons" (Lyotard 1991, 4). Rossi seems to echo Lyotard when he discusses his interest in analogy: "I encountered something similar to this in Juan de la Cruz's ascent of Mount Carmel: the representation of the mountain in his magnificent drawing/writing brought me back to my initial perception of the Sacri Monti, where the most difficult things to understand always seemed to me the meaning of and reason for the ascent" (1981, 81). He states this more clearly in other childhood reflections: "This is a strange memory or experience of modern architecture, but it is also always accompanied by the awareness that aspects of reality can only be apprehended one at a time; I mean that *rationality or the smallest degree of lucidity permits an analysis of what is certainly reality's most fascinating aspect: the inexpressible*" (Rossi 1981, 52). (Emphasis added.)

13. Although Rossi (1981) rejects his critics' accusation of neo-Enlightenment rationalism, his sympathy and admiration of Boullée's position are telling. In relation to his gestalt framework, the simple binary is also the structure of "forgetting architecture," i.e., architecture and "life." Grahame Shane (1976) discusses various aspects, and some of the complexities, of the gestalt figure/ground concept in the Italian rationalist movement in the 1950s.

TM: *…or the will-to-abstraction, the ascetic ideal, or an architecture-without-qualities.*

AF: *I'm interested in how this desire, and attendant uneasiness with ambiguity, can be utilized progressively. Are there ways to manipulate the familiar constructs of type to provide a sense of order without sacrificing change or progressive design thinking?*

JB: *Is type as an instrument of order, as technology, producing an erasure of technique in the sense of the Greek* techne *(making appear)? Is concealment the historical and mechanical basis of architectural production?*

JK: *…or, does it create that which does not? (argument about limits, prohibitions…)*

MF: *Appearance erases (displaces) structure. In fact, doesn't Rossi try to push his work to the moment, this edge, the space and time of the event?*

Sixteen

Type reveals a predisposition or desire for order, clarity, simplicity. Such a desire is fulfilled by, or at least manifest in, a yearning for technique. Type "becomes an apparatus, an instrument for analysis and measure" (Eisenman 1982, 7) and for production. Such a desire overcomes and displaces the tension of the confrontation with the inexpressible or the "unpresentable" which is made unacceptable by naming it as "error" or "mythical."

Seventeen

Poststructuralists, especially deconstructivists, harbor a certain abhorrence for method or technique because these presume principles that institute certain metaphysical presuppositions (Knesl 1988).

Eighteen

Technique has complex relationships with ideology. It inscribes itself into thought and production (Baudrillard 1981). It also makes possible and inscribes a particular subjectivity, i.e., it participates in shaping our character, our values, and our view of the world (Hollier 1989). It inscribes a particular kind of order. Any method or goal-oriented behavior, including type as an apparatus or instrument for design action, is a technique. Rossi states that a "passion for technique is very important for my projects and my interest in architecture" (1981, 37–38). He carries this to a surreal limit, perhaps, by asking: "Is happiness perhaps a technique?" (1981, 55).

Nineteen

Function as technique: idea versus experience. If the nineteenth- and twentieth-century city were a *cité parlante*, it would be replete with objects whose specific function would be optically evident. The city would become a matrix of utility, a *machine à habiter*, both in terms of serving designated purposes and serving the will to understand through classification and naming.[14] It would provide the means of controlling architectural production, symbolism, and its reading. It would serve a certain population, one that takes pleasure in accounting for what is owned and owed, for what is controlled through various economies. *Architecture parlante* participated in the making of such a city — a place exhaustively defined in terms of use — and in the servicing of a collective subjectivity interested in a utilitarian visuality.

JK: ...*if imposed from above/outside.*

LS: *To have no method or technique also presumes principles.*

TM: *The denial of technique is itself a (radical) technique.*

MF: *Perhaps freedom in the deconstructivist's critique is sited in the pauses that link, the gaps between strategies, the opportunity to reassess, twist the critique. Moments of choice.*

AF: *This statement is obviously true and extremely important. I would love to see the idea expanded to include some discussion of how this relationship is viewed and how it can be exploited to come to terms with the ideological basis of design.*

TM: *Here tragedy is the technique in Rossi's architecture of anticipation.*

JK: *What are the connections between techniques and desire...*

12-4
Cemetery of San Cataldo, Modena, Italy, Aldo Rossi, 1974

JK: *Not vacant but uninhabited.*

NCM: *The cemetery figure seems the embodiment of the dream state — beyond the tangible; such is death.*

LS: *Or the equation is problematic and isolative?*

MF: *What about madness? Madness effectively demonstrates presence of absence. Madness would effortlessly violate the logical causality of this statement.*

EC: *Do you mean he uncovers the idea of "type" or he uncovers the set of types (forms — yes?) from memory?*

TM: *…paradoxically reconstructing a document of subjective inscriptions and foregrounded technique(s).*

MF: *Because he believes he is part of a collective, a populous.*

JB: *Is not memory, as a residue of experience, itself a process of contingency?*

NCM: *Dreams are real, entirely rational in another sense.*

Twenty

The use of the human figure in the Modena Cemetery attests to Rossi's rationalist convictions and his interest in analogy: if the proof of existence is thought — *cogito, ergo sum* — then death is its absence. The vacant building — the head of this body located at the entrance to the cemetery — testifies to the equation of life with thought. Is this evidence (1) that the Tendenza's[15] analyses of the city did not arrive at an understanding of the compositional strategies; (2) that such analyses and results were inappropriate for a cemetery; (3) that Rossi had abandoned at least some of his earlier convictions?

> Rossi's work develops and transforms the classical mode. His projects evolve from images sketched from his memory of building types found in the city… the act of drawing from memory filters out the contingent, giving the image a stripped-down, essential presence (Editors 1985, 9).

What is the basis for Rossi's belief that drawing from memory is a legitimate basis for the uncovering of "type" and what type of type emerges from this practice? Why would Rossi assume that his drawn memory is type?[16]

---

14. Vidler states that type "was readily assimilated by architectural theorists concerned to distinguish between kinds of building. To talk of a building type then, implied not only its search for original validation… but also its specific aspect, the form that enabled it to be read as to its purpose at first glance" (1977, 97).

AF: *La Marche is referring to the crucial relationship between type and architectural character here, i.e., the ways in which type allows us not only to read the functions of specific buildings but also their ideological and political meanings. At the core of* architecture parlante *was a desire to make typological conventions, and mimetic forms, function in a revolutionary culture, i.e., with reformulated and progressive meaning substituted for conventional and conservative order.*

15. For a brief review of the group known as the Tendenza, to which Rossi belonged, see Filler 1980.

16. Frances Downing discusses many of the questions surrounding the issues of memory and drawing in this book.

Twenty-one
How does drawing from memory uncover type? In addition, how can Rossi employ this strategy given the fact that the Tendenza rejected willfulness and self-consciousness as legitimate bases for the production of architecture? We must conclude from these two apparently antithetical conditions that memory is as scientific and objective as structuralist propensities demand, or that it operates in a universal, structuralist manner.[17] If so, it fulfills the goal, and becomes one of the primary conditions, of the definition of legitimacy: if all humans process information, as in seeing difference over seeing sameness, what Rossi re-members through his drawings is what anyone else would remember. What this argument omits and obscures, however, is the architectural training in drawing and thinking, his specialization, the transformations of which he recognizes elsewhere:

> Architecture and architectural theories, like everything else, can only be described according to concepts which are neither absolute nor neutral, and these, depending on their importance, have the potential to modify man's way of seeing profoundly (Rossi 1982, 165).

JK: *Because, in his method, it generates an absolutized form complex (no scale).*

JB: *Does drawing in this way make of him the author and not the representative of the collective?*

MF: *In selecting comments, authorial presence is (re)affirmed. In their questions, the voices remain spectators. This is the "technique" or method of this text.*

LS: *His argument also overlooks his place in culture; he has a location as a human and a man, not just as an architect.*

□ □ □

Twenty-two
The dominance of specific interpretations of type changes over time, e.g., its movement in the late eighteenth century from symbolist to materialist (Vidler 1977). In certain histories type is specifically a term grounded in visuality; in others it is spatiotemporal, constructional, functional. Does the shifting pattern of dominant concepts of type attest to a movement of focus from the visual to the phenomenal experience? Does history of type as idea move between these two and other possibilities, tracing a cats cradle in the space of cultural transformation? Which others? If so, is the array of potential human experience in architecture limited, or limited to these specific possibilities? Or is it that architecture cannot eviscerate the history that we construct of it?

MF: *Are we (the readers/writers) moving in and out of type?*

EC: *Architecture can/cannot disembowel the history of architecture.*

Twenty-three
The varieties of types make type appear to be as flexible in relation to its definition as it is to "model." There are, for Anthony Vidler (1977), three Enlightenment types — those of origins, of characteristic form of a classified species, and of symbolic mark.

17. The emergence of typology in post-World War II architectural theory parallels the work of Claude Lévi-Strauss, whose major work, *Structural Anthropology*, disseminated his conviction concerning, and attempt to uncover, universal mental structures, an endeavor which came to be known as structuralism. Some of the prominent criticisms of structuralism (that it exhaustively homologized and allowed for no chaos), or Sartre's criticism that it was "remote from human existence and even denies its fundamental condition – that is, freedom" (Kurzweil 1980, 24) can also be levied against the concept of type as it emerged in the post-World War II European context. Charles Levin expands on this: "As John Fekete puts it: in structuralism, 'attention is shifted away from the ways in which human beings have altered and do alter and may yet alter their objectifications; in consequence, structuralism finds nothing to investigate but order, the codes of order, reflections upon order, and the experience of order'" (1981, 10).

TM: *This transience of function may not preclude "truth"; it perhaps posits a relativism that flows into and through "types," filling them with difference.*

TM: *Is this occurring dialectically or teleologically?*

NCM: *An experiential typology?*

TM: *...or "anti-perspectival" readings?*

KF: *Certainly all theory presupposes and forms a particular mode of beholding. This is as true of Eisenman as Christopher Alexander.*

LS: *One of the characterizations of type is that its categories overlap and collide rather than being mutually exclusive as by incision and boundary.*

JK: *Type: clearly an attempt to* define, *to subordinate differences, to identify by test of possessing certain* properties *and also to work out difference to an* other *type.*

JK: *Wider: type related to power (political, cultural — who defines what type something is to belong to...).*

TM: *Let us not forget the logic of the scar — a residual trace of a previous incision operating over time to erode and transgress the incision, to create the "other" of the incision (and the body).*

Twenty-four
Types of type: functional, formal, image, style, constructional, compositional, conceptual. All are related at times and in certain ways. Rossi's type is specific; he admired Mies van der Rohe and agreed substantially with his argument concerning "universal space:" buildings change their function over time and, therefore, for a building to be an honest expression, the only truth is its structure, its construction, and its making room for unforeseen events and activities. Thus Rossi's "city" is a materialist city seen in terms of type-forms, a typology of forms based on the constant repetition of certain constructions.[18]

Twenty-five
The idea of type changes focus historically from visual to functional, from optical to phenomenal. The variety is evident in the different typological projects in the postmodern world such as Michael Graves's work starting in the late 1970s, Peter Eisenman's early projects, Rob Krier's postmodern taxonomies, and the work of Mario Botta and Steven Holl, to mention only a few.

Twenty-six
The idea of type operates at different "scales." Christopher Alexander's *A Pattern Language* (1977) attempts to ascribe to architectural "fragments" the status of type, thus moving the instrumentality of type as technique to a more intimate and experiential scale. This shift in scale demonstrates the migration of boundary conditions which move between dimensionalities and foster different perspectival readings.[19]

Twenty-seven
Type emerges along the boundaries, the incisions that we make, in terms of informational processing in both a biological and a logical context.

Twenty-eight
Each text presents a landscape of surfaces and edges that delineate the metaphysical conditions embedded in its forms and boundaries.[20] The edges and boundaries are lines inscribed by ideas, language, and subjectivity.

Poststructuralist writers "reject both the earlier humanism, with its idea of a subject in control and at the center of the world, of a history with an origin and an end, and also the extension of humanism into the idea of a structure with its own center… It may be said that all these authors search for ways to accept materiality without relying on the authority of interpretive systems" (Knesl 1988, 163). This does not necessarily mean that poststructuralism can be exhaustively understood as a radical materialism. Questioning interpretive systems cannot reduce the world to simple materialist reality; questioning does not in and of itself imply a denigration of that which is questioned.

Is there an architecture to resist the architectural production of subjectivity? Is there an architecture that produces/supports a subjectivity other than that which architecture currently promotes? Hollier (1989) discusses the possibilities of an architecture that does not provide the "space" for the creation of subjectivity; he claims that such an architecture was attempted in Bernard Tschumi's Parc de la Villette. Tschumi (1983) implies that such a pre-subjective architecture is possible; he suggests that, if one critiques assumptions concerning the relationship between form and function, there are three possibilities: they agree, they conflict, or they are indifferent to one another. (What is an architecture like in which spaces and events have little to do with one another?) Knesl discusses subjectivity specifically in relation to Rossi's concept of memory which "belongs to a collective city body… a material body that can resist the modern power techniques that develop 'subjects' and 'things' into resources" (1988, 170).

These lines of subjectivity are generated, maintained (protected against disassembly), and nurtured by the metaphysical. The metaphysical and these lines are held in place by each of us alone or in concert by means of the sustenance of conviction: an architecture of faith.

TM: *Are there no texts without metaphysics? Does Rossi, when he denies metaphysical contamination of his work, therefore not write the type, or write the not-type?*

NCM: *Is there a place here for metaphysics?*

MF: *I think this is what motivates "I think, therefore I am," as opposed to the causality of logic.*

TM: *The modernist projects of negation, erasure, and disappearance point towards such an exclusion of subjectivity, but not exclusively outside the boundary lines delimiting "type."*

NCM: *Whose faith, whose truth? Is there a greater truth than "us"?*

JK: *Maybe we are being convicted and collude with it as well.*

TM: *Is this a recurrent monasticism, or scholasticism?*

18. Knesl argues that the "Tendenza's quest for the so-called autonomy of architecture did liberate architectural form but only insofar as it rebelled against the functionalistic appropriation of architecture by social and cultural engineering" (1988, 163).

JB: *Is origin necessary?*

TM: *Is the origin knowable?*

JB: *Martin Heidegger argues that "boundary is not that at which something stops but, as the Greeks recognized, the boundary is that from which something begins its presencing" (Heidegger 1975, 154). How is the concept of boundary in this sense related to* techne *as revelation, and is type, as ground, a negation of the boundary condition?*

LS: *Question of reversal — what does type do to us, not just to the world?*

MF: *Identity is assumed here unless it is merely in the language of the "structure," e.g., so far "above and to the right" of another fixed point.*

19. Such a boundary difference appears in relation, for example, to the binaries that are the bases of autonomies: some are defined as a condition of difference between form and meaning (Rossi), some between form and function (Eisenman, Tschumi, Mies), etc. In addition, one position might be based on a different spatial perspective. For example, the concepts of "layering" (the frontality and purist layering in Le Corbusier's work) and superposition (Tschumi's Parc de la Villette) could be based on a "radial" metaphorical structure that could be re-structured as concentric circles.

20. I am using the term *metaphysical* in the sense that John Knesl uses it. Specifically, it is his interpretation of the Derridean objective if one can say of deconstruction that it "hunts down the metaphysical, since it is the metaphysical that supports the act of assigning meaning and value that is performed by the will that brings itself to life in the strategy in/of a text" (Knesl 1988, 164).

21. In relation to the history of the city, Rossi's assumptions are not only, nor primarily, concerned with origins; he is more concerned with that which is repeated over time. Repetition is proof of significance.

Twenty-nine

The first line makes its appearance between, and establishes, sameness and difference. Because of this initial appearance, the first and every subsequent differentiation is into sameness and difference. Knowing and being are partially, and perhaps only temporarily, controlled by the residual effects of origin.[21]

> The metaphysical rests in the idea that a system (made up of hierarchically ordered oppositions) is founded on a vindicating, authorizing power center, a presence from which emanates meaning… Structure is to tame the difference that is the movement of the becoming of the world at every instant, so that it will play the role of a mere difference of position [spatial metaphor structures] *within* a system that enforces unity from above or from behind and relies on identities based on the structure as ultimate referential… In this, architecture has clearly played a principal role by forcing this kind of memory of the identical on "us," thus making us into subjects for whom identity is a necessary constituent (Knesl 1988, 164).

Thirty

Structuring assigns everything a place. Even that which is excluded, defined as outside, as different, is controlled.

Thirty-one

It is the interpretation and/or characterization of sameness or difference that is different in different systems.[22] Each system and all modifications mirror and are structured by the same origin and each constructs another framework and another metaphysical.

Thirty-two

The structure is a network that is a piece of a larger construct, a *weltanschauung*. Its simplest form is one that is exponentially binary *ad infinitum*. This ladder of structuration invents and maintains a unity, a singularity, an identity. The content that takes place in the structure is culturally imbued with value by means of the dominant/subordinate hierarchical relationships (up and down, left and right, in and out). The stability of the structure is enforced by the binary sets, each of which contains and maintains hierarchical relations. How does structuring invent or maintain?

Thirty-three

Each binary set is construed along the lines of what is "elementary," "essential," "natural." These terms reveal the incision that defines the limits beyond and behind which the theoretical position cannot go.

Thirty-four

Language is the basis for the characterization of the content and quality of the binary but not its form. The content also shares in the residual effects.

Thirty-five

We become aware of sameness and difference at the moment we map this binary system onto/into/in the experience. The characterization of the binary is invented at that moment. Because of its nature, both of the "terms" used to characterize the binary are coterminous and coexistent. They share a closed set in which there are no other possibilities; two is the only number.

TM: *Where each attempt to resolve the dilemma merely increases the dilemma's proportions?*

JK: *Singularity resists structural order which later leads to its own identity as encompassing all difference.*

JB: *Is there architecture outside of structure?*

LS: *Is binary considered oppositional or can it be complementary as well?*

EC: *The binary pair always seems to be read as one better and one worse, but this must be culturally specific and thus not structural.*

JK: *This is unexpected to me: on reflection there could be something there worth expanding because: "undoing" the division (in which ways does this become farther reaching) then means undoing structure (and hierarchy).*

JK: *"Interrogation" or "deconstruction" can go "behind?"*

JB: *How are these limit concepts defined?*

JK: *I would have thought the opposite? Is it possible to maintain this binary context/form without "deconstructing" it?*

JB: *Is metaphysics a purely two-dimensional order?*

MF: *What about poetics — what is latent and brought to the surface? This is a coming into presence both beyond and within language (one of numerous facets of "structure"). It is a naming of limits that exceed structure in the manner they are sited.*

JB: *Do we need to make a picture in order to displace experience or are we looking for a picture to confirm our displaced experiences? Should we aim at shedding the refuse in order to arrive at the basic core of type? Are we willing to face the other which Homi Bhabha finds in the most intimate place? "The 'other' is never outside or beyond us; it emerges forcefully, within cultural discourse, when we think we speak most intimately and indigenously 'between ourselves'" (Bhabha 1990, 4). Are we capable of accepting or even admitting to the existence of the unpresentable?*

JK: *To displace death, fear of death:... to what extent, how might that be in Rossi's types?*

EC: *This assumes that there is such a thing as experience apart from the what-we-make-sense-of.*

JB: *Who is we?*

JK: *(Collusively?) generated by interpretation...*

LS: *What are the options to radical relativism?*

Thirty-six
At some moments in the flow of experience seeing is purposefully focused. At such moments are the tendencies to include and exclude and to make the assignments that attend perception, personal or cultural, self-generated or enculturated? Einstein stated that we "make a picture of the world" and use that picture as a means of making sense of, and displacing, experience.[23]

Thirty-seven
We "write" the structure of experience. It cannot be conceived as exclusively empirical; we have never been capable of exhaustively defining an objective or materialist "reality" that is not subject to interpretive systems. Yet these are also inconclusive unless we accept a radical relativism. "[W]here can one go after this fundamental metaphoricity of all meaning has been demonstrated?" (Knesl 1988, 164).

> Yet in the end, the very notion of structure may be metaphor itself, dependent on the will to forget the rhetorical status of the very concept of structure (Knesl 1988, 163–4).

□ □ □

---

22. For another interpretation of the issues of sameness and difference, see Baudrillard (1993), especially "The Hell of the Same" and "The Melodrama of Difference," pages 113–23 and 124–38, respectively.

23. The nature of experience is too complex to explore here. See La Marche (1992, 1993) for discussions of one possible means of engaging the different positions in architectural theory and their consequences for the material production that results from them.

Thirty-eight

"Type" is subject to the same consequences as other concepts such as "history" or "self" which have become unclear and disturbed, to the point of disappearing or being banished from discourse. Their presence is sliding into absence, disappearing across the horizon of theoretical control. If they remain, however, their content will slide, transforming their meaning.

Thirty-nine

Typological shift: renaming attempts to shift the particular cut of name as in the shift from house to residence. The contours of the particular cut transform variety into a series (it orders), difference into sameness (Baudrillard 1993), many into one. Visuality, and the body in general, is changed by modern technology (the computer, television, video, film, cyberspace, etc.) and, therefore, thinking will change and displace the particular cuts or connections that we currently make. Changes in perception and visuality affect association, memory, the body as well as the structure of experience.

Forty

Type privileges constancy and sameness. It supports these in re-presentation and re-production, in duplicities and repetitions that institute the ideological content of the re-production, the choice of political continuation.

Forty-one

Given his political convictions, Rossi can only use type if, as he maintains, form has lost all its meaning. This conviction is one of the sources of the tragic and the sublime in his work.

TM: *Isn't theory always control?*

TM: *As an uncanny conceptual "doppler effect," where barely recognizable blurs on the periphery of our "horizon of theoretical control?"*

TM: *Are not the body and technology always mutually inscribing/rewriting each other, frequently through the discourse of architecture?*

NCM: *The constant and fixed versus the ephemeral, transitions ongoing.*

EC: *Not if the multiple meanings of type that you noted before still hold.*

LS: *What about the work of reconstruction? Does type, does history become* absent*? Or only reinscribed into absence (binary always)?*

JK: *Except, and this is crucial, that the form will have been elected, reaffirmed by what remains unnamed ("life").*

TM: *Ironically, "life" reinhabits these forms, the eternal return of the same.*

AF: *Rossi's approach to type is based, it seems to me, on the sense of multivalent meaning in type forms, i.e., the notion that deep meaning, psychological response, and cultural convention can be understood differently and manipulated accordingly. Stripping away conventional meaning (with its specific cultural connotations) is a different exercise from denying that form has any meaning at all. Rossi's project seems far less nihilistic than La Marche proposes.*

JK: *But they do not represent a life: this is the difference to the nineteenth century and historicism.*

BG: *I'm not sure how you're using the term "historicism." Architects usually use it to refer to the ransacking of history for images, while Popper uses it to refer to teleological theories of history such as those of Marx or Hegel. Rossi, I suppose, would be interested more in the Heideggerean sense of a force of tradition that unifies diverse ways of Being, or perhaps just an interrelated series of events. I'm also uncertain about what you mean when you speak of the move from one form of thought conditioning (science) to another (history). If these were both very powerful in the nineteenth century, how can it be that we are moving from one to the other? Do you mean that the history-conditioning is eclipsing the science-conditioning? To me the legitimacy of the 300-year-old scientific paradigm is* **the** *crucial issue of our time.*

24. Note Karl Popper's (1957) differentiation, in *The Poverty of Historicism*, between synchronic and diachronic historicism. I am speaking of the latent power of the move from one form of thought conditioning, science, to another, history, which were both very powerful conditions of nineteenth century thought. Are we living the final stages of nineteenth century thought?

Forty-two

Concerned with a history of life, Rossi's analyses and early architecture are appropriate for our historicist era.[24] History is what we have turned to in the wake of the erosion of modernist prescriptions. Yet whose lives are overlooked in the specific history which we accept?

12-5
The Cabins at Elba,
Aldo Rossi, 1975

Forty-three

"Type" is subject to the same consequences as other concepts such as "history" or "self" which have become unclear and disturbed, to the point of disappearing, or being banished, from discourse. Their presence is sliding into absence, disappearing across the horizon of theoretical control. We are in a deconstructive free-fall. In his critique of deconstruction, Knesl suggests that what we might need is a technique of forcing a spatial typology to play out its secret allegiances, ideas, and values. A deconstruction of typologies would range through all levels of structure, from the obvious — say, the facade of a city hall and its relation to the state, or the apartment house and its relation to the palace, to the deeper levels, e.g., the urban grid and its connection to market and exchange (Knesl 1988, 170–1).

TM: *You seem to have a fascination for the "deconstructivist free-fall" (or is it the ascent of the Challenger?). Is there an end? It appears unclear whether there is an attempt to deny closure or signify incompletion.*

KF: *There are, it seems, two perennial themes running through your discourse, the* anti-metaphysical, *and the* anti-subjective, *or in Eisenman's terminology, the* anti-anthropomorphic. *These positions are sought after in order to arrive at an absolute degree zero of bourgeois consciousness. And with this* deserted *landscape, what should we now make? It seems to me essential, politically and otherwise, to re-instate the subject and above all the* inter-subjective, *and also the inescapability of* metaphor *and metaphorical thought, in all culture.*

JB: *The postmodernist iconoclastic position that lies at the core of this work is related to Rossi's ideas of type in an analogous way to what Heinrich Wölfflin saw in "the difference between a rococo decoration and a renaissance ornament." In Wölfflin's own words, "[t]he elementary phenomenon is this — that two totally different architectural effects are produced according to whether we are obliged to perceive the architectural form as something definite, solid, enduring, or as something over which, for all its stability, there plays an apparent, constant movement, that is, change" (Wölfflin 1950, 63). The fundamentally baroque character of postmodernist criticism, explained here as a movement of the becoming along boundaries and edges, is also possible: "The baroque neutralizes line as boundary, it multiplies edges, and while the form in itself grows intricate and the order more involved, it becomes increasingly difficult for the individual parts to assert their validity as plastic values; a (purely visual) movement set going over the sum of the forms, independently of the particular viewpoint. The wall vibrates, the space quivers in every corner" (Wölfflin 1950, 65). Are we in a deconstructive free-fall or are we erecting a neobaroque paradigm?*

MF: *How does one step outside of a system that spawns pairs, projects images that presume to be vacant but can only be different? In the pause between negation and affirmation we might slip away, forget. If you are mad, have you lost your will? Is this the only way to escape our efforts to double, being trapped in a system that will not dissolve? If one is mad and exercises free will, perhaps one is perfectly free.*

References

Alexander, C., S. Ishikawa, and M. Silverstein. 1977. *A Pattern Language: Towns, Buildings, Construction*. New York: Oxford University Press.

Baudrillard, J. 1981. Design environment or how political economy escalates into cyberblitz. In *For a Critique of the Political Economy of the Sign*, translated by C. Levin, 185–203. St. Louis, Mo.: Telos Press.

———. 1993. *The Transparency of Evil: Essays on Extreme Phenomena*. Translated by J. Benedict. New York: Verso.

Bernasconi, R. 1992. No more stories, good or bad: de Man's criticisms of Derrida on Rousseau. In *Derrida: A Critical Reader*, ed. D. Wood. Cambridge: Blackwell.

Bhabha, H. K. 1990. *Nation and Narration*. New York: Routledge.

Colquhoun, A. [1967] 1986a. Typology and design method. In *Essays in Architectural Criticism: Modern Architecture and Historical Change*, 43–50. Cambridge, Mass.: MIT Press.

———. 1986b [1978]. Form and figure. In *Essays in Architectural Criticism: Modern Architecture and Historical Change*, 190–202. Cambridge, Mass.: MIT Press.

Derrida, J. 1988. *The Ear of the Other*. Edited by C. McDonald and translated by P. Kamuf. Lincoln, Neb.: University of Nebraska Press.

Editors. 1985. Editorial: autonomous architecture. *The Harvard Architecture Review* 3 (Winter): 6–12.

Eisenman, P. 1975a. Cardboard architecture: House I. In *Five Architects*, 15–23. New York: Oxford University Press.

———. 1975b. Cardboard architecture: House II. In *Five Architects*, 25–37. New York: Oxford University Press.

———. 1982. Editor's Introduction. In *The Architecture of the City* by Aldo Rossi. Translated by D. Ghirardo and J. Ockman. Cambridge, Mass.: MIT Press.

———. 1987. Interview by author, 3 April, Columbus, Ohio.

Ellul, J. 1964. *The Technological Society*. New York: Vintage Books.

Filler, M. 1980. Rossi secco and Rossi dolce. *Art in America* (March): 100–106.

Goodwin, B. 1980. Architecture of the id. *Architecture + Urbanism* (June): 112–24.

Greenberg, C. 1973. Modernist painting. In *The New Art*, rev. ed., ed. G. Battcock, 66–77. New York: Dutton.

Heidegger, M. 1975. Building dwelling thinking. In *Poetry, Language, Thought*, 145–61. New York: Harper & Row.

Herdeg, K. 1983. *Decorated Diagram: Harvard Architecture and the Failure of the Bauhaus Legacy*. Cambridge, Mass.: MIT Press.

Hollier, D. 1989. *Against Architecture: The Writings of Georges Bataille*. Translated by B. Wing. Cambridge, Mass.: MIT Press.

Knesl, J. 1988. Postclassical *Poesis*. *Pratt Journal of Architecture* 2 (Spring): 163–75.

Kurzweil, E. 1980. *The Age of Structuralism: Levi-Strauss to Foucault*. New York: Columbia University Press.

Lacan, J. 1981. *The Four Fundamental Concepts of Psycho-Analysis*. Edited by J.-A. Miller and translated by A. Sheridan. New York: Norton.

La Marche, J. 1992. The desire of our eyes. *Person-Environment Theory Series* 16. Berkeley, Calif.: University of California.

———. 1993. Self and surface: the mirror of architecture. *Person-Environment Theory Series*. Berkeley, Calif.: University of California.

Levin, C. 1981. Translator's Introduction. In *For a Critique of the Political Economy of the Sign* by Jean Baudrillard. St. Louis, Mo.: Telos Press.

Libeskind, D. 1980. "Deus ex machina"/"machina ex deo": Aldo Rossi's theater of the world. *Oppositions* 21 (Summer): 2–23.

Lyotard, J-F. 1991. *The Inhuman: Reflections on Time*. Translated by G. Bennington and R. Bowlby. Stanford, Calif.: Stanford University Press.

Moneo, R. 1976. Aldo Rossi: the idea of architecture and the Modena Cemetery. *Oppositions* 5 (Summer): 1–34.

———. 1978. On typology. *Oppositions* 13 (Summer): 22–45.

Panofsky, E. 1991. *Perspective as Symbolic Form*. New York: Zone Books.

Popper, K. 1957. *The Poverty of Historicism*. London: Routledge & Kegan Paul.

Rossi, Aldo. 1976. The blue of the sky. *Oppositions* 5 (Summer): 31–4.

———. 1981. *A Scientific Autobiography*. Translated by L. Venuti. Cambridge, Mass.: MIT Press.

———. 1982 [1967]. *The Architecture of the City*. Translated by D. Ghirardo and J. Ockman. Cambridge, Mass.: MIT Press.

———. 1988. Architetture Padane. *Pratt Journal of Architecture* 2 (Spring): 40–43.

Shane, G. 1976. Contextualism. *Architectural Design* 11: 676–9.

Tschumi, B. 1983. Spaces and events. *Themes* 3: 6–11.

Vidler, A. 1976. The third typology. *Oppositions* 7: 1–4.

———. 1977. The idea of type: the transformation of the academic ideal, 1750–1830. *Oppositions* 8: 95–115.

Wölfflin, H. 1950. *Principles of Art History: The Problem of the Development of Style in Later Art*. New York: Dover Publications.

Young, J. E. 1992. The counter-monument: memory against itself in Germany today. *Critical Inquiry* 18 (2): 267–96.

Chapter 13

Memory and the Making of Places

Frances Downing

In order to be significant, architecture must be forgotten, or must present only an image for reverence which subsequently becomes confounded with memories.
   Aldo Rossi 1981, 45

Memories float, waltz, and flash into our consciousness, welcome or not, infiltrating thought and powering imagination. Memory presents a realm of past experience – emotional, sensuous, and sometimes objective – that can simultaneously haunt our existence and help us imagine our future. Rather than a simple repository of experience, memory is dynamic, often seeming to form and reform experience without our conscious permission. However, while admitting the often uncontrolled creative input of memory to the imagination or its uncalled-for interference, humans can learn to understand the usefulness of memory and, to a certain degree, order its expressive presence. Type is one useful construct for ordering the complexity of memory.

   The construct of type is used in this essay to structure a theory of memory and imagination in the act of design. As a mechanism of classification and organization, type may seem too rigid for modeling the complexity of memory. However, while memories seem to present themselves to consciousness in a less than ordered fashion, this does not prevent a conscious organization of informa-

Included with the text of this essay are drawings made by students involved in a junior-level design studio. The students were asked to remember a powerful landscape place from their youth. The images ranged across cornfields, orchards, rice paddy fields, piney woods, river bottoms, aspen meadows, jungle beaches, backyard paths, canyons, and pastoral landscapes. They were asked to model the place abstractly by picking the most potent physical attributes. At first it was difficult for the students to stand back from their remembered experiences and dissect attributes, meaning, or pattern. However, as they worked at modeling, then drawing, their memorable places, they were able to find order, dimension, shape, form, and organization that could prove useful for structuring their assigned design task.

tion contained within memorable experiences. And, while evidence exists that our minds function by categorical ordering of new experience through existing templates (Edelman 1992), this theory does not assume that the mind is incapable of recategorization of memorable experience or unable to reconstitute the same experience through several categories simultaneously. Type is a construct that provides a framework for identifying different kinds of places and events in memorable experience, for indicating the ways in which these experiences may be used during design inquiry, and for distinguishing between forms of innovation.

In this essay, sources for design ideas are ordered into six categories of mental images, forming a catalogue of past experience. During the act of design these experiences are aligned to the project at hand through two types of referential comparisons, prototypical and precedential. These referents become constructions through which the designer imagines and manipulates the design of a future place. This chapter explores how innovation occurs as an outcome of analogous or metaphoric thinking during design inquiry.

The use of past experience as a template for understanding future possibilities is not exclusive to designers (Ghiselin 1952; Black 1962; Rugg 1963; Ahsen 1982; Mac Cormac 1985). It is evident in all people as a basic condition of human thinking (Richardson 1983). The design process would benefit by more precise knowledge of the natural workings of the human mind, its abilities to connect seemingly unrelated phenomena and experiences, and the possibilities that arise from dealing with mental imagery more openly as a basic condition of inquiry. The ability of the designer to form and then adjust categories, reinterpreting place and event experiences in order to gain needed information, suggests a kind of flexible thinking necessary for successful inquiry during the design process.

Many of our processes of thinking and feeling occur as involuntary responses. However, when new experience is encountered that does not fit existing constructs held subconsciously, a conscious effort is made to align the new experience with some past construction in order to define and control the situation. There is much evidence that the conscious use of mental imagery as a way to define and control inquiry is a capability upon which designers rely (Korobkin 1976; Lawson 1980; Rossi 1981; Littlejohn 1984; City of Phoenix 1985; Downing 1992a). Manipulation of the image during design also means that the original experience may be redefined or understood in a different light as a response to active contemplation. This reflective awareness of the manipulated mental image is at the heart of design inquiry and engages memory as the basic repository of raw data.

13-1
Out of the Jungle, Patricia Revollo
(memory of jungle and beach)

JLM: *Even if all people use past experience, this does not guarantee that all people have the same set of mental images.*
FD: *Image banks are absolutely idiosyncratic. Given the range of experiences and texture in our own lives, it is phenomenal that we can communicate at all. But we do communicate, although in varying degrees of clarity. It is our ability to understand each other that indicates the existence of a kinship underlying our experiences.*

JLM: *But what architects are trained to "see" teaches them to edit the experience of the world differently.*
FD: *It is true that architects are often trained to see and understand formal attributes and for a time this way of thinking may prove dominant. But this kind of training does not eradicate informal assessments of place that are relatively common and shared with society and culture. See the references at the end of this chapter for my articles on imagery.*

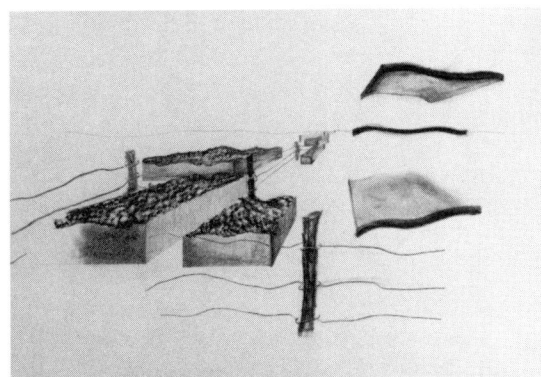

13-2
Sporadic Boundaries,
Suzanne Corman
(memory of rice paddy fields)

Mental Imagery and the Shaping of Experience

Mental images are an active, vital repository of information gathered through sensual experience – through sight, sound, smell, touch, and taste. A mental image presents more than an initial remembered percept to the mind; it contains multiple versions of involvement that stretch beyond the experiential to the emotional and intellectual realms (Ahsen 1982; Downing 1992b). For instance, the memory of a small, overgrown pavilion in grandmother's garden can evoke experiential dimensions of shade and shadow, the smell of roses, or a vista of the garden. In addition to these sensual experiences, the memory may evoke emotional dimensions of belonging and safety, of cultural identity or individual expression. Objective dimensions of scale and detail, identification of elements, and rules of assembly may also be derived from this experience. The immediacy and power of the mental image in memory suggests that the image does not lose ground to a maturing and more abstract understanding of the world. It continues to order the world and, within its own structure, retains meaningful detail and complexity.

However powerful a mental image may seem in memory, it does not include all the environmental information contained in any particular place or event experience. Instead, the mental image presents a *version* of experience that is most important to the individual or situation at a particular moment in time (Antrobus 1968; Mandler 1975; Marks 1977, 1983). Designers exhibit a capability to "select" versions of experience in a conscious effort to rehearse potential experiential, emotional, or objective criteria for the design of a future place.

Although all humans cultivate known experience upon encountering something new or different, very little research relating to this capability has been generated. After a long period of languishing under the shadow of positivist definitions of what was suitable to study through empirical research (Hebb 1968; Sheehan 1972; Neisser 1976), studies addressing the structure, function, and role that mental imagery plays in people's mental and physical life were undertaken in the 1960s. Unfortunately, most of the research on mental imagery in the last 30 years is not applicable to this essay. Much of it addresses the biological structure of mental manipulations of imagery, or expounds theoretical positions on the form that imagery takes in the mind. Formal empirical research has tended to study and debate the function and characteristics of mental imagery rather than the complexities of imagination. Before the 1970s those who practiced psychoanalysis were the only group to explore the realm of mental imagery's shaping of experience. Formulation of research that undertakes the study of the meaning and function of mental imagery in people's day-to-day lives has been left to clinical psychiatry and psychology. Such studies often are regarded as less reliable than laboratory research, but it is the clinical "in the field" operations that show some kinship with design inquiry.

Children engage in shaping experience, or make-believe play, in an almost continual manner that is characterized by transformations (Caplan and Caplan 1973). Anyone who watches a child at play can observe the use of empty boxes as all kinds of vehicles, the space under the table as a miniature house, and the tree house as a kingdom. While engaged in this kind of play, children use found props and fill in the details through their own imagination (Singer and Singer 1977). Imagination for the child involves duality: the child transforms the self, objects, and social roles while simultaneously maintaining an awareness of their original identity and function (Qualls and Sheehan 1983). This ability to shape experience through mental imagery is also a necessary part of an architectural designer's capabilities. In design, bridging from past place experience to the shaping of an imagined future is similar to the child's make-believe play. It is through *imagination* rather than simple mental imagery that the designer applies and tests ideas. Application of a mental image to a future place does not necessarily mean that the past place experience will be altered, although it is certainly possible. If a child can "imagine" a box as a car while simultaneously acknowledging the reality of the box, there is every reason to believe that a designer can retain the original experience independently of its simultaneous manipulation during design inquiry.

Mental images are the tools of design that Aldo Rossi recalls as past experiences etched in memory, stored and awaiting use as templates for design inquiry:

> Perhaps the observation of things has remained my most important formal education; for observation later becomes transformed into memory. Now I seem to see all the things I have observed arranged like tools in a neat row; they are aligned as in a botanical chart, or a catalogue, or a dictionary. But this catalogue, lying somewhere between imagination and memory, is not neutral; it always reappears in several objects and constitutes their deformation and, in some way, their evolution (Rossi 1981, 23).

The cataloguing of experience is a natural, biological requirement for humans (Smith and Medlin 1981). It is through this cataloguing and typing of complex experience that concepts are formed and used in the act of designing.

13-3
Density, John Allen
(memory of piny woods)

Memory and Design

The process of design is as complex and enigmatic as any creative act and has never been successfully transferred to established method. An architect must determine a client's desires from the ideas and images relayed through discussion, and in many cases from a formal program. However, the client's desires are not always stated initially nor are these desires expressed in a list of required spaces. A traditional portrayal casts the architect as listening carefully to the descriptions and statements made by the client concerning the kind of place desired. After examining the program, functional necessities, and pertinent research, the architect begins the task of design, only to be faced at every point of decision with an anomaly, something which does not yet ring with clarity. The architect, however, must present to the client a clear manifestation of a design that responds to the client's stated desires. It is often only after the client has perused an initial design response that a true realization of what is wanted begins to emerge. After seeing what is possible, what is desired becomes clearer. Clients usually respond to initial designs by elucidating their needs to achieve clarity. In other words, clients often understand better what they want after they have been presented with design responses they *don't* want.

The initial stages of negotiation through ideas and drawings between designer and client is a definition-seeking process. Much like a doctor probes a patient's history and body to reach a diagnosis, the designer must probe the client's ideas and the nature of a proposed project for constructions of meaning that may not be clear initially. This process of clarification, examination, and interpretation continues long past the initial schematic phases of design. It often continues as far into the process as the design of details and the beginning of construction. The problem of two or more minds coming to some understanding takes a great deal of insight on the part of responsive designers and their clients.

The designer might not have had firsthand experience of all the circumstances and components of a proposed project the client names as pertinent. Yet, the categorical nature of the human mind, which seeks to transform the unknown

AF: *How does this concept of "niche" relate to the notion of conventional behavior or "scripted behavior"? Is part of the architect's role to intervene in the process of social and architectural conformity?*

FD: *My purpose in labeling the process of understanding the unknown through the known as finding a "niche" does not assume that either the original unknown experience the designer is struggling to understand, or the template of personal known experience through which the designer assigns meaning, involves either conventional or scripted behavior. For that matter, the experience the designer is attempting to understand could be quite unusual.*

It was never my inclination to wander into the battlefield of political ramifications in design, although I recognize this as an impossible and naive fantasy. As for the architect's "role" beyond the desire to understand and design, intervention (or design) of any kind cannot escape addressing social convention or architectural conformity, whether or not this is the designer's intention. However, this chapter sidesteps the politics of motive in favor of exploring the structure of memory.

AF: *How can these (filters?) be analyzed in ideological terms? This concept has to be theorized if the discussion of type is to move from description of processes to analysis and intervention.*

FD: *My response depends on whether ideology is defined as "the study of ideas, their nature and source" or "the body of ideas on which particular political, economic, or social system is based" (Webster). I think, based on your first comment, that your question assumes the second definition, while I am absorbed by the first.*

Filters simply exist in every individual. Most likely they are formulated through complex interweavings of deterministic environmental factors and internal, idiosyncratic free will. As such, filters could neither be static and one dimensional, nor based in first-order logic (male-female, liberal-conservative, old-young, open-closed, etc.). In this spirit, ideologies as "bodies of ideas" change with environment, choice, and time. I prefer to spend my time puzzling over very basic, timeless structural components of memory, thinking, and process.

JLM: *Or it could imply that there is a common point of departure to which we can return — to share — after weaving or hacking our way through the "heteroglossia" that surrounds "objects" and images as objects.*

into the known, suggests that the designer must find a "niche" for client needs and desires within the designer's experience. The designer does this through discussing and sharing pertinent mental imagery with the client and other designers. These discussions, shared images, and private images evolve into drawings or some other physical medium of expression. All participants in the design process bring their specific experiences with them to formulate a collective understanding of what is wanted. The designer often reformulates information gathered from his or her own mental images that in some way displays kinship to what the client describes as a needed feature, feeling, or experience. Mental images can present a variation on themes — intellectual, emotional, or experiential — where a kernel of essential meaning is understood by all parties but is colored differently by each participant's own filters (Downing 1992b).

As designers rehearse with clients the physical, experiential, and emotive possibilities of a future place, both parties become more and more adept at *seeing* the consequences of paper architecture. The eloquence of description and enticement that a mature, successful designer displays while convincing a client of the relative merits of a particular design response suggests that the designer not only has the ability to manipulate and control imagery as a part of inquiry, but that some shared mnemonic experiences are also present between designer and client. The client participates in the mental rehearsal in order to be convinced of a direction the designer wishes to take regarding a future place. The sharing of mental imagery between designer and client implies multiple versions of similar memorable experiences, otherwise the discussions between participants would not have any common point of departure. The managing of memory imagery reflects the abilities of the designer, as well as the client, to apply consciously, and learn from, past experience (Richardson 1983). Memory can and does work subconsciously as well, but most mature designers seem to be aware of the mental imagery they are using to frame or define the problem, along with the reasons why it might be applicable to the task at hand (Hillier, Musgrove, and O'Sullivan 1972; Darke 1978; Downing 1992a).

The need to come to some common understanding drives the use of mental imagery and the ideas derived from mental images of experience. The designer or client often begins the design process with descriptions of what the future place should be "like." Designers draw upon memory for sources of design images and ideas from six categories. These are: specific places, specific events, place types, scripted behavior, concepts, and essential constructs. They are a designer's source

13-4
Density, John Allen
(memory of piny forest)

Sources of Design Images

Specific places are those places that can be named. The history of architecture is an obvious source for designers but is often unfamiliar to clients. Historical references are generally recognized as places that are formally "designed," or places vernacular in nature but representative of a certain era or style. In contrast to more formally recognized "architecture," designers and clients carry a range of idiosyncratic experiences of informal, common, or personal places that are memorable for reasons less easy to identify or understand because they are shrouded by more complex connections and reverberations. Specific places, therefore, can range from grandmother's garden to Frank Lloyd Wright's Fallingwater. For Rossi, specific memorable places are both named and examined for useful design inquiry:

> The Hotel Sirena is so fundamental to my Architecture that someone may think of it as my invention, as one of my projects. I might add that because of its courtyard typology, it also embodies an aspect of my architectural analysis of building volumes... In reality, though, it is not the typological aspect of the hotel which has influenced my work, but its color – certainly from the point of view of the marvelous (Rossi 1981, 25).

Specific events are much like specific places. They are events that can be named. Memorable events do not have to have a strong spatial component to prove useful in design. Designers and clients can use the memories of a particular occasion to help define the emotions and experiences that are necessary to some future function. Specific events can also be formal, as in rituals, or informal, as in occurrences. These kinds of images can range from father's burial to an evening spent reading *Swann's Way*. In response to a question about traffic control for special events in his design for the Phoenix Municipal Center, competitor Barton Myers introduced an event image:

> I just went through that in New York yesterday. You know, the United Nations is having this big show going on and [the] President... arrived, and for security reasons there were a series of [street] closures all through Manhattan, so that no one knows exactly where he is going to be and obviously it throws traffic into a turmoil. Yet, there is a sense of excitement about that, that New York is suddenly a different city. You know, you have to go this way or that way, not that way, because the President is coming, and that is the kind of thing we want to do here (City of Phoenix 1985, 51).

material and often act as communication tools in discussions between client and designer or among designers. A mental image of past experience can fall into more than one category or move from category to category depending upon the context of its use. It is the circumstances of a particular design inquiry, at a particular time and place, and interactions between particular people, that frame how an experience might be remembered, conceptualized, and used during the design process.

Aldo Rossi, in his *Scientific Autobiography* (1981), gives abundant examples of memorable places and events that he has used for design inquiry throughout his career. Examples clearly fall within the categories named in this essay. Another set of rich examples can be culled from the transcript of the winning competitor, Barton Myers, presenting his ideas for the Municipal Center Building Design Competition to a design board and the general public (City of Phoenix 1985). The six categories for the sources of design images are presented below with examples from these sources.

JLM: *This is structuralism!!! It is seriously undermined by criticism levied against structuralism.*
FD: *No, I don't believe it is a structuralist statement. It is a logical argument concerning how experience is abstracted in order to form analogic or metaphoric linkages between phenomena. This reference comes from an introduction to a symbolic logic text.*

Langer's writings do not suggest any connection to structural linguistics which Copleston defines as "the study of the unconscious infrastructure of linguistic phenomena, concentration on the relations between terms, exhibition of the structures of phonemic systems (systems of vocal sounds), and the discovery of general laws which would formulate basic necessary relations" (1974, 414). Nor do Langer's writings show any kinship to Lévi-Strauss' structural anthropology. Her work has never suggested a priori categories of formal structures or patterns which frame all forms of mental life. I have always thought of Langer's work as fundamentally phenomenological, as presented in such works as Feeling and Form *(1953).*

In addition to specific places and events, memory can also be accessed through more abstract interpretations of experiences. Abstractions are defined by Susanne Langer as "the consideration of a form apart from any contents" (Langer 1967, 33). She stretches the meaning of "form" beyond its common connotation of shape to include anything that may be said to follow a pattern or structure of any sort. This kind of definition allows for such things as music, ritual, or etiquette to have form. In abstraction it is the logical form or structure which interests us and not the particular medium. In this essay, the abstraction of logical form from experience can be identified in the sources of place type, scripted behavior, concepts, or essential constructs.

Place types are places linked together as group, class, or taxonomy identifiable through shared attributes, rules of formation, or cultural manifestation. An example would be New England connected farmhouses (Hubka 1984). These farmhouses all have similar structure, not just in the literal sense of heavy timber built structure, but also in organization, orientation, and materials. In addition, the history of connected farmhouses represents a clear development of rules, both physical and social. A designer need not refer to a specific attribute of a specific farmhouse if an understanding of *some* aspect of connected farmhouses (such as a modified U-shaped courtyard formed by addition, or the definition of "front" and "back" through a variation in cladding materials) frames a possible solution to his or her inquiry about what a future place should be like.

Rossi conveys a sense of historical value in reference to place types that define for him the concept of dwelling:

> Yet in speaking of the forms in which human life is manifested, I ought to elaborate further on some of those structures with which this sense of life has been associated for me and which have impressed me from an archaeological and anthropological point of view ever since my early youth. I have mentioned the *corrales* of Seville, the courtyards of Milan, in particular the courtyard of the Hotel Sirena; and the balconies, arcades, corridors, as well as the literary and actual impressions made on me by convents, schools, barracks. In a word, those forms of dwelling – together with that of the villa – are stored in the history of man to such a degree that they belong as much to anthropology as to architecture. It is difficult to imagine other forms, other geometric representations, precisely because we do not already have examples of them (Rossi 1981, 71).

13-5
Tunneled Perception, Kurtis Koop
(memory of river bottom)

Scripted behavior is a portrayal of an abstracted, normative response to typical situations (Bower, Black, and Turner 1979). Scripted behavior is present in the mind as schematic "scripts" for response in situations that are familiar. The scripts, therefore, include abstracted understandings of appropriate behavior dictated by cultural and societal norms. One example of scripted behavior is the interactions of a patron in a restaurant. The patron interacts with the host or hostess, with the server, with other patrons, and so on. Deviation from normal behavioral responses throws the situation outside of the script and into a specific event no longer dictated by the norm. Designers and clients alike rehearse scripted behavior in their minds as they come to some understanding of the program or walk through paper designs.

If abstraction reduces our complex everyday experience to logical form, it therefore assists us in developing concepts. *Concepts*, in this essay, refer to a person's understanding of logical forms that are manifested in different types of places (like an axis down the middle), or events (like people gathering in a circle for a discussion). These concepts are based in experience but have become so abstracted or generalized that they exist as independent ideas. Concepts can act as referents for framing design inquiry. The conceptual response of creating an axis down the middle as a way of controlling design inquiry need not initially relate to a specific place or place type. Nor does the conceptual idea of gathering in a circle for discussion need to be tied to a specific event or scripted behavior. Generally, however, a designer can align abstract concepts with specific memories of places or events in order to exemplify what a place or experience should be like. Mental images enrich a concept and allow the designer to become subjectively involved in an inquiry. Here, Rossi describes how an abstract organizational grid, a concept for ordering space, is understood through a specific place experience:

> I wish only to emphasize how a building, how architecture may be a primary element onto which life is grafted. This idea… was made particularly clear to me by several "urban artifacts" at Seville, especially the enormous encampment of the summer holidays, rigorously laid out like a Roman city, with its lots divided into the minimal dimensions for the little houses, and with its huge triumphal portals. This encampment forms the weak but very precisely jointed skeleton of an unsettled and convulsive body, one that is destined to the short, intense life of the holidays (Rossi 1981, 20).

AF: *Isn't "scripted behavior" a social convention? Is the designer meant to record and accommodate or interrogate these processes? Obviously the answer carries political meaning. But whatever the answer, the question has to be asked.*

FD: *Yes, scripted behavior could be thought of as social convention. However, theorists and researchers in this area suggest that scripts are abstractly stored in our memory, or subconscious, as "forms" of behavior. We rely on these forms to know how to behave in situations which are familiar but not exact duplicates of past experience.*

As to whether the designer's role is to accommodate or interrogate these processes, I do not believe there are any rules of engagement. Each design situation varies from the last. Clients are different, the site is different, the problem may vary, time has passed, and the designer has probably changed as well. With this many variables involved there is no formula as to whether a design situation calls for compliance to or challenge of conventional, scripted behavior.

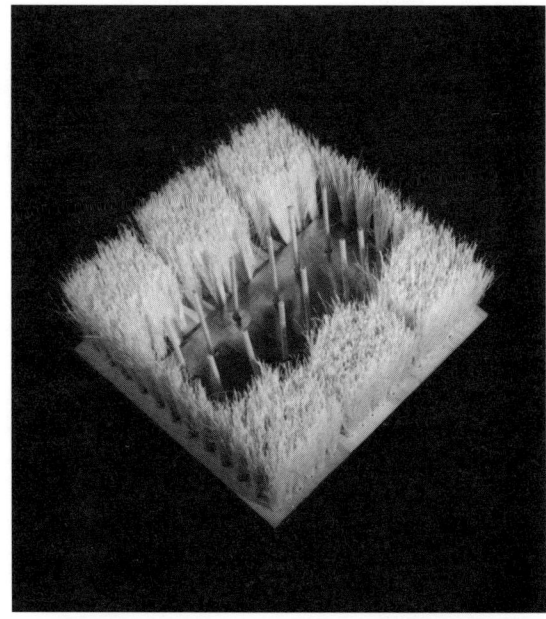

13-6
Two Orders, Jennifer Green
(memory of cornfield and orchard)

JLM: *Doesn't this process have a value somewhat the opposite of that of controlling experience? Design would depend on finding a pattern of a multitude of examples and in reverse finding a multitude of examples that satisfy the pattern we wish to manifest?*

FD: *Yes. Multiple images and ideas are the rule. A good designer will organize multiple ideas hierarchically or thematically, otherwise they would all compete with each other for prominence. When multiple images are present and contain some pattern of information, it is the designer's task to identify the pattern.*

> **JLM:** *Thematic, yes!! But essential?*
> **FD:** *Yes, essential — meaning elemental in nature. Basically, this kind of involvement with the problem/project focuses on the meaning of phenomena rather than the particularities of experience.*

AF: *If meaning is contained in the nature of the project, how can we make room for a variety of meanings and a variety of audiences? Architectural form is, after all, a process of representation, and like literary representation should be subjected to analysis in terms of convention, audience, etc.*

FD: *The assumption latent within "essential" is that the meaning is so inherent to the project that it can be said to be a shared construct. For example, Kahn, in the design of the Salk Institute, discerned that the nature of scientists at work consisted of doing and dreaming, and thematically designed the project around the juxtaposition of those two realms (plus fantastic site, plus materiality). Essential constructs are meant to be so deeply embedded in the project as to actually* be *the defining nature.*

I do not believe that architectural form is representation. I like to think of form, space, and order as a presentation *of ideas captured within the experience of architecture. As such, if the designer is very good at the craft of thematic presentation of ideas in form, space, and order, essential constructs would generate deeply felt presence.*

This act of aligning logical forms to actual experience is what Langer refers to as interpretation. Langer suggests that the interpretation of an abstract form (concepts of pattern, structure, or organization) is a process of looking for kinds of things to which a certain form belongs. The "things" this essay addresses are mental images of place and occasion. Langer argues that our ability to identify many phenomena as exemplars of the same "logical form" makes it possible for us to control the incredible variations in our experiences. Once we have abstracted concepts, scripted behavior, or place type from actual experience, we can reverse the process through interpretation. Interpretation begins with an abstraction and seeks some specific place, place type, or occasion that embodies it. Designers need to summon an exemplar from their own experience to help structure a deeper understanding of an abstraction.

Essential constructs are generally taken from the meaning contained in the nature of the project. Built forms can present us with their meanings, the connotations of which must be carefully teased from obvious physical and specific denotations of place. At the beginning of many design projects, the designer, whether cognizant of it or not, is often involved in the search for meaning or the true essence of the project. Through the negotiation of ideas the designer and client set the "tone" or "theme" that can guide future physical manipulation of the design. The idea of *democracy* was used to challenge architects involved in the Phoenix Municipal Center Competition and is an example of a thematic, essential construct. Myers writes:

> [In response] to the Mayor's very vigorous introduction to the team several months ago... for an open democratic society [our concept is] that essentially the building should be accessible. There should be a certain informality... The idea of accessibility is very much [a] part of this democratic idea, and to provide [it] we were the only scheme [with an] original idea of making a great public room... I call a City Room, and from that room, all of the [city offices] are essentially accessible [to the people]... (City of Phoenix 1985, 36).

When an essential construct is used as a source, the designer struggles to discover the underlying form, or pattern, or structure, that might satisfy the construct. For Myers, the essential construct of democracy was referenced through the concept of accessibility. In turn, he displayed to the public and design board many examples of places, or "city rooms" as he called them, from Greek agoras to large Italian and Mexican town plazas. Although essential constructs do not, in themselves, suggest physical attributes, designers need only refer back to their own bank of experiences to align the essential construct to a concept and perhaps to a more specific place or event. Aldo Rossi discusses his own struggles with the construct of death and the artifacts society builds as a response to this inevitable occurrence:

> In the project for the cemetery at Modena, as I have said, I sought to resolve the youthful problem of death through representation. I know very well that this may not be the best way to begin an explanation of a project, nor is the skeletal mediation or meditation on bones which I have already mentioned. Beyond these things, though, there still clearly existed in this project a mediation between the object and its representation, a mediation which somehow vanished from subsequent projects. The central concept of the cemetery was perhaps my realization that the things, objects, buildings of the dead are not different from those of the living. I have referred to the Roman tomb of the baker, an abandoned factory, an empty house; I also saw death in the sense of "no one lives here anymore" and hence as regret, since we do not know what our relations with this person were, and yet we still search for him in some way (Rossi 1981, 38-9).

Essential constructs relate to the designer's desire to define the "meaning" inherent to a specific project. The design of a house might allow the designer to consider essential constructs of *protected intimacy* outlined in Gaston Bachelard's *The Poetics of Space* (1964). The design of a city hall and municipal buildings might require the designer to consider the nature of *democracy* (City of Phoenix 1985). For Rossi, the form of death initially took on the physical structure of a body. He then proceeded to link the idea of death to the emptiness of things. Rossi's juxtaposition of death with skeletal forms moves away from the essential to the abstract concept of a physical form. His understanding of death evolves from the memory of bombed-out buildings at the end of World War II. This mental image or group of mental images present the essential construct of *death* to his consciousness. This search is only a part of Rossi's growing understanding of his design inquiry for the cemetery at Modena. Yet his understanding follows a course of linking an essential construct with concepts and mental images from memory. The direction of this linkage, that is, whether Rossi started with the essential construct or with images that evoke the construct, is not critical to untangle. It is the act of linkage that is critical for the designer.

The use of essential constructs to find a lucrative physical referent for the task at hand is common in the world of design. Essential constructs eventually lead the designer to search for places and events that embody meaning. Essential constructs remain in the background during the active manipulation of places or events as a sort of qualitative check for the design. Aldo Rossi admits that his past experience forms the basis for exploring design possibilities. These experiences are deformed, or reinterpreted, as they are engaged in design inquiry through manipulation and evolution.

The fundamental nature of physical "types" of places has also been a source of inspiration and guidance for Rossi (1981), not only because they represent functional and formal physical attributes, but because type suggests the "nature" of place and dwelling – the nature of humanity. In the *Autobiography*, he continued to find complex layers present in each experience that could be mined for data and direction during design. The significance of sources in Rossi's exploration of architecture goes far beyond the moments of creation. The storage of mental images as a function of memory locates a bank of experience that, in part, constitutes individual, societal, and cultural identity.

Designers use their sources of mental imagery to formulate responses to abstract, word-oriented project statements or undefined design situations. There is no "correct" way for the designer to proceed. It is possible that a stored experience can range across the six categories named here depending upon particular circumstances of design inquiry, seemingly unrelated intellectual activity, or serendipity. Instead of each experience residing in one categorical area, there exists a framework in memory that identifies specific places and events, place types, scripted behavior, concepts, and essential constructs as temporary hooks upon which an experience can be hung and understood in a particular light for a

13-7
Extended Horizons, Matt Widmer (memory of pastoral landscape)

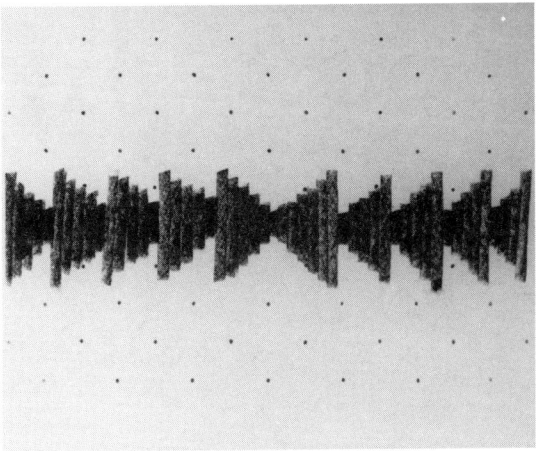

13-8
Two Orders, Jennifer Green
(memory of cornfield and orchard)

JLM: *What about architectural precedents? Are you including these in the "experience" of the designer? And, if so, how does the experience of the precedent (as a slide in a history class, a postcard received from a friend, an "on-site" experience...) get remembered and how does this effect final design?*

FD: *Oh yes. Our imaginations are quite incredible. Whether or not we imagine the place as it objectively exists, what is important are the qualities, attributes, and fantasies we conjure for ourselves from these various experiences. During the act of design it may be less important for the memory of place to be formally correct and more important for it to be powerful and useful.*

period of time. When needed, the same experience might be reformulated to fit within a different category. A designer or a client could begin to think using one source category, then weave his or her way through related images in other categories, proceeding to puzzle through to some useful end.

Memory and Design Conjectures

Beginning in the 1960s the traditional design process was scrutinized and subjected to various critiques. Interest in the design process and design knowledge was fueled by well-known failures of modern design such as the Pruitt Igoe public housing project (Stevens 1990). Complaints about the traditional design process centered around what was perceived as most designers' lack of real evidence concerning how people responded to environments. At the time the existing design process was berated as enclosed in a black box, where designers depended upon idiosyncratic knowledge of behavior in space. Systems theory, which touted a more "scientific" method that depended upon more detailed research of human behavior, was developed (Alexander 1971; Cross 1977). While the attempt to make design more scientific was laudable for some well-intentioned reasons, it was completely unworkable in the business world of design (Darke 1978). The suggested processes were too time-consuming and arduous for most practitioners to consider seriously as a replacement for more familiar, traditional processes.

It was not until the 1970s that research on the design process began to illuminate the intuitive process of design. In 1972, Bryan Lawson examined the problem solving process as exemplified by two different groups: students of architecture and students of science (Lawson 1980). An experimental designlike problem was used to test whether differences existed. The problem solving process that worked for students in science was found to be ineffective for design students; the results indicated that the science students used a problem-focused process while design students favored a solution-focused process. Problem-focusing was time-consuming in that it involved learning as much as possible about the structure of the problem before attempting a solution. Solution-focusing involved the immediate identification of a solution based upon some match made in the designer's mind between the problem statement and an exemplar stored in his or her own experience. Evaluation of the solution was accomplished by the examination of the exemplar against the background of programmatic criteria and other forces that had an impact on the design problem.

Armed with the failure of systems theory in practice, plus a new understanding of the intuitive process, design methodologists began to formulate a new model. The model needed to account for a designer's tendency to use subjective knowledge, with a more objective accountability for behavior research, program information, and evaluation (Hillier, Musgrove, and O'Sullivan 1972). In this model conjecture is an "if" statement and is based on knowledge of problem/solution relationships. Analysis is the "then" response, referring to the manipulation and adjustment of principles found in the conjectured solution to test for "fit" to the design problem (Korobkin 1976). In the *conjecture-analysis* model, design becomes a series of "if-then" speculations (Schön 1983). Conjectures are a form of stating hypotheses, perhaps more tentative and action oriented than most scientific hypotheses. Conjecture represents a momentary "if" statement meant to address a particular problem linked with a particular solution to which a "then" evaluative response is necessary. These conjectures run the gamut from encompassing ideas that initially frame the design problem to figuring out the appropriate details of a structure. In any case, the conjecture is often formulated through mental images stored within memory. The conjecture-analysis model accounted for the use of personal place and event experiences, place types, scripted behavior, a large range of abstracted concepts of space, form, and order, as well as essential constructs.

In her research concerning architects' public housing designs, Jane Darke (1978) explores design processes in order to account for the presence of value systems expressed by designers prior to initial design decisions. She discovered that in the course of design, architects had not only used conjectures of a solution-oriented nature in formulating their responses to design projects, but that they also relied on a hidden agenda she called the *primary generator*. The primary generator is a set of values held by the designer or client that generates the initial conjectures concerning what a future place might be like. In Darke's particular research, the "generator" was the high value placed on the site that, in turn, influenced all major conjectures that guided design responses. The primary generator narrows the range of considerations a designer must initially address. With the evidence obtained, Darke was able to remodel the process into a *generator-conjecture-analysis*.

13-9
Transparent Boundaries, Mike Harris (memory of bounded backyard)

JLM: *Yes, but this is not necessarily readily available to others, or is that an important issue here?*
FD: *It depends upon the design situation. Some of these images may be initiated by the clients or users as well as by the designer. In other situations the "if/then" process goes through iterations of unsuccessful references before a successful referent is aligned. The designer controls whether or not to make this process "available" to others.*

AF: *The "primary generator" is a set of values held by the designer or client that generates the initial conjectures concerning what a future place might be like. Again, this way of approaching the problem helps me to understand the points at which designer intervention can have meaning. Rather than accept these values unquestioningly, should we not at least examine the ways in which they encode power, i.e., class and gender relations?*
FD: *Absolutely.*

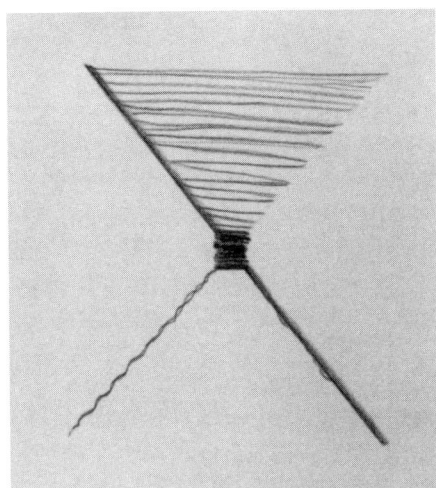

13-10
Canopy, Lana Medina
(memory of back yard path)

In the design process, when conjectures are solution-oriented, the "if" part of the statement represents an experience applied as a template to an as yet undefined design problem. The referenced image provides a framework for the design problem, giving the situation immediate structure and meaning. The "then" portion of the process occurs when the designer considers the consequences of the concepts conveyed by the referent. Conjectures that pose the known experience in order to understand the unknown future can be stated as either a prototypical or precedential referent.

Prototypes and Precedents

Mental images, whether the source be specific places or events, scripted behavior, place types, concepts, or essential constructs, present themselves in the designer's mind as raw data to be used. The *way* memories are used as tools in design is through the act of reference. Two basic referent strategies for comparing image to task is through the use of prototype and precedent. These two referent types allow the designer to compare or contrast information, feeling, or sensation derived from past experience to an unfocused or unformed design task at hand.

Prototypes are defined as: "the first or primary type of anything; the original [thing or person] of which another is a copy, imitation, representation or derivative, or to which it conforms or is required to conform; a pattern, model, standard, exemplar, archetype" (*Oxford English Dictionary* 1971). This definition is reiterated in various forms in the architectural literature as a set of places that are linked functionally or formally in a group, typology, or taxonomy (Glassie 1975; Gulgonen and Laisney 1982; Williams and Scofido 1983). To use prototype as a template for "seeing" a future place is a strategy of comparing like phenomena. Prototypes are more *similar* than dissimilar to the kind of place the designer is struggling to understand and frame. In Barton Myers's explanation of additional uses of the "City Room," he described, and displayed in slide form, a type of place and experience that can be found in many American, European, and Mexican cities:

> We could have Saturday markets... a place where produce can (be brought) in... I know a number of examples like that where [sales] are simply done off [the backs of] trucks. You drive the truck in, there is a little pipe rigging. Each truck opens its back door to a canvas piece and it creates aisles, right of way, and you have... interesting truck farms instantly. We can do that. We can have public addresses. If the President comes and wants to address people of Phoenix outdoors, then this is the place for him to do that. You finally have a (city) room that is appropriate for that kind of ceremony (City of Pheonix 1985, 43).

Precedent is defined as: "preceding in time; existing or occurring before something expressed or implied; previous, former, antecedent; or previous instance or case which is or may be taken as an example or rule for subsequent cases, or by which some act or circumstance may be supported or justified" (*Oxford English Dictionary* 1971). To use a precedent as a template for "seeing" a future place is a strategy of comparing unlike phenomena. Precedents are more *dissimilar* than similar to the kind of place that the designer is struggling to understand and frame. Precedents can be built places that are not obviously similar to the task at hand. However, in the act of referencing between precedent and future place, the designer identifies some kinship, a relationship discovered in form, space, or order that suggests design directions to be explored. Precedents can also be derived from natural forms, objects, or abstract social situations. Rossi displays this ability to find patterns of significance in seemingly unrelated phenomena:

The paintings of Angelo Morbelli, like *Il Natale dei remasti* and *Pio Albergo Truivulzio*, had always impressed me: I had observed them with fascination, not knowing how to judge them. Now they served me as the plastic and figurative means for this project [the Cemetery at Modena]. The study of light, the great bands of light that fall on the benches filled with old people, the precise shadows cast by the geometrical forms of these seats and by the stove, seem to be taken from a manual on the theory of shadow (Rossi 1981, 12).

For Rossi experiences are deformed, or perhaps reinterpreted, as they are engaged in active inquiry through manipulation and evolution. Rossi names many referents for various design projects. He uses common objects such as coffeepots to explore the containment of space, and the act of setting a table, preparing food, and arranging food on the table as a metaphor for the unfolding events in architecture. Rossi has also used a child's game, the "goose game," as a precedent for a table he designed. As Langer (1967) suggests, these referents represent different "contents" that may display some underlying, shared logical form.

While the definition of prototype and precedent may seem clear on paper, during the act of design inquiry there are few "rules" or "definitions" that are held consciously. The distinction between these forms of conjecture sometimes get blurred in the frenzy of design. Often it is difficult even to classify the template as either precedent or prototype. For instance, if a designer is designing a public library and chooses to use a courthouse as an initial conjecture about what the library could be like, is the courthouse a precedent or a prototype? It seems obvious to say that a courthouse can only be a precedent because it does not have the specific function of libraries. However, one could argue that the courthouse and library are both civic buildings, and therefore have formal attributes in common. A mental image might be used as a prototypical template in one design circumstance and as a precedential template in another. The classifications of prototype and precedent have fuzzy edges and can clearly be twisted into many "deformities," as Rossi puts it. The two strategies for comparing and contrasting images to task are only clearly distinct as the poles on a continuum between similar and dissimilar referents.

13-11
The Ravine, Kayce McLish
(memory of the ravine)

JLM: *But Rossi's work isn't intended as contrast, or is that what you are saying? (Perhaps he is amazed at the multiple possibilities for content that certain forms might support?)*
FD: *Contrast is meant here simply to denote that successful references can be made between images of dissimilar source (as when Rossi uses a two-dimensional painting of strong shade and shadow as a source for design). The contrast is in using a precedent, a painting, to inform the design of a building. The contrast is in reference type (painting/building) not in content (shade/shadow). In this case the contrast is relatively mild. Other referential duos, as when Rossi uses the "goose game" as a reference for the design of a table, are more extreme.*

I think you are partially right. Rossi does seem delighted, perhaps amazed, at the rich content of memory and multiple uses that can be made from memorable imagery. Multiple versions and multiple dimensions of emotion, experience, and quasi-objective information are suspended within the image. It is the designer's task to find and utilize aspects of the memory that may be appropriate to the task at hand.

JLM: *The linguistic analogy might be more metaphor than analogy; and as with all metaphors, there are limits to the congruency between the two things brought into a relationship through such rhetorical traps. In addition, the relationship is made significant perhaps if and only if we maintain the assumptions concerning images and concepts, a set of assumptions that I am not certain is popularly grounded and that might represent the last attempts by the profession of architecture to maintain its Albertian status.*

FD: *Yes and no. Although there are many theories about how conjectures are formed through the use of reference, there is very little hard evidence. At this time there is some evidence that points to our ability to imagine an image and reality simultaneously (the child imagining the box as a car). But there is very little evidence for the process this ability suggests. There may be some interesting possibilities for explanation on the horizon (like chaos theory).*

If you mean, by Albertian status, that the structure behind appearance is rationally (mathematically) organized, and this knowledge is controlled by architects — no, this reference does not relate to the exploration presented in this essay. If you mean, by Albertian status, that this attempt to explain the relationship between memory and design is meant to make architecture and/or process as objective as possible — not completely. My agenda is on the table: I would like to "unlock" some of the mystery of memory and make it a teachable source material. The images included with this essay come from the memory banks of my students. They seem to present, to the student remembering, a rich array of meaningful place experiences. These memories are subjective and when we objectify — or make a drawing — the purpose is to tease out information that might be useful for the design task they have been assigned. I am guilty of believing that we can, to a limited extent, understand and use our subjective memories in a more productive way.

Memory and Innovation

Innovation in design is intimately tied to the manipulation of mental images. Because no experience is ever repeated exactly, the use of past knowledge to frame present or future situations necessarily demands abstraction, adjustment, and evolution of ideas, emotions, and experience derived from the past as it is applied to a possible future. Innovation refers to the amount of adjustment or manipulation necessary to bring ideas into some alignment with the functions and desires embedded in the present design situation. When a solution to a design problem resides within some knowledge of *similar* referents, the need for innovation is local, that is, it relates to the specifics of context, site, client, materials, etc. When a solution to a problem resides within some comparison of *dissimilar* referents, the need for innovation increases as the two referents are seen as related in an obscure or less direct way. Dissimilarity of referents between past experience and a possible future raises more questions and demands — more innovation — if the two are to be held in conscious thought at the same time (Mac Cormac 1985).

This distinction between similar and dissimilar referents is evident in language as the difference between analogy and metaphor. The difference between analogy and metaphor is a matter of the degree of dissimilarity: referents that differ substantially are metaphoric, while referents that display more similarity are considered analogous (Mac Cormac 1985). Like prototypes and precedents, analogies and metaphors form a continuum of similar to dissimilar referents.

The evolution of language and the ideas embedded within linguistic expression can be attributed to metaphoric thinking. Mac Cormac (1985) explores a nonrigid hierarchical organization of semantic development by proposing a semantic theory of levels. First is a surface level in which metaphors appear in linguistic form, then a deeper level of linguistic explanation, and finally, the deepest level of cognitive activity. It is in the deepest level that metaphoric thinking occurs. When a metaphoric statement is continually used as an expression, it works its way from a deep level of cognition to a surface level of accepted meaning. As a metaphoric expression becomes the accepted norm, it loses the emotive tension which first accompanied it as an exploratory vehicle. Although imagistic conjectures are not linguistic in form, they might travel this same path as they move from tension to acceptance. The evolution of ideas from initial emotional tension to acceptable norm is the framework for change in the physical world as well as the semantic world. The juxtaposition of concepts not generally held in common represents a fast moving innovation and evolution of ideas that is as important to understand in the manipulation of the physical world as it is in the evolution of ideas in semantics.

The discipline of architecture has evolved through metaphoric juxtaposition, as has language. For example, the use of social models of democracy and equality as metaphoric referents is what fueled part of the early modern movement in architecture. This innovative approach caused much debate as it suggested physical adjustments to traditional space, form, organization, and materials. These innovations began at the cognitive level for the inventors of these juxtapositions, slowly moved into acceptance, and then degenerated into style. The same process is true of many other initially innovative metaphors for built form. The machine metaphor returns with each new technological era – the steam engine, power plants, electrical conduits, the inside-out machine, the computer, and many more to come. Each manifestation loses its innovative character as acceptance grows into stylistic manipulations.

There are dangers in using a semantic theory to explain the nature of innovation in design inquiry. Language does not have to suggest spatiality, but the visual or kinesthetic image requires a spatial component. The act of comparing referents, however, can be made through language or through the mental image (Black 1962; Langer 1967; Kuhn 1970; Mac Cormac 1985). The nature of analogous and metaphoric comparison is the same for both modes of communication. The channels of thought may prove to be different, but the act of comparison has functional significance for both kinds of thinking.

Some theorists believe that it is the tension between referents that leads to creative endeavors (Mac Cormac 1985). When other buildings are used as referents for design, even when they have no typological or functional relationship to the specific design problem, the tension that is created is relatively mild because both referents are built forms. Natural forms, machinery, biological systems, social models, or any idea or physical referent can also be used in design to frame a problem. The use of a non-building as a precedent naturally creates more tension between referents. This use of precedent could be thought of as more novel: the tension between referents is produced by comparing dissimilar phenomena.

Innovation is possible with either analogous or metaphoric thinking. The measure of innovation necessary is its appropriateness to the task at hand. Using prototypes as imagery conjectures for design can be seen as generally maintaining a status quo, innovation being relegated to smaller moves of adjustment and fit.

Precedents as imagery conjectures for design allow a much greater opportunity for possible innovations. The combination of known constructs not normally thought of as related can generate new perceptions, new relationships, and unmask the fear of the unknown. Because the metaphoric conjunction can cross modalities and features, like comparing death to emptiness or democracy to accessibility, the opportunity for innovation through metaphoric precedent can lead not only to innovation, but to the rapid evolution of ideas. There are no rules for when, or under what conditions, analogic or metaphoric thinking should be applied to a particular design inquiry. It is a question of appropriate use that is inevitably tied to the character of a project and its contextual situation.

Conclusion

Knowledge of type in the physical world introduces the design community to a deeper understanding of societal and cultural form, space, and order. Similarly, knowledge of sources of design ideas and the types of referential conjectures made during design inquiry gives the design community access to rich repositories of experience and strategies for innovation.

While categories, definitions, and constructs may be necessary to a formal explanation and understanding of design inquiry, these efforts do not describe the *nature* of inquiry. The designing mind displays a dynamic fluidity in pursuit of flexible, complex associations of images and ideas (Downing 1992b). This fluency is fundamental to thinking and produces both intentional and serendipitous integrations of experience, emotion, and information. The classification of mental imagery as specific places and events, scripted behavior, place types, concepts, and essential constructs, is not meant to imply that barriers exist that keep experience tightly constrained. If these categories were viewed as a framework to which the "tools" of experience could be attached and reattached, it would be more in keeping with the complexity of human thinking. Rossi writes:

> A design pursues this fabric of connections, memories, images, yet knowing that in the end it will have to be definitive about this or that solution; on the other hand, the original, whether in its true or presumed state, will be an obscure object which is identified with its copy (Rossi 1981, 35).

AF: *Isn't memory colored by identity and in particular by the perception of power relations? Memory (the crucial repository of meaning for type) is obviously structured by identity of the individual and his/her perception of status, agency, and power.*

AF: *How can knowledge of type introduce the design community to a deeper understanding of societal and cultural form, space, and order? This is the key question. The analysis should be pushed at points like this.*
FD: *Patterns repeated in time present an underlying, essential fabric for behavior. Patterns may change as time passes, but change in meaningful patterns is slow and methodical. It is these patterns that deserve our attention and contemplation.*

In addition, the same image content can be used at different times or under different conditions. The design situation is dynamic and ever changing as information impacts the designer's thinking process. The same mental image could be imagined as a specific place in one design situation and as belonging to a place type in another. The same mental image could be used as a prototypical referent in one design situation and as a precedential referent in another.

The construction of categories and definitions in this essay represents a framework to which designers can "hang" a mental image, for the moment, for consideration as a part of design inquiry, or for intellectual curiosity and development. It is not the categorization that would generally be apparent to the designer in the act of design. However, knowledge of this framework of categories and the potential for fashioning a way to see a possible future could assist designers. Knowledge of the different strategies that are possible when prototypes or precedents are engaged in design inquiry could lead the designer through the conjecture stage more effectively, allowing more comparisons, and developing a broader range of conceivable avenues to pursue and evaluate.

The elasticity of the designer's mind, his or her ability to adjust one mental image to many different circumstances, is a necessary condition for the ability to "imagine" in design. Rossi states that "in my projects, repetition, collage, the displacement of an element from one design to another, always places me before another potential project which I would like to do but which is also a memory of some other thing" (Rossi 1981, 20). The ability to transcend our own experiences, use them to imagine other people and places, to discover something new and surprising, and to deepen a thought, describes the power and the rich potential for memory in the making of places.

References

Ahsen, A. 1982. Principles of imagery in art and literature. *The Journal of Mental Imagery* 6: 213–50.

Alexander, C. 1971. *Notes on the Synthesis of Form.* Cambridge, Mass.: Harvard University Press.

Antrobus, J.S. 1968. Information theory and stimulus-independent thought. *British Journal of Psychology* 59: 423–30.

Bachelard, G. 1964. *The Poetics of Space.* Boston: Beacon.

Black, M. 1962. *Models & Metaphors: Studies in Language and Philosophy.* Ithaca, N.Y.: Cornell University Press.

Bower, G.H., J.B. Black, and T.J. Turner. 1979. Scripts in memory for text. *Cognitive Psychology* 11: 177–220.

Caplan, F. and T. Caplan. 1973. *The Power of Play.* New York: Doubleday.

City of Phoenix. 1985. *The Municipal Center Building Design Competition.* Transcript. Phoenix, Ariz.

Copleston, F. 1974. *The History of Philosophy: Volume IX.* Garden City, N.Y.: Image Books.

Cross, N. 1977. *The Automated Architect.* London: Pion.

Darke, J. 1978. The primary generator and the design process. In *Proceedings: EDRA 9*. Tucson: University of Arizona.

Downing, F. 1992a. The role of place and event imagery in the act of design. *Journal of Architectural and Planning Research* 9 (1): 64–80.

———. 1992b. Conversations in imagery. *Design Studies* 13 (3): 291–319.

———. 1992c. Image banks: Dialogues between the past and the future. *Environment and Behavior* 24 (4): 441–69.

Edelman, G.M. 1992. *Bright Air, Brilliant Fire*. New York: Basic Books.

Fink, R.S. 1976. The role of imaginative play in cognitive development. *Psychological Reports* 39: 895–906.

Ghiselin, B. 1952. *The Creative Process*. New York: New American Library.

Glassie, H. 1975. *Folk Housing in Middle Virginia*. Knoxville: University of Tennessee Press.

Golomb, C. and C.B. Cornelius. 1977. Symbolic play and its cognitive significance. *Developmental Psychology* 13: 246–52.

Gordon, R. 1972. A very private world. In *The Function and Nature of Imagery*, ed. P.W. Sheehan. New York: Academic Press.

Gulgonen, A. and F. Laisney. 1982. Contextual approaches to typology of the Ecole des Beaux-Arts. *The Journal of Architectural Education* 35: 26–28.

Hebb, D.O. 1968. Concerning imagery. *Psychological Review* 78: 466–77.

Hillier, B., J. Musgrove, and P. O'Sullivan. 1972. Knowledge and design. In *Environmental Design: Research and Practice*, ed. W.J. Mitchell. Berkeley, Calif.: University of California.

Hubka, T. 1984. *Big House, Little House, Back House, Barn: The Connected Farm Buildings of New England*. Hanover N.H.: University Press of New England.

Korobkin, B.J. 1976. *Images for Design: Communicating Social Science Research to Architects*. Cambridge, Mass.: An American Institute of Architects Research Report, Architecture Research Office.

Kuhn, T.S. 1970. *The Structure of Scientific Revolutions*. Chicago: University of Chicago Press.

Langer, S.K. 1953. *Feeling and Form*. New York: Scribner's Sons.

———. 1967. *An Introduction to Symbolic Logic*. New York: Dover Publications.

Lawson, B. 1980. *How Designers Think*. London: Architectural Press.

Littlejohn, D. 1984. *Architect: The Life and Work of Charles W. Moore*. New York: Holt, Rinehart & Winston.

Mac Cormac, E.R. 1985. *A Cognitive Theory of Metaphor*. Cambridge, Mass.: MIT Press.

Mandler, G. 1975. Consciousness: respectable, useful, and probably necessary. In *Information Processing and Cognition: The Loyola Symposium*, ed. R. Solso. Hillsdale, N.J.: Lawrence Erlbaum Associates.

Marks, D.F. 1977. Imagery and consciousness: a theoretical review from an individual differences perspective. *Journal of Mental Imagery* 2: 275–90.

———. 1983. Mental imagery and consciousness: a theoretical review. In *Imagery*, ed. A. Sheikh. New York: John Wiley & Sons.

Neisser, U. 1976. *Cognition and Reality*. San Francisco: Freeman.

Oxford English Dictionary, The Compact Edition. 1971. New York: Oxford University Press.

Qualls, P.J. and P.W. Sheehan. 1983. Imaginative, make-believe experiences and their role in the development of the child. In *Mental Imagery and Learning*, eds. M.L. Fleming and D.W. Hutton. Englewood Cliffs, N.J.: Educational Technology Publications.

Richardson, A. 1983. The voluntary use of memory imagery as an aid to learning and performance. In *Mental Imagery and Learning*, eds. M.L. Fleming and D.W. Hutton. Englewood Cliffs, N.J.: Educational Technology Publications.

Rossi, A. 1981. *A Scientific Autobiography*. Cambridge, Mass.: MIT Press.

Rugg, H. 1963. *Imagination*. New York: Harper & Row.

Schön, D.A. 1983. *The Reflective Practitioner: How Professionals Think in Action*. New York: Basic Books.

Sheehan, P.W. 1972. A functional analysis of the role of visual imagery in unexpected recall. In *The Function and Nature of Imagery*, ed. P.W. Sheehan. New York: Academic Press.

Singer, D.G., and J.L. Singer. 1977. *Partners in Play*. New York: Harper & Row.

Smith, E.E. and D.L. Medlin. 1981. *Categories and Concepts*. London: Harvard University Press.

Stevens, G. 1990. *The Reasoning Architect: Mathematics and Science in Design*. New York: McGraw-Hill.

Williams, T. and T. Scofido. 1983. Typology and primary elements. *The Journal of Architectural Education* 35: 29–32.

Part V

TYPE IN SCHOLARSHIP

Chapter 14

Type and the Possibility of an Architectural Scholarship

Guido Francescato

Il faut un antecédent à tout.
(Everything must have a precedent).
    Quatremère de Quincy

This chapter is written in response to the recently renewed interest in the concept of architectural type, interest of which this volume is but one example. Discourse on type concerns architecture as a whole but seems particularly relevant for those fields variously labeled as environmental design research, architectural and planning research, environment/behavior studies, or environmental psychology.[1]

The focus of this chapter is on architectural scholarship. My purpose is to clarify the nature and role of nontechnological research in architecture, especially in view of the current limited application of environmental design research findings in actual design practice. My point of departure is the question: Can the idea of type suggest which characteristics are unique to architectural knowledge as opposed to knowledge in other domains of human experience? My central assumption is that the answer to this question points to research directions more likely to address designers' central concerns than those currently being pursued, and thus will result in application.

But no question can be asked about architectural scholarship that does not involve the nature and methods of architecture itself. Surprisingly, as Saegert (1987) and Rapoport (1990), among others, have noted, comparatively little attention has been paid to this point by the environmental design research community. I will endeavor to avoid this oversight by examining three intimately interrelated issues: the nature of the *process* through which architecture is made, the nature of the *objects* it produces, and that of the *knowledge* it depends upon. At first glance, these may seem academic and abstract issues. They are not, because implicitly or explicitly they influence not only how designers go about making environments, but also how the public, critics, and researchers view both the design professions and the buildings and spaces that result from their activities.

---

1. In this chapter, the term *architecture* is used broadly to encompass not only architecture but other environmental design fields (e.g., urban design, landscape architecture, interior design). There are, of course, acknowledged differences in the specific tasks and operations that each of these fields addresses, but the general principles with which this chapter deals seem, by and large, applicable to all.

One of the most focused examinations of the relationship between architecture and research is Lang's (1987) work on architectural theory and the behavioral sciences. However, his approach moves in a direction fundamentally contrary to that suggested in this chapter. In effect, Lang argues that architectural theory and practice can – and should – be transformed not by evolving and sharpening their own paradigms, but by the contribution of behavioral science research.

Another compelling proposal for a reexamination of the links between scholarship and design is that of Rapoport (1990). In many ways, some of the points that will be made in this chapter parallel his work, in particular the value of learning from history and the need to develop more useful methods of historical analysis. However, by his own admission, Rapoport (1991) concerns himself not with current design practice, but with the blueprint for a new and different kind of environmental designer who would conform with a new theory of design based on "environment/behavior studies" and a "scientific metaphor."

Lang's, Rapoport's, and similar approaches are useful because they lead us to question a number of ill-debated professional assumptions in both architecture and the human sciences about, for example, scholarship, rigor, "congruence" of environments and social behavior, and differences between descriptive and prescriptive theories. But if a nondesign discipline is to make an effective contribution to the praxis – whether understood as architecture or, more broadly, as environmental design – it must start not from its own theories, worldviews, values, and methodologies, but from those of design itself. Although architecture, as any other human activity, is affected by the culture of the times, and thus cannot escape the propensity of our age for privileging scientific knowledge, it cannot be expected to become what it is not, to embrace a view of itself that would fundamentally change its nature and *raison d'être*.

I take a different approach from those outlined thus far. I develop the argument that scholarship based on central ideas in architecture's *own* conceptual basis, rather than on those of the social and behavioral sciences, is more likely to address architects' fundamental concerns and therefore to be embraced by designers as an essential source of knowledge. The concept of *type* is such an idea, pertinent to making architecture (praxis), thinking about architecture (theory), and knowing in architecture (research).

For the purpose of focusing on the concept rather than on the specific entities that may be involved in designing particular buildings or spaces, I use the singular *type* whenever possible throughout the chapter even though in the design of an environment a number of types are usually brought together. The term *typology*, though strictly speaking the study of types, is often found in the literature as a synonym of *type*. Here it refers to a collection or group of types, or to a process centered on type.

What Is Type?

In order to entertain a discourse on type, the term must first be defined. Not unlike other useful concepts, type has acquired many different meanings. In everyday speech, it is synonymous with *class* and *category*; hence a tendency to misunderstand its usage in architecture and design merely as a term of classification. In the professional literature one finds interpretations of type that range from the relatively straightforward to the more ambiguous and abstract. Examples of definitions along this spectrum can be found in a number of chapters in this book.

When associated with general categories of use or construction, type is easily understood as a term of functional or structural taxonomy. For example, professional journals routinely classify their coverage of building types with such expressions as "libraries," "hospitals," or "shopping centers." Likewise, the technology employed in a building, such as "passive solar" or "precast concrete," offers another accepted classification system.

Attributes of form are not central to these uses of type. Although there is an expectation that hospitals should not look the same as shopping centers, or that precast concrete will impart certain distinguishable formal aspects to buildings,

14-1
The main square of Telč, Czech Republic. Buildings surrounding the square all have similar formal and functional characteristics, even though each is unique. As examples of a *building type*, they belong to a common class of preindustrial buildings, the shop-cum-residence. But as examples of a *relational type*, they embody this multifunctional character in a specific *idea of form*, to which they all belong but of which each individual building is a unique manifestation. (photo by author)

AVM: *I am uncomfortable with the use of the terms* type *and* architectural type *in this chapter. I think* typology *or the study of type is a better word for what is being discussed. The word* type *seems to indicate that there is a method, or overall philosophy, about type in architecture, which is certainly not the case. So* type *should be qualified as* a *type, or* the *type, or* types.

GF: *This chapter is about the* idea *of architectural type, not about the study of type. It posits that this idea holds the key to clarifying the nature of architectural knowledge, that is, knowledge central to the generation of form. In my view, moreover,* architectural *type is not the same as* building *type. As discussed later in this section, building types are used to classify buildings across functions they are designed for (e.g., schools, single-family housing, etc.). Architectural type however, denotes a more inclusive idea linking function to form, and suggests, as you point out, a method or overall philosophy (a theory, really; see also the beginning of the section of this chapter entitled "For an Instrumental Scholarship of Architecture"). That is why the term is used not only in this chapter (the title of which is intended to reflect that of the recent Midgård Monograph* Type and the (Im)possibilities of Convention*) but also in many of the works cited. In the last paragraph of the introduction, I acknowledge that* type *and* typology *are often used synonymously in the literature and that* typology *is also frequently employed to mean a collection of types or a process centered on type.*

MS: *I cannot understand why this argument applies only to architecture, and not, for example, to coffeepots which Aldo Rossi also designs.*

GFL: *Indeed it does. Architecture, construed broadly as environmental design (as I posit in this chapter), deals with more than just buildings. For instance, Quatremère himself writes that "a great number of pieces of furniture, utensils, seats, and clothes have their necessary type in the use one makes of them, and the natural habits for which one intends them (Quatremère 1977, 150)." In a typological discourse, these "great numbers" of objects therefore include coffeepots as well as buildings, urban spaces, and the built landscape.*

there are all kinds of differences in form among hospitals or shopping centers and among precast concrete structures. The purpose of these kinds of typologies is to categorize buildings by function or structural technology, not by form.

On the other hand, form is an essential constituent of type at the opposite end of the definitional spectrum. It is at this end where ambiguity is the greatest, but also where the most useful notions of type are found. But even here type retains an aspect of classification; that is, it incorporates the invariant characteristics of a group of architectural works each of which is, in detail, different from the others. While different authors have offered different definitions, two main classes of concepts can be discerned: one in which type is thought of as a geometric property of form, the other in which type is viewed as a relational attribute of form connected with its historical development and use.

Geometric typologies are easily understood as classifications based on configurations, on Euclidean characteristics of form. An example might be Passanti's (1963) interpretation of Guarini's oeuvre, in which he distinguishes four types: (1) a central space surrounded by subordinate spaces; (2) a linear space articulated in sectors; (3) interwoven domes; and (4) overlapping domes.

As a descriptive tool, geometric typologies are undoubtedly very useful. Historical texts on architecture would be inconceivable without references to the geometry of plans, facades and, above all, spaces. (It is impossible to examine and analyze architecture without realizing that the articulation of spaces is at the core of the making of architecture; Zevi 1948, 1960; Giedion 1967). But geometric typologies are not unique to architecture; they do not distinctively characterize its nature. For example, they are equally applicable to other art forms, such as painting and sculpture, and to a gestalt of general form (Eco 1968).

Relational typologies, the subject of this chapter, are less straightforward. *Relational* connotes the idea that type epitomizes the relationship between architectural form and utility. This connection is distinctive of architecture and lies at the core of its enterprise, but it has been difficult to identify and to describe how type embodies it. Indeed, a great deal of puzzlement about what is meant by type stems from the interpretations given to relational typologies by architects and critics alike, which prompts some authors to label type as a "confusing" notion (e.g., Pérez-Gómez 1991). In general though, two main classes can again be identified. The first represents the highly personal views of type espoused by such designers as Aldo Rossi and the Kriers. Leon Krier, for example, seems to think of type as a formal property of the elements of a composition, the finished building being the result of a process of assembling a typology of selected components. This is explicitly shown, for example, in his plans for a school in St. Quentin en Yvelines.

Rossi (1982) merges a similar notion of type with what has been called an "autobiographical" approach, which depends on "personal experiences, memories, even fleeting impressions" (Doordan 1989, 59) and "on the juxtaposition of memory and reason" (Moneo 1978, 36). The result is a vigorous, evocative, but highly idiosyncratic architecture, perhaps the inevitable consequence of a view of type that depends so strongly on a personal interpretation of history (Figure 14-3). Indeed, Moneo suggests that Rossi's work is based on types born in the architect's imagination, reflecting "a past that may not have existed" (1978, 37). This is a crucial insight, because, as I will discuss later, the canonical view of type holds that its foundations are to be sought in history — and there can be no history of a past that did not exist.

Krier's and Rossi's notions of type (and similar ones) are highly prescriptive; that is, they express the view that contemporary architects must recover forms from the past, especially urban forms, that have been lost through the antihistorical posture of the Modern Movement and the profit-making orientations of capitalist societies. In this sense, their view is certainly nostalgic. But even though in many ways it is responsible for muddying the waters of a general discourse on typologies, it is nevertheless important — no matter how problematic the interpretations and the actual projects that emerged from it. The reason is that these designers view architectural objects as the result of a process that begins by considering entities (types) already possessed of formal *and* functional aspects. This stands in sharp contrast to the cause-and-effect relationship of programmatic requirements and architectural form that had been postulated by functionalism, and affords a linkage to more descriptive ideas of type.

The second class of interpretations of relational type reaches back to the formulations proposed originally by Quatremère de Quincy in his well-known, seminal, but frequently misinterpreted article for the *Encyclopédie méthodique* ([1825] 1977). Quatremère's article was firmly founded on the Neoplatonic ideas of Laugier's (1753) "primitive hut" as the root-principle or origin of architecture (Vidler 1977, Lavin 1992).[2] This article was intended as a manifesto extolling the virtues of the neoclassical tradition and opposing the perceived excesses of baroque and rococo and the pre-Romantic symbolism of such architects as Boullée and Ledoux. Moreover, the notion of art as mimesis, as imitation of nature, hovers in the background of Quatremère's argument, though it must be recognized that he was not bound to the notion of imitation in a positivistic sense; on the contrary, he criticized literal interpretations based on a pedestrian reproduction of preexisting form.

A contemporary reading must strip Quatremère's essay of its Neoplatonic overtones and prescriptive qualities, which were relevant to the polemics of the time but are not germane to the debates of the present. Regrettably, this has not often been the case, which has led to critiques of the notion of type as a prescription for banal and reductive convention (Bandini 1984; Pérez-Gómez 1991) or as a rigidly ideological principle that requires adherence to the concept of origin or primitive cause (Bell 1991).

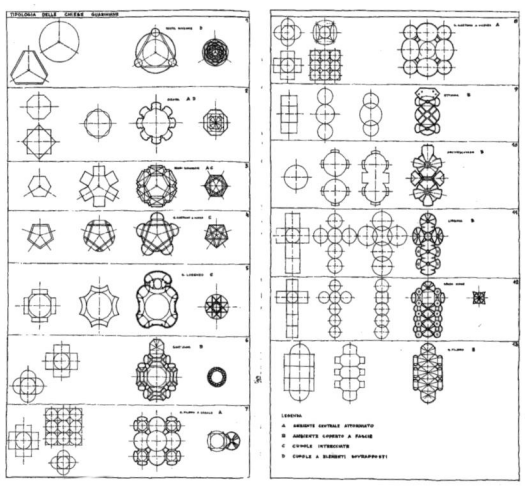

14-2
Geometric typology of Guarini's churches according to Passanti (source: M. Passanti 1963, *Nel mondo magico di Guarino Guarini*, Toso)

2. Quatremère himself was an intellectually conservative, if not downright reactionary, man. Jacques and Vidler (1977) report that students at the Ecole des Beaux-Arts twice rioted and had to be evicted by the police during his eulogies for architects Bonnard and Delabarre, respectively. It is then ironic that Quatremère's view of type was resurrected by Argan (1963, 1965), surely a most refined and progressive historian, and taken up and further developed by a number of architects who have been in the forefront of the critique of both the Modern Movement and contemporary consumer society, especially in Italy.

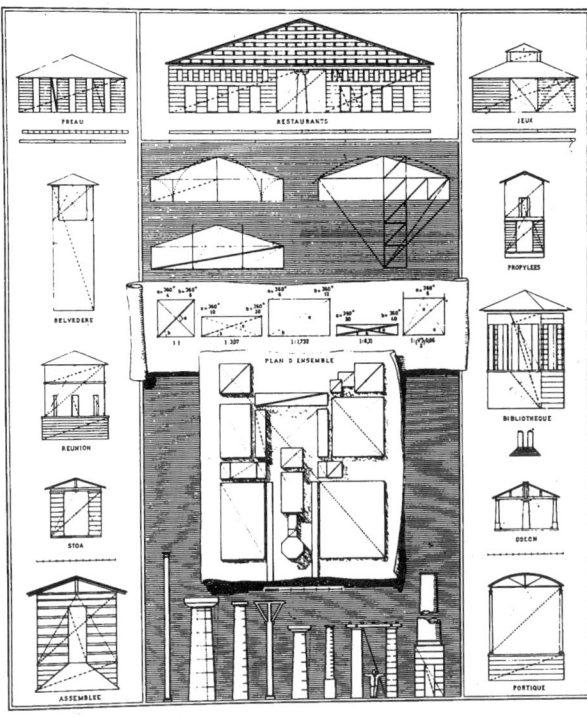

14-3
Drawing showing the compositional elements and plan for a school in St. Quentin en Yvelines, designed by Leon Krier. Functional labels have been affixed to elements of classical architecture as if they were a formal property of each element. (courtesy of Leon Krier)

14-4
Aldo Rossi. Scale model of the South Bronx Academy of Art, New York City (photo by M. Adelman)

Quatremère's discussion of type is articulated around the following themes: (1) a careful distinction between *type* and *model*; (2) the recognition of the inescapable relationship between objects and their *historical precedents*; and (3) an emphasis on the connection between *form* and *use*.

The first theme is crucial not only for understanding Quatremère's paradigm, but also for addressing a number of recent critiques objecting to the perceived restrictiveness of type. Quatremère writes that "all is precise and given in the model; all is more or less vague in the *type*" ([1825] 1977, 148). In his view, the *model* is clearly a form to be repeated, copied, and imitated, and therefore more appropriate to the crafts or, in our time, to the technologies of industrial production, than to architecture. The word *type*, on the other hand, suggests "the idea of *an element which ought itself to serve as a rule for the model... an object after which each [artist] can conceive works of art that may have no resemblance* [to the model]" ([1825] 1977; emphasis added).

Second, the relation between objects and their historical precedents represents, beyond the Neoplatonic ideas of "origin and primitive cause," the recognition that form is not the product of the artist's imagination unfettered by knowledge of prior forms. On the contrary, form results from operations performed on prior forms, or better, on ideas of prior forms – that is, on relationships embodied in prior forms. Hence, history becomes the necessary underpinning of the generation of form.

Finally, the third theme in Quatremère's discussion links the historical evolution of a type to the use for which an object is intended, suggesting that there are forms that tend to support a specific function, while others, whatever their aesthetic merits, are simply inimical or inappropriate to the intended purpose. Not surprisingly, this is the theme that already in the nineteenth century, through Durand's (1805) theories, began the process that eventually led to the programmatic determinism of the Modern Movement.

In Quatremère's thinking one already finds the germ of the important idea that type is both limiting and liberating: limiting, because designers cannot avoid the constraints imposed by social use and the physical environment, which are the initial *raison d'être* of their work; liberating, because they are not compelled to slavishly repeat historical models. The significance of this thought becomes apparent when dealing with the dilemma designers constantly face: whether to produce forms to which the public is already accustomed and which it presumably "wants" (Michelson 1968) or to invent new forms.

For Quatremère, then, type represents at the same time the architectural intention or purpose ("the original reason of the thing"), the generator of form ("an element which... serve[s] as the rule for a model"), and the container of tested functionality ("has... its type in use and nature") ([1825] 1977, 148–50). Although type belongs to the domain of visual form, it is not a mere icon or image but a composite of form and function. And precisely because it contains the relationship between form and use (or better, one possible such relationship), it is also a carrier of architectural knowledge ("a sort of nucleus about which are collected... the development and variations of forms to which the object is susceptible") (148).

This is undoubtedly a highly abstract, complex, and somewhat ambiguous formulation. But it is also evocative and persuasive precisely because, in its intricacy and vagueness, it reflects the absence of certainties, the complex interplay of nonexplicit and frequently conflicting goals, and the difficulty of predicting outcomes that so essentially characterize design. It suggests that knowledge in architecture is likewise uncertain but is also attainable (through the study of precedent) and communicable (by means of historical analysis). The ambiguity of Quatremère's formulation need not be construed in a negative sense. For example, Kahn (1991) has proposed an interpretation based on contemporary concepts of metaphorical structure, which points out the critical value inherent in the tensive relationship between such perceived opposites as convention and innovation or likeness and difference. She suggests that this relationship is indeed essential to the production of form.

Argan (1963, 1965) is credited with reproposing Quatremère's definition of type. However, Moneo (1978) submits that Argan's interpretation was, in an important aspect, diametrically opposite to Quatremère's. While the latter, true to his Neoplatonic orientation, thought of type as an *a priori* entity, Argan viewed it largely as the result of a search for commonalities among real works of architecture, therefore as an *a posteriori* examination aimed at uncovering the "inner formal structure" of a series of such works. Argan, as a historian, was primarily interested in the descriptive and taxonomic qualities of type and only incidentally in those that may affect the generation of form.

Argan made a distinction between "the moment of the typology," which he regarded as a link between the architect and historical precedent, a sort of passive form-receiving by the designer, and "the moment of formal definition," which he viewed as the active, form-giving stage in the production of architectural works. He seemed to imply that form was the result of operations outside the domain of typology, operations still ruled by the logic of function and economics as "determinants" of form. Moneo indicates that, in this, "he revealed his respect for Modern Movement orthodoxy" (1978, 36), that is, for the doctrine that viewed form as the result of operations performed on the functional requirements of the architectural program, not of operations performed on an entity – the type – which already contained a formal response to those requirements.

It is important to understand that Argan's emphasis implies a notion of type that focuses mainly on the formal aspects of architecture. In his writings, for example in an examination of the relations between the social, economic, and intellectual climate of the Weimar Republic and the work of Gropius and the Bauhaus, he eloquently links the formal aspects of that work to the cultural context in which it was produced, as the best historians have always done (Argan 1951). But this is not the same as explicating the connection between form and use, which would have been the corollary of a view of type consistent with Quatremère's definition. In the case of the Bauhaus and its architectural production, and particularly in the instance of the *siedlungen* in Dessau-Törten and Berlin-Siemensstadt, exploring the connection between form and use would have led him to analyze the public meaning and social acceptance of that work and, ultimately, what Robinson (1991) calls its "political and moral consequences."

Still, though Argan seems to have misread one of Quatremère's principal points, it was he who reopened the discussion of type and redefined it as the "generator of form" (*progetto di forma*). In so doing, in fact, he began to turn the focus of architectural discourse away from a purely functional perspective and opened the door to the rethinking of the design process that was to follow.

Type and the Design Process

It remained for Rogers (1965) to extend Argan's interpretation, and at the same time to complete the break with functionalist orthodoxy, by suggesting that the design process not only *starts* with type, but in fact *consists* of operations on type. For Rogers, functional appropriateness is intrinsic to, though not necessarily insured by, a process explicitly and consciously based on typological transactions. Clearly, this view of the design process was in complete opposition to the then prevalent theories advanced by the methodologist school (e.g., Alexander 1964; Jones 1970). For example, in his well-known analysis of an Indian village, Alexander had described the process of identifying, ranking, and grouping functional requirements, and deriving a topological diagram from them. At the point

14-5
The *Torre Velasca* in the Milan skyline. Designed by Ernesto Rogers (BBPR Studio), it houses offices in its narrower portion and apartments in its wider top and may be viewed as an attempt to generate a new type for a set of functions that coexist in other buildings without formal differentiation. (photo by author)

In Rogers's perspective, on the other hand, functional requirements, along with the precise *topos*, climate, society, and culture in which the building is to be built, shape the architect's judgment of which particular type to call forth. From this initial judgment to the completion of the design, all subsequent operations are operations on the selected type, because type is presumed to respond to use, to fit the requirements, at least to an extent. When this presumption is doubted, the architect chooses a different type or attempts to modify the type, occasionally to the point that the initial one is no longer recognizable and a new one is invented. When a completely new type is proposed, the danger is high that it will not be accepted because the users will not find it sufficiently familiar. Thus if architects are conscious of the role of type, they will have a check against excessive deviations from already tested typologies. This will increase the likelihood that the building or space will be socially accepted, even when embodying a modified type, because it will have evoked recognition of types embedded in the culture.

For the methodologists, fit between form and functional requirements was the object of the design process. If the requirements were set forth with precision and were analyzed in a systematic manner, form would necessarily fit, like the pieces of a well-assembled puzzle. Underlying this paradigm was the idea that functional fit is a property inherent in form, that certain configurations are per se an appropriate response to the building program. It goes without saying that in this view the question of public acceptance does not even emerge, functional appropriateness being virtually guaranteed by the rigor of the procedures used in analyzing the requirements. But for Rogers, functional suitability is the outcome of a historical process in which real buildings (the history of architecture) are used by specific cultures (human history). Because designers participate in the making of history by making new forms, they cannot rely on the comfort of guaranteed fitness; they inevitably run the risk of making inappropriate forms.

Central to Rogers's theory is the idea that architectural knowledge is generated and transmitted through typologies – that the architect knows by type. If, as Quatremère had proposed, type is a formal structure intended for a specific use and is the result of the interaction of society and nature, identifying a type that would solve the problem proposed by the program is the way in which architectural knowledge is brought to bear on that problem. By the initial choice of type, architects extend their roots into society, make a connection with human needs, and begin the process of transforming an abstract type (Argan's "*progetto di forma*") into a specific, concrete reality.

of having sketched the diagram, he stopped, implying that the "synthesis of form" had thus been achieved. Form, in Alexander's view, appeared to be the outcome of a reductive process based on analysis of the linkages or "interactions" among "functional sets" of programmatic requirements. This process was only tenuously connected with architectural history and precedent, and then only through relationships that such requirements may have had with prior requirements, not with prior forms.[3]

3. As is well known, Alexander later changed his views and advocated a different approach based on "pattern language." Pattern language may appear closer to a typological view of design because it is, at least in theory, based on precedent and research. But its normative structure and the assertiveness of its prescriptions seem to suggest formulaic and conforming solutions.

Argan's and Rogers's ideas about type owe much to the work of Muratori (1959), who, probably independently of the reexamination of Quatremère de Quincy's formulation, had evolved a methodology of urban design based on what he called "instrumental history" of the city (*storia operante*). Muratori maintained that systematic historical analysis of a city would yield a typology of urban form on which to base both urban growth and interventions in the existing urban fabric. In spite of the often hermetic aspects of his writings, the importance of Muratori's contribution lies not only in his strong sense of history as a usable repository of types, but also in his insistence on their specificity. For instance, in his analysis of the historical development of Venice, the urban types that he studies and describes are not the generic ones of streets, alleys, and squares, but the distinctively Venetian ones of *calli*, *corti*, and *campi*.[4]

At about the same time as Rogers, Colquhoun (1967) also became interested in an alternative to the theories of the methodologists. In a critique of their argument that type-based procedures are nothing but vestige of the age of craft, he noted that objects of use, such as buildings, continue to have not only a "use" value but a "message" value as well, even in postindustrial societies. This message, in Colquhoun's view, is tied to the purpose of architecture, which is that of making a "representation" of the objective world available to society. He suggested that the design process involves adapting past typologies to present needs.

In addition to supporting Rogers's formulation, Colquhoun's ideas point to the intersection of the concept of type with that of meaning. This intersection is important for a discourse on type because use necessarily implies communication, as Barthes (1964) stresses. In his discussion of the difference between linguistic signs and those pertaining to objects of use (of which buildings and urban spaces are major examples), he notes that the latter, which he calls sign functions, did not develop for the primary purpose of signifying something, but rather in response to a functional need. Still, because "*as soon as there is a society, every usage is converted into a sign of itself*" (Barthes 1964, 41), they acquire meaning through an inevitable process of semanticization. Applying Barthes's terminology to our discourse, architectural objects can be seen as the "substances" that are realizations of "a significant form," that is, realizations of a type. The designed environment becomes a whole having formal, functional, and signifying dimensions. Type becomes a carrier of coded meaning expressly because of its genesis through social use. The parallel with Rogers's and Colquhoun's views is obvious.

From Quatremère to Moneo, the discourse on typology describes the design process neither as an ineffable leap of creativity supported by intuition, nor as a codified sequence of transformations and reductions of functional requirements, nor even as an interplay between processes of image making and processes of practical problem solving. Rather, architectural objects begin their lives in the mind of the architect as choices among types. Types are the vehicle of architectural knowledge because they embody the unity of form, function, and meaning transmitted by history and transformed through it by the dialectical encounter between architecture and society. Once made, the initial choice can be questioned, and later be discarded, but as long as the choice remains in effect it governs and informs the entire process.

Following the generational rules embedded in the type, this "idea of a formal structure" (Moneo 1978) takes on more precise features suggested by the characteristics of the project site, by the social, cultural, and economic context, and by the designer's own experience and attitudes toward society. This process of transformation may lead to a simple adaptation of an existing type or to a more or less radical elaboration. In the first case, the type in question will be restated, its validity for the present corroborated, even though the specific form of the final product may significantly depart from past forms. In the latter, the original type will be altered in response to contextual conditions that challenge its appropriateness. In sum, the architect's task is viewed as one of performing operations on typologies to produce environments that either accept and develop a particular type or in varying degrees diverge from it and, at the limit, generate a new one.[5]

---

4. While at first glance there seems to be some similarity between Muratori's ideas and those recently put forth by Rapoport (1990), the former's insistence on the specificity of type is directly contrasted by the latter's quest for generalizability. Rapoport seeks to uncover general "lessons and principles," in turn derived from "historical data" fed into "constructs, concepts, models and theories" of environment/behavior science; these are to become the "precedents" (Rapoport 1990, 30) on which to base new designs. But for Muratori the precedents are the spaces and buildings themselves — a certain type conveying their invariant characteristics and thus a degree of generalization, to be sure, but primarily embodying their connection to the specifics of purpose, *topos*, society, and culture.

Type and the Nature of Architectural Objects

In any domain, research has the purpose, first of all, of understanding the domain itself and the phenomena with which it deals. In this sense, it is sufficient that it be illuminating. However, in professional fields the purpose of research is also to generate practical knowledge; it must also be *useful* in effecting a "better product;" it must have an instrumental character. But what is the nature of the architectural product? If type is a composite of architectural intention, form-generating rules, and tested functionality, and if the design process consists of operating on type to produce a certain object, can the concept of type help define the nature of this object? Is it merely a utilitarian article, an object of use, albeit a sign-function invested with meaning through a process of semantization, essentially no different from the products of crafts or industry? Or, because of its obvious individuality, uniqueness, and distinct communication content, is it really an art object embodying and expressing the artist's *weltanschauung*, the architect's view of the world?

Moneo (1978) begins to frame an answer to these questions when he suggests that designing consists of casting the idea of a formal structure, or type (in which, as Quatremère had remarked, "all is more or less vague"), into the concrete, specific form of the work. If architects know by types, they are initially bound to the configurations that a particular type encompasses. But because types do not represent models to be imitated, or standards that will ensure cultural acceptance and functional appropriateness, from this point on architects are free to propose deviations from the formal structure of the initial type.

In acting on type, architects inevitably rely on their own ideologies, worldviews, memories, personalities, and individual creativity. These are bound to impart expressive and representational qualities to specific architectural objects. Consequently, the creative process in architecture is no different from that of other aesthetic endeavors. However, the starting point of the process *is* different because architectural type has no counterpart in those arts whose essence is not related to use. Hence, from a typological perspective, there is no reason why architectural objects should be any less unique than works of art in the sense of possessing the singularity that distinguishes them from other works.[6] Yet because their genesis begins with a utilitarian purpose in addition to a communicative/aesthetic one, works of architecture (and objects of use) are also uniquely different from other works of art.

AVM: *Do architects produce "objects" or "objective space"? Hillier and Hanson, for example, make a distinction between object and building.*

GF: *Of course there are objects that are not buildings. I use the term* object *in its broadest sense of "thing placed before eyes or presented to sense" (Concise Oxford Dictionary). I use the adjective* architectural *to restrict the domain of all such objects to those that result from a process of designing environments. Designed space cannot come before our eyes or our other senses unless the construction of an object has occurred. In the section "What is Type?" I point out that the articulation of spaces is indeed at the core of the architectural task.*

---

5. For a discussion of the concepts of operator and operations, see Mitchell (1990). His treatment of the relationship between design and computation includes a section on type.

6. The recent reconstruction of Mies van der Rohe's pavilion for the 1929 exhibition in Barcelona, in spite of the continuing existence of many other works by this architect, is an example of the uniqueness of the architectural object.

As noted earlier, the architect is free to propose deviations from a specific type. Indeed, to propose altogether new types is often to make one's mark in the profession and to ensure one's place in its history. To make architecture is at the same time to draw from the past, through types, and to subject the past to a critical examination from which deviations from a type and ultimately new types are to emerge. To the extent that developing new types involves questioning society's values and structure, architecture, like any other art, also engages in a critique of the present.

But unlike other arts, which propose either new worldviews or new views of themselves, architecture proposes new ways of living in the environment. Also unlike other arts, architecture partakes of a number of aspects that characterize not art but mass communication:

> Its discourse is persuasive... and promotional (as it seeks to induce people to live in new ways)... is consumed unthinkingly (like television viewing or comics)... allows for aberrant meanings without loosing its essential ones (for instance, by permitting one to use a cathedral as temporary shelter from a sudden rain)... is subject to rapid obsolescence and re-signification (as in fashion)... and is immersed in the mercantile world (Eco 1968, 228).

In this regard, it is interesting to note the parallel between a typological view of the design process and contemporary theories of rhetorical discourse, especially those that regard rhetoric not as a repository of worn arguments effective only on naive audiences, but rather as "the study of the general conditions of persuasive discourse" and as "a generative technique based on a dialectic between information and redundancy" (Eco 1968). The parallel is interesting because rhetoric, like architecture, oscillates between the new and the known. In order to generate information, rhetoric must, on the one hand, provide novelty; it must play on that which the audience did not know or expect. But on the other hand, because the completely new and unexpected is by definition meaningless, it cannot generate information unless it starts from something that the audience already knows and wants; it must be based on the redundancy of the familiar.

Likewise, because architecture plays on the users' expectations of difference from the known, of variance from forms to which they have become accustomed and which have been consumed, it must avoid using a type as a model and delivering the familiar, the trite, the cliché. But because it also plays on the users' recognition of expected general relations derived from the social use of architectural forms, it must at the same time avoid offering forms that completely transform a type beyond recognition – or face the possibility of society's rejection.

In sum, the concept of type suggests that the architectural object is still a single and unique event but not in the same way as other works of art unbound by the world of utility. By stressing alterations to a type as the central feature of the design process, the typological approach sets out "more demanding conditions and premises," but it does not unduly restrict or deny creativity to the point where design becomes just another service (Oechslin 1986). In this optic, the architectural object stands in a class by itself, neither work of art nor craft, neither technological application of scientific discovery nor industrial commodity. Should not then research that seeks to contribute knowledge useful in making architectural objects also have unique characteristics that reflect the nature of those objects? Should it not be based on those aspects that make architecture different both from other visual arts and from the sciences?

Architecture and Research

In the previous two sections, I presented a typological view of the design process and of the nature of its products. In this section, I ask the question: How closely is this view supported by the current paradigms and methods of environmental design research and architectural history?

As is well known, the interest in design methodology that emerged in the 1960s and early 1970s was paralleled by the emergence of architectural research or, more broadly, environmental design research. This is not the technologically oriented research of a long tradition in architecture, which comprises studies in structural, mechanical, and constructional systems. Rather, it is research based on the social and behavioral sciences and aimed at generating knowledge about the interaction of people and the built environment; hence the terms environment/behavior studies, person/environment relations, architectural or environmental psychology, environmental sociology, and human or social ecology, often used to describe the field.

As the field grew, and more and more studies were produced, much attention was given to the general scarcity of applications of research findings in the practice of architecture (e.g., Kantrowitz 1985; Proshansky 1987; Sommer 1987). Indeed, the well-known metaphor of the "gap" and the perceived need for "bridging the gap" between research and practice grew out of the continuing disappointment with the minimal effect of social and behavioral research on design praxis.

The rationale for environmental design research stems from dissatisfaction with architects' perceived inability to predict the performance of their buildings. This suggests that designers depend on a knowledge base that is inadequate either because there is little knowledge or because existing knowledge is unreliable (or both). The methods of science clearly hold the lure of rigor, expressed in the requirements that findings be tested for reliability and validity. When this requirement is met, one can place confidence in the predictions one makes. In environmental design research, the assumption has been that knowledge derived from social and behavioral science research can improve prediction of the congruence between design and use. For example, Lang writes:

> If the gap between designers' predictions or claims of how their designs will work and how they *do* work is to be reduced, the quality of the knowledge base for design action needs to be considerably enhanced. This is particularly true in addressing the claims that designers make about the impact of their work on people's lives (Lang 1987, vii).

The need for more reliable prediction was also emphasized by Zeisel (1981). His view of the design process, certainly a refinement over that of the methodology school, consists of an iterative, cyclical interplay of what he calls "image formation" (the invention of form) and "test information" (design guidelines and research findings), aimed at bringing the image within the "domain of acceptable responses." In turn, this domain of acceptability is defined by knowledge of the predictable consequences, the "effects and side effects" of a design.

It is difficult to dispute the desirability of gaining a more dependable sense of how designs will perform once built. But to rely on scientific methods for this purpose is to overlook both the limitations of science and the fact that prediction, in the classical sense of explicating cause-and-effect relationships, is not invariably its goal. It is outside the scope of this chapter to examine this issue in detail. It is sufficient to point out that science has been extremely successful in explaining phenomena in some realms of human activity but not in others. One has only to think of economics or political science. Furthermore, prediction is not the only mode of science. The recent emergence of the mathematics and physics of chaos implies that prediction does not necessarily follow from rigor. An entirely new scientific perspective on the description and intelligibility of real-world phenomena became possible when Lorenz (1979) suggested that any physical system that behaves nonperiodically is unpredictable. Thom (1991) goes further in pointing out that "to predict is not to explain." In the social sciences, there are also examples of approaches that do not depend on prediction. For instance, Altman and Rogoff (1987) emphasize the aleatory quality of human events. Gergen recalls Whilhelm Wundt's idea that

> the metaphor for social psychology [is] not that of natural science, but rather of historical analysis... the function of social psychology [is] not that of making predictions... Rather than prediction, the goal of the social psychologist [is] to render the world of human affairs intelligible (Gergen 1982, 174).

In more general terms, the scarcity of research applications in design has been imputed to perceived general differences between architects and researchers. On the one hand, architects are seen as visually oriented, intuitive, subjective, nonsystematic, often socially irresponsible, occasionally even perverse in their refusal to integrate research results in their work. Researchers, on the other hand, are viewed as verbally oriented and possessed of qualities that represent the opposite of the architects' traits. In a less judgmental perspective, there remains the widespread view that the two groups are fundamentally different in their purposes and attitudes: architects are out to change the world, human scientists only to explain it.

Beneath these perceptions lies a conception of architecture very different from that suggested by the typological perspective. Central to that conception is the notion that the products of design should not conform to the designer's intention, only to the users' expectations. Architectural objects are seen as primarily utilitarian artifacts, though with some admission that these may become charged with meaning through semanticization processes. This perspective views architecture more as a service industry than as "perhaps the only and last humanistic profession," to use Eco's (1968, 245) words. Hence, for example, Rapoport's statement that

> [in architecture,] the decision about what to do and why must be based on the best available information, on a body of literature, on research on man-environment interaction, on theory, rather than on the likes and dislikes of designers. In fact I have argued that in its strong form this position may involve designing something that the *designer dislikes or even detests* (Rapoport 1984, 100, emphasis added).

This certainly defines in the starkest terms the dilemma that would face the architect that Argan and Rogers had in mind, not to mention the one whom Rossi and the Tendenza exemplify. For if the architect knows through type, this surely implies a certain *einfühlung*, an empathy with specific typologies, developed from an affective as well as a cognitive study of history and thus very definite likes and dislikes. In fact, Rapoport's argument contradicts the canonic notion of design as that enterprise through which we order space. What does this ordering consist of? In fact, it involves conferring reality to the built environment by endowing form with meaning, a process underscored by Barthes's reminder that "there is no reality except when it is intelligible" (1964, 42). This process involves both designers and users, not just users. To follow Rapoport's precept would be to reduce designers to minions who, as Eco puts it, "would obey the sociological and 'political' decisions of those who decide for them, and who would furnish the 'words' to say 'things' that do not belong to them and about which they can make no decision" (1968, 246).

Type implies choice among formal-functional entities. If type is socially and contextually based, as Quatremère suggested (rather than based on personal memory, as Rossi seems to believe), this choice is not arbitrary or frivolous but, on the contrary, represents the outcome of learning grounded in historical precedent. Lang recognizes the inevitable centrality of the architect's choice among types, but clearly regards it as a handicap, rather than the essential component of the process, when he writes:

> Most decision theorists... agree that the [design] process involves much adjustment of preconceived types to the present situation (46)....
> Designers frequently refer to generic solutions and types in examining present problems.... The classification and use of types is based on perceptions of what problem a designer is addressing. *This is a value-laden choice* (Lang 1987, 62, emphasis added).

Rapoport's and Lang's statements (several similar ones could be cited) reflect a conviction that "traditional" models of architectural praxis are inadequate, not to describe what current practice is (which Lang, albeit grudgingly, concedes they do), but to prescribe what it ought to be.[7] This is a curious outcome for a current of thought that arose originally from the view that architectural theories were too normative, hence unlikely to reliably account for the praxis. It is difficult to escape the conclusion that in fact the theories, hypotheses, and methods of the environment/behavior researcher are no less "value laden" than those of the architect.

Nothing said here should be taken as criticism or indictment of environmental design research, a field that has been making important contributions to general knowledge of the interactions of people and environments, and to the solution of some problems that arise from that interaction. This research has had an effect in special situations or at the policy-making level in regard to legislation and regulations that ultimately do have a major effect on the built environment. For example, standards and regulations pertaining to building accessibility for people with physical impairments have been formulated and are now law. Pre- and post-occupancy evaluations have been used successfully to write programs for complex buildings or to guide interventions aimed at solving problems in existing environments. And some of the techniques and methods that have been developed in this work could be used in studies focusing on type.

Furthermore, holistic perspectives such as the transactional approach in environmental psychology are being proposed (Altman and Rogoff 1987), and a recent review of the literature (Lawrence and Low 1990) suggests that a new focus on culture and history is emerging in environment/behavior research. As the field further develops and matures, it gains a broader outlook and its work becomes potentially even more useful. Still, because its paradigms are derived from those of its constituent disciplines in the social and behavioral sciences, it is unlikely that it will be able to generate type-centered knowledge. Perhaps the most important value of this type of research will remain its role as a gadfly, its continuing questioning of designers' assumptions about the users' expectations, values, and preferences. This is certainly not a trivial function, but it does not lie at the core of the enterprise I described in the section on the design process.

At this point, it is possible to ask a number of questions. Is it really desirable or even possible for architecture to fundamentally alter its very nature and *modus operandi* in order to meet society's or, more accurately, social scientists' perceptions of the public's needs and expectations? Is environmental design research, in its present form of knowledge generation and dissemination, likely to provide a

---

7. That the design process starts with type is beginning to be recognized not only by behavioral science researchers but also in the literature of the methodologist school. See, for example, Hawkes (1976) and, for some empirical evidence, Schön (1988).

stronger conceptual base for architecture than traditional theory? Will it enhance our ability to predict how architectural objects will "work"? Will it yield greater social relevance, hence public acceptance of architectural production, than has been the case so far?

If a typological theory of architecture rather than an artistic or scientific one better reflects the true nature of the profession, the answer to these questions has to be negative. Neither can architectural praxis fundamentally change without, in effect, destroying itself, nor is it reasonable to expect that the current mode of environmental design research, hitherto so ineffectual in causing its findings to be applied in design practice, would significantly reduce the architects' need for relying on typological knowledge.

I have noted that such knowledge is, by definition, precedent based. Can one then look for it in the scholarship of architectural historians? Lang (1987) asserts (correctly, in my view) that traditional research in the history of architecture is "not very helpful" in providing knowledge for theory building or form making. But his explanation (shared by Rapoport 1990) that this is so because historical research has focused on monuments and "high design" rather than everyday environments seems only partially correct. The fact is that most historical research, just like most environment/behavior research, is based on the theories, methods, and values of a field other than architecture itself, in this case those of art history. The result is, more often than not, an iconic history of architecture, or what Oechslin (1986), writing about Pevsner's work (1936, 1976), has called a "lapidary history."

Traditional architectural history, apart from its own purpose as a humanistic discipline, is certainly closely bound up with design practice. Indeed, architects derive a large part of their typological knowledge from historical scholarship. After all, even the work of the most revolutionary among them takes shape against the backdrop of architectural history, or at least against a certain view of that history. One need only remember the Le Corbusier of the *Sketchbooks* (1981) or of *Précisions* (1930) to confirm the profound presence of architectural history in his work at the same time as he presented his ideas and proposals as a rejection of historical precedents. Moreover, architectural history has not escaped the recent surge of interest in the social consequences of design. For example, the writings of Kostof (1985) suggest a new interest in going beyond the formal aspects of architecture to linking them with aspects of use and users, to some extent reflecting the influence of the *Annalistes* school of historiography and especially of Braudel.

Scuri's (1990) study of the skyscraper as a building type is another example of this interest. And Gowans's recent *Styles and Types of North American Architecture* (1992) takes one step in the direction of use by examining the relationships between formal types and the institutions they serve or symbolize. Yet architectural history remains essentially concerned with, and bound by, its own aims and paradigms, as indeed it should if it is to fulfill its roles and the orientations of its field.

Thus, neither environmental design research nor architectural history seems likely to provide knowledge that would centrally reflect the views of the design process and of the nature of architectural objects that have been set forth in this chapter. This is perhaps incongruous in the case of environmental design research, because the field emerged as a response to a perceived lack of applicable design knowledge. But by and large environmental design research has not confronted the issue of the nature of that knowledge. Its scarce utilization by designers should therefore not surprise us.

The situation could appear even more puzzling in architectural history because its methodology is founded on the study of precedents. But precedents can be examined for different purposes, and the aim of architectural history is only tangentially related to investigating the connections between designers' intentions and environmental use. Therefore we should not be shocked when historical precedents are regarded more as a source of iconic "quotations" than as collective experience of form-in-use.

Should one conclude then that architectural knowledge is ineffable, that architecture and scholarship are mutually exclusive, destined forever to move in worlds that have little that is useful to say to each other? Not if the idea of type can suggest a new kind of scholarship, one founded on systematic and intensive inquiry of the three interrelated facets of type outlined earlier: architectural intention, form-generating rules, and use.

For an Instrumental Scholarship of Architecture

If the typological view of the design process is correct, it represents a descriptive, not a normative, theory. In this perspective, architects inevitably operate typologically, indeed cannot choose to create form on the basis of anything else but type. Therefore, from a typological viewpoint, any attempts to elaborate theory and scholarship based on processes and methods outside of architecture, whether aesthetic or scientific, are doomed from the start. This does not mean that traditional typological knowledge absorbed through one's experience and exposure to history is by itself sufficiently robust to perform two of type's most important functions: that of fostering a design culture in which use becomes as important an aspect of design as the designers' intention; and that of alerting the architect to the potential for public acceptance or rejection of a design.

Lang observes that "the design professions have a poor history of scholarship" (1987, 1). By and large this is true, but it is not inevitable. Architecture can attain a more stable and more communicable knowledge base than that currently available if it can develop its own scholarship based on constructs that are at the core of its endeavor. Following Muratori's (1959) terminology, this could be called *instrumental* scholarship, by which I mean that it should be conceived as a tool for the central task of architecture, the generation and development of form.

As with any endeavor that has not yet been tested with empirical work, it is difficult to predict what form this type of research would take, or to set clear and exhaustive criteria in advance for developing its methodology. Because environment/behavior research concentrates on use and architectural history privileges form, it would be tempting to envision a combination of approaches and methods from the social sciences and art history. To some extent this may be possible and indeed desirable. But because the task at hand relies on different paradigms, it seems more likely that it will require new and different procedures. However, there should be no doubt about the essence of the enterprise – it should be a kind of historical analysis. It should focus on the study of typologies embodied in precedents, that is, on the study of form/use transactions in historical time (including the history of what has been built in this century). Keeping this in mind, there are a number of implications of taking a typological view of scholarship.

First, if architects know through type, one of the most important tasks would be that of articulating and conveying useful findings of existing research by means of typologies. As Moudon (1989) observes, some environmental design researchers (e.g., Newman 1980; Cooper Marcus and Sarkissian 1986; Lawrence 1986) have, at least in part, organized their work on this basis. As a result, their findings have received some acceptance among designers. But the necessarily analytical format of guidelines that such work often follows seems more useful as a checking device at advanced stages in the design process than as central information in the form-generation stage.[8]

Because type conveys information about form and form is visual, there needs to be a concentration on more advanced techniques of visual presentation of information than are customarily used. In this area, graphic and multimedia computer technology may offer opportunities that were unavailable until recently. Solid modeling, virtual reality, interactive modalities, cd-ROM technology, and similar developments could be used effectively for this task. However, it would be a mistake, in my view, to consider visual formats only a matter of communicating results. The research itself should be modeled on these formats.

Second, it seems clear that typologies are synthetic entities. Thus, research paradigms and methods that depend on holistic, rather than analytical, modes are more likely to yield the desired results. This presents great obstacles because analytical modalities are well known, can be used with rigor and precision, and can be tested against generally accepted criteria of reliability and validity. Holistic approaches, on the other hand, tend to appear to the scholarly mind as arbitrary, or at the very least, ineffable. They are difficult to describe and to communicate, and for this very reason they are difficult to apply consistently. Again, these obstacles represent challenges for this type of research, but they are not necessarily insurmountable.[9] After all, historical methods, even when relying on analytical techniques for documentation and other research tasks, are in essence synthetic. With the caveats noted earlier, some procedures from both scientific and humanistic fields can be adapted to the needs of typological scholarship, as long as a general synthetic mode is preserved.

Third, because type is a formal-functional entity shaped by history and therefore an entity molded by social and cultural *change*, one of the essential components of type-centered scholarship must be a focus on time. Until the recent emergence of transactional approaches (Altman and Rogoff 1987), the concepts of time and change have not been at the center of the discourse of environmental design research. To be sure, time-series and longitudinal studies have been long-accepted, though not often practiced, research designs in this field. But even when time has been taken into some account, its significance in architectural terms has not.

A reason for this stems from the fact that buildings and spaces tend to last longer than the historical situation in which they are conceived; therefore, the architectural work can fail even when it initially met public expectations, guidelines, or programmatic requirements. Architectural form lives on, often acquiring new meanings and uses in a constantly changing social, cultural, and political milieu, even with the accelerated physical destruction of buildings that characterizes contemporary society.[10] Hence the need for much greater attention to the aspect of change, for intensive and sustained concern with what Altman and

14-6
Marne-la-Vallée. Central space of a housing development by architect E. Girard (photo by author)

8. Architects tend to be instinctively antagonistic to guidelines. For example, Refuerzo and Verderber's guidelines for renovation and construction of public health facilities were criticized as "terribly prescriptive: the corridors must be, this must be, that must be... it actually kills the possibility of making architecture" (Saitowitz 1992, 94–5).

9. Mitchell's (1990) *The Logic of Architecture* is a thorough discussion of design aspects that may be explicitly and rigorously defined. Discussions such as this may serve as bases on which to build a modality of type-centered research. For a less illuminating, but nevertheless useful, treatment, see also Thiis-Evensen (1987).

10. Reuse is central to a discourse on type and on changing relationships because it demonstrates the nondeterministic links between form and function. The making of a former office building into a museum, or of a former factory into a shopping center, are operations of reutilization of no longer functional buildings, as for example in the National Building Museum in Washington or Ghirardelli Square in San Francisco. Reuse in fact re-semanticizes old building types and generates new types, recoding new uses and new meanings that make obsolete forms both intelligible and usable in new ways. It is in reuse where the dynamic dimension of the idea of type can perhaps be best appreciated.

Rogoff (1987) call "*the changing* relations" among psychological, social, cultural, economic, and architectural/environmental aspects of human events.

Fourth, while type is an architectural concept, its very nature requires that any typological study include the urban fabric of which the individual building or space is but one component. In describing the genesis of urban typological studies, especially with the work already cited of Muratori (1959) and that of Aymonino (1966), Moudon (1989) notes the need for type-oriented research to consider not isolated buildings, but the urban whole consisting of buildings, streets, spaces, and other elements of the environment – and not only "high-style" works, but also lesser structures and vernacular buildings.

Finally, and most important, the focus of an instrumental scholarship of architecture must be on uncovering, documenting, and communicating the essential characteristics of type: that of embodying relationships among form, use, and meaning; that of expressing commonalities among certain works of architecture while maintaining the specificity of time, place, and culture in which they were conceived and used; and that of exposing the inner formal structure of buildings and spaces.

An example that suggests the kind of research envisioned here emerged during an investigation of urban housing complexes built in Europe after World War II (Francescato 1987). Some of the housing that appeared most successful when judged by the degree of residents' satisfaction, general upkeep, and occupancy rates exhibited many of the site design features characteristic of a housing type developed in Austria in the 1920s and early 1930s, known as the Viennese Superblock, which in turn was an evolution of the German tenement known as *mietkaserne*. These characteristics include bringing the exterior facades of the buildings to the street line, thus preserving street continuity; creating a landscaped central space devoted to recreational activities, especially for children; and providing entrance to this space only through clear gateways. In recent housing developments in France and the Netherlands in which these features were replicated, there were indications that the appropriateness of their design was to a degree dependent on specific proportions of the central open space, on the height of the surrounding buildings, on the overall scale of the complex, and on the activities provided for in the central space. These characteristics seemed to come very close to those form-generating rules that form an important aspect of the idea of type.

At the time, these observations represented only an embryonic intimation. But in the context of the scholarship described here, they suggest that studying the relationship of form and function in this type of environment could yield knowl-

14-7
Noisy-le-Grand. Le Théâtre, a housing complex by Ricardo Bofill. The layout reflects the same overall choice of a central space surrounded by housing units as in the example of Figure 14-6. But this is the only similarity, suggesting a wide typological distance between the two examples. (photo by author)

14-8
Noisy-le-Grand. Les Arènes de Picasso. Housing designed by architect M. Nunez. Another central space in a large housing development, yet very different spatial qualities from the examples in Figures 14-6 and 14-7. (photo by author)

edge useful to designers of urban housing. They also hint at the possibility of a history of twentieth-century housing based on architects' search for new typologies reflective of perceived social, economic, and political change. At the very least, such a history would generate a potentially valuable taxonomy of housing types that have been successful under specific circumstances of use.

Conclusion

Insistence on architecture itself as the subject of scholarship, on a more sophisticated understanding of the aspects of time and change, and on the application of such understanding to the design process should not be interpreted as a call for the continuation of the status quo in which personal aesthetics, individual whim, and social irresponsibility often dominate environmental design. On the contrary, a serious discourse on type cannot but emphasize the need for a higher level of social accountability on the part of the design professions. This observation underscores the fact that, like all descriptive theories, the typological perspective inevitably introduces a prescriptive aspect. Acknowledging the complexity, ambiguity, and inevitable subjectivity of design is not the same as adopting the view that architecture is only about architecture and therefore need not concern itself with use and social acceptance. Recognizing the importance of personal memories and experience and the inevitable *einfühlung* that individual architects have for certain forms and styles is not the same as espousing private and idiosyncratic application of historical precedent whether appropriate or not.

Nor is my plea for a scholarship internal to architecture meant to suggest that architecture should continue on the current path of professional debate, which some critics see as largely parochial, and "remove [itself] from humanity" (Portoghesi 1991, 21). Quite the contrary, by evolving and enhancing a use-and-time-centered scholarship, designers would come closer to fulfilling the vital social and cultural roles of architecture, which are so clearly at the core of the idea of type. It is doubtful, in my view, that designers can achieve this goal without social accountability, and accountability is not just a question of roles and values. It also depends on shared, communicable knowledge derived from purposeful and robust scholarship.

Of course, there should be no illusion that in architecture, as in any other area of professional practice, knowledge per se would eliminate the need for the professional to make *choices* and therefore run the risk of making the "wrong" choice. This is, after all, the difference between a profession and a mere occupation. In spite of sometimes brilliant contributions to our built environment, in many ways as compelling and significant as those of the past, architecture as a profession has been in a condition of crisis for some time and for reasons that often have very little to do with the appropriateness of its scholarship. As Gutman (1988) has so thoroughly described, many practical factors unrelated to the issues discussed here impinge on the profession and shape its activities. Moreover, I have observed elsewhere that professional ideologies play a strong role in the decision-making process not only of architects, but also of other groups responsible for the built environment (Francescato 1987). Not infrequently, these ideologies override factual information and knowledge.

But, if designers' choices are among types, an instrumental scholarship of architecture would yield a number of important benefits. It would provide knowledge directly usable in the central architectural task of form making. It would support the profession's claim to a preeminent role in the creation of the *entire* built environment, not just its high-style monuments, by illuminating the need for socially acceptable design to be based on recognizable precedent. It would make it easier for architects who understand this limit to develop and maintain successful practices because they would be less likely to make idiosyncratic, frivolous, or simply unworkable design choices. Finally, it would clarify the reasons for the application gap in current modes of environmental design research. And this could only strengthen the field by sharpening the definition of both its possibilities and its limitations.

I thank the editors for their questions which pressed me to sharpen my own thinking about type. I am also grateful to Juan Pablo Bonta, Isabelle Gournay, and Piera Scuri for their insightful comments on earlier drafts.

References

Alexander, C. 1964. *Notes on The Synthesis of Form*. Cambridge, Mass.: Harvard University Press.

Altman, I. and B. Rogoff. 1987. World views in psychology: trait, organismic, and transactional perspective. In *Handbook of Environmental Psychology*, vol. 1, eds. I. Altman and D. Stokols. New York: John Wiley & Sons.

Argan, G.C. 1951. *Walter Gropius e la Bauhaus*. Turin: Giulio Einaudi Editore.

———. 1963. On the typology of architecture. *Architectural Design* 33 (12): 564–5.

———. 1965. *Progetto e Destino*. Milan: Il Saggiatore.

Aymonino, C. 1966. *Il Significato della Città*. Bari: Laterza.

Bandini, M. 1984. Typology as a form of convention. *AA Files* 6: 73.

Barthes, R. 1967. *Eléments de Semiologie*. Paris: Editions du Seuil. English trans. 1967. *Elements of Semiology*. New York: Hill and Wang.

Bell, D. 1991. Nomads. In *Type and the (Im)possibilities of Convention*. Midgård Monographs 2: 19–31.

Colquhoun, A. [1967] 1969. Typology and design method. Reprint in *Meaning in Architecture,* eds. C. Jencks and G. Baird. New York: George Braziller.

Cooper Marcus, C. and W. Sarkissian. 1986. *Housing as if People Mattered*. Berkeley, Calif.: University of California Press.

Doordan, D.P. 1989. Changing agendas: architecture and politics in contemporary Italy. *Assemblage* 8: 69.

Durand, J.N.L. 1805. *Précis des leçons d'architecture données à l'Ecole politéchnique*. Paris: Chez l'Auteur.

Eco, U. 1968. *La Struttura Assente*. Milan: Bompiani.

———. 1976. *Theory of Semiotics*. Bloomington, Ind.: Indiana University Press.

Francescato, G. 1987. Housing planning and design: learning from three decades of experience and research. In *Public Environments*, eds. J. Harvey and D. Henning. Washington, D.C.: Environmental Design Research Association.

Gergen, K.J. 1982. *Toward Transformation in Social Knowledge*. New York: Springer-Verlag.

Giedion, S. 1967. *Space, Time and Architecture: The Growth of a New Tradition*. 5th ed. Cambridge, Mass.: Harvard University Press.

Gowans, A. 1992. *Styles and Types of North American Architecture*. New York: HarperCollins, Icon Editions.

Gutman, R. 1988. *Architectural Practice: A Critical View*. Princeton, N.J.: Princeton Architectural Press.

Hawkes, D. 1976. Types, norms and habit in environmental design. In *The Architecture of Form*, ed. L. March. Cambridge: Cambridge University Press.

Jacques, A. and A. Vilder. 1977. Chronology: the Ecole des Beaux-Arts, 1671–1900. *Oppositions* 8: 151–7.

Jones, J.C. 1970. *Design Methods: Seeds of Human Futures*. New York: Wiley-Interscience.

Kahn, A. 1991. Toward a nonoppressive interpretation of the concept of type. In *Type and the (Im)possibilities of Convention*. Midgård Monographs 2: 107–13.

Kantrowitz, M. 1985. Has environment and behavior research made a difference? *Environment and Behavior* 15 (3): 311–22.

Kostof, S. 1985. *A History of Architecture: Settings and Rituals*. Oxford: Oxford University Press.

Lang, J. 1987. *Creating Architectural Theory: The Role of the Behavioral Sciences in Environmental Design*. New York: Van Nostrand Reinhold.

Laugier, M.A. 1753. *Observations sur l'architecture*. Paris: Desaint.

Lavin, S. 1992. *Quatremère de Quincy and the Invention of a Modern Language of Architecture*. Cambridge, Mass.: MIT Press.

Lawrence, D.L. and S.M. Low. 1990. The built environment and spatial form. *Annual Review of Anthropology* 19: 453–505.

Lawrence, R.J. 1986. *Le seuil Franchi... Logement populaire et vie quotidienne en Suisse romande 1860–1960*. Geneva: Georg Editeur.

Le Corbusier. 1930. *Précisions sur l'état présent de l'architecture et de l'urbanisme*. Paris: Crès & C. English trans. 1991. *Precisions on The Present State of Architecture and City Planning*. Cambridge, Mass.: MIT Press.

———. 1981. *Le Corbusier Sketchbooks*. New York: Architectural History Foundation.

Lorenz, E.N. 1979. On the prevalence of aperiodicity in simple systems. In *Global Analysis*, eds. M. Gremela and J. Mardsen. New York: Springer-Verlag.

Michelson, W. 1968. Most people don't want what architects want. *Transaction* (July–August): 37–43.

Mitchell, W.J. 1990. *The Logic of Architecture*. Cambridge, Mass.: MIT Press.

Moneo, R. 1978. On typology. *Oppositions* 13: 23–45.

Moudon, A. 1989. The role of typomorphological studies in environmental design research. In *Changing Paradigms*, eds. G.J. Hardie, R. Moore, and H. Sanoff. Washington, D.C.: Environmental Design Resarch Association.

Muratori, S. 1959. *Studi per una Operante Storia Urbana di Venezia*. Rome: Istituto Poligrafico dello Stato.

Newman, O. 1980. *Community of Interest*. Garden City, N.J.: Anchor Press/Doubleday.

Oechslin, W. 1986. Premises for the resumption of the discussion of typology. *Assemblage* 1: 37–53.

Passanti, M. 1963. *Nel Mondo Magico di Guarino Guarini*. Turin: Toso.

Pérez-Gómez, A. 1991. Architecture is not a convention. In *Type and the (Im)possibilities of Convention*. Midgård Monographs 2: 11–18.

Pevsner, N. 1936. *Pioneers of the Modern Movement: From William Morris to Walter Gropius*. London: Faber & Faber.

———. 1976. *A History of Building Types*. Princeton, N.J.: Princeton University Press.

Portoghesi, P. 1991. Progettare l'architettura ascoltando. *Domus* 723: 21–6.

Proshansky, H.M. 1987. The field of environmental psychology: securing its future. In *Handbook of Environmental Psychology*, vol. 2, eds. D. Stokols and I. Altman. New York: John Wiley & Sons.

Quatremère De Quincy, A.C. [1825] 1977. English trans.: Vidler, A. 1977. Type. *Oppositions* 8:147–50. Published originally in Architecture. *Encyclopédie Méthodique*, vol. 3. Paris: Panckoucke.

Rapoport, A. 1984. Architectural education: there is an urgent need to reduce or eliminate the dominance of the studio. *Architectural Record* (October): 100–103.

———. 1990. *History and Precedent in Environmental Design*. New York: Plenum.

———. 1991. Studying practitioners of environmental design professions. Oral presentation at the 22nd Conference of the Environmental Design Research Association, March 12–15, Oaztepec, Mexico.

Robinson, J. 1991. Premises, premises: architecture as a cultural medium. In *Type and the (Im)possibilities of Convention*. Midgård Monographs 2: 11–18.

Rogers, E. 1965. *L'utopia della Realtà; Un Esperimento Didattico sulla Tipologia della Scuola Primaria*. Bari: Leonardo da Vinci Editrice.

Rossi, A. 1982. *The Architecture of the City*. Cambridge, Mass.: MIT Press.

Saegert, S. 1987. Environmental psychology and social change. In *Handbook of Environmental Psychology*, vol. 1, eds. D. Stokols and I. Altman. New York: John Wiley & Sons.

Saitowitz, S. 1992. Jury Comments. *Progressive Architecture* (January): 92–94.

Schön, D.A. 1988. Designing: rules, types and worlds. *Design Studies* 9 (3): 181–90.

Scuri, P. 1990. *Late-Twentieth-Century Skyscrapers*. New York: Van Nostrand Reinhold.

Sommer, R. 1987. Dreams, reality, and the future of environmental psychology. In *Handbook of Environmental Psychology*, vol. 2, eds. D. Stokols and I. Altman. New York: John Wiley & Sons.

Thiis-Evensen, T. 1987. *Archetypes in Architecture*. Oxford: Oxford University Press.

Thom, R. 1991. *Predire n'est pas expliquer*. Paris: Eshel.

Vidler, A. 1977. The production of types. *Oppositions* 8: 93.

Zeisel, J. 1981. *Inquiry by Design*. Monterey, Calif.: Brooks/Cole.

Zevi, B. [1948] 1974. *Architecture as Space*. Translated by M. Gendel. London: Oxford University Press.

———. 1960. *Architettura in Nuce*. Venice-Rome: Istituto per la Collaborazione Culturale.

Chapter 15

Type as Analytical Tool: Reinterpretation and Application

Roderick J. Lawrence

Type commonly refers to a kind, class, or category of people or things that have some characteristics in common. Hence it is possible to identify particular types of objects, events, settings, and people with respect to specific characteristics. These characteristics underline the general form, plan, or design of each type and enable one or more to be distinguished from others.

According to the *Oxford English Dictionary* (1989), a type refers first and foremost to "that by which something is symbolized or figured; anything having a symbolic signification." From this perspective typology refers to "the study of symbolic representation; of the origin and meaning of Scripture types" as well as "the study of classes with common characteristics; the classification, especially of human products, behavior, characteristics, etc., according to type; the comparative analysis of structural or other characteristics."

These definitions of type and typology are included to emphasize their multidimensional nature, including the subtle, symbolic layering of their meaning. These subtle layers of meaning include tacit, cognitive structures as well as explicit institutional and material structures. Given that these two sets of structures mutually define architectural types, they ought to be studied in order to identify the multidimensional nature of building types in precise localities. It is argued that if this approach is applied to the study of built environments, then architectural type can be used as an analytical tool. In order to achieve this goal, type in architectural and urban studies can be interpreted as a corpus of shared knowledge: social conventions and rules that constitute societal types in general, and building types in particular. This interpretation stems from an overview of discourse on type and typology in several disciplines of the natural and social sciences (Lawrence 1986).

In principle, societal types and building types are contextually defined (Lawrence 1987). They are expressed and transmitted by both tacit and manifest structures that enable and constrain individuals and groups to produce and reproduce human culture in general, and building types in particular. The practices of individuals and groups can be related to the roles, responsibilities, and obligations of sets of people in society, including the designers, the makers, the owners, and the users of the built environment. Lawrence (1986) illustrates this multidimensional interpretation of type with a study of the development of urban rental housing in the French-speaking cantons of Switzerland. The theoretical framework applied in this study has been presented in Lawrence (1993). This illustration of the application of type as analytical tool led to the formulation of principles for future theoretical and applied research in architectural and urban studies.

Type as Analytical Tool

Theories and applications of type and typology have a long history in several disciplines including philosophy, linguistics, and the natural sciences. Since antiquity, humans have sought to organize their observations in the natural sciences, including botany, geology, and zoology. Aristotle explicitly referred to 400 animal species which he categorized into types, or classes. Since then, the recognition and classification of a growing number of species have reflected not only the growth of human knowledge but also the elaboration of typologies that result from the systematic classification of the constituents of ecosystems.

The interpretation of organic types commonly applied today stems largely from contributions like that of Etienne Geoffrey Saint-Hilaire (1772–1844) in the natural sciences, as well as Bertrand Russell (1872–1970) in philosophy, and Max Weber (1864–1920) in the social sciences. What these contributors share is their interpretation of type as an analytical tool for the application of systematic methods of study. Although these kinds of contributions are rarely cited in architectural discourse on type, they merit close attention for a number of reasons.

First, these contributions collectively show that *principles of classification* are used by scholars in diverse fields or disciplines to identify order in the world according to distinct sets of categories. From this perspective, classes or types are denoted by implicit, cognitive structures that define and demarcate conceptual boundaries between categories of people, settings, objects, and events. Consequently, all types (not just architectural ones) are constructed by humans. Durkheim and Mauss (1903) are generally recognized as being the first to apply this concept of type to identify the human ordering of both material and nonmaterial components of their milieu. Durkheim and Mauss were primarily concerned with the symbolic classifications of a religious and moral kind and their relationship to kinship and descent systems, as reflected in clans, marriage classes, and moieties in specific societies.

Second, although their contribution appears to have little relevance for the development of our comprehension of built environments, it is appropriate to underline the little known, yet far reaching, impact of the contribution of Durkheim and Mauss on a small group of scholars who have examined symbolic classifications associated with the spatial order, meanings, and uses of buildings (Needham 1973; Markus 1987). Some other authors have interpreted social classifications as the foundation of types or classes of people, settings, objects, and events. Tambiah's ethnography of the village of Baan Phraan Muan in northeast Thailand is one example. The study describes and interprets how three sets of human and nonhuman classifications, namely marriage and sex rules, spatial categories in the house and village, and sets of forest and domesticated animals, relate to the organization and use of behavioral, conceptual, spatial, and temporal boundaries in and around the orthodox layout of the village buildings. Tambiah analyzes the system of explicit ideas which the villagers have about their dwellings, animals, and other possessions:

> The house categories which refer to the physical arrangement of the rooms and floor space have for the villagers a direct association with the human series and also a relevance for the manner in which the domesticated and forest animals are conceived. The architecture of the house thus becomes a central grid to which are linked categories of the human and animal world (Tambiah 1969, 429).

This ethnography shows that human actions, plans, and products related to the construction and use of the built environment encompass a wide range of societal dimensions including social organization and systems of classification. The approach used by Tambiah enables us to identify and study some of the implicit and explicit anthropological dimensions of type. Hence, the material characteristics of building types can be explicitly related to the more subtle meanings shared by people who constructed and/or used specific built environments. When this approach is applied in architectural and urban studies, it can enrich our current understanding of architectural type, which is too frequently interpreted only in terms of stylistic, morphological, and functional criteria.

The above-mentioned contributions can help to reorient and enrich interpretations of architectural type. Nonetheless, the majority of them present a synchronic interpretation, in contrast to a diachronic one that can account for both continuity and change over time. A temporal perspective is necessary in order to identify *whether* (and if so, *how*) systems of social classification provide a fixed framework while simultaneously enabling the interpretation of daily life in terms of dynamic processes.

Histories of the human-made environment, and of buildings in particular, indicate that from the late eighteenth century, specific kinds of internal and external spaces were explicitly commissioned and constructed for precise groups of people and human purposes. During the same period, biological theories and taxonomies about evolution developed. They illustrated a broad societal concern for

1. The study reported in Lawrence (1986) identified how specific terms such as *logement ouvrier* (workers' housing), *petit logement* (small dwellings), *logement économique* (economical housing), *logement à bon marché* (low-cost housing), and *logements pour les personnes peu aisées* (housing for persons with low incomes) were commonly used in public debate from the mid-nineteenth century. Then, with the growing impetus of the housing reform movement, other terms were used, such as *logement hygiénique* (hygenic housing), *logement salubre* (healthy housing), and *logement amélioré* (improved housing). These terms were complemented by others that specifically referred to the volume of residential buildings: when a building was relatively large the term *immeuble de rapport* (a building yielding a return on investment) was used to underline the financial incentive of the property owner. Or the term *caserne locative* was used pejoratively to infer that the building was like a military barracks. In contrast, when there was only one residential building, the term *logement individuel* was used to refer to a detached, semidetached, or a row house.

KAF: *With new kinds of objects, the image may not be shared until after the object is made and its use demonstrated. This can be a problem in architecture when the new building seems overly novel. Guido Francescato and Tom Markus discuss this problem in their chapters.*
RL: *I agree. The case of the houses at Pessac by Le Corbusier is a well known example.*

novel forms of social classifications. This proliferation of the building stock led to a growing interest in the classification of specific buildings in relation to aesthetic, functional, material, and other criteria, including the social class of the groups of building users. For example, within one functional type of building — housing — specific terms were gradually formulated and applied in order to classify the type of housing that each residential building was intended to include. In essence, as Lawrence (1986) shows, social classification and discrimination became increasingly conveyed by nomenclature applied to distinguish between the increasing number and kinds of housing units, as well as the groups of people they were intended to accommodate.[1]

Such studies illustrate how social classifications are commonly used either implicitly or explicitly to convey ideas, values, and intentions about human products and processes in general, and residential buildings in particular. Moreover, when the concept of type is defined in this way, it can be used as an analytical tool to identify both the tacit and manifest interrelated dimensions of shared knowledge and social conventions associated with the spatial ordering, meanings, and uses of the built environment. This analytical approach can lead to a contextual understanding of the multiple dimensions of architectural and urban types in precise locations, as shown by the historical study of the development of urban residential buildings in Switzerland (Lawrence 1986).

Type as a Corpus of Shared Knowledge

Designing produces a representation of something that is to be made. This representation of an object by a formal design template (e.g., a text, a model, or a drawing) can be contrasted with the conventional image of that class or type of object. The image must be shared and understood by both the makers and the users of objects if it is to serve its intended purpose. In the absence of a design document, the image serves as the template that is reproduced each time a new object is made. Consequently, image and reality, process and product are explicitly associated in the realization of any human-made object. This association occurs implicitly or explicitly between the tacit, cognitive structure — the mental representation of an object — and the manifest, formal material characteristics of that same object, be it a building, a window, or an item of furnishing within the building. It is noteworthy that Habraken has related the concept of type to conventional images and shared knowledge of material culture. He suggests that types embody both functional and formal properties that are classified according to societal customs:

The concept of type, I suggest, is much more than a means for classification and more than a way to indicate the historic origins of a form. It is a complex form that lives within a social body: a knowledge, familiar to a group of people by common experience. Types come and go with societies and their cultures. They are, to a large extent, those cultures (Habraken 1985, 25).

Habraken states that the concept of type cannot account for the genesis of human products or the rationale of their formal properties. However, he does not refer to the *principles of classification* that structure implicit and explicit meanings attributed to types in accordance with societal conventions. These principles serve as vehicles for the expression and transmission of that implicit knowledge which constitutes the meaning and use of architectural types in general and housing types in particular. If this wider perspective is adopted, the concept of type is not merely descriptive or prescriptive, as most architectural interpretations claim, but, above all, type is a corpus of shared knowledge and conventions that structure knowledge, action, and material culture. Hence, in order to understand the multiple dimensions of type it is necessary to identify and study the shared knowledge and social conventions of diverse groups of people in society. Habraken (1985) notes this includes *the designer* (who controls the formal characteristics of objects), *the maker* (who controls the transformation of matter into the object), and *the user* (who controls the usage of the object).

In most industrialized societies today, the designer, the maker, and the user are different people. Consequently, the image, the representation, and the product require chains of information transfer. This is particularly the case with respect to the built environment. Moreover, "the user" is a term that frequently camouflages a range of people from diverse cultural, socioeconomic, religious, and professional backgrounds who use particular buildings. Likewise, the term "designer" often conceals the fact that several people can be attributed tasks during the design process. Finally, the term "maker" does not account for the number of people involved in the production of objects. Analysis of the responsibilities and obligations of these parties enables us to identify some of the implicit nonmaterial dimensions of building types in precise localities.

This discussion serves to illustrate that it is necessary to question the applicability of broad monolithical interpretations of concepts such as architectural type for architectural research (Lawrence 1987). Such broad interpretations tend to obscure rather than reveal the essence of social processes and cultural ideals.

KAF: *This concept of type as a corpus of shared knowledge is very useful for highlighting the way types help structure knowledge, action, and material culture. I don't think this aspect of type is sufficiently recognized or understood by researchers or designers.*

TM: *To what extent, and how, is the understanding of a type culturally determined? Are there universal types?*
RL: *Types are contextually defined. Therefore, although monuments are a type of human-made structure found in all human societies, their purposes and meanings vary rather than being universal.*

TM: *The distinction between history and culture is dangerous. A culture is a "materialization" of history over time — no?*
RL: *Your reading of a "distinction" between history and culture is unfortunate and unintentional on my part. Moreover, I do not think that culture should be equated only with material culture as you imply. It is necessary to distinguish between a synchronic analysis of cultural predispositions, and their constancy and change over time, in order to identify what constituents of culture are applicable for deciphering the meanings and uses of the built environment in precise localities.*

These characteristics of human societies should be examined in order to comprehend the multidimensional nature of architectural types in precise situations by intensive analyses that define not only those parameters operative in a specific context, but also the reciprocal relations between them. In order to achieve this objective, human actions, intentions, and plans associated with the construction and use of the built environment can be related to a wide range of societal dimensions, including social organization and interpersonal communication. Hence the localized structure and functioning of human societies can be related to the rights, responsibilities, and obligations of individuals and groups. These can be illustrated by studies of the ownership, control, and use of property (in general) and buildings (in particular). From this perspective it is possible to bypass the traditional, generalized distinction between public and private in order to identify and comprehend the number and kinds of parties (e.g., landlord, leaseholder, caretaker, tenant), as well as the division of responsibilities between the parties (e.g., individual, collective, public), and the definition of rules and conventions between the parties (e.g., administrative, mandatory, formal, conventional, informal, optional). Together, these characteristics define the claims and responsibilities of individuals and groups across diverse scales or levels of society. These claims and responsibilities may be tacit and conveyed by unwritten conventions, or they may be explicit and prescribed by regulations. Consequently, they can both enable and constrain individual action and group practices in the housing sector across different levels of society.

This reinterpretation of type as an analytical tool interrelates implicit cognitive structures and explicit societal structures, either with respect to an individual or group, or in relation to the less tangible cultural and historical context to which each individual and group are inevitably associated. On the one hand, the historical context not only provides an abstract temporal framework for human action, but defines and is defined by the tacit and manifest meanings attributed to people, settings, objects, and events in relation to implicit and explicit structures. On the other hand, the cultural context provides a framework for individual and group actions and plans, including active, process-oriented knowledge and societal rules and conventions, such as institutional power and control. Collectively, these constituents of culture enable and constrain daily affairs including the definition and use of architectural types at a specific point in time.

Research Application: Urban Housing and Domesticity in Switzerland

The kind of analytical approach outlined in this chapter has been applied in a longitudinal study of the development of urban rental dwelling units in three French-speaking Cantons of Switzerland between 1860 and 1960. This study has used both synchronic and diachronic perspectives in order to show how shared knowledge, social conventions, and rules are associated with the layouts, meanings, and uses of urban residential quarters in Geneva, Fribourg, and Le Locle, three towns with divergent cultural, economic, geographical, and political backgrounds (Lawrence l986). The research comprises two interrelated studies.

The first study is an historical analysis of the evolving design, meaning, and use of public, collective, and private spaces and facilities in residential quarters built between 1860 and 1960, including a longitudinal study of household size and composition, the local housing stock, and housing tenure during this period. This longitudinal study involved an analysis of three sets of sources, including: (1) a sample of the 100 sets of architectural plans of extant and non-built housing schemes (such as projects for competitions) in Geneva, Fribourg, and Le Locle, descriptions and articles by architects on housing, and site visits to existing buildings; (2) a sample of official publications, including reports of government agencies, philanthropic societies, health and housing reformers, and examples of building regulations and tenancy agreements; and (3) some novels, autobiographies, brochures, and newspapers.

The second study includes ongoing research with 525 households in the Canton of Geneva from a representative sample supplied by the government statistics office. A survey includes plan analysis of residential buildings and their immediate surroundings; documentation of changes to the layout and furnishing of dwelling units; an interview with directed, semidirected and open-ended questions about the daily activities of the household and each respondent, both inside and outside the dwelling unit; his or her residential biography; and questions about the dwelling unit, the residential building, the immediate surroundings, and the neighborhood and its facilities and services. As the results of this study are still being processed, the remainder of this chapter will focus on some of the findings of the historical study enriched by initial results emerging from the second study.

Analysis of Building and Dwelling Layouts

Analysis of the architectural plans following site visits to all existing residential buildings indicate that it is possible to classify the dwelling types in this study according to one or more of the following criteria:

(1) Stylistic conventions related to the composition of building facades (e.g., classical, neo-Gothic, modern). These criteria account for the explicit professional knowledge of architects and builders which is frequently recorded in pattern books or other professional publications. There is rarely any consideration of the point of view of lay people.

(2) Socioeconomic variables related to the income and professional status of the inhabitants (e.g., working class or middle class, blue- or white-collar workers). People in all walks of life are generally aware of their position in society when it is defined according to these criteria.

(3) The number, size, and layout of dwelling units on each floor level of residential buildings (e.g., two or three rooms, a through floor plan, or only one facade with fenestration). These criteria are frequently used by architects, property owners, and estate agents to classify and assess urban house types.

(4) The layout and construction of the buildings (e.g., timber framed, brick or stone walled), which is not only used by professionals to interpret the nature of physical boundaries (e.g., walls, fenestration, door openings), but also by lay people to attribute social values to residential buildings.

(5) The spatial organization of the floor plan in relation to the means of access from the public realm of the street to the private realm of each dwelling unit (e.g., passing through a private outdoor space, a shared external space, and/or an internal space).

Using these criteria, I elaborated a typology of urban rental housing constructed in Fribourg, Geneva, and Le Locle between 1860 and 1960. This included an analysis of 100 architectural plans of residential buildings constructed in each of the three towns during the period of study, according to the methods shown in Figure 15-1. Particular attention was given to the spatial layout of these buildings, the names attributed to internal and external spaces, and the intended and actual usage of them.

Some recent morphological interpretations of the spatial layout of the built environment stem from the development of systematic methods for comparing diverse buildings by the topological analysis of their floor plans (Steadman 1983). In this approach, a graph comprises a set of points called nodes which are connected by lines. Each internal space is represented by a node, and the possibility of movement between spaces is represented by a line, as shown in Figure 15-1. The graph can represent all interior spaces of buildings and the surrounding external spaces. Using this method, a number of buildings that appear to have different configurations can be shown to have a shared spatial pattern. This was ably illustrated by March and Steadman (1971) in their topological analysis of three houses designed by Frank Lloyd Wright. This example confirms that this approach is not only a means of visual representation, but also a method of studying the spatial organization of buildings.

15-1
Text, floor plan, and topological analysis illustrating the application of the analytical method for the study of one residential building in this study.

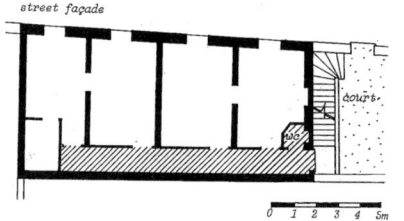

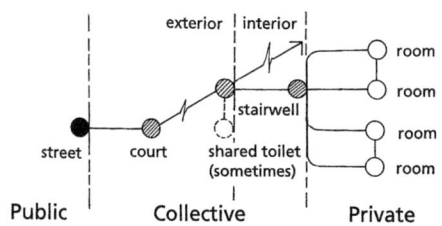

- ● street/public space
- ○ collective space
- ○ private space
- — access between spaces
- ⤢ stairs between levels

Case GE 1:
Ruelle du Midi, 14
A semi-detached residential building constructed around 1860 with a ground floor level and one upper floor level. Each floor level comprises 5 habitable rooms that can be rented as 2, 3 or 4 separate dwelling units. One shared toilet is accessible from an internal corridor that provides access to each dwelling.

Location
A residential neighborhood of buildings aligned in continuous rows along streets. Windows are only included in one facade, that overlooking the street.

Architectural features:
There is no aesthetic decoration on the external facade. There is no decoration inside the building. Rooms are of minimal dimensions. The building is aligned along the footpath without any transition space.
Access to the building is through a gate that opens into a small courtyard.
A door to the building provides access from the courtyard to an internal corridor, each dwelling unit, and one shared toilet at ground level.
There is no change of floor level between the courtyard and the ground level of the building.
An external staircase provides access from the courtyard to an internal corridor, the dwelling units and one shared toilet at the upper level.
The entrance door to each dwelling opens directly into a room.
A flexible use of rooms to form one-, two-, or three-roomed flats on each floor level is possible by closing connecting doors between rooms.

Documents:
There is no archival records of landlord-tenant agreements for this building.

NB:
The volume of this building and the spatial organization of rooms are probably borrowed from buildings that were used to accommodate agricultural workers. Such examples are not very common in Geneva.

Nonetheless, the mere act of transforming the two-dimensional representation of a building from a traditional scale drawing of the floor plan to a graph does not provide any information about cultural, societal, or psychological dimensions related to the meaning and use of that building. Yet Hillier and Hanson (1984) claim that the topological analysis of diverse buildings indicates how human relations are embodied in the spatial configuration of the built environment. These authors try to establish formal properties of buildings and external spaces that reflect the ways in which interpersonal contact between individuals and groups is encouraged or inhibited. They maintain that the position or depth of a space on a topological graph, and its relationship to adjacent spaces, reveal whether strangers have easy access to that space.

This generalization requires several qualifications. In the different context of rented and owner-occupied dwellings, for example, although the spatial organization of these kinds of dwellings can be represented by a graph, the accessibility to any space is not determined solely by architectural factors but also by legal rights and obligations, and societal customs and rules. In principle, the topological analysis of diverse housing units may highlight the similarities and the differences between their spatial organization but, alone, it cannot yield information about their multidimensional meaning and use. The meaning and use of dwellings units are not just expressed materially because they are also ordered by behavioral, legal, and symbolic dimensions that may be transient in kind (Lawrence 1987). Therefore this kind of analysis is only informative about the spatial characteristics of the built environment when it was initially constructed. In this respect buildings are interpreted as fixed objects by a static abstraction that ignores their life history. What if internal changes or additions were made to the structure or functions of specific buildings? How are different spaces classified and used over time? Such questions relate to the design, meaning, and use of the built environment. They cannot be answered satisfactorily by a topological analysis. Rather, this approach should be used in a complementary way with other analytical methods, as illustrated in this chapter.

Bearing these qualifications in mind, a topological analysis of the residential buildings included in this research preceded studies of the relationship between the functional labels ascribed to spaces and the relative positions of them, and the interface between the private domain of each tenement and the shared, collective spaces providing access from each tenement to the public domain of the street. These methods are illustrated in Figure 15–1, and presented in detail in Lawrence (1986). After these methods were applied the following typology was formulated:

Type 1: Tenement buildings, like those shown in Figure 15–2, that were constructed in urban quarters with an internal or external circulation corridor providing shared access to several dwelling units on each floor level; each tenement receives daylight from only one facade, either that orientated toward the street or the back court; each tenement has two or three rooms of similar size; there commonly is sequencing of rooms; and there usually is one shared toilet at each floor level.

Type 2: Tenement buildings, like those shown in Figure 15-3, that were constructed in new urban quarters with a shared internal daylit lobby, staircase, and landing providing access to two, three, or more tenements on each floor level (two usually having a through type plan). Each tenement comprises two or three rooms of similar size which are independently accessible from a central passageway or distribution space. These dwellings were usually not self-contained before 1900; thereafter they were, and they commonly included an additional room plus a bathroom.

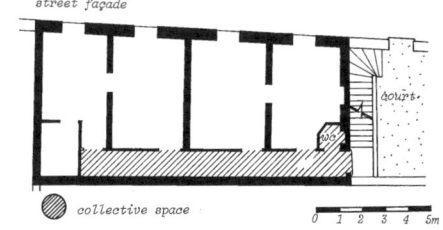

15-2
Example of house type 1, constructed at the Ruelle du Midi, in Geneva, around 1860
a. view of building facade overlooking the street
b. floor plan with shared space indicated

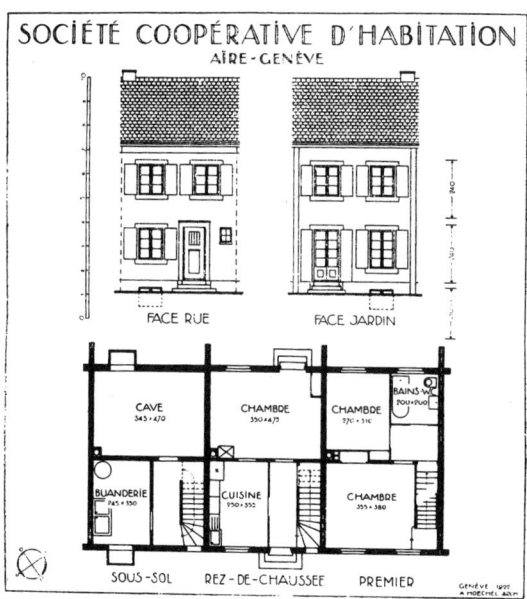

15-4
Example of house type 3, constructed in the suburb of Aire, in Geneva, during the 1920s (courtesy of Centre d'iconographie genovoise)

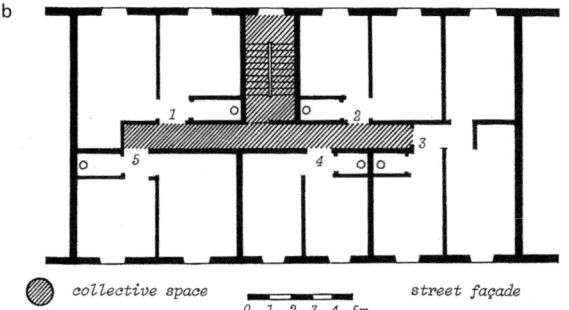

15-3
Example of house type 2, built at the Boulevard Carl-Vogt, in Geneva, in 1897
a. view of building facade overlooking the street
b. floor plan with shared space indicated

Type 3: Dwelling units, of the kind shown in Figure 15–4, that were built on suburban sites rather than in urban quarters, comprising two or three floor levels with a through type floor plan, built-in terraces and accessible from the street through a private outdoor space. These dwellings were self-contained, but shared the boundary wall with each neighboring unit.

Type 4: Flatted dwellings, like those shown in Figure 15–5, with a through type floor plan, each tenement comprising three or more rooms which are accessible from an external gallery at each floor level, usually with a shared laundry accessible from each gallery. Prior to 1900 this type of tenement was not self-contained, indicating that collective space and facilities were available beyond the private realm of each dwelling unit.

Type 5: Cottage dwellings, of the kind shown in Figure 15–6, with a through type floor plan, either detached or semidetached, commonly with one or two floor levels (sometimes three) and completely self-contained or demarcated from nearby dwellings.

Although this typology of urban rental housing is representative of dwelling units that were constructed between 1860 and 1960, several qualifications must be made. First, examples of all these types were built concurrently at the end of the nineteenth century and did not follow a chronological sequence. Second, the relative numbers of each housing type varied considerably; for example, the second type is predominant throughout the whole period of this study. Third, with respect to all but the fifth housing type, it became increasingly common from

15-5
Example of house type 4, built between 1930 and 1932 at the Cité Vieusseux, in Geneva
a. view of the building facade showing the external, shared circulation gallery
b. view of facade overlooking shared garden
c. floor plan with shared space and laundry indicated

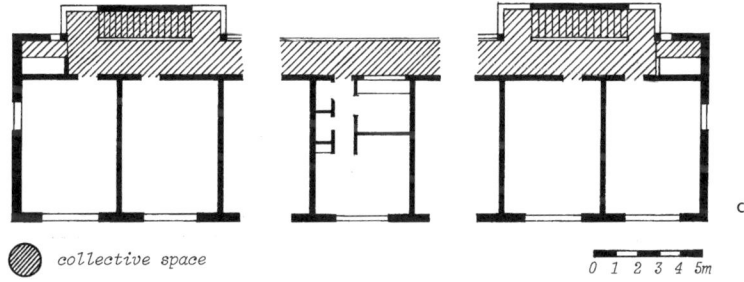

◯ *collective space*   0 1 2 3 4 5m

KAF: *These five types serve as a good framework for understanding your research and the many changes that you document. It is important that we recognize that they were generated from that research rather than posited in an a priori manner. It would be beneficial for more researchers to adopt such an approach.*

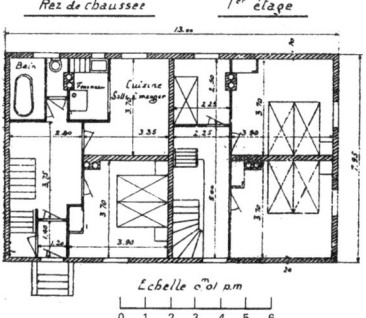

15-6
Example of house type 5, built in 1920 at the suburb of Charmilles in Geneva (courtesy of Centre d'iconographie genovoise)

1900 to provide each dwelling unit with its own sanitary and cooking facilities, whereas during the nineteenth century these were commonly shared, being accessible from the interior, collective space. Fourth, although the design and layout of these five types of dwelling units vary considerably, the tenure status of all the occupants is the same: they are tenants who have prescribed rights and obligations concerning the use of collective and private spaces and facilities, as defined in tenancy agreements (Lawrence 1986). For this and other reasons, including their vocation, the tenants share the same socioeconomic status. Finally, this typology is based on the architectural, stylistic, and functional characteristics of dwelling units, such as the lack of decorative ornament on building facades and interior spaces, the rare provision of balconies, and the total lack of rooms for maids (which were commonly provided in dwellings for the middle and upper classes). Although these characteristics do not account for the meaning and use of residential buildings, the latter are explicitly integrated into the following analysis which summarizes several chapters of the original study (Lawrence 1986).

During the period of this study, the small increase in the size of urban dwelling units can be contrasted with the significant improvement in the provision of private domestic services, and a marked decline in the number of persons per household. Hence, demographic, socioeconomic, and technological factors have been implicated as much as architectural ones in the decline of residential densities and changes to the use of public, collective, and private spaces and facilities. In this respect, the development of an integrative typology, in which architectural and societal characteristics are explicitly interrelated, can provide a comprehensive understanding of the social transformations of the layouts, meanings, and uses of buildings over time.

In principle, given the limited number of rooms inside the five types of urban rental housing, the activities of each member of the household are restricted spatially and temporally because the use of a few small rooms requires a chronological rather than a simultaneous ordering of activities. There is little possibility for domestic activities to occur simultaneously in a small dwelling unit compared with other dwelling units with many more rooms, or with one very large room, such as the traditional farmhouse kitchen, in which a range of domestic activities can occur simultaneously. In general, this means that, during the nineteenth century, in the majority of urban tenements in Geneva, Fribourg, and Le Locle, there were explicit physical and temporal boundaries between domestic activities. These characteristics of urban house types meant that residents applied unwritten conventions about the use of collective and private spaces and facilities. These conventions were tacit rules and codes of conduct that were shared by tenants of the same building.

Developments in the layout and use of these five types of urban rental housing can also be considered in terms of private or shared domestic services for ablutions, laundry, and cooking activities. During the last half of the nineteenth century, the debate about the minimum standard of an urban dwelling for "the working classes" in Switzerland (and many other European countries) focused on the definition and design of self-contained tenements, with private facilities and a separate bedroom for parents and children of different gender over ten years of age. The implications for house planning were explicit: the design and layout of rooms for specific household activities, and the controlled liaison between rooms by architectural boundaries, were intended to generate a reform of lifestyle and the instigation of sanitary living conditions. This architectural and moralistic concept linked the design of dwellings to moral well-being. The quest for improved housing conditions in urban areas led to the inclusion of a private toilet and

KAF: *This is very important. It is one example of type as a "corpus of shared knowledge." These tacit rules and codes of conduct help constitute the urban house types.*
RL: *This is an essential principle underlying the thesis of this chapter. Unfortunately types are frequently formulated by architects and urban designers only in relation to stylistic, construction, or use characteristics, and implicit meanings and diverse kinds of behavior are not considered.*

kitchen, then a bathroom, in each dwelling unit. Although household laundry activities still occurred in a collective or public space, they were relegated to the basement. The content and use of the five types of urban rental housing evolved over the course of time; consequently, the spatial and temporal demarcations between public, collective, and private space and facilities became more explicit than they had been before. This trend warrants further consideration.

Apart from changes in the design and use of private, interior spaces and facilities in urban residential buildings, there were also significant transformations in the design and use of external and internal shared spaces and facilities during the same period of time. Analysis of floor plans and fieldwork shows that collective interior spaces (such as the lobby at ground level, and the staircase and its landings at the upper levels) were significantly redesigned from the late nineteenth century on. There was a reduction in size and decoration, the suppression of natural daylight from windows and/or skylights, the elimination of subtle changes in floor level, and the privatization of shared facilities, especially for ablutions. These trends have transformed the collective spaces that linked the front doorstep of each dwelling unit to the public realm of the street into a passage of minimal dimensions meant to serve no purpose beyond pedestrian circulation. Consequently, residents could no longer personalize the space adjacent to the front doorstep of their dwelling units; children could no longer play in these shared spaces during inclement weather; and thus it became increasingly unlikely for neighbors to meet informally. It is instructive to examine why this occurred.

According to our research, the catalysts for the transformation of internal collective spaces and facilities in all types of urban housing were numerous, so they can only be summarized here. First, they included architectural and technical developments, especially the introduction of the elevator as the principal means of vertical circulation. Over an extended period of time, the stair became a fire escape. Second, innovations in domestic technology, as well as the distribution of public services (e.g., the supply of gas, electricity, and water), meant that private facilities for ablutions, cooking, and laundering were promoted.

Last, but not least, a fundamental idea shared by many housing reformers of the late nineteenth century was that different spatial relationships in urban dwellings should engender different degrees of human interaction. This idea became the foundation of a principle of domestic culture that architects, landlords, estate agents, and reformers upheld and applied for the construction and management of urban dwelling units:

(1) Reducing the size of shared space and facilities, notably sanitary services, in order to maximize the amount of rentable space within each building, reduce the maintenance costs of nonleased spaces and services, and minimize interpersonal contact between residents.

(2) Providing private facilities in each dwelling unit, which could be charged to the tenant by increasing the rent. The tenancy agreement stipulated that the tenant was responsible for the maintenance and repair of these facilities, and concurrently, that domestic activities should not occur in the shared, interior spaces.

15-7
Views of rental housing units in Fribourg. These two views illustrate the redefinition of outdoor space, especially the contrast between the direct link to the street and the complete demarcation from it.
a. some rental housing units built about 1900
b. some rental housing units built in 1960

(3) Prescribing how both interior and external spaces and facilities ought to be used by tenants. These prescriptions included written codes of conduct that were explicitly intended to regulate behavioral and temporal boundaries that defined the daily lives of tenants. Often caretakers were employed to insure that the residents did not transgress these prescribed boundaries.

Beyond the realm of interior collective spaces and facilities, immediately outside and around all types of urban residential buildings, there were also other significant changes during the period of study. Both fieldwork and plan analysis show that during the last decade of the nineteenth century it became increasingly common for all types of buildings to be set back from, rather than aligned along, streets, alleys, and courts, as had been the custom in Swiss towns until that time. This gradual change (which increased after the First World War) meant that the residential building was no longer directly linked to the public realm of the street. It has been observed that the external space between the building and the street was initially a small garden. However, since the 1930s it has increasingly become a

KAF: *Do the residents, landlords, or real estate agents have a name for this space between the dwelling units and the street? Do they think it serves any purpose? Because of its physical features and its frequency, this is a* type *of space even though it may have no name or clear purpose.*
RL: *There is no name for it. The lack of a label indicates that people have a problem identifying with this space. Consequently it is not used.*

TM: *But none of this explains how* external *space, like the vast "no-man's-land," came into being.*
RL: *Earlier in this chapter I wrote that "the catalysts for the transformation of internal collective spaces and facilities were numerous, so they can only be summarized here." I mentioned architectural, technical, public health, and social reform factors. The same approach has been used to study the morphogenesis of the external space around residential buildings, as discussed in a chapter of the original study (Lawrence 1986).*

KAF: *All of these additional changes in space, form, and regulations contributed to the creation of new housing types. Types are generated and transformed by a multitude of different actions and interests. Hemalata Dandekar analyzes some of these forces in her chapter on the development and transformation of the midwestern farm and farmscape in the United States.*
RL: *Yes, it is the "multitude of different actions" that ought to be emphasized here as well as the interrelations between these actions.*

vast, landscaped area, sometimes with space for parking, that frequently encircles all four sides of residential buildings, as shown in Figure 15-7. This outdoor space is neither "public" in the sense of a street nor "private" in the sense of the garden of a villa. It is a collective space, which is commonly not demarcated from the public realm of the street. Consequently, the residents interpret it as an ill-defined space between their dwelling unit and the street. Furthermore, owing to the fact that this space is rarely used for leisure activities (if these are permitted by the tenancy agreement), it is attributed, at best, a neutral value, and, at worst, an anonymous value. And, if it is not well maintained by the caretaker or housing authority, it not only becomes abandoned but also vandalized.

Research has indicated that no building or town-planning regulations prescribed these changes, nor did government or local populations intervene in an attempt to suppress them. Therefore, the underlying reasons for these changes evoke the need for further research, which cannot be achieved solely by the study of building plans and fieldwork. In this case, a study of diverse documentary sources has also been completed in order to identify the interrelations between the implicit societal and the explicit architectural dimensions of these house types.

Analysis of Documentary Sources

The content of many parliamentary papers and the publications of architects, property owners, estate agents, and health and housing reformers record the concern of politicians and members of benevolent and learned societies to resolve the problem of accommodating the increasing urban population in sanitary dwellings at a reasonable rent. There was a debate about the merits and shortcomings of tenements and cottages, and about associated and self-contained dwellings. It was generally accepted that tenement buildings with self-contained units had to be built to meet quantitative demand as economically as possible.

The ambitious intentions of benevolent societies and reformers to accommodate several households in one building while still providing autonomous dwelling units produced a dilemma for landlords and speculators, who wanted to minimize maintenance costs and maximize economic yield on investments in the housing stock, yet provide a sanitary building. This dilemma prompted the regulation of the use of internal space by explicit written codes of conduct, like those still applicable today, shown in Figure 15-8. These codes were introduced by landlords and estate agents in Geneva from 1893, in Le Locle from 1932, and in

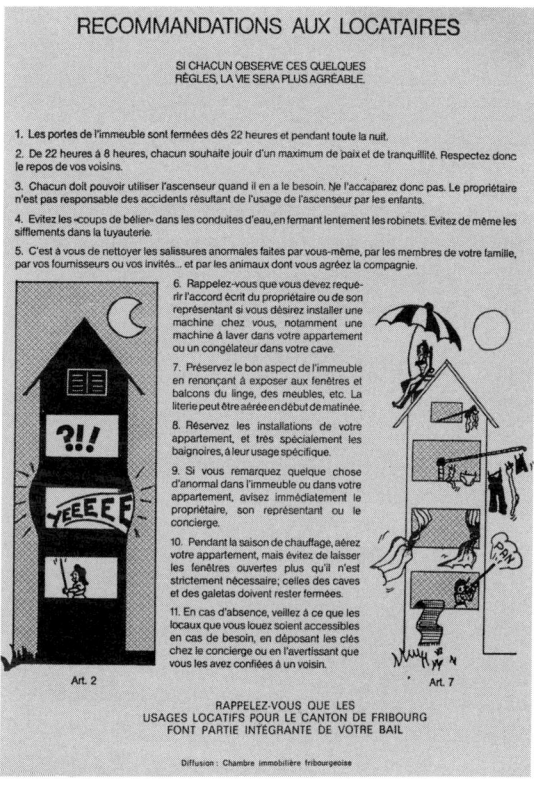

15-8
One example of tenancy agreements still enforced today with written prescriptions about the use of private and shared spaces and facilities in tenement buildings. These regulations were first introduced in Geneva in 1893 by landlords and estate agents. (courtesy of Chambre immobilière fribourgoise)

Fribourg from 1943 (Lawrence 1986). They were explicitly intended to regulate behavioral, spatial, and temporal boundaries, notably the occurrence of specific activities (especially children's play, drying clothes, and cleaning household wares) in the interior collective space. That these activities were intentionally prohibited suggests that they occurred regularly (as shown in Figure 15-9), thus contradicting the behavioral, spatial, and temporal boundaries imposed by landlords and estate agents in all types of urban rental housing.

Analysis of the tenancy agreements indicates the power and strategy of landlords and estate agents. They intended the interior collective space of rented dwelling units to be only a pedestrian passage between the inside and the outside, devoid of any other latent or manifest functions. Therefore, the daily activities of tenants had to be regulated; this was achieved by both architectural and administrative interventions, which transformed both the design and intended use of the interior collective space. It remains to explore how the residents were affected by transformations of this kind: how they valued the space and facilities provided, and how they appropriated them in relation to the explicit structures that were intentionally provided.

Deciphering the Residents' Connotation and Use of Space

The two preceding sections illustrate how the analysis of house types is a systematic way of studying the design of residential buildings by considering a range of factors implicated in their development. Now, attention will focus upon the lifestyle and values of the residents, specifically the meanings and uses attributed to particular spaces in past times. An analysis of narratives has been completed in order to decipher the activities and values of the residents during the whole period of this study.

Text analysis of autobiographies, diaries, and novels enables the design, meaning, and use of residential quarters to be examined. These sources concur that during the nineteenth century, the definition of those architectural boundaries delimiting public and private space and facilities was not explicit, because the layout and use of collective spaces and facilities in each building or court enabled the enlargement of the dwelling unit beyond the architectural, legal and symbolic borders defined by the entrance door to each flat. It has been noted that it was commonly at the border between the private and collective spaces (by the entrance door, or at the windows) that residents enacted their behavior toward kith and kin. These thresholds were appropriated with decorated wares, and collective spaces were used for diverse activities (such as household chores and children's play), as shown in Figure 15-9. Such practices tempered the stark physical boundaries of each dwelling. Spatial meaning was expressed by unwritten social rules and conventions about who could, and when one could, enter the private domain of each dwelling unit. Some codes of conduct would have been interpreted from different spatial dispositions, like the main door to each dwelling unit being left ajar (a code for access to the private domain) or the bedroom door remaining shut (a code for nonaccessibility). These rules and conventions were known to the residents. This implicit knowledge was not only an important characteristic of the domestic lifestyle and culture of the residents, but also an expression of their interpretation of the predominant urban house types.

15-9
A view of a public courtyard in the old town of Geneva around 1900, showing collective stairs and galleries providing access to tenements. Note the display of goods for sale by women. (courtesy of Centre d'iconographie genovoise)

KAF: *This shared knowledge and the spatial practices helped to create the house types. Here the types consist of characteristic architectural and spatial features* and *the pattern of uses and meanings that became associated with them.*
RL: *I agree. In principle I maintain that types are multidimensional with both tacit and manifest dimensions.*

KAF: *The spatial reorganization alone could not generate the type of use the caretakers desired. Patterns of use and meaning may be linked to spatial organization, and they can be influenced by it, but they cannot be fully determined by it.*
RL: *I agree. However there is some contemporary housing research which upholds a determinist interpretation, for example see Alice Coleman (1985),* Utopia on Trial: Visions and Reality in Planned Housing, *London: Hilary Shipman.*

TM: *My main concern is that you discuss the questions of language (and the types it establishes), conceptual structure, and meaning only in a cursory manner, if at all. The great emphasis you place on empirically observable data (in buildings, documents, and interviews) hides the basic fact that such empirical observation can only be carried out by selection from the infinite field which is observable and that this selection is based on a theoretical framework. What is the theoretical standpoint? It is implicit but not clearly set out. Meaning is often referred to in the text, but never explored. Hence "type" as a way into understanding the meaning of social relations is not used.*
RM: *In principle, the study of language (or the spatial layout of buildings) is only one way of examining how diverse groups of people endow buildings with meanings. In contrast to you, I maintain that any one-dimensional approach is incomplete. Rather, multiple sources of data should be used in an integrative way. This kind of approach can establish whether different parties (not "the social") endow buildings with divergent meanings that may be conflicting at one point in time or over a period. Moreover, any divergence between intended and actual use cannot always be interpreted from spatial layouts. Therefore, a content analysis of the rules and regulations about the intended use should be compared with records of the actual use of buildings.*

This interpretation illustrates that the meaning and use of space cannot be prescribed by deterministic associations between human activities and the spatial organization of buildings. In principle, there is no one-to-one relationship between architectural and behavioral boundaries that express explicit, material structures and implicit, cognitive structures. This is why the spatial reorganization of tenement buildings had to be supplemented by the introduction of written tenancy agreements and the surveillance of the residents by caretakers. Collectively, these components of domestic culture were intentionally used to challenge the tacit rules and conventions that were a constituent of the residents' daily life, and to impose architectural, administrative, and legal prescriptions that are still enforced today.

Implications for an Integrative Interpretation of Type

The study of urban housing presented above illustrates many of the theoretical and methodological principles presented earlier in this essay. It also shows indirectly that most contemporary debate in architectural and urban studies is too restrictive in its interpretation of type (Lawrence 1986). In contrast to these recent contributions, the study reported here confirms a number of principles presented in earlier sections of this essay.

First, principles of social classification underlie the conceptual boundaries that are used implicitly and explicitly to define and delimit categories of all kinds, including the spaces, facilities, and people accommodated in urban housing. Therefore, when researchers employ the concept of type in architectural and urban studies they need not limit their analysis a priori to sets of stylistic, functional, and morphological dimensions. Rather, they should also account for other subtle dimensions that are defined, at least partly, by the implicit cognitive structures and the explicit institutional and material structures discussed in this chapter. Hence it is necessary to apply an integrative approach, rather than a selective one, in order to identify and understand both the tacit and the manifest dimensions of type.

Second, the multidimensional nature of urban house types is contextually defined from the point of view of diverse groups of people including architects, property owners, estate agents, caretakers, and tenants. Consequently, it is instructive to examine the aesthetic and spatial dimensions used by architects – the designers' professional knowledge and shared conventions used to design and construct buildings. Then it is revealing to compare these dimensions with the economic and functional ones used by property owners, estate agents, and building caretakers who administer the built environment using explicit knowledge, rules, and conventions. Both these sets of dimensions can be compared to the conceptual, behavioral, and symbolic dimensions that form an integral part of the daily lives of the residents – their tacit knowledge and shared conventions with which they interpret and use house types. This comparative approach was applied in the study reported here because the design, meaning, and use of house types are grounded in human values and ideals, which may vary over the course of time. Consequently, the values and ideals of diverse groups of people should be considered both synchronically and diachronically. Using this approach it is also plausible to identify any conflicting activities, intentions, and values of individuals or groups involved in the construction, management, and use of specific buildings. From this perspective, there is no inherent reason to assume that implicit social knowledge is consensual and thus reflected in, or conveyed by, the architectural characteristics of urban house types.

Third, types serve a threefold capacity that can be identified in relation to urban housing *if* the layout and use of buildings are considered simultaneously in terms of both tacit and manifest structures. From this perspective type is:

(1) A conceptual template that serves as an instrument for architects, builders, and landlords to classify space, objects, and people in relation to the design, construction, and use of the built environment. Moreover, the template also serves for the transmission of professional knowledge about the characteristics of particular settings.
(2) An instrument for the explicit ordering of space, objects, people, and time by both professionals and lay people so that human activities can be located and regulated according to explicit and implicit social conventions and customs, or imposed norms and prescriptions.

The method and results of this study question recent contributions in the fields of architectural and urban studies, especially those that have sought to apply an analytical method of studying architectural and urban types solely in terms of stylistic, functional, and morphological dimensions. This kind of interpretation has a long history which stems, at least in part, from the contribution of Quatremère de Quincy (1832), who explicitly linked building morphology to intended use. During the twentieth century this kind of interpretation has been applied at a different scale in order to formulate and apply a method for the study of the interrelationships between building typology and urban morphology. Rossi (1966), for example, maintained that the concept of type can be used to bridge the gap between the scales of buildings and urban quarters. From this perspective, architectural typology was meant to be a tool for understanding the urban environment, largely in terms of formal, functional, and historical dimensions. Yet this contribution contains significant limitations, including the assertion that urban house types have not changed through the course of history since antiquity. Rossi's claim, based only on his interpretation of the formal characteristics of urban house types in a limited number of Italian cities, ignores the relevance of context. Consequently, he overlooks the pertinence of geographical location and scale, of cultural meaning, and the complexity of a temporal perspective. This limited view of type can be contrasted to the study of house types in this chapter, which shows the layers of interpretations evident when one accounts for cultural, societal, and individual human factors which are context-dependent. If one overlooks these dimensions then there is no account of the tacit and manifest rules, conventions, and meanings attributed to people, settings, objects, and events. Yet these are the essence of shared knowledge and conventions that are implicated in the roles, responsibilities, and obligations of the designers, the makers, the owners, and the users of the built environment.

Recurrent interpretations of architectural type indicate that there is no core definition of type in contemporary architecture and urban studies (cf. Collins 1965; Pevsner 1976; Rossi 1966). Type as a classificatory device, or type as an operative tool for design practice, or type as a bridge between diverse geographical scales, are the mainstreams of contemporary debate. Yet the definitions and interpretations of specific contributions within each of these sets of interpretations are rarely founded on consensus.

In general, it is noteworthy that the recurrent interpretations of architectural type mentioned above commonly consider architectural and urban design as inanimate material culture, whereas the built environment is socially constructed. Consequently, a topological analysis of one or more buildings provides a systematic yet incomplete means for interpreting the meanings and uses of architectural types. In principle, this kind of method cannot provide information of this kind, either at one point in time or over an extended period. Buildings and neighborhoods are not just created materially, because they are simultaneously ordered by behavioral, legal, and symbolic dimensions that may vary over time. Meanings do

KAF: *Whether house types, or other types, have changed over time or not depends upon which attributes of the types and what level of generality are being considered. In terms of some formal and general spatial and morphological features, one could say that a given type has not changed. Part of the value of types, as analytical and design tools, is precisely that they can be applied to different levels of generality and to different kinds of characteristics. The "house types" you have defined and studied are different types from those Rossi referred to and they serve a different purpose.*

RL: *I agree that the spatial and morphological features of house types may not change over time. But there are also use characteristics and tacit dimensions including meanings. I argue that the method I use for deciphering the multidimensional nature of house types is essentially different from the approach used by Rossi.*

not reside in material objects. Rather, all human-made objects, including buildings, are endowed with meanings by people. Meanings are construed in accordance with sets of rules and conventions that are context-dependent and may change over time. Therefore, it is essential to identify and understand them. This essay has suggested and illustrated how type can be used as an analytical tool that accounts not only for the material characteristics of buildings but also those subtle, implicit constituents that include the societal dimensions of the built environment. This integrative approach focuses on the corpus of shared knowledge and social rules and conventions that define and are mutually defined by implicit cognitive structures and explicit material and institutional structures. Hence the approach presented in this essay is not merely a different architectural or anthropological interpretation of type, but an innovative interpretation of the human milieu. After all, the built environment is not only thought and lived thought, but also *lived*.

References

Collins, Peter. 1965. *Changing Ideals in Modern Architecture 1750–1950*. London: Faber and Faber.

Durkheim, Emile and Marcel Mauss. 1903. *Primitive Classification*. Translated and edited by R. Needham. London: Cohen and West.

Habraken, John. 1985. *The Appearance of the Form*. Cambridge, Mass.: Awater Press.

Hillier, Bill and Julienne Hanson. 1984. *The Social Logic of Space*. Cambridge: Cambridge University Press.

Lawrence, Roderick. 1986. *Le Seuil franchi… logement populaire et vie quotidienne en Suisse romande 1860–1960*. Geneva: Georg Editeur.

———. 1987. *Housing, Dwellings and Homes: Design Theory, Research and Practice*. Chichester, U.K.: John Wiley & Sons.

———. 1993. Reinterpretation of cognitive, institutional and material structure in an integrative historical perspective. *The Quarterly Newsletter of the Laboratory for Comparative Human Cognition* 15 (1): 16–23.

March, Lionel and Philip Steadman. 1971. *The Geometry of Environment*. London: Royal Institute of British Architects.

Markus, Thomas. 1987. Buildings as classifying devices. *Environment and Planning B* 14 (4): 467–84.

Needham, Rodney, ed. 1973. *Right and Left: Essays in Dual Symbolic Classification*. Chicago: Chicago University Press.

Pevsner, Nicholas. 1976. *A History of Building Types*. London: Thames & Hudson.

Quatremère de Quincy, Antoine. 1832. *Dictionnaire historique d'architecture comprenant dans son plan les notions historiques, descriptives, archéalogiques, bibliographiques, théoriques, didactiques et pratiques de cet art*. Paris: Editions de Paris.

Rossi, Aldo. 1966. *The Architecture of the City*. Translated by D. Ghirardo and J. Ockman. Cambridge, Mass.: MIT Press.

Steadman, Philip. 1983. *Architectural Morphology: An Introduction to the Geometry of Building Plans*. London: Pion.

Tambiah, Stanley. 1969. Animals are good to think and good to prohibit. *Ethnology* 8 (4): 423–59.

Chapter 16

Getting to Know the Built Landscape: Typomorphology

Anne Vernez Moudon

The concept of type is in good currency in the fields of planning and design in North America: streets, buildings, open spaces, neighborhoods, etc., are commonly organized in classes.[1] Yet the theories framing the nature, purpose, and applications of type in these fields remain vague and flawed with ambiguity. The definition and use of type to characterize urban form, its buildings, and open spaces are particularly weak; most rely on functional or aesthetic criteria (Moudon 1987). In a strident critique of the use of type in North American architecture, Bandini called typological work a collection of "easily appropriated icons" – a potpourri of images of buildings randomly selected by architects who find them inspiring (Bandini 1984, 81). This apparent shallowness contrasts with the numerous and complex definitions of urban form and building type that have been debated and refined in Europe for several centuries (Goode 1992, Tice 1993). Clearly, serious gaps in interpretation have occurred as the concept is transported from one continent to the next, translated from one language and culture to others, and transformed from discipline to discipline. These gaps characterize a state of affairs that this chapter begins to unveil. The focus is on typomorphology, an area of study by European architects and geographers which now spans the past four decades.

Typomorphological studies reveal the physical and spatial structure of cities. They are typological and morphological because they describe urban form (morphology) based on detailed classifications of buildings and open spaces by type (typology). Typomorphology is the study of urban form derived from studies of typical spaces and structures.

Typomorphology is an unusual approach to urban form. First, it considers all scales of the built landscape, from the small room or garden to the large urbanized area. Second, it characterizes urban form as a dynamic and continuously changing entity immersed in a dialectic relationship with its producers and inhabitants. Hence, it stipulates that city form can only be understood as it is produced over time. Typomorphology accounts for what Italian urbanist Saverio Muratori called an "operational history of urban form," because it is a record of actions taken by planners, designers, and builders, both lay and professional, as they mold city

---

1. See for instance Downing [1850] 1969; Pevsner 1976; Myers and Baird 1978; Rowe and Koetter 1978; Groth 1981, 1988; Upton 1981; Hull 1982, 1983; Boyer 1985; and Schön 1988, to cite a few cases in a broad range of applications.

form (Muratori 1959, Muratori et al. 1963). Typomorphology offers a working definition of space and building types, and serves as a rich launching ground for studying the nature of building design, its relationship to the city, and to the society in which it takes place.

A typomorphological approach to defining type differs from other approaches in three ways. First, type in typomorphology combines the volumetric characteristics of built structures *with* their related open spaces to define a *built landscape type*.[2] This approach is in opposition to the monumental, siteless typology of Durand, for instance. The element that links built spaces to open spaces is the lot or parcel, the basic cell of the urban fabric. Second, the inclusion of land and its subdivisions as a constituent element of type makes land the link between the building scale and the city scale. Third, the built landscape type is a morphogenetic, not a morphological, unit because it is defined by time – the time of its conception, production, use, or mutation.

This chapter reviews the work of three schools of thought on typomorphology which I have identified and researched following my own work *Built for Change* (Moudon 1986).[3] Centered in Italy, in France, and in England, these three schools have generated lively debates among students of the built landscape with architects, planners, sociologists, geographers, and others participating. For the most part, these disciplines and professions in North America have ignored or misinterpreted the deliberations on typomorphology in Europe and England.

The typomorphological schools of thought make different contributions to knowledge of the built landscape. They address different disciplinary and cultural issues and use different methods of inquiry. Until recently, the schools have had little contact with each other (Choay and Merlin 1986, Whitehand and Larkham 1992). Together, however, these schools elaborate the exciting beginnings of a scholarly approach to the built landscape which complements established design research. They outline a way of learning how cities are produced and built that can support the further development of design and planning theory.

Muratori and Caniggia in Italy

In Italy, typomorphological studies began in the 1940s at the instigation of Saverio Muratori (1910–1973), an architect who was profoundly disturbed by the devastating effects of modern architecture on existing habitats and cities. Muratori and his principal follower, Gianfranco Caniggia (1933–1987), analyzed the city building process in traditional Italian towns, making this analysis the foundation for a theory of design. Their analyses rest on extensive classifications of buildings and related open spaces extending from their original state to their various mutations over time. Muratori's and Caniggia's work had a major impact on design theory and practice in Italy and, indirectly, on the use of building types in architectural design in North America.

Muratori

Saverio Muratori saw that the roots of architecture lie not in the fantastic projections of the modernists, but within the more continuous tradition of city building which prevailed from antiquity until the 1930s. Teaching at the University of Venice in the 1950s, and then at the University of Rome after 1964, Muratori made the morphological study of existing cities a first, mandatory step in his architectural design studios. As a philosopher, researcher, and practitioner, he is recognized as the early pioneer of the typomorphological trend in Italian architecture, and the spiritual father of such well-known architects as Aldo Rossi and Carlo Aymonino. Muratori's course syllabus soon became seminal for Italian architects who, to this date, see urban morphological analysis as a necessary preparatory step for design (Muratori [1959] 1985). He also published two extensive "operational histories," one of the city of Venice and the other of Rome (Muratori 1959, Muratori et al. 1963).

For Muratori, the structure of cities could only be understood historically, with building typology as the basis of urban analysis. Urban form and structure, he stipulated, are an aggregate of many ideas, choices, and actions which are mani-

---

2. I use *built landscape* as an umbrella term that includes urban form, city form, built environment, etc. Built landscape is attractive because it marries concepts of built and open spaces (which "built environment" does not), and because it connotes concrete material space (while "urban form" is more abstract). Italian and French architects often refer to "architecture" with a small "a" to depict the same phenomena.

3. This chapter is adapted from a manuscript in progress, tentatively entitled *City Building*. The research was initiated in 1987 under an Individual Fellowship from the National Endowment for the Arts (Moudon 1987).

fested in given buildings and their surrounding spaces (gardens, streets, etc.). These buildings and spaces, called *edilizia* in Italian and loosely translated as the built landscape, can be classified by *type*, which summarizes the essence of their character. These different types become a *tipologia edilizia,* or a typology of buildings and related open spaces, which defines the essence of the building fabric.

Muratori's early emphasis on the typological process as the tool to understand city building explains why, in recent years, ideas and debates about building typologies have been developed more fully in Italy than anywhere else (Gerosa 1986). Unfortunately, however, much of the interesting polemic following Muratori's legacy has been lost to non-Italian audiences. Specifically, the elaborate work of Gianfranco Caniggia, one of Muratori's early assistants and the principal heir to the Muratorian tradition, remains little known outside of Italy. And even there, it has been kept out of the limelight for reasons that will be discussed in the next section.[4]

Caniggia

Gianfranco Caniggia first published an operational history of the city of Como in 1963, *Lettura di una città: Como*, with an introduction by Muratori. The research for the book had been conducted in Muratori's Centro Studi di Storia Urbanistica (Caniggia [1963] 1984b). Caniggia subsequently carried out numerous empirical studies of cities in Italy, Sicily, North Africa, and northern Europe, often in collaboration with other planners and architects and as preambles to preservation efforts.[5] However, Caniggia's is the work of an architect, not a historian. His own publications seek not to document the historical process of a city's development, but to isolate the fundamental principles of city making (Caniggia 1984a, [1976] 1985; Caniggia and Maffei 1979). They are meant to teach these principles to guide the identification of the elements and rules that mark the genesis and then the transformation of the city fabric.

Caniggia explains the human environment as made of "built objects," all related one to the other. He identifies built objects at four different scales: the building (*edificio*), the group of buildings (*tessuto* or building fabric), the city (*città*), and the region (*territorio*).[6] Each object is described as a complex entity made of elements, structures, systems, and organisms. Thus the built environment is an organism made of components that are themselves organisms. Caniggia

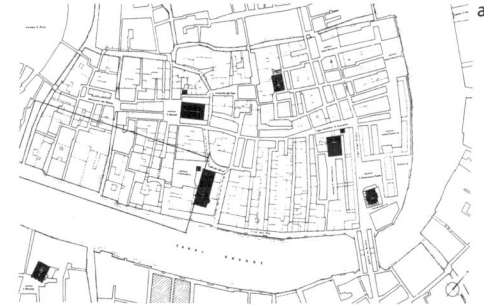

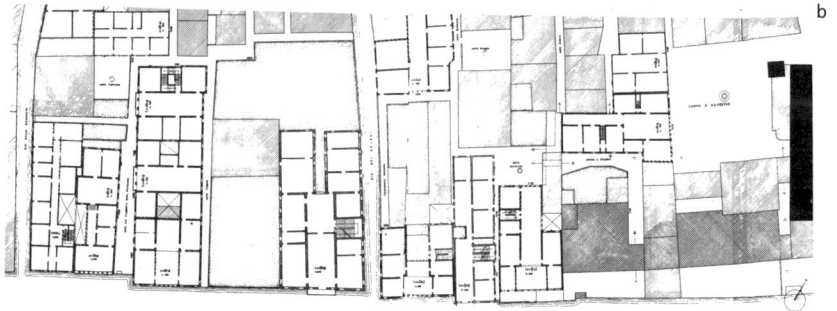

16-1
Caniggia's objects-organisms (source: M. Maretto, 1986, *La casa veneziana nella storia della città, dalle origini all'ottocento*, Marsilio Editori, pp. 82–3)
a. A partial plan of Venice shows the fabric (*tessuto*) of streets, canals, plazas, parcels, and churches.
b. An enlarged piece of the plan shows the interaction between built and open spaces. Zooming into the buildings themselves (*edificio*), one sees the organization of rooms, circulation spaces, and courtyards.

---

4. Such influential Italian historians as Leonardo Benevolo and Manfredo Tafuri only paid lip service to Muratori's work and ignored Caniggia's until after the mid-1980s (Tafuri 1989).

5. Published volumes of this work are available for the town of Venzone (Sartogo n.d.), the cities of Naples (Ciccone 1984), Florence (Maffei 1981; Malfroy and Caniggia 1986), and Venice (Maretto 1986). Caniggia was also an active practitioner; he had an office in Rome in partnership with Francesca Sartogo (Caniggia 1984c).

6. Caniggia also studied the development of pre-Etruscan settlements in various regions of Italy. His theories explaining the pattern of these settlements go beyond the concerns of this chapter, but they do establish further links between urban and regional form.

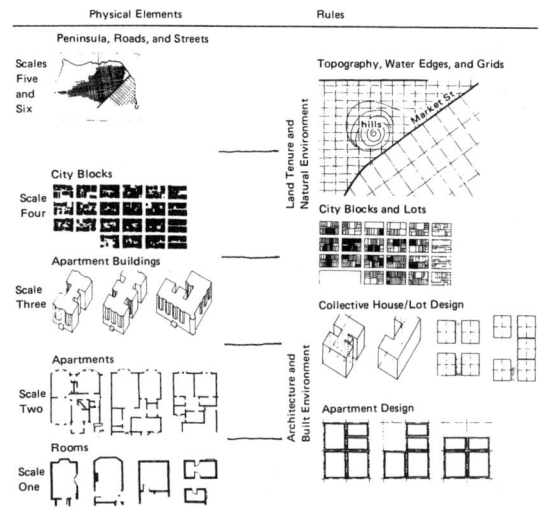

16-2
Modularity in the built landscape (source: A.V. Moudon 1986, *Built for Change: Neighborhood Architecture in San Francisco*, MIT Press, p. 124). This diagram shows how a typical turn-of-the-century apartment building in San Francisco fits into its host fabric. Reading from the bottom up: Rooms are grouped to form apartments, which are then grouped to form the apartment building; the land subdivision pattern organizes the position of buildings within the block; blocks fit into the city according to the layout of the streets; and the network of streets fits into the landscape.

stresses the modularity of the environment (how objects fit one into the other) and its scalar dimension (how objects-organisms at one scale fit into objects at other scales) as two important principles of the structure of the environment. Objects relate one to the other, and must be understood in relation to other objects at different scales. All built objects that are affected by planning and design activity must be studied from the scale of the single building to the scale of the territory within which buildings are set.

Caniggia stands out in the group of typomorphologists introduced here because he clearly states that the physical city is not an object but a process: cities are built incrementally with many small elements being juxtaposed. An understanding of the formation and transformation of cities is guided by the analysis of the mutation of the type through both time and space. For him as an architect, the analysis of urban form proceeds from the small to the large elements of the environment (Caniggia and Maffei 1979, 57–74, 122–65).

Caniggia, like Muratori, does not use the word *morphology*, because, in his theoretical construct of the human environment, urban form per se is *not* an object of study. Instead, he calls himself a "*tipologo*," because he believes that the establishment of *procedural typologies* (*tipologia processuale*) is the basis for understanding the making and hence the design of the city and its architecture. He defines *type* as the *conceptual* existence of an object in the form of the "experience of this object," apart from its physical existence or its phenomenological being ("experience" meaning cultural experience, and *not* the individual experience of an existential nature which is a more commonly used definition in Anglo-Saxon cultures).

Procedural typologies can be defined at all scales of the human environment: for buildings and their ancillary spaces (*edilizia*), the urban fabric, the city, and the territory. Caniggia focused on the scale of the *edilizia*.[7] There, a base type is identified in terms of its volumetric characteristics, its position relative to the street, and its solar orientation. The base type is then reviewed over time for possible mutations or adaptations. The type is therefore defined in formal terms, in terms of its

16-3
Caniggia's typological process (source: P. Maretto 1986, *La casa veneziana nella storia della città, dalle origini all'ottocento*, Marsilio Editori, pp. 29–30). This diagram illustrates the progressive transformation of the elementary domus and its ancillary spaces into a medieval courtyard house. Starting at top left and reading across: the basic domus type was perpendicular to the street with a side court; depending on the solar orientation of the lot, an alternative type has a front court parallel to the street; mutations through the thirteenth century include the addition of porches, the building of new stories, and the infill of side yards along the street to form L-shaped courtyards.

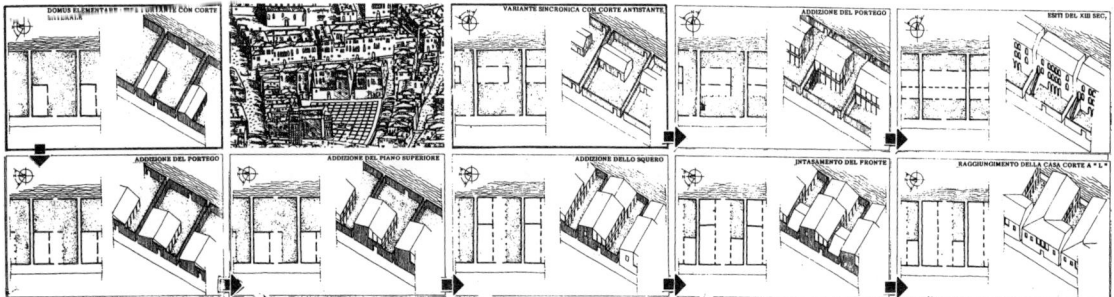

7. Caniggia's work on the types of elements that make up buildings and on the spatial organization of roads and settlements is not included in this discussion.

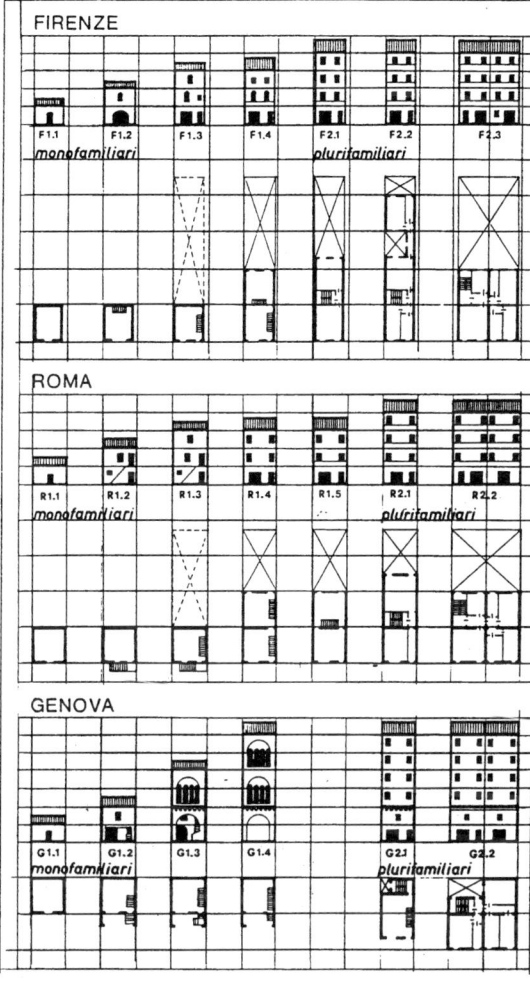

16-4 Human action and environmental reaction (source: G. Caniggia and G.L. Maffei 1979, *Composizione architettonica e tipologia edilizia, 1. Lettura dell'edilizia di base*, Marsilio Editori, p. 101). The diachronic mutation of house types in Florence, Rome, and Genoa is reconstructed in a schematic way.

8. Functionalism, the prevailing approach to architectural design in the postwar period, stipulates that architecture is best understood and practiced in a multidisciplinary context: the psychological, social, and economic components of buildings have to be considered as external forces, to be handled by the appropriate professionals.

relation to scales above and below, and in terms of its evolution over time. Most types of buildings in Italy have roots in the Etruscan or Roman cities, and their mutations are reconstructed through medieval times. Caniggia identified the elementary Roman *domus* as the base type which evolved into a courtyard house, then into a row house, and finally into a linear house.

Focusing on the processes by which cities are made, Caniggia portrays an extremely dynamic picture of the built world, whose production is the result of a dialectic, or an active relationship, between human action and "environmental reaction." According to him, this human action is directed either by a "spontaneous conscience" (*coscienza spotanea*), which is an immediate understanding of what is necessary to make a building, or by a "critical conscience" (*coscienza critica*), which is a self-conscious thought process guiding the building activity which may not refer to cultural heritage. The spontaneous conscience yields *basic structures* (read: vernacular, common houses), while the critical conscience leads to *specialized structures* (read: monuments) (Caniggia and Maffei 1979, 39–57).

Debates Surrounding the Muratorian School

The relative obscurity of the Muratorian School beyond Italian borders contrasts with the immense influence it has had on an entire generation of architects who became internationally known. It was Muratori who led Rossi, Aymonino, Scolari, Gregotti, and others to the historical city as a source of knowledge and inspiration. Muratori's condemnation of the modernist city was an early subject of research by architects Aymonino (Aymonino et al. 1966, Aymonino 1976) and Rossi (1981, [1966] 1982). They established that the modernist and the traditional city differed in at least two areas: in the ways individual buildings related to the city as a whole, and in the ways individual buildings were designed. (Interestingly, however, none of the Italian typomorphologists analyzed the modernist city systematically.)

Rossi continued Muratori's argument against buildings designed to respond directly and solely to programmatic needs, advocating instead a formal composition of space based on materials and on generic functions and related spatial needs. Rossi's principal concern was to demonstrate the power of what he called the autonomy of architecture. Elaborating on Muratori's case against functionalism,[8] he claimed that built forms are themselves embodiments of people and their societies, and therefore can be understood, and ultimately shaped, outside of the realm of the social sciences.[9]

GETTING TO KNOW THE BUILT LANDSCAPE 293

Aymonino shed light on what he termed the "reversed" relationship between building and city which modernism introduced. Explaining how the existence of the city was based on a dialectical relationship between building typology and urban morphology, he noted how the compact building types of the medieval city are the "servants" of urban form – pieces of space defining a collective fabric. As the modern city develops, however, new building types emerge that are largely independent of urban form (e.g., theaters, libraries). In the modern city, he claimed, the relationship between typology and morphology has been reversed, with building types defining individual environments that do not serve a collective urban form, such as malls and office parks (Aymonino 1976).

Aymonino's and Rossi's work clearly empathized with Muratori's and Caniggia's thinking. However, these famous students did part from their master in their interpretation of the crisis of modernism. Aymonino and his colleagues accepted the reversed relationship between building and city as part of an irreversible change in the socioeconomic forces that shaped the city. Muratori and Caniggia, on the other hand, saw it as an aberration, a temporary crisis in the way cities are produced. This difference in interpretation led to a parallel, yet irreconcilable, difference in the way urban analysis related to the development of a design theory. If, according to Aymonino and his colleagues, the relationship between building and city has been broken in the contemporary city, then the analysis of the traditional city can no longer inform the design of new buildings. But if, according to Muratori and Caniggia, the traditional relationship between building and city must be restored in the contemporary city, then the design of new buildings must rely on the analysis of the traditional city. This disagreement generated an intense debate on the nature of building typology and its value to architectural design and theory. The basic question became: Can there be and should there be any continuity between existing and new building types?

Building Typology and Design Theory

Historian Guilio Carlo Argan (1965) structured the debate by highlighting what he identified as the two "moments" in the design process: (1) the *typological moment*, when the rules of design and building used in the past (and thus yielding types which have been called *a posteriori*) are identified and understood, and (2) the *moment of invention*, when the artist answers the historical and cultural questions through a critical approach (yielding so-called *a priori* types). Muratori and Caniggia scorned a priori building types as arbitrary inventions by architects; they believed that the architect's creative work must be harnessed by common building traditions. But Aymonino, Rossi, and others thought that designers, in creating anew, were free to interpret the historical city as they wished. Justifying the architect's freedom from past conventions, Aymonino wrote:

> [U]rban analysis does not provide a structure for architectural intervention. In fact, it is wrong to assume a direct relationship of cause and effect between the two: this leads to the academic embalming of architecture, shown clearly in the projects of Muratori's and his School (Aymonino 1976, 176).[10]

In contrast, Muratori and later Caniggia defined architectural design intervention as conditioned by what they call preexisting structures. These include the existing built environment as well as the building traditions and living practices which shaped it. Caniggia specifically stated that the architect is a *technician* organizing the *human* environment *(tecnico della structurazione del spazio antropico)*. As a technician, the architect must fit his work into the growth and transformation processes that take place in any city, and witness the dialectic between buildings and their fabric. He believed that architects and planners need to overcome the crisis of modern architecture through a critical examination of the process of formation and transformation of the human environment. This critical examination cannot be based superficially on style and experience, but must rely on knowledge of the historical processes shaping urban form.

---

9. Rossi is not interested in the systematic study of the city's origins and evolution or in its operational history. Theoretical or methodological aspects of typology or morphology by and large are absent from *The Architecture of the City* (Lawrence 1985). Rossi wants to break away from the Muratorian tradition; the "master" is not mentioned in the book.

10. Argan's own position is ambiguous. He says that a building typology is not a mere classification but the definition of an aesthetic purpose. The classification of buildings has three dimensions: the shape of the building, its major building elements, and its decorative elements. He argues that in studying typology, the designer considers history as a source of information for the new project to be "naturally connected to the past." Yet in this process, the designer has freed himself from the conditioning influences of the past as a model, accepting it instead as a completed process: precedents need to be understood, not copied mindlessly (Argan 1965).

These distinct positions lead to two radically different approaches to design theory: one that rests entirely on the history of city building and its analysis, and the other that is defined solely by the architect, and which may or may not borrow from this history.

So far, in Italy and in other parts of Europe, the strict disciplinarian doctrine which Muratori and Caniggia advocated and practiced has been less popular in design circles than the liberal stand of Aymonino and his colleagues. The commercial success of the designs of Rossi and Gregotti have no doubt precipitated this trend. Today, Muratorian urban analyses are performed by designers primarily as a predesign exercise for sensing the logic and tradition of the site. But only in cases of preservation projects do urban analyses have an actual impact on the designs proposed.

Interpretation of the Italian Work in North America

The intricacies and subtleties of the Italian discourse never reached North America. Early reviews of the work sidestepped the heart of the debate. Historian Anthony Vidler and architect Rafael Moneo focused on the use of building typology in architecture.[11] They did not dwell on the relationship between building types and urban form. Nor did they discuss the tension between analysis and design and the two moments of the design process described by Argan (Vidler 1976, Moneo 1978). Vidler pointed to three stages in the definition of typology which culminated with Aldo Rossi's writings.[12] He saw Rossi's primary contribution as having designed building types that were no longer based on concepts of functional organization (which the French School calls the abstract plan types of the modernist approach), but on actual constructions found within the traditional city fabric (which the French call consecrated types).

Concentrating on the downfall of modernism and interested in the consequences of neorationalist proposals for architectural design, Vidler was particularly curious about replacing the functionally-based building types of the moderns with form-specific types of traditional buildings. Moneo was less impressed with what he called functionally indifferent building types, and complained that the Italian work emphasized the attributes of urban form and "reduced" typological studies to the field of urban analysis (Moneo 1978, 35–36). Thus by limiting their inquiries to the architectural scale, these writers missed an opportunity to introduce the breadth of typomorphological studies to the Anglo-Saxon world and to begin exploring the relationships between buildings and cities in this context.

The subsequent notoriety of Rossi's *The Architecture of the City* (published in English in 1982, 16 years after its publication in Italian, and six years after Vidler's discussion of this work) also contributed in oversimplifying the typomorphological debate. In spite of its provocative views, Rossi's book remains a personal statement about understanding the city through its architecture. *The Architecture of the City* principally influenced architects in English-speaking countries and generated only curiosity about the relationship between buildings and cities; it did not demonstrate convincingly the value of systematic urban analysis for urban design. And by the 1980s, Rossi's projects and drawings had become more prominent in architectural circles than the theoretical underpinnings first described in the book (Moudon 1987).

The plan and implementation strategy of the City of Bologna's restoration work did capture the attention of the few North American architects and planners

---

11. Although Vidler's and Moneo's writings were most influential, other writings in the architectural literature do refer to the Italian typological work. See entire issues of the *Journal of Architectural Education* in 1982 and *Casabella* in 1985; Colquhoun 1969; Ungers 1979; Anderson 1982; Castex and Panerai 1982; Porphyrios 1984; Brown 1986; and Broadbent 1990.

12. Vidler traces the first typology back to the Enlightenment, when architectural typologies exemplified by the work of Abbé Laugier classified the different elements of buildings as geometric forms related to natural elements (the column as a tree, for instance). These types were *archetypes* or ideal types to be emulated. Later on, Durand expanded the notion of type to describe special public programs, their different plan configurations and facade compositions, from which designers could choose. The second typology belonged to the modernists who advocated building types fit for mass production. Theirs were *prototypes* or first expressions of a type. A third typology identified by Vidler and Moneo (although Moneo did not use the term) was developed in the 1960s by the Tendenza, the then little-known neorationalist group championed by Aldo Rossi. The Tendenza identified building types based on urban vernacular traditions.

with community development interests (Cervellati et al. 1977, Comune di Bologna 1979). The project was the labor of Italian architects who collaborated with Caniggia and hence operated within the theoretical tenets of a typomorphological approach and beyond the particular case study. However, the impact of this work remained small, limited as it was by the perceived uniqueness of the city, and its particular social and historical heritage.

The Legacy

The most important contribution of the Muratorian School lies in its attempt to build a theory of design based on traditional processes of city building. It reads city form as a historical settlement process, a territorial conquest to control space with materials and building techniques. The research identifies basic organisms (elements and processes) that underlie the formation and transformation of the built landscape. It recognizes that sociopolitical forces shape the design and production of cities and act as a framework within which architects and planners must work. The approach is based on the notion of a dynamic relationship between human action and environmental reaction which matches in an interesting way the one used in studies of person-environment relations in English-speaking countries.

Muratori's and Caniggia's primary publications serve as textbooks for architecture students to read and analyze the city building process before they begin the design process. Caniggia's texts are synthetic and abstract, centered on the typological process as a tool to record the mutation of a base type of *edilizia*, the smallest element of the built landscape, over time. The typological process therefore becomes a link between analysis and design: as types of buildings and territories are shown to have permeated centuries of urbanization, they are proven to be generic and therefore must be continued in contemporary design.

While Muratori is increasingly recognized as the father of typomorphology, his work as well as Caniggia's remains little known outside of Italy. In Italy itself, the work has been trivialized in many ways by architects who have treated the traditional building of the city as an anachronism. A few young historians of the city are emerging, however, whose research is based on Caniggia's teachings. Gian Luigi Maffei and Paolo Maretto have published challenging histories of the building of Florence, Venice, and Genoa which add a new, scholarly dimension to Caniggia's work (Maffei 1990a, 1990b; Maretto 1986). These exemplary books illustrate the power of applying the typomorphological approach to the history of cities.

Conzen and the Urban Morphology Research Group in England

M.R.G. Conzen's work is available in English, and hence accessible to readers of this volume. However, because its significance has yet to be fully appreciated in either geographical or design and planning circles, the work needs to be an integral part of this chapter.[13] Conzen's contribution is especially important in the context of typomorphology because it excludes the prescriptive dimension of planning and design which underlies the Italian and French work. The focus is strictly on research intended to describe, analyze, and explain how urban form is made.[14] As a geographer, the freedom Conzen gained from not having to concern himself directly with the future city and its design has allowed him to concentrate fully on studying the actual city, the processes for building it, and on developing methods for analyzing it. As a result, his approach offers the most thorough, detailed, and systematic typomorphological method of the three schools.

Conzenean Philosophy and Method

M.R.G. Conzen first studied cultural geography at the Geographical Institute of the University of Berlin, where urban morphology became a subject of study in the late nineteenth century (Whitehand 1981). He later trained as a town planner in England, where he practiced as such until he accepted an academic position in geography at the University of Newcastle upon Tyne.

---

13. Fortunately, Conzenean ideas have recently been enjoying a revival in England. Yet the work remains largely unknown in France, Italy, and the United States. Geographer James Vance at the University of California, Berkeley, is one of the few proponents of Conzen's method, and the historian Spiro Kostof, on the same campus as Vance, referred to Conzen in his publications (Kostof 1991, 1992).

14. In principle, geographers are charged with studying elements of the landscape and generating knowledge that designers and planners can then use. However, this particular focus generally has been neglected by the discipline, leaving a gap that only a few social scientists and designers have been attempting to fill. Why geographers have left this gap and why designers have not moved into this field more forcefully is worth another paper. Aspects of this subject are addressed by Whitehand (1981, 1987).

16-5
Conzen's fundamental elements of the town plan (source: J.W.R. Whitehand, ed. 1981, "The Urban Landscape: Historical Development and Management, Papers by M.R.G. Conzen." In Institute of British Geographers, special publication no. 13, p. 26)

Conzen's townscape is a palimpsest of society and culture on which features of particular periods stand out while others are obliterated over time. His empirical research has focused primarily on the reading of the town plan. However, he describes his complete method as three pronged, to include the *town plan* (primarily a two-dimensional cartographic representation of a town's physical layout), the *building fabric* (made of buildings and related open spaces), and the pattern of *land and building utilization* (detailed land use) (Conzen 1968, 113–16). All three analytical components are interrelated genetically and functionally. The corresponding documents needed to explain urban form include: the town plan, the distribution plan of urban building types, and the distribution plan of urban land uses. Conzen's work itself has concentrated almost exclusively on the study of the town plan. In spite of representing a town in only two dimensions, the town plan embodies, for all intents and purposes, all the essential characteristics of urban form.

In an approach he calls *town-plan analysis*, Conzen identifies three fundamental elements of the town plan: the streets, the plots, and the buildings, which all fit one into the other as a precise puzzle. Caniggia, and later the Versailles School, also use the town plan and its elements in their research, yet Conzen's clear identification of the plan and of its basic elements as analytical tools sets an important point of departure for typomorphological analysis.

According to Conzen, the town plan is to be analyzed over time in an evolutionary fashion. The fundamental unit of analysis is the individual plot. It is the basic element of the pattern of land subdivision and acts as an organizational grid for the urban form. Conzen further introduces the concept of *compositeness* of the town plan to describe the variations in the forms, uses, and configurations found in different parts of the city. The composite town plan is made of different units called *plan units*, which are best noted in the variations typically found in street, lot, building size, and shape. Thus the different plan units are due to differences in the socioeconomic roots of the settings as well as to the different periods of building. Plan units contribute to the stratification of the townscape, *stratification* meaning literally storage into layers, the formation and deposit into strata.

The definition of the plan unit as a unique combination of types of street patterns, buildings, and lot configurations is also an important contribution. In Conzenean terms, the plan unit itself identifies a type of what Caniggia calls the urban fabric (Caniggia has not, however, spelled out clearly the characteristics of its components). Conzen and Caniggia's research thus become complementary, with Caniggia providing an approach to the definition of building types and Conzen to the types of urban fabrics.

Conzen's own studies focus primarily on medieval towns, and they reach a climax in the analysis of the town of Alnwick, Northumberland (Conzen 1960), which covers the origin of the city and its growth and transformation until the twentieth century. The study illustrates Conzen's methodological contributions. Regional soil structure, ancient road network, the old town's site, topography, and surrounding field structure all explain the town's layout. Urbs, suburbs, and original plot structure – still readily visible in today's fabric – are reconstructed as well. At the center of the analysis is the formation of the *burgage,* the basic plot of land that is narrow and deep. A detailed study of a burgage along one of Alnwick's

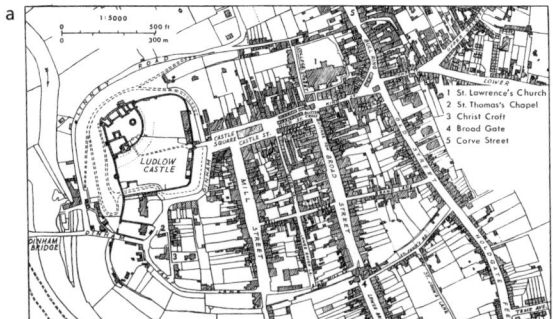

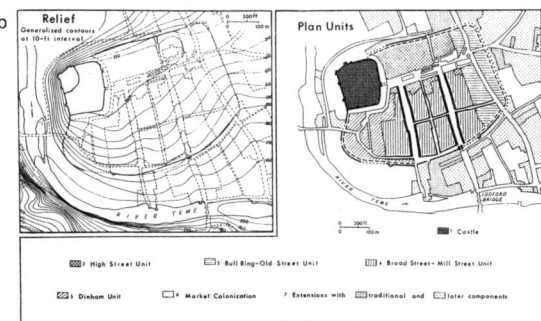

16-6
Conzen's plan units and the compositeness of the town plan (source: H.J. Dyos, ed. 1968, *The Study of Urban History*, St. Martin's Press, pp. 123, 125)
a. Ludlow town plan 1926; lays out streets, lots, and building footprints
b. Topography and plan units; demonstrates how the town plan emerged in response to topographical conditions and to the gradual accretion of seven plan units

The compact medieval towns we know today are an aggregate of areas (plan units) built over time. The case of Ludlow shows how an original castle area was consolidated into a town. Focusing on the walled core, the successive addition of plan units reads as follows: The High Street unit (unit number 2) is laid out on axis with the castle (unit number 1). The Bull Ring Old Street (unit number 3) is developed perpendicularly to the main axis, along the main access road. Units number 4 and 5, Broad Street and Dinham units, come next. While the Broad Street unit is clearly a planned addition with regular streets laid out perpendicularly to High Street, the Dinham unit fits into space left over in the walled city. It comes last because its rugged topography made building difficult and costly.

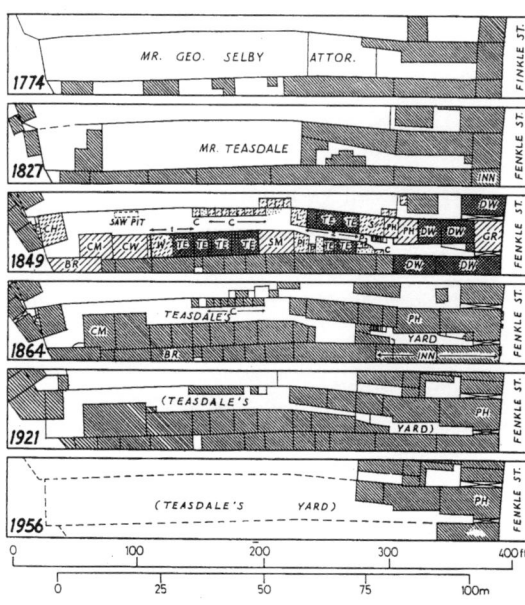

16-7
Conzen's burgage cycle: Alnwick (source: M.R.G. Conzen 1960, "Alnwick, Northumberland: A Study in Town-Plan Analysis." In Institute of British Geographers Transaction, publication No. 27, p. 68). Detail of the transformation of a burgage between 1774 and 1956 shows that it was filled in gradually with structures until 1921. Major demolition took place after that to eliminate out-of-date and hazardous structures.

streets illustrates many of the transformations that are apparent in subsequent studies of other medieval towns.

Conzen also introduces the concepts of *market colonization*, or the gradual development of the original open-air marketplace at the center of town, and *fringe belt*, a zone of atypical buildings and land uses on either side of a town's walls. These concepts encapsulate phenomena that can be found in other cities in other times. Fringe belts are common occurrences around areas of intense development such as contemporary downtowns, and market colonization is visible today in many commercial malls. These phenomena occur at the scale of the plan unit because they engender special types of urban fabrics.

The Urban Morphology Research Group

Following Conzen's research contributions, several historical geographers in the 1980s formed the Urban Morphology Research Group at the University of Birmingham. The Group's mission is to conduct research in urban morphology

16-8
Conzen's burgage cycle: Newcastle (source: J.W.R. Whitehand, ed. 1981, "The Urban Landscape: Historical Development and Management, Papers by M.R.G. Conzen." In Institute of British Geographers, special publication no. 13, p.45). The study of a group of burgages shows the cumulative effect of their transformation on the urban fabric. Although structures were not cleared in Newcastle (presumably because they were of acceptable quality), new streets were inserted into the fabric from the 1900s on to alleviate congestion.

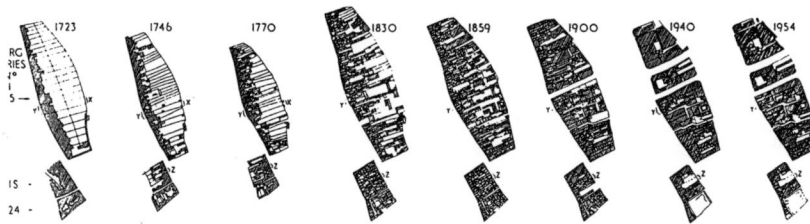

and to integrate it with more traditional concerns in the field of geography. It has also worked to facilitate access to M.R.G. Conzen's writings and graphic studies that have not been widely distributed.

Individuals in the Urban Morphology Research Group have different specialties. T.R. Slater's focus is closest to Conzen's in its emphasis on the town-plan analysis of medieval towns (Slater 1987). J.W.R. Whitehand is concerned about the effects of the building and development industries on urban form (Whitehand 1987, 1992). His prolific writings on the fringe belt and building cycle concepts rely on the identification of transformation of building types – the mutations of existing types or the emergence of completely new types.[15] He and P.J. Larkham are now turning to the study of suburban areas, thus testing Conzenean methods on more recent urban forms. P.J. Larkham has applied the method to preservation projects. He and others have assembled a glossary of terms used in Conzenean analysis which illustrate the group's commitment to morphological study (Jones and Larkham 1991).

International and Interdisciplinary Outreach

To broaden the scope of the Conzenean approach, and, in so doing, to affirm the importance of studying urban morphology, the Birmingham Group is seeking to expand the number of towns studied, to extend research to more recent cities, and to pursue cross-cultural comparisons (Whitehand 1988). This outreach program, if continued, would assemble material on the variety of extant building, space, and urban fabric types and would be the first international and longitudinal data base on the city building process. It would be rich ground for research and would further strengthen the links between morphological research and planning and conservation practices (Slater 1984).

T.R. Slater (1990) has edited a book, *The Built Form of Western Cities*, which includes analyses of industrial towns, and makes several references to research in Italy and the United States.[16] A chapter by M.P. Conzen reports on comparative studies of nineteenth-century American towns, using some of the concepts developed by his father. Discussing the nature of the morphology of these towns, M.P. Conzen reiterates the importance of the cadastre and the building fabric in understanding the town plan. He notes how little detailed empirical work has been done on town morphology in the United States: the few studies of extant building types (notable exceptions including Kniffen's work [Upton and Vlach 1986]) have generally been eclipsed by the more popular, but a-morphological work on the spatial structure of urban *land uses* (see also Conzen 1980).

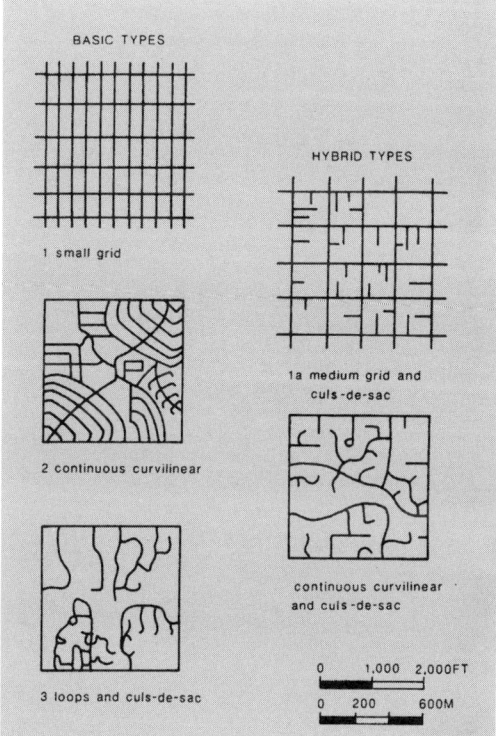

16-9
Elements of U.S. suburban residential forms: houses, lots, and streets (source: A.V. Moudon 1992b, "The Evolution of Twentieth-Century Residential Forms: An American Case Study." In *Urban Landscapes: An International Perspective*, eds. J.W.R. Whitehand and P.J. Larkham, Routledge, pp. 173–6)
These illustrations show two levels of resolution in the built landscape. The simple lines and shapes outlining houses, lots, and streets illustrate a low level of specificity in describing the types.
a. Houses and lots
b. Street pattern

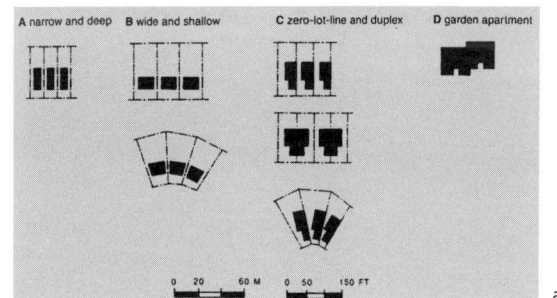

15. The connections that Whitehand establishes among traditional measures of urban development, economics, and resulting city form are important for explaining the city-building process. Certainly, the descriptive powers of morphological studies can only be complemented and reinforced by economic arguments. Whitehand's pioneering work begins the difficult task of relating real estate and community development practices to city planning and design theory.

16. In 1987 Slater also began editing a newsletter which now reaches an impressive number of individuals and groups in Ireland, Germany, Spain, Switzerland, Poland, Austria, the United States, and elsewhere.

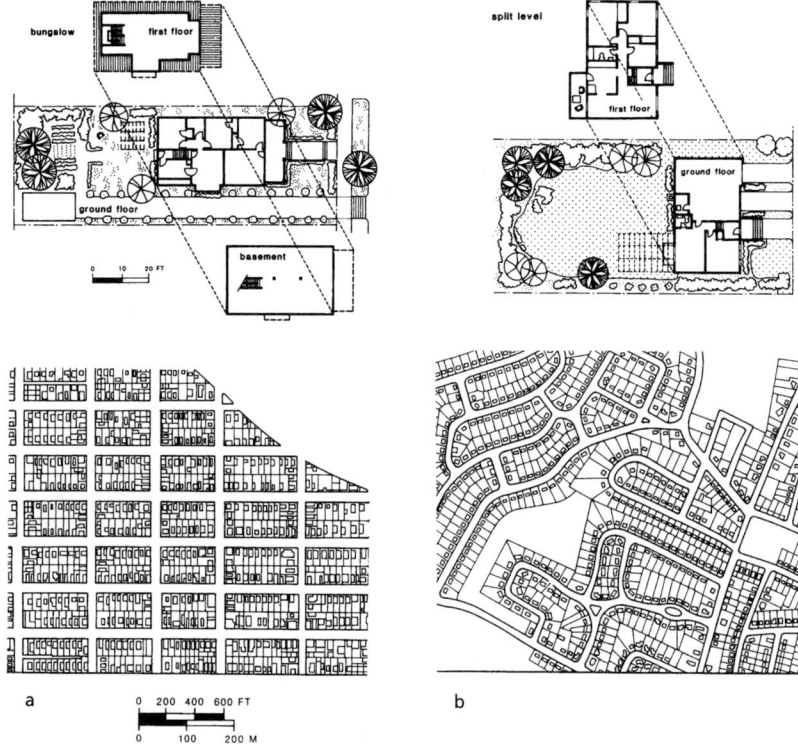

16-10
Elements of U.S. suburban residential forms: plan units (source: A.V. Moudon 1992b, "The Evolution of Twentieth-Century Residential Forms: An American Case Study." In *Urban Landscapes: An International Perspective*, eds. J.W.R. Whitehand and P.J. Larkham, Routledge, pp. 182, 185)
a. Plan unit and house plan typical of suburban residential development until the 1930s. It integrates Street Type One (small grid) and House Type A (narrow and deep) shown in Figure 16–9.
b. Plan unit and house plan typical of development between the 1930s and the 1960s. It combines Street Type Two (continuous curvilinear) and House Type B (wide and shallow). A higher level of specificity in defining types is used than in Figure 16-9: double lines describe the width of streets, and details of the material quality of buildings and related open spaces are included.

J.W.R. Whitehand and P.J. Larkham (1992) recently edited a second international volume, *Urban Landscapes: An International Perspective*. A chapter by D. Holdsworth reconstructs the development of office buildings in downtown Manhattan using computer simulation techniques. My own chapter offers a typology of U.S. suburban residential form, identifying basic house and street types as well as suburban plan units.

Finally, a doctoral thesis sponsored by the Group compares Conzen's method with the work of Caniggia at the scales of the building and the urban fabric (Kropf 1993). Beyond the obvious importance of making parts of Caniggia's contribution accessible to English-speaking readers, the thesis makes methodological headway in the definition of type. Kropf clarifies the distinction between levels of *resolution* (the different scales which are clearly recognizable in the built landscape) and levels of *specificity* (the different levels of detail at which type can be defined). For instance, elements such as streets, buildings, and open spaces are at one scale or level of resolution and plan units or urban fabrics are at another. Types of streets can be established at different levels of specificity. For instance, street width and block size may be the characteristics used to differentiate one type of street from another, or those characteristics plus the number of vehicular lanes, arborization, drainage, etc. could be used to identify the types. Kropf introduces the notion of *outline* as a tool for defining type in the built landscape. Building types are commonly identified by their graphic outline, as are most other elements such as rooms, streets, yards, lots, and so forth. Outlining appears to be a standard means of describing various types of spatial elements in the built landscape.

The Legacy

Conzen's approach has been called morphogenetic rather than morphological because it stresses not only the elemental structure of the city but its temporal dimension and its evolution. Morphogenesis and the morphogenetic approach are more accurate terms for describing the methods used than typomorphology. They are accepted in geography (Vance 1977, 1990).

Conzen's methodological contribution lies in the strength of the town-plan analysis, the definition of its elements and plan units. It confirms and clarifies the work of French and Italian typomorphologists. Their methods and findings being similar, they begin to define a systematic way to describe the built landscape. Recent efforts to expand the scope of cities studied and to spur comparative work all begin to consolidate a bona fide field of morphogenetic analysis of the built landscape which promises to provide practical applications in city planning and design. So far, however, assessments of Conzen's work by the few urban designers and planners who know it remain mixed. They lament the work's thoroughness, and question its direct usefulness to design beyond the management of the historic urban landscape (Samuels 1988, 1990; Bandini 1988, 1992).

The Birmingham Group clearly is looking for applications of the morphogenetic approach which transcend historic landscapes and address general issues of what they term "townscape management," an activity akin to, yet different from, urban planning. With its emphasis on managing the existing city according to its historic evolution, townscape management is the city planning equivalent of adaptive reuse of buildings. The Conzenean approach begins to provide an analytical basis for facilities management planning, which is itself a growing subfield of city planning.

The Versailles School in France

The Versailles School of Architecture emerged from the widespread institutional reform that took place after the students' and workers' riots in 1968.[17] The school followed the Muratorian philosophy which had preceded it, believing that modernism had created an unmendable break from the past and that the roots of architecture had to be rediscovered in past traditions. However, the French work emerged in a special intellectual climate. Whereas debates in Italy and in England involved, respectively, architects and geographers, in France, sociologists, historians, geographers, and planners all worked together with architects to achieve an improved understanding of the city. The resulting approach to typomorphology is not only oriented to issues of design and geography but also can incorporate literary and social science perspectives. In this sense, the Versailles School stands between the Italian and the British schools, and addresses issues of both design and the city-building process.

Intellectual Climate Contributing to the Formation of the School

The work of the Versailles School is part of France's long history of applying typological study to architectural design. Quartemère de Quincy, Abbé Laugier, and Durand were the first to experiment with architectural types. French hegemony in the field of urban geography and the legacy of a Lavedan and a Poëte left important marks in the design community as well.[18] The Cartesian thinking necessary for good classification still remains ingrained in the culture. But the relationship between building types and urban form was not established in France until the early 1970s.

French intellectuals of the 1960s became highly critical of the institutions and professions responsible for the reconstruction of the war-damaged country. A policy of massive housing production based on selected aspects of modern design theories devastated the French urban landscape, perhaps more so than anywhere else in Europe. Twenty years after the end of World War II, thousands of HLM (*habitations à loyer modéré*) grouped in so-called satellite towns on the periphery of cities, and of Paris in particular. Sociologist-philosopher Henri Lefebvre was strongest in condemning the focus on housing production, with all its paraphernalia of efficiency and pseudoscience, as destructive of French social practices (Lefebvre 1968, 1970).[19] Lefebvre was first to claim that appropriation, or the domination of material space including the city itself, was the ultimate goal of social life. He argued that contemporary construction and house production

---

17. After 1968, reforms changed the education of architects and urbanists, and supported the development of an infrastructure to support extensive design and historical research. The old Ecole des Beaux-Arts was replaced by some eight *unités pédagogiques* (UP), still scattered around the periphery of Paris. Each *unité* represents an autonomous school of architecture, housing not only the staff to teach studios and other architectural subjects, but person-environment studies, urban design, and urban studies. The Versailles School of Architecture is known as UP 3, or third Unité pédagogique.

18. Recently, the works of geographers Roncayolo and Rouleau have reinforced the focus on urban historical architecture (Rouleau 1983, 1985).

19. Lefebvre taught at the Institut d'urbanisme of the University of Paris, where he influenced a number of designers and planners with a kind of urban sociology that included fundamental aspects of anthropology. Another influential person at the Institut d'urbanisme is philosopher Françoise Choay, whose seminal publications have focused on the roots of urban design theory but not on the city.

methods crushed people's natural instincts for appropriation and weakened the relationship between people and their environments.[20]

Lefebvre influenced many students, particularly architects and urbanists who turned to the traditional city for theoretical inspiration. Among them were Jean Castex (an architect), Philippe Panerai (an architect-urbanist), and Jean-Charles Depaule (a sociologist) who constituted the original core of the Versailles School of Architecture.[21] Lefebvre's teachings fostered interdisciplinary work and a *rapprochement* with the social sciences, and encouraged the search for a socially responsive and responsible architecture.

Work in urban history also influenced urban morphology at the time of the 1968 reforms. Historian André Chastel and his team headed by Françoise Boudon were the first to focus on how ordinary buildings are built and rebuilt over long periods of time (Boudon et al. 1977). Subsequent research in the provinces as well as in Paris continues this tradition (see, for instance, *Typologie opérationnelle de l'habitat ancien* 1979; Fortier 1986).

LADRHAUS: A Dual Purpose

The Versailles team's work now spans two decades of uninterrupted research and includes four books, as well as studies of many cities, and critical essays on urban design and practice. The original group of researchers expanded and formed LADRHAUS (Laboratoire de recherche: Histoire architecturale et urbaine – Sociétés or Research Laboratory: Architectural and Urban History – Societies).[22] The French work is broader than the Muratorian and the Conzenean schools' in terms of both the subjects studied and the methods used. Of the four books produced by the group, one is a critical analysis of the roots and effects of the modern movement in the recent history of city building (Castex et al. 1977). This critique relies on the comparative study of carefully selected projects tracing the evolution of urban form from traditional, pre-nineteenth century street-and-block architecture to the straight, linelike architecture of the modern movement.[23] Two other books focus on individual cases studies: the City of Versailles (Castex et al. 1980) and the Bastides new towns (Divorne et al. 1985). These studies are explicit applications of typomorphological analysis. One book is a compendium of philosophical and methodological issues related to typomorphology (Panerai et al. 1980).

This published work is historical and descriptive, and thus in the same vein as Conzen's. Case studies rest on the explicit documentation of the evolution of

20. Lefebvre was also the director of the Institute of Urban Sociology, which conducted an influential study published in 1966 as *L'habitat pavillonnaire (The single-family detached dwelling)* (Raymond et al. 1979). Object of planners' and architects' derision, yet object of desire for 82 percent of French men and women at the time, the *pavillonnaire* symbolized the conflicts between people's choices and the values of professional urbanists.

21. In UP 8, founding member Henri Raymond was one of the researchers and authors of *L'habitat pavillonnaire*. Another founding member, Bernard Huet, had spent a year at the Polytechnic in Milan, and was aware of Italian work in typomorphology. He became editor of the *Architecture d'Aujourd'hui* in 1974, at which time his student, Christian Devillers, published "Residential Typology and Urban Morphology." A few years later Huet himself published a small manifesto in favor of historically grounded architecture (Huet 1978).

22. LADRHAUS keeps in close contact with groups having similar interests in Spain and Latin America. Many of the team's case projects have used environments that are familiar to the researchers: Versailles, various Parisian neighborhoods, and the Parisian fringe. Field trips with students led to special investigations, with several small projects carried out in Italy where the team also retains close intellectual ties. Over the past decade, Panerai and Depaule have been immersed in research on Cairo, Egypt, and other towns in North Africa.

23. The case studies include Haussmann's Paris, London's garden cities, Amsterdam's extensions, Ernst May's Frankfurt, and Le Corbusier's Cité Radieuse.

typical buildings and their corresponding fabrics, as well as on analyses of their social history. The work is different from Muratori's and Caniggia's who, in their more direct search for a prescriptive design theory to set future design activity in the proper direction, could forgo explicitness in their descriptive work. Hence, in comparison with the French work, the early studies of Venice, Rome, and Como read as designers' reconstitutions of the city building process. Drawings are personalized, chronologies missing, and explanatory texts remain vague in their historical reference and laced with abstract theoretical design discussions. Indeed, in most of their publications, Muratori and Caniggia used their case study research to identify the basic principles and rules which, in their minds, were most useful as natural guides for the design of the future city.[24]

The French research, however, is also motivated by the need to identify the ingredients of good city design. Like Muratori and Caniggia, Castex and Panerai teach and periodically practice architecture and urban design. Hence the research addresses issues of urban design, particularly in the face of modernity and the urban crisis. This preoccupation is apparent in the identification of *architectural models,* defined as basic concepts governing the organization of urban space, which starts in the first book, *Formes urbaines: De l'îlot à la barre (Urban Forms: From the Block to the Slab)* (Castex et al. 1977) and continues in the case studies of the Bastides and Versailles.

The dual purpose of descriptive research and identification of design models permeates all of the French work and adds complexity to the field of typomorphology. It calls for the development of an applied discipline to study the city as a physical entity – or, what is often called the city as "architecture."[25] And it demands that lessons be drawn from this discipline to serve the practice of urban design – to assess the effectiveness and the impact of different design approaches and theories on the city and urban life.

The attempt to treat typomorphology as a new and separate discipline, an eminently modern stand, contrasts with the more reflective and personal writings of Muratori's and Caniggia's. It also differs from Conzen's work; as a social scientist, he could relate directly to the existing fields of geomorphology and cultural and urban geography. The Versailles School had to justify a new discipline in the light of other, established disciplines. And it had to prove its relevance to the practice of design to satisfy the design and planning professions. So, on one hand, the book *Eléments d'analyse urbaine (Elements of Urban Analysis)* (Panerai et al. 1980) stipulates that the knowledge derived from urban analyses enhances the ability to describe and discuss the city as a sociophysical phenomenon, and thus sets the design of the city within the broad, multidisciplinary intellectual framework of the humanities and the social sciences. And on the other hand, the case study research is carefully targeted to critique design theory in the context of how cities have been built.

Outlining a Discipline for Understanding the City and its Design

The Versailles team is aware that theirs is the first attempt in France to document how "architecture" fares as a discipline in the analysis of the "urban crisis" already well documented in philosophy, sociology, psychology, and economics. Although their quest parallels Rossi's argument for the autonomy of architecture, their stand is less polemical than exploratory, relying on the close ties with Lefebvre, who early on advocated the need to know material space as well as the people inhabiting it. The multidisciplinary background of the Versailles team members allows them to recognize that the city can be read in many ways, including the architectural way, even if it has yet to gain approval as a legitimate route to understanding the city.[26] Confronting these questions, *Eléments* (Panerai et al. 1989) is the principal work that engages directly with issues of historiography as well as methods in the social sciences.

In this work, the relationship between built space and social space is described as a dialectic between urban form and social action (discussed by Caniggia as well, but in less detail). Identifying built space as conceptually separate from social space, the authors explain how physical space is assumed, invested in, qualified, named, and eventually "practiced" by people in everyday life (much like a musical instrument, it would seem). They argue that while physical space has its

---

24. The strength of recent research by Maretto and Maffei is changing the nature of Italian work in typomorphology, bringing its scholarship up to par with the Conzenean and the Versailles schools (Maffei 1990a, 1990b; Maretto 1986).

25. This generalized use of the term "architecture" is now common in many parts of Europe to describe material space. Other terms such as built environment or landscape are often avoided because they are deemed to emphasize social rather than material space or to connote a narrow focus on the aesthetics of space.

own logic and organization, which are uncovered by morphological analysis, it becomes real and takes on meaning through social action. There are also discussions of the newly identified phenomenon of the consumption of space which has inspired a number of research projects since then (Croizé, Frey, and Pinon 1991).

The study of material space, as it evolves and changes over time, introduces a social dimension to an otherwise static object. Social forces are embedded in the changes recorded in built space. For example, houses that are typical of a given period are inevitably transformed over time to respond to social change. Transformed house types in turn reflect the social forces at work. Thus the historical dimension of typomorphological studies insures the definition of a built landscape that integrates material space with the social forces that produce it.

Eléments critiques traditional macroscopic approaches in geography because they divide the city artificially into suburbs, center city, and fringes, and focus only on major, dominant land uses, disregarding the smaller scale at which the built landscape is actually produced and experienced.

An entire chapter in *Eléments* acknowledges the positive early influence of both Sitte's and Lynch's approaches. Called *picturesque analyses* (evidently because they are based on perception and firsthand experience), these approaches are thought to complement the understanding of urban form. With the exception of M.P. Conzen who, in a 1978 article, discusses the parallel existence of the objective (material) and subjective (perceived, experienced) structure of form without favoring one over the other, no other typomorphologist surveyed has discussed explicitly the possible interrelationships between these two analytical approaches.[27]

Method of Typological Analysis

In *Eléments*, the methodological components of typological analysis are framed within the historical evolution of the method and includes recent Italian work. The reader is exposed to the different ways of establishing types, whereas both Conzen and Caniggia promote only their own. A type is defined as an "abstract object built through analysis" that reproduces the properties that are deemed essential by the analyst of a family of *real* objects. Second, building classification systems can be used to two different ends: to seek *exemplary* specimens or to define *groups* or *families* of similar specimens. The identification of groups of similar specimens yields elements that are common to all (e.g., a California bungalow), while exemplars represent outstanding specimens within the groups (e.g., a house by architects Greene and Greene).

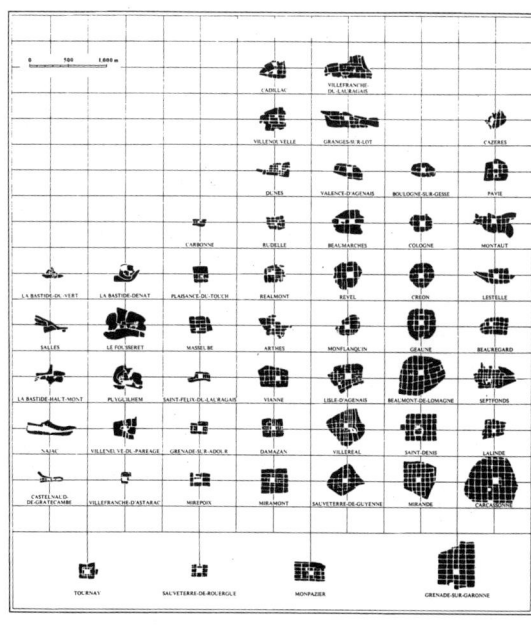

16-11
Type as group of specimens and exemplar (source: Ph. Panerai in F. Divorne, et al. 1985, *Les Bastides d'Aquitaine, du Bas-Languedoc et du Béarn, essai sur la regularité*, Editions des Archives d'Architecture Moderne, p. 41).
The Bastides are shown as families of towns with central plazas and city blocks. Four groups of plans are identified: small towns with regular or irregular blocks, and medium-size towns with blocks with or without alleys. At the same time, each plan is presented as an exemplary specimen.

26. They realize that their work will be questioned because it does not correspond to traditional disciplines and to commonly accepted categories of inquiry: "too historical for the theoretician, not mathematical enough in the methodologist's eyes, too empirical for the historian's taste ..." (Castex et al. 1977, 7). They add: "Hence the apparent ambiguous nature of our work: a morphological study, yet one based on examples that are approached historically; an architectural study, yet one carried out at the scale of the urban fabric; a spatial study, yet one based on social concerns" (Castex et al. 1977, 9).

27. Conversely, proponents of the study of urban structures *as they are perceived* usually ignore or even dismiss the utility of "objective" urban form as a mere "geometric" exercise, which gives the false impression that urban form can be discussed "objectively," that is to say in its "true" dimension (Lynch 1981; Goodey 1985; Moudon 1992a).

Completing the historical argument started by Vidler, the Versailles School notes that modern classification techniques date from the Enlightenment when the natural sciences embarked on systematic observations of the plant and animal worlds.[28] The first industrial revolution then brings the Encyclopedists and, among them, Quatremère de Quincy, who first made the important distinction between the type as a *model* to be replicated, and the type as a *rule* to be followed. The differences between a posteriori and a priori types are stressed. While early classifications of buildings and parts of buildings are descriptive, resting primarily on formal and stylistic criteria, by the end of the eighteenth century the French *polytechnicien* J.N.L. Durand proposed building typologies that are both *descriptive* of the characteristics of extant buildings and spaces and *analytical* or critical of these characteristics.[29] In what constitutes a further breakthrough, Durand's typologies become *generative*: guiding the reinterpretation of building types described and applying the concepts to other sites and contexts.[30] For the first time in history also, buildings are conceived as separate from their site and context. Durand emerges as an eminently modern thinker (a point made less clearly by Vidler in his "Third Typology" [Vidler 1977]).

The Versailles School identifies two categories of building types in use today. There are *consecrated types* of buildings that can be found repeatedly in various periods of history, such as Roman villas and cathedrals. They correspond to Vidler's first and third typologies (the archetypes and the traditional urban types). These types are a mix of basic functional programs and specific spatial configurations. And there are *typical plans*, Vidler's second typology (the prototypes). Trademarks of modernism, typical plans are standards or norms meant to guide replication, related not to tradition but to future production. Consecrated types include not only vernacular settings (called *architecture banale*), but also high-style architecture (called *architecture savante*). Consecrated types thus can be monumental, but they differ from typical plans in that they always relate to the fabric of the city. Furthermore, they are form specific and often functionally indifferent (as per Moneo 1978).[31]

As illustrated by the work of Durand, the move from consecrated types to typical plans or standards occurred gradually, over a long period of profound changes in the practice of architecture and building. It included an enlargement in typological scale which has been particularly significant since the nineteenth century, and is evident in the emergence of mass-produced terraced buildings in England and large public buildings in France following the French Revolution.

The process of defining types is addressed, albeit succinctly. It includes four steps. The first step is the choice of the scale at which the analysis will be conducted. The level likely to be the most appropriate for architectural design is the building or the parcel. Another level includes the group of buildings and related parcels, as, for instance, the city block or group of blocks (this is similar to Caniggia's *tessuto* and elaborated by Conzen's concept of *plan units*). The choice of level or scale of the typological analysis will necessarily limit the scope of the study.

A second step is the classification of building types, which involves the selection of criteria on which the typological process rests — for example, volume, function, architectural style, etc. The classification process that follows is the result of trial and error usually based on comparisons and analyses of analogues. A third step elaborates on the tools available for refining the classification process: exemplars, rules, and variations are introduced as concepts that support the analogous and comparative classification process. And a final step relates one type to the other, thus generating a *typology*.

---

28. The work of Carl von Linnee Linnaeus stands out as illustrative of this period. Applications of classification techniques in architecture are illustrated in the work of the Abbé Laugier, who did borrow from the natural sciences.

29. Durand's 1801 *Recueil et parallèle des edifices de tout genre anciens et modernes* is a catalogue of buildings that represent the "basis of architectural culture" at the time (Panerai et al. 1980, 76).

30. In Durand's second volume, *Précis des leçons d'architecture données à l'Ecole polytechnique (1802)*.

31. Saverio Muratori is noted as a pioneer in the quest to abandon typical house plans in favor of consecrated types. Further, Muratori's novel approach to typology, which anchors the common building to its site and groups parcels to define the elementary organization of the building fabric, is recognized as the first approach to establish a dialectic between building types and urban form.

A Critical History: The Other Side of Design Theory

Review of the hand-picked case studies suggests a new approach to design theory. The Italians debated the relationship between typomorphological analysis and design theory, whereas the French critique the history of design theory. Whether they followed the Muratorian tradition or not, Italian architects generally shared a dialectical view that opposed the traditional to the modern city. When they asked what the contemporary city can and should be, and what architects and urban designers should do, the answer was either continuity or discontinuity between past and present. Although sparked by the same angst that the Italians experienced about the mission and role of the architect, French researchers differ from the Italians in that they identify many different kinds of traditional cities — as for instance, the Bastides as planted towns and Versailles as a new town with both monumental and traditional characteristics. As a result, they do not consider modernism only in opposition to the traditional city. Modernism is not a temporary state of crisis, but a set of new design principles that have gradually infiltrated the city-building process over a relatively long period of time. For the Versailles School, the present is not a complete break from the past, and the past offers several different models for the future. In this sense, the French work does not associate issues of continuity or discontinuity in the built landscape with past and future. Since both states have existed in the past, both are likely to be possible in the future.

The differences between the Italian and the French contributions can now be illustrated simply by building on Argan's argument. The Italians only distinguished between a posteriori and a priori types, the former representing the traditional way of making the city and the latter being primarily the concoction of elite designers to shape the future. The French argue that there exist types which today are a posteriori but originated as a priori types. They reflect explicit, elite theories, as for instance the residential tower. These types thus represent discontinuities which occurred in the past. They must not only be included in urban analysis, but they must be evaluated for their relative effectiveness. This pluralistic view complicates the study of history: it demands that city building be studied along with the history of design theory. And it demands that the history of design theory be not only operational, as Muratori claimed, but also *critical*.

While the history of design theory is a well-developed subject in Italy, the focus on the history of urban design theory is particularly strong in France thanks to the work of Françoise Choay (1965, 1980). However, whereas Choay's interest

16-12
Critical history of city design: short-lived Versailles pavilion (source: J. Castex, et al. 1980, *Lecture d'une ville: Versailles*, Editions du Moniteur, pp. 54, 57, 62, 63). In the new suburban city a new housing type was introduced for the nobility: detached pavilions lining the main boulevards.
a. Late seventeenth-century view of the castle and pavilions lining the boulevards (Plan by Israël Sylvestre, ca. 1674)
b. The prototypical Versailles pavilion stood in a walled open space, facing the boulevard, with entry only from the boulevard. (drawing by LADRHAUS)
c. A reconstruction of several actual pavilion designs shows the inability of the type to accommodate inconspicuous service areas. Traditional housing at the time separated formal spaces (entry court, gardens, etc.) from service spaces (secluded court, gardens, stables with their own service access in the back of the parcel, etc). In the Versailles pavilion, not only was it difficult to shield these service areas from view, but service access was through the ceremonial entry. Castex et al. speculate that the conflict between formal and service spaces led to the abandonment and eventual demise of the type. (drawing by LADRHAUS)

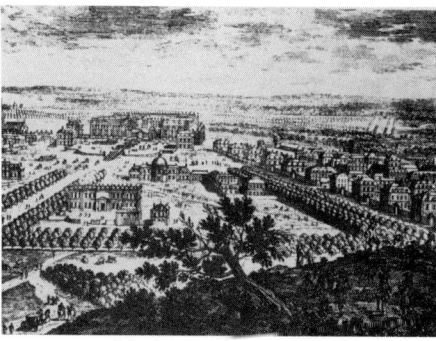

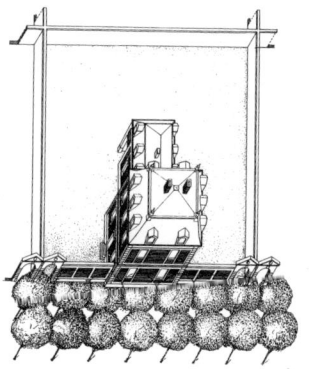

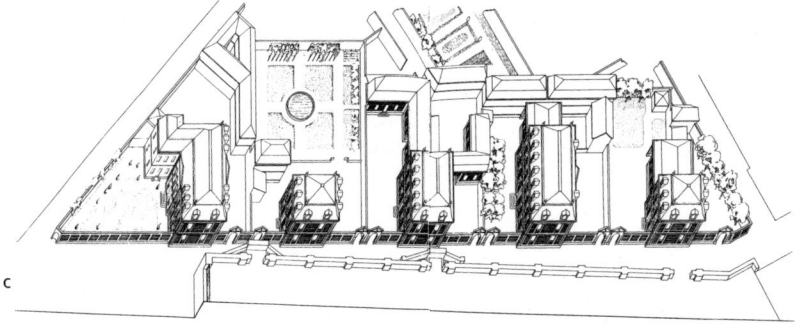

lies in the history of consciously articulated ideas and concepts about the city, the Versailles School focuses on the history of applications of design theory. Thus the critical history of design theory has itself two dimensions: the history of *design theory as ideas* (e.g., one can refer here to the Athens Chartes or to the Cité Radieuse as the ideals and principles of modernist design) and the history of *design theory as practiced* (e.g., the case of the Unité d'habitation, or any of the new towns built according to the modernist principles).[32]

The Versailles School studies theories that are culturally defined and theories that are elite driven (for instance, the theories behind the design of the Bastides and the popular neighborhoods of Versailles, versus those used in the monumental Versailles of the king and his court). These two different origins of theories generate different architectures. One is ordinary, the aforementioned *architecture banale* or the architecture of everyday life, and the other is scholarly, *architecture savante*, or high-style architecture. They deplore the fact that elite architectures all tend to sever their relationship to the city and to become monumental, a phenomenon that they recognize in the study of the City of Versailles as well as in the study of the emergence of the modern movement (Castex et al. 1977).

32. Historian Corboz's terminology helps explain further the scope of the Versailles School (Corboz 1992). He differentiates between the *city of the geographer* (the Conzenean and the Versailles School's interest) and the *city of ideas* (Choay's primary interest). The city of the geographer is both built and used; its design is often governed by two, sometimes conflicting, processes. One is a set of culturally-bound traditions and the second is theories consciously elaborated by one of several elites (architects, bankers, etc.). The Versailles School studies both types of design processes and considers them both part of the history of design theory.

33. This concurs with Rossi, who denies the value of urban design in the term's narrow sense of designing the city because the city should evolve, rather than be designed (Rossi 1982, 116).

The particular cases studied show that good models used to design the city oscillate back and forth between the need to control and provide order in city design and the need to create environments that respond to the needs and actions of their immediate inhabitants. This puts in question the value of a global composition of the city (an underlying concern and general direction in the evolution of urban design theory), proposing instead an emerging definition of city form through the incremental acts of many people.[33] The search for formal models which allow this incremental, participatory process of designing the city points to simple urban blocks subdivided into several parcels. Street hierarchies work well as long as the superblocks created are further subdivided into autonomous blocks with clear, legible public access and their own sets of independent parcels.

The Legacy

The Versailles School favors a separate discipline for studying the built landscape that serves to evaluate design theory. The novel aspect of this stand forces the School to discuss methods and philosophy in a multidisciplinary context, which neither the Conzenean nor the Muratorian schools had to do. The development of an applied discipline paves the way for a systematic approach to design evaluation. Also, the simultaneous investigation of traditional and elite city-building processes invites a critical review of design theory in light of its actual achievements. The work recognizes the need for mixing tradition and innovation in the way cities are designed, and for keeping monumentality under control.

The Versailles work has taken solid roots in both design practice and research in francophone countries. Typological and morphological investigations are fully integrated into the growing discourse on the built landscape and its design. However, for all its outreach into the disciplines involved in the urban crisis, and in spite of its multidisciplinary origins, the Versailles work has made slow progress in the field of urban planning – a field that is separate from architecture in post-World War II France. When the Institut d'urbanisme of the University of Paris undertook a major research project on urban morphology and its applications to planning in 1985, it did not include any of the Versailles faculty, even though architects from other countries were invited to contribute to the project (Choay and Merlin 1986). Since then, however, both Panerai and Castex have been teaching urban history and morphology at the Institut, and the final edition of the Institut's research on morphology contains further references to the Conzenean School (Merlin et al. 1988).

Conclusion

The three schools of typomorphology offer an intellectually challenging framework for thinking about the built landscape within the historical context of the city. Italy's provides a theoretical foundation for planning and design within age-old traditions of city building. England's offers a scholarly approach to researching how the built landscape is produced. And France's outlines a new discipline that combines the study of the built landscape with a critical assessment of design theory. Together these schools suggest an order for a formidable agenda of research, planning, and design that takes into account the relationships between space, time, habitat, and culture. In this order, type provides the essential conceptual framework for understanding the built landscape and intervening in it.

All three schools claim that the built landscape must be understood in three fundamental dimensions: time, form, and scale. The built landscape is in a constant state of evolution and change, subject to sociocultural forces constructing, using, and transforming space. So all typological work must be linked to a measure of time. Built and open spaces together constitute form. They are persistent; they dominate the definition of the built landscape as use and function come and go according to changing social practices and related needs. Since elements of form are highly sensitive to sociocultural forces operating over time, they are morphogenetic rather morphological. And several scales permeate the structure of the built landscape from the inhabited room to the city as a whole, and the block and district in between.

Together these three dimensions of time, form, and scale weave an intricate web of relationships between fields and disciplines which all too often remain separate. A focus on the formal dimension of the built landscape facilitates linkages between analysis and design, linkages that are tenuous when urban analyses address primarily economic or social dimensions. Yet, by the same token, the time dimension insures that form remains linked to sociocultural and historical forces. The marriage of space and time is the marriage of architecture and history, and architecture and the social sciences as advocated by Porter and Tigerman (1992). And the scalar dimension of the built landscape demands the integration of architectural and city planning approaches (Goode 1992).

Debates about typomorphology in the three schools illuminate the use of type in design theory. The schools differentiate between descriptive, analytical, explicative critical, and generative types. They are therefore able to separate conceptually the description, analysis, and critique of the historical and the existing city from the projection of the future city. They can learn to know the built landscape, to explain it, and to theorize about its production without worrying about its future design. The three schools provide the tools to monitor the emergence of new types and to relate them to theory, whether it is tradition-bound and cuturally defined or consciously articulated. And they can evaluate the actual effects of past design theories on the existing built landscape.

The intellectual framework sketched out by the three schools is propitious for research and teaching about the built landscape (Moudon forthcoming). Further, this material offers a basis for what the Birmingham Group defines as townscape management. Managing the built landscape is an ongoing process that includes planning, designing, and construction as continuous tasks performed by many different actors. A typomorphological approach yields a data base on the built landscape that can be used by various public entities charged with maintaining, upgrading, and modifying it. Public regulatory and capital improvement agencies responsible for urban planning and design, public works, transportation, parks and open space, housing, and community development need to work together to build on the wealth in urban infrastructure and amenities already in place. A shared data base can inform and guide future intervention.

This intellectual framework should also prove useful to such practitioners as Daniel Solomon (1992), Andres Duany and Elizabeth Plater-Zyberk, Peter Calthorpe (Katz 1994), Stanford Eckstut, John Kriken, and others who, in an intuitive way, have come to believe that solutions to good community design lie within the broad context of making the city. Their town plans, street and land subdivision layouts, and building codes as architectural strategies to balance community and individual needs belong together under the theoretical umbrella of typomorphology. The three schools of typomorphology offer such practitioners a rich data base on forms and form making processes. And more importantly, morphogenetic research grounds this design work in the history of city building. Types no longer need to be arbitrarily borrowed icons. They are structuring concepts which have been tested in the reality of city building. They are place-bound and time-bound, responding and adapting to new social, economic, and technological circumstances.

References

Anderson, Stanford. 1982. Types and conventions in time: toward a history for the duration and change of artifacts. *Perspecta* 18: 109–18.

Argan, G.C. 1965. Sul concetto di tipologia architettonica. *Progetto e Destino*: 75–81.

Aymonino, C., M. Brusatin, G. Fabbri, M. Lena, P. Loverro, S. Lucianetti, and A. Rossi. 1966. *La Città di Padova, saggio di analisi urbana*. Rome: Officina edizoni.

Aymonino, Carlo. 1976. *Il significato della città*. Bari: Laterza.

Bandini, Micha. 1984. Typology as a form of convention. *AA Files* 6 (May): 73–82.

———. 1988. La contribution britannique à la morphologie urbaine. In *Morphologie urbaine et parcellaire*, eds. P. Merlin, E. d'Alfonso, and F. Choay, 81–86. Paris: Presses universitaires de Vincennes.

———. 1992. Some architectural approaches to urban form. In *Urban Landscapes: An International Perspective*, eds. J.W.R. Whitehand and P.J. Larkham, 133–69. London: Routledge.

Boudon, Françoise, André Chastel, Hélène Couzy, and Françoise Hamon. 1977. *Système de l'architecture urbaine: le quartier des Halles à Paris*. Paris: Editions du Centre National de la Recherche Scientifique.

Boyer, Christine C. 1985. *Manhattan Manners: Architecture and Style 1850–1900*. New York: Rizzoli.

Broadbent, Geoffrey. 1990. *Emerging Concepts in Urban Space Design*. New York: Van Nostrand Reinhold.

Brown, Denise Scott. 1986. Invention and tradition in the making of American place. *The Harvard Architecture Review*: 162–71.

Caniggia, Gianfranco. 1984a. *Composizione architettonica e tipologia edilizia, 2. Il projetto nell'edilizia di base*. Venice: Marsilio Editori.

———. [1963] 1984b. *Lettura di una città: Como*. Como: Edizione New Press.

———. 1984c. *Moderno con moderno*. Venice: Marsilio Editori.

———. [1976] 1985. *Strutture dello spazio antropico*. Florence: Ed. Alinea.

Caniggia, Gianfranco and Gian Luigi Maffei. 1979. *Composizione architettonica e tipologia edilizia, 1. Lettura dell'edilizia di base*. Venice: Marsilio Editori.

Casabella. 1985. Issue on typology. 49 (January/February).

Castex, Jean, Jean-Charles Depaule, and Philippe Panerai. 1977. *Formes urbaines: de l'îlot à la barre*. Paris: Dunod.

Castex, Jean, Patrick Céleste, and Philippe Panerai. 1980. *Lecture d'une ville: Versailles*. Paris: Editions du Moniteur.

Castex, Jean and Philippe Panerai. 1982. Prospects for typomorphology. *Lotus International* 36: 94–99.

Cervellati, Pier Luigi, Roberto Scannavini, and Carlo de Angelis. 1977. *La nuova cultura della città. La salvaguardia dei centri storici, la riappropriazione sociale degli organismi urbani e l'analisi dello sviluppo territoriale nell' esperienza di Bologna*. Milan: Mondadori.

Choay, Françoise, ed. 1965. *L'urbanisme: utopie et réalités, une anthologie*. Paris: Editions de Seuil.

———. 1980. *La règle et le modèle, Sur la théorie de l'architecture et de l'urbanisme*. Paris: Editions du Seuil.

Choay, Françoise and Pierre Merlin. 1986. *A propos de la morphologie urbaine*. Tome 1, rapport de synthèse. Laboratoire "Théorie des mutations urbaines en pays développés," Université de Paris VIII, Institut d'urbanisme de l'Académie de Paris, E.N.P.C, mars.

Ciccone, F. ed. 1984. *Recupero e riqualificazione urbana nel programma staordinario per Napoli*. Milano: Dott. Antonino Giuffrè Editore, August.

Colquhoun, Alan. 1969. Typology and design method. In *Meaning in Architecture*, eds. C. Jencks and G. Baird. New York: George Braziller.

Comune di Bologna. 1979. *Risanamento Conservativo del centro storico di Bologna*. Bologna: Graficoop.

Conzen, M.P. 1978. Analytical approaches to the urban landscape. In *Dimensions of Human Geography*, ed. K. W. Butzer, 128–65. Chicago, Ill.: University of Chicago Department of Geography, Research Paper 186.

———. 1980. The morphology of nineteenth-century cities in the United States. In *Urbanization in the Americas: The Background in Comparative Perspective*, eds. W. Borah, J. Hardoy, and G. Stelter, 119–41. Ottawa: National Museum of Man.

———. 1990. Town-plan analysis in an American setting: cadastral processes in Boston and Omaha, 1630–1930. In *The Built Form of Western Cities*, ed. T.R. Slater, 142–70. Leicester, U.K.: Leicester University Press.

Conzen, M.R.G. 1960. Alnwick, Northumberland: a study in town-plan analysis. Publication No. 27. London: Institute of British Geographers.

———. 1968. The use of town-plans in the study of history. In *The Study of Urban History*, ed. H.J. Dyos, 114–30. New York: St. Martin's Press.

Corboz, André. 1992. *L'urbanisme du XXe siècle, esquisse d'un profil*. Genève: Fédération des Architectes Suisses.

Croizé Jean-Claude, Jean-Pierre Frey, and Pierre Pinon, eds. 1991. *Recherche sur la typologie et les types architecturaux*. Paris: L'Harmattan.

Devillers, Christian. 1974. Typologie de l'habitat et morphologie urbaine. *Architecture d'Aujourd'hui* 174 (July).

Divorne, Françoise, Bernard Gendre, Bruno Lavergne, and Philippe Panerai. 1985. *Les Bastides d'Aquitaine, du Bas-Languedoc et du Béarn, essai sur la régularité*. Brussels: Editions des Archives d'Architecture Moderne.

Downing, Andrew Jackson [1850] 1969. *The Architecture of Country Houses*. New York: Dover Publications.

Durand, J.N.L. 1801. *Recueil et parralèle des edifices de tout genre anciens et modernes, remarquables par leur beauté, par leur grandeur ou par leur singularité, et dessinés sur une même échelle*. Paris: An IX.

———. 1802. *Précis des leçons d'architecture données à l'Ecole polytechnique*. Paris: An X.

Dyos, H.J., ed. 1968. *The Study of Urban History*. New York: St. Martin's Press.

Fortier, Bruno. 1986. La rue Réaumur. *Les annales de la recherche urbaine* 32: 23–28.

Gerosa, Pier Giorgio. 1986. Sur quelques aspects novateurs dans la théorie urbaine de Saverio Muratori. *Collection: Urbanisme et Sciences Sociales* 6. Strasbourg, France: Université des sciences humaines, Ecole d'architecture de Strasbourg.

Goode, Terence. 1992. Typological theory in the U.S.: the consumption of architectural autheticity. *Journal of Architectural Education* 46 (1): 2–13.

Goodey, Brian. 1985. The current condition of urban design: the significance of Lynch's final question: "How to make public the analysis of local place quality?" Unpublished paper based on a presentation to the seminar *L'analisi de 'luogo'*, 23 March Istituto di Architettura e Urbanistica, Università degli Studi di Napoli, Italy.

Groth, Paul. 1981. Streetgrids as frameworks for urban variety. *The Harvard Architectural Review* 2 (Spring): 68–75.

———. 1988. Generic building and cultural landscapes as sources of urban history. *Journal of Architectural Education* 41 (3): 41–44.

Holdsworth, Deryck W. 1992. Morphological change in Lower Manhattan, New York, 1893–1920. In *Urban Landscapes: An International Perspective*, eds. J.W.R. Whitehand and P.J. Larkham, 114–32. London: Routledge.

Huet, Bernard. 1978. Small manifesto. *Rational Architecture Rationelle*. Brussels: Archives de l'Architecture Moderne 54.

Hull, Steven. 1982. *Alphabet City*. New York: Pamphlet Architecture.

———. 1983. *Rural & Urban Houses in North America*. New York: Pamphlet Architecture.

Jones, A.N. and P.J. Larkham. 1991. Glossary of urban form. Historical Geography Monograph No. 26. London: Institute of British Geographers.

Journal of Architectural Education. 1982. Issue on typology in design education. 35 (2).

Katz, Peter, ed. 1994. *A New Urbanism*. New York: McGraw-Hill.

Kostof, Spiro. 1991. *The City Shaped: Urban Patterns and Meanings Through History*. Boston: Little, Brown.

———. 1992. *The City Assembled: The Elements of Urban Form Through History*. Boston: Little, Brown.

Kropf, Karl S. 1993. *The Definition of Built Form in Urban Morphology*. Ph.D. dissertation, vols. 1, 2. Department of Geography, University of Birmingham, England.

Laugier, P. 1754. *Essai sur l'architecture*. Paris: Duchesne.

Lavedan, Henri. 1926. *Qu'est-ce que l'urbanisme?* Paris: Que sais-je.

Lawrence, Roderick J. 1985. Architecture of the city reinterpreted: a critical review. *Design Studies* 6 (3): 141–49.

Lefebvre, Henri. 1968. *Droit à la ville*. Paris: Editions Anthropos.

———. 1970. *Du rural à l'urbain*. Paris: Editions Anthropos.

Lynch, Kevin. 1981. *Theory of Good City Form*. Cambridge, Mass.: MIT Press.

Maffei, Gian Luigi. 1981. *La Progettazione edilizia a Firenze 1910–1930*. Venice: Marsilio Editori.

———. 1990a. *La casa fiorentina nella storia della città*. Venice: Marsolio Editori.

———, ed. 1990b. *La casa rurale in Lunigiana*. Venice: Marsolio Editori.

Malfroy, Sylvain and Gianfranco Caniggia. 1986. *L'approche morphologique de la ville et du territoire*. Zurich: Eidgenössische Technische Hochschule, Lehrstuhl für Städtebaugeschichte, October.

Maretto, Paolo. 1986. *La casa veneziana nella storia della città, dalle origini all'ottocento*. Venice: Marsilio Editori.

Merlin, Pierre, E. d'Alfonso and F. Choay, eds. 1988. *Morphologie urbaine et parcellaire*. Paris: Presses universitaires de Vincennes.

Moneo, Raphael. 1978. On typology. *Oppositions* 13 (Summer): 23–45.

Moudon, Anne Vernez. 1986. *Built for Change: Neighborhood Architecture in San Francisco*. Cambridge, Mass.: MIT Press.

———. 1987. The research component of typomorphological studies. AIA/ACSA Research Conference, Boston, November.

———. 1992a. A catholic approach to organizing what urban designers should know. *Journal of Planning Literature* 6 (May): 332–49.

———. 1992b. The evolution of twentieth-century residential forms: an American case study. In *Urban Landscapes: An International Perspective*, eds. J.W.R. Whitehand and P.J. Larkham, 170–206. London: Routledge.

———. forthcoming. Teaching urban form. *Journal of Planning Education and Research*.

———. Manuscript in progress. *City Building*.

Muratori, Saverio. 1959. *Studi per una operante storia urbana di Venezia*. Rome: Instituto Poligraphico dello Stato.

———. [1959] 1985. *Una lezione di seminario per la preparazione alla missione di architetti e per la formazione di docenti in una scuola di architettura*. Transcribed by Guido Marinucci. Edizione dei Corsi di Composizione Architettonica di R. e S. Bollati, Facoltà di Architettura di Reggio Calabria.

Muratori, Saverio, Renato Bollati, Sergio Bollati, and Guido Marinucci. 1963. *Studi per una operante storia urbana di Roma*. Rome: Consiglio nazionale delle ricerche.

Myers, Barton and George Baird. 1978. Vacant lottery. *Design Quarterly* 108.

Panerai, Philippe, Jean-Charles Depaule, Marcelle Demorgon, and Michel Veyrenche. 1980. *Eléments d'analyse urbaine*. Brussels: Editions Archives d'Architecture Moderne.

Pevsner, Nikolaus, Sir. 1976. *A History of Building Types*. London: Thames and Hudson.

Poëte, Marcel. [1929] 1967. *Introduction à l'urbanisme*. Paris: Editions Anthropos.

Porphyrios, Demetri, ed. 1984. Leon Krier – houses, palaces, cities. *Architectural Design* 54 (7/8).

Porter, William L. and Stanley Tigerman. 1992. Administrators' essays on architectural history. *Journal of Architectural Education* 46 (1): 46–50.

Quatremère de Quincy, A.C. 1977. Type. With an introduction by Anthony Vidler. *Oppositions* 8 (Spring): 147-150.

Raymond H., N. Haumont, M.G. Raymond, and A. Haumont. 1979. *L'habitat pavillonaire*. 3d ed. Paris: Centre de Recherche d'Urbanisme.

Rossi, Aldo. 1964. Aspetti della tipologia residenziale a Berlino. *Casabella-continuità* 288 (June): 10–20.

———. 1981. *A Scientific Autobiography*. Cambridge, Mass.: MIT Press.

———. [1966] 1982. *The Architecture of the City*. Cambridge, Mass.: MIT Press.

Rouleau, Bernard. 1983. *Le tracé des rues de Paris, formation, typologie, fonctions*. Paris: Editions du Centre Nationale de la Recherche Scientifique.

———. 1985. *Villages et faubourgs de l'ancien Paris, Histoire d'un espace urbain*. Paris: Editions du Seuil.

Rowe, Collin, and Fred Koetter. 1978. *Collage City*. Cambridge, Mass.: MIT Press.

Samuels, Ivor. 1988. La morphologie urbaine: de la recherche à la profession. In *Morphologie urbaine et parcellaire*, eds. P. Merlin, E. d'Alfonso, and F. Choay, 87–93. Paris: Presses universitaires de Vincennes.

———. 1990. Architectural practice and urban morphology. In *The Built Form of Western Cities*, ed. T.R. Slater, 415–35. Leicester, U.K.: Leicester University Press.

Sartogo, Francesca. n.d. *Venzone come e perché*. Roma: Alba Centro Stampa.

Schön, Donald A. 1988. Toward a marriage of artistry and applied science in the architectural design studio. *Journal of Architectural Education* 41 (4): 4–10.

Slater, T.R. 1984. Preservation, conservation and planning in historic towns. *The Geographical Journal* 150 (3): 322–34.

———. 1987. Ideal and reality in English Episcopal medieval town planning. *Transactions of Institute of British Geographers* 2: 191–203.

———. ed. 1990. *The Built Form of Western Cities*. Leicester University Press.

Solomon, Daniel. 1992. *ReBuilding*. New York: Rizzoli.

Tafuri, Manfredo. 1989. *History of Italian Architecture 1944–1985*. Cambridge, Mass.: MIT Press.

Tice, James. 1993. Themes and variations: a typological approach to housing design, teaching, and research. *Journal of Architectural Education* 46 (3): 162–75.

Typologie opérationnelle de l'habitat ancien (1850–1948). 1979. Collection Actes des Colloques. Paris: Plan Construction.

Ungers, Oswald Mathias. 1979. Architecture of the collective memory: the infinite catalogue of urban forms. *Lotus International* 24: 5–11.

Upton, Dell. 1981. Ordinary buildings: a bibliographical essay on American vernacular architecture. *American Studies International* 14 (2): 57–73.

Upton, Dell and John Michael Vlach, eds. 1986. *Common Places: Readings in American Vernacular Architecture*. Athens, Ga.: University of Georgia Press.

Urban Morphology Research Group. 1987 to present. *Urban Morphology Newsletter*. Birmingham: University of Birmingham, Department of Geography.

Vance, James E. 1977. *This Scene of Man: The Role and Structure of the City in the Geography of Western Civilization*. New York: Harper's College Press.

———. 1990. *The Continuing City*. Baltimore, Md.: Johns Hopkins University Press.

Vidler, Anthony. 1976. The third typology. *Oppositions* 7.

———. 1977. The idea of type: the transformation of the academic ideal, 1750–1830. *Oppositions* 8 (Spring): 93–113.

Whitehand, J.W.R., ed. 1981. The urban landscape: historical development and management, papers by M.R.G. Conzen. Special Publication No 13. Institute of British Geographers. New York: Academic Press.

———. 1987. The changing face of cities: a study of development cycles and urban form. Special Publication No. 21. Institute of British Geographers. Oxford: Blackwell.

———. 1988. Recent developments in urban morphology. In *Urban Historical Geography, Recent Progress in Britain and Germany*, eds. D. Denecke and G. Shaw, 285–96. Cambridge: Cambridge University Press.

———. 1992. The making of the urban landscape. Special Publication No. 26. Institute of British Geographers. Oxford: Blackwell.

Whitehand, J.W.R. and P.J. Larkham, eds. 1992. *Urban Landscapes: An International Perspective*. London: Routledge.

Part VI

TYPE AND SOCIAL PRACTICE

Chapter 17

Typification and the Building of Society: "The Absent Patron"

David Vanderburgh

Now buildings become shells occasionally used by people who want to be restored to health, to bathe, learn, read, or buy. These buildings cannot be identified with one personality; they belong to everyone and therefore to no one. The absent patron is not replaced by the poetry in a theater, the science in a school, the hygiene in a public bath…

  Paul Frankl, *Principles of Architectural History*

Like a Second Empire salon, the western nineteenth century was stuffed with a seeming overabundance of ideas, inventions, and artifacts. Among the objects that strained its seams were its new building types, "buildings for every conceivable purpose, most of them adapted to requirements which have never before arisen in history…" (Henry van Brunt in Pevsner 1976, 9). The new buildings themselves, in images and descriptions of the time, seemed to swell and bustle with activity: visitors thronged the glass-skinned halls of international exhibitions, merchandise weighed down the display shelves of arcades and department stores. It is strange, then, that Paul Frankl's assessment should so insist on images of emptiness, speaking of "shells occasionally used," belonging to "no one" in the void left by the "absent patron." Were the century's new building types empty or full, and of what?

17-1
The Crystal Palace, London: Is the building empty, as it appears in this rendering, or full, as its "contents" would imply? (Sir Joseph Paxton, 1850–1851. Courtesy of Bibliothèque Royale, Brussels)

The Age of the Many

France provides intriguing figures for these abundances and absences. The Revolution of 1789, whatever its other effects, introduced the age of the Many: the bourgeoisie became more numerous and more vocal; government became a function of list making, cataloging, and monitoring, giving shape and number to *le peuple* through the work of a shapeless and numberless bureaucracy. Production gradually left the artisan's shop for the factory, providing props by the thousands for the spectacle of mass consumption. Migrant hordes invaded the cities, traveling farther and faster and more frequently than ever before. Yet the advent of the Many displaced the One, whether temporal or spiritual: absolutism was decapitated along with Louis XVI. Revolutionary legislators redrew the national map as a geographical vivisection of the *ancien régime*. And the space left by the banishment of the One was dramatically concrete: aristocrats abandoned their châteaux and went into exile, and the clerics were chased from their churches and monasteries.

The French thus began the nineteenth century with a host of new needs and a collection of vacant buildings. For many years after the Revolution, officials, architects, and entrepreneurs worked to bring functions and buildings together, to fill these shells with, indeed, "every conceivable purpose." They changed convents into poorhouses and police stations, monasteries into factories and prisons, châteaux into offices, workshops, courthouses, or anything else they could imagine.[1] It was not only a matter of economy; sometimes, when it would have been cheaper to build anew, they converted and remodeled anyway (Petit 1991, 128-9). The builders of the new regime needed, it would seem, to reoccupy the space of the dethroned, to expose the reliquary as the simple box that it was.

But even as they began to build new buildings, they emphasized containment over representation. Architects of government buildings were sworn to the simple; grander gestures, like Paris's train stations, markets, and exhibition halls, were above all grand in how much they could hold. Hence a tentative answer to the empty-or-full question: the new building types were empty, as Frankl implied, of the symbolic content of monarchy, aristocracy, and church; but they were full, on the other hand, of new intentions, new technologies – and new inmates.

Society and Social Architecture

The inmates were a special architectural problem for the new nation, a particular incarnation of the Many. For the first time, government took on the task of sequestering *all* those who fell below, above, or outside certain developing norms.

AK: *This is a nice metaphor. But between the One and the Many, weren't there also the Few?*
DV: *Yes, a good point. The Few were those who spoke for the Many and also repressed them when they got too restless…*

17-2
A new institution for the poor: people bringing collateral in order to borrow money from a state-run pawn shop, in "Intérieur du Mont-de-Piété de Paris, au Marais." *Monts-de-piété,* first permitted late in the *ancien régime* and expanded after the Revolution, lent money to the poor at high interest to the profit of state social projects. This ambiguous gesture at once lent the poor a new status and allowed for certain predictable abuses. (Andrew, Best, & Leloir from a drawing by K. Girardet, *Magasin Pittoresque,* 1842. Courtesy of Bibliothèque Royale, Brussels)

Criminals, the insane, and the poor were recognized as new social types who required new building types. Social scientists, themselves a new social type, helped harden the lines between the types that made up the Many, and at the same time reinvented the displaced One as Society. From then on, though France still had kings and clerics, it was in the name of Society that the nation built its prisons, asylums, hospitals, and later its schools, public housing, and new towns (Rabinow 1989).

It was a profoundly contradictory enterprise. As early critics recognized, one consequence, or concomitant, of segregating Society architecturally by building types was a segregated Society – not One and indivisible, but Many and divided. Reformers in favor of this segregation could be broadly divided into optimists and pessimists.[2] Optimists invoked the convenient fiction of social uplift, arguing that those segments singled out in prisons, poorhouses, etc., would through that very experience be brought back into the fold. This answer had long roots in Christian notions of redemption, and in Rousseauist views of human nature. It was further supported by the new literary form of the novel, where individual characters were often seen to develop beyond their social and moral backgrounds (Bender 1988). The pessimist answer relied on various biological and military metaphors to demonstrate that these diseased, belligerent, or otherwise intractable members of the body politic must be cut off for the good of the rest. This latter argument derived increasing empirical support from the successive waves of civil unrest and epidemics that shook the nineteenth century from beginning to end.

Optimists and pessimists were sometimes bitterly opposed, but they tended to agree on the necessity for social/architectural sequestration – or, as it will be called here, *typification*. The adoption of typification as a long-term strategy in the building of a modern state was overdetermined by the diverse cultural currents that supported it. Government was in favor of typification as an efficient means of administration and repression: public building for the socially marginal, with proper distinction between types, was integral to French administration from the Revolution onward. The century's myriad social reformers, with the occasional exception of socialists, believed typification provided the proper framework for reform, at once representing and housing Society's concerns. And the increasingly powerful bourgeoisie, which overlapped with the previous two groups, simply demanded typification for its own protection. For the bourgeoisie, placeless people were by definition threatening. A case in point was the recurrent hysteria over vagabondage, despite the evidence that vagabonds did not pose any real threat to life or property (Petit 1990).

At the same time, the very breadth of the enthusiasm for typification entailed deep ideological divisions among its proponents. Because there was so little agreement on what, beyond containment, should happen to the human objects of typification, the social technologies proposed were rarely deployed to their full extent. Despite experiments with model projects, especially in prison design, "social" building types reverted, again and again, to their minimal function as containers.

This insight allows a more developed answer to the question of whether the new building types were empty or full. First, one might add a nuance to Frankl's observation by noting that, while the patron, the One, was indeed absent, most sought to replace him with a collective symbolic investment in Society. But Society in the age of the Many was inescapably diverse, which militated against such investment. Moreover, the vexing question remained as to whether this Society should include the subjects of typification or not: were they to be reclaimed or simply excluded? The "empty" container remained as the only common ground between opposing conceptions, a kind of placeholder for the absent resolution.

But the major contradiction in the project of typification was that the container, by dint of being empty, or emptied, was also increasingly full of unresolved decisions, full of inmates who might or might not belong there, and full of contradictions. A box made of stone and iron was the physical and conceptual locus of one of modernity's central debates, and in this sense "contained" contradictions.

---

1. The Archives Nationales in Paris retains a large collection of drawings of these projects under the rubric "F^{21}- Beaux-Arts." They were the subject of a general study by Georges Teyssot (n.d., 1988), and were the basis for substantial portions of the author's dissertation (Vanderburgh 1993).

2. The distinction between optimism and pessimism as drawn here, though it could be compared with technical debates in social philosophy, as between Lockean and Hobbesian views of Society, is meant to be quite broad. It is invoked only to suggest the range of attitudes and antecedents in the reform community. In practice, the two tendencies were sometimes hard to distinguish, and individual advocates were capable of expressing both sorts of opinions. Indeed, as the reform movement gained momentum, this sort of distinction became submerged in debates over more precise questions of treatment, budget, and architecture. Many scholars (Goffman 1961; Rothman 1971; Foucault [1975] 1979; Ignatieff 1978; Nye 1984) have covered this contradictory territory, with as many resulting ways of explaining it.

Yet, more and more, it was a cul-de-sac on the century's chimerical road to social reform. The tension between competing theories, as well as that between theories and social practices, exhausted attempts to wed architecture and social amelioration (Evans 1982).

Given these weaknesses, it would not be surprising had typification simply gone the way of the nineteenth century's other forgotten inventions. What happened instead was a striking persistence of typification as a social and architectural technology, notwithstanding the broad perception that it had failed. Whatever the possible reasons — some of which are discussed below — typification, alongside urbanization and industrialization, retains a prominent role in the structuring of social space, in France and across the West.

AK: *This happened not only in the West. "Typification" — not least the prison — was a prime instrument in the European project of colonization.*

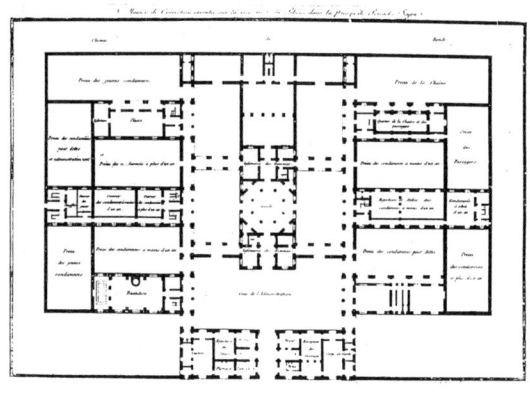

Typification and the Bourgeoisie

To typify, as the word is most commonly used, is to be the example that defines a quality, a state, or a genre. But it can be used in another sense: to emphasize that it is the observer, the typifier, who endows the object with its typical status. To look for the typical in something or someone is to enact a reduction whereby the object becomes its ostensible quality. Most often, this reduction reflects a desire for control on the part of the typifier; such was certainly the case for the nineteenth-century typifiers of new "social problems." Typification in this sense is fundamental to culture, and to the power relations within a culture, because it is the principal basis for naming things.

In France, the period immediately following the Revolution of 1789 was a particularly fertile one for naming and re-naming. In keeping with the Revolution's leveling spirit, everyone was given the same new title, *citoyen* ("citizen," *citoyenne* for women) in place of the old honorifics. When the *ancien régime* provinces were dismembered, the new "departments" were named after ostensibly neutral geographical features (Figure 17-4), and the calendar was re-invented using secular and didactic names for the days and months. Prisons, in keeping with a new role in the justice system, were differentiated into *maisons d'arrêt* (literally "houses of arrest"), *maisons de correction*, and *maisons de justice*, among others. In domains other than political geography, the apparent life span of these changes was short: aristocrats' titles and privileges returned quickly, the calendar was switched back under Napoleon, and the various *maisons* were hopelessly intermixed for many years.[3]

AK: *Both here and elsewhere I am struck by the contrast between a process of spatial transformation promoted by the state compared to its transformation by the market.*

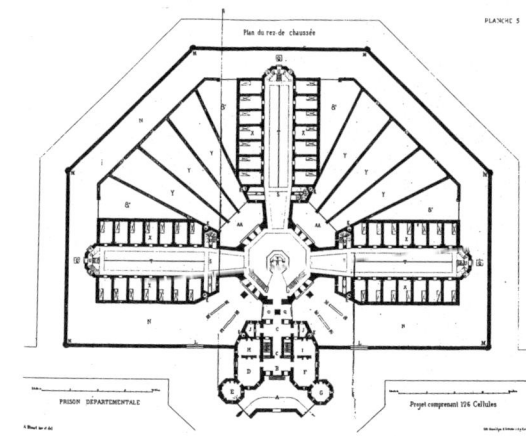

17-3
Cycles of prison design in nineteenth-century France. During the 60 years between 1820 and 1880, the French government changed its prison program four times, alternating between the simple and inexpensive "congregate" system, shown in (a), which confined inmates in groups, and the "cellular" system, shown in (b), which required expensive individual cells.
a. prison at Lyon: ground floor plan
  (L.-P. Baltard, 1820s. Courtesy of Bibliothèque Nationale, Paris)
b. provincial cellular prison: sample ground floor plan (G.-A. Blouet, 1841. Courtesy of Ministry of Justice, Paris)

AK: *Wasn't it rather that a semifeudal system based on "orders" was being replaced by a more capitalist one based on "class"?*

DV: *One could say that, although the change you speak of had already been going on for more than a century in most of Europe. In another sense French society still includes both: orders based on certain kinds of hereditary privilege, and classes that are based on common interests.*

17-4
Map of France: one lasting change brought by the Revolution of 1789 (drawings by author)

a. French provinces before the Revolution

b. French "departments" after the Revolution

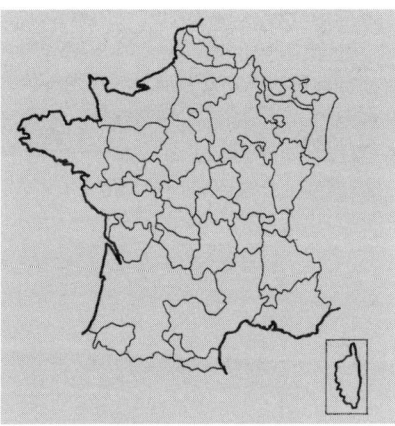
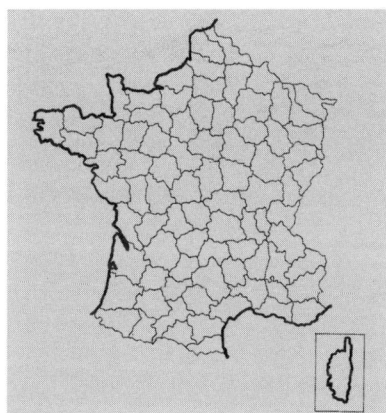

3. Moreover, in terms of cultural attitudes and political behavior, even the *ancien régime* division of the territory remained quite meaningful well into the twentieth century (Le Bras and Todd 1981; Vanderburgh 1993).

4. L'Abbé Sieyès, the author of the pamphlet cited, was also one of the best known proponents of a plan to redivide France using a perfect square grid, ignoring entirely the existing traditional boundaries.

As with most such exercises, however, the Revolutionary re-naming accompanied some lasting changes in social practices. The pre-Revolutionary elites would never again be so secure, nor the lower classes so subdued. The whole class structure was in flux. The most dramatic evidence of this dynamism was the emergence of a new *middle* class, politically active, socially prominent, and growing. This new element was also radically diverse: its members ranged from far left to far right in politics, and from the very top to quite near the bottom of the economic scale. However, its efforts at self-definition made one characteristic stand out: if the class as a whole was somewhat confused as to where its interests lay, it was nonetheless determined — and well placed — to defend them.

This determination was a proximate cause of the Revolution. In the 1789 session of the ancient institution of the Estates General, it was the so-called Third Estate, representing mostly the bourgeoisie, that provoked a legitimation crisis in French government, challenging the primacy of the first two Estates, those of the clergy and aristocracy. This was framed explicitly as a question of political and social identity. A famous pamphlet asked, "What is the Third Estate? Everything. What has it been until now? Nothing. What does it want? To become something" (Augé 1933, 1359).[4]

The desire of this awkward stepchild of the old regime to "become something" forced, one might say, everything else to become something else. The Third Estate's blanket challenge to traditional authority opened the way to a questioning of values that produced both an important affirmation of basic human rights and the absurdity of the Revolutionary Calendar.

Still, for the present purpose, the defining characteristic of the middle classes was anxiety, an anxiety with both spatial and temporal components. Because this amorphous group lacked the traditional status of those above and below, it had to create for itself a social space in the politics of the new nation. But the middle classes were also concerned about physical space: fear of the disease and disorder of the lower classes made them wish to be separate from these others. Alain Corbin (1986), for example, has pointed out that it was with the birth of the middle classes that smells and odors became an issue in public and private life. The newly sensitized bourgeois nose retreated from the great unwashed behind clouds of perfume and fragrant oils, adding olfactory to spatial distance.

The temporal component of the middle classes' anxiety stemmed, on the one hand, from their disengagement from aristocratic history, the wars and successions of the *ancien régime*, and, on the other, from the correct intuition that revolution could break out at any moment. Even in their personal lives, in business and the professions, the middle classes were subject to brusque changes in fortune. Capitalism had not yet mastered its attendant risks, and there was no separation of personal and commercial assets until late in the century (Smith 1981, 42-3). Professionals had no liability insurance – architects and engineers, for example, could see their careers and fortunes ruined by a single failure or collapse (Van Zanten 1989).

The bourgeoisie, trying to limit its risks and increase its gains, was thus ready-made to sympathize with the paradoxical tenets of Enlightenment utilitarianism. Jeremy Bentham, who was well known to the French Revolutionaries, proposed that human nature sought a maximum of pleasure with a minimum of pain, and that the goal of the state should be to provide the greatest good for the greatest number, with the minimum expenditure of resources. Bentham was an obsessive systematizer, and a persistent critic of what he perceived as inefficient administration in his native England. His own foray into typification, beginning in the 1780s, was the well-known Panopticon, an all-purpose building type that could serve, with minor variations, as a school, a factory, a prison, a workhouse, or any other building where efficient supervision was important (Bentham 1791).

Early in the Revolution, before the Terror of 1793–4, the French showed particular enthusiasm for the Panopticon, perhaps because it resonated with Rousseau's dream of an open or transparent Society (Bentham [1791] 1977, 16). But the most important lasting influence of the Panopticon in France was its marriage of the physical and the social. Even the most idealistic of Revolutionaries realized that they faced an enormous task in retraining oppressed monarchical subjects to behave as free citizens. They welcomed the notion that a "simple idea in architecture," as Bentham called it, could be the single motor that drove a multitude of initiatives, from education to punishment. And though the Panopticon itself was only taken up later, Bentham's strict calculus of cost and benefit remained at the root of French public architecture from the Revolution onward.

Architecture and the Functional Type

Among architectural theorists, building type had always been a central topic of discussion. Debates about the proper use of the classical orders were one kind, Laugier's notion of the primitive hut another. But these efforts revolved around a search for origins, for *urtyp* rather than functional type. They tended to assume a

17-5
Bourgeois space and time: *"maison à trois étages"* ("four-story house"). This imaginary cross section of a nineteenth-century French apartment building shows the range of middle-class fortunes in both space and time. Any middle-class individual might expect to live on any or all of the three middle levels depicted here within the course of his or her lifetime. (J. Quarterly from a drawing by K. Girardet, *Magasin Pittoresque*, 1847. Courtesy of Bibliothèque Royale, Brussels)

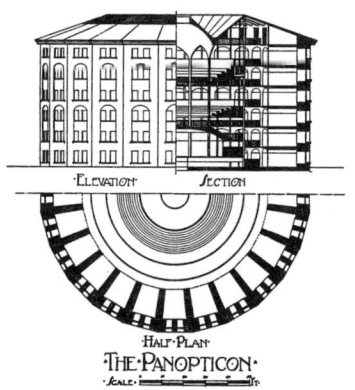

17-6
The Panopticon: elevation, section, half plan (Jeremy Bentham, 1790s, drawing by R. Newcomb in A. Hopkins, 1930, *Prisons and Prison Building*, Courtesy of Bibliothèque Royale, Brussels)

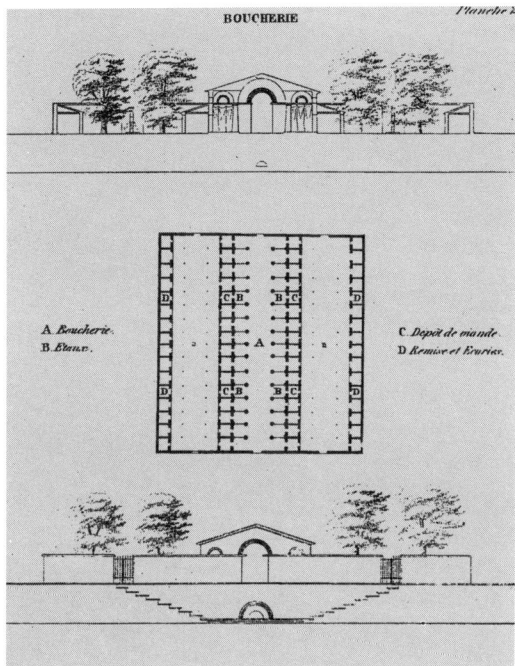

17-7
Durand's prototypes: *"Boucherie"* ("Slaughterhouse"): section, plan, and elevation. A modest building given the same visual status as any other type shown in the *Précis*. (*Précis*, 1840–1841. Courtesy of Bibliothèque Royale, Brussels)

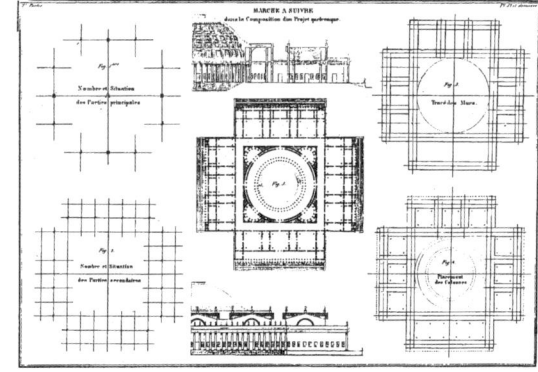

17-8
Durand's compositional method: *"Marche à suivre dans la Composition d'un Projet quelconque"* ("Procedure to Follow in the Composition of any Project"). (*Précis*, 1840–1841. Courtesy of Bibliothèque Royale, Brussels)

5. Still, as more than one scholar has proposed (e.g., Vidler 1987), these discussions provided the opening for a more radical vision of type.

fixed hierarchy of building function based in a particular reading of history. Theoreticians were less interested in accommodating new functions than in finding a solid basis for enclosing traditional ones.[5]

It is J.-N.-L. Durand, a professor at France's elite post-Revolutionary engineering school the Ecole polytechnique, who is usually credited with the formulation of the modern functional type, the architectural component of typification. In order to teach architecture efficiently to engineers (who at that time often received architectural commissions), Durand developed a simple method of composition that varied plan-forms within a limited range to accommodate, theoretically, any possible use (Durand 1809). Durand's teachings spread widely beyond his classroom, and became a fundamental element of the teaching of architectural design at the Ecole des Beaux-Arts in Paris (Szambien 1982; Pérez-Gómez 1983).

Basing his method on the same egalitarian grid that underlay the new French administrative geography, Durand promoted a model of design as the repetition and recombination of basic architectural elements. His simple prototypes, which were echoed in architectural production throughout the nineteenth century, were formal analogues to the desanctifying impulse of the Revolution, rejecting the mystical authority of the *ancien régime*.

The prototypes were intended to support Durand's contention that *disposition*, or the combination and assembly of architectural elements, was "the only thing to which the architect must attach himself" Durand (1809, 1:23). From a good *disposition* would naturally result all of the desired qualities of architecture, even beauty itself. He emphasized the plan as the generative idea, from which would follow the section and, only after these, the elevation (1809, 1: 89-90).

More important for the present discussion, Durand's demystification extended to the relation between the different functional types. There was to be no more hierarchy of functions. There were simply needs to be fulfilled in the service of the new nation: the engineers he taught, and the architects he influenced, would take the same approach in laying out a prefecture, a prison, or a stable. Moreover, Durand justified his work in explicitly utilitarian terms, claiming architecture's goal as the minimization of inconvenience and expenditure for the maximum benefit (1809, 1:15).

Durand's method responded well to the spatial anxieties of the middle classes. Architecture, both between and within buildings, was to provide the separation they demanded, admitting a healthy dose of light and air to its discrete and economical volumes. The essence of this logic was classificatory. Spaces were

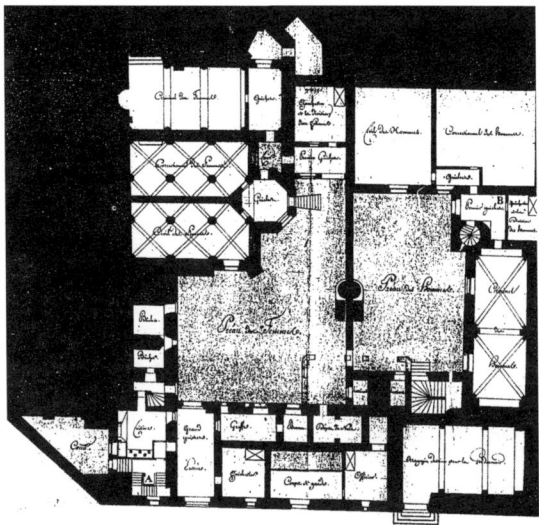

17-9
A typical commission for Durand's contemporaries: conversion of an ecclesiastical building to a prison at Narbonne (Aude), France, ground floor plan, 1799. (Courtesy of Archives Nationales, Paris)

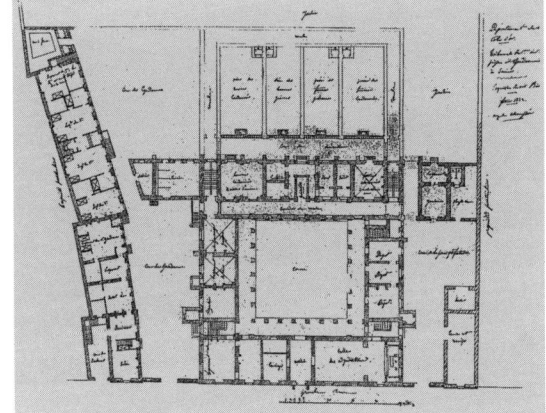

17-10
Functional mixing: project for conversion of a convent or château to various public uses at Semur (Côte-d'Or), France, ground floor plan (Flamand, 1832. Courtesy of Archives Nationales, Paris)

monofunctional so that one would always know what was there: Durand's program envisaged no spaces for disease or dangerous social mixing, and at the same time simplified the connection between space and activity.

However, the method was less helpful in addressing *temporal* anxiety. Although the practice of spatial classification ensured that proper distinctions were made to begin with — between the clean and the dirty, the loud and the soft, etc. — it could not insure against their later abuse. More tellingly, in his approach to history, while Durand displayed a willingness to derive formal lessons from buildings of the past, the passage of time and the problems it presented were completely denied. He reduced the force of history, as in the continued use of classical orders, to what one historian has termed "force of habit" (Rykwert 1982, 16). In his *Recueil...* (1801), a volume of old and recent buildings and projects redrawn to the same scale and sorted by functional type, Durand's strategy was somewhat like that of a manufacturer who buys a competing invention in order to keep it out of circulation. Rather than allowing the threatening insight that buildings themselves were sites of cultural contestation over time, Durand preferred to anchor them firmly in a timeless two-dimensional grid of plan-forms.

Ironically, during the time of Durand's greatest influence, most public architectural commissions underscored the contested character of France's built space. For the first 30 years of the nineteenth century, building activity was overwhelmingly concentrated on the transformation of the *lieux sacrés* ("sacred places," in this case both literally and figuratively) of the aristocracy and the church — even, after Napoleon's defeat, on the restoration of some of these buildings to their original state. Graduates of Durand's curriculum and of the Beaux-Arts found their training confronted with the inevitably time-bound and symbolically loaded monuments of the past.

These buildings were opposed in both form and conception to Durand's prototypes: they were often irregular, accretive constructions dating from centuries before; many still bore the traces of a distinctly unrestrained decorative hand; and their thick walls and small spaces were highly resistant to the entry of light and air. And, whereas Durand's prototypes were intended to be universally applicable, the *ancien régime* relics were specific to their sites and periods of construction.

The very size of these monasteries, convents, and châteaux made it difficult to limit them to one function per building. Provincial architects were often compelled by local administrations to produce projects combining the most widely divergent uses under the same roof, sometimes reproducing the same degree of functional mixing found in the buildings' original programs. A château of any size, for example, would originally have combined living quarters, stables, offices, chapel, storage, administrative offices, and perhaps a cell or two in a dungeon or keep. Projects for the reuse of such a building, especially in less wealthy or popu-

AK: *I'm prompted here to ask about the forms of historically constructed social phenomena that make up a "type." And how does that process relate to the distribution of power in society?*

DV: *Difficult questions! As regards the* functional *type, at any rate, the two horns of its dilemma are* specificity to function *and* universality of application. *By presuming that these two contradictory criteria could be met at once, the promoters of the functional type (government, reformers, architects) came up against the resistance of local officials, builders, and users, whose habits ran more towards* generality of function *and* specificity of application. *In this situation, power relations became very apparent.*

17-11
"Rationalizing" a provincial project: The Conseil des Bâtiments Civils' intervention in a project for a courthouse/prison/gendarmerie at Arcis-sur-Aube (Aude), France, elevations (Courtesy of Archives Nationales, Paris)
a. local architect's project of 1819   b. Conseil des Bâtiments Civils' revision of 1820

lated areas, might try to accommodate as many as possible of the new post-Revolutionary administrative needs: subprefecture, chamber of commerce, courthouse, prison, gendarmery, town hall, and school might all end up in the same volume.

The Conseil des Bâtiments Civils, an advisory board that answered to the Interior Ministry, was frequently the first party to see these projects after they left the drawing board. Its members, products of the Beaux-Arts and usually winners of the Prix de Rome, were dismayed by what they saw. From the early years of the century, the Conseil's philosophy was close to Durand's; but provincial architects, with different backgrounds and different concerns, were rarely in step with Paris. And even if they were, they had to satisfy provincial legislatures' own version of utilitarianism, which laid more emphasis on parsimony than on the "greatest good" (Vanderburgh 1993).

In its criticisms of reuse projects, the Conseil argued first for economy and functional adequacy, second for formal regularity and symmetry; the wording of its decisions often gave the reader to understand that it did not expect much beyond that. Under the Conseil's guidance, especially during the 1810s and 1820s, some relatively remarkable operations were performed on existing buildings, leaving them with a strong resemblance to Durand's models (Figure 17-11). The Conseil also intervened in the few new projects built before 1830, and these came to reflect a "rationalist" bent. But this was a drastically abbreviated version of Durand's lavish minimalism. Small urban sites only rarely permitted the spacious courtyards and narrow pavilions of Durand's preference. Time and history, in the form of property rights, heavy walls, and constrained sites, forced themselves back into the elegant but fragile equation of nascent functionalism.

History, Careers, and Machines

As a delayed building boom hit France in the 1830s, the problem of history came back to architectural consciousness in other forms as well. Most obviously, the revival of the Gothic style became a problem to be confronted both within and outside the Beaux-Arts system. By the end of the decade, "restoration" of France's medieval buildings was enough of an issue that Prosper Mérimée, a Romantic writer and polemicist, was appointed to the Conseil des Bâtiments Civils as its expert on restoration and preservation. But the fascination and fear of history went much deeper than matters of decoration. As reformist architects like Eugène Viollet-le-Duc proclaimed, formal style was only one aspect of a whole way of living that included, but was not limited to, the production of buildings. Viollet-le-Duc took pains to emphasize that the conditions of existence of medieval craftsmen were central to the perceived power of their work, and that the weakness of contemporary work was tied to what he saw as a deteriorating quality of life.

Environmental determinism, the belief in a causal relationship between social and physical space, was the order of the day. Just as Viollet-le-Duc believed that social problems were the cause of bad buildings, there were others who believed that inadequate buildings were the cause of social problems. But unlike Durand and his sympathizers, who had sought to parry the thrust of history by reducing it to a set of conventions, a new generation of reformers recognized the power of history and wanted to exploit it.

The most committed environmental determinists in politics had come to power in the July Revolution of 1830. These men, who had agitated in the 1820s for reform of institutional architecture on principles of hygiene and secular humanitarianism, included such figures as Alexis de Tocqueville, the famous observer of American prisons and democracy. Although a revolution had brought them to power, the notables of the July Monarchy could not ignore the possibility that one might happen again, as indeed one would in 1848. History was still not under control, but it was exhibiting some regularity (as Marx noted sardonically after Napoleon's nephew engineered a coup just like his uncle's, 50 years later).[6]

Broadly speaking, there were two concepts available for the taming of time: the career and the machine. The idea of the career made it possible to thematize social progress in the person of an upwardly mobile individual; the machine would become the incorruptible, inexorable means to that end. Together, these two elements released typification from the grip of Durand's antihistorical matrices into the possibility of mass-produced redemption, holding out a difficult dual promise of security for the upper classes and change for the lower.

Already under Napoleon's doomed expansionism, some members of the bourgeoisie had begun to transmute their collective desire to "become something" into a quest for individual advancement. The pursuit of careers in the military and the bureaucracy allowed those of relatively humble origin to distinguish themselves quickly, as had Napoleon himself. After 1830, most professions formed organizations in order to provide a secure path into the future for their members. Even reformers, abandoning the aristocratic model of disinterested charity and *bienfaisance*, were becoming professionalized through the developing bureaucracy of social welfare (Perrot 1991).

At the same time, other circumstances began to require that the upper levels of Society address the "careers" of their social inferiors. Until that time, various forms of classification, more or less on the model of medical quarantine, had guided reform principles. As Durand had implied, it should be sufficient to separate out the different elements, and a "cure" would follow – if not for those so sequestered, then at least for Society at large. But the cholera epidemic of 1832 brought chaos to the medical understanding of contagion, and at the same time introduced new tensions between the classes. Members of all classes were touched by the epidemic: the bourgeoisie and aristocracy developed a renewed fear of the lower classes, whom they viewed as having somehow generated the disease through their filthy habits, while the poor widely believed they had been poisoned by the rich and the doctors (Evans 1988, 121–7).

Classification was not a defense against the maladies now ostensibly confronting Society. The bad health habits of the poor were no longer simply unpleasant, but actively threatening. And a growing literature of novels and popular broadsheets described gangs and rings of organized criminals, who even had their own language: criminals, too, were becoming professionalized.

The implication, a part of Bentham's thinking that had remained latent in France, was that the poor, criminals, the illiterate, and other marginal citizens must be retrained – forcibly if necessary – and begin a new sort of moral career (Foucault [1975] 1979). Helping to aliment this new view was the bourgeois's own origin myth, that of the poor but honest merchant or tradesman who rose from his low class position through talent and hard work. It was easy enough for those who had lived through this, or believed themselves to have done so, to imagine the same possibility for others – and to doubt the worth of those who failed or chose the wrong path.

However, the numbers were virtually overwhelming: for instance, with the beginning of statistical studies in the 1820s, reformers and administrators realized that the great majority of the country's citizens were illiterate, and well over half of these spoke French as a second language, if at all. In order to reorient the careers of thousands of potential subjects, then, one could not rely on the fatherly

---

6. Marx's trenchant analysis of Napoleon III's rise to power in *The Eighteenth Brumaire of Louis Bonaparte,* (1852) is the source of his famous remark about history repeating itself, the first time as tragedy, the second time as farce.

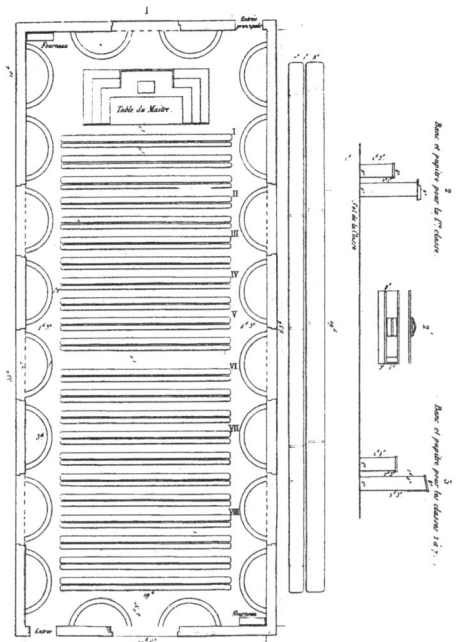

17-12
Plan of a Lancasterian school
(*Méthode Lancastérienne*, 1816.
Courtesy of Bibliothèque Royale,
Brussels)

17-13
Pupils at recitation in a Lancasterian school (*Méthode Lancastérienne*, 1816. Courtesy of Bibliothèque Royale, Brussels)
a. correct behavior of monitor and pupils
b. incorrect, disorderly behavior

chats and personal epiphanies that studded the narratives of the self-made. One needed something efficient and powerful, like a machine. Once set in motion, like the new steam locomotives, it would continue to do its work at a predictable pace, requiring only periodic tending by a few relatively unskilled technicians. Then, perhaps, imprinted with the strict regularity of the machine, the re-careered citizen would go and deviate no more.

The Old Soul of the Machine

A century before Le Corbusier coined his famous phrase, French architects were being called upon to design a whole panoply of "machines for training in." The architectural importance of the metaphor, both for the time and for what followed, cannot be underestimated. A fascination with the autonomous, locomotive character of machinery, from eighteenth-century automatons to twentieth-century war machines, is after all constitutive of modernity. But for the architecture of typification, the machine was already both means and end — not so much yet for its aesthetic qualities as for its power to accomplish repetitive tasks, and as a symbol of effectiveness.

This attitude began to emerge, for example, in schools following the system of *enseignement mutuel* ("mutual teaching"), known in English as the Lancasterian or Monitorial System. The system, which involved using students as assistants to a principal instructor, had been first promoted in England by educators Andrew Bell and Joseph Lancaster, but was quickly embraced by the French, who sought a means to carry out the unfulfilled Revolutionary mandate for universal education. Although a network of teachers' colleges was already in place, these were not intended to provide the personnel for widespread primary education. The French were easily persuaded that the only way to make education available on a large scale was to use students themselves as educators.

The functioning of a Lancasterian school was explicitly mechanical, in that the action of a single source of power, the teacher, was propagated through the secondary actions of his student monitors, to result finally in the education of the pupils. The system was criticized for reducing education to acts of memorization that could easily be transmitted by the monitors; but this was also seen as a virtue by its promoters, who believed memorization to be the essence of primary education. A Parisian theatrical comedy of 1818 poked fun at the method and its peasant subjects, as well as the potential double meaning of "mutual teaching":

> *Julien*: Everyone has to do the same thing at the same time… Just so you know, I'm the monitor.
> *Lucas*: Say, the *Monitor* [*Le Moniteur*, a government newspaper], isn't that the big sheet of paper the Mayor gets?
> *Julien*: No, shut up and do like the others, everything I do… First, to get a good start, I kiss the girl across from me… (*He kisses Toinon, and each boy kisses a girl…*) (Brazier, Dumersan, and Delestre-Poirson 1818, 20)

17-14
Provincial Panopticon: prison at Autun (Saône-et-Loire), France, aerial view (A. Berthier, 1847–1856. photo by author)

The architecture of the Lancasterian school, in keeping with its mission of efficiency, was as reductive as the lessons. The system required only that the classroom contain enough space to accommodate the benches and recitation spaces called for in the program, and that this space be uninterrupted for surveillance. In his French-language promotional tract on the method, Lancaster (1816) included a sample plan, as well as engravings showing good and bad use of the arrangements. Here, despite the plan's simplicity, the machine was powerfully latent.[7] Pupils and monitors would flow predictably through the classroom's internal articulations, forming and re-forming the same arrays of interchangeable units under the master's surveillance.

By the 1830s, as the Lancasterian System was reaching the peak of its popularity, the Panopticon enjoyed a revival in France, serving as a lightning rod in the debates over prison design. As a building design, the Panopticon had remained unresolved in many details (Evans 1982). But French architects produced numerous versions of it, from a small circular prison built in the Burgundy region to enormous, hypertrophied projects that could probably not have been built at the time. In view of the prominent architect L.-P. Baltard's (1829) authoritative criticism of the idea (and in general of the English "mechanistic spirit") it is difficult to understand why the Panopticon should have been so suddenly accepted in France.

But it is important to remember that architects themselves were members of the bourgeoisie – with a very few exceptions above and below – and were hence struggling with the same questions of personal, professional, and class identity as their peers (Jacques 1986). With public interest in prison architecture at a fever

17-15
Panopticon-type project: *Projet de Pénitencier*, view from a cell toward the central observation tower (Harou-Romain the younger, 1840. Courtesy of Bibliothèque Nationale, Paris)

7. The paradigms of military and factory organization (cf. Foucault [1975] 1979) were also latent, both in terms of the discipline imposed and in terms of spatial distribution. Mechanization, militarization, and industrialization were all "available" at the beginning of the nineteenth century.

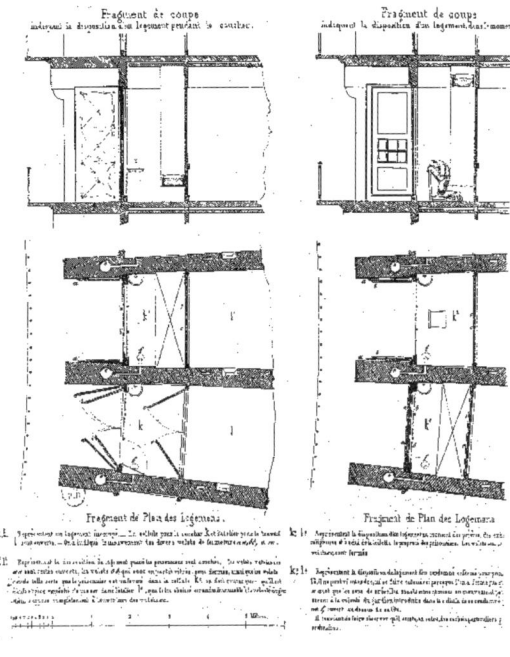

17-16
The machine-prison: *Projet de Pénitencier,* cell details. Doors and bed are retractable, nearly every furnishing swings or slides to accommodate various activities. Harou-Romain even provided for an early version of "white noise" during sleeping hours, to be distributed by pipes marked "f" in the plan. (Harou-Romain the younger, 1840. Courtesy of Bibliothèque Nationale, Paris)

AK: *This seems to be just a further step in the removal of punishment from the realm of the public to that of the private, which is what the prison itself represented — bringing hanging and public executions indoors.*

---

8. The other model that caught the French imagination during this time was the well-known Eastern State Penitentiary at Philadelphia, designed by John Haviland and constructed during the 1820s and 1830s. In the 1830s, the system followed there was the basis for an ambitious French government reform for provincial prisons, which attempted to combine the Philadelphia system with elements of the Panopticon (Petit 1990; Vanderburgh 1993).

pitch, and social conflict mounting, both architects and others were led to make extravagant claims: one reformer called the prison architect "the primary executor of the sentence" (Petit 1991, 243). For architects, to furnish what was asked of them was at the same time impossible and imperative. They could not, faced with the competition of engineers and contractors, turn away from such a tempting opportunity, even if the prospects of success were doubtful.

Hence the popularity of the Panopticon, a building supposed virtually by itself to reform human character. There was no other model with such an ambitious program and such a resonant form.[8] French architects accompanied their Panopticon-inspired prison projects with long explanatory texts combining extracts from the most diverse sources, perhaps hoping to cover all the political bases (Charpentier 1838; Harou-Romain 1840).

By and large, the Panopticon's presumed functioning had been passive, a simple matter of the distribution of spaces. In this way it was not a machine so much as a framework for observation. However, Bentham's version had envisaged a few mechanical details for ventilation, aural surveillance, and security. French architects tried to improve on Bentham with the newer techniques at hand, festooning their projects with sliding doors, folding beds, retracting shades, and mechanical ventilation. Harou-Romain's projects are particularly noteworthy in this regard.

Unlike the Lancasterian schools, which were simply articulated containers, the prisons themselves began to move. And although most of these mechanisms required human power to move them, they usually worked by action at a distance, through levers and pulleys and systems of gears. This, like the guillotine, gave an impression of removing human agency by one step. Though mechanism's major purpose was to facilitate the work of the guards, it also introduced a certain distance into the relation between the guard and the punishment. This was especially appealing to administrators, who lamented the poor training and discipline of the guards. They were happy to imagine that a machine-prison could replace, even in part, the administration's fallible agents.

But prisons were only the first to take this step away from direct material responsibility: hospitals, train stations, hotels, and even houses began to bristle with mechanisms as well (cf. Banham 1984). The thousands of alternative devices invented and abandoned have given collectors and historians a great deal to catalogue. And though one often views such artifacts with a smile of nostalgia, there was an edge of desperation in that outpouring of energy. It was as if these inventors were trying, by a collective effort of will, to make architecture take on a role, or at least a content, for which it was fundamentally unsuited.

By filling the manifestly empty container with machinery, ostensibly the better to streamline its function, the ruling middle class was attempting an emergency reanimation on a body that had never lived. The class felt some responsibility for the marginal and "less fortunate," as witnessed by its hearty participation in public debates on the subject. But the right-thinking bourgeois would have liked nothing better than to see the task in someone or something else's capable, steam-powered hands.

Architects, preening in the glow of the spotlight, could not take a step backward without falling off the stage. They themselves had been typified, or typecast, as saviors, as the medium through which Society could at last be unified and the plot of history resolved. Expecting perhaps a *machina ex deum* – a machine from God, the absent patron – architects found themselves instead with a particularly flagrant *deus ex machina*. Their machine-buildings failed with monotonous regularity, and by the end of the century architects were widely mistrusted. Flaubert's characterization of the architect as "an imbecile who always forgets the stairs" was among the most innocuous of the critiques they endured (Jacques 1986, 42).

Conclusion

Although it is a topic for another essay, it is worth asking how architects should address present demands for new typifications, in the form of shelters, transitional housing, and, of course, more prisons. They are no longer dazzled by the spotlight, but they are still waiting on a darkened stage, doing a bit of what actors call "business" *en attendant*. The last 40 years have seen repeated questioning, from both within and outside the profession, of the architect's role in the ambiguous spectacle of social reform. But few architects can successfully avoid the feeling that Society is in the audience, watching.

Architects are still preoccupied with the empty-or-full question, and it shows, if nowhere else, in their drawings. Whether in the calculated animation of a Charles Moore, or the calculated emptiness of an Aldo Rossi, the container is often masked or dissembled by the presumption of a content that can be suggested, but not shown with the means at hand. This suggested content is sometimes a kind of fulfillment or wholeness, perhaps a descendant of the One that was banished by the Many. Or, as in recent work of a more anticlassical bent, the content may be an energetic assertion that there never was One.

If Moore's work depends for its appeal on a fictive reading of contemporary culture – that collective public life is one long festive occasion – it is nonetheless an agreeable one that many would like to share. And if Rossi's beautiful but eery projects are somehow more true to present conditions, as Manfredo Tafuri implies in using a Rossi drawing for the paperback edition of his dark manifesto, *Architecture and Utopia* (1976), it is still not a truth many desire to face. Richard Ingersoll, speaking of Rossi's projects in a recent essay, writes that these "tombs for the living… are the painful pleasures representing a world that is dependent on but disgusted by its own modernity" (1991, 13).

Tombs are, in a somewhat lugubrious sense, both full *and* empty. However, they are also almost exclusively symbolic (apart from a residual role in urban hygiene), a distinction enjoyed by very few building types. In the meantime, most other buildings have more complicated briefs to fulfill, mostly revolving around the difficult notion of function. And, as argued above, the very idea of differentiating buildings according to function is in part a response to another problem – or, as it were, another function.

The middle classes of the nineteenth century invented Society as a replacement for the lost traditional order, and to secure their own place within the new one. Confronted with the temporal and spatial anxieties raised by their own changing consciousness, they successfully introduced a new spatial and temporal architectural order, substituting pattern for patron. The most problematic elements of this order, brought into being by a process of social and architectural sequestration, or typification, were and are those directed toward so-called social purposes.

Expecting architectural space to represent and reinforce the new order, Durand and his many descendants introduced the universalizing logic of classification, but lost control of history. Time, no longer cyclic but linear, became a threat because each of the infinite number of points along the line could be the point of departure for revolution.[9] At the same time, members of the middle class were only too aware that the life path of an individual could just as easily lead downward as upward.

---

9. Of course, for some this was precisely the promise of linear history: groups of new millenialists saw that they need not wait for some preordained date. The millenium was always now, or very soon, and could be witnessed through the proscenium of the next modern building/manifesto.

AK: *I would say that tombs are 50 percent symbolic (above ground) and 50 percent functional (below ground). Thinking about the difference is productive.*

AK: *But was (is?) an architectural problem ever defined only in such narrow terms?*
DV: *Rarely, indeed, which is what gives rise to the third problem.*

Perhaps machines were embraced not because of their novelty but because they were cyclic and reassuring. By reconceiving buildings as machines, the power of linear time could be harnessed back to a predictable rhythm of production. In contrast to unpredictable, history-prone humanity, machines only did what they were set in motion to do. By articulating the life stream of inmates with the cogs of a social engine, the new machines would reduce Revolution to revolutions per minute.

But the analogy worked too well – the container turned into a boiler, and the gears ground down as fast as they could be made. Inexpertly tended by exhausted social engineers, the relics of typification remind one that machines can wear out, as has the public housing apparatus of recent years. And contemporary prisons still undergo crises regularly enough to prove that containment is only a prelude to explosion.

Thus, the question that begins this essay runs the risk of setting up a false problem: if the architecture of typification is both empty and full, then perhaps it is also neither. If Society is still perturbed by certain lacks and abundances, then it may be wise to look beyond typification, and beyond architecture, for their resolution. Designing new building types may absorb more energy than it liberates, as in the oxymoronic new crop of "homes" for the homeless. Often enough, mixing an architectural problem with a social problem seems only to create a third.

References

Augé, Claude, ed. 1933. *Nouveau petit Larousse illustré*. Paris: Larousse.

Baltard, L.-P. 1829. *Architectonographie des prisons…* Paris.

Banham, Reyner. 1984. *The Architecture of the Well-Tempered Environment*. 2nd ed. Chicago: University of Chicago Press.

Bender, John. 1988. *Imagining the Penitentiary*. Chicago: University of Chicago Press.

Bentham, Jeremy. 1791. *Panopticon; or, the Inspection House…* 3 vol. London: T. Payne.

———. [1791] 1977. *Le Panoptique, précédé de L'oeil du pouvoir, entretien avec Michel Foucault, Postface de Michelle Perrot*. Paris: Pierre Belfond.

Brazier, Dumersan and Delestre-Poirson. 1818. *L'école de village, ou L'enseignement mutuel, comédie en un acte, mêlée de vaudevilles*. Paris: Ladvocat.

Charpentier, Théodore. 1838. *Projet de Maison Pénitentiaire*. Paris.

Corbin, Alain. 1986. *The Foul and the Fragrant: Odor and the French Social Imagination*. Leamington Spa, U.K.: Berg.

Durand, J.-N.-L. 1801. *Recueil et parallèle des édifices de tout genre, anciens et modernes*. Paris.

———. 1809. *Précis des leçons d'architecture données à l'Ecole polytechnique*. 2 vols. Paris.

———. 1840–1841. *Précis des leçons d'architecture données à l'Ecole polytechnique*. Pirate edition of Durand's revised, enlarged edition of 1813. 2 vols. Liège.

Evans, Richard J. 1988. Epidémies et révolutions: le choléra dans l'Europe du XIXe siècle. In *Peurs et terreurs face à la contagion*. Edited by Jean-Pierre Bardet et al. and translated by Françoise Lehenand, 107–35. Paris: Fayard.

Evans, Robin. 1982. *The Fabrication of Virtue*. Cambridge: Cambridge University Press.

Foucault, Michel. [1975] 1979. *Discipline and Punish: The Birth of the Prison*. Translated by Alan Sheridan. New York: Vintage Books.

Frankl, Paul. [1914] 1982. *Principles of Architectural History: The Four Phases of Architectural Style, 1420–1900*. Translated and edited by James F. O'Gorman. Cambridge, Mass.: MIT Press.

Goffman, Erving. 1961. *Asylums: Essays on the Social Situation of Mental Patients and other Inmates*. Garden City, N.Y.: Anchor-Doubleday.

Harou-Romain. 1840. *Projet de pénitencier*. Caen: Lesaulnier.

Ignatieff, Michael. 1978. *A Just Measure of Pain: The Penitentiary in the Industrial Revolution*. London: Macmillan.

Ingersoll, Richard. 1991. Four works by Aldo Rossi in Italy: building is forgetting. *Concrete* 2 (Fall): 10–13.

Jacques, Annie. 1986. *La carrière de l'architecte au XIXe siècle*. Les dossiers du Musée d'Orsay 3. Paris: Réunion des musées nationaux.

Lancaster, J. 1816. *Méthode lancastérienne, ou Système d'éducation britannique*. Translated by Th.F.A. Jouenne and J.R. Jones. Brussels: P.J. De Mat.

Le Bras, Hervé and Emmanuel Todd. 1981. *L'invention de la France*. Paris: Librairie Générale Française.

Middleton, Robin, ed. 1982. *The Beaux-Arts and Nineteenth-Century French Architecture*. Cambridge, Mass.: MIT Press.

Nye, Robert A. 1984. *Crime, Madness, and Politics in Modern France: The Medical Concept of National Decline*. Princeton, N.J.: Princeton University Press.

Pérez-Gómez, Alberto. 1983. *Architecture and the Crisis of Modern Science*. Cambridge, Mass.: MIT Press.

Perrot, Michelle, ed. 1991. *From the Fires of Revolution to the Great War*. Vol. 4 of *A History of Private Life*. Edited by P. Ariès and G. Duby and translated by Arthur Goldhammer. Cambridge, Mass.: Harvard University Press.

Petit, Jacques-Guy. 1990. *Ces peines obscures: La prison pénale en France, 1780-1875*. Paris: Fayard.

———. ed. 1991. *Histoire des galères, bagnes, et prisons, XIIIe-XXe siècles: Introduction à l'histoire pénale de la France*. Paris: Privat.

Pevsner, Nicolas. 1976. *A History of Building Types*. Bollingen Series XXXV 19. Princeton, N.J.: Princeton University Press.

Rabinow, Paul. 1989. *French Modern: Norms and Forms of the Social Environment*. Cambridge, Mass.: MIT Press.

Rothman, David J. 1971. *The Discovery of the Asylum: Social Order and Disorder in the New Republic*. Boston, Mass.: Little, Brown.

Rykwert, Joseph. 1982. The Ecole des Beaux-Arts and the classical tradition. In *The Beaux-Arts and Nineteenth-Century French Architecture*, ed. R. Middleton, 8–17. Cambridge, Mass.: MIT Press.

Smith, Bonnie G. 1981. *Ladies of the Leisure Class*. Princeton, N.J.: Princeton University Press.

Szambien, Werner. 1982. Durand and the continuity of tradition. In *The Beaux-Arts and Nineteenth-Century French Architecture*, ed. Robin Middleton, 18–33. Cambridge, Mass.: MIT Press.

Tafuri, Manfredo. 1976. *Architecture and Utopia: Design and Capitalist Development*. Translated by B. Luigia La Penta. Cambridge, Mass.: MIT Press.

Teyssot, Georges. n.d. La ville-équipement: la production architecturale des bâtiments civils, 1795–1848. *Architecture Mouvement Continuité* 45: 87–92.

———. 1988. Type, program and regularity: the diffusion of architectural principles in the Conseil des Bâtiments Civils. *Canon: Princeton Journal Thematic Studies in Architecture* 3: 119–37.

Vanderburgh, David. 1993. Cultures of public architecture in nineteenth-century France: Re-forming the provincial prison. Ph.D. dissertation, University of California, Berkeley.

Van Zanten, David. 1987. *Designing Paris: The Architecture of Duban, Labrouste, Duc, and Vaudoyer*. Cambridge, Mass.: MIT Press.

———. 1989. Nineteenth-century French government architectural services and the design of the monuments of Paris. *Art Journal* 48 (1): 16–22.

Vidler, Anthony. 1987. *The Writing of the Walls: Architectural Theory in the Late Enlightenment*. Princeton, N.J.: Princeton Architectural Press.

Chapter 18

Just Not My Type:
Gender, Convention, and the Uses of Uncertainty

Alice T. Friedman

Much has been written in recent years about the concept of type in architecture. Beginning with the rather specialized critical and historical investigations of the 1970s[1] the debate has, appropriately, expanded to include an assessment of the meaning and relevance of typology in architectural design as it is generally taught and practiced in the United States and Europe. The recent publication of a new study of the work of Quatremère de Quincy (Lavin 1992) as well as a substantial collection of essays on the theory of type (Rockcastle 1991) testify to the high level of interest in the ongoing discussion and investigation.

Notions of type as symbol, as linguistic category, or as cultural and social convention have all received considerable critical and scholarly attention. Yet it should come as no surprise to observers of the architectural subculture that the role played by gender in the formation and experience of architectural types has hardly been mentioned. In part this may be seen as the result of resistance to concerns of "outsiders" by the members of a close-knit and hierarchical community, but, more problematically, it seems to be also a function of the narrow and abstract terms around which the debate has been structured. More concerned with form than with function or experience, and with heroic creativity over political effect, most writers have focused on the understanding of type in the profession and the schools rather than on the meaning and experience of architecture for those outside of this hermetic world.

The goals of this essay, then, are twofold: to introduce gender as a term in the discourse on the theory of type, and to expand the scope of the discussion to include both plan and program, moving the

FD: *I agree with your observation that "form" has taken precedence over function or experience in studies of type. My own research of American bungalows suggests that the history of change in style and aspects of form shows a relatively fickle attitude on the part of the American homeowner – that is, in the last 100 years rapid change is evident. At the same time, relatively slow adjustment in the plan of houses, or the juxtapositions of rooms, suggests that function may have some deeper significance than form. Perhaps the way we move through space and relate spaces to each other possess a different set of values? Meanings? The question remains as to what degree this paradox of change is controlled by clients, builders (I am referring to builder houses, not designer houses), society, or culture.*

debate away from its exclusive focus on form and linguistic symbolism to examine some aspects of the social relations of architecture. The first two parts of this essay focus on a historical overview of architectural education and design theory, while the last section concentrates on two significant building projects built for women clients. These case histories suggest some of the ways in which type forms, conventions of social practice, cultural values, and especially gender, structure all aspects of architectural design.

□ □ □

Two realms of experience, individual and cultural, are brought to bear on the interpretation of architectural form. Shared memories within a particular culture and the repetition of familiar images and sensations produce the matrix of conventional norms (social, spatial, and visual) against which individual ideas are measured and given meaning (Ladd 1977; Rossi 1982). The strategies of representation, effortlessly transparent in their cultural protective coloration, depend on this process and on the notion that what we share with those in power, at the level of intuition, is fundamental and natural. Yet the meaning of a specific image for an individual seems to result from how it is plotted on a series of *overlapping* memory grids configured by culture, ideology, and personal experience: individual attributes of gender, class, race, and ethnicity refract and redefine images to create the broad spectrum of different meanings produced by any single event or image. The contradiction produced by the simultaneous existence of an ideal or authorized reading of an image and the changing, particularized, and localized meanings produced by individual experience obviously undermines any claim to universality, and yet this is precisely the starting point from which the discussion of types begins. In the history of western architecture, it has been the job of the professional, the educator, and the critic to narrow the conceptual gap produced by this contradiction; that is, through the power of professional authority (and the reinforcing ubiquity of approved forms) to erode the authenticity of the personal and shore up the dominant culture's claims of universality and "naturalness," replacing individuality with community and ambiguity with certainty.

Although social conventions (notably gender relations) and artistic or typological conventions are arbitrary, specific, and value laden, they are often made to appear natural, neutral, and universal. The ideological structures that produce them also "feel" natural because they have been approved and internalized to such

FD: *You believe that power, status, and controlling worldviews are at the heart of the establishment of type. I feel that there is something yet to be argued concerning universality. Communication between humans, although sometimes feeble, requires more than convention. Communication requires that we have some basic experiences in common. The interpretation of meaning may be a point of departure, but the fact that we can argue and debate our views implies sharing, exchanging, intercourse. I do not yet want to give up the correlation between individuality and communion.*

1. The exhibition on "The Architecture of the Ecole des Beaux-Arts," presented in 1975 at the Museum of Modern Art in New York, served as a catalyst for the inquiry into type.

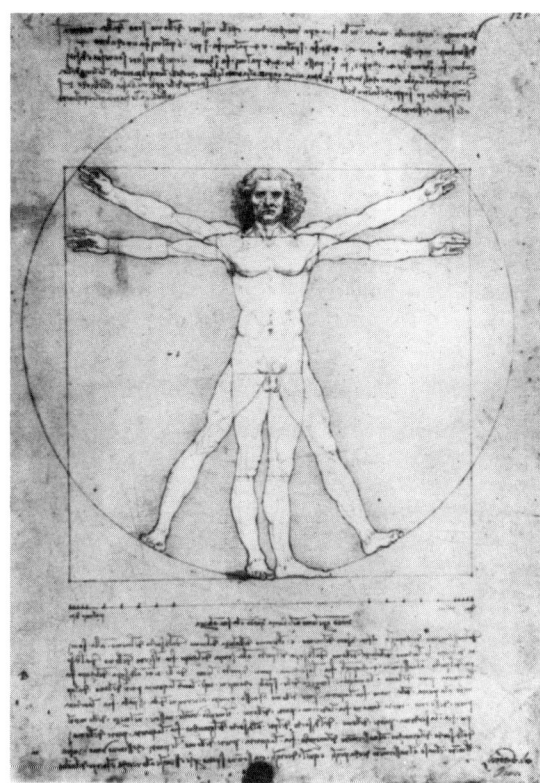

18-1
Vitruvian Man, drawing by Leonardo da Vinci (Venice, Galleria dell'Accademia; photo courtesy of the Harvard University Library)

Convention and imitation are the mainstays of professional education. According to the academic approach to design (Drexler 1977; Egbert 1980), approved models are available to the student through the study of architectural history, and the principles of design are learned through memorization of visual images and absorption of rules derived from universally accepted precedents. As explained by L.-P. Baltard, Professor of Theory at the Ecole des Beaux-Arts in 1839, this was accomplished through "frequent consultation" with a corpus of types drawn from ancient and Renaissance sources, i.e., through study of such masterworks as the Pantheon, the Colosseum, and the Palazzo Farnese. For Baltard and his colleagues at the Ecole, imitation of these "generally accepted" models was the only way to achieve design of quality. As Baltard wrote: "In architecture, there is no innovation possible... the work of genius consists of making choices and of the satisfactory application of generally accepted architectural elements" (Baltard 1839, 10–11). This position proved remarkably durable despite contemporary social and political upheaval because it conjured up such a powerful and reassuring image of consensus and stability. One might argue over the choice of examples – indeed, the very institutions that architecture was called upon to serve might change completely – but classicism continued to be viewed as a system that made sense.

Confidence in the revealed laws of Nature, and in the universality of these laws, was the foundation on which academic theory ultimately lay. The Platonic ideal, given an architectural application by Vitruvius's description of the perfect coherence of human (i.e., European male) form and geometric form, structured academic classicist discourse around notions of universality, coherence, and order from the Renaissance onward. Yet Nature validated the forms and rules of classicism in other ways as well. For example Abbé Laugier, in his *Essai sur l'architecture* (1753), described how people's first attempts to provide themselves with shelter produced a rational and simple solution – the primitive hut consisting of four tree-columns and a pitched roof of tree branches – and claimed that this simple form provided the type for all architectural design:

> Such is the course of simple nature; by imitating the natural process, art was born. All the splendors of architecture ever conceived have been modeled on the little rustic hut I have just described. It is by approaching the simplicity of this first model that fundamental mistakes are avoided and true perfection is achieved (Laugier [1753] 1977, 12).

a degree that they are experienced intuitively. The language of architectural form not only derives meaning through such an interpretive process, but, since the architectural profession, like all sanctioned institutions, serves those in power, architecture has been and continues to be an effective ideological tool. Nevertheless, to suggest that we can or should dispense with type and design completely new forms misses the point. Since our experience of form and space has been structured by type (as historical precedent and as cultural convention), the most radical gestures will surely grow out of an understanding and awareness of it rather than utopian (and individualistic) efforts to transcend or reject it.

In Laugier's view, then, Beauty consisted in the elegant simplicity and the economy of means by which structural problems were solved (Rykwert 1972, 44). Laugier's formulation gained wide acceptance, like the Vitruvian concepts of symmetry and proportion based on the idealized image of Man inscribed within a circle and a square, because of its apparent rationality and intuitively accessible naturalism.

It is significant that the emphasis on function that underlay Laugier's discussion of the primitive hut as a type form did not extend to his treatment of the plan. On the contrary, Laugier remained committed to the idealist principles of symmetry and geometry in architectural design, and he thus insisted that the type forms of the plan were to be found in the storehouse of regular geometric figures. "Forms are determined by plans," he declared (sounding curiously like a Bauhaus-inspired modernist), insisting that "the only way to make forms look pleasing is to avoid ordinary and hackneyed plans"; thus he advised his readers "to take advantage of regular geometrical figures, from the circle to the most elongated ellipse, from the triangle to the many-sided polygon" (Laugier [1753] 1977, 65). Symmetry was an absolute requirement, a far more powerful factor in design than anything having to do with function or circumstance. When Laugier takes up the issue of "convenience" at some length, he includes the following discussion of the entrance to the *corps de logis*:

> Many people no longer want it [the entrance]... to be in the center because they say it means giving up the best room in the house in order to turn it into a vestibule which is after all only a place to pass through. Therefore, they decide to move the entrance into one of the corners or to one of the wings. This idea has always shocked me. It results in a great inconvenience; a stranger, entering the courtyard, is obliged to ask for the entrance to the house. Once the doorway has been placed in a corner it becomes necessary for the sake of symmetry to simulate an identical one at the opposite corner (Laugier [1753] 1977, 85).

Obviously there is no question of thwarting the rules of symmetry for functional convenience. This example suggests that Laugier's contribution to the discussion of type is more complex than it at first appears: while the primitive hut, representing the pragmatic lessons of Nature and history, furnished the model for the treatment of structure, the type forms of design – both the plan and the resulting massing of a building – were to be drawn from a limited selection of geometric figures yielded up by the idealized Nature of the classical tradition.

JLM: *"Proportion" is also a source for gender bias, if the proportional system is derived from the body of "man." (Although I disagree with her interpretation of the use of the term "man" in the past, see Diana I. Agrest 1988, "Architecture from without: body, logic and sex," in* Assemblage *7: 29–41). It is also a scopic characterization that is body-biased: for those who do* not *identify with, find comfort or fulfillment in, their body or their relationship to it, systems of proportion will not register or achieve the ends toward which such aesthetic convictions aim.*

18-2
The Primitive Hut
(source: Marc-Antoine Laugier,
Essai sur l'architecture, Paris;
photo courtesy of the
Harvard University Library)

Such notions were barely disturbed by the French Revolution or by the political and cultural upheavals of the nineteenth century. Even the Romantics, who claimed to reject the corpus of self-authenticating theory, conceived of architectural invention in terms of originary principles. And, like the Modernists after them, they relied heavily on their own experiences and intuitions – as men and as members of the educated middle class – to reveal the meaning of form. According to A.-L.-T. Vaudoyer, an architect and teacher whose *atelier* produced some of the foremost architects of the nineteenth century (including his son Leon Vaudoyer and Henri Labrouste), the expression of character in architecture was achieved through the study of Nature and its effects on human emotions. Following Boullée, Vaudoyer wrote that the creation of this abstract architectural language was the true Art of architecture; the "science of architecture" was something far more mundane, having to do with recording and responding to the utilitarian demands of function, local customs, and materials. Thus Vaudoyer's *Dissertation sur l'architecture* (1832) described invention as the art of expressing sensations inspired by Nature through imitation of effects rather than through replication of types. This process was one of abstraction rather than mimesis; it was not a matter of mere manipulation of architectural conventions but of learning the universal language by which Nature itself achieved expression (Friedman 1985).

Rejecting the conservative notion of typological imitation put forward by contemporary Beaux-Arts theorists like Baltard and Quatremère de Quincy (Vidler 1977), Vaudoyer instructed his readers to stop studying their pattern books and to delve "into the hearts of men and observe the effects of different places and conditions on their spirits" (Friedman 1985, 116–19). Thus, according to Vaudoyer, when the architect is called upon to invent, he immerses himself in his subject, studies its properties, and chooses a mode, embarking on an imaginary journey of discovery in his own imagination:

> Then his spirit takes fire and he is transported into a domain of elevated and vivid illusions. His heated imagination produces in him a kind of delirium, or better, an ecstasy; he penetrates new and unknown places, he passes through magnificent palaces, enchanted gardens, cool and mysterious grottoes, and like a second Poliphilus, he experiences successively diverse sensations as if in a dream. Here a rich and imposing architecture causes him to recognize a Temple of Deity; further on, there is a majestic building, but much simpler, severe in character, open and easy of access – here he discovers the seat of Justice (Vaudoyer 1832, 19).

For Vaudoyer the types of architecture could only be learned from direct observation of Nature's own moods and from the experience of a wide range of architectural traditions. As he confronted each new sight, the architect would look upon his own moods as a guide for interpreting the effects of various formal languages. The assumption for him, as for his teachers, was that his own intuition was the way to gain access to what was natural and universal. Thus he stopped short of rejecting the classical style in which he had himself been schooled, claiming that "experience, taste and analytical study" showed that Greek, Roman, and Egyptian architecture were preferable to "Gothic, Chinese, Persian, Moorish, Arab, etc." (Vaudoyer 1832, 63). By relying heavily on his own thoroughly conditioned and well-educated imagination for such judgments, he not only paid tribute to his academic roots (and, of course, revealed his allegiances: he was the *secretaire*-archivist of the Ecole des Beaux-Arts for many years), but he also contributed to architectural conservatism by successfully enlisting Reason and Nature once again in the cause of classicism.

□ □ □

Reason and Nature were again called to serve by the theorists of the Modern Movement in an effort to justify the creation of an entirely different architectural vocabulary – a vocabulary which was, however, no less culturally specific and no more universal than that which it replaced.

Further, with the development of the significant social and economic agendas to which the modernists subscribed, the requirements of program in the broadest sense of the term took on a new importance for architectural design, and here too it was to the dictates of logic (the logic of social and political transformation), rather than to history or convention, that architects were told to look. Architectural design was to be created *de novo* in response to materials, technology, local conditions, and, above all, the requirements of program (Banham 1960; Herdig 1983). This approach, with its obvious currency in our own time, gives the impression of freedom from the constraints of type and from the conservatism of the schools. Yet just as modern architects underestimated the tenacity of formal typology and the resistance to change of an audience conditioned to accept its authority (a major factor in the success of conservative postmodernism and of the patronage of the political right) so too did they misjudge the powerful hold of the spatial arrangements and power relations dictated by what we might call spatial typology – i.e., the plans and patterns of living structured by gender and class relations. Far less arbitrary than conventions of form in three dimensions, conventions of planning, because of their relationship to systems of values and relationships of power, proved difficult to alter in any significant (much less architecturally meaningful) way.

Yet belief in the ability of architecture to play a significant role in engineering social change was, and remains, strong. Reflecting the optimism of the Modern Movement, the architectural historian James Ackerman suggested, under the heading of "Architecture" in the 1966 edition of the *Encyclopedia Brittanica*, that:

> the types of architecture are established not by architecture, but by society, according to the needs of its different institutions. Society sets the goals and assigns the architect the job of finding the means of achieving them (Ackerman 1966, 311).

Despite its apparent simplicity, this approach contained a contradiction that impeded genuine social and architectural change. Although it appears logical and even socially progressive to follow the dictates of utility rather than the conventions of the past, it ignores and conceals the fundamentally conventionalized nature of "program" itself, since this expresses and accommodates entrenched relations of power based on class, gender, or race. Rejecting the dictates of architectural typology is clearly quite a different project from cutting oneself adrift from the fundamental organizational models that pattern both architectural culture (education, economics, and social relations) and the dominant culture-at-large. Thus while the modernists could make significant changes in the appearance and construction of buildings (and even made genuine attempts to use architectural planning to alter patterns of living in such experiments at the housing projects of socialist Vienna), they and their patrons were continually pulled back to the familiar, to what they knew intuitively about both buildings and people.

In *The Production of Space*, Henri Lefebvre describes the difficulties encountered in the formation of a *critical* approach to spatial relations because of the tenacity of memory, the transparency of representation, and their mesmerizing effects:

> The error – or illusion – generated here consists in the fact that, when social space is placed beyond our range of vision in this way, its practical character vanishes and it is transformed in philosophical fashion into a kind of absolute. In the face of this fetishized abstraction, "users" spontaneously turn themselves, their presence, their "lived experience" and their bodies into abstractions too. Fetishized abstract space thus gives rise to two practical abstractions: "users" who cannot recognize themselves within it, and a thought which cannot conceive of adopting a critical stance towards it (Lefebvre [1974] 1991, 92).

The fact remains that the role of the architect in service of the client tends to favor conservatism. Neither the successful architect nor the wealthy and powerful client (namely, individuals whom the society has rewarded for conformity with dominant beliefs and behaviors) will be motivated to challenge the status quo in fundamental terms. In the same way, the developer/contractor and the "typical" consumer also conform with and promote these values as normative. Indeed, it is *their* values which are encoded even in the most abstract forms. As Ackerman put it in the *Encyclopaedia Brittanica*:

> Architecture is created to fulfill the specifications of an individual or group. Economic law prevents architects from emulating their fellow artists in producing works for which demand is nonexistent or only potential. So the types of architecture depend on social formations or may be classified according to the role of the patron in the community (Ackerman 1966, 311–12).

Since these "social formations" – and the resonant memories of the types that accommodate them – typically structure the professional and psychological world of the architect and the client, it is not surprising to find that their values frequently intersect. Indeed, these intersecting values *empower* them and permit them both to function as actors on the architectural stage. Yet these values are not often made explicit; on the contrary, they are blurred by notions of intuition and naturalism. Simply put, one might say that if it works (i.e., for me, for us), it must be right. This condition has obviously fostered continuity and impeded change, providing a liberal rationale for the exclusion of women and people of color from the decision-making process.

While some critics seem to have been quite skeptical of the possibility that "society" or "the architect" could ever really be free of the past, this kind of pessimism remains an unpopular position. As Alan Colquhoun (1967) pointed out in his essay "Typology and Design Method," since both the academic and the rationalist rely on memory and intuition, both are inexorably tied to the fundamental conservatism by which architecture perpetuates cultural institutions. It would be better to understand the effects of these inherited categories and try to use them

FD: *I seriously doubt that architects have as much power as you claim. Some, yes. Actually, I think modern builder/developers have more power because they rely upon traditional markets (and have not yet recognized that the "family" has metamorphosed).*

18-3
Hollyhock House, West front, Frank Lloyd Wright, Los Angeles 1919–21
(photo courtesy of the Security Pacific Photo Collection, Los Angeles Public Library)

to produce new forms and new meanings. Most theorists, however, remain confident in the ability of the profession, and of individuals within it, to create genuinely original form.

Recent discussions of type in the pages of *Oppositions* and *Assemblage* have focused on the appeal of a modified system such as that described by Adolf Loos in the 1910s: typology not as a straight jacket of rigid models but as a guide; not a "frozen mechanism" but "a frame within which change operates," as Rafael Moneo paraphrased Loos in his article on type. Among other things, this view helps provide legibility to the essentially abstract forms of modernism (Moneo 1978, 27).

Yet the conservatism of this line of inquiry becomes apparent when Loos is made the apologist for an approach in which convention appears intuitively correct because of its cultural *expediency* (utility masquerading in 1980s drag?). "The primary problem [of the architect] should be to express the three-dimensional character of architecture clearly in such a way that the inhabitants of a building should be able to live the cultural life of their generation successfully" (Anderson 1986, 15). Here again the architect appears to be merely serving his client by interpreting the "cultural life" of his generation in built form. Yet he is clearly promoting a specific system of values (which were, of course, made explicit in Loos's own writings) and an exclusive hierarchy of power relations in which he, as a professional, retains control. Social *transformation*, in which access to power, critical language, and form making would be available to others outside of the professional world, is obviously well beyond the scope of anticipated results. Rare are the theorists — and rarer still the architects or clients — who, like Henri Lefebvre, describe their "project" in terms of social change, or his goal as the creation of "a different society, a different mode of production, where social practice would be governed by different conceptual determinations" (Lefebvre [1974] 1991, 419).

□ □ □

The inhibiting effects of convention and the liberating effects of uncertainty on both social and architectural form become evident when one seeks out and examines projects in which either program or design appear to depart from the norm. In domestic architecture in particular (but in other types of buildings as well), unconventional programs seem to give rise to significant innovations in formal language: for example, Frank Lloyd Wright's Hollyhock House, built for Aline Barnsdall (1919–22) in Hollywood, California, or Mies van der Rohe's Farnsworth

House (1946–51) in Plano, Illinois. Both were commissioned by unmarried professional women who headed their own households; the original responses reveal what can result from typological uncertainty. These cases also suggest the high interpersonal price paid by both architect and client when power relations in the social and professional sphere are destabilized by unfamiliar gender relations (Smith 1978, 1992; Friedman 1992). Barnsdall and Farnsworth were both economically and socially powerful women employing successful architects, and they insisted on playing a decisive role in the development of their own projects. Yet their architects, because of their fame and power as heads of successful design firms, were accustomed to playing the dominant role with both men and women, perhaps even more than most men of their generation. Thus gender was a significant factor in structuring both the approach to type forms and the terms of interpersonal negotiation.

The complexity of these relationships, and the myriad manifestations of gender ideology in social relations and cultural production, requires us to define our terms and categories precisely. To point to the constraining effects of gendered social relations on architectural design and design typology, or, for that matter, to point to the influence of gender on architect/client relations, *does not* imply the absence of women as participants in the design process or the lack of female influence on design decisions. On the contrary, an analysis of gender in specific historical circumstances helps us to understand how relationships between men and women were (and are) understood, mediated, and structured. Ideas about gender, i.e., the constellation of attributes assigned to men and women by specific cultures, not only can be, but almost always are, equally shared by both men and women in any given society. Gender ideology, the system of values, social structures, and power relations which develop as a result of these sex-based attributes, is pervasive within cultures. Indeed, ideas about gender help to define, structure, and differentiate cultures. According to Joan Scott, writing in "Gender: A Useful Category of Historical Analysis," gender can be defined as:

> a constitutive element of social relationships based on perceived differences between the sexes, and... a primary way of signifying relationships of power (1988, 42).

Thus she suggests gender as a tool for analyzing a range of social and artistic products: "culturally available symbols," "normative concepts" based on perceived sex differences, social institutions and organizations, and subjective identity (Scott 1988, 43–44).

While it is obvious that gender is a decisive factor in the outcome of design projects in which either the client or the architect is a woman, it is no less a factor in cases in which no woman plays a prominent role. Architectural typology, as a product of culture, is constructed in gendered terms; absence (from institutional participation, from positions of power, etc.) is as significant as presence. The typology of domestic architecture – with its direct connection to the family and to reproduction – is only the most obvious instance of the overlapping significance of sexuality and gender relations; other type forms are also affected. Lefebvre underscores the particular significance of domestic space with the term "genitality":

> As a substitute for the monumentality of the ancient world, housing, under the control of a state which oversees both production and reproduction, refers us from a cosmic "naturalness" (air, water, sun, "green space"), which is at once arid and fictitious, to *genitality* – to the family, the family unit and biological reproduction... Familial space, linked to naturalness through genitality, is the guarantor of meaning as well as of social (spatial) practice (Lefebvre [1974] 1991, 232).

18-4
Hollyhock House and Olive Hill
(Photo courtesy of Security Pacific Photo Collection, Los Angeles Public Library)

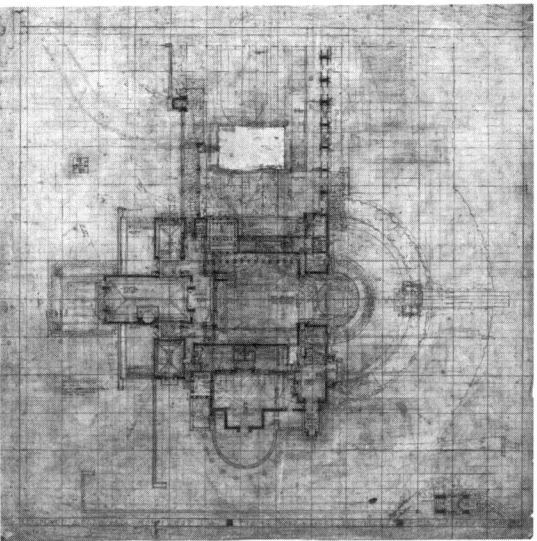

18-5
Hollyhock House. First floor plan, working drawing, 1919 (courtesy of Frank Lloyd Wright Foundation)

When the *idea* of home – that highly charged social, spatial, and ideological nexus of received opinion, individual memory, and ideology – is destabilized by the inversion or disruption of gender roles, the results are potentially revolutionary.

Confronted with the unfamiliar experience of working with a woman client, and with the unfamiliar programs which the condition of the female-headed household implied, both Wright and Mies initially seem to have seen their projects as opportunities for experiment and innovation. Wright was at a turning point in his career, and for him southern California represented a new landscape, a place in which, as his *Autobiography* made explicit, he could experiment with a new form of "organic architecture." Mies, too, had been recently transplanted to an unfamiliar place and culture, the midwest of the 1930s and 1940s, a very different world from that of his European past. More important, without the constraints imposed by conventions of architect/client relations – typically a dialogue between men with a "counterpoint" provided by the wife, mother, or lover of the client – both architects felt free to approach the problem of the house in a new way. Wright, for example, described the Barnsdall project in his *Autobiography* as a "Romanza," comparing it to a musical composition in which the composer is not constrained by the rules, but is free to follow his imagination.

Further, for both men, the design process seems to have involved psychological, and to some extent real, projection of themselves into the role left vacant by the absent husband. In a double sense, these houses were *their* houses – they were both the creators of them and in some respects their owners. Since no man would live in them, the houses could be seen as purely architectural exercises, serving the artistic and imaginary needs of their designers. An extreme case of this phenomenon is, of course, Adolf Loos's house for Josephine Baker, an unbuilt project representing the architect's fantasy of glamour and pleasure in which he would be free to watch Baker uninhibitedly, to see her not only in his mind's eye as the inhabitant of a house that *he* designed for her, but also as he projected himself into the scenario together with other male visitors – to watch her sleeping, eating, and swimming in an indoor pool, complete with porthole-shaped peepholes (Colomina 1992). Here power relations based on professional expertise and gender were further complicated by racial difference. In light of the phenomenon of projection, it is not surprising that Loos's building was to be boldly striped in black and white, an image not only of bold ornamental "primitivism," but an emblem of the union of the white European architect and the African-American woman whom he imagined as the occupant of the house.

Wright and Mies both employed the imagery of marriage in describing these projects, using words suggestive of partnership and referring to the buildings as offspring. While both Barnsdall and Farnsworth readily accepted the role of patron and cultural innovator, and both saw themselves as participating in the birth of a new form of architecture in America, Farnsworth seems to have been more willing to accept the maternal and accessory position in relation to the architect's patriarchal stance. As Farnsworth wrote in her memoirs, describing her visit to the Museum of Modern Art exhibition in which a model of her house was exhibited: "I was happy as I boarded the train back to Chicago reflecting that our project might well become the prototype of new and important elements in American architecture" (Farnsworth II, Chapter 11). Farnsworth's close personal relationship with Mies and her place in the office "family" gave her a special role in bringing this new prototype to life. Her status as a successful Chicago doctor enhanced her ability to formulate this identity, i.e., by preparing her to assume the traditionally male role of patron. But, as a woman, she was also drawn to, and encouraged to assume, the role of mother and muse.

In both cases, program, more than personality, represented a significant break from convention. Barnsdall's home was to be the center of an extensive theatrical community on Olive Hill, a vast tract of land – an entire city block – in the heart of Hollywood (Smith 1992). The house itself was intended to accommodate the domestic needs of the client, her daughter, and their guests, and to provide significant outdoor terraces and gardens (including an outdoor theater) for use by both family and visitors. Wright's thinking thus had to extend well beyond the patterns established in his experience as an architect of houses, drawing on various earlier projects for other building types, including the Imperial Hotel and the Midway Gardens.

Farnsworth's program called simply for a weekend house in the country for one person; she seems to have suggested little else to her architect (Schultze 1986). This was a rare opportunity for Mies, an architect whose unbuilt projects included a number of radically innovative glass houses (e.g., the Hubbe House of 1935) which appeared virtually uninhabitable in the real world, while his executed commissions (the Tungendhat House of 1928–30, for example) appear tame by comparison. In a sense, Farnsworth's needs seemed so simple and so vague that hers was a house without a program, a perfect vehicle for the sort of open planning and "universal space" with which Mies was experimenting.

Both projects resulted in buildings of major importance in the history of architecture. Both represent a major turning point not only in the careers of their architects but in the course of twentieth-century architecture. Yet it is also significant that in both cases the architects and their clients were unable to sustain their personal relationships or the client's confidence in the project. At the end, heated arguments and bitter recriminations erupted over varying interpretations of form, both social and architectural, and both ultimately resulted in court cases. The problem was both interpersonal and professional, and, indeed, the two were in both cases hopelessly intertwined. Barnsdall felt that Wright gave too little attention to her project and too little respect to her ideas, blaming his failure in both areas on the fact that she was a woman. An ardent feminist, Barnsdall refused to play the role of wife or muse, instead confronting the architect with sharp criticisms when his behavior or his designs seemed lacking. Wright responded to this with anger, hurt, and recrimination, and ultimately, to his credit, with respect. The two remained lifelong friends.

Barnsdall's house proved unsatisfactory to her as well. Originally conceived in response to an unconventional program, it was nevertheless formal and monumental in a way she found intimidating. While she had originally intended the house to serve as her own semipublic residence at the center of an extended theatrical community, she was nonetheless disappointed to find that it lacked privacy and warmth. She "never felt at home there," perhaps because, as a home, it conformed to none of the Arts and Crafts Movement ideas of domesticity with which she and her architect had grown up. Clearly then, despite its evident success as an innovative architectural statement in a new style, Hollyhock House did not fully resolve the problem of having been designed "against type," especially because this meant leaving the certainty of categories and conventions for a vast, anxiety-provoking wasteland of formal and interpersonal possibilities.

18-6
Farnsworth House, Ludwig Mies van der Rohe, Plano, Illinois, 1946–51
(photo courtesy of Mies van der Rohe Archive, the Museum of Modern Art, New York. Gift of the architect)

The problem was even more extreme in the Farnsworth House with its open spaces and walls of glass. The close personal relationship between architect and client, a connection that sustained Farnsworth's role as disciple and her faith in the experiment, dissolved sometime late in 1950, about the time that Farnsworth moved into her new home. Cost overruns and structural problems can only have contributed to the breakdown of communication between the two. Suddenly, what had seemed to be a partnership bound by a shared commitment to confront convention and lead the world to a new architectural level appeared to be a cruel hoax perpetrated on an unsuspecting "woman alone" by a smooth operator who used his professional power and foreign background to dupe his client. As Farnsworth wrote: "Perhaps it was never a friend and collaborator that he wanted but a dupe and a victim" (Farnsworth II, Chapter 12). Their personal relationship fell apart just as the architect, his project completed, was poised to move on.

Farnsworth's complaints about the house, while magnified perhaps by her sense of pain and abandonment, were nonetheless real. Ultimately she focused on issues of privacy and domesticity, precisely those aspects of Mies's architecture in which her experience as a woman and nonprofessional was entirely removed from Mies as architect and theorist. In her memoirs, she describes her disappointment and perplexity about the interior arrangement. There was a "guest bathroom" (back-to-back with the "private bathroom") but no bedroom. "We would co-habit a sort of three-dimensional sketch, I in my 'sleeping space' and he in his – unless sheer discomfort and depression would drive us together" (Farnsworth, III, Chapter 13). This would suggest that, ultimately, it was Farnsworth who lacked the courage to break with the typology of the conventional home, i.e., to live with the reality of the new program which she had defined. But I believe it was Mies's failure to respond fully to this program that destroyed the project in the client's eyes. Seizing the opportunity to exercise his power as a man and as an architect/artist, Mies psychologically and formally obliterated both client and program at one stroke, retreating to the fantasy world of heroic architecture, a Laugier-inspired primitive hut of pure form devoid of content and client. It is hardly surprising that the breakdown of the architect/client relationship, and of the client's relationship to the house, was articulated in terms of the client's body: her sexuality (or lack of it), her need for privacy (or lack of it), her individual proportions (or lack of conformity with the universal), and her personal history (or lack of ability to participate in the timelessness of the artistic product).

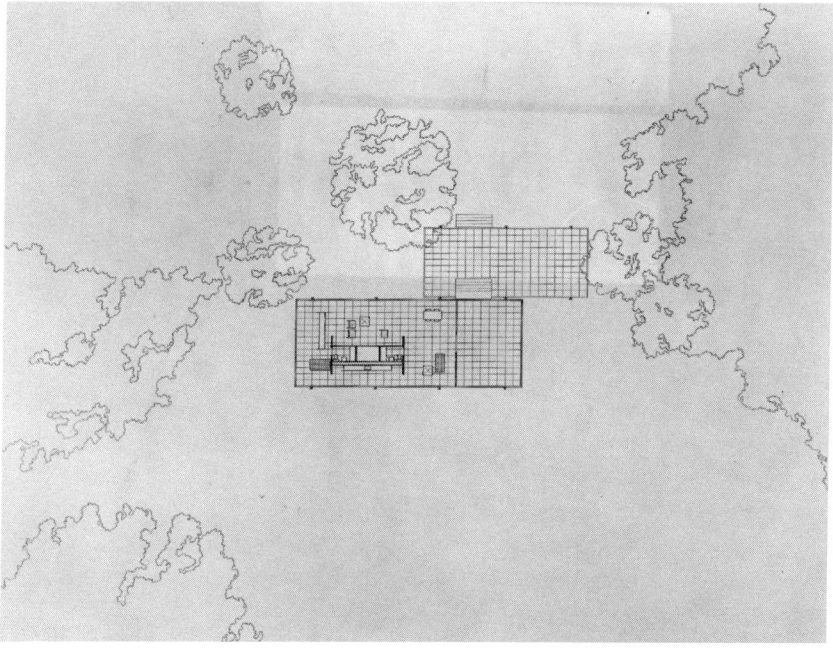

18-7
Farnsworth House plan
(courtesy of Mies van der Rohe Archive, the Museum of Modern Art, New York. Gift of the architect)

Though a radical in architectural language, Mies remained a typological ultraconservative, using built form to approximate a mental image of static, unchanging, and ideally uninhabited architecture. Farnsworth, on the other hand, moved in the opposite direction, seeking out a sense of place and an image of homey domesticity in which her femaleness – her conformity with "appropriate" gender roles – would be celebrated. Alone in her house at Plano, she even went so far as to replace Mies's furniture with her own family antiques, placing a pair of stone lions on the terrace by the door.

Mies's notions of intrinsic order (Neumeyer 1991), his references to Laugier's archetypal hut and to the classical system of proportions and geometries were, by this point, completely lost on Farnsworth. While Mies gazed coolly at a perfect form in glass and steel, his client was complaining of being the object of the gaze of passersby and neighbors. Airing her complaints in an article in *House Beautiful*, Farnsworth poignantly made clear the chasm that separated her experience from that of her architect:

> Do I feel "implacable calm"? she repeated. The truth is that in this house with its four walls of glass I feel like a prowling animal, always on the alert. I am always restless. Even in the evening. I feel like a sentinel on guard day and night. I can rarely stretch out and relax (Barry 1953, 266).

For Farnsworth, now an outsider, the promised freedom gained from confronting tradition and type in architecture had evaporated into thin air, leaving her with a very expensive, transparent house which she no longer saw as Architecture but simply as a very poor excuse for a home.

These examples expose the very real problems inherent in attempts to confront convention, not simply in formal or programmatic terms, but in architect-client relations and issues of professional authority. When gender relations are destabilized in either area, old patterns of thinking and interacting no longer apply, yet they are forced into high relief. The absence of the familiar engenders conflict, tension, and suspicion. Nevertheless, originality, albeit at a high price, is often the result.

If received tradition and convention inhibit formal innovation, perhaps we should look for the most creative alternatives at the very margins of social and architectural practice, i.e., not within the professional world but well outside of it. What lessons can be learned from the interventions made to conventional spaces – workplaces, apartments, houses – by those men and women for whom these conventionalized building types afford little usable space? For example, newly built "developer" houses intended for the typical buyer, with "master bedrooms," "dens," and three-car garages, obviously have little relevance to the lives of divorced mothers and children, to gay couples (with or without children), or to older men and women who have taken in boarders to pay the rent. Indeed, they solve few problems for the household in which two (or more) adults work both outside the home and at in-home offices as well. What sorts of changes are being made to these buildings to make them more habitable?

18-8
Farnsworth House under construction
(photo courtesy of Mies van der Rohe Archive, the Museum of Modern Art, New York. Gift of the architect)

If we are to thoroughly investigate the interrelationship between convention and originality, we should be looking at those places where real changes are being made to accommodate diverse experiences and lifestyles. Further, as a number of successful new living arrangements are proposed and tried – cohousing, congregate housing for single parents and the elderly, single-room occupancy hotels – a number of significant modifications to notions of type can be made. Looking at the successes and failures of these in conjunction with the grass-roots architectural design undertaken by residents will no doubt provide significant information to those architects and planners attempting to broaden their own ideas about the types of house and home (Franck and Ahrentzen 1991; Weisman 1992).

On the front line of architecture, where convention, memory, and lived experience are in daily confrontation, new types are being generated, new relationships are being formed. It is here, in the realm of the uncertain and unexpected, that we should look for the tools of social and architectural transformation, not to be free of the past, or of the conventions of culture, but to understand them better and make them work for us.

LS: *The fascinating question you frame is what happens when cultural expectations/conventions are violated as in the case of these two modern examples… an uncommon "family" requesting an atypical house. How far can architecture go in these circumstances? You demonstrate that from a formal perspective, the architectural response can transform the "cultural expectations" of what it will "look like." Uncertainty does change program and form. But a new form doesn't challenge the context of design – the relationship between client and architect. The gender power relationships were not contested… a dislocation in one aspect of the architectural domain, formal type, doesn't confront other conventions which maintain their conservative power. Must we step outside of the usual professional framework, to both understand how these types and conventions work, and to make them work for us? This question must be taken seriously by architects.*

References

Ackerman, James S. 1966. Architecture. *Encyclopaedia Britannica* 14th ed., Chicago: Encyclopaedia Britannica, 310–12.

Anderson, Stanford. 1986. Critical conventionism in architecture. *Assemblage* 1: 7–23.

Baltard, Louis-Pierre. 1839. *Introduction au cours d'architecture*. Paris.

Banham, Reyner. 1960. *Theory and Design in the First Machine Age*. New York: Praeger.

Barry, Joseph A. 1953. Report on the American battle between good and bad modern houses. *House Beautiful* 95 (May): 172–3; 266-73.

Colomina, Beatriz. 1992. The split wall: domestic voyeurism. In *Sexuality and Space*, ed. B. Colomina, 73–130. New York: Princeton Architectural Press.

Colquhoun, Alan. [1967] 1981. Typology and design method. In *Essays in Architectural Criticism: Modern Architecture and Historical Change*, 43–50. Cambridge, Mass.: MIT Press.

Drexler, Arthur, ed. 1977. *The Architecture of the Ecole des Beaux-Arts*. Cambridge, Mass.: MIT Press.

Egbert, Donald D. 1980. *The Beaux-Arts Tradition in French Architecture*. Edited by D.V. Zanten. Princeton, N.J.: Princeton University Press.

Farnsworth, Edith. *Memoirs*. Unpublished Manuscript, 3 vols., Newberry Library Archives.

Franck, Karen A. and Sherry Ahrentzen, eds. 1991. *New Households, New Housing*, New York: Van Nostrand Reinhold.

Friedman, Alice T. 1985. Academic Theory and A.-L.-T. Vaudoyer's *Dissertation sur l'architecture*. *The Art Bulletin* 67 (1): 110–22.

———. 1992. A house is not a home: Hollyhock House as "art-theatre garden." *Journal of the Society of Architectural Historians* 60 (3): 239–60.

Herdig, Klaus. 1983. *The Decorated Diagram: Harvard Architecture and the Failure of the Bauhaus Legacy*. Cambridge, Mass.: MIT Press.

Ladd, Florence. 1977. Residential history: you can go home again. *Landscape* 21 (2): 15–20.

Lavin, Sylvia. 1992. *Quatremère de Quincy and the Invention of a Modern Language of Architecture*. Cambridge, Mass.: MIT Press.

Laugier, Marc-Antoine. [1753] 1977. *An Essay on Architecture*. Translated with an introduction by Wolfgang and Anni Hermann. Los Angeles: Hennessey and Ingalls.

Lefebvre, Henri. [1974] 1991. *The Production of Space*. Translated by D. Nicholson-Smith. Oxford: Blackwell.

Moneo, Rafael. 1978. On typlogy. *Oppositions* 13: 22–45.

Neumeyer, Fritz. 1991. *The Artless Word: Mies van der Rohe on the Building Art*. Cambridge, Mass.: MIT Press.

Rockcastle, Garth, ed. 1991. *Type and the (Im)Possibilities of Convention*. New York: Princeton Architectural Press.

Rossi, Aldo. 1982. The structure of urban artifacts. In *The Architecture of the City*. Translated by D. Ghirardo and J. Ockman. Cambridge, Mass.: MIT Press.

Rykwert, Joseph, 1972. *On Adam's House in Paradise: The Idea of the Primitive Hut in Architectural History*. Greenwich, N.Y.: New York Graphic Society.

Schultze, Franz. 1986. *Mies van der Rohe*. Chicago: University of Chicago Press.

Scott, Joan. 1988. Gender: a useful category of historical analysis. In *Gender and the Politics of History*. New York: Columbia University Press.

Smith, Kathryn. 1978. Frank Lloyd Wright, Hollyhock House and Olive Hill, 1914–1924. *Journal of the Society of Architectural Historians* 38 (1): 15–33.

———. 1992. *Frank Lloyd Wright: Hollyhock House and Olive Hill: Buildings and Projects for Aline Barnsdall*. New York: Rizzoli.

Vaudoyer, A.-L.-T. 1832. *Dissertation sur l'architecture*. Unpublished manuscript. Royal Institute of British Architects, London.

Vidler, Anthony. 1977. The idea of type: the transformation of the academic ideal. *Oppositions* 8: 95–113.

Weisman, Leslie. 1992. *Discrimination by Design: A Feminist Critique of the Man-made Environment*. Urbana and Chicago: University of Illinois Press.

Wright, Frank Lloyd. 1943. *An Autobiography*. rev. ed. New York: Duell, Sloan and Peance.

Chapter 19

Types Are Us

Karen A. Franck

Society, with the aid of architects and many others, creates *types* of places, not just places. Clients do not simply ask for *a* building or *a* place; they ask for a particular *kind* of place, usually named, such as a "school," a "park," or a "memorial." Many additional types frame subsequent choices during design and construction: an elementary school, a courtyard plan, brick construction, and categories from the zoning ordinance and building code. The types that are physically created support and promote the values, social relationships, and patterns of activities that are dominant in that society at that time. It is through the development, repetition, and modification of types that "physical and spatial forms... constitute as well as represent social and cultural existence" (King 1992, 130).

Types are *categories of places* that we group together because the places are alike in some way, and types are *specific places* that we treat as members of categories. Types organize our thinking, communicating, and acting in all domains of life. Without repeated, recognizable kinds of places, no coordination or predictability of actions and meanings would be possible. In entering and occupying a place occupants recognize, however unconsciously, what type of place they are in and act according to the customary pattern of uses and relationships associated with that type in that society. What we do in a church differs from what we do in a school or a library. In this sense, we occupy and experience the place through the type to which it belongs. Particular attributes of the type, such as its plan, guide our activities and relationships; other attributes may impart particular meanings.

RL: *But we experience and occupy the place through type only if the type is known. (If I enter a mosque, I do not know the customary behavioral rules.)*
KAF: *If you are not a Moslem, you may not know the specific movements, dress, prayers, and so on. But you may very well know that a mosque is a place of worship and that you should be quiet, behave respectfully, and so forth. Even if you do not know the type called mosque, in observing its form and the ongoing activities, you may well deduce that it is a place of worship. We refer to whatever understanding we have of place types to make sense of our surroundings.*

Types are conceptual categories that we use to order places mentally in daily life, design, research, and regulation, and they are the material places that we physically create, observe, and experience in the world. These two ways of considering type may not always overlap; there are ways of classifying that include categories of places that do not exist in the material world, and there are probably types of places that exist but have not been named or represented as categories.

Like spiderwebs, types are created *and* inhabited. As our designed and named habitats, they are both outside of us — as products — and extensions of us. The web — either the individual place or the type of place — is both the product of human intention and action and the necessary support for human intention and action. We spin the webs from ourselves: the types that a society creates further that society's dominant purposes and values. Understandably then, as the purposes, values, and patterns of activities and relationships change, so do types. Similarly, if we wish to alter the dominant values and patterns, we need to change the types.

Since types are so much a part of daily life, we take them for granted and fail to recognize their many interrelated attributes, the power they have, or the questionable purposes and values they may serve. This chapter seeks to make types visible and problematic. The first section describes types as mutable webs composed of form, use, and meaning attributes. The second section critiques current types in light of the purposes they are designed to serve and presents changes in types that address new or modified purposes. The last section reviews emerging cultural shifts that challenge current types and warrant new orientations for planning, designing, and studying them.

There are many different ways of defining types. This chapter focuses on both material places and ideas about them that connect use and meaning to form. After the first section below, I use the term *use types* to distinguish this view of type from others and to emphasize the importance of use in this approach to type.

Types as Mutable Webs

We make sense of the world in many different ways, and for different purposes as well. From the vast array of attributes of the material and other worlds, we select some attributes to connect and combine, to mold and transform, and to imbue with meanings. Typing, or the recognition and construction of similarities and differences between places, is one way we do this. Which attributes are recognized, conceived, or constructed to form a type varies tremendously; that is one of the advantages of typing. From a possibly *infinite* array of qualities one place might share with others, a *few* become the ones that characterize that type of place and distinguish it from other types. The name, image, or other representation of the type highlights those attributes and ignores other ones.

The place called "Notre Dame" possesses a multitude of properties; the type called "church" captures some of them and groups other places that have those same properties in the same category with Notre Dame. The type called "cathedral" captures other properties and forms a different, but overlapping, category; the type called "Gothic-style cathedral" captures others. As indicated by this example, type works at different levels of specificity; Gothic-style cathedral is more specific than cathedral, which is more specific than church. Each of these three types suggests attributes of form, use, and meaning that are woven together in multilayered, mutable webs. The worlds we inhabit are very dense fabrics from which we make, or recognize, webs composed of particular properties.

The concept of type as *web* calls attention to several important features of place types. It points to the importance of the interconnections between form, use, and meaning, and the mutability and differing strengths of these connections. "Web" suggests that types are human creations that are extensions of us, not independent objects. Without types of some kind we could not survive; at the same time, the particular kinds of types we create have significant implications for the kinds of lives we lead.

Linking Form, Use, and Meaning

For ease of discussion, only three kinds of attributes of place types are distinguished here, although each kind comprises a great variety of characteristics. *Form* attributes include *all* the material, spatial, structural, and geometric properties of designed places, both fixed and movable. This means all the physical interventions, both long-lasting and temporary, that have been made in the landscape to create and furnish a place either indoors or outdoors.

Use attributes comprise *all* aspects of use, including actions that are largely generic to most settings (entering, leaving, circulating) and actions that are more specific to that particular kind of place. The latter are often called "function" and usually involve the performance of specific tasks that are housed by that type.[1] Frequently, the generic activities are performed in a particular manner to carry out the functions specific to that type. In a museum, we circulate in a particular

TM: *I do not like your trilogy of form, use, and meaning. Form and use (or function) have or are given meanings; if they don't they are not worth discussing. Meaning is a meta-category, not to be equated with form and function, or any other property of buildings you could add.*
KAF: *First, I distinguish use from function and I do not like to equate them. Second, my purpose in separating meaning from form and use is precisely to show that attributes of form, use, and meaning are connected to each other and that together they form types. I do not mean to imply that they have equal status or that they are the same kinds of things. As groups of characteristics, how they are different from each other is still an open question for me.*

RL: *My reservation about the spiderweb analogy is that it is a direct transfer of a biological analogy to cultural/human artifacts. Is the spider preprogrammed? Is each web following a generic pattern? And so on. Personally I would talk about lattices, grids, or networks rather than spiderwebs, but you must decide, bearing in mind the consequences.*
KAF: *I agree that this analogy is problematic, but some of its biological connotations are intended. Grids, networks, and lattices all suggest fixed, relatively hard objects with regular features, and objects that are separate from and independent of their makers and users. I wish to suggest change, fluidity, irregular features, and close interdependencies between types and their makers/users. The dichotomy we create between nature and culture is one of the problems we need to tackle. (See Schneekloth's chapter.)*

1. The words "function" and "functional" are often used in a pejorative sense in architectural discourse in the United States. Hence, I have chosen the word "use" because it is more neutral, and because it is more inclusive, referring to human occupation — bodily movement and generic actions — and to specific tasks (or functions).

way, with particular movements and postures, in order to view the art works on display. Circulating is generic while viewing art works is an activity specific to museums (and galleries, private collections, and displays for auctions). The bundle of use attributes also includes the kinds of users, their particular roles or tasks, their relationships to each other, and the implicit and explicit rules behind the use of the type.

Meaning attributes comprise the practical and symbolic messages that are conveyed by aspects of form and use or that are more loosely associated with that type. These include the latent and manifest purposes of a designed place and the philosophy or ideology behind its construction and occupation. While many aspects of form and use are directly observable, most aspects of meaning must be inferred or interpreted. Like use and form attributes, meanings can be generic, even universal, or they can be more specific to a particular type and to a particular period and culture. Thus, any opening in a wall that accommodates the passage of a human body may be understood to be for entry or exit in any culture. Its meaning as "doorway," conveyed by its form attributes, is universal. In contrast, the door to a church will carry additional meanings beyond generic entry and exit and additional cues for how it is to be used that are understood by people in cultures that have churches.

Attributes of form, use, and meaning may be more or less loosely woven together. This variety in the connections between and among attributes is an advantage of types and typing. It is valuable for creating new exemplars of an existing type, for modifying types, for creating new types, and for occupying all types. This looseness means that when we occupy, observe, or contemplate a place, the web of attributes does not determine our actions and interpretations but rather encourages certain ones and constrains others. The type guides uses and meanings, rather than fixing them. The web is always and unavoidably loose and filled with holes; unforeseen uses and meanings can develop. The planned, the existing, or the conventional uses and meanings are only some possibilities; others develop and become associated with a place or a type.

The looseness of some connections allows new meanings and new uses to become associated with existing types without any modification of the form attributes. Alternately, some form attributes can be changed without significantly changing meanings and uses. Other changes in form attributes have a significant impact, sometimes enough to constitute a new type. We may agree easily on what the form attributes of a given place are — often we can point to them. However, there may be significant differences of opinion about the meanings or appropriate uses of a type. Meanings and uses may be highly contested before and after places are created or modified. The controversy often revolves around differing interpretations of what type the new or modified place actually is, or whether it is the appropriate type for that location. It is precisely because of the lack of one-to-one correspondence between many attributes of meaning, form, and use that such conflicts can, and do, arise.

Some of the links between form, use, and meaning are very strong and are unlikely to generate differences in interpretation. This is particularly true of generic form types. For example, even when the particular function of a form is not determined, as in the types called "doorway" and "tower," particular kinds of human habitation and circulation are implied – they are unavoidably linked to the form attributes of these types. The doorway suggests moving through or looking through. The tower suggests moving up or down, looking up, looking down, looking over the landscape, or looking toward the structure from the landscape. These are generic or universal actions and postures that are intimately and inescapably linked to generic or universal forms. Indeed, they make the forms very potent devices for designing and experiencing the built landscape.

When the tower is part of a church or a prison, the form, use, and meaning attributes of the tower, now embedded in a larger and more functionally specific type, become more delimited and more specific. When the tower is a minaret next to a mosque, or a spire of a medieval cathedral, or a lighthouse on the coast, the attributes of form, meaning, and use become even more specific. The context of the type in the material world, which often consists of larger and more inclusive place types, helps define its meanings and uses. This speaks, again, to the connectedness of types; they are composed of attributes connected to each other and to their context.

Naming, Representing, and Changing Types

The example of different towers illustrates one way that the name, visual image, or other representation of a type highlights particular form and use attributes and downplays or excludes others. The more specific the name or the image, the more specific and delimited the attributes that are implied. The type "housing" suggests a very general and inclusive set of form, use, and meaning attributes, whereas "perimeter block housing" suggests a more specific set, particularly relating to form. "High-rise public housing" suggests even more specific attributes, which in the United States include form and location characteristics, kinds of uses

TM: *There is never a tower as such, even if it is by itself in a desert. It is always in context.*
KAF: *Granted, in the material world the tower is always in a physical context. In our imaginations, in other forms of representation such as poetry or drawing, the physical context may be highly ambiguous or not specified at all. And, in the design process, architects take form types from one context and place them in a very different one. During that process, while the architect decides whether to use the type in the new context and/or to transform it first, the form type is relatively free of context (see Downing's chapter). This fluidity and malleability of type is very important.*

2. Architects often emphasize form attributes while environmental design researchers are more likely to emphasize use attributes. Some attributes of form are necessarily embedded in the types the latter consider, although they may be very general, just as the use aspects considered by architects may be very general. It is precisely this lack of specificity about use, according to design researchers, and the lack of specificity about form attributes, according to designers, that contributes to the frustration each discipline experiences with the other. Greater specificity and thoroughness in describing or exploring the particular form, meaning, and use attributes of a given type and their links to each other would be of great benefit to both design and research. It would also be beneficial to recognize that both disciplines are concerned with form, use, and meaning, and to adopt a less oppositional approach to each other and to form or use.

TM: *"Form types" always carry meanings, as do "use types." On the other hand, "meaning types" only work because form and use carry meanings.*
KAF: *I agree and have therefore eliminated any reference to "meaning types." I also believe, as I say in the text, that form types always have some use attributes. Types, as I view them, always link at least some attributes of form, use, and meaning.*

and residents, and a specific set of meanings that are predominantly negative. Thus types in name, image, and actuality are incredibly rich in the form, use, and meaning information they convey.

Some names, images, or classifications of types refer primarily to attributes of form or use. "Perimeter block" suggests form attributes; "housing" implies the kinds of activities to be housed. Other attributes of these types, although not directly communicated by these names, are implied. "Perimeter block" is a class of places that possess a common attribute of form. Although the specific use for this type (such as housing) is not named, certain generic kinds of use, including the pattern of circulation, are implied by the form. Similarly, "housing" highlights domestic activities, and in a particular culture and period it may also suggest the manner in which these activities will be carried out and general form attributes associated with those activities.

The capacity to attend to certain attributes of types and to ignore others is extremely valuable for the design process, for studying design alternatives, and for classifying existing places. A systematic and explicitly typological method is frequently used to display the form or use differences between the exemplars of a type, as in schools (Stuebing 1992), apartment buildings (Holl 1980), or courtyard housing (Polyzoides et al. 1992). When we name or otherwise represent types in ways that emphasize either form or use attributes, it may appear as if the links between form and use have been severed; usually they have not been, and cannot be. Once we consider places for human occupation, it is very difficult to name or visually represent them in ways that do not carry some implicit information about form, use, and meaning.[2]

Names, images, or classifications of places that highlight form attributes may usefully be called *form types,* whereas those highlighting use attributes can be called *use types.* Thus perimeter block, concrete block buildings, tower, gate, field, and courtyard are form types because it is primarily attributes of form that have been used to designate them. Church, museum, park, and bedroom are use types because aspects of use more than form, particularly function or task, have been used to designate the types. Some types seem to imply both form and use equally, such as high-rise housing and basilica plan church, but for simplicity I call them use types.

The naming, and representing, of places according to use occurs in many domains – in daily life, in the design work of architects, in real estate listings, in building codes and zoning ordinances, in land use planning, and so on. The name of the type of place is extremely significant in the making, regulating, modifying, preserving, and occupying of places. In all cases, knowing the name of the place type influences, even helps determine, a wide array of subsequent actions.

Use types are invented, modified, discarded, and, sometimes, rediscovered. The form, use, and meaning attributes associated with a use type such as hospital (Forty 1980), park (Cranz 1982), restaurant (Thorne 1980), cemetery (Sloan 1991), or apartment building (Cromley 1990) emerge and change even though the name of the type remains the same. Previous use types that were once deemed socially unacceptable may be rediscovered and adapted to more contemporary circumstances and requirements, as with single-room occupancy housing in the United States (Franck 1989a). The adoption of a "new" type with its own name, such as transitional housing for single-parent families, may be explicitly encouraged, and the form, use, and meaning attributes may be described and explained to architects, policymakers, and the public in order to teach the audience what the new type is or can be. However, the new type may possess no form attributes in its outward appearance that distinguish it from existing use types; it may not *look* like a new type. Sometimes it may be beneficial if it does not.

Neither the web of attributes nor the various ways of naming types are fixed. Frequently the name as well as the meanings and uses associated with the name may be grounds for disagreement and conflict. The classification of a whole array of spaces into types, as in the zoning of neighborhoods, is similarly the object of debate and legal challenges. What the use type in question is, or should be, is not fixed any more than its form or use attributes are fixed. There is room, even much room, for further discussion, conflict, and change.

Revealing the Webs

Types are us because use types support and reinforce our patterns of activities, relationships, and beliefs. They do not simply reflect who we are as individuals, families, and society; they help make us who we are. Today however the types we occupy are not usually ones that we ourselves have built; they may not even be ones we have freely chosen to occupy or use, or ones that we would choose if there were other options. Instead, they are constructed and their proliferation ensured by dominant groups whose goals and interests we may not share. In one way or another, use types may be forced upon us either because few alternatives have been built or because we do not have access to those alternatives. They may not be the types we want or need; they may not be the types that support the activities, relationships, and values that we believe are, or could be, *us*.

If we wish to change the dominant patterns of actions and beliefs in society that are supported by current use types, we need to change the types. Many use types are repeated in highly conventional, standardized, and unexamined ways, and new use types are often adopted without critical reflection. The links between form, use, and meaning are either unrecognized or treated as unbreakable bonds, and the purposes that use types serve and the consequences they have are either invisible or taken for granted. As architects or members of allied professions, we help to make the webs and support their continuation. We have the ability and the obligation to uncover and critique the links between existing form and meaning attributes, to consider the consequences they have, and to suggest new links.

Revealing the existing webs of use, form, and meaning and proposing new ones is a sticky business since we all occupy the webs of place and type and are, in some sense, part of them. This makes it difficult for us to recognize all or even many of the attributes or to propose alternatives: we cannot see what is part of us. There are several possible approaches to this problem. Two are explored here: considering how the overall organization of the built landscape into use types has changed over time in this society, and exploring the purposes that use types serve at the present time and how they do so.

Segmentation and Standardization

One of the reasons for having any use types at all is to organize daily life by locating particular activities in particular places or kinds of places. Use types allow us to assign meanings and activities to space, to map them onto the material world. This is done by *separation* and *connection*. Some uses are physically separated by distance, by physical barriers, or by both. Some uses are connected because they occur in the same space or near each other. Not all use types possess a high degree of separation from other use types or elaborate physical interventions in the form of specialized buildings or rooms. In some cultures, the meanings and uses of different kinds of spaces are mapped onto the landscape with many overlapping categories and with minor or temporary physical markers. In other cultures, the categories are much more independent with a high degree of separation between uses housed in specialized forms. What is included and what is excluded in use types, how much overlap there is, how specialized they are, and how they are made physically manifest in the world, are all subject to wide variation and change.

The organization of the landscape into discrete, separate, and highly bounded place types devoted to single uses, which we now take for granted, began in

19-1
Photomontage, Martha Rosler, 1967

TM: *Yes, but the change is not so rapid. See massive evidence from anthropology about stability of culture – concepts, language, categories – and what happens when these connections are ruptured.*
KAF: *While the framework provided by categories and concepts as represented by their names does continue over time (man/woman, city/country, public/private), much of the content of the categories and how they are made manifest in the landscape or in our actions and expectations seem to me to change quite rapidly.*

Europe in the Renaissance. J.B. Jackson compares the character of this landscape (Landscape Two) to that of earlier times (Landscape One).

> Unlike Landscape One, which mixed all kinds of uses and spaces together, Landscape Two insists on spaces which are homogeneous and devoted to a single purpose. It makes a distinction between city and country, between forest and field, between public and private, rich and poor, work and play; it prefers the linear frontier between nations rather than the medieval patchwork of intermingled territories (Jackson 1984, 152).

During the eighteenth and nineteenth centuries, interior spaces were increasingly devoted to single uses for which they were intentionally designed: a room just for sleeping and dressing, a room just for dining, a building just for producing fabric, a preserved piece of land – a park – for strolling, and so on. This distinction and separation between uses and the physical construction of specialized types to house the uses and users have steadily increased ever since, creating a segmentation and compartmentalization of contemporary everyday life (Tuan 1982).

Today places that support different activities are often quite distant from each other. Imagine a New England farm before industrialization: a single house, outbuildings, and land were the site of most of a family's activities during a week, a year, and a lifetime, including being born, growing up, working, playing, growing old, and dying. Within the town most of life's other activities were supported. Then imagine the conventional suburban house and neighborhood, which are the ultimate examples of separation and segmentation of uses and users. Most of the activities that occurred in the New England farm now occur in many different, discrete use types, all removed from the home and neighborhood and all designed for particular uses.

We have built a landscape based on a whole series of conceptual dichotomies – public/private, old/young, built/natural, dead/alive, work/leisure, family/not-family, rich/poor. We have tried to keep the contents of these categories as separate as possible, seemingly to prevent some kind of contamination between them. These efforts and the proliferation of specialized use types dedicated to single classes of uses and users have helped create the sequestration of experience that Giddens (1991) describes as one of the features of modernity. Those who are relatively well-to-do, healthy, and able do not, for the most part, encounter or interact with those who are poor, ill, old, or frail. Because we do not encounter the problems of others we do not experience any sense of responsibility for them. Indeed, their problems may seem completely alien to us. Giddens writes that "the

19-2
Photomontage from *Bring the War Home: House Beautiful*, by Martha Rosler, 1971

sequestration of experience means that for many people direct contact with events and situations which link the individual life span to broad issues of morality and finitude are rare and fleeting" (1991, 8). In the modern era, the sequestration of experience afforded by use types has led to a moral impoverishment of daily life.

Use types also organize daily life by incorporating those form attributes that accommodate a specific *manner* of use and pattern of relationships among occupants. These attributes become common to all exemplars of that type and help define the type. Both single-family houses and army barracks are dwelling places, and both have spaces for sleeping and personal hygiene, but the attributes of these spaces — and of these types more generally — establish a very different manner of use and pattern of relationships. This makes sense because the type of occupant and their spatial practices differ significantly. A type becomes standardized when *all* the form and use attributes become the same, or nearly the same, in all exemplars of the type. The modern era has witnessed a greater and greater standardization of exemplars.

The development and elaboration of use types in Western Europe and the United States since the eighteenth century has followed the assumption that particular uses require specific form attributes. Much attention is still paid to what those form attributes should be. What is the single best form for a hospital, a prison, a house, or a park? This search for the best solution during a particular historic period encourages the adoption of a single solution which is then repeated in a standard fashion. So not only are many use types dedicated to single uses, but all exemplars of that type often possess the same form attributes, supporting the same manner of use and relationships. There is little attention paid to the possibility of multiple purposes and multiple uses within a single use type, and little attention to the possibility of diversity of form and use attributes across exemplars of that type.[3]

So, not only is the single-family home and neighborhood purged of nondomestic activities and of nonfamily households in the drive toward separation and segmentation, but many of the houses within a neighborhood possess the same attributes. Even houses in another region or country may possess the same attributes. This standardization is taken to a greater extreme in chain restaurants, airports, hotels, and stores that may look exactly the same in all parts of the world. Standardization recognizes no differences in culture, geography, climate, or the occupants' needs and desires. By eliminating architectural, cultural, and experiential diversity, standardization of use types enforces a single universal manner of use, pattern of relationships, and set of meanings and purposes. The drive toward a single, universal reality acknowledges only the needs, desires, and contributions of the dominant cultural and gender groups and neglects, or represses, those of other groups.

Purposes of Use Types

The power of use types in producing and reproducing the dominant social order lies largely in the purposes, and thereby the interests, that use types promote. By focusing on these purposes, this role of use types is revealed; the prob-

3. Although use types are often used to create standardized places and to segment and compartmentalize the built landscape, there is nothing inherent in the idea of use types, or type more generally, that requires either segmentation or standardization.

lematic character of current use types becomes much clearer, and the value of new or modified use types is illustrated. Some of the purposes of use types may be quite obvious, particularly when only one use type is studied, i.e., a prison is for removing and controlling criminals. Other purposes are implicit, if not hidden, embedded in the images and ideology of the use type. These purposes are easier to identify if we examine an entire landscape of use types and uncover the common purposes that quite disparate types are designed to serve.

Of the myriad purposes of use types, six are discussed here: (1) for removal and control; (2) for retreat or escape; (3) for protecting and honoring; (4) for producing and controlling capital; (5) for public service; and (6) for enabling and empowering. Any use type may serve more than one purpose, and exemplars of the same type may differ in the purposes they serve. The predominance of some of these purposes over others and the ways use types are designed and regulated to serve these purposes have fueled the segmentation and standardization of use types in the modern landscape.

For Removal and Control. Some use types are intended to remove, and through the attributes of the particular type, to control certain activities and people. Often the ostensible reason for this removal is the solution or amelioration of a social problem; the types become a means of social reform. Persons occupying these types are in a kind of quarantine, isolated from those who are deemed healthy; responsibility for the occupants is shouldered by the staff of those types. Many of the use types that signal the emergence of specialized building types in the modern period – schools, prisons, hospitals, and asylums – were developed because they were recognized as a tool for the control and reform of deviance. The tendency to invent or adopt a use type to address a social problem continues unabated in the present, with transitional housing for mothers with children and single-room occupancy housing for the homeless mentally ill.

Of all use types, those intended for removal and control have contributed most significantly to the modern sequestration of experience and the removal of moral dilemmas from daily life. Contamination and responsibility, literally and metaphorically, are avoided. The "problem" and any responsibility for it are removed from the daily lives and experiences of people fortunate enough not to be in these types. Those who are "here," who have not been removed, do not have to see or think about those who are "there." "There" are prisons, asylums, nursing homes, public housing projects, housing for the homeless, hospitals, hospices, and funeral homes. Again, before industrialization, a New England farm was often the site of birth, illness, death, and preparation of the dead for burial. And the household might have included orphans and indigents placed there by the state. Today, even when we are "there," as visitors or patients in a hospital, for example, we still may be sequestered from the experience of birth, illness, or death by the form attributes or spatial practices of the type.

By emphasizing control, these use types place occupants (other than staff) in a passive, if not subservient, position, denying them rights and responsibilities they would have outside these institutions. They become the objects of actions; their own subjectivity is denied. In recent years in the United States the rights of mental patients, hospital patients, prisoners, and residents of public housing have been widely discussed and some rights have been restored. Sometimes the institution has been removed altogether: for instance, large state mental hospitals were closed throughout the United States in the 1970s and 1980s on the basis of cost and changes in therapeutic philosophy. And some attention has been given to creating attributes of form and use that give residents more responsibility for their environment and their lives, for instance in public housing and in group homes for the mentally ill. However, the underlying assumption that the use type itself, even

19-3
Mixed City, Nancy Wolf, 1976 (photo by Paul Kennedy)

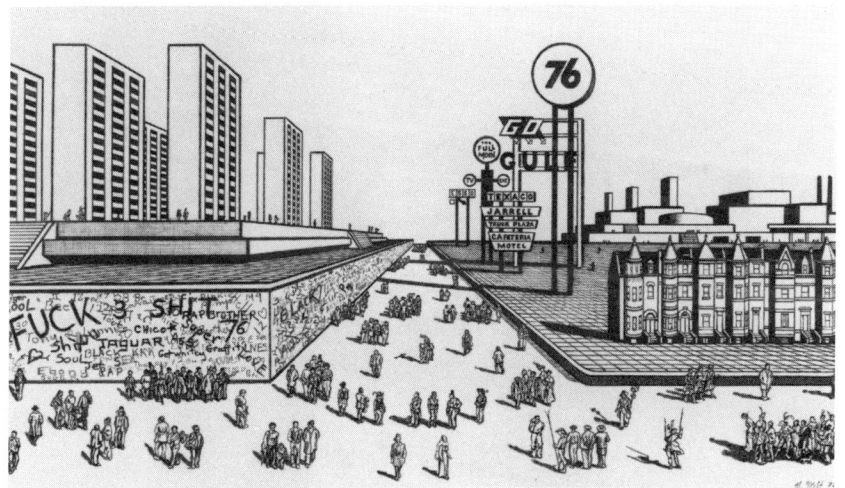

when modified, is primarily for control and removal is not sufficiently questioned, nor is the separation of that type of person from other types. The separation and segmentation continue.

Although institutions are the prime examples of use types for removal and control, this purpose operates for other types and at other scales of the environment as well, notably in zoning. In the United States, zoning ordinances often separate places of wage work and commerce from places of domestic life and divide different kinds of households from each other. In residential neighborhoods such zoning is geared to preventing a kind of contamination by certain kinds of people or activities deemed unacceptable (Perin 1977). The zoning serves two purposes simultaneously: removing some uses and users (the poor, the elderly, commerce, wage work), and creating a retreat for others (nuclear families, relatively young, able, and wealthy people, domestic life).

The more general goal of control can be detected in the design of many current use types where all manner of activity is predetermined and enforced and there is little opportunity for choice or change. Once allowed in, occupants, as in traditional prisons or hospitals, are cast in passive, subservient roles, are carefully watched, and are forced to follow certain procedures and rules. This occurs in expensive and exclusive subdivisions, in elegant office towers and shopping malls, as much as in public housing. The increasing segmentation and standardization of use types in modern times has allowed, and fueled, greater and greater control of activities and actors.

For Retreat and Escape. A second purpose of use types is to create a retreat from daily life, to offer a place that is different from the mundane, which one is not required to visit or occupy as part of daily task-oriented routines. These may be places of leisure or entertainment: parks, restaurants, cafés, theaters, nightclubs, health clubs, resorts, hotels, amusement parks, theme parks, museums, beaches, spas, golf courses, and shopping malls. Other types, such as churches or libraries, may also serve the purpose of retreat; certainly convents and monasteries do.

For many years, the urban park has been viewed as a place of retreat, a way of escaping the harsh, grim atmosphere of the workaday city. Evidence of work, production, of anything not associated with leisure of either a bucolic or athletic nature, has no place in such a retreat (Cranz 1982). Today shopping malls are designed as escapes and retreats with lush trees, fountains, music, and an atmosphere of leisure. By being completely enclosed, by forbidding activities that might be intrusive such as begging, campaigning, or proselytizing, and by maintaining high levels of security and cleanliness, the malls try to create a "better" world than the one outside (Crawford 1992). This imperative of creating architecturally uniform enclaves for leisure has been pursued in the redevelopment of urban settings as well so that entire urban neighborhoods become "variations on a theme park" (Sorkin 1992).

Like a park to live in, the American suburban community of single-family homes is also portrayed and designed as an escape – from the city, from all commerce and wage work, and from all persons who are not part of the image of retreat. The house and neighborhood are expected to form an idyllic retreat that is

19-4
Winter Garden, World Financial Center, New York City (photo by author)

not compromised or contaminated by the presence or apparent presence of work, economic interests, human hardship, or human failings. The image of the idyllic retreat requires that the domestic realm appear to be exclusively a place of leisure, even though hard work does occur there. Mixtures of different kinds of activities or people are perceived as potentially disruptive. The house and neighborhood are envisioned, designed, built, and regulated only for the times when all family members are healthy and able-bodied, for the times when they are happy and get along well with each other, and for when the household can afford to pay all housing costs from income earned elsewhere.

Residents depend on commercial and other services, but these also must be located elsewhere. A place of idyllic retreat cannot accommodate long-term illness, an extended loss of income, a possibility of earning income, or support services for other individual or family needs. People must resolve these problems or meet these needs on their own without even appearing to have them. Zoning enforces these exclusions and insures that the houses, yards, and streets will possess the form and use attributes that match the image of retreat.

Recent modifications to the ideal of the single-family house and community alter the preoccupation with retreat and escape by accommodating nondomestic activities, services, or wage work in the dwelling or the neighborhood. Service-enriched housing is being developed for single parents, for the homeless mentally ill, and for other groups with special needs (Sprague 1991; Franck forthcoming). Private houses and apartments are modified to accommodate wage work and sometimes whole developments are designed with such uses in mind (Ahrentzen 1991). At the neighborhood level there is increasing pressure for zoning that allows the incorporation of accessory apartment units and possibilities for family day care and other services in communities of single-family homes. Mixing commercial and residential uses is seen as a way to make urban neighborhoods safer and more viable (New York City Planning Commission 1993). In planning future suburban developments, Duany and Plater-Zyberk (1991, 1992), Solomon (1992), and Calthorpe (1993) all advocate versions of the American town where the feeling of retreat created by houses, trees, lawns, and parks does not require the exclusion of commercial and service uses or public transit.

Offering places for retreat is important. Problems arise when the interpretation of retreat is so closely coupled with escape and distance that they overwhelm other purposes, or when the creation of retreat for one group of people means the control and degradation of other places and other groups. The experience of retreat does not require solitude or distance from other kinds of places. Relaxation and the visual and sensual pleasure that the idea of retreat suggests could well be considered in the design of use types that currently are preoccupied with issues of efficiency, practicality, and control. Airports and contemporary train stations are prime examples. Unfortunately, when pleasure is considered an important aspect of such public places, it is translated into consumerism, as in the renovation of Pennsylvania Station in Washington, D.C. It is possible to imagine gardens, galleries, or conservatories as part of such use types, as the artist Robert Irwin did in his proposal to redesign the Miami airport (Weschler 1993). Experiencing retreat on our way someplace else, or even "at work," can transform our sharp distinctions between work and leisure, between journey and arrival.

For Protecting and Honoring. A third purpose served by use types is to protect and honor the use and users who are included or represented in the type. Examples are churches, synagogues, mosques, cemeteries, memorials, monuments, battlefields, museums, historic landmarks and districts, wilderness areas, national parks, city halls, state and national capital buildings, courthouses, and possibly libraries and universities.

By having places specifically designed for an activity such as for worship, or for memorializing an event or a person, we are giving continuing public significance to those activities, events, or persons and the meanings attached to them. J.B. Jackson sees the lack of such long-lasting markings in the landscape as a significant difference between the medieval and renaissance landscapes. In the latter, Landscape Two,

> the function of space... is to make us visible, allow us to put down roots and become members of society. Land in Landscape One meant being a member of a working community; it was a temporary symbol of relationships. In Landscape Two land means property and permanence and power (Jackson 1984, 152).

In one sense, *any* use type with form attributes protects the housed activity and its meanings. In the United States without some observable markings in the landscape in the form of buildings or other design interventions, both the activities and the place in which they occur are highly vulnerable. This is exemplified in recent court cases in which Native Americans have attempted to protect sacred sites where ritual activities occur but which are unmarked (Baum 1992). The dominant culture expects such activities and meanings to be embodied in physical design. Thus, urban parks and national parks are intended to protect the land they contain from development or other uses. The design interventions that are made in creating them help signify the kinds of activities that are to take place and the meaning the park is to have. Without such design intervention in the landscape, the dominant culture in the United States literally cannot recognize or help protect the activities and meanings parts of the landscape may have.

Ironically, a use type also can make its users and activities *less* protected since they are more clearly identifiable. Lesbian bars, while providing a place for lesbians to meet and enjoy each other's company in the hope of less interference from others, make the patrons vulnerable to attack inside or near the site even when the bars are not marked by signs or other identification (Wolfe 1992). The same is true of abortion clinics, and churches, cemeteries, or memorials associated with particular ethnic or religious groups. Urban parks and national parks, in being kept free of complete development, remain forever vulnerable to continuing pressures *for* development.

The most obvious use types for protecting and honoring are probably museums, monuments, and memorials. What or who is to be honored, and how, have become difficult questions. This was the case with the Vietnam Veterans Memorial in Washington, D.C., where the intended and appropriate meanings became the subject of intense and bitter debate. Maya Lin's design of two black granite walls carving a wide angled V in the land and listing, chronologically, the names of all who died or are missing was initially seen by critics as a place of shame and grief, not a place that expressed pride and honor, as war memorials conventionally do. To counter this criticism, a sculpture of three GIs and the American flag were added at some distance from the wall. This constellation of objects with such different meanings expresses several points of view rather than a single, overriding one.

There is increasing recognition that the monuments and memorials we have built in the United States segment and sequester, standardize and privilege as much as any other use types by recognizing the contributions only of the dominant group, usually white middle or upper class men who have performed some conventionally heroic or otherwise honorific act, sometimes at the expense and to the detriment of others. There is a growing concern that we recognize and honor the contributions and experiences of those who are not members of the dominant class and culture and who have long been excluded from recognition or denigrated. The Power of Place is a nonprofit organization that has begun to identify and celebrate places that mark the history of women, ethnic minorities, and working

19-5
Vietnam Veterans Memorial, Washington, D.C. (photo by Tony Holmes)

people (Hayden 1990). One of their projects in Los Angeles, "Biddy Mason: Time and Place," designed by Sheila de Brettville, portrays the history of an African American woman who worked as a midwife, raised a family, and started numerous community organizations. Similarly, the National Park Service is now seeking to take a less biased view of the events that occurred at Wounded Knee in North Dakota and Little Big Horn in Montana. Once called "Custer's Battlefield," the latter has been renamed "Little Bighorn National Battlefield" and a monument is to be built honoring the Native American warriors who died there.

Although it is neither a memorial nor a monument, the single-family detached house in a suburban community has been viewed, and is designed, to honor and protect. It gives protection and almost sacred significance to a single kind of household: father, mother, and their young children. Indeed, in much nineteenth-century writing about the value of a secluded domestic life for parents and their children there are numerous references to the sanctity of the home, and to its purpose as both a sanctuary and a place of retreat. If the home is to protect and honor the nuclear family, then it and its occupants must be separated from other households, from nonfamily members, and from nondomestic activities. The separation between families (or any other households) in the single-family house and community is now being questioned in the United States, particularly in the recent development of cohousing communities.

For Producing and Controlling Capital. During the same period that many of the use types for removal and reform were invented, types dedicated to producing and controlling capital were also introduced. Industrialization brought the development of indoor markets, factories, mills, mines, warehouses, railroad stations, banks, office buildings, and stock exchanges. The rise of consumerism brought department stores and subsequently shopping centers and malls. The pressure for real estate development made the grid system an easy way to divide property in New York City. Late capitalism has brought large office complexes, industrial parks, "edge cities," and large, industrialized farms.

In late capitalism, the production of capital becomes an ever more ubiquitous and powerful goal, served by an ever widening array of use types whose form attributes and manner of use are increasingly determined by that goal alone. The production and control of capital originally generated a number of use types specifically geared to that goal, particularly the production, circulation, and marketing of goods and materials. As space and place become increasingly powerful tools of consumer capitalism, this purpose infiltrates and dictates the design and use of other use types as well, modifying them to fulfill their new purpose on a very large scale. Thus large suburban subdivisions, industrial parks, and industrialized farms are developed, designed, owned, and managed by large corporations whose decisions are continuously guided, and constrained, exclusively by their profit-making imperative. In doing so, they neglect other purposes of these use types, and reject form and use attributes that are not perceived to be directly related to profit.

The imperative to produce capital has made land and buildings merely tools that have little value or importance in and of themselves; they are manipulable, disposable. The desire and the opportunities to purchase, build, destroy, convert, modify, and sell places overwhelm opportunities or desires to conserve, preserve, or cherish them. The landscape becomes not only more segmented but more temporary (Jackson 1984, 155).

Many use types for recreation and leisure have been made places of consumption as a way of producing capital. In Disney World, Club Med, Quincy Market in Boston, or South Street Seaport in New York, one purchases a prepackaged activity and experience, as well as consumer items. Retirement communities and suburban subdivisions are similarly presented: places of retreat and leisure where you purchase both a product and a predesigned lifestyle, as well as a host of consumer items to support that lifestyle. In all these cases, the place itself is a kind of product and becomes highly standardized across all locations and regions. This is most noticeable with chain restaurants and hotels, but also clearly apparent in office buildings, industrial parks, suburban subdivisions, and shopping malls.

As more and more standardized, consumerist places have been built, other kinds of leisure places, such as the corner bar or the local coffee shop, that were oriented to the customer, not the consumer, have disappeared (Oldenburg 1989). Relatedly, more and more places for recreation and leisure require a fee for entry. At Disney World, you pay a large fee simply to enter; at Coney Island entry into the amusement park was free, and one paid only for the rides. In the past, many of

19-6
Tom's Restaurant, Brooklyn (photo by Tony Holmes)

the places enjoyed for leisure, including parks, streets, and squares, were truly in the public domain, whereas today shopping malls, a prime location for leisure in suburban areas, are privately owned and managed and place restrictions on uses and users.

More attention is now being paid to the ways that economic interests mold the built landscape (Frieden and Sagalyn 1989; Davis 1991; Garreau 1991; Zukin 1991), and the extent to which corporate interests drove the architecture of the 1980s (Barna 1992; Goode 1992). However, the power that the goals of capital production and accumulation exerts over the form and use attributes of a multitude of use types is not yet sufficiently understood, much less challenged or restrained. Indeed, a developer's interest in purchasing land and developing, or redeveloping, is still too often welcomed by local authorities with few conditions or restraints imposed. The environment is fast becoming one large corporately owned landscape of guarded subdivisions, industrialized farms, "edge cities," supermalls, highways, and city fortresses with toxic waste sites, devastated neighborhoods, and deserted main streets scattered in between. Development, however, does not require the large scale, or the standardization, sanitization, and privatization of places that corporations now impose. Nor does it require that all decisions regarding form, use, and meaning be left to the developer or serve only the goal of profit. Other goals and concerns, other attributes, can also be addressed.

For Public Service. Many use types are intended to provide a service to the public, whether they are publicly or privately owned. Examples include all retail stores and commercial services (cleaners, hairdressers, laundromats), as well as streets; sidewalks; highways; parking lots; train, bus, and subway stations; airports; banks; schools; hospitals; clinics; libraries; day-care centers; and post offices. Indeed, much of our environment consists of use types generally accessible to the public, providing services or goods that are part of daily life.

Use types that are most public – publicly owned and accessible to all without charge, such as streets and squares and parks – have long been the sites of public communication and debate so crucial to democracy. Public spaces have been sites for campaigning, proselytizing, begging, and other forms of confrontal communication. They are places of demonstrations, rebellions, revolutions, and other actions to contest the dominant order. In all these ways, the most public of spaces have been the least amenable to continuous control, although control may be harshly exerted when the dominant interests of society are contested in those spaces, as in the demonstrations in Tiananmen Square in May 1989. At other times it is in public spaces that the dominant interests are overturned, as in more successful revolutions.

Today the openness of public space to the many meetings of differences, confrontational or not, is being curtailed in several ways in the United States. Many public places where people encounter each other in daily routines are now privately owned. In urban and suburban malls, large office complexes, and privately owned plazas or recreation areas, many uses and users are forbidden in order to maintain a particular atmosphere of harmony, homogeneity, and apparent safety. Both control and the maintenance of a retreat from the more unpredictable world of the street and the city are paramount. With the rise of industrialization and capital production, market forces have generated more and more use types that offer a public service and are open to all members of the public, much like streets and squares. However, whether these places – such as airports, train stations, and bus stations – are public in the same way that streets are is under debate. The U.S. Supreme Court has struggled with the question of whether airports and bus stations are "public forums" and therefore whether political or other forms of debate, including religious proselytizing, can take place in them.

Some publicly owned spaces, once accessible to all, are now subject to restrictions. In efforts to reduce crime and fear of crime, residential streets in Bridgeport, Connecticut, Chicago, and Los Angeles are being restricted to residents only and in many places developers are building gated and guarded subdivisions (Guterson 1992). Public parks have adopted rules to prevent the homeless from occupying benches overnight or living in the park, and may be redesigned to remove squatters and to reduce, or repress, conflicts over use. In other cities, attempts have been made to limit homeless people to certain parts of the city either by law or through design interventions.

Simultaneous with the increasing privatization of public space is an increase over the last 30 or so years in the variety and frequency of public events occurring in streets and parks, particularly in cities. Free concerts and other forms of entertainment, fairs, markets, parades, demonstrations, and religious rituals all speak to the continuing, if not increasing, vitality of public space. Social movements dedicated to ending the Vietnam War; establishing the rights of blacks, women, gays and lesbians; ending nuclear armament; and protecting the environment have also used public events in public space to make their identities and concerns known. As pointed out by Young these events often involve the theatrical, including skits, costumes, puppets, music, and dancing. The demonstration of different histories and different interests, as well as the expressive elements, are part of an "emancipatory politics" that challenges the Enlightenment ideal of a civil public that prizes unity, equality, and rationality over difference, particularity, and emotion. In such a public, "consensus and sharing may not always be the goal, but the recognition and appreciation of differences, in the context of confrontation with power" (Young 1986, 399).

Public use types can operate as an antidote to the imperatives of control, retreat, and capital accumulation, but such a possibility is reduced when the latter three purposes encroach upon use types that were once open to alternative, and possibly contested, uses. Fortunately, restrictions on the use of public space are being contested in the courts, and public events of various kinds seem to be increasing in number and variety. Also, new use types are emerging that challenge the definition of what is public. Some add an international dimension, such as the Seebruge Maritime Terminal for channel ferryboats designed by Rem Koolhass. Frederick Jameson suggests that the terminal is an "interspace" between all the countries it serves, "outside of the public spaces" of any of them (Jameson and Speaks 1992, 35).

For Enabling and Empowering. Quite a different purpose for use types is to enable and empower occupants. Libraries, schools, universities, town halls, state and national capitols, religious buildings (including monasteries and convents), and buildings for fraternal organizations and charities may all serve this purpose, although not all exemplars of each do so. Many capitol buildings seem to disempower the public and empower only those already powerful. Some transitional housing for mothers and children is intended more for the removal and reform of residents while others are intended for, and managed with a view to, empowering the occupants (Sprague 1991).

The idea of enabling and empowering can be a heuristic device to uncover other purposes for use types, particularly when one considers who is empowered and how. The single-family house and suburban community may have empowered the wage-earning husband who could treat the home as his evening and weekend retreat and feel proud of his success in owning it. The proliferation of this use type empowered developers and manufacturers of certain consumer products by producing profits. But by isolating women and children from public life, it disempowered them. Such critiques raise important questions for how the suburban house and neighborhood can be reenvisioned to empower all occupants.

New use types that have been developed, or modified, to serve the purpose of large-scale capital production disempower consumers and small businesses. Cooperative food stores, local green markets, community gardens, community workshops, incentive programs for small businesses, and the control of large-scale commercial development are all attempts to counter this trend. Similarly, urban renewal, large public housing projects, and downtown redevelopment programs of the 1970s and 1980s addressed goals of removal, control, and production of capital, but did nothing to empower local residents, local businesses, or existing neighborhoods. More recent programs for urban revitalization, community development banks, and some cities' requirement that banks make loans to local organizations all focus attention on the circumstances of residents, not on the interests and goals of those located elsewhere. And more attention is being paid to a range of needs — for housing, stores, services, education, employment, and safety.

19-7
Pike's Place Market, Seattle (photo by Lynda Schneekloth)

The greater attention given to the goals of removal and control, retreat and escape, and producing capital rather than to empowerment indicates how much use types serve the dominant interests in society, which for the most part are not furthered by empowering others. Several of the innovative designs presented below seek to empower some of those others. As we recognize how more and more use types are primarily a means for producing capital, perhaps the goal of empowerment will grow as a counteractive force, a tool for critique and change.

Planning and Designing Webs, Not Containers

Although use types are like webs, they are most often envisioned, planned, created, and regulated as discrete, independent objects – as *containers*. Spaces (indoors or outdoors) are seen as and made to be separate and autonomous, self-sufficient and complete, contained and fixed. Use types become cells for predetermined kinds of uses and users, making ever finer distinctions between them. Separation and segregation are given far more attention than connection and overlap. By being placed in containers, users are seen and treated as passive objects, not active, participating subjects. Places become so standardized that regional and local identities are almost invisible. Various forces, including financing and regulating, severely constrain any diversity or flexibility. Although this happens most easily with buildings and rooms because they are physically constructed, it also happens with outdoor places such as farms or parks and with plans for development and redevelopment.

Control and removal, retreat and escape become more important than providing public service or enabling and empowering, and the production and control of capital becomes the overarching imperative. The characteristics of existing types at all scales of the environment, ensured by building codes and zoning ordinances, make the built landscape a complex of fixed compartments, a kind of prison. In presenting the ideas of Georges Bataille, Hollier writes:

> Architecture, formerly the image of social order, now guarantees and even imposes this order. From being a simple symbol it has now become the master. Architecture captures society in the trap of the image it offers, fixing it in the specular image it reflects back... Architecture does not express the soul of society but rather smothers it (Hollier 1989, 47).

It is also possible to plan and design places so that they are more like webs and less like containers. Webs are open and have no hard or fixed boundaries; they have holes and extend outward, touching their surroundings. Webs are made up

TM: *Isn't daily life divided into these categories? Is the distinction between sickness and health disappearing? Or between young and old? Perhaps for intellectuals but surely not for ordinary folk? In fact one could argue that many distinctions were only recently created – e.g., child and childhood, or privacy.*
KAF: *I completely agree that many distinctions were only recently invented, many of them around the same time that the increasing segmentation of the built landscape began. However, I do believe that many distinctions are no longer clear for any of us. People are now living for many years with AIDS or cancer and alternating between periods of sickness and health. (Or are they ever "healthy"?) There are serious medical and ethical questions regarding when "life" begins and ends; and there are increasing expectations that people who are chronologically "old" should be active, vital, and athletic and in these ways more like "young" people (see particularly Cole 1992). The contemporary blurring, or questioning, of categories that were only recently treated as more distinct is a fascinating topic. (Other examples include male and female, culture and nature, waste and not-waste.)*

RL: *I don't think we should discuss "architecture" in these terms. The built environment does have an architectural input, albeit a very small one, and architects are not autonomous actors but the agents of developers, etc.*
KAF: *In this passage from Hollier, I think the reference to "architecture" is more inclusive than buildings designed by architects. Granted, if "input" is the percentage of buildings designed by architects, the input can be considered small. But if input is the culture of architecture – the ideas, images, beliefs, and preferences that architects offer in built projects, drawings, testimonies, books, competitions, exhibitions, magazines, and so on that are then drawn upon, transformed, and used in many different, and sometimes unintended, ways – then the input is much larger and richer. Of course architects are not autonomous but that does not mean that they have no influence, either in these more indirect ways or in designing buildings for developers or others.*

of many different, connected strands. They can be added to and repaired. Unlike containers, webs suggest connections not separations, interdependence not autonomy, multiplicity not singularity, variety not standardization, and the possibility of activity and change. By designing, planning, and regulating use types as webs, we can support and promote these values and participate in a cultural shift that has already begun in many domains.

Relational, Overlapping Worlds

The segmentation of daily life by use types reinforces the conceptual dichotomies of built/natural, work/home, private/public, family/not-family, sick/healthy, and young/old. In order for the environment to enhance and not obstruct daily life, which is not clearly divided into such independent categories, and in order for us to alter conditions that are harming people and the earth, both the dichotomies and the use types that enforce them must be changed. Such a shift requires a different view of reality, one that recognizes and prizes relationship and connections, not autonomy and separations. Kenneth Gergen sees relational reality as part of a "new vocabulary of being" that stresses the interdependence, not the autonomy, of individuals. "One chooses not between relationship and individual autonomy but between varying forms of interdependence... " (1991, 242). The same can be said of a shift in our construction of categories of types, uses, and people.

The conceptual dichotomies between built and natural, culture and nature, and city and country are all being questioned and modified. We are beginning to acknowledge that buildings and what we consider parts of nature (air, land, resources, energy, our bodies) affect each other in significant ways and that our ways of designing and occupying buildings should take these interactions into account. This means conserving energy, planning for the recycling of materials during construction and occupancy, and creating healthful interiors.

Dichotomies between work and leisure, constructed city and bucolic nature, and consumption and production are transcended in parks that include river runoff, wastewater treatment facilities, agricultural activities, and canning factories (Cranz 1992). In their design for Olympia Fields, a "productive park" in Illinois, Galen Cranz and David Robinson made a recycling center the heart of the project and incorporated community gardens, a greenhouse, a windmill, a composting earthwork, and storage for gardening supplies and equipment for local residents along with baseball, basketball, and tennis courts and places for strolling

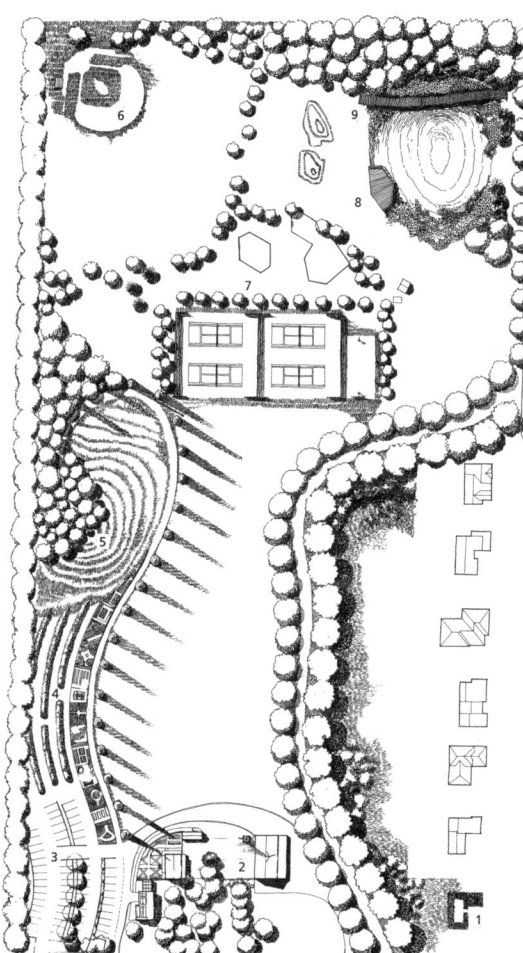

19-8
The Productive Park, Galen Cranz and David Robinson: site plan (Competition for Olympia Fields Park for the 21st century, 1992)
1. phantom house of prairie grass
2. recycling center; demonstration and catering kitchen; office and public toilets, storage; greenhouse
3. parking
4. community gardens, compost mounds, shredder
5. prospect/refuge
6. existing baseball diamond
7. existing tennis courts
8. platform for viewing marsh
9. elevated walkway

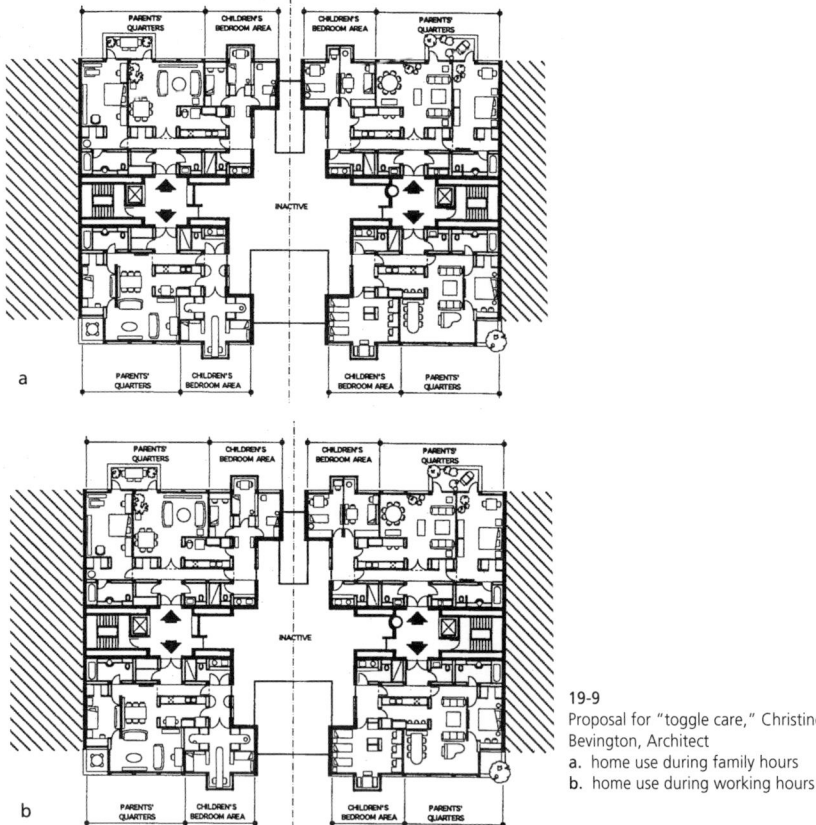

19-9
Proposal for "toggle care," Christine Bevington, Architect
a. home use during family hours
b. home use during working hours

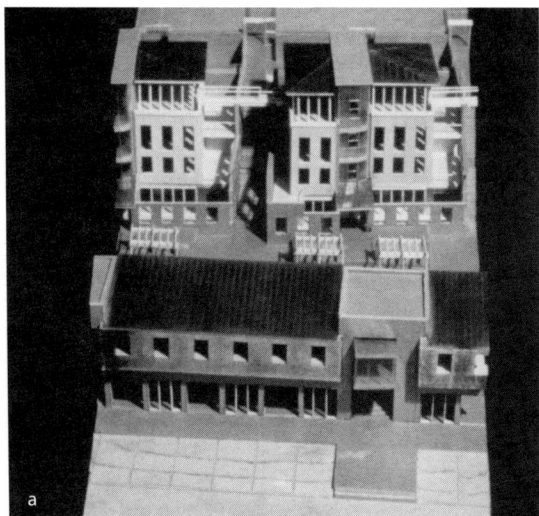

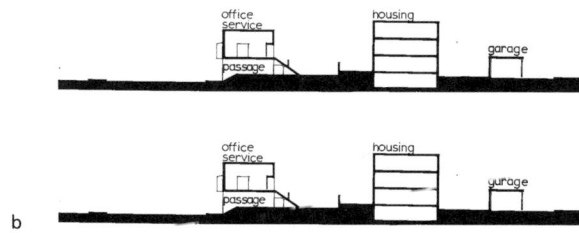

19-10
Proposal for collective home/work settlement, Jeff Speck
a. model. Work center with parking in front; courtyard and housing in back
b. diagrammatic site section. Offices and workshops are divided into appropriately sized units by service spaces above and passages below linking parking to courtyard.

and pausing in the landscape. Through its facilities and the educational activities they can house, the productive park would demonstrate resource management while also offering conventional opportunities for recreation. For Cranz and Robinson the design demonstrates a new purpose for parks: to celebrate the conservation of resources.

The split between home and work is bridged in projects that incorporate opportunities for wage work or various kinds of services for residents into housing. In Christine Bevington's proposal for "toggle care" there is space for child care that is an immediate extension of several apartment units. During the daytime when the space is being used for day-care activities, there is direct access from the space into part of each of the adjacent apartments so that children can use their own bedrooms but do not have access to the living room, kitchen, or adults' bedrooms. At night, each apartment becomes a complete and separate dwelling again, with the day care space closed off. Not only is a support service brought into a close relationship with dwellings, but a series of distinctions replaces the usual single separation, and both the boundaries and the content of the spaces that are separated change over the course of the day.

Home, wage work, and day care are all brought closer together in Jeff Speck's proposal for a collective home/work settlement that combines a housing development with its own neighborhood work center of offices, workshops, and commercial space. Not only is wage work placed adjacent to residents' own homes in a suburban setting, but interaction between the domestic and work realms is envisioned by locating a shared court between the housing and the work center. Speck places the project right on the suburban strip and maintains the conventional arrangement of roadway, parking, and linear commercial building. He accepts the idea of commercial strip but significantly alters both its anticipated uses by residents and its relationship to housing. The kinds of modifications in current use types that can create connections and overlaps need not be radical typological changes, as demonstrated by both Bevington's and Speck's proposals.

The same can be said of cohousing, where the isolation of individual households in single-family homes is reduced by softening the division between private and public and creating a way of life, as well as spaces and amenities, that bring households together. The privacy and independence of each household are still preserved since each household has its own complete dwelling. But close relationships and daily interactions with other households are intentionally sought and encouraged, both in the design of the community and in the sharing of preparing and eating evening meals together in a common house (McCamant and Durrett 1988).

The segmentation of use types and efforts to arrange our lives and landscapes into independent categories have allowed many of us to avoid conflict, to escape demanding or unpleasant experiences, to remain ignorant of the problems of others, and to conceal or deny our own. We have not only escaped, we have been anesthetized. Douglas Darden (1993) challenges this condition and our feelings of complacency by proposing buildings that reverse conventional expectations: for instance, that architecture is confrontation, not accommodation or that a monument is for forgetting, not remembering. Darden reveals what is usually hidden, connects what is usually separated. His Oxygen House celebrates the dying-while-living of his client, whose oxygen tent is part of the visible structure of the house, and his eventual death, which is signaled by the tomb that is part of the house. It is a house for living and dying, together.

Multiple, Diverse Realities

The alternative to standardization and a single universal reality is multiple and diverse realities. The shift to multiplicity and diversity Gergen calls the "free play of discourses," as opposed to the earlier totalizing discourse that promulgated a single truth (1991, 247). The cultivation of diversity and multiplicity can be seen in bioregionalism, architectural regionalism, contextualism, historic preservation, and the recognition of the importance of cultural identity in the landscape.

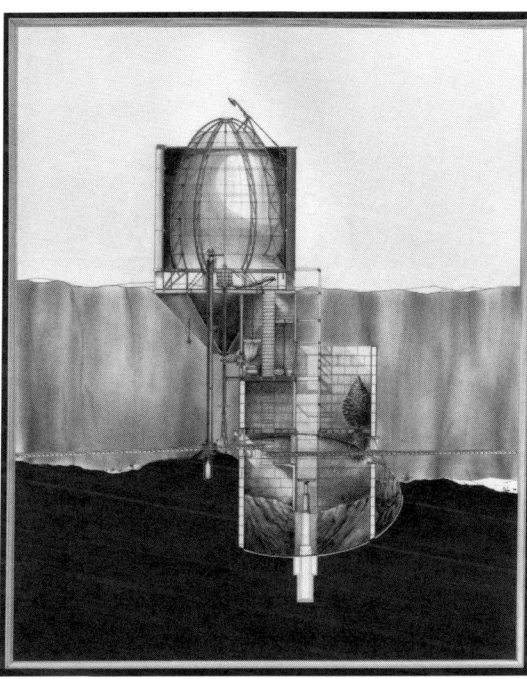

19-11
Oxygen House, Douglas Darden: anatomical section

The variety of kinds of transitional housing for women and children in terms of philosophy, program, and physical design that has evolved is beneficial, and continued variety should be encouraged (Sprague 1991). In housing generally, a greater variety of floor plans to accommodate different kinds of households and relationships between households and between household members needs to be developed (Franck and Ahrentzen 1989).

An array of alternative floor plans to suit different kinds of households appears in Katrin Adam's proposed renovation of Greenpoint Hospital in Brooklyn into housing for women. An apartment for two single women provides two separate living spaces, each with its own entrance, and a shared kitchen and bath. Similarly, an apartment for two single-parent families provides separate entrances to two suites of bedrooms and baths, with a shared kitchen and dining and living spaces in the center of the apartment. And an apartment for a family incorporates an adjacent efficiency apartment for a single person, possibly a relative, who could have a close relationship with the family, but also could retain her own privacy and independence. In all Adam's plans, some degree of privacy and independence for households is preserved without adopting the isolated sanctuary model of conventional apartments.

The choice of diversity and variety over singularity and uniformity was made in the controlled redevelopment of Pikes Place Market in Seattle. The mix of uses, people, and architectural styles has been retained and preserved so that upscale restaurants, shopping, and housing coexist with the original fish and produce markets, low-cost housing, soup kitchens, secondhand clothing stores, and unusual services such as tattooing (Frieden and Sagalyn 1990). The market is busy and messy; activities of delivery and unpacking are highly visible; vagrants and graffiti are tolerated. The atmosphere is lively and informal.

A similar choice of multiplicity over a single, standardizing form of development was made in Manteo, North Carolina. There the preservation of a network of places that support the existing lifestyle and values of residents and the controlling of development have resulted in a "healthy tension between the town's traditional aesthetics… and the more ordered signs of new development" (Hester 1993, 294). However, these places had to be discovered through research with residents: the marshes surrounding the town, a local restaurant, a local soda fountain, a gravel parking lot near the waterfront, and other sites did not initially appear to be important enough to be preserved. Their significance and the explanation of their significance had to be revealed and explained. These places are "sacred" because they "exemplify, typify, reinforce and perhaps even extol the everyday life patterns and special rituals of community life" (Hester 1993, 279).

Recognizing multiple realities also means remembering events and experiences we might prefer to forget; it means acknowledging pain, error, and even cruelty rather than repressing or sanitizing them. The existence and design of such places raises many difficult questions, as evidenced in discussions of the preservation of Nazi concentration camps (Langenbach 1992) and the building of the Holocaust Museum in Washington, D.C. (Gourevitch 1993). What painful events, significant to the history of peoples or communities, should be marked and how should this be done in ways that do not sensationalize or trivialize the past? Where there are multiple interpretations of the same event, as of the battle/massacre at Wounded Knee in North Dakota, how can this multiplicity be acknowledged? Designing for a single, universalizing reality avoids these questions completely.

19-12
Proposed scheme for Neighborhood Women Renaissance Housing, Katrin Adam, Associates (Katrin Adam, principal, with Barbara Marks)
a. schematic floor plan: second floor, West building
b. schematic floor plan: third floor, West building

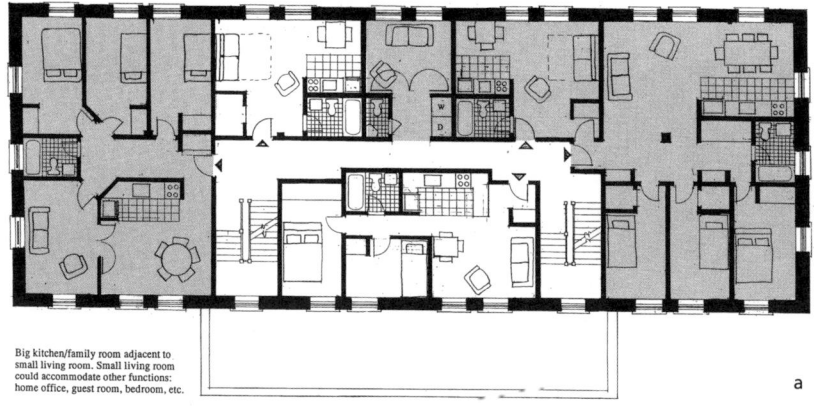

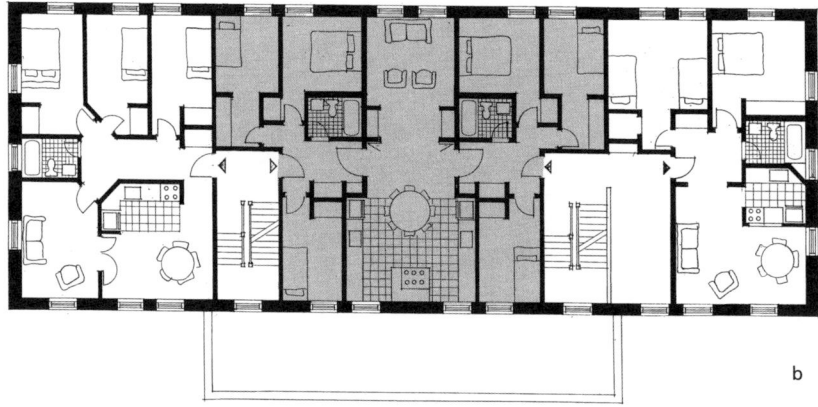

Current use types and the purposes they serve help shape self and community identities in ways that are consonant with the dominant social order and with its single universalizing truth, causing us to repress experiences and desires that conflict with that order and that truth. Uncovering these repressed experiences and desires requires a kind of *excavation*. In order to do this with our experience of homes, Harvey Sherman has developed a bodywork process that involves deep focused breathing, voice work, movement, and responding verbally to large, projected photographic images of places one has lived. Called "building community from the body," the process is intended to uncover memories and hidden aspects of identity that may have implications for the design of houses and communities (Sherman 1993).

These examples indicate the beginnings of a shift that we must encourage and work hard to promote. To pursue any of them requires that many obstacles be overcome and difficult questions be resolved. Katrin Adam's proposed renovation to Greenpoint Hospital was not acceptable to city agencies that preferred more conventional, standardized floor plans. Without research and advocacy planning, the "sacred" places of Manteo would have been lost in the redevelopment of the town (Hester 1993). When projects are built, or plans adopted, the difficulties are not over; the projects may continue to generate controversy or require continuing efforts to preserve them.

If diversity, multiplicity, and the pairing of opposites are to be prized, then a certain amount of conflict may not only be inevitable but desirable. A monument against fascism erected in Hamburg was designed by Jochen and Esther Gerz for viewers to add their own names and messages to the monument. Along with names and inscriptions, swastikas have appeared. Many have criticized the design of the monument for encouraging such responses, but this may be a new purpose of memorials – to allow the expression of feelings, usually hidden, even when they are deplorable (Freiman 1993). Indeed, in acknowledging multiplicity, architecture may sometimes confront rather than accommodate.

Active Subjects

In emphasizing the purposes of control, escape, and capital production, and in creating a built landscape of segmented and standardized use types, we place ourselves, the inhabitants of these places, in a passive role. We are the objects of these manipulations as much as the landscape is. What we need, what we should do or experience, are decided and arranged for us; indeed our experience is directed and manufactured as much as the place. This contributes to the sequestration of experience in the modern period, to our alienation from our own bodies and feelings. Those use types dedicated to control and removal make the passivity of occupants most obvious, but a similar compliance is expected in other use types as well. One alternative is design that supports people's full engagement in activities and experiences as active *subjects*.

Bianca Lepori's analysis and design of a space for giving birth illustrate this alternative (Lepori 1992). She considers each birth a unique event that cannot, and should not, be molded to fit a standard model. Instead, the space and the furniture she proposes allow for a variety of possibilities that sustain the woman's freedom of movement and her power to choose different positions and different actions during labor. Instead of a bed placed in a dominant position either in the middle of the room or in the center of a wall, the center of the room is left open and a low platform, easy to get on and off, is placed to one side. Other items of furniture offer many different opportunities for stretching, hanging, leaning, squatting, pressing, and reclining.

19-13
Various positions and movements during labor, Bianca Lepori, Architect

The intention is to support, not to control, the natural process of delivery. In a conventional birthing room in the United States, the bed is the focus of the room, suggesting that the best way to give birth is lying down. Here the role of the woman is passive; she is the recipient of the actions and decisions of others. In Lepori's design the choice of positions and movements and the very encouragement of *activity* puts the mother, physically and emotionally, in control and places the staff, both symbolically and actually, in a supportive role. Lepori's design is not intended to replace existing spaces and spatial practices for giving birth but rather to add another option, to increase the range of possibilities. And these new options are to be placed within a hospital setting so that all of the medical technology that is presently available could be used if necessary.

A very different example is found in the Vietnam Veterans Memorial in Washington, D.C., a structure that also invites active participation and engagement in the experience of visiting. Visitors look for particular names as they move along the wall: they touch or trace the names of those they have come to remember; they stand and reflect; they cry; they embrace; and they leave flowers, flags, and mementos. The Memorial has also become the site for veterans to express their concerns publicly about issues such as the situation of the MIAs. As Griswold (1992) notes, these activities do not occur at other memorials. In her design Maya Lin envisioned a new and different purpose for a memorial: to acknowledge loss and to bring about healing; the subjectivity and the movements and feelings of visitors are central to such a purpose.

In contemporary society, self-identity is not simply given but is actively and continuously created through reflexive actions (Giddens 1991). The self has a body that is not simply an entity but an "action-system, a mode of praxis... its practical immersion in the interaction of day to day life is an essential part of the sustaining of a coherent sense of self identity" (Giddens 1991, 49). The acknowledgement of self-identity as an ongoing, creative process involving both reflexivity and a body performing actions underscores the value of designing for active subjects who make choices, who participate fully and freely in the occupation of places.

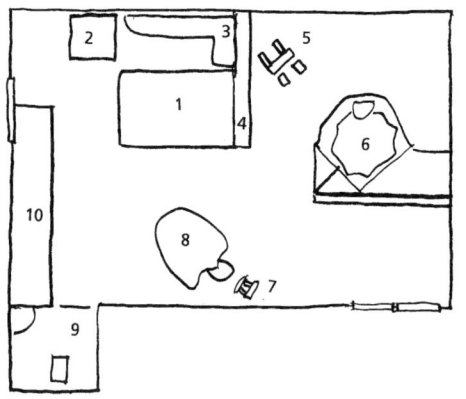

19-14
Plan of labor and delivery room for natural childbirth in a hospital setting: experimental project, S. Gerardo dei Tintori Hospital, University of Milan, (Bianca Lepori, Architect)
1. platform bed
2. mat, rungs mounted on wall
3. bench
4. low wall
5. balancing stool
6. bath
7. birthing stool
8. mat, fabric rope hanging from ceiling
9. bathroom
10. cabinet

19-15
Parc de la Villette, Paris
(photo by author)

LS: *Current practice in urban design is to create urban structures that can accommodate many different functions. This way of working is a critique of the modernist notion of a close fit between form and function. The practice results in a strong, traditional urban fabric that has the potential to rebuild cities and make places that have a sense of place. This is important work! But I also feel a real discomfort with the practice because the real client for the structure is capital — the only truly mobile element of postmodern culture. Do we really want to be about the business of designing for capital that moves in, out, and through our cities with no respect for the place, the people, or the region?*

KAF: *Yes, this is a dilemma. The open frame certainly does accommodate the mobility of capital to come and go, and it is rare that capital is required to respect the character of local activities and places, but it is happening more often in both rural and urban locations. And it will happen more often as more people realize it is possible to have both* development *and* preservation. *The particular frame that is adopted may be quite explicit, and quite restrictive, in preventing certain kinds of places and uses while encouraging others, and residents can determine what that frame should be. That is also important work!*

TM: *The argument for your web rather than container, for paradox, contradiction, openness, etc., I completely accept. But what such a web, etc. needs is a rich set of clearly defined, subtle terms that can be combined in an infinite variety of new ways. In spoken language the fact that we have well-defined words, and rules of grammar for combining them, has never prevented anyone from saying something new.*

In use typology one has the elements, and the words, to create an infinitely rich web of places and meanings, but only because "school," "classroom," "map corner," etc. have already provided a generative lexicon each item of which has clear meanings. Clarity is not rigidity; in fact the liberal-sounding plea for flexibility could result in destroying the very substance that allows creativity.

KAF: *But new words are invented all the time; existing words develop new meanings and old words fall into disuse. And language is not always perfectly clear. Moreover, the ambiguities in meaning can be both beneficial and problematic. I would say the same about use types and the words that name them. I do favor change and ambiguity over stability and clarity, when the former serve purposes I can endorse.*

Open Frames

Diversity, choice, and active engagement are constrained, if not prevented, by the creation of tight fixed relationships between use and form attributes. Many use types are designed to be complete and finished and do not welcome choice or modification. They prescribe which activities should occur where, and how they should be performed, leaving little opportunity for other options or for change.

One alternative is to create a frame where choices, additions, subtractions, and modifications can be made with greater ease. Here form and use attributes are not tightly bound to each other; the designer has intended uses in mind but avoids fixing them to a limited set of form attributes. Thus one avoids the lock-step connection between form and use that is perpetuated by a more stereotyped repetition of use types. In its very best sense, that is what deconstructivism in architecture can do, as when Bernard Tschumi realized a new kind of park at la Villette in Paris, new in its array of uses, given by the program, and new in the form attributes and their links to those uses, which he devised (Tschumi 1987).

The opportunity for choice and change allows for more diversity and serves the multiple realities we are now beginning to recognize. The site plan and follies of Parc de La Villette provide a clear and cohesive frame to accommodate a variety of uses that can change over time. The frame of form attributes is fixed; the uses vary. The urban codes developed by Duany and Plater-Zyberk (1991, 1992) also incorporate flexibility within a clearly organized frame. Rather than fixing and restricting uses as most zoning ordinances do, the code fixes the form attributes of different areas within a town and allows uses to vary. With an open frame, what is envisioned and built, or in the case of planning and zoning what is envisioned and encouraged, is a field of possible links between form and use. The possibilities have been thoroughly considered so that the frame that is provided can accommodate them.

When the open frame is adopted, relatedness, diversity, and possibility for change may all be incorporated, as in Barbara Knecht's (1993) proposal of four housing models for the formerly homeless mentally ill. In the Transitional/Permanent model, residents in a transitional program participate in program activities but live in a building with other permanent residents. The funds for the transitional program are tied to the person or to the unit, not to the building. In the Satellite model, participants develop supportive relationships with other program participants in transitional housing and then move as a group to permanent housing. In the Linkages model, the transitional program is a day treatment center combined with a transitional housing center, operating in close connection with nearby permanent housing so that participants maintain their relationship to that program after they move to the permanent housing. And in the Convertible model, the building and the residents together convert from a transitional program to permanent housing. In all models the building becomes permanent housing with community services after a specified period of time.

These models support and encourage relationships – between participants, between participants and staff, and between project and neighborhood; they see both buildings and services as facilitating relationships rather than as categorizing people and needs. They address a diversity of needs that change over time. And they have disconnected the conventionally tight and fixed links between a person's needs and the use and form attributes of a particular use type. These usually insure that a person moves from one kind of facility to another (and possibly back again) as his or her needs change while the attributes of the facilities remain the same. Instead, Knecht makes all the links – among programs and services, persons with particular needs, and buildings – looser and more flexible so that both programs and buildings can change when people change.

The open frame supports choice and change however the possible options are envisioned; they are not left to chance. While there is diversity and looser links between form and use, there is still a degree of certainty and predictability. The frame, although open, is fixed.[4]

Uncertainty, Ambiguity

A more radical approach is to design for greater uncertainty and more fluidity, to invite chance occurrences. One example is Diana Agrest's and Mario Gandelsonas's vision plan for the city of Des Moines, Iowa. Unlike a traditional "master plan" that would present a complete and thorough guide mapping out future development for a city, their vision plan proposes a few key locations for reinvigoration. These points or "moments" are chosen to reinforce the existing physical and social configuration of the city and, like sensitive points in the body

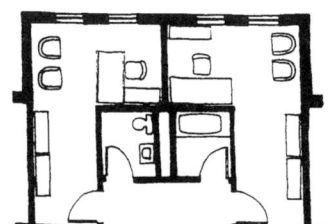

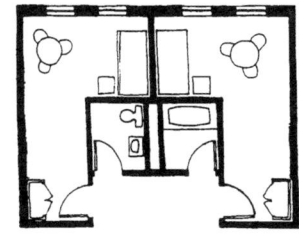

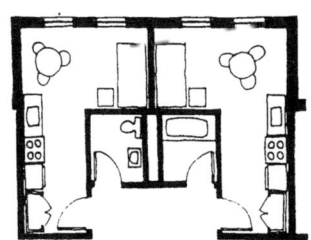

19-16
Plans of alternative uses Barbara Knecht (source: *Flexible Housing Models: Proposals to House Homeless Mentally Ill People*, prepared for the Corporation for Supportive Housing, 1993).
a. transitional phase: offices
b. transitional phase: private sleeping units
c. permanent phase: SRO units with kitchens

4. In either case, fixing the range of options or envisioning an open-ended future, the building or landscape is viewed and designed to be transformative rather than stable.

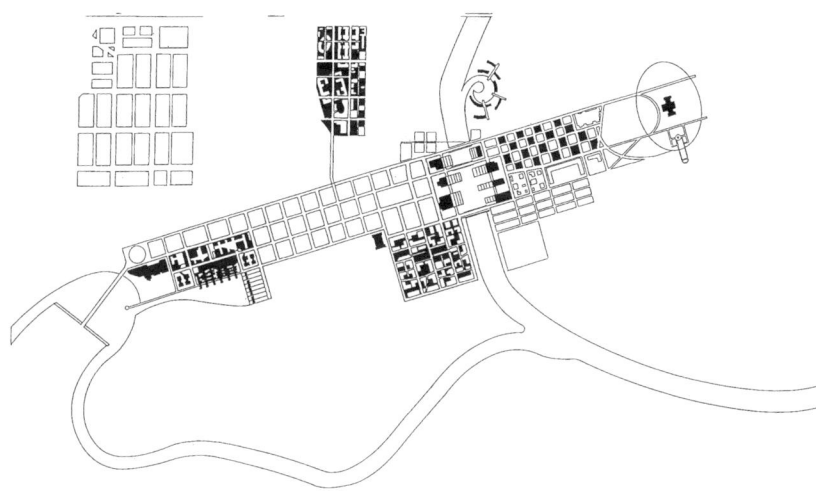

19-17
Vision Plan for Des Moines, Iowa: "Moments" in downtown, linear reading
(Diana Agrest and Mario Gandelsonas, Architects).
  From left to right: Gateway with proposed lake and new Waterfront residential neighborhood, incorporating some existing buildings; new Hillside neighborhood; new Court Avenue residential neighborhood, incorporating all existing buildings; Riverfront civic place, extending existing buildings into river; new Marina neighborhood; new Eastside mixed-use neighborhood; existing State Capitol building

TM: *One reason I like this chapter is that in many ways it creates a useful polarization from my, and I suspect a number of the other authors', views and will thus generate useful debates and discussions.*

KAF: *My goal for working on this book was to understand the meanings of type more fully by reading, and responding to, what my colleagues had to say. That goal has been met. Reviewing your drafts and those of Julia Robinson, Guido Francescato, Marsha Ritzdorf, and Roderick Lawrence in particular helped me develop and clarify my own ideas, as did comments and suggestions from Lynda Schneekloth. I see quite a few commonalities, as well as differences, among all the chapters, including yours and mine.*

touched by acupuncture, will generate energy around them (Agrest and Gandelsonas 1994). The exact content of this subsequent development around and between these points is intentionally not predicted; chance is incorporated into the plan. The process is also open: several alternative proposals for the way to invigorate these points are made to the community and the one chosen is developed with community participation. Extensive media coverage of the proposals and their development is welcomed, and received.

The randomness built into the vision plan recognizes the unpredictability of future events and circumstances. It does not present the architecture of buildings and neighborhoods as a protection against uncertainty, as some kind of tranquilizer to quell the fear of not knowing. Indeed, instead of fully answering the question "What will be?" it poses that question, answers it partially, and invites additional answers in the form of future actions by others. The creation of relational worlds, multiple realities, and looser links between form and use all pose more questions than answers. The categories overlap; their boundaries and content change, bringing ambiguity and uncertainty. What at first may seem messy or confusing will soon be experienced as lively and invigorating, sometimes mysterious, always rich in possibilities for activity and participation.

Such a world asks more of us, the occupants; sometimes it may ask us to experiment. Lebbeus Woods (1992) portrays a "free space architecture" to which he assigns no meanings or uses. The uses will be created by those who choose to occupy the free spaces. These inhabitable structures, as in the Zagreb Free Zone Project, are inserted into existing cities where they can remain for any length of time. Spaces without designated uses and meanings, with a mysterious appearance, leave us perplexed. We are not told what to do or believe; we are left to our own devices.

Conclusion

Use types are all around us. We occupy them, refer to them, build and modify them every day. Because the ways they link form, use, and meaning are so deeply embedded in our daily lives, we take use types for granted and assume that they are given. We forget that use types are social and physical inventions, often made and changed to serve purposes we may question, most recently consumer capitalism. The mutability of use types, even over short periods of time, indicates how very possible it is to make self-conscious modifications of existing types and to develop new ones.

To create a more socially just, ecologically sound, and life-enhancing built landscape, we can no longer take use types for granted or allow them to become ever more segmenting and standardized, serving primarily the purposes of control, escape, and capital production. We need to *see* the use types that surround us and to imagine different ones. To do this we must welcome a wide array of methods and proposals, as shown by the examples in this essay. We can uncover existing webs through various kinds of research; through art; through self-reflexive, almost therapeutic techniques; and through the design of new use types. We can work toward changing the existing webs with the same variety of approaches.

In proposing change one may start with existing use types and propose physical or spatial modifications that, although not radical in themselves, make a radical difference in the uses and meanings of the type, as in the projects by Bevington, Adam, Speck, and Knecht. Or the modification may be substantial enough to suggest an altogether new use type as in Cranz and Robinson's design of a productive park, or Lepori's alternative birthing room. In either case, the attributes of the existing use type, along with attributes from other sources or other types, are treated as an array of elements from which to pick and choose, keeping some attributes and discarding others, to forge a new configuration. The designer treats use types as what they are: mutable webs of form, use, and meaning to be unraveled and rewoven in order to support new patterns of living, working, and inhabiting the earth.

In proposing change one may also *avoid* existing use types and begin inquiry and design elsewhere, for instance, with intended uses but independently of the types formally dedicated to those uses. Bianca Lepori did this when she interviewed women who had given birth at home. Another possibility is to imagine places and scenarios not with an eye to building them but to exploring forms, uses, and meanings under only those constraints one chooses to adopt. Architects like Lebbeus Woods and Douglas Darden do this by drawing places without referencing the use types that we already know.[5] This exploration of ideas and possibilities through an imaginary architecture challenges what *is* by imagining what is *not*.

With any stretching of the web, we see anew the use types that we know and occupy. We begin to recognize how much they mold what we do and believe, what we are. And we begin to ask what we want to be.

19-18
Balanced Stones, Sam Taylor and Rob Logan (photo by Tony Holmes)

5. In a course I teach on architecture for utopia, students imagine places that do not exist and write stories and draw images of these places and the experiences, activities, and meanings they associate with them. In doing this they discover their own wishes (and fears) of a different world and of the present one. In another course students invent rituals and the spaces for their enactment; this often reveals what is missing from our current ways of living and what could be made, and done, differently.

TM: *Of course one has to account for changes of use, of experience, and of language. But this will occur by increasing and refining typological language, not by doing "without" types. That stance is, for me, individualistic and not socially based.*

KAF: *New words that are invented may not be derived from existing words but may be quite independent of them; so too with new use types. How new use types are proposed, how modifications to existing types are suggested, and how we gain insight into existing use types and their problems should not be limited to particular methods or particular kinds of contributions to the discourse, such as those that are "socially based." We need more proposals, more insights, and more varied ones, not fewer or more restricted ones. Which ideas are then adopted or which projects are built is another question, one to which a variety of criteria should apply. But even then, a project that is "individualistic" may appeal to a wide range of people because, perhaps unexpectedly, it meets a need or desire they did not know they had. There is much dis- and uncovering to be done!*

References

Agrest, D. and Gandelsonas, M. 1994. *Agrest and Gandelsonas, Architects*. New York: Princeton Architectural Press.

Ahrentzen, S. 1991. *Hybrid Housing: A Contemporary Building Type for Multiple Residential and Business Use*. Milwaukee, Wis.: Center for Architectural and Planning Research, University of Wisconsin.

Barna, J. 1992. *The See-Through Years: Creation and Destruction in Texas Architecture*. Houston, Tex.: Rice University Press.

Baum, D. 1992. Sacred places. *Mother Jones* (March/April): 32–38.

Calthorpe, P. 1993. *The Next American Metropolis*. New York: Princeton Architectural Press.

Cole, T.R. 1992. *The Journey of Life: A Cultural History of Aging in America*. New York: Cambridge University Press.

Cranz, G. 1982. *The Politics of Park Design*. Cambridge, Mass.: MIT Press.

———1992. The principles of sustainable development can and must shape our cities and parks. Paper presented at Environmental Design Research Association Conference, Boulder, Co., April, 1992.

Crawford, M. 1992. The world in a shopping mall. In *Variations on a Theme Park*, ed. M. Sorkin, 3–30. New York: Noonday Press.

Cromley, E.M. 1990. *Alone Together: A History of New York's Early Apartments*. Ithaca, N.Y.: Cornell University Press.

Darden, D. 1993. *Condemned Building*. New York: Princeton Architectural Press.

Davis, M. 1991. *City of Quartz: Excavating the Future in Los Angeles*. New York: Vintage Books.

Duany, A. and E. Plater-Zyberk. 1991. A town plan for Seaside. In *Seaside: Making a Town in America*, eds. D. Mohney and K. Easterling, 86–107. New York: Princeton Architectural Press.

———. 1992. The second coming of the American small town. *Wilson Quarterly* (Winter): 19–48.

Forty, A. 1980. The modern hospital in England and France. In *Buildings and Society*, ed. A. King, 61-93. London: Routledge & Kegan Paul.

Franck, K.A. 1989a. Overview of single room occupancy housing. In *New Households, New Housing*, eds. K.A. Franck and S. Ahrentzen, 245–62. New York: Van Nostrand Reinhold.

———. 1989b. Towards a feminist architecture. In *Architecture: A Place for Women*, eds. E.P. Berkeley and M. McQuaid. Washington, D.C.: Smithsonian Institution Press.

———. forthcoming. Questioning the American Dream: housing innovations in the United States In *Housing Women*, eds. R. Woods and R. Gilroy. London: Routledge.

Franck, K.A. and S. Ahrentzen.1989. *New Households, New Housing*. New York: Van Nostrand Reinhold.

Freiman, Z. 1993. The sorrow and the pity. *Progressive Architecture* (February): 75–76.

Frieden, B.J., and L.B. Sagalyn. 1989. *Downtown, Inc.: How America Rebuilds Cities*. Cambridge, Mass.: MIT Press.

Garreau, J. 1991. *Edge City: Life on the New Frontier*. New York: Doubleday.

Gergen, K. 1991. *The Saturated Self: Dilemmas of Identity in Contemporary Life*. New York: Basic Books.

Giddens, A. 1991. *Modernity and Self Identity*. Stanford, Calif.: Stanford University Press.

Goode, T. 1992. Typological theory in the United States. *The Journal of Architectural Education* (September): 2–13.

Gourevitch, P. 1993. Behold now behemoth: the Holocaust Memorial Museum. *Harpers* (July): 55–62.

Griswold, C. 1992. The Vietnam Veterans Memorial and the Washington Mall. In *Critical Issues in Public Art*, eds. H. Senie and S. Webster, 71–99. New York: HarperCollins.

Guterson, D. 1992. No place like home. *Harpers* (November): 55–64.

Hayden, D. 1990. Using ethnic history to understand urban landscapes. *Places* (Fall): 11–17.

Hester, R.T. 1993. Sacred structures and everyday life. In *Dwelling, Seeing and Designing*, ed. D. Seamon, 271–98. Albany, N.Y.: State University of New York Press.

Holl, S. 1980. *The Alphabetical City*. New York: Pamphlet Architecture.

Hollier, D. 1989. *Against Architecture: The Writings of Georges Bataille*. Cambridge, Mass.: MIT Press.

Hubbard, W. 1987. A meaning for monuments. In *The Public Face of Architecture*, eds. N. Glazer and M. Lilla, 124–41. New York: Free Press.

Jackson, J.B. 1984. *Discovering the Vernacular Landscape*. New Haven, Conn.: Yale University Press.

Jacobs, J. 1961. *The Death and Life of Great American Cities*. New York: Vintage Books.

Jameson, F. and M. Speaks. 1992. Envelopes and enclaves: the space of post-civil society, an architectural conversation. *Assemblage* 18: 32–37.

King, A. 1992. Building institutionally significant histories. In *Changing Places: ReMaking Institutional Buildings*, eds. L.H. Schneekloth et al., 124–36. Fredonia, N.Y.: White Pine Press.

Knecht, B. 1993. *Flexible Housing Models for Mentally Ill Homeless People: Final Report to Corporation for Supportive Housing*. New York: Barbara Knecht, Inc.

Langenbach, R. 1992. The good and the evil: the preservation of monuments with a negative symbolic image. In *Changing Places: ReMaking Institutional Buildings*, eds. L.H. Schneekloth et al., 159–95. Fredonia, N.Y.: White Pine Press.

Lepori, B. 1992. *La Nascita e i suoi Luoghi*. Como, Italy: Red Studio Adazionale.

McCamant, K. and C. Durrett. 1988. *Cohousing: A Contemporary Approach to Housing Ourselves*. Berkeley, Calif.: Habitat Press.

Newman, O. 1972. *Defensible Space*. New York: Macmillan.

New York City Planning Commission. 1993. *Shaping the City's Future: New York City Planning and Zoning Report*. New York: Department of City Planning.

Oldenburg, R. 1989. *The Great Good Place*. New York: Pantheon Books.

Perin, C. 1977. *Everything In its Place: Social Order and Land Use in America*. Princeton, N.J.: Princeton University Press.

Polyzoides, S., R. Sherwood, and J. Tice. 1992. *Courtyard Housing in Los Angeles*. New York: Princeton Architectural Press.

Ritzdorf, M. 1986. Women and the city: land use and zoning issues. *Urban Resources* (Winter): 23–27.

Sennett, R. 1970. *The Uses of Disorder: Personal Identity and City Life*. New York: Knopf.

Sherman, H. 1993. The body in the house: restimulating bodily memory as a means to reclaim the identities of our bodies in the environment. In *Body, Technology and Design*, eds. M. Underhill and M. Underwood. Washington, D.C.: American Collegiate Schools of Architecture Press.

Sloan, D. 1991. *The Last Great Necessity*. Baltimore, Md.: Johns Hopkins University Press.

Solomon, D. 1992. *ReBuilding*. New York: Princeton Architectural Press.

Sorkin, M. 1992. *Variations on a Theme Park: The New American City and the End of Public Space*. New York: Noonday Press.

Sprague, J.F. 1991. *More Than Housing: Lifeboats for Women and Children*. Boston: Butterworth Architecture.

Stuebing, S. 1992. *The Seattle Public Schools' School Design Notebook*. Newark, N.J.: School of Architecture, New Jersey Institute of Technology.

Thorne, R. 1980. Places of refreshment in the nineteenth century city. In *Buildings and Society*, ed. A. King, 228–54. London: Routledge & Kegan Paul.

Tschumi, B. 1987. *Cinegramme Folie: Le Parc de la Villette*. New York: Princeton Architectural Press.

Tuan, Y.F. 1982. *Segmented Worlds and Self: Group Life and Individual Consciousness*. Minneapolis, Minn.: University of Minnesota Press.

Weschler, L. 1993. In a desert of pure feeling. *The New Yorker*. July 7: 80–91.

Wolfe, M. 1992. Invisible women in invisible places: lesbians, lesbian bars and the social production of people/environment relationships. *Architecture and Behavior* 8 (2): 137–58.

Woods, L. 1992. *Anarchitecture: Architecture is a Political Act*. New York: St. Martin's Press.

Young, I.M. 1986. Impartiality and the civic public. *Praxis International* 5 (4): 381–401.

Zukin, S. 1991. *Landscapes of Power*. Berkeley, Calif.: University of California Press.

Contributors

MIKE BRILL is Professor of Architecture at the State University of New York in Buffalo and President of BOSTI, the Buffalo Organization for Social and Technological Innovations, Inc., a design research organization. He teaches architecture as if it were a "natural language" inherent in us all. Since his Bachelor of Architecture degree from Pratt Institute, he has worked as an architect, teacher, and researcher for some 30 years, and is the author of numerous articles, monographs, and book chapters on the effects of design on behavior, human performance and satisfaction, and on public life and public places. He is also the author of a two-volume work, *Using Office Design to Increase Productivity* (Buffalo, Bosti, 1984-85).

PATRICK M. CONDON is Associate Professor and Director of the Landscape Architecture Program at the University of British Columbia. He received his Masters of Landscape Architecture from the University of Massachusetts in 1981. He worked as a city planner and in private practice before taking a teaching position at the University of Minnesota in 1985. His work focuses on design theory for landscape architecture and has been published in *Landscape Journal* and *Midgard Journal*. He guest coedited the special spring 1991 edition of *Landscape Journal* entitled "The Avant-Garde and the Landscape – can they be reconciled?" In addition to the work included in this volume, his works on typology have been published in *Midgard Journal* and in an NEA-sponsored monograph entitled *A Designed Landscape Typology*. He maintains an active practice with much of his present design work performed on behalf of Upper Iowa University in Fayette, Iowa.

HEMALATA DANDEKAR is Professor of Urban Planning at the University of Michigan in Ann Arbor. She received her Bachelor of Architecture at the University of Bombay, her Masters of Architecture at the University of Michigan in Ann Arbor, and her Ph.D. in Urban Planning from the University of California at Los Angeles. She has worked as an architect and urban planner and has published her research on rural development in India and the changing farmscape of the United States, as well as other articles and chapters on research methods in planning, and women and shelter.

FRANCES DOWNING is Associate Professor of Architecture at Texas A&M University. She received her Bachelors and Masters of Architecture from the University of Oregon and her Ph.D. in Architecture from the University of Wisconsin at Milwaukee. She has published articles and chapters on the use of memorable place imagery during design inquiry, the meanings assigned to memorable place images by designers, and the structure of the design process.

GUIDO FRANCESCATO is Professor of Architecture at the University of Maryland, College Park. He received his Masters Degree in Architecture from the University of Illinois at Urbana-Champaign. He has designed buildings and urban spaces in the United States and abroad. His most recent publication is the chapter "Meaning and Use: A Conceptual Basis" in *The Meaning and Use of Housing* (ed. E.G. Arias, Avebury, 1993). He is currently assisting the Office of the Chief Architect of Bratislava in developing strategies for the humanization of the Petrzalka mass housing project built by the former socialist regime in the Slovak capital.

KAREN A. FRANCK is Associate Professor at the New Jersey Institute of Technology in Newark, where she holds a joint appointment in the School of Architecture and the Department of Social Science and Policy Studies. Her Ph.D. in Environmental Psychology is from the City University of New York. She has previously written about single-room occupancy hotels, other forms of alternative housing, and feminist architecture. With Sherry Ahrentzen, she edited *New Households, New Housing* (Van Nostrand Reinhold, 1989). Her research on innovative housing, funded by the National Science Foundation, and on the history of public housing design, funded by the National Endowment for the Arts, has contributed significantly to her ideas about type.

ALICE T. FRIEDMAN is Professor of Art and Co-Director of the Architecture Program at Wellesley College. She is currently working on a book entitled *The Best Laid Plans: Architecture, Gender and the Making of the Modern House*, an analysis of architect/client relations, gender ideology, and architectural design based on in-depth case studies of twentieth-century domestic architecture in Europe and America. She is the author of *House and Household in Elizabethan England: Wollaton Hall and the Willoughby Family* (University of Chicago Press, 1988) and of numerous articles on English Renaissance architecture and social history.

ANTHONY D. KING is Professor of Art History and of Sociology at Binghamton University, State University of New York. He received his Masters Degree in History from the University of Sheffield and his Ph.D. in Social Sciences from Brunel University. He is the author of several books including *Global Cities: Post-Imperialism and the Internationalization of London* (Routledge, 1990), *The Bungalow: The Production of a Global Culture* (Routledge & Kegan Paul, 1984), and the editor of *Buildings and Society: Essays on the Social Development of the Built Environment* (Routledge & Kegan Paul, 1980).

JEAN LA MARCHE is Associate Professor of Architecture at the State University of New York at Buffalo. He received his Bachelor of Architecture from Lawrence Technological University in Michigan and is completing his Doctorate at the University of Michigan in Ann Arbor. He is a practicing architect and has won several design awards, including an honorable mention in the 1990 National Peace Garden Competition. His work has been displayed in numerous exhibits including the National Architectural Museum in Washington, D.C. His articles on architectural theory have appeared in several publications, including the Berkeley PETS series. He is developing a cross-disciplinary project for urban installations in the city of Buffalo, New York.

RODERICK LAWRENCE is Master of Teaching and Research at the Centre for Human Ecology and Environmental Sciences at the University of Geneva. He received a Bachelor of Architecture Degree with First Class Honors from the University of Adelaide (Australia), a Master of Letters Degree from the University of Cambridge (England), and a Doctorate of Science from the Ecole Polytechnique Fédérale in Lausanne (Switzerland). He has served as a Consultant to the Committee on Housing, Building, and Planning of the Economic Commission for Europe, as well as to the Urban Affairs Division of the OECD. He is the author of two books: *Le Seuil franchi... logement populaire et vie quotidienne en Suisse romande, 1860–1960* (Georg Editeur, Geneva, 1986); and *Housing, Dwellings and Homes: Design Theory, Research and Practice* (John Wiley, Chichester, U.K., 1987).

THOMAS MARKUS is Professor Emeritus at the Department of Architecture and Building Science, University of Strathclyde, Glasgow. He received his B.A. (Honours Architecture) from Manchester University in 1949, and his M.A. from the same university in 1953; he received a Masters of Architecture from the Manchester Institute of Technology in 1955. A Fellow of the Royal Society of Arts, he is also the author of numerous articles and books, and a co-author and editor of *Order in Space and Society: Architectural Form and its Context in the Scottish Enlightenment* (Mainstream, Edinburgh, 1982). He most recently authored *Buildings and Power: Freedom and Control in the Origin of Modern Building Types* (Routledge, London, 1993).

ANNE VERNEZ MOUDON is Professor of Architecture, Landscape Architecture, and Urban Design and Planning at the University of Washington, Seattle. She is Associate Dean for Academic Affairs and Director of the Graduate Certificate Program in Urban Design. Dr. Moudon holds a B.Arch. from the University of California, Berkeley, and a Doctorate of Science from the Ecole Polytechnique Fédérale of Lausanne, Switzerland. Her research focuses on urban form analysis, neighborhood and street design, and pedestrian planning. Her published works include *Built for Change: Neighborhood Architecture in San Francisco* (MIT Press, 1986) and *Public Streets for Public Use* (Columbia University Press, 1991).

MARSHA RITZDORF is Associate Professor of Planning, Public Policy, and Management at the Virginia Polytechnic Institute and State University in Blacksburg. She received her Masters of Urban Planning from the University of Oregon and her Ph.D. at the University of Washington in Seattle. Her specialty as a researcher and a professional planner is women and land use planning, and she is currently writing a book on that topic.

JULIA ROBINSON is Professor of Architecture at the University of Minnesota in Minneapolis. She received her Bachelor of Architecture and her M.A. (Anthropology) from the University of Minnesota. She is the author of numerous articles and monographs including "Architecture as a Medium for Culture" in *Culture, Housing and Design* (eds. S. Low and E. Chambers, University of Pennsylvania Press, 1988). She is author of the forthcoming book *Architecture Through the Looking Glass: Beyond Institution and Home* (Van Nostrand Reinhold).

LYNDA H. SCHNEEKLOTH is Associate Professor at the School of Architecture and Planning, State University of New York at Buffalo, and is a partner in The Caucus Partnership, Consultants on Environmental and Organizational Change. She received her Masters of Science in Landscape Architecture from the University of Wisconsin in Madison. Her earlier research on the construct of building type was supported by a grant from the National Endowment for the Arts. She recently edited *Changing Places: Re-Making Institutional Buildings* (The White Pine Press, 1992) with Marcy Feuerstein and Barbara Campagna, and is co-author with Robert G. Shibley of *Placemaking: A Critical Practice* (John Wiley and Sons, forthcoming).

MARTIN SYMES is Professor of Urban Renewal and Head of the Department of Architecture at Manchester University in England. He studied architecture at Cambridge University and planning at the Architectural Association, later taking his Ph.D. at the Bartlett School. He has contributed numerous articles on architecture, urban design, and the human environment to books and journals, was joint editor of "Urban Waterside Regeneration" (Ellis Hillman, 1993), and is currently working on an international study of urban strategies and projects for the French government.

DAVID VANDERBURGH is a Killam Postdoctoral Fellow at the School of Architecture, University of British Columbia, Vancouver. He received Masters and Ph.D. degrees in Architecture from the University of California, Berkeley, in 1990 and 1993. Among his recent publications are "Urbino: Planning, Preservation, and Polyculture" in *Places* magazine, summer 1992, and "Pandora's Black Box: The Cellular Prison in France, 1830–1880," in Marc Angelil (ed.), *On Architecture: The City and Technology*," Butterworth Publishers, 1991. He is currently working on a book on nineteenth-century architecture and social reform in Europe and North America.

NANCY WOLF is an artist and lives in New York City. She received her BFA from the Rhode Island School of Design in Providence, Rhode Island. The relationships of people to modern technological environments, cities, and contemporary architecture has been the subject of her art for the past 20 years. Her drawings, paintings, and prints are visual critiques of modernist, postmodernist, and deconstructivist architecture. Her experiences living and traveling in Europe, Asia, and Africa have influenced her thinking about new technologies and the creation of humane spaces in which to live. She exhibits her work at the Marsha Mateyka Gallery in Washington, D.C.

Index

A
Adam, Katrin, 363–65, 370
Agrest, Diane, 368–69
Alexander, Christopher, 223, 258, 259
Allé, 76, 92
American Dream, 19, 32, 33, 35, 117, 122
    See also Single-family housing, Single-family neighborhood, Suburb
Ancien régime, 316, 318, 319, 321–22
Animate world, 45–48, 58
Apartment building(s), 25, 182, 349
Appleton, Jay, 66, 89
Argan, Guilio, 258, 260, 294
Archetypes, 17, 20, 29, 76
    and charged places, 62–63
    as dialectic of tones, 69–71
    forms, 76
    and imaginal types, 31
    landscape, 66, 88–93
    as mythic themes in places, 67–68
    as "natural language" for place making, 61–78
    of our original places, 67
    theory-stories of, 64–67
    and type, 76
    using in design, example of, 72–77
    value of thinking about, 76–77
    See also Landscape archetypes
Architect and client, 236–38, 337–41, 344
    See also Architectural practice
Architects and lay people, 184–85, 191
Architect's Dilemma (Wolf, drawing), 198, 200
Architectural practice, 166–78, 307
    case studies of:
        Adelaide Road, 170–72
        Northwick Park Hospital, 172–74
        Riding Center for the Disabled (RDAvon), 174–76
    design/build, 174–76
    participatory design, 170–72
    See also Architecture, professional practice

Architecture:
    and basic types, 182–85
    and classificatory types, 185–86
    deconstructivist, 204, 205, 367
    forgetting, 209–10, 214
    and functional type, 320–28
    imaginary, 370
    instrumental scholarship of, 265–68
    modern, 197, 198, 200–3, 243, 290, 294–95, 306, 335, 336, 337
    Modern Movement, 185, 256, 257, 258, 302, 335–36
    "paper", 30
    postmodern, 10, 29–30, 125, 200, 203–4, 335
    professional practice, 12, 166–78, 268–89
    social, 30, 316–318
    vernacular, 195, 201, 207, 305
Architecture banale, 305, 307
Architecture parlante, 220, 221
Architecture savante, 305, 307
Asylum(s), 153, 157, 353

AT&T Building (New York), 203, 204
Aymonino, Carlo, 267, 293–95

B
Bachelard, Gaston, 65, 67, 71, 242
Backyard, 90–91
Baker, Josephine, 339
Baltard, L.P., 326, 333
Barn, 98–100, 107, 109, 110
Barnsdall, Aline, 337–38, 340–41
Barnes, Edward Larrabee, 204
Barthes, Roland, 260, 264
Basic types, 180, 181–85, 190–92
Beauty/beautiful, 83–84, 87, 93, 334
Bell, Andrew, 325
Bentham, Jeremy, 320, 324, 327
Berry, Thomas, 45, 55, 56
Bevington, Christine, 362, 370
"Biddy Mason: Time and Place" (project), 356
Billboard Dreams (Wolf, drawing), 205, 206
Birthing room, 365–66
Bishop, Peter, 35, 50, 51, 5

Blondel, 22, 151, 157
Body, 62, 64 – 65, 72, 228, 365, 366
Bonds, 149 – 150, 152
Bosque, 76, 84 – 85
Boullée, E., 151, 256, 335
Boundaries, 31 – 32, 41 – 42, 47, 57, 68, 141, 181, 184, 223, 284 – 85, 360 – 61, 369
Building fabric, 291, 297, 299, 300
Building form, 126, 127, 128
Building type(s), 18, 22, 127 – 28, 148, 179, 181 – 82, 271, 305
   image and, 29, 182, 349
   new, 315, 317, 350
   of origin, 188, 189, 190
   See also Basic types, Names of types, Language of function
Building typologies:
   and design theory, 294 – 95
   and social practices, 147 – 63
Built landscape typology, 67, 79 – 94, 290
   dialectical landscape, 80 – 88
Burke, Edmund, 71, 80, 83, 87
Burrell Art Gallery (Glasgow), 155 – 56
Butler, Octavia, 49 – 51

C

California Coastline (Wolf, drawing), 196, 197
Calthorpe, Peter, 33, 308, 355
Caniggia, Gianfranco, 290, 291 – 93, 294, 296, 300, 304
Capitalism, 357 – 58, 360
   See also Market forces
Castex, Jean, 302 – 4
Categories, 10, 17, 31 – 32, 182, 254
Change of type(s), 28, 32 – 35, 125 – 26, 158 – 63, 179, 181 – 82, 221, 228, 280 – 83, 336 – 37, 367 – 68
Chaos, 64, 68, 85 – 86
Charged places, and archetypes, 62 – 63
Choay, Françoise, 306 – 7

Cities, 18, 215 – 216, 220, 223
   contemporary, 293, 294
   contemporary, classification criteria, 141 – 42
   modern/modernist, 141 – 42, 197 – 98, 200
   traditional, 141 – 42, 306
   typologies of, 138 – 42
Class, 254
Class (socioeconomic), 22, 130, 132, 135 – 38, 155
   middle, 118, 119, 125, 279, 320 – 21, 328
Classicism, 151, 159, 160, 333, 334, 335
Classification, 17, 21 – 23, 31, 138 – 40, 142, 154, 305, 324
   of environments, 185 – 86
   imaginal content of, 22 – 23
   principles of, 272, 274, 285
   See also Classificatory types
Classification systems, 17, 127, 129, 130, 139, 142, 154
Classificatory types, 23, 180, 181, 185 – 86, 189, 190 – 92
Cloister, 76, 87 – 88
Cochrane, Willard, 101, 102, 103, 111
Cohousing, 26, 363, 343
Colquhoun, Alan, 218, 260, 336 – 37
Community, 196, 207, 364, 365
   speech/language 130, 136, 152
Concept, 240
Conceptual types, 11, 28
   aspects of, 17, 21 – 23
Conflict, 24, 122, 358 – 59
Conjecture-analysis model, 244
Convention, 332, 342 – 43
Conzen, M.P., 299, 304
Conzen, M.R.G., 296 – 302, 304
   international/interdisciplinary outreach, 299 – 300
   legacy, 300 – 301
   philosophy and method, 296 – 98

   Urban Morphology Research Group, 298 – 99
Corporate farms, 113 – 14
Cranz, Galen, 354, 361, 370
Crystal Palace, 159 – 60
Culture, 129, 130, 142, 155, 191 – 92, 264, 332, 337
   and basic types, 164 – 65, 191
   and dwelling types, 130, 132 – 38

D

Danford, S., 181
Darden, Douglas, 17, 363, 370
Darke, Jane, 244
Das Haus Im Haus (Wolf, drawing), 202 – 3
de Bretteville, Sheila, 356
Deconstructivist architecture, 204, 205, 367
Delicate Balance (Wolf, drawing), 204, 205
Derrida, J., 210, 224
Design/build, 174 – 76
Design images:
   sources of, 238 – 43
      essential constructs, 241 – 42
      place types, 239
      scripted behavior, 240 – 41
      specific events, 238
      specific places, 238
Design process, 233 – 49
   analysis of, 243 – 45, 248, 263, 264
   and innovation, 247 – 48
   and memory, 236 – 46
   and type, 258 – 61
Design theory, 308
   and building typology, 294 – 95
   evaluation of, 307
   historically based, 294, 296, 306 – 7
Dialectics, 11, 69 – 72, 81, 84
   See also Landscape, dialectical
Dinan v. Town of Stratford, 121
Disabled, 174 – 76, 188

Disneyworld/Disneyland, 331, 357
Duany, Andres, 33, 305, 355, 367
Dubos, René, 66, 89
Durand, J.N.L., 22, 160, 301, 305, 321 – 23, 324, 328
Durkheim, Emil, 372
Dwellings/dwelling types, 72, 125, 126, 128, 130 – 38
   classifying, 130 – 38
   and social class, 135 – 36
   social/cultural/historical meanings, 130 – 38
   types of, 131 – 38

E

Earth, 11, 44 – 45, 48, 49 – 50, 52, 55 – 58, 60
Eco, Umberto, 152, 262, 263, 264
Ecological imagination, 51 – 54, 58 – 60
Ecology, 41, 42
Eighteenth century, 20, 22, 152, 157, 272, 305, 351, 352
Eisenman, Peter, 211, 219, 223, 224
Eléments (Panerai), 303 – 4
Eliade, Michel, 64, 68, 80
Enlightenment, 34, 84, 151, 215, 222, 305, 320, 359
Enseignement mutuel, 325
Entrance to the City (drawing), 196
Essential constructs, 241 – 42
Extinction, 50

F

Family:
   defined, 117, 121, 123 – 24
   ideal, 118 – 121, 124
   policies regarding, 119 – 21, 126
Farm, 18, 72, 97 – 116
   barn, 98 – 100, 107, 109, 110
   early, in Michigan, 105 – 7
   and ethnicity, 100

and family labor, 107
farmhouse, 106, 109
government policies/actions:
    early settlement period, 102
    modern and corporate farming, 110–14
    railroads and commercial architecture, 107–9
    technology and scientific education, 109–11
land survey ordinance (1785), 103–4
silos, 109–11, 113–14
transformations in, 98–99
type analyses of buildings, 99–101
Farnsworth, Edith, 337–38, 340–41, 342
Farnsworth House, 337, 338, 339, 341–42
Fiction:
    literature, 43, 49–51
    media, 46–48, 52–53
    myths, 41–43, 45, 53, 55, 58–60, 68–69
    See also Science Fiction, Myths, Stories
Forest, 18, 32, 54, 83–84
Form, 151, 254–55, 257–59, 266, 308, 331, 334–35, 337
    complexity of, 185–86
    and function, 157, 158–59
    and function, space, and meaning, 152, 153, 163
    interpretation of, 332–33
    logical, 241
    and meaning, 215, 347, 348
    sterility of, 200
    type as generator of, 257, 258, 305
    and use, 258–59, 347–49, 367–69
Form attributes of types, 254–55, 346–47, 349, 352, 367
Form types, 76, 349
Frankl, Paul, 315, 316, 317
Frazer, George, 89

French Revolutions, 151, 158, 305, 316, 317, 318, 319, 320–22, 324, 335
Foucault, Michel, 21, 44, 138
Frontier, 44–46, 52, 55–57, 59
Function, 151–53, 161, 203, 255, 256, 258, 259, 266, 328, 331, 346
    and form, 157, 158–59, 259
    and form, space, and meaning, 152, 153, 163
    language of, 148–49, 153–63
Functionalism, 256, 293, 323
Functional space, 137
Functional types, 18, 171, 223, 320–28
Future City #5 (Wolf, drawing), 196

G

Gandelsonas, Mario, 368–69
Gardens, 18, 26, 72
Gender, 9, 13, 22, 118–119, 125, 142, 155, 331–32, 338–42, 352
Generator-conjecture-analysis, 244
Genius loci, 45
Geometric typologies, 255, 256
Gergen, Kenneth, 263, 361, 363
German Museum of Architecture (Frankfurt), 202
Gerz, Jochen and Esther, 365
Giddens, Anthony, 351, 366
Gilpin, William, 80, 83
God(s), dieties, 44–45, 68, 85
Gowans, A., 265
Grid, 138, 197, 207, 240, 357
Group home, 28, 35, 186–90

H

Habraken, John, 273–74
Hanson, Julienne, 22, 152–53, 186, 187, 191, 277
Harries, Karsten, 65, 67, 70

Harrison, Robert, 55, 57, 59
Hart, John, 102, 104
Hidden Longings (Wolf, drawing), 201
High-rise, 198, 204
High-rise office tower, 25, 71
Highways, 18, 33
Hillier, Bill, 22, 152–53, 186, 187, 191, 277
Hillman, James, 20, 27, 46, 58
History, 55, 214, 229–30, 257–60, 265, 321–25, 332–35
    of city building, 292–94, 296, 301–3
    and design theory, 306–7
    instrumental, 260, 265–67
    and type, 257
Hollyhock House, 337, 338, 339, 340
Holocaust Museum (Washington, D.C.), 205, 364
Home, 55–57, 339, 341, 342
Homelessness, 25, 44–48, 51, 55–56, 329
Hospitals, 24, 26, 153, 168, 172–74
House, 16–17, 181, 182, 185, 187, 202, 339–40
    See also Single-family house/housing
Housing:
    basic types, 187–88
    classifying, 130–32
    English dwellings, 133–38
    single-family, 11, 117, 119–20, 122, 125, 179, 351–52, 354–55, 356–57, 359
    social and cultural categories, 129–38
    transitional, 367–68
    types, 119, 135, 276–79
    urban (Switzerland), 275–87
    See also Dwelling types
Housing market, 128, 131–32
    and advertisements for housing, 132–138
    and dwelling types, 128, 131–32
Hubka, Thomas, 99
Hudson, John, 108
Husserl, 147, 149

I

IBM Building (New York), 203, 204
Ideal types, 17, 20, 181
    and imaginal types, 31
Image, 352, 180, 182, 348–50
    See also Design images, Mental imagery
Imaginal types, 16, 17–18, 25, 27–30, 36, 41–43
    aspects of, 19–21
    power of, 33, 42
Imagination, 30, 63, 79, 161, 234, 236, 249, 257
    See also Design images
Industrialization, 35, 108, 112–14, 358
Industrial Revolution, 151, 155
Innovation, 125–26, 163, 184, 247–48, 337, 342–43
Institutional building(s), 187, 188, 190, 353–54
    See also Asylums, Hospitals, Prisons, Typification

J

Jackson, J.B., 351, 355
Jahn, Helmut, 205
Johnson, Philip, 203
Journey to a New Place (Wolf, drawing), 198–99

K

Kahn, Andrea, 258
Knecht, Barbara, 367–68, 370
Knesl, John, 214, 220, 224, 225, 227, 230
Knowledge, 12, 15–16, 34, 61, 249, 263
    and power, 15, 23
    place as form of, 205
    social construction of, 127, 128, 139–42
    structure, 28, 34
    type as corpus of, 273–75
    type as structuring, 13, 15
    type as vehicle of, 259–60, 266
    and typologies, 259

Kostof, Spiro, 265
Krier, Leon, 255–56

L

LADRHAUS, 302–3
Lancaster, Joseph/Lancasterian School, 325–27
Land, 91–92, 102–105
Landscape, 17, 18
   built, 67, 79–94, 290–91, 308
   dialectical, 80–88
   economic forces of built, 357–58
   management of built, 291, 308
   typology of built, 67, 79–94, 290
Landscape archetypes, 66, 88–93
   dimensions of model for, 91–93
      clearing to the forest continuum, 91
      human relations to nature continuum, 91–92
      landform continuum, 92
      social dimension, 90–91
   forest and clearing, 89–90
   land, 90
Landscape space:
   defined, 80
   designed, 90
   rooms, 80–83
   typology of, 11, 91–93
      backyard, 90–91
      bosque, 84–85
      clearing, 80, 83–84
      cloister, 76, 87–88
      orchard, 85–87
      promontory, 91–92
      single tree, 76, 87–88
Landscapes of Peril design project, 72–77
   Black Hole, 74
   Forbidding Blocks, 75
   Landscape of Thorns, 73
   Menacing Earthworks, 74
   Rubble Landscape, 75
   Spike Field, 75
   Spikes Bursting through Grid, 74
Landscape types, 17, 18, 66, 191–93
   See also Landscape space, typology of
Land use, 117–26
Lang, John, 254, 264–66
Langer, Suzanne, 239, 241
Language, 12, 72, 79, 147–48, 226, 247–48
   of function, 148–49, 151, 153–63
   natural, 11, 61, 73
   See also Names of types, Terminology
Larkham, P.J., 299, 300
Laugier, Abbé, 256, 301, 320, 333–34, 341, 342
La Ville Radieuse, 196
Lawson, Bryan, 243
Le Corbusier, 20, 82, 185, 196, 215, 265, 325
Lefebvre, Henri, 127, 301–2, 303, 334, 336, 337, 338–39
Lepori, Bianca, 365–66, 370
Lin, Maya, 356, 366
Little Bighorn National Battlefield, 356
Loos, Adolf, 337, 339

M

Mac Cormac, E., 247
Market forces, 131, 357–58
   See also Capitalism, Housing market
Markets, 72, 108–9, 112
   global, 112–13
Markus, Thomas, 23
Marx, Karl, 80, 81, 86, 150
Material types, aspects of, 17–19, 23, 27, 32–33
Meaning(s), 12, 18, 32, 62–63, 76, 227
   attributes of types, 347
   convergence of, 156–57
   of dwelling types, 128, 130–31, 135–38
   and form, 163, 152, 153, 215, 347, 348
   shifts in, 32–35, 158–61, 162
Memorial(s), 345, 356, 364, 365
Memory, 211, 221–22, 332, 343
   and design, 236–43
   and design conjectures, 243–45
   and innovation, 247–48
   and place making, 233–50
Mental imagery:
   designers' use of, 236, 238, 241–43, 249, 340
   and shaping of experience, 235–36
Merleau-Ponty, Maurice, 80, 81, 86–87
Metaphor, 128, 246, 247–248, 258, 325
Modena Cemetery, 217, 221, 242
Modern architecture, 197, 198, 200–3, 243, 290, 294–95, 306, 335, 336, 337
Modern farms, 110–13
Modernism/modernity, 31, 35, 51, 55, 81–82, 211, 229, 351
Modern/modernist city, 141–42, 197–98, 200
Modern Movement, 185, 256, 257, 258, 302, 335–36
Moneo, Rafael, 211, 216, 217, 256, 258, 295, 337
Moore, Charles, 328
Morphogenesis, 290, 300, 307, 308
Morphology, 90, 290, 292, 300, 307, 308
Municipal Center Building (Phoenix), 238, 241, 242, 245
Muratorian School, 290–94
   building typology and design theory, 294–95
   debates surrounding, 293–94
   interpretation in North America, 295–96
   legacy, 296
Muratori, Saverio, 260, 266, 289, 290–91, 292, 293–95, 296
Myers, Barton, 238, 241
Myth(s), 42–43, 45, 53, 55, 58, 60, 67–68
   common, 68
   cultural, 68
   science fiction, 44–60
   See also Fiction, Stories

N

Names of types, 25–27, 29–30, 32, 41, 180–81, 182, 184, 318, 345, 348–50,
   power of, 25–27, 34–35, 142
   and typification, 318–19
   See also Language of function, Terminology
Napoleon, 324, 332
Nature, 18, 33, 52, 53–55, 57–58, 80–88, 333–35, 361
Neoclassical language, 161–63
New Realities (Wolf, drawing), 204
Nineteenth century, 22, 108, 118, 122, 138, 141, 216, 279, 281, 305, 316, 321, 322, 335, 351
Noble, Allen, 99
Nominalism, 35
Not-us, 41–43, 48, 52, 59

O

Objective, 21
Office buildings, 18
Olmsted, Frederick Law, 83, 85, 86
Olympia Fields Park, 361–62
One Liberty Place (Philadelphia), 205
Orchard, 85–87
Other, 41–60
Oxygen House, 363

P

Palo Alto Tenants Union v. Morgan, 121
Panerai, Philippe, 302–4
Panopticon, 20, 320, 326–27
Parc la Villette (Paris), 160–61, 367
Parks, 18, 32, 345, 354, 356, 358–59, 360–61, 367
Participatory design, 174–76

Perfect Order (Wolf, drawing), 10, 18, 20, 203
Perin, Constance, 118, 119, 354
Picturesque, 83–84, 304
Pike's Place Market (Seattle), 364
Pilgrimage (Wolf, drawing), 207
Piranesi, 161
Place:
    beloved, 56
    charged, 11, 61–63, 76–77
    essential qualities of, 68–69
    sacred, 3, 68, 84, 255–56, 322, 364
Place making:
    and archetypes, 61–78
    and memory, 233–50
Place types, 9, 15, 16, 17, 25, 41–42, 239
    conceptual, 17
    in human experience, 16–18
    imaginal, 16, 17
    material, 17, 18, 21–22
    representations of, 29–30
Plan unit, 297, 305
Plater-Zyberk, Elizabeth, 33, 308, 355, 367
Postmodern architecture, 29, 200, 203–4, 335
Postmodernism, 142
Poststructuralist, 224
Power, 127, 129, 142, 149–50, 152, 159, 203, 332–33, 338, 339
    empowerment, 336, 359–60
    of expression, 80
    and knowledge, 15, 23
    of memory, 249
    of mental image, 235, 249
    of naming, 25–27, 34–35, 142
    of type, 181–83
Power of Place (organization), 356
Practice:
    architectural, 12, 165–78, 307
    professional, 12, 166–67, 268–69
    social, 13, 15, 147–63, 150–55, 303–4, 319, 337
    spatial, 15, 16, 23–26, 30, 284
Praxis, 34
Precedent, 186, 245–46, 247, 248, 249, 257
Prescriptive texts, 155–56
    See also Program
Prescriptive type, 179, 256, 268
Price, Uvedale, 80, 83, 84
Primary generator, 244
Prime directive, 52–54, 58
Primitive hut, 320, 334, 341
Prison(s), 153, 157, 318, 327
    type as, 30–36
Prisoner to a Grid (Wolf, drawing), 197, 202
Privacy, 189, 280–82, 284, 341, 363
    gradient, 187, 189–90, 341
Program, 152, 155–56, 172–74, 259, 335, 336, 337, 340–41
    See also Prescriptive text
Promise, type as, 30–36
Promontory, 91–92
Prototype, 179, 245–46, 247, 249, 305, 321
Public space, 187, 200, 280–82, 283, 358–59

Q

Quatremère de Quincy, 20, 76, 256–61, 264, 286, 301, 305, 331, 335

R

Railroads, 107–9
Railway stations, functional typology for, 160, 169
Rapoport, Amos, 253, 254, 263, 264–65
Reason, 79–80, 335
Representation, 29–30, 42–43, 348–49
Research
    architectural, 191, 262–65, 267, 285–86
    environmental design, 263–65
    urban, 303–4, 138–42, 307
    See also Scholarship
Robinson, David, 361, 370
Rogers, E., 358–59, 260
Rossi, Aldo, 88, 209–14, 216–19, 221–24, 228–29, 238, 239, 240, 242, 246, 249, 255–56, 286, 289–311
Rossler, Martha, 30
Rules, 246, 283–84, 257
    to generate form, 161, 186, 246, 248
Russell, Bertrand, 272

S

Sacred places, 3, 68, 84, 255–56, 322, 364
Sainsbury Center (University of East Anglia), 159
Saint-Hilaire, Etienne Geoffrey, 272
Scholarship, 12
    instrumental, 266–68
    and type, 253–70
    See also Research
Schön, Donald, 27, 167, 182, 244
Schools, 18, 24, 325–26, 345, 349
    functional typology for, 169
Scuri, P., 265
Segmentation, 350–51, 360–62
Self/selves 149, 195, 364, 366
    place distinction, 41–42, 55
Sequestration, 316, 328, 351–53
    See also Typification
Seventeenth century, 44
Shane, Grahame, 214, 215, 217, 219
Sherman, Harvey, 365
Silos, 110–11, 113–14
Single-family house/housing, 11, 117, 119–20, 122, 125, 179, 351–52, 354–355, 356–57, 359
Single-family neighborhoods, 120–25, 342, 351–52, 356–57, 359
Single tree, 76, 88–89
Slater, T.R., 299
Smithson, Robert, 80, 81–86

Social practice, 13, 15, 303–4, 319, 337
    and architectural discourse, 150–55
    and buildings, 148–49
    and building typologies, 147–63
Social production, 19, 138
Social relations, and buildings, 149–50, 152–53, 157, 162
Soul, 44–45
Spatial practice, 15, 16, 23–26, 30, 284
Spatial structure(s):
    analysis of, 188–90, 152–53, 276–80
    defined, 152
    desired distribution of power in, 152–53
    as form of knowledge, 15
Species, 11, 22, 50, 52–54, 64
    endangered, 54, 57
    human, 41–43, 53, 55–56, 62, 64, 72
Speck, Jeff, 362–63, 370
Spirit, 63–64, 66–67, 70, 82, 83, 88, 89, 203, 207
Standardization, 350–52, 353, 354, 360
Stark, William, 155
Star Trek: The Next Generation, 47–48, 52–54
Steadman, Philip, 276
Stories, 66, 93
    See also Fiction, Theory
St. Pancras Station (London), 160
Street, 90, 300, 307, 358–59
Strip development, 32, 362–63
Sublime, 81, 83–84, 93, 217
Suburb, 33, 118, 123, 196, 197, 203, 351, 354–55, 356–57, 359
Subjective, 21, 224, 240
Subjects/subjectivity, 147–48, 150, 157, 353
    active, 365–66
    See also Self/selves

T

Tax Court (Wolf, painting), 198
Taxonomies, 130

of cities, 138–42
of English regional dwellings, 133–35
folk, 127, 129, 130
Technology, 41, 89, 109–11, 139, 160, 327–28
Tempietto of San Pietro Inside the Walls (Wolf, drawing), 202
Terminology, 11, 127–28, 142
of city types, 138–42
of dwelling types, 130–38
See also Language, Names of types
Text(s), 11, 12, 23, 42, 57, 148–49, 209–10, 224
prescriptive, 155–56
Theater Royal (Plymouth), 157–58
Theory
architectural, 209–30
landscape, 66–67, 80–86, 89–93
stories of archetypes, 64–67
See also Design Theory
Thiis-Evensen, T., 65
Third Estate, 290, 319
Time, 67, 141, 142, 268, 272, 286, 308, 322, 324, 329, 368
Tones, 69–71
aspiration, 71
contentment, 71
nurturance, 72
risk, 71
Torre, Susana, 97, 125
Tower, 348, 349
Town plan, 297
analysis, 297, 300
Train stations, 327
Tschumi, Bernard, 160–61, 224, 225, 367
Tversky, B., 183
Twentieth century, 11, 35, 44, 50, 53, 100, 118, 123, 138, 139, 214, 268, 340
Twenty-first century, 125
Type attributes:
form, 254–55, 346–47

meaning, 347–48
use, 346–48
Type operations, 23–30
imaging, 27
inventing/modifying, 27–28
naming, 25–27
occupying, 23–25
representing, 29–30
Type(s):
as analytical tool, 271–87, 305
as answer, 179, 184
archetypes, 17, 20, 29, 76
arguments of, 28
artist's perspective on, 195–208
base, 292–93, 296
basic, 180, 181–85, 190–92
boundaries between, 31–32
building, 18, 22, 127–28, 148, 179, 181–82, 271, 305
changing, 28, 32–35, 125–26, 158–63, 179, 181–82, 221, 228, 280–83, 336–37, 367–68
classificatory, 23, 180, 181, 185–86, 189, 190–92
classlike, 31–32
conceptual, 17, 21–23, 28
connection between image and, 27, 29, 182
consecrated, 295, 305
as container, 316, 317, 360
as corpus of shared knowledge, 273–75
defined, 9, 10, 15, 20, 126, 180, 212, 234, 254–58, 271, 286, 345, 346
and the design process, 258–61
discourse in U.S., 289, 296–97, 331, 336
dwelling, 131–38
farm, 99–101
form, 76, 349
functional, 18, 169–70, 223, 320–28
as generator of form, 257, 258, 305

housing, 119, 135, 276–79
ideal, 17, 20, 31, 181
imaginal, 16, 17–18, 19–21, 25, 27–30, 33, 36, 41–43
landscape, 17, 18, 66, 91–93
as limiting and liberating, 257
as machine, 325–29
material, 17–19, 23, 27, 32–33
and model, 257, 305
as multidimensional, 275, 285–86
names of, 25–27, 29–30, 32, 41, 180–81, 182, 184, 318, 345, 348–50
and the nature of architectural objects, 261–62
negotiating, 12, 28, 165
new, 259, 262, 350
new work on, 34–36
a posteriori, 258–59, 294, 305, 306
precision of, 168
prescriptive, 179, 256, 268
a priori, 258–59, 294, 305, 306
as prison and promise, 15–36
and professional practice of architecture, 166–70
as question, 12, 179, 186–90
as repressive and transformative, 32–34
as structure/vehicle of knowledge, 13, 15, 259–60, 266
and terminologies, 127–44
in urban analysis, 290–91
use, 346–47, 352–60
as web, 13, 346–48, 350–51, 360–61
Typification, 315–30
and age of the Many, 316–18
and the bourgeoisie, 318–20
defined, 317
and functional type, 320–28
and social architecture, 316–18
Typing, 9, 13, 15, 34–35
Typological analysis, 17, 22, 304–5

Typological evolution, 157
Typological moment, 258, 294
Typological process, 296, 305
Typological thinking, 165–78, 168
Typologies, 15, 17, 21–22, 168, 305
in architectural practice, 168–70, 176–78
of cities, 138–42
defined, 254, 271
of dwellings, 131–38
geometric, 255
landscape, 11, 91–93
new, 161–63
outdated/redundant, 169
procedural, 292
relational, 255–56
as synthetic entities, 266
Typomorphology, 289–311
defined, 289–90
in England, 296–302
in France, 302–7
in Italy, 290–95

U
Unconscious, 62–63, 75, 76
Unger, O.M., 192
Urban fabric, 267, 294, 297–300
Urban housing (Switzerland), 275–87
building/dwelling layouts, analysis of, 276–83
residents' use of space, 284–85
tenancy agreements in, 284
Urban Morphology Research Group, 298–99
Urban planning, 197, 205, 307, 308
Urban renewal, 198, 202, 359
U.S. Department of Energy, 72
Use, 186, 268, 346, 352
and form 258–59, 347–49, 367–69
Use attributes of types, 346–48, 367
Use characteristics of types, 186
Use types, 349–50

as containers, 360
defined, 346, 349
purposes of, 352–60
    for enabling/empowering, 359–60
    for producing/controling capital, 357–58
    for protecting/honoring, 355–57
    for public service, 358–59
    for removal/control, 353–54, 360
    for retreat/escape, 354–55, 360
relational, overlapping worlds, 361–69
segmentation of daily life by, 361
as webs, 360–61
Us/place relationships, 42–43, 57
    in science fiction, 44–60
        ecological imagination, 51–54, 58, 59
U.S. Tax Court (Washington, D.C.), 198

V
Van de Rohe, Mies, 82, 337–38, 339–41
von Eckhardt, Wolf, 207
Vaudoyer, A.L.T., 335
Vernacular architecture, 195, 201, 207
Versailles School of Architecture, 301–8
    critical history, 306–7
    formation of, 301–2
    LADRHAUS, 302–3
    legacy, 307
    typographical analysis, method of, 304–5
Vidler, Anthony, 20, 88, 167, 221, 222, 295, 305
Viennese Superblock, 267
Vietnam Veterans Memorial (Washington, D.C.), 356, 366
Village of Belle Terre v. Boraas, 120–21
Village of Euclid v. Ambler Realty Co., 119
Viollet-le-Duc, 323–24
Vitruvius, 333

W
Walter, E.V., 65
Waste, 41, 55, 58
    radioactive, 72–75
Web, 13, 346, 370
Weber, Max, 141, 272
Whitehand, J.W.R., 299, 300
Willems, E.P., 181
Wolf, Nancy, 20
Woods, Lebbeus, 369, 370
Wright, Frank Lloyd, 13, 97, 337–38, 339–40

Z
Zagreb Free Zone, 369
Zeisel, John, 263
Zoning, 10, 11, 21, 31–32, 117–126, 354, 367
    and cultural differences, 122–25
    defined, 117
    family, cultural ideal of, 118–19
    and family type, 117–26
    housing categories, 124
    law, judicial perspectives on meaning of family, 119–21
    single-family vs. multifamily, 124–25
    Village of Belle Terre v. Boraas, 120–21
    Village of Euclid v. Ambler Realty Co., 119